Religious Celebrations

Religious Celebrations

AN ENCYCLOPEDIA OF HOLIDAYS, FESTIVALS, SOLEMN OBSERVANCES, AND SPIRITUAL COMMEMORATIONS

Volume Two

L-Z

J. Gordon Melton, Editor

with
James A. Beverley
Christopher Buck
Constance A. Jones

Santa Barbara, California • Denver, Colorado • Oxford, England

Library of Congress Cataloging-in-Publication Data

Religious celebrations : an encyclopedia of holidays, festivals, solemn observances, and spiritual commemorations / J. Gordon Melton, editor, with James A. Beverley, Christopher Buck, Constance A. Jones.

p. cm.

Includes bibliographical references and index.

ISBN 978–1–59884–205–0 (hard copy : alk. paper) — ISBN 978–1–59884–206–7 (ebook)

1. Fasts and feasts—Encyclopedias. 2. Festivals—Encyclopedias. 3. Holidays—Encyclopedias. 4. Sacred meals—Encyclopedias. I. Melton, J. Gordon.

BL590.R46 2011

203′.6—dc23 2011018594

ISBN: 978–1–59884–205–0

EISBN: 978–1–59884–206–7

15 14 13 12 11 1 2 3 4 5

This book is also available on the World Wide Web as an eBook.
Visit www.abc-clio.com for details.

ABC-CLIO, LLC
130 Cremona Drive, P.O. Box 1911
Santa Barbara, California 93116-1911

This book is printed on acid-free paper ∞

Manufactured in the United States of America

Contents

List of Entries

Main Religion Entries are indicated by **boldface**.

'Abdu'l-Bahá, Ascension of

Abhidhamma Day

Aboakyer Festival

Acorn Feast

Adalbert of Prague, Saint's Day of St.

Adi Da Samrajashram, Anniversary of Adi Da's First Footstep on

Advent

African Methodist Quarterly Meeting Day

Agnes, Feast Day of St.

Agua, La Fiesta de

Ahoi Ashtami

Airing the Classics

Aizen Summer Festival

Aki Matsuri

Akshay Tritiiya

Akshay Tritiya (Jain)

Aldersgate Day

Ali ibn Abi Talib, Commemoration Days for

All Saints Day

All Souls Day

Alphabet Day

Alphonse de Ligouri, Saint's Day of St.

Amalaka Ekadashi

Amarnath Yatra

Ambuvachi

Amitabha's Birthday

Anant Chaturdashi

Anapanasati Day

Andrew, Saint's Day of St.

Anne, Feast Day of St.

Annunciation, Feast of the

Ansgar, Saint's Day of St.

Anthony of Padua, Saint's Day of St.

Aparecida, Feast of Our Lady of

Asalha Puja Day

Ascension Day

Ashokashtami

Ashura

Ash Wednesday

Assumption of the Virgin

Auditor's Day

Augustine of Canterbury, Saint's Day of St.

Augustine of Hippo, Saint's Day of St.

Aurobindo, Birth Anniversary of Sri

Avatar Adi Da Samraj's Birthday

Avataric Divine Self-Emergence, Day of

Ayyám-i-Há (Bahá'í Intercalary Days)

Báb, Festival of the Birth of the

Báb, Festival of the Declaration of the

Báb, Martyrdom of the
Babaji Commemoration Day
Baba's Day
Bahá'í Calendar and Rhythms of Worship
■ **Bahá'í Faith**
Bahá'í Fast
Bahá'u'lláh, Ascension of
Bahá'u'lláh, Festival of the Birth of
Balarama, Appearance Day of Lord
Baptism of the Lord, Feast of the
Bartholomew's Day, Saint
Basket Dance
Befana
Beltane
Benedict of Nursia, Saint's Day of St.
Benedict the African, Saint's Day of St.
Bhairava Ashtami
Bhaktisiddhanta Sarasvati Thakura, Appearance Day of
Bhaktivinoda Thakura, Appearance Day of
Bhishma Ashtami
Bhumanandaji Paramahansa, Birthday of Swami Guru
Bible Sunday
Black Christ, Festival of the
Black Nazarene Festival
Blajini, Easter of the
Blessing of the Fleet
Bodhi Day
Bodhidharma Day
Bok Kai Festival
Boniface of Germany, Saint's Day of St.
Boun Ok Phansa
Bridget, Saint's Day of St.
Brigid of Kildare, Saint's Day of St.
■ **Buddhism**
Buddhism—Cycle of Holidays
Buddhist Churches of America Founding Day
Burning of Judas
Butter Lamp Festival
Calendars, Religious
Cannabis Day
Casimir, Saint's Day of St.
Catherine of Siena, Saint's Day of St.
Celebrity Center International
Chair of St. Peter, Feast of the
Chaitra Purnima
Chandan Yatra
Chaturmas Vrat
Che Kung, Birthday of
Chichibu Yomatsuri
Children's Day
Chinese New Year's (Preliminary Festival)
Chinese New Year's Day
■ **Chinese Religion**
Chinese Religion—Annual Cycle of Festivals
Chinmayananda, Commemoration Days for
Chittirai Festival
Chokhor Duchen
Chongmyo Cherye
■ **Christianity**
Christmas
Christ the King, Feast of
Circumcision, Feast of the
Clement of Ohrid, Saint's Day of St.
Columba, Saint's Day of St.

Common Era Calendar
Common Prayer Day
Confucius, Anniversary of the Death of
Confucius's Birthday
Conversion of St. Paul, Feast of the
Corpus Christi, Feast of
Counting of the Omer
Covenant, Day of the
Cyprian, Saint's Day of St.
Cyril and Methodius, Saint's Day for Sts.
Czestochowa, Feast Day of Our Lady of
Dalai Lama's Birthday
Danavira Mela
Daruma Kuyo
Darwin Day
Dasain
Data Ganj Bakhsh Death Anniversary
Dattatreya Jayanti
Day of All Things
Days of Awe
Death of Jean-François Lefevre de la Barre
Dhan Teras
Dhyanyogi's Mahasamadhi
Dianetics, Anniversary of
Divine Holy Spirit Festival
Divine Mercy Sunday
Divino Rostro, Devotion to
Diwali
Diwali (Jain)
Doll Festival
Dominic, Saint's Day of St.
Dosojin Matsuri
Double Ninth Festival
Double Seventh Festival
Doukhobor Peace Day
Dragon Boat Festival
Duruthu Poya
Easter
Easter (Ethiopian Church)
Easter Monday
Eastern Orthodoxy—Liturgical Year
Ecclesia Gnostica—Liturgical Year
Elephant Festival
Elevation of the True Cross
Ember Days
Eostara
Epictetus the Presbyter and Astion, Saint's Day of Sts.
Epiphany
Eshinni-Kakushinni Memorial
Ethiopian Church—Liturgical Year
Eucharistic Congresses
Evtimiy of Bulgaria, Saint's Day of Patriarch
Expectation of the Birth of the Blessed Virgin Mary, Feast of
Fall Equinox
Fasinada (Montenegro)
Fast of Gedaliah
Fast of the First Born
Fatima, Feast Day of Our Lady of
Feast for the Three Days of the Writing of the Book of the Law
Festival of Light (Rosicrucian)
Festival of the Tooth
Festivus
Fiesta dos Tabuleiros
First Night of the Prophet and His Bride
First Salmon Rites

Florian, Saint's Day of St.
Flower Communion
Forgiveness, Feast of
Forty Martyrs' Day
Founders' Day (Salvation Army)
Founders' Day, the Church of Perfect Liberty
Francis Xavier, Saint's Day of St.
Fravardegan
Freethought Day
Gahambars
Ganesh Chaturthi
Ganga Dussehra
Gangaur
Gathemangal
Gaura Purnima
Genna
George, Feast Day of St.
Giant Lantern Festival
Gita Jayanti
God's Day
Good Friday
Good Remedy, Feast of Our Lady of
Govardhan Puja
Great Buddha Festival
Great Full Moon Festival (Korea)
Gregory the Great, Saint's Day of St.
Grotto Day
Guadalupe, Feast of Our Lady of
Guan Yin, Renunciation of
Guan Yin's Birthday
Guru Gobind Singh's Birthday
Guru Granth Sahib, Celebration of the
Guru Purnima
Gyana Panchami
Hadaka Matsuri
Haile Selassie I, Birthday of Emperor
Hajj
Hala Shashti
Halloween
Hana Matsuri
Hanukkah
Hanuman Jayanti
Harikuyo
Hari-Shayani Ekadashi
Haru Matsuri
Higan
■ **Hinduism**
Hinduism—Festivals and Holidays
Holi
Holy Days of Obligation
Holy Family, Feast of the
Holy Innocents' Day
Holy Maries, Festival of the (La Fête des Saintes Maries)
Holyrood or the Feast of the Triumph of the Holy Cross
Holy Week
Hoshi Matsuri
Hubbard, Birthday of L. Ron
HumanLight
Human Rights Day
Hyakujo Day Observance
Id al-Adha
Id al-Fitr
Image Not-Made-by-Hands, Feast of the
Imbolc
Immaculate Conception, Feast of the
Immaculate Heart of Mary, Feast of the
Indivisible Day

Indra Jatra
Ingersoll Day
I'n-Lon-Schka
International Association of Scientologists Anniversary
International Day of Prayer for the Persecuted Church
International Religious Freedom Day
Islam
Islam—Annual Festivals and Holy Days
Iwashimizu Matsuri
Jainism
Jainism—Cycle of Holidays
James the Greater, Feast Day of St.
Janaki Navami
Janardanji Paramahansa, Commemoration Days of Swami Guru
Janmashtami
Jhulan Yatra
Jizo Bon
Joan of Arc, Saint's Day of St.
Jogues, John de Brébeuf and Companions, Saint's Day of St. Isaac
John the Baptist, Beheading of
John the Baptist, Nativity of
John the Evangelist, Day of St.
Joseph, Feast Day of St.
Jubilee Year
Judaism
Judaism—Festivals of the Year
Juhannus
Kaijin Matsuri
Kamada Ekadashi
Kamakura Matsuri
Kanmiso-sai
Kartika Purnima
Kartika Purnima (Jain)
Kartika Snan
Karwa Chauth
Kataklysmos
Kathina Ceremony
Kaza-Matsuri
Kodomo no Hi
Kojagara
Koshogatsu
Ksitigarbha's Birthday
Kumbha Mela
Kwan Tai, Birthday of
Kyoto Gion Matsuri
Laba Festival
Lahiri Mahasaya, Commemoration Days for
Lammas
Lantern Festival (China)
Laozi, Birthday of
Laylat al-Mir'ag
Laylat al-Qadr
Laylat ul Bara'ah
Lazarus Saturday
Lent
Lha Bab Duchen
Lingka Woods Festival
Linji/Rinzai Day Observance
Liturgical Year—Western Christian
Lorenzo Ruiz, Saint's Day of St.
Losar
Lotus, Birthday of the
Lourdes, Feast Day of Our Lady of
Lucy, Saint's Day of St.
Madeleine, Fête de la
Magha Puja Day

Magha Purnima
Maghi
Mahashivaratri
Mahasthamaprapta's Birthday
Mahavir Jayanti
Maiden Voyage Anniversary
Makar Sankranti
Mani, Commemoration of the Prophet
Manjushri's Birthday
Mardi Gras
Margaret of Scotland, Saint's Day of St.
Martin de Porres, Saint's Day of St.
Martin Luther King Jr., Birthday of
Martinmas
Martyrdom of Guru Arjan
Martyrdom of Guru Tegh Bahadur
Mary—Liturgical Year of the Blessed Virgin
Mary Magdalene, Day of the Holy
Mauna Agyaras
Maundy Thursday
Mauni Amavasya
Mawlid an-Nabi
Mayan Calendar
Mazu Festival, Goddess
Medicine Buddha's Birthday
Meher Baba, Commemoration Days of
Meskal
Michaelmas
Mid-Autumn Festival
Mid-Pentecost, Feast of
Miracles, Feast of Our Lady of
Misa de Gallo
Mokshada Ekadashi
Monkey King, Birthday of the
Monlam, the Great Prayer Festival
Montségur Day
Most Holy Name of Mary, Feast of the
Most Precious Blood, Feast of the
Mother, Birthday of the
Mothering Sunday
Mother's Day
Mount Carmel, Feast Day of Our Lady of
Mudras
Muktananda, Birthday of Swami Paramahansa
Munmyo Ceremony
Nagapanchami
Nagasaki Kunchi
Nanak's Birthday, Guru
Narak Chaturdashi
Narasimha Jayanti
Narieli Purnima
National Bible Week
National Brotherhood Week
National Day
National Day of Prayer
National Day of Reason
National Founding Day (Scientology)
Native Establishment beyond East and West
Nativity of Mary
Natsu Matsuri
Navaratri
Navpad Oli
Naw-Rúz, Festival of
Nehan
Neri-kuyo
New Church Day
New Year's Day

New Year's Day (India)
New Year's Day (Jain)
New Year's Eve (Scientology)
Nichiren's Birthday
Nicholas, Saint's Day of St.
Nine Emperor Gods, Festival of the
Nineteen-Day Feast (Bahá'í)
Nino, Saint's Day of St.
Nirjala Ekadashi
Nityananda Trayodasi
Niwano, Nikkyo, Centennial of (2006)
Nossa Senhora dos Remédios, Pilgrimage of
Nowruz
Nyepi
Obon Festival(s)
Oeshiki
Olaf, Saint's Day of St.
Onam
Onbashira
One Great Hour of Sharing
Orthodoxy, Feast of
Osho (Rajneesh), Birthday of
Pak Tai, Birthday of
Palm Sunday
Parents Day
Parshurama Jayanti
Paryushana
Passover
Patotsav
Paush Dashami
Peace and Good Voyage, Feast of Our Lady of
Peñafrancia, Feast of Our Lady of
Penitentes
Pentecost
Perpetual Help, Feast of Our Lady of
Pesach
Peter and Paul, Saint's Day of Sts.
Peter Baptist and Companions, Saint's Day of St.
Peter Chanel, Saint's Day of St.
Peter Claver, Saint's Day of St.
Peter of Alcantara, Saint's Day of St.
Phang Lhabsol
Pilgrimage of Sainte Anne d'Auray
Pilgrimage of the Dew
Pitra Paksha
Ploughing Day
Pooram
Posadas, Las
Poson
Potlatch
Prabhupada, Appearance Day of A. C. Bhaktivedanta Swami
Prabhupada, Disappearance Day of A. C. Bhaktivedanta Swami
Prasadji Paramahansa, Birthday of Swami Guru
Presentation of Jesus in the Temple, Feast of the
Presentation of Mary, Feast of the
Procession de la Penitencia, La (Spain)
Procession of Penitents
Procession of the Cross
Procession of the Fujenti
Procession of the Holy Blood
Prompt Succor, Feast of Our Lady of
Pure Brightness Festival
Purim

Purnanandaji Paramahansa, Commemoration Day for Swami Guru
Putrada Ekadashi
Queenship of Mary, Feast of
Race Unity Day
Radhashtami
Raksha Bandhan
Ramadan
Ramakrishna, Birthday of Sri
Ramana Maharshi, Birthday of
Rama Navani
Ratha Yatra
Reformation Sunday
Religious Freedom Day
Riḍván, Festival of
Rishi Panchami
Rogation Days
Romeria of La Virgen de Valme
Rosary, Feast of Our Lady of the
Rose of Lima, Saint's Day of St.
Rosh Hashanah
Rukmini Ashtami
Rushi Pancham
Sacred Heart of Jesus, Feast of the
Sai Baba of Shirdi, Birthday of
Saint John Lateran, Feast of the Dedication of
Saint Patrick's Day
Saint Stephen's Day
Saint Stephen's Day (Hungary)
Saints (Roman Catholic Tradition)
Saints, Celebrating the Lives of (Protestant Tradition)
Saints, Veneration of (Roman Catholic Tradition)
Sakura Matsuri
Sakya Dawa Festival
Samantabadhara's Birthday
Samhain
Sanghamitta Day
Sankt Placidusfest
San Sebastian Day
Sarada Devi, Birthday of
Satchidananda, Birthday of Swami
Sava, Saint's Day of St.
Schneerson, Anniversary of the Death of Rabbi Menachem Mendal
Schutzengelfest
Schwenkfelder Thanksgiving
Scientology, Holidays of the Church of
Sea Org Day
Sechi Festival
Seijin no Hi
Seton, Saint's Day of Mother Elizabeth
Setsubun
Shankaracharya Jayanti
Sharad Purnima
Shavuot
Sheetala Ashtami
Shemini Atzeret/Simchat Torah
Shichi-Go-San
Shikinensengu
Shinran Shonin, Birthday of
■ **Shinto**
Shinto—Cycle of Holidays
Shravava Mela
Shuni-e (Omizutori)
Siddha Day
Sigd
Sivananda Saraswati, Birthday of Swami

Skanda Shashti
Snan Yatra
Solemnity of Mary, Feast of the
Songkran
Sophia, The Descent and Assumption of Holy
Sorrows, Feast of Our Lady of
Spring Dragon Festival
Spring Equinox (Thelema)
Spring Equinox (Vernal)
Stanislaus, Saint's Day of St.
Sukkot
Summer Solstice
Surya Shashti
Takayama Matsuri
Tam Kung Festival
Tatiana, Saint's Day of St.
Teej Festivals
Tejomayananda, Birthday of Swami
Templars, The Day of the Martyrdom of the Holy
Tenjin Matsuri
Tens of Thousands of Lanterns Ancestral Memorial Service
Thaipusam
Theophany
Thérèse of Lisieux, Saint's Day of St.
Third Prince, Birthday of the
Thomas Paine Day
Three Hierarchs, Day of the
Three Kings Day, Native American Pueblos
Timkat
Tirupati Brahmotsava Festival
Tisha B'Av
Tohji-Taisai
Transfiguration, Feast of the
Trinity Monday
Trinity Sunday
True Parents' Birthday
Tsagaan Sar
Tsong Khapa Anniversary
Tu B'Shevat
Tulsidas Jayanti
Ullam-bana
■ **Unbelief**
Unification Church, Holidays of the
Up Helly Aa
Uposattha Observance Day
Urs Festival
Vaikuntha Ekadashi
Vaitarani
Valentinus, Feast of the Holy
Valmiki Jayanti
Vamana Jayanti
Varaha Jayanti
Vartan's Day, St.
Vasant Panchami
Vassa
Vata Savitri
Virgen de los Angeles Day
Vishwakarma Puja
Visitation, Feast of the
Vivekananda, Birthday of Swami
Vladimir, Saint's Day of St.
Walpurgisnacht
Week of Prayer for Christian Unity
Wesak/Vesak
White Lotus Day
White Sunday

■ **Wicca/Neo-Paganism Liturgical Calendar**
Willibrord, Saint's Day of St.
Winter Solstice
World Communion Sunday
World Community Day
World Day of Prayer
World Humanist Day
World Invocation Day
World Peace and Prayer Day
World Peace Ceremony (Tibetan Buddhist)
World Religion Day
Yogananda, Birthday of Paramahansa
Yogananda, Mahasamadhi of Paramahansa
Yom HaAtzmaut
Yom HaShoah
Yom HaZikaron
Yom Kippur
Yom Yerushalayim (Jerusalem Day)
Yukteswar, Commemorative Days of Swami Sri
Yule
Zaccheus Sunday
Zarathustra, Commemorative Days of
Zartusht-no-diso
■ **Zoroastrianism**

L

Laba Festival

The Laba Festival is a Chinese celebration that seems to have its roots in an ancient harvest festival, held to celebrate a bumper crop in hopes of having another the following year. Over time, however, it evolved into a celebration of one's ancestors. The contemporary festival remains as a building block in the Chinese veneration of ancestors. In the fifth century CE, the government decreed the eighth day of the 12th lunar month (January in the Western calendar) as the day for the Laba Festival.

As Buddhism was transmitted and grew in China, it identified the eighth day of the 12th lunar month as the day that Gautama Buddha gained enlightenment sitting under the Bodhi Tree. The accompanying story told of how the Buddha had reached a point of discouragement and hunger in his practice. About to give up the pursuit, he encountered a shepherd girl who shared her porridge and rice with him. Revived and refreshed, he continued his meditation and eventually became enlightened.

Over succeeding centuries, the Buddhist and traditional Chinese celebrations merged, and however an individual thought of it, all participated in the essential actions of preparing, sharing, and eating porridge. By the 11th century, it became a national holiday. The Chinese ruler would give Laba porridge to their underlings and send rice and fruits to the Buddhist monasteries. All families would make porridge, share it with their ancestors and neighbors, and then share it with their gathered family. It would be a good sign when all had eaten their fill and there were leftovers.

The Laba porridge is made with eight (for luck) main ingredients (including beans and grains) and eight supplementary ingredients (for sweetness and flavor). Preparation of the food begins the day before. The offering of the food to the ancestors and the distribution to neighbors (and of course, the poor and needy) is done before noon on the eighth, and then the family gathers to partake in what can be, depending on the importance placed on preparation, a most delicious meal.

J. Gordon Melton

See also Chinese New Year's Day; Double Ninth Festival; Double Seventh Festival; Lantern Festival (China).

References

Guoliang, Gai. *Exploring Traditional Chinese Festivals in China.* Singapore: McGraw-Hill, 2009.

Latsch, Marie-Luise. *Traditional Chinese Festivals*. Singapore: Greaham Brash, 1984.
Liming, Wei. *Chinese Festivals: Traditions, Customs, and Rituals*. Hong Kong: China International Press, 2005.

Lahiri Mahasaya, Commemoration Days for (September 26 and 30)

Lahiri Mahasaya (1828–1895) was a 19th-century Indian spiritual teacher (guru) born as Shyama Charan Lahiri. As a young man, he married and took a position with the British government in the Military Engineering Department. He also began to pursue various yoga disciplines. In 1861, he encountered a mysterious yogi whom he came to know through some honorific titles as Mahavatar Babaji. This mysterious teacher initiated him into the secret practices of kriya yoga, a spiritual discipline that involves the awakening of the kundalini energy that is pictured as lying coiled at the base of the spine.

Following Babaji's instructions, Lahiri began to gather disciples and write books. Among those attracted to him was Sri Yukteswar Giri (1855–1936), who would pass the lineage to his student Paramahansa Yogananda (1893–1952). Yogananda would bring it to the United States early in the 20th century and become the founder of the Self-Realization Fellowship (SRF), a pioneering Hindu organization in the West.

As the SRF grew and developed worship centers in southern California, Yogananda instituted annual commemorations of those who had initiated and perpetuated the kriya yoga lineage that he had inherited. Two services were added to the movement's annual schedule relative to Lahiri Mahasaya—September 26, in commemoration of his mahasamadhi or death, and September 30, in remembrance of his birthday.

On each of these commemoration days, the centers of SRF will hold a special service, usually in the evening, to celebrate the life and teachings of Lahiri. The service includes chanting, readings of texts concerning Lahiri, and a liturgy. Attendees are asked to bring a flower and an offering to the commemoration service as symbols of their devotion and loyalty to the Fellowship and the SRF gurus. These commemorations have been passed to several groups that originated out of SRF such as the Ananda Church of Self-Realization.

J. Gordon Melton

See also Babaji Commemoration Day; Yogananda, Birthday of Paramahansa; Yogananda, Mahasamadhi of Paramahansa; Yukteswar, Commemorative Days of Swami Sri.

References

Satyananda Giri, Swami. *A Collection of Biographies of Four Kriya Yoga Gurus*. Lincoln, NB: iUniverse Inc., 2006.

Yogananda, Paramahansa. *Autobiography of a Yogi*. Los Angeles: Self-Realization Fellowship, 1971.

Lammas (August 1)

Lammas is a holiday celebrated by the modern Neo-Pagan and Wiccan community, those groups expressive of the contemporary revival of ancient pagan religion of Northern and Western Europe. The revival, largely developed in response to the effort of Gerald B. Gardner (1884–1964) in the 1950s, spread from England to various parts of Europe and across North America. Gardner proposed eight evenly spaced holidays anchored in the two solstices and equinoxes, with four additional days equally between them. Lammas, also called Lughnasadh, is held in late summer between the summer solstice and the fall equinox.

The Pagan festivals are related to the agricultural seasons, and Lammas is a corn festival, literally meaning loaf festival. It was designed to celebrate the first fruits from the corn that had been growing through the summer and the first bread baked from the freshly gathered ears. It would be a symbol of a coming fruitful harvest and thus herald a time of rejoicing. There would be food for the winter for man and beast, and a variety of products for the home. One additional product of the corn harvest would have been corn whisky, a necessary item for the harvest-time celebrations.

Lammas also has its negative side. It is a sign that the land that blossomed with new life and strength in the spring has given of that life to produce the food, and the life force is in a waning stage of its cycle. In olden times, this life force was identified with the king, and it would be a time for the king to sacrifice himself to the goddess for the life of the land. In modern times, of course, no such sacrifice is need, expected, or allowed, and many modern Pagans object to other associated activities of the season, such as fox hunting. Lammas is, however, related to the Irish Celtic deity Lugh, pictured as a legendary ancient king. He is seen as a warrior who possessed many supernatural weapons, a poet, and a historian, and numerous stories are told of his life and exploits. He is also said to have initiated a harvest fair in memory of his foster mother. Amid the Lammas celebration, many stories of Lugh are available for the modern bard to recount.

Modern Pagans also focus attention on the goddess as bountiful mother who is transitioning to Crone, and see in the harvest the continued transitions in the life cycle. Lammas would have been a time to reap the first fruits of the harvest, celebrate, and then return to complete the harvest—wheat, barley, and rye—and await the end of harvest celebration at Samhain, the end of the year and the death of the land. Today, Lammas is a time to pause and enjoy the pleasant summer, celebrate with fellow believers, and consider the changing times.

J. Gordon Melton

See also Beltane; Eostara; Fall Equinox; Imbolc; Samhain; Spring Equinox (Thelema); Spring Equinox (Vernal); Summer Solstice; Winter Solstice; Yule.

References

Benson, Christine. *Wiccan Holidays—A Celebration of the Wiccan Year: 365 Days in the Witches Year.* Southfield, MI: Equity Press, 2008.

Cabot, Laurie, with Jean Mills. *Celebrate the Earth: A Year of Holidays in the Pagan Tradition.* New York: Delta, 1994.

Crowley, Vivianne. *Principles of Paganism.* London: Thorsons, 1996.

Harvey, Graham. *Contemporary Paganism: Listening People, Speaking Earth.* New York: New York University Press, 1997.

Lantern Festival (China)

The Chinese Lantern Festival had its roots in the ancient past, possibly as early as the Shang dynasty, which came to an end around 1046 BCE. The festival occurs on the 15th day of the first lunar month. As the lunar months are calculated from new moon to new moon, the 15th day is coincidental with the full moon. Thus, the Lantern Festival celebrates the light of first full moon after the New Year celebration heralding the coming spring. At times, the New Year's spring festival would be stretched out for two weeks, with the Lantern Festival bringing it to a close. In a day before electricity, the festival celebrated the declining darkness of winter and the ability of the community to move about at night with human-made light. Lanterns were the popular mode of illumining the dark, and villagers threw their artistic skills into the making of highly decorative lanterns. In recent times, temples and social groups would hold contests for the most beautiful and interesting lanterns.

The Lantern Festival took on a religious connotation from the Taoist concept of three worlds (which was, in turn, rooted in Buddhist thought). The Lantern Festival celebrated the heavenly realm, while the later Double Seventh Festival celebrated the earth realm and the Double Ninth Festival the human realm. Another account, from the Han dynasty (202 BCE–220 CE) tied the festival to the North Star. The Lantern Festival honored Ti Yin, the god of the North Star, who was seen as the balanced embodiment of the two opposing universal principles of yin and yang. He never changes his position in the sky.

Over time, as the meaning of the Lantern Festival changed, its essence remained as a way of asserting authority over darkness and a time for the general public to demonstrate its artistic creativity with unique, comical, and beautiful lanterns. The festival has lost much of its purpose with the coming of electricity and continues largely as a time for leisurely frivolity often expressed with fireworks and lion dancing.

One custom has survived—the posing and answering of riddles. This began with scholars amusing their students and friends by hanging lanterns outside their homes on which they had written riddles. This action was later generalized into a popular custom of posing riddles as part of the broader celebration.

J. Gordon Melton

See also Double Ninth Festival; Double Seventh Festival; Laba Festival.

References

Guoliang, Gai. *Exploring Traditional Chinese Festivals in China.* Singapore: McGraw-Hill, 2009.

Kaulbach, B, and B. Proksch. *Arts and Culture in Taiwan.* Taipei: Southern Materials Center, 1984.

Latsch, Marie-Luise. *Traditional Chinese Festivals.* Singapore: Greaham Brash, 1984.

Liming, Wei. *Chinese Festivals: Traditions, Customs, and Rituals.* Hong Kong: China International Press, 2005.

Lanterns, Festival of (Korea). *See* Wesak/Vesak

Laozi, Birthday of

Taoism traces its beginning to Laozi (or Lao-tzu, in the older "Wade-Giles" system of transliteration), who according to tradition lived during the sixth century BCE. He is preeminently identified with the *Daodejing* (*Tao-te ching*), commonly translated as the "Classic of the Way and Virtue," a classic text whose ideas permeate Chinese culture. That being the case, it is unfortunate that little to nothing is known of Laozi's life, and many contemporary scholars even doubt his very existence as anything more than a creature of legend. On the other extreme, religious Taoists revere him as a deity.

The *Daodejing* teaches of the Tao or "Way" which is manifest in "virtue" (*de*), expressed as "naturalness" (*ziran*) and "nonaction" (*wuwei*). These basic concepts may be taken as espousing a mystical way or given a more ethical slant, the tension between the two accounting for many of the differences that divide Taoists.

The formation of organized religious Taoism in the second century CE traditions about Laozi began important in a religious context. The Tao was seen as a divine reality, and Laozi revered as the personification of it. Even earlier, during the Han dynasty (206 BCE–220 CE), a court historian named Sima Qian (c. 145–86 BCE) had written the *Shiji* (Records of the Historian) which included biographical reflections on Laozi. Then during the Tang dynasty (618–906 CE), the ruling Li family began to claim descent from the semidivine philosopher and today, Laozi's "birthday" is still celebrated in many parts of Asia.

Laozi, also known as Lao-tzu, is the founder of Taoism and credited with authoring the *Daodejing*. (Jupiterimages)

Laozi is remembered on the 15th day of the second lunar month in the Chinese traditional calendar (February–March on the Common Era calendar).

J. Gordon Melton

See also Chinese New Year's Day; Confucius's Birthday.

References

Bokenkamp, Stephen R. *Early Daoist Scriptures*. Berkeley: University of California Press, 1997.

Kohn, Livia, ed. *Daoism Handbook*. 2 vols. Leiden: Brill, 2000.

Pas, Julian F. *Historical Dictionary of Taoism*. Lanham, MD: Scarecrow Press, 1998.

Robinet, Isabelle. *Taoism: Growth of a Religion*. Stanford, CA: Stanford University Press, 1997.

Laylat al-Mir'ag

In the first verse of the 17th chapter of the Qur'an, reference is made to a journey taken by Muhammad:

> Glorified be He Who carried His servant by night from the Inviolable Place of Worship to the Far distant place of worship the neighborhood whereof We have blessed, that We might show him of Our tokens! Lo! He, only He, is the Hearer, the Seer. (Pickthal translation)

Toward the end of his earthly life, Muhammad is awakened from his sleep in the mosque at Mecca, mounts the horse known as Buraq (a mythical steed with the head of a woman), and rides to Jerusalem, where from the Temple Mount, he ascended into heaven accompanied by the angel Gabriel. While in heaven, he met the previous prophets—Adam, Joseph, Enoch, Abraham, Aaron, Moses, John the Baptist, and Jesus. While there, he came into the presence of Allah. Allah spoke the words that are now recited in the prayers repeated daily by the observant Muslim. The ascent is also important in substantiating Muslim claims to the Temple Mount in Jerusalem as its sacred space. Details of what occurred are elaborated upon in the Hadith (stories of Muhammad told by his companions), and an early biography of the Prophet by Ibn Ishaq (eighth century).

The ascension to heaven occurred around 620 in the Islamic month of Rahab, on the night of the 26th/27th. Many Muslims remember this event by attendance at the mosque, a period of self-examination and prayer, the reading of the Qur'an, and attention to the 12 commands given by God to Muhammad during his visit (and mentioned in the 17th chapter of the Qur'an). These commands are: Be a servant only to Allah; be kind to your parents; respect the rights of others; avoid spend thriftiness; do not kill your children (as a means of escaping poverty); do not commit adultery; do not kill; be kind to orphans; fulfill your promise; be fair in your dealings; do not be suspicious of others; and do not be arrogant.

James A. Beverley

See also Ashura; Data Ganj Bakhsh Death Anniversary; Hajj; Id al-Adha; Id al-Fitr; Islam—Annual Festivals and Holy Days; Laylat al-Qadr; Laylat ul Bara'ah; Mawlid an-Nabi; Ramadan; Urs Festival.

References

Algül, Hüseyin. *The Blessed Days and Nights of the Islamic Year.* Somerset, NJ: Light, 2005.

Busse, Heribert. "Jerusalem in the Story of Muhammad's Night Journey and Ascension." *Jerusalem Studies in Arabic and Islam* 14 (1991): 1–40.

Gruber, Christine, and Frederick Colby. *The Prophet's Ascension: Cross-Cultural Encounters with the Islamic Mi'raj Tales.* Bloomington: Indiana University Press, 2010.

Laylat al-Qadr

Laylat al-Qadr (Arabic), also known as Sab-e Qadr (Persian) or the Night of Destiny (or Power), is a Muslim holy night that occurs during the month of Ramadan. It is referenced in the Qur'an 97:1–3 (Pickthal translation):

1. Lo! We revealed it on the Night of Predestination.
2. Ah, what will convey unto thee what the Night of Power is!
3. The Night of Power is better than a thousand months.
4. The angels and the Spirit descend therein, by the permission of their Lord, with all decrees.
5. (The night is) Peace until the rising of the dawn.

Neither the Qur'an nor the collected sayings of Muhammad reveal the exact day upon which the Night of Destiny should be observed, but from the different references to it, the Sunni Muslims have generally concluded that it is the 27th day of Ramadan and the Shi'as that it is the 23rd.

This passage from the Qur'an is also been tied to the reception of the book by Muhammad. Here, early commentators disagreed. Some saw it as describing that Muhammad received the entire Qur'an at one time from angels delivering it to him. This perspective did not conform, however, to the accounts of Muhammad receiving the Qur'an gradually over a number of years. Commentators have reconciled these two views by suggesting that the angels took the text from its ultimate source and brought it to the lowest level of heaven as a total volume, but only gradually did the angel Gabriel reveal it to Muhammad.

Drawing on the various comments on this night, and its reference as a Night of Destiny, many Muslims see this night as the moment when Allah decrees each person's destiny for the year ahead. According to the Hadith, the collection of writings considered most holy next to the Qur'an, Allah will forgive the sins of all who engage in prayer and good deeds on this night.

Shi'a Muslims have additional reasons to observe this night, as they believe it to be the anniversary of both the birth of Muhammad's daughter Fatima (c. 605–633) and the day of the assassination of her brother Ali Ibn Abi Talib (d. 661).

Devout Muslims will go to the mosque on this night and spend it in prayer and listening to recitations from the Qur'an, in many cases staying up until dawn in this endeavor. In a lesser number of cases, given the inexactness acknowledged in identifying the day on which the night of Destiny or Power should be observed, some Muslims will go on a 10-day retreat that continues through the last 10 days of Ramadan.

James A. Beverley

See also Ashura; Data Ganj Bakhsh Death Anniversary; Hajj; Id al-Adha; Id al-Fitr; Islam—Annual Festivals and Holy Days; Laylat al-Mir'ag; Laylat ul Bara'ah; Mawlid an-Nabi; Ramadan; Urs Festival.

References

Algül, Hüseyin. *The Blessed Days and Nights of the Islamic Year.* Somerset, NJ: Light, 2005.

Al-Jibouri, Yasin T. *Fast of the Month of Ramadan: Philosophy and Ahkam.* Falls Church, VA: International Islamic Society of Virginia, 1994.

Majahid, Abdul Malik. "16 Things You Can Do on the Night of Power." Posted at http://www.soundvision.com/info/ramadan/10.16things.asp. Accessed July 15, 2010.

Maulana, Muhammad Ali. *The Religion of Islam: A Comprehensive Discussion of the Sources, Principles and Practices of Islam.* 6th ed. Lahore: Ahmadiyya Anjumun Isha'at Islam, 1990.

Laylat ul Bara'ah

Laylat ul Bara'ah, or the Night of Freedom from Fire, is a Muslim holy day observed on the 15th day of the Islamic month of Sha'ban. It is one of several days to celebrate the giving of the revelation of the Qur'an, and many commentators see it referred to in the Quran 44: 2–4.

> By the Scripture that maketh plain. Lo! We revealed it on a blessed night! Lo! We are ever warning! Whereon every wise command is made clear. (Pickthal translation)

This day is seen by most Muslims as the moment when the Qur'an was sent from heaven to the skies of this world in preparation for its revelation over a period of time to the Prophet Muhammad. The Night of Power, Laylat al-Qadr, was the beginning of the revelation of the Qur'an to Muhammad. It is also the day that Muhammad completed a process of asking for the ability to intercede for the nation. He asked on Sha'ban 13 and received the ability to intercede for a third of the nation, for another third on the 14th, and on the 15th, for all the nation.

On the night of Sha'ban 15, observant Muslims will attend the mosque, read or listen to readings from the Qur'an, and engage in activities appropriate to repentance and self-reform. Prayer on this night not only is conducive to personal reform, but benefits the whole community.

James A. Beverley

See also Ashura; Data Ganj Bakhsh Death Anniversary; Hajj; Id al-Adha; Id al-Fitr; Islam—Annual Festivals and Holy Days; Laylat al-Mir'ag; Laylat al-Qadr; Mawlid an-Nabi; Ramadan; Urs Festival.

References

Algül, Hüseyin. *The Blessed Days and Nights of the Islamic Year.* Somerset, NJ: The Light, 2005.

Lazarus Saturday

Although the New Testament character of Lazarus is well known throughout all Christian church bodies, he has attained a special place in the Eastern Orthodox churches, where a special day has been accorded to acknowledging him and his importance in the history of salvation. The story of Lazarus is recounted in the Gospel of John, where he is pictured as the brother of Mary and Martha, three siblings who had a close personal relationship with Jesus during his earthly life. Upon learning of Lazarus's death, it was noted that Jesus felt grief and that he wept. He was then challenged by the two sisters who knew of his healing powers. Upon arriving in Bethany, Jesus ordered:

> "Take away the stone."
>
> Martha, the sister of him that was dead, said to him, "Lord, by this time the body is decaying; for he has been dead four days."
>
> Jesus said unto her, "Said I not unto you, that, if you believed, you should see the glory of God?" So they took away the stone. And Jesus lifted up his eyes, and said, "Father, I thank You that You heard me. And I knew that

> You always hear me: but because of the multitude that stands around I said it, that they may believe that You did send me." And when he had thus spoken, he cried with a loud voice, "Lazarus, come forth."
>
> He that was dead came forth, bound hand and foot with grave-clothes; and his face was bound about with a napkin. Jesus said unto them, "Loose him, and let him go."
>
> Many therefore of the Jews, who came to Mary and beheld that which he did, believed on him. (11: 39–45)

This story is widely told as a demonstration of Jesus's power, messiahship, and divinity. Theologically, it was taken as a sign that God would resurrect the dead in the Last Days. In the Eastern Church liturgy, a day to celebrate the raising of Lazarus was inserted into the liturgical calendar on the Saturday before Palm Sunday. This important event has Jesus confirming the resurrection of humankind prior to the events of Holy Week and his own suffering, death, and resurrection.

Lazarus Saturday brings to an end the fast time of Lent a day early and has a unique status as the only day when a focused celebration of the resurrection is not on a Sunday.

The Eastern churches also have their own tradition as to what happened to Lazarus, who drops from the biblical story after it is noted that some officials in Jerusalem actually conspired to kill Lazarus—the implication being that he needed to move from Bethany. Tradition suggests that he moved to Cyprus, the city of Kittium (known today as Larnaca) and that when the Apostle Paul and his companion Barnabas arrived in Cyprus on their missionary tour, they consecrated Lazarus as the first bishop of Kittium. He is honored in the city with the diocesan cathedral dedicated to him. Western churches are generally unaware of this tradition.

J. Gordon Melton

See also Easter; Lent; Palm Sunday.

References

Esler, Philip Francis. *Lazarus, Mary and Martha: Social-Scientific Approaches to the Gospel of John*. Minneapolis, MN: Fortress Press, 2006.

North, Wendy E. S. *The Lazarus Story within the Johannine Tradition*. Sheffield, UK: Sheffield Academic Press, 2001.

Taylor, John W. *The Coming of the Saints: Imaginations and Studies in Early Church History and Tradition*. London: Methuen, 1906. Reprint ed. Whitefish, MT: Kessinger Publishing, 2006.

Lent

For six weeks prior to Easter, Christians have customarily undergone a time of penitential prayer, fasting, and almsgiving to prepare for the celebration of the resurrection of Jesus on Easter Sunday. This season of Lent originally was also a time of preparation for baptismal candidates and those separated from the Church who were rejoining the community.

In Latin, this season of the Christian year was called *Quadragesima*, referring to 40 days. With the shift to the vernacular in the Middle Ages, the word "Lent" replaced the Latin term. Lent originates from the Teutonic root for "long" and refers to spring, the time of the year when days lengthen.

Originating in the fourth century of the church, Lent spans 40 weekdays, reminiscent of the 40 days of temptation Jesus spent in the wilderness preparing for his ministry. In the Western church tradition, Lent begins on Ash Wednesday and ends on Holy Saturday, the last day of Holy Week before Easter Sunday. Since Sundays celebrate the resurrection of Jesus, the six Sundays that occur during Lent are not considered part of the 40 days of Lent, and are referred to as the Sundays "*in*" Lent. In the Eastern Orthodox tradition, the 40 days are calculated differently: the fast begins on Clean Monday, Sundays are included in the count, and it ends on the Friday before Palm Sunday.

Ash Wednesday, the seventh Wednesday before Easter Sunday begins Lent. The name refers to the ancient practice of drawing a cross of ashes in oil worshippers' foreheads to demonstrate humility before God and mourning for death caused by sin.

There are other holy days within the season of Lent: Clean Monday, the first day of Lent in Eastern Orthodox Christianity; the fifth Sunday of Lent, which begins Passiontide; Palm Sunday, the beginning of Holy Week; Spy Wednesday, recognizing the day Judas betrayed Jesus; Maundy Thursday, in commemoration of the Last Supper; and, Good Friday, commemorating Christ's crucifixion and burial.

Throughout Lent, observers fast, though not necessarily every day. Historically, there has been great divergence regarding the nature of the fast. However, traditionally, days of fasting include taking one meal a day, in the evening. Often fasters will abstain from meat and wine, and the common law of the Roman Catholic Church is to avoid meat, milk, cheese, and eggs. During Holy Week, or at least on Good Friday, it is common to restrict the diet to dry food, bread, salt, and vegetables. Consequently, the custom arose to give eggs for Easter to break the fast, thus leading to the concept of Easter eggs.

During Lent, the color purple or violet dominates the sanctuary to denote the pain and suffering of Jesus and the world under sin. As well, purple is also the color of royalty, befitting Jesus as the King. Some churches use gray for Ash Wednesday or for special days of fasting and prayer. Commonly, church traditions change the sanctuary colors to red for Maundy Thursday. As well, Good Friday and Holy Saturday may utilize black to symbolize the powers of sin and death overcome by the death of Jesus.

On the local level, Lent includes a number of lesser-known religious holidays such as Carling Sunday (Scotland). It is preceded in primarily Roman Catholic

The devil tempts Jesus on a mountaintop in this bible illustration of *The Temptation of Christ* by Gustave Doré in 1866. (Time Life Pictures/Getty Images)

areas by a spectrum of pre-Lenten celebrations (Carnival, Mardi Gras) often characterized by their overindulgence in things normally eschewed during the Lenten fast.

Kevin Quast

See also Ash Wednesday; Easter; Eastern Orthodoxy—Liturgical Year; Good Friday; Holy Week; Liturgical Year—Western Christian; Mardi Gras; Maundy Thursday; Palm Sunday.

References

Adam, Adolf. *The Liturgical Year: Its History and Its Meaning after the Reform of the Liturgy*. New York: Pueblo, 1981.

Regan, Patrick. "The Three Days and the Forty Days." *Worship* 54 (1980): 2–18.

Senn, Frank. *Christian Liturgy: Catholic and Evangelical*. Minneapolis, MN: Augsburg Fortress, 1997.

Stevenson, Kenneth. *Jerusalem Revisited: The Liturgical Meaning of Holy Week*. Washington, DC: Pastoral Press, 1988.

Stookey, Laurence Hull. *Calendar: Christ's Time for the Church*. Nashville, TN: Abingdon, 1996.

Talley, Thomas J. *The Origins of the Liturgical Year*. 2nd ed. Collegeville, MN: Liturgical Press, 1991.

Thurston, Herbert. "Lent." *The Catholic Encyclopedia*. Vol. 9. New York: Robert Appleton Company, 1910.

Lha Bab Duchen

Lha Bab Duchen is one of the Tibetan celebrations of the major events in the life of the Buddha, in this case the Buddha's descent from the heavens. Seven years after his enlightenment, during the rainy season when the monks had ceased to travel about the countryside, the Buddha reputedly visited his deceased mother in heaven (Tusita). Each evening for seven days, he preached the Abhidhamma to both his mother and the assembly of the heaven's divine and semidivine beings for whom he had developed some compassion. The preaching activity continued through the three months of the Indian rainy season.

Upon completion of his work, he sought permission of the king of the celestial realm to return to his work in the human realm. On hearing this, the king made available three stairways, one of silver, one of ruby, and one of gold, and the Buddha chose the middle (ruby) stairway. He descended in the accompaniment of devas who played musical instruments and fanned him as he descended to earth. Brahmins on the silver stairway held a white umbrella to shade the Buddha.

As he returned, those awaiting his return were able to see the heavenly beings who accompanied him and the celestial world they inhabited, while the heavenly beings saw the humans who had gathered to welcome the Buddha home.

Tibetan Buddhists believe that all virtue and non-virtue is multiplied 10 million times during this day. Thus, virtuous practice and activity on this day can enhance the believer's capacity both to deepen practice and to benefit others. Lha Bab Duchen falls on the 22nd day of the 9th lunar month on the Tibetan calendar (usually November on the Common Era calendar). Theravada Buddhists celebrate the Buddha's descent on Abhidhamma Day. There is a shrine at Sankasia, Uttar Pradesh, India, where the Buddha is believed by some to have first touched down when he made his descent.

J. Gordon Melton

See also Abhidhamma Day; Chokhor Duchen; Sakya Dawa Festival; Wesak/Vesak.

References

Bagchee, Moni. *Our Buddha.* Kuala Lumpur, Malaysia: Buddhist Missionary Society, 1999.

"Lha Bab Duchen: *Tendrel Nyesel* Practice. Posted at http://www.ironknot.org/event-iron-knot-lha-bab.php. Accessed July 15, 2010.

Thomas, E. J. *The Life of Buddha as Legend and History.* London: Routledge & Kegan Paul, 1956.

Lingka Woods Festival

The Lingka Woods Festival has been a high point of the summer season in Tibet, a land with a harsh winter followed by a spring in which it remains cold and windy. However, the summer is generally a pleasant time and Tibetans enjoy the outdoors, being outside in the lingka (various translated as garden, park, or forest) or camping in the countryside by a river being popular pastimes. The essence of the festival is the direct enjoyment of nature.

The 15th day (the full moon) of the fifth lunar month on the Tibetan calendar has been designated the World's Incense Burning Day, or the day of the Lingka Woods Festival. Buddhists trace the celebration to a legend concerning Padmasambhava, popularly known as Guru Rinpoche, or Precious Teacher, the eighth-century monk and missionary credited with introducing Buddhism into Tibet from India. It is said that Padmasambhava finally conquered all evil and completed that task in the fifth month of the Tibetan year.

In Lhasa, the day has been the occasion for Buddhists to gather for prayer at Jokhang Temple/Monastery to burn incense, hence its alternate designation as Incense Burning Day. They would also scatter glutinous rice cakes, salt, and *chhaang*, a beer-like beverage made from barley, symbolizing their prayers for peace and happiness. Those unable to go to Lhasa would go to their local temple.

The Lingka Woods Festival marks the midpoint of the Tibetan summer that begins with the Sakya Dawa Festival that celebrates the birth, enlightenment, and mahanirvana (death) of Gautama Buddha, and ends with the Bathing Festival in the eighth month (August). Outside of Tibet, the Lingka Woods Festival has lost much of its significance as a summer holiday.

J. Gordon Melton

See also Chokhor Duchen; Losar; Monlam, the Great Prayer Festival; Sakya Dawa Festival.

References

Osada, Yukiyasu, Gavin Allwright, and Atushi Kanamaru. *Mapping the Tibetan World*. Tokyo: Kotan Publishing, 2001.

Linji/Rinzai Day Observance (January 10)

Chinese Zen master Linji Yixuan (d. 866) began his study of Buddhism at an early age, finally settling with the Chan master Huángbo Xiyun (720–814). In 851, Linji moved to a temple in Hebei, China, which eventually assumed his name and became the dissemination point for the Linji form of Chan. Part of the larger community of meditative Buddhism, Linji Chan became most successful during the Sung dynasty (860–1279) and then was introduced to Japan in the 13th century.

Linji is remembered for his iconoclastic approach to Buddhism. He urged his students to free themselves from the binding influence of masters and to push doctrinal concepts aside, as they searched to discover their own individual true nature (or Buddha Nature). Zen is distinguished from other forms of Buddhism by its emphasis on meditation toward enlightenment, as opposed to the study of Buddhist sutras and other texts, or the Pure Land emphasis on repeating the name of Amida Buddha to reach the Western Paradise. Rinzai is distinguished from Soto Buddhism by the latter's use of word puzzles called koans, to assist the process of realizing enlightenment.

The remembrance of Linji has been perpetuated by the Rinzai groups in Japan and passed to their affiliated centers and independent Rinzai centers around the world. On Rinzai Day, Rinzai Zen Buddhists, never known for elaborate rituals or staged celebrations, commemorate the founder of their lineage with a special if relatively subdued ceremony through which practitioners acknowledge their gratitude for his teachings. These commemorations will be held wherever Rinzai Buddhists gather for their regular meditation sittings.

J. Gordon Melton

See also Bodhidharma Day; Hyakujo Day Observance.

References

Schloegl, Irmgard. *The Zen Teaching of Rinzai*. Berkeley, CA: Shambhala Publications, 1976.

Watson, Burton, trans. *The Zen Teachings of Master Lin-Chi: A Translation of the Lin-chi lu*. New York: Columbia University Press, 1999.

Welter, Albert. *The Linji Lu and the Creation of Chan Orthodoxy: The Development of Chan's Records of Sayings Literature*. New York: Oxford University Press, 2008.

Litha. *See* Summer Solstice

See Summer Solstice

Liturgical Year (Western Christian)

From as early as the second century CE, the Christian Church, following earlier Jewish tradition, has used the seasons of the year to mark sacred times. Around these times, it has established festivals and holidays set aside to worship God and mark special moments in salvation history. While Jewish celebration revolves around the Exodus from Egypt, the Christian Church year focuses on the life and ministry of Jesus.

The Christian calendar is organized around two major feasts: Christmas and Easter. Advent ushers in Christmas, and the season ends with the feast of Epiphany. Easter is preceded by Lent and leads to Pentecost. The periods of the year surrounding these two major seasons are known in the liturgical calendars as "Ordinary Time" and focus on various aspects of the Christian faith, particularly the mission of the church in the world.

The timing of all of the other moveable feasts in the Christian year revolves around Easter. The date of Easter itself is set according to a lunar cycle that changes annually. Consequently, seasons in the liturgical calendar vary in length and calendar dates. As well, the Eastern Orthodox tradition, for example, uses the revised Julian calendar (proposed in 1923 and adopted by most Orthodox churches over the next several decades) rather than the Common Era calendar, which has evolved over the last century from the Gregorian calendar. The major events of the Liturgical Year are as follows:

Advent (*First Sunday of Advent through December 24*): The beginning of the Christian Liturgical Year in Western churches, Advent marks the four Sundays before Christmas. The word "advent" comes from the Latin "adventus," which means "coming." This season just before Christmas is associated with the "coming" of Jesus as Messiah and marks a time of penitence, preparation, and anticipation.

Advent always contains four Sundays, beginning on the Sunday nearest to November 30 (the feast of Saint Andrew the Apostle). Consequently, Advent may begin as early as November 27 but always ends on December 24. If Christmas Eve is a Sunday, the last Sunday of Advent falls on that day, as Christmas Eve begins at sundown.

Christmas (*December 25 through to Epiphany*): The Christmas season begins with the celebration of the birth of Jesus, Christmas Day, or as a vigil on Christmas Eve. The *Feast* of Christmas lasts 12 days, until Epiphany. The Christmas season is a time of rejoicing in the Incarnation. Christmas probably originated in the Roman culture, which celebrated the winter solstice on December 25, the shortest day of the year. It was a Pagan celebration of the birth of "The Invincible Sun" as it began its annual journey back north from its southernmost point. It is likely that Christians began celebrating the birth of Jesus at this time as an alternative to the Pagan observance of the winter solstice.

Epiphany: Falling on January 6, Epiphany is a Christian feast that celebrates the revelation of God in human form in the person of Jesus Christ. In Greek, the word "epiphany" means "manifestation," and in Eastern Christian tradition, the event is called "Theophany," which means "manifestation of God." In the Eastern tradition, it falls on January 19. Roman Catholics will often celebrate it on the Sunday closest to January 6.

The Western observance commemorates the visitation of the Biblical Magi to the child Jesus, stressing the appearance of Jesus to the Gentiles. In many Hispanic and European churches, it is also known as "Three Kings Day." Eastern Christians include the baptism of Jesus in their celebration, highlighting Christ's revelation to the world as the Son of God.

Marking the 12th day of Christmas, Epiphany brings to an end the Advent and Christmas seasons.

Ordinary Time after the Baptism (Monday after the Epiphany through to Lent): This season focuses on the early life and childhood of Christ, and then on his public ministry.

Lent (*Ash Wednesday through Holy Saturday*): The season of Lent begins with Ash Wednesday and lasts until the final Saturday before Easter, Holy Saturday. It includes "Holy Week," the week before Easter. For six weeks preceding Easter, it is a time of penitential prayer, fasting, and almsgiving to prepare for the celebration of the resurrection of Jesus on Easter Sunday. This season of Lent originally was also of a time of preparation for baptismal candidates and those separated from the Church who were rejoining the community.

Holy Week, the last week of Lent, commemorates the last week of the earthly life of Jesus Christ. It covers the events of his triumphal entry into Jerusalem, the last supper, the arrest, and his death by crucifixion. Beginning with the sixth Sunday of Lent, Holy Week includes Palm Sunday, Spy Wednesday, Maundy Thursday, Good Friday, and Holy Saturday.

Easter (*Easter Vigil through Pentecost*): The high feast of the Christian church, Easter celebrates the resurrection of Jesus Christ. Even churches that typically do not follow the liturgical calendar observe Easter. Easter Sunday begins a 50-day season of "Eastertide" that includes Ascension Day and leads to Pentecost.

The Easter Vigil is celebrated after night falls on the evening before Easter Sunday. It incorporates a "new light" ceremony in the form of candle lighting and, often, an outdoor sunrise service. Typically, new converts to the church are baptized on Easter Sunday.

Six weeks into Easter, the church celebrates Ascension Day, a commemoration of the bodily ascension of Jesus into heaven. Until recently, this holy day fell on the sixth Thursday after Easter Sunday, the traditional 40 days between the resurrection and ascension in the biblical narrative. However, some Roman Catholic provinces have moved the celebration to the following Sunday to facilitate the obligation of the faithful to receive Mass as part of the Feast.

The last day of the Easter season is Pentecost, the festival that marks the birth of the Christian church by the power of the Holy Spirit as recorded in the biblical book of the Acts of the Apostles 2:1–41. The word "Pentecost" means "50th day" and is so named because it is celebrated 50 days after Easter Sunday.

Ordinary Time after Pentecost (*the day after Pentecost through the final day before Advent*): The second period of Ordinary Time is the longest liturgical season. Ordinary Time resumes after Pentecost and runs until the final Saturday before Advent. This period of Ordinary Time focuses on Christ's reign as King of kings, and on the age of the Church. It is meant to be a time of growth as the church meditates on the teachings of the Bible and their application to the Christian life. This is the present time between the age of the Apostles and the age of Christ's second coming. The final Sunday in Ordinary Time is the Feast of Christ the King; the Saturday after this feast is the final day of Ordinary Time. The cycle repeats itself with the beginning of Advent.

Kevin Quast

See also Advent; Ascension Day; Calendars, Religious; Christmas; Common Era Calendar; Easter; Epiphany; Holy Week; Lent; Pentecost.

References

Adam, Adolf. *The Liturgical Year: Its History and Its Meaning after the Reform of the Liturgy.* New York: Pueblo, 1981.

Bonneau, Normand. *Ritual Word, Paschal Shape.* Collegeville, MN: Liturgical Press, 1998.

Bradshaw, Paul F., and Lawrence A. Hoffman, eds. *Passover and Easter: Origin and History to Modern Times.* Notre Dame, IN: University of Notre Dame Press, 1999.

Fink, Peter E., ed. *The New Dictionary of Sacramental Worship.* Collegeville, MN: Liturgical Press, 1990.

Lathrop, Gordon W. *Holy People: A Liturgical Ecclesiology.* Minneapolis, MN: Fortress Press, 1999.

Martimort, Aime Georges, ed. *The Church at Prayer: An Introduction to the Liturgy.* Vol. 4, *The Liturgy and Time.* Collegeville, MN: Liturgical Press, 1986.

Nocent, Adrian. *The Liturgical Year.* Collegeville, MN: Liturgical Press. 1977.

Senn, Frank. *Christian Liturgy: Catholic and Evangelical.* Minneapolis, MN: Augsburg Fortress, 1997.

Stookey, Laurence Hull. *Calendar: Christ's Time for the Church.* Nashville, TN: Abingdon, 1996.

Taft, Robert. "Towards a Theology of the Christian Feast." In *Beyond East and West: Problems in Liturgical Understanding.* Washington, DC: Pastoral Press, 1984.

Talley, Thomas J. *The Origins of the Liturgical Year.* 2nd ed. Collegeville, MN: Liturgical Press, 1991.

West, Fitz. *Scripture and Memory: The Ecumenical Hermeneutic of the Three-Year Lectionaries*. Collegeville: Liturgical Press. 1997.

Lorenzo Ruiz, Saint's Day of St. (September 28)

Lorenzo Ruiz (c. 1600–1637), was born in Manila, Philippines, of a Chinese father and a Filipino mother. He was raised a Roman Catholic and received his education from the Dominicans, during which time he gained a reputation as a calligrapher. He married and had three children. He appeared to be heading for a relatively uneventful life as a devout lay member of the Binondo Roman Catholic Church in his hometown.

Then in 1636, his life was turned upside down when he was falsely accused of killing a member of the Spanish elite that ruled the Philippines at the time. Fearing for his life, he left his community bound for Japan on board a ship with some of his Dominican acquaintances. The ship made its way to Okinawa, but upon their disembarkation, Ruiz and all the Dominican brothers were arrested and taken to Nagasaki. Here, with no chance to defend themselves, they were tortured in various ways to force them to recant their faith. Several did, but Ruiz and those who remained faithful were finally taken to a spot execution and hung upside down. Two days later, on September 29, Ruiz died. His body was cremated and the remains thrown into the sea.

It would be several centuries before Ruiz's martyrdom was recognized by the church. Finally, as part of his visit to the Philippines, on February 18, 1981, Pope John Paul II (r. 1978–2005) held the first ceremony outside of Rome for the beatification of a future saint. Ruiz was canonized in Rome in ceremonies in 1987. He became the first Filipino whose saintly status was recognized by the church.

The international Filipino community began to promote devotion to San Lorenzo. In the United States, credit has been given to Fr. Erno Diaz, a priest in the New York in the 1980s who organized an annual Mass at Saint Patrick's Cathedral on his feast day, September 28. Fr. Diaz went on to become the director of Manhattan's the Chapel of San Lorenzo Ruiz, the first chapel in America formally designated for the use of Filipino Americans.

J. Gordon Melton

See also Forty Martyrs' Day.

References

Carunungan, Celso Al. *To Die a Thousand Deaths: A Novel on the Life and Times of Lorenzo Ruiz*. Manila: Social Studies Publications, 1980.

De la Pena, Ordanico, and Dani de la Pena. *The Birth of the Catholic Philippines in Asia*. Princeton, NJ: Xlibris Corporation, 2001.

Delgado, Antonio C. *The Making of the First Filipino Saint*. Manila: The Ala-Ala Foundation, 1982.

Villarroel, Fidel. *Lorenzo Ruiz, the Protomartyr of the Philippines, and His Companions*. Manila: Saint Paul Publications, 1979.

Losar

Losar, the Tibetan New Year, begins the annual cycle of religious celebrations for Tibetan Buddhists. As the Tibetans have a lunar calendar not unlike that of the Chinese, Losar is generally in the month of February on the Common Era calendar. It usually coincides with the Chinese New Year, but may vary by as much as a month. Every three to four years, a 13th month is added to the calendar to keep the lunar calendar in sync with the solar year. Months begin with a new moon.

Losar seems to have originated as an autumn festival celebrated at different times relative to the local harvest in pre-Buddhist times. Following the emergence of Buddhism in the eighth century CE and its subsequent growth to a position of religious dominance, it evolved into a Buddhist celebration. In the 13th century, Lama Drogon Choegyal Phagpa advocated the setting of the New Year on the present date. The date was subsequently accepted by the Buddhist leadership and became the dominant practice, though divergent Losar celebrations continued locally into the 20th century. Losar is celebrated in Tibet (now the Tibet Autonomous Region of the People's Republic of China), Bhutan, and among adherents of Tibetan Buddhism in India and worldwide. The second-largest group of Tibetans now resides in China apart from Tibet.

Losar begins on the first day of the first month and officially lasts for 15 days (new moon to full moon), though the major celebration occurs on the first three days. The celebration of Losar has been radically affected by the incorporation of Tibet into the People's Republic of China in the 1950s and the accompanying exile of the Dalai Lama, as an important site for the traditional celebration was the Potala Palace, the Dalai Lama's residence in Lhasa, Tibet.

Prior to the 1950s, Losar began in the early morning with the gathering of the monks at of Namgyal Monastery (a part of the Potala Palace), where a ritual would ensue honoring the Dharma protector Palden Lhamo, a goddess who is considered the protector of Tibet. The ceremony would be led by the Dalai Lama, and the leading lamas (considered reincarnated emanation of the various deities) and various government officials would join in the ceremony. Following the service, all would gather in the Excellence of Samsara and Nirvana halls to exchange New Year's greetings. Since the relocation of the Dalai Lama to Dharamsala, a new Namgyal Monastery has been constructed along with branches in various countries in which a Tibetan Buddhist community has developed. Namgyal Monastery in Ithaca, New York, for example, serves as the North American seat of the present Dalai Lama.

Following the assumption of authority by the Chinese in Tibet, the celebration of Losar fell as part of the general suppression of Tibetan Buddhism that included widespread destruction of the many monasteries and disbanding of monastic communities. In the years since the Cultural Revolution, Tibetan Buddhism has revived, and many of the monasteries have been rebuilt. Losar is now celebrated, though without the former ceremonies surrounding the person of the Dalai Lama. In the new century, the celebration has been somewhat politicized and muted as monks have used it to make statements about their wish that Tibet regain its independence and that the Dalai Lama be allowed to return. Currently, the majority of Tibetans (four million out of seven million) reside outside their homeland.

The festivities of the first day of Losar continued with the offering of well wishes to the Dalai Lama symbolized in small cakes made from roasted barley that would be presented by the abbots of the three major Tibetan monasteries and other high officials. Entertainment of the assembled dignitaries would include dancing performances and a lively theological debate by the monks, and a ceremony bidding farewell to the Dalai Lama as he retired for the evening to his residence. Various aspects of the traditional day may be repeated in Dharamsala, while dancing, theological discourses, and general festivities will occur in Tibetan Buddhist temples worldwide.

The second day of Losar was traditionally a more secular political occasion, recognizing that the Dalai Lama was also the head of state of Tibet. The day featured a gathering again in the Excellence of Samsara and Nirvana halls, where the Dalai Lama and various high religious officials received and exchanged greetings with the ambassadors of those countries bordering Tibet—China, India, Bhutan, Nepal, and Mongolia. This event now occurs in Dharamsala.

The third day of Losar launches two weeks of general festive activity with times for parties, special foods, and drink. While Tibetan Buddhism generally frowned upon the consumption of alcohol, two alcoholic drinks—*chhaang*, a beer-like beverage made from barley and *raksi*, a distilled beverage made from millet—were often consumed during this time.

While ceremonies and rituals are being enacted at the higher levels of the religious community, the majority of the people has their own festive activities. These usually begin on New Year's Eve with a cleansing and decoration of the home to drive away any accumulated evil influences. A variety of actions, including the use of fireworks, aim at driving off evil spirits. The first day of Losar is a time to light lamps (fueled with butter) to the deities and on the second day to begin visits to one's neighbors and relatives.

On the fourth day, the two weeks of Losar festivities begin to overlap with a second important Tibetan Buddhist holiday celebration, the week of Monlam, the Great Prayer Festival (see separate entry), and until the full moon, both holidays will be celebrated simultaneously. Losar culminates with the Butter Lamp Festival on the full moon (15th day of the first lunar month).

J. Gordon Melton

See also Butter Lamp Festival; Lingka Woods Festival; Monlam, the Great Prayer Festival; New Year's Day; Sakya Dawa Festival.

References

Kelly, Elizabeth. *Tibetan Cooking: Recipes for Daily Living, Celebration, and Ceremony.* Ithaca, NY: Snow Lion Publications, 2007.

Richardson, Hugh. *Ceremonies of the Lhasa Year.* Chicago: Serindia Publications, 1994.

Salden, Venerable. "The Story of Losar." Posted at http://www.buddhapia.com/tibet/newyear.html. Accessed March 15, 2010.

Lotus, Birthday of the

Amid their love of flowers in general, the Chinese single out the lotus for special consideration, with content for the honoring the flower with its own birthday celebration coming from all the Indian and Chinese lore that have allowed it a special place in both the religious and secular community. In Hinduism, out of which Buddhism sprang, the goddess Lakshmi emerged from a lotus that came from Vishnu's forehead, while Vishnu himself holds in his four hands a conch, a wheel, a mace, and a lotus. Enlightenment is often described as the opening of a lotus. While yogis sit in the lotus position, the Buddha is often depicted sitting on a lotus and/or grasping a lotus in his right hand.

The Chinese have designated the sixth moon of their lunar calendar the Lotus moon. They celebrate the birthday of the lotus on the 24th day of the sixth month. In Beijing, people will visit the Winter Palace to view the large pink lotuses blooming in the lakes. Ancient lore suggests the blooming lotus signifies that the Dragon-Prince has answered numerous prayers, especially those for sufficient rain to produce an abundant harvest.

Earlier in the year, the Chinese have celebrated a birthday for all flowers during the second lunar month on the 12th (in Beijing), or on the 15th elsewhere.

J. Gordon Melton

See also Flower Communion; Mother's Day; White Lotus Day.

References

Burkhardt, V. R. *Chinese Creeds and Customs.* Hong Kong: South China Morning Post, 1982.

"The Lotus: Flower of the Month of July." *School of the Seasons.* Posted at http://www.schooloftheseasons.com/flowers/lotus.html. Accessed March 15, 2010.

Lourdes, Feast Day of Our Lady of (February 11)

In 1858, Lourdes, a small town in southern France near the Spanish border, became the site of the most well-known modern apparition of the Blessed Virgin

Pilgrims come to view and pray at the shrine of Our Lady of Lourdes in Lourdes, France. (Bernadette Rigal-Cellard)

Mary. That year, a young girl named Bernadette Soubirous (1844–1879) had visions of the Virgin over a period of six months. The initial vision occurred on February 11, a few days after she had received her first communion at the local church, her village being a Roman Catholic community. As she searched for wood near a grotto, her attention was drawn to a moving rosebush, and shortly thereafter, what she would described as a young and beautiful woman appeared above the bush. Bernadette immediately dropped to her knees and began to pray and was joined by the woman. The woman then disappeared without saying anything.

The lady, eventually established to be the Virgin Mary, appeared on 18 subsequent occasions over the next six months. Bernadette first heard her speak during the third apparition. Her ninth appearance became a key event, as she instructed Bernadette to dig in the ground. Water would emerge, and she was to drink from and bathe in that water. At the spot she dug, a spring began to flow. That spring would then be seen as flowing with healing water available for all. The lady finally instructed Bernadette to see to the building of a chapel at the grotto.

The local priest, who saw Bernadette as naïve and somewhat ignorant, pressed her to inquire of the identity of the lady she was seeing and with whom she was conversing, especially after the request to build the chapel was made. Finally, in her last appearance, the lady identified herself as the Immaculate Conception. At the time, Catholic theologians of the day were pursuing a full inquiry into the viability of the concept of Immaculate Conception, the idea that the Virgin Mary had been born without original sin. (Among non-Catholics, the idea of the

Immaculate Conception is often confused with Jesus's birth from a virgin, rather than Mary's birth without sin.) That Bernadette came forward with this somewhat sophisticated idea served to convince the parish priest that she was, in fact, in contact with the Virgin.

The increasingly secularized French public and government officials did not accept Bernadette's claims as readily as the priest. Evan as Lourdes gained fame as a healing shrine, government officials occasionally moved against it and, at one point, closed it for several years. In 1862, however, the local bishop declared that the faithful were "justified in believing the reality of the apparition." A basilica church was built, and in 1873, the large pilgrimages were inaugurated. In 1876, the basilica was consecrated and the statue of Our Lady of Lourdes was crowned.

Meanwhile, Bernadette lived quietly and during this time suffered from a spectrum of illnesses. Her health having become an obstacle to her entrance into a religious order, the local bishop put pressure in the Sisters of Nevers, who eventually found a place for her at the Convent of Saint-Gildard. She lived only a short time and passed away on April 16, 1879, at the convent's infirmary.

After remaining on view for three days, her body was placed in a coffin on April 19 and it was sealed in the presence of a number of witnesses, and on May 30, 1879, the coffin was transferred to the convent's chapel. In 1909 the coffin was opened, and officials discovered that her body had remained uncorrupted. This discovery merely added to her reputation. To this day, her body remains on view at the Nevers chapel.

During Bernadette's stay at the convent, the spring continued to flow and the grotto of the apparitions became the source of a growing number of reported cures. Tens of thousands of reported cures were claimed, though only a small percentage passed the very strict standards of the medical bureau that was established to examine different cases and assemble records of those that appeared to be medically unexplainable.

In 1883, the foundation was laid for a second larger church that was finished and consecrated in 1901 as the Church of the Rosary. Pope Leo XIII (r. 1878–1903) authorized a special office and a Mass to commemorate the apparitions. Six years later, Pope Pius X (r. 1903–1914) extended the observance of this feast, which came to be observed on February 11, to the entire Church.

In 1933, Pope Pius XI (r. 1922–1939) canonized Bernadette. A new church, the Basilica of Saint Pius X, was dedicated by Angelo Cardinal Roncalli (1881–1963) then the Papal Nuncio to France and later known as Pope John XXIII. The innovative building, largely underground, can accommodate a crowd of 30,000.

In 1992, Pope John Paul II (r. 1978–2005) inaugurated the annual celebration of the World Day of the Sick, as a day to listen and reflect on the mystery of pain and illness. This new celebration was specifically tied to the commemoration of Our Lady of Lourdes on February 11 beginning in 1993.

J. Gordon Melton

See also Fatima, Feast Day of Our Lady of; Immaculate Conception, Feast of the; Rosary, Feast of Our Lady of the.

References

Carrel, Alexis. *The Voyage to Lourdes*. New York: Harper, 1950.

Crawford, Kerry. *Lourdes Today: A Pilgrimage to Mary's Grotto*. Ann Arbor, MI: Servant Books, 2008.

John Paul II, Pope. *Letter Instituting the World Day of the Sick*. May 13, 1992, n. 3.

McEachern, Patricia. *A Holy Life: The Writings of St. Bernadette of Lourdes*. Ft. Collins, CO: Ignatius Press, 2005.

Neame, Alan. *The Happening at Lourdes: The Sociology of the Grotto*. New York: Simon and Schuster, 1967.

Taylor, Therese. *Bernadette of Lourdes: Her Life, Death and Visions*. London: Burns & Oates, 2003.

Lucy, Saint's Day of St. (December 13)

The day of Saint Lucy, or Lucia's Day, is the annual commemoration of a young woman about whom almost nothing is known. Lucy (283–304) lived in Syracuse, a city of eastern Sicily, at the beginning of the fourth century. All that is known is that she turned back a suitor as she wished to remain a virgin, and in his disappointment, he accused her of being a Christian. She was then executed in the year 304 CE, during the widespread persecution of Christians by the emperor Diocletian, for her faith, and was subsequently remembered as a saint martyr.

Modern scholars relate Lucy's story to pre-Christian Paganism. Lucy's name means "light." There was a Sabine (central Italy) deity named Lucina who was the goddess of light. She is on occasion shown carrying a plate of cakes and a lamp. She was related to Juno, the wife of Jupiter, who as Juno Lucina was the goddess of childbirth. As the winter solstice came and went, Juno Lucina could be seen as the midwife of the miraculous sun-child born at Yule.

Drawing on the older account of Lucy's martyrdom, Christians embellished her story. They told of a suitor admiring her beautiful eyes. She responded by cutting them out and sending them to him with a request that she be left alone. She was subsequently been designated the patron saint of eye diseases and the blind. She would later be depicted, like Sabine, carrying a plate, but with eyeballs on it instead of cakes.

The celebration of Saint Lucy's Day is generally identified with the various Scandinavian countries—formerly Catholic, but now largely Protestant. It appears that the veneration of Lucy emerged in strength in the Middle Ages, and though it continued into the years of the Protestant Reformation in the early 16th century, it gradually died out. The celebration of the day was reborn in Sweden in the late 18th century by families in the area of Lake Vanern, north of Göteberg. What began as a family celebration evolved in the early 20th century into a more public celebration in which a young woman is selected to portray Lucia, dressed in a white robe with a wreath with candles in her hair and a selection of similarly clad attendants, each of whom carries a candle. While the girl chosen to portray Lucy is the center of attention, the modern celebrations offer roles for many young people and the procession around which the celebration is built but the start of a wide range of wintertime and Christmas-related activities.

The popularity of Saint Lucy's Day spread from Sweden to the neighboring Scandinavian countries and the diaspora communities in North America. It seems to have resonated with the desire for light through the long dark winter in far northern climes, where in the dead of winter, daylight may be cut to a few hours or less. It has been an especially popular occasion for school-based parties, a last time to celebrate with classmates before the Christmas holidays.

In many Catholic and Anglican countries, Saint Lucy's Day signaled the arrival of one of the four sets of Ember Days, solemn fast days on the following Wednesday, Friday, and Saturday.

J. Gordon Melton

See also Agnes, Feast Day of St.; Christmas; Ember Days; Florian, Saint's Day of St.; George, Feast Day of St.

References

Elkstrand, Florence. *Lucia, Child of Light: The History and Traditions of Sweden's Lucia Celebration*. Bloomington, MN: Skandisk, 2004.

Johnson, Ebba. *Lucia: A Legacy of the Past*. Minneapolis, MN: American Swedish Institute, 1969.

Kelly, Aidan, Peter Dresser, and Linda Ross. *Religious Holidays and Calendars*. Detroit, MI: Omnigraphics, 1993.

Lughnasad. *See* Lammas

Mabon. *See* Fall Equinox

Madeleine, Fête de la (July 22)

Among the many tales that became attached to Mary Magdalene is that soon after the crucifixion of Jesus, she joined a circle of Jesus's close followers and left Palestine in a boat that eventually arrived in Provence, France. Once landed, the groups separated and went to various locations to evangelize the country. Two of the female followers on the trip, Marie Jacobe, the sister of the Blessed Virgin Mary, and Marie Solomé, the mother of the apostles James and John, would settle in Provence near the landing site and work among the local people, including the Romany people. Their burial site would occasion the building of the Church of Notre Dame de la Mer, and the celebration of the Festival of the Holy Maries (La Fête des Saintes Maries) every May.

Meanwhile, Mary Magdalene, who is also identified as the Mary who is the sister of Martha and Lazarus (whom Jesus raised from the dead) of Bethany, as well as the woman taken in adultery (Luke 7:37) and thus in need of penitence, wandered from the landing spot eastward to the forest of the cave (la fôret de la Baume). Once in the forest, some angels took her to a cave/grotto on a hillside. Here, covered only by her long hair, with a psalm book and crucifix, she lived the next 33 years (symbolic of the 33 years of Jesus's life). She survived on a diet of roots and berries. Occasionally, she was visited with visions of the Virgin Mary.

As she approached her death, she was transported by angels to the oratory of Saint Maximin, the church founded by Saint Maximin, the first bishop of Aix-en-Provence and one of the people who fled to France from the Holy Land. In 1279, a sarcophagus with the reputed relics of Mary Magdalene (by this time considered a saint within the church), was found, and a short time later, a large basilica was constructed (1295–1296), together with the adjacent Dominican convent.

Since the 14th century, pilgrims have flocked to the church to view the relics, and today, a reliquary with Mary Magdalene's skull may be venerated in the basilica's crypt. They will also visit the cave where she lived for so many years. The largest number of visitors will arrive at the church and cave on July 22, the anniversary of Mary Magdalene's feast day.

Over the years, pilgrims have included a number of young couples who sought the saint's help in building a united marriage and young women seeking a mate.

J. Gordon Melton

See also Holy Maries, Festival of the (La Fête des Saintes Maries); Mary Magdalene, Day of the Holy.

References

Nantes, Georges de. "Did Saint Mary Magdalene Come to Provence?" *Catholic Counter-Reformation in the XXIst Century*. Posted at http://www.crc-internet.org/CCR/2009/82-Mary-Magdalene.php. Accessed March 15, 2010.

Spicer, Dorothy Gladys. *Festivals of Western Europe*. New York: H. W. Wilson Company, 1958.

Magha Puja Day

Magha Puja Day (or Sangha Day) is a Southeast Asian Buddhist celebration that recalls an occasion during the earthly life of Gautama Buddha. During the first year after he had received his enlightenment and following the lengthy retreat during the rainy season that had been held at Sarnath, the Buddha traveled to Rajagaha, the capital of the ancient Indian state of Magadha city. The mountain that rises above Rajagaha, known as Vulture Peak, would often be chosen by the Buddha as a spot from which to deliver his discourses, and the king gave the Buddha a park, the Bamboo Grove, as a place where his monks could stay. As many as 1,250 monks along with two of his principal disciples, Sariputta and Moggalana, visited him at the monastery in the Bamboo Grove. The Buddha took this occasion to deliver his discourse on the Vinaya (i.e., the rules governing the monastic order). Magha Puja Day is now celebrated on the full moon of the third lunar month on the Buddhist lunar calendar (late February or early March on the Common Era calendar).

On the day in question, the monks, all ordained by the Buddha, listened to a discourse in which he summarized his teachings around three principles—to do good, to abstain from evil actions, and to purify one's mind. While the year is unknown, it was said to have been delivered in the third lunar month under the full moon.

It is also unclear as to the manner in which Buddhists commemorated this event over the years. What is known is that a new celebration of it began in the 19th century under the Siamese king Rama IV (1804–1868) and expanded during the lengthy reign of his successor King Rama V (1853–1910). Rama IV ordered the celebration of the Magha Puja Ceremony at the famous Temple of the Emerald Buddha in Bangkok in 1851 and established it as an annual celebration. The image of the Emerald Buddha and its presence in Bangkok is tied directly to the emergence of the Thai royal family.

Under Rama V, the ceremony spread throughout the kingdom and to neighboring lands. On that day, believers go to a temple for various ceremonies and, in the evening, participate in a candlelit procession led by the monks under the full moon. The king of Thailand generally participates in the activities at the Emerald Buddha Temple.

Although Magha Puja Day is celebrated most extensively in Thailand, where it is a national holiday, the practice has spread throughout Southeast Asia and among Theravada communities in the West. One popular practice at Buddhist temples is the lighting of 1,200 candles in memory of those who gathered at the Bamboo Grove.

J. Gordon Melton

See also Abhidhamma Day; Asalha Puja Day.

References

Bagchee, Moni. *Our Buddha*. Kuala Lumpur, Malaysia: Buddhist Missionary Society, 1999.

Chadchaidee, Thanapol. *Essays on Thailand*. Bangkok: Thaichareunkanpem, 1994.

Roeder, Eric. "The Origin and Significance of the Emerald Buddha." *Explorations in Southeast Asian Studies* 3 (Fall 1999). Posted at http://www.hawaii.edu/cseas/pubs/explore/eric.html. Accessed March 15, 2010.

Magha Purnima

The day of the full moon during the Indian Hindu month of Magha (January–February on the Common Era calendar) is considered, as are all full moon days, an auspicious time for religious endeavors—a bath in one of the holy rivers, the engagement in meditation, japa yoga (repetition of mantras), fasting (*upvaas*), or doing meritorious deeds. Each purnima has a distinct emphasis, however, and thus activity around it for observers varies. Guru Purnima is, for example, a time to remember one particular ancient guru, Bhagwan Ved Vyas, and also to pay homage to one's own contemporary religious teacher.

On Magha Purnima day, believers pay special homage to one's favorite deity, possibly with a visit to their temple to make an offering. For Saivite Hindus, it is a day to worship the goddess Parvati, the wife of Shiva and/or the deity Bruhaspati (or Brahmanaspati) He is also known as Deva-guru, as he is the teacher of the Devas, one set of deities in Hindu mythology. Shiva granted him this position in the hierarchy of deities.

While Magha Purnima may be observed at most any temple, its celebration is more emphasized in Tamil-speaking areas of the country (and among Tamil people now scattered around the globe), Magha Purnima is celebrated as Teppotsavam, the float festival. Its celebration is centered on the large famous Saivite Meenakshi Sundareshvarar temple at Madurai. This two-millennium-old temple is dedicated to the goddess Meenakshi (a manifestation of Parvati) and Shiva as the beautiful Lord (Sundareshvarar). On Magha Purnima, the statues of Meenakshi and Lord Sundareshvarar are taken in procession to the nearby Lake Teppakolam. Once there, the idols are seated on a small, elaborately decorated boat which then becomes the focus of worship.

Teppotsavam originated in the 17th century when the local ruler, King Thirumala Nayaga, built the lake to accompany his new palace. In the middle of the lake, he built a palace to Ganesh, the son of Parvati. His birthday was Magha Purnima (or Thai Purnima, as the full moon day of the Tamil calendar is called in Thai). He began holding the Teppotsavam festival as a means of celebrating his new palace and his birthday. Also called Thaipusam, it continues to be celebrated by Tamil communities around the world, and most elaborately in Singapore and Malaysia.

Magha Purnima also is celebrated in a noteworthy manner at the Kateel Durga Parameshwari Temple near Mangalore in Karnataka, where the goddess Durga is the center of attention. This ancient temple is located on the banks of the River Nandini and Magha Purnima is observed as the anniversary of the river's descent from the heavens.

Some women also celebrate Magha Purnima as Dattatreya Jayanti.

Constance A. Jones

See also Dattatreya Jayanti; Guru Purnima; Thaipusam; Vaitarani.

References

Fuller, Chris. *A Priesthood Renewed: Modernity and Traditionalism in a South Indian Temple*. Princeton, NJ: Princeton University Press, 2003.

Harman, William P. *The Sacred Marriage of a Hindu Goddess*. Bloomington: Indiana University Press, 1989.

"Magha Purnima or Maha Maghi—Importance and Spiritual Significance." *Hindupad—Everything about Hinduism*. Posted at http://hindupad.com/tag/magh-purnima/. Accessed April 15, 2010.

Maghi

Maghi, a holiday for Sikhs, commemorates the martyrdom of the Chali Mukte, or Forty Immortals. The remembered incident occurred on December 29, 1705. Today, using the new Sikh Nanashahi calendar, the event is celebrated annually on January 13.

The founding of the Khalsa, the Sikh military order, by Guru Gobind Singh had alerted the Mughal (Muslim) rulers who controlled the Punjab at the time of the growing strength of the Sikhs and the correlative power of their leader. The Hindu leadership also felt threatened. The initial attempts to suppress the Khalsa were unsuccessful. Much of 1705 was spent fending off the much larger Muslim forces and found the Sikhs in what amounted to a strategic retreat. In December, Gobind Singh was visited by a group of 40 Punjabi Sikhs. During their visit, he received word of the imminent approach of a Mughal army led by Wazir Khan. The 40 decided that they could not at that moment support him and they moved away, taking a position by the side of a small body of water. As the army became visible, however, they reassessed their situation and turned to face the oncoming force. By sunset, all 40 were dead or seriously injured, and the Mughal forces retreated. Guru Gobind Singh blessed them as *muktas*, or emancipated ones, and changed the name of the place to Muktsar in their honor.

The largest celebration of Maghi is at Muktsar, where an annual fair is held. Around the world, however, Sikhs visit their *gurdwaras* for *kirtan* (hymns), stories of the martyrs, and an end-to-end recital of the holy Guru Granth Sahib, the Sikh holy book.

Maghi is celebrated on the first day of the month of Magh in the Hindu lunar calendar. It follows on the heels of the Hindu midwinter Lohri festival when bonfires are lit in Hindu fields and yards. The next morning Hindus see as an auspicious occasion to go for a brief swim in a local river or pond.

J. Gordon Melton

See also Calendars, Religious; Guru Gobind Singh's Birthday; Guru Granth Sahib, Celebration of the; Makar Sankrati; Martyrdom of Guru Tegh Bahadur.

References

Kapoor, Sukhbor Sing. *Sikh Festivals*. Vero Beach, FL: Rourke Publishing Group, 1989.

Singh, Bhagat Lakeshman. *Short Sketch of the Life and Work of Guru Govind Singh, the Tenth and Last Guru*. Ottawa, Ontario, Canada: Laurier Books, 1995.

Mahashivaratri

On the 14th day of each month of the Hindu lunar calendar, the god Shiva (or Siva), one of the three major deities of the Hindu pantheon, is acknowledged, and the day is called Sivaratri. However, the 14th day of the Hindu month of Magha is designated as Mahashivaratri, and became a national Hindu holiday celebrated throughout India and the Indian diaspora. It is a solemn occasion in which leaves of the Bael tree, believed to have medicinal value, are offered to Lord Shiva, and people fast and engage in an all-night vigil.

Mahashivaratri recalls an old story of the Asuras (power-hungry demons) and their half-brothers, the gods. The demons had much power, but because of their lack of piety—they neglected the making of sacrifices and did not visit holy places—they did not acquire great powers within themselves. Meanwhile, the gods made sacrifices, dealt truthfully with each other, visited holy places, and thus increased in power within themselves.

Both the Gods and the Asuras knew that they could gain the Amrit, the Water of Life, if they churned up the Ocean of Milk that encircled their world. With the mountain Mandara for a churning pole and the giant serpent Vasuki for a churning rope, the gods and the Asuras churned the Ocean of Milk. As they churned, Vasuki spat venom from each of his many heads. The venom broke the rocks around the

Festival participants stay awake through the night in a vigil to honor the Hindu god Shiva. (*Hinduism Today* Magazine)

ocean, creating openings for the ocean to flow over creation, threatening destruction to the worlds of both gods and men.

At that point, Shiva stepped forward, gathered the venom in a cup, and drank it. His wife Parvati, fearing for his life, grabbed his throat so the poison would not enter his stomach. And the burn on his throat is still seen to this day as a dark blue marking. His action, however, saved creation and allowed the gods to gain more powers than the demons.

As the churning continued, wondrous things emerged from the primordial Milk Ocean. Surabhi, the wish-fulfilling cow, came forth. Shri, the goddess of prosperity and fortune, and Dhanvantari, the physician of the gods, came forth. Then, the Kaustubha gem that always adorns Vishnu's chest emerged. Finally, the nectar of immortality appeared, and knowing that the demons would want to seize the nectar of immortality, Vishnu took the form of the enchantress Mohini. While the demons were mesmerized with her beauty, she served the nectar to the gods alone. Thus, only the gods gained immortality, and when the demons attacked they were routed and the world was once again in the hands of the gods.

Since that time, Shiva dwells in woodland filled with flowers. He keeps near him a spear with which he will destroy the worlds at the end of an age, a bow, a battle-axe, and a trident. At one point, his wife Umā covered his eyes with her hands. As a result, the world sunk into darkness. Again to save the world, Shiva developed a third eye on his forehead. When he opened that eye, the light returned to the world. But Shiva's throat remains blue from the venom that he drank.

Mahashivaratri is unique as the major Hindu celebration not accompanied by revelry and gaiety. It is rather a solemn event that emphasizes restraint and vows of forgiveness, truth telling, and noninjury to others that must be kept for the full 24 hours. Fasting and staying awake to worship Shiva during the entire night fill the hours of observance. One is to recite the mantra of Shiva, *om namah shivaya*, and prayers for forgiveness during the evening vigil. If the rites are performed faithfully, one is rewarded with worldly success and the heavenly realm of Shiva.

Constance A. Jones

See also Ashokashtami; Chaitra Purnima; Navaratri.

References

Harshananda, Swami. *Hindu Festivals and Sacred Days*. Bangalore: Ramakrishna Math, 1994.

Mukuncharandas, Sadhu. *Hindu Festivals (Origin, Sentiments and Rituals)*. Amdavad, India: Swaminarayan Aksharpith, 2005.

Sharma, Nath. *Festivals of India*. New Delhi: Abhinav Publications, 1978.

Welbon, Guy, and Glenn Yocum, eds. *Religious Festivals in South India and Sri Lanka*. Delhi: Manohar, 1982.

Mahasthamaprapta's Birthday

Mahasthamaprapta (Bodhisattva Great Power, known in Japan as Seishi Bosatsu) is a Mahayana Buddhist bodhisattva best known within the Pure Land Buddhist tradition as a close associate of Amitabha and the Western Paradise. She is most often depicted sitting or standing beside Amitabha, along with Avalokitesvara (Guan Yin). This popular group is known as the Three Saints of the Western Paradise. Mahasthamaprapta's halo of wisdom permeates all creation. She is often seen in feminine form, and recognized by the water pitcher on her crown and the lotus bud in her hand. The lotus bud is meant to be used to guide the elect to the Pure Land.

In the *Surangama Sutra*, he is pictured as praising Amitabha. He notes that in the remote past, he was taught by a Buddha associated with Amitabha, called the called the Buddha Whose Light Surpassed that of the Sun and Moon, to call upon the name of Amitabha, which led to realizing Samadhi (the meditative state in which the mind is totally concentrated and achieves complete bliss). He ends his brief discourse by declaring that he will "help all living beings of this world to control their thoughts by repeating the Buddha's name so that they can reach the Pure Land. As Buddha now asks about the best means of perfection, I hold that nothing can surpass the perfect control of the six senses with continuous pure thoughts in order to realize Samadhi."

Mahasthamaprapta's birthday is celebrated on the 13th day of the seventh month in the Chinese lunar calendar, just two days before the Ullam-bana Festival. In Japan, it is held on July 13. Japanese Pure Land practitioners make note of the fact that Shinran (1173–1263), the founder of the larger Pure Land group, had a vision of Mahasthamaprapta whom he identified with Honen (1133–1212), the founder of Pure Land Buddhism in Japan and Shinran's teacher.

J. Gordon Melton

See also Amitabha's Birthday; Guan Yin's Birthday; Ksitigarbha's Birthday; Manjushri's Birthday; Samantabadhara's Birthday, Shinran Shonin, Birthday of; Ullam-bana.

References

"The Bodhisattva That Shinran Knew in Person." The Way of Shinshu Buddhism. Posted at http://www.shinranwasan.info/jw19.htm. Accessed May 15, 2009.

Boheng, Wu, and Cai Zhuozhi. *100 Buddhas in Chinese Buddhism*. Translated by Mu Xin and Yan Zhi. Singapore: Asiapac books, 1997.

"The Gentility of the Dharma." The Way of Shinshu Buddhism. Posted at http://www.shinranwasan.info/jw118.htm. Accessed May 15, 2009.

The Seeker's Glossary of Buddhism. New York: Sutra Translation Committee of the United States and Canada, 1998.

Vessantara. *Meeting the Buddhas: A Guide to Buddhas, Bodhisattvas, and Tantric Deities*. Birmingham, UK: Windhorse Publications, 1998.

Mahavir Jayanti

Mahavira, the founder of Jainism, is generally seen as living between 599 and 527 BCE, while the Jain scriptures place his birth as having occurred on the 13th day of the waning moon of the Hindu month of Chaitra (March–April of the Common Era calendar). Mahavira was the son of Siddhartha of the Jnatri clan and Trishala, the sister of the local king. They named him Vardhamana, or "He who brings prosperity."

The two main Jain groups disagree on details of his life. They agree that his parents were followers of the earlier Jain Tirthankara Parshvanatha and that Mahavira had an aversion to worldly matters from an early age. The Shvetambaras and Digambaras, however, disagree about his pre-renunciation life. The Shvetambaras believe he married a princess called Yashoda and fathered a daughter called Priyadarshana. The Digambaras believe that Mahavira never married.

When Mahavira was 30 years of age, he renounced the world. The Digambaras suggest that he removed all his clothes, pulled out all his hair in five bunches, and became a naked ascetic. The Shvetambaras largely agree, but suggest that he kept on his small loincloth, which he wore until it fell from him. He then lived as a

Jain devotees watch a dancer as they celebrate the anniversary of the birth of Lord Mahavira in Allahabad, India. (AP/Wide World Photos)

naked or "sky clad" mendicant. He began a life of wandering, often fasting and ignoring bodily pains or pleasures. Digambaras believe he observed a vow of silence for 12 years. The Shvetambaras believe that the ascetic Makkhali Gosala asked to become his disciple. They were companions for a while but eventually parted ways on less than cordial terms.

After 12 years of austerities, Mahavira attained complete enlightenment and became the 24th and final Tirthankara (saint) of this era. Though he made no effort to create it, the Jain community began to form around him. He lived another 30 years and traveled widely throughout India. He then entered the afterlife, where he exists now as an arihant in a state of unlimited consciousness and eternal bliss.

Mahavir Jayanti commemorates the birth, and on this day Jains gather together to focus upon him and his message. This commemoration also falls in the midst of the observance of Navpad Oli and its time of meditation upon the spectrum of Jain leadership, Mahavira being an arihant of the first order. Thus while keeping the fast and meditational intent of Navpad Oli, the story of Mahavira is added. The statue in the temple of Mahavira will be ceremonially bathed (abhishek) and if a moveable statue is present, it will be rocked in a cradle. In many places, especially in India, the statue may also be processed through the streets of the community around the temple. In some states in India, such as Gujarat, where Jains are especially concentrated, this day is a public holiday. Many people will travel to the Jain sacred sites in Gujarat on this day.

J. Gordon Melton

See also Akshay Tritiya (Jain); Diwali; Gyana Panchami; Kartika Purnima; Mauna Agyaras; Navpad Oli; New Year's Day (Jain); Paryushana; Paush Dashami.

References

Dundas, Paul. *The Jains*. London: Routledge, 1992.

Jaini, P. S. *The Jaina Path of Purification*. Delhi: Motilal Banarsidass, 1990.

Singh, Narendra K., ed. *Encyclopedia of Jainism*. 30 vols. New Delhi: Anmol, 2001.

Wiley, Kristi L. *Historical Dictionary of Jainism*. Lanham, MD: Rowman & Littlefield, 2004.

Maiden Voyage Anniversary (June 6)

Scientology is a religion that shares its teachings with members in progressive stages as they master more introductory and intermediate levels of beliefs and practices. The very highest levels of instruction (called OT VIII) are presented to the more advanced members aboard a luxury liner owned by the church and docked in the Caribbean nation of Curaçao. The maiden voyage of that ship, the *Freewinds*, began and the release of the materials for OT VIII occurred on June 6, 1988. The OT (or Operating Thetan) levels represent the highest teachings of Scientology.

Scientology is organized as a Western Esoteric religion. It teaches that humans are essentially not their body or mind, but their spirit (the Thetan), which has been trapped in the body due to its forgetfulness of its true nature. Scientology teaches people about the true nature of the self—body, mind, and spirit—and offers instructions on how to return the mind to full functionality, how the spirit may be freed from the many aberrations (called *engrams*) that it has accumulated over the eons of multiple embodiments, and how the Thetan may be freed to develop its full potential. The early stages of Scientology attempt to rid the individual of the effects of the reactive mind (which acts without consciousness or thinking), and the early OT levels focus upon ridding the self of accumulated engrams. OT VIII is the first level to concentrate on developing the individual Thetan's positive abilities (as opposed to simply removing obstacles to development). Instructions for OT VIII (the first of a set of OT levels yet to be released) are currently offered only on the *Freewinds*.

One must have finished the work for OT VII before proceeding to OT VIII, and only those who have finished OT VIII may deliver the materials to the new students of that level. These individuals form the elite and dedicated core of Church of Scientology members. Only they are invited aboard the *Freewinds*, and only on the *Freewinds* are OT VIII and the related courses offered. Annually, graduates of the OT VIII courses gather in Curaçao for a four-day event to celebrate the first voyage of the *Freewinds*, the release of OT VIII, and to hear about and discuss at the highest levels the international development and future of the Church of Scientology and its outreach into the world.

J. Gordon Melton

See also Hubbard, Birthday of L. Ron; Scientology, Holidays of the Church of.

References

What Is Scientology? Los Angeles: Bridge Publications, 1998.

Makar Sankranti (January 14)

Makar Sankranti is a festival held across India, under a variety of names, to honor the god of the sun, Surya. Though often relegated to a secondary position relative to the three prominent Hindu deities—Brahma, Vishnu, and Shiva—Surya was a key figure in the ancient Hindu texts, the Vedas, and is the subject of one of the most repeated texts of Hindu liturgy, the Gayatri Mantra. Many devout Hindus chant this mantra daily as part of their morning rituals.

Makar Sankranti also heralds the end of winter and the arrival of spring throughout the Northern Hemisphere. Through the next six months, called the Uttarayana period, the days will become longer and warmer, and the whole period is considered an auspicious time. The day is also tied to the just-celebrated Bhishma Astami, which remembered the death of the hero Bhishma from the ancient Hindu epic the *Mahabharata*, who chose to die just as the Uttarayana period began.

Makar Sankranti is observed in the month of Magha as the sun enters Capricorn (on or near January 14 on the Common Era calendar). Being a solar date, it will vary from year to year on the Hindu lunar calendar. It is also celebrated as Uttarayana Punyakalam, Pongal (in Tamil Nadu), and Pedda Panduga (in Andhra Pradesh).

A variety of stories are told of Surya, which have implications for observance of this day(s). The sun god, for example, had a number of children, among them the Lord Shani, one the nine primary celestial beings in Hindu astrology; Shani is identified with planet Saturn. When Shanti was born, it is said, an eclipse of the sun occurred. It is also said that Surya and Shani have their differences, but always on Makar Sankranti, Surya visits with Shanti—thus should fathers visit with their sons. Food, especially sweets, will be prepared using *til* (sesame seed oil), which is valued for its stickiness or binding quality. Thus, the sweets that people will give those close to them are a symbol of being bound together, whatever differences might arise.

Makar Sankranti is also fraught with implications for the early phases of the agricultural cycle. It is a time to pray for a prosperous growing season and a good future harvest, and a time to bathe one's cows, so essential to all aspects of agricultural production. It is a time to remember ancestors and, in the evenings, to celebrate around bonfires.

Hindu women draw patterns on the ground using rice flour as a form of prayer during Makar Sankranti. (*Hinduism Today* Magazine)

The largest gathering for Makar Sankranti is on Sager Island in West Bengal at the point the Hooghly River, a branch of the Ganges as it spreads out approaching the Indian Ocean and meets the Bay of Bengal. Each January, several hundred thousand pilgrims gather on the island for the beginning of spring. Makar Sankranti occurs in the middle of the lengthy Kumbha Mela and Magh Mela celebrations and is a high point within them.

Kite flying has become a popular activity in India, and for the more secular-minded, it has become the dominant aspect of this day. The city of Delhi holds an annual Kite Flying Day festival on January 14, and the celebration has spread across the country.

Constance A. Jones

See also Kumbha Mela; Surya Shashti.

References

Kelly, Aidan, Peter Dresser, and Linda Ross. *Religious Holidays and Calendars*. Detroit, MI: Omnigraphics, 1993.

Rajendran, Abhilash. "What Is Makar Sankranti?" Hindu Blog. Posted at http://www.hindu-blog.com/2007/01/what-is-makar-sankranti.html. Accessed April 15, 2010.

Mani, Commemoration of the Prophet (April 25)

The prophet Mani (c. 216–276 CE) was the founder of a religious movement named for him, Manichaeism, a post-Gnostic dualist faith. Manichaeism reached its greatest expansion around the seventh century, by which time followers could be found from the Mediterranean basin to China. Today, the major Manichaean community is the Mandeans of Iraq (and its diaspora).

Mani offered a vision of a world engaged in a cosmic struggle between good and evil, a spiritual world of light, and a material world of darkness. Humans may identify with either, through an ongoing process that takes place in human history; light is gradually removed from the world of matter and returned to the world of light from which it came. Mani shared a belief with the Gnostics that the human soul lives as an exile captive, trapped in matter, and that its real home is with the supreme Entity (God), to which it will eventually return.

Contemporary Gnostics, such as those associated with the Ecclesia Gnostica, revere Mani as a major figure in the Western Gnostic tradition. It has assigned April 25 as a day to remember him and commemorate his birth. The worship that day includes a prayer to him, and readings from Manichean writings.

J. Gordon Melton

See also Ecclesia Gnostica—Liturgical Year; Valentinus, Feast of the Holy.

References

Ecclesia Gnostica: Liturgical Calendar. Posted at http://gnosis.org/eghome.htm. Accessed March 15, 2010.

Greenlees, Duncan. *The Gospel of the Prophet Mani*. San Diego: Book Tree, 2007.

Tardieu, Michael. *Manichaeism*. Translated by Malcolm DeBevoise. Urbana: University of Illinois Press, 2009.

Manjushri's Birthday

Manjushri (in Japan as Monju-bosatsu) is pictured in the Buddhist sutras (holy books) as the leader of the bodhisattvas. Regarded as a symbol of the perfection of wisdom, he is often pictured, along with Samantabadhara, in attendance upon Gautama Buddha—most notably in the Flower Garland (Adornment) Sutra. He is generally pictured riding a lion and holding a sword symbolic of the sharpness of his discrimination.

Manjushri is said to manifest himself on Mount Wutai, in China's Shanxi Province. Stories tell of the visit of an Indian monk in the first century CE who reported a vision of the bodhisattva. Wutai Mountain and the Wisdom Buddha Manjushri are also the subjects of various Buddhist scriptures, sutras, and tantras. Mahayana Buddhism began arriving on Wutai Mountain quite early in its transmission to

Statue of Manjushri, the Buddhist leader of the bodhisattvas. (J. Gordon Melton)

China, and the first temple was constructed during the reign of Emperor Ming Di (r. 58–75 CE). Literally hundreds of monasteries were built over the next centuries. The associations of the mountain with Manjushri were significantly strengthened in the eighth century with the visit of arrival Padmasambhava, who was spreading Vajrayana Buddhism through nearby Tibet. Manjushri is especially dear to Vajrayana Buddhists. Then in the 12th century, the Mongolians of the Yuan dynasty, as part of their kingdom building, intruded into Tibet and left the Dalai Lama in charge of the country. As the development of Vajrayana Buddhism was encouraged, the Gelugpa school became established at Mount Wutai. The various Buddhist temples that remain on Mount Wutai hold two major celebrations. The first, the Assembly of the Sixth Month, is a time for pilgrims to visit. The second and more important occurs over four days in the fourth month. It focuses on rituals held in 10 of the mountain's largest temples. This ritual cycle marks Manjushri's birthday on the fourth day of the fourth lunar month.

In Japan, celebrations to honor Manjushri can be traced back to the ninth century CE. His veneration is still practiced in Japan and draws on stories of Manjushri appearing in the guise of beggars. Believers prepare food and drink on this day to feed all beggars. Meanwhile, in the temples, the names of Manjushri and the Medicine Buddha were recited 100 times each, each day. Today this ritual survives in only two temples. Manjushri is one of the characters in the Medicine Buddha Sutra.

J. Gordon Melton

See also Amitabha's Birthday; Guan Yin's Birthday; Ksitigarbha's Birthday; Mahasthamaprapta's Birthday; Samantabadhara's Birthday.

References

Boheng, Wu, and Cai Zhuozhi. *100 Buddhas in Chinese Buddhism*. Translated by Mu Xin and Yan Zhi. Singapore: Asiapac books, 1997.

Einarsen, John, ed. *The Sacred Mountains of Asia*. Boston: Shambhala, 1995.

"Sacred Mountains of China." Places of Peace and Power. Posted at http://www.sacredsites.com/asia/china/sacred_mountains.html. Accessed May 15, 2009.

The Seeker's Glossary of Buddhism. New York: Sutra Translation Committee of the United States and Canada, 1998.

"Wutai Mountain Pilgrimage: Manjushri Empowerment, Teachings and Buddhist Qigong." Sacred Journeys. Posted at http://www.sacredjourneys.org/schedule/a_wutai.html. Accessed May 15, 2009.

Vessantara. *Meeting the Buddhas: A Guide to Buddhas, Bodhisattvas, and Tantric Deities*. Birmingham, UK: Windhorse Publications, 1998.

Mardi Gras

Mardi Gras, also known as Carnival, is the name given to the celebrations that precede the beginning of the Lenten fast in Roman Catholic countries. Lent, the 40-day period of preparation leading to the celebration of Easter, originated in the wake of the church's rise to a place of dominance in the Roman Empire. With the shift of secular power to Constantinople, the church in Rome arose as the strongest international organization in the West. Through the medieval period, as the population accepted Christianity and the communal practice of the Christian year became pervasive, the weeks between Epiphany (January 6) and the beginning of the Lenten season, usually in February, became a time to remove those food items from the home that were banned during the fast—especially meat and related products such as butter, milk, and eggs. The actual week prior to Lent became a time to indulge in the forbidden items—including alcohol and sex. The turning of such indulgence into the occasion for a community celebration also resonated with prior spring celebrations in pre-Christian European cultures, but came to focus on the day prior to Ash Wednesday, which became known as Fat Tuesday (or Mardi Gras) and Carnival (from a Latin word meaning to take away meat).

Mardi Gras is thus not so much a religious celebration as an irreligious celebration that immediately precedes a lengthy period of somber religious observance. The excess that began to mark Mardi Gras was related to the seriousness with which the Lenten season was practiced. European celebrations spread from Rome to communities across southern Europe. In Roman Catholic countries, Fat Tuesday is also known as Shrove Tuesday, a reference to the requirement that Roman Catholics should make formal confession to a priest immediately before Lent begins. The most famous European Carnival evolved in Venice, but many local celebrations also emerged across Europe, especially in France, Spain, Portugal, and England. Most of these celebrations did not survive in those countries that came to be dominated by Protestantism, the celebrations in Denmark being a notable exception. Pastries became a popular indulgence in northern Europe at this time.

Mardi Gras/Carnival was transferred from Europe to the Americas by the French (to New Orleans) and the Portuguese (to Brazil). When Jean Baptiste Le Moyne de Bienville (1680–1767), landed on the Gulf Coast of Louisiana in 1699, he named the spot, "Pointe du Mardi Gras." Three years later, he established Fort Louis de la Louisiane, at what is now Mobile, Alabama. The first Mardi Gras was actually celebrated in Mobile in 1703. New Orleans was established in 1718, and by the 1730s, records show that Mardi Gras was being regularly celebrated but in a much more subdued manner, relative to what it would become. The first parades were recorded in the 1830s, and the event had grown to the point that a list of festive activities was announced in the newspapers. Floats constructed in France were imported for the Fat Tuesday parade. It became a legal holiday in Louisiana in 1872, and from that time grew steadily into an elaborate communal party that faced a major setback only by the flood following Hurricane Katrina in 2005 (which fortunately did not reach the old French Quarter, where much of the Mardi Gras celebration has been centered).

Today, the most famous Mardi Gras/Carnival celebrations are staged in Venice, Rio de Janeiro, and New Orleans, but smaller ones are also held in other Gulf communities such as Galveston, Texas; Biloxi, Mississippi; Mobile, Alabama; and Pensacola, Florida. In the last half of the 20th century, numerous Mardi Gras celebrations have appeared as part of the tourist economy in many cities, large and small, across the United States. In Miami, Florida, the Majic City Carnival is sponsored by the Church of the Incarnation (Episcopal), one of a miniscule number of celebrations that have any religious base. Polish Americans, most of whom are Catholic, in the northern urban centers of Chicago and Detroit celebrate Mardi Gras on Fat Thursday (the Thursday before Ash Wednesday) as Pączki Day, named for the doughnut-like pastry that is consumed amid the music and parties. Pancakes and rich pastries are a ubiquitous element of the Mardi Gras season across North America and Europe.

J. Gordon Melton

See also Easter; Epiphany; Lent.

References

Goldman, Albert. *Carnival in Rio*. New York: E. P. Dutton, 1978.

Kinser, Samuel. *Carnival, American Style: Mardi Gras at New Orleans and Mobile*. Chicago: University of Chicago Press, 1990.

Mitchell, Reid. *All on a Mardi Gras Day: Episodes in the History of New Orleans Carnival*. Cambridge, MA: Harvard University Press, 1999.

Tallant, Robert. *Mardi Gras . . . As It Was*. Gretna, LA: Pelican Publishing, 1989.

Vidaling, Raphaale. *Venice: A Day in Carnival*. London: Periplus Publishing, 2004.

Margaret of Scotland, Saint's Day of St. (June 10)

Saint Margaret (c. 1045–1093) was the daughter of a Scottish exile living in Hungary and a distant relative of Saint Stephen, the Hungarian ruler. Her father returned in 1057 and was warmly received by Malcolm III (d. 1093), who would eventually make Margaret his wife. Margaret has become quite religious and used her influence as queen to help reform the Scottish church. She had several churches built, including the Abbey at Dunfermline, constructed primarily to house an important relic she had acquired, a piece of the True Cross. She predicted the day of her death, November 16, 1093, shortly after that of her husband.

Her body was entombed at Dunfermline. Following her canonization in 1250, a shrine was constructed and her relics reburied. As the Protestant Reformation moved through Scotland, and the Catholic churches voided of their relics, Mary Queen of Scots, a staunch Catholic, gained possession of Margaret's skull, which was later transported to France and lost during the French Revolution. The rest of the remains were shipped to King Philip II (1556–1598) of Spain. In the 19th century, the Catholic bishop James Gilles of Edinburgh (r. 1838–1863) asked Spain for the return of Margaret's relics, but no one could locate them.

Margaret's Day was for many years celebrated on June 10, but in 1969, it was moved to November 16, the anniversary of her death. She has been named one of the patron saints of Scotland. Her saintliness is also celebrated by the Episcopal Church of Scotland. Bishop Gilles founded a convent named in her honor.

J. Gordon Melton

See also Saint Stephen's Day (Hungary); Willibrord, Saint's Day of St.

References

Dunlop, Eileen. *Queen Margaret of Scotland*. Edinburgh: NMS Enterprises, 2005.

Forbes-Leith, William. *Life of St. Margaret Queen of Scotland by Turgot, Bishop of St Andrews*. Edinburgh: St. Margaret's Catholic Church, 1884.

Huneycutt, L. L. "The Idea of a Perfect Princess: The *Life of St. Margaret* in the Reign of Matilda II (1100–1118)." *Anglo-Norman Studies* 12 (1989): 81–97.

The Miracles of St. Abba of Coldingham and St. Margaret of Scotland. London: Clarendon Press, 2003.

Martin de Porres, Saint's Day of St. (November 3)

Martin de Porres, among the first Africans in the New World to be canonized by the Roman Catholic Church, was born in Lima, Peru, in 1579, the illegitimate son of a Spanish knight and a black free-woman. Martin was raised in poverty. As a youth, he learned to cut hair and assist a physician in the then-common practice of bleeding patients.

In his 15th year, he became associated with the Dominicans and eventually became a professed lay brother. He tended the sick in the monastery infirmary and assumed responsibility for the daily distribution of food to the needy. During these years, he became acquainted with the Dominican nun Rose of Lima. Martin became known of his humility, and was constantly reminded of his illegitimate birth.

Martin became known for his prayer life, and his fellow monks reported on instances in which he was seen to levitate and stories abounded of his passing unhindered through locked doors and bi-locating to assist a ill person. Gradually, people began to seek him out for spiritual counseling. He was ill through most of 1639, at times in some degree of pain, alleviated by a variety of vision of the Blessed Virgin Mary and several saints and angels. He died on November 3, 1639. The priests who knew him praised his saintliness, and he was deemed worthy to have a final resting place among the priests of the order. Knowledge of the miraculous events throughout his life was widespread. It was reported that so many people who came to view his body prior to his burial took pieces of his robe as a relic that his body had to be redressed three times before the burial.

Numerous letters were sent to Rome asking for his beatification, but the process moved very slowly. In 1763, Pope Clement XIII (r. 1758–1769) issued a decree affirming the heroism of his virtues. In 1937, Pope Gregory XII (r. 1831–1846) beatified him, but not until 1962 did Pope John XXIII (r. 1958–1963) oversee his canonization. The Episcopal Church in the United States honors Martin (along with Rose de Lima and Toribio de Mogrovejo, a contemporary of Martin who was bishop of Lima) with a feast day on August 23. Lutherans honor him on November 3.

J. Gordon Melton

See also Benedict the African, Saint's Day of St.; Dominic, Saint's Day of St.; Peter Claver, Saint's Day of St.; Rose of Lima, Saint's Day of St.

References

Cavalini, Giuliana. *St. Martin De Porres*. Charlotte, NC: St. Benedict Press/TAN Books, 2009.

Garcia-Rivera, Alex. *St. Martin de Porres: The "Little Stories" and the Semiotics of Culture*. Maryknoll, NY: Orvis Books, 2008.

Kearns, John C. *The Life of Blessed Martín de Porres, Saintly American Negro and Patron of Social Justice*. St. Louis, MO: P. J. Kenedy & Sons, 1937.

Orsini, Angela M. "St Marin de Porres—Patron of Social Justice." Posted at http://www.martindeporres.org/about.htm. Accessed May 15, 2010.

Martin Luther King, Jr., Birthday of (January 15)

Martin Luther King, Jr., Baptist minister and leader of the civil rights movement in the United States in the 1960s, was born Michael King in Atlanta, Georgia, on January 15, 1929. His father was a prominent African American minister and pastor of the Ebenezer Baptist Church in Atlanta. In 1933, the elder King had both his name and his son's name changed to Martin Luther King.

The younger King attended Morehouse College, where he experienced a call to the ministry, and after his college years enrolled at Crozier Theological Seminary in Chester, Pennsylvania, where he initially became aware of the nonviolent philosophy of the recently martyred Mahatma Gandhi (1869–1948).

He completed his graduate studies at Boston University (PhD, 1955). While there, he married Coretta Scott (b. 1927). They settled in Montgomery, Alabama, where he had become the pastor of the Dexter Avenue Baptist Church. Before the year was out, Rosa Parks was arrested for refusing to give up her seat to a white patron of the local bus system. Following her conviction for breaking the local laws segregating the races, a boycott of the city buses by African Americans ensued, and King was selected to lead the Montgomery Improvement Association, an organization formed to guide the boycott. The boycott's success led to the formation of the Southern Christian Leadership Council (SCLC). In 1959, King visited India and, upon his return, resigned from his pastorate, moved to Atlanta, and devoted most of his time to SCLC.

In the early 1960s, the focus of the civil rights movement turned to Birmingham, Alabama, where King was arrested during demonstrations aimed at desegregating the city. While in jail, he wrote one of his most memorable pieces, "Letter from a Birmingham Jail," explaining his actions. He followed by leading the 1963 march on Washington in support of new civil rights legislation, during which he gave his oft-quoted "I Have a Dream" speech. In 1964, he was named *Time* magazine's Man of the Year and received the Nobel Peace Prize.

Ultimately, the passing of national civil rights legislation presented King with decisions about broadening the movement to include northern urban centers and about applying the nonviolent philosophy to the growing war in Vietnam. He also decided to throw his support behind poverty concerns and selected Memphis, Tennessee, where a strike of garbage workers was ongoing. In Memphis, on April 4, 1968, King was assassinated while standing on the balcony of his motel.

King emerged in the years after his death as both an international Christian figure inspiring a scope of efforts to liberate the poor, oppressed, and outcast of the world, and a controversial figure among many white people in the United States. After much debate, on November 2, 1983, President Ronald Reagan signed the bill that established the federal holiday honoring King. It would initially be celebrated on January 20, 1986, the Monday following his birthday. In 1992, President George H. W. Bush proclaimed Martin Luther King Day as a national holiday to be observed on the third Monday of January each year. Several states resisted accepting the proclamation, and it would be 2000 before it became officially commemorated in all 50 states.

Most Protestant churches do not have a mechanism for establishing a new holiday, and have chosen to join in the various local public celebrations rather than organize competing events. The liturgical churches, especially the Lutherans and Anglicans, were also in a quandary as whether to celebrate King's life on January 15 or April 4, the day of his death, it being usual to commemorate saints on their death day. Lutherans have tended to favor January 15, especially as the civil holiday is rarely on that date. Episcopalians and Methodists have tended to favor April 4.

In 1993, the U.S. government created the Corporation for National and Community Service to coordinate a number of agencies that nurture volunteer action and community services. In 1994, Congress supplemented the legislation creating the new corporation by passing the King Holiday and Service Act that mandated establishing Martin Luther King Day as a day of service. Subsequently, the corporation has pursued efforts of mobilizing volunteers to give a day to their community on Martin Luther King Day.

J. Gordon Melton

See also Benedict the African, Saint's Day of St.; Martin de Porres, Saint's Day of St.; Martinmas; Race Unity Day.

References

Albert, Peter J., and Ronald Hoffman, eds. *We Shall Overcome: Martin Luther King, Jr., and the Black Freedom Struggle*. New York: Pantheon Books, 1990.

Baldwin, Lewis V. *There Is a Balm in Gilead: The Cultural Roots of Martin Luther King, Jr.* Minneapolis, MN: Fortress Press, 1991.

Colaiaco, James A. *Martin Luther King, Jr.: Apostle of Militant Nonviolence*. New York: St. Martin's Press, 1993.

Pfatteicher, Philip H. *New Book of Festivals and Commemorations: A Proposed Common Calendar of Saints*. Minneapolis, MN: Fortress Press, 2008.

Martinmas (November 11)

Martinmas, the feast day within the Roman Catholic Church for Saint Martin of Tours (c. 316–397) honors the life of the fourth-century pioneer of monasticism. Martin was born in what is now Hungary and raised in a Pagan home. His family later moved to Italy, where at the age of 15 he was drafted into the Roman army. Though he had had some brushes with Christianity during his teen years, his conversion followed a vision of Christ he had in 337. He had encountered a beggar who was a suffering from the cold, and he tore his own cloak into two pieces to share with the man. In the vision, Christ wore the cloak he had given away. He completed his time in the army, returned to Italy, and joined a monastic community.

His quiet life in Milan would be altered when he met Hillary of Poitiers (315–368), another convert from Paganism who around 350 was named bishop of Poitiers (France). Hillary became a bishop while the controversy concerning the teachings of Arius, who denied the doctrine of the trinity, still raged. Amid the back-and-forth of controversy, Hillary aligned with the position of Athanasius against Arius. As a result, he was exiled from Poitiers to the Eastern Mediterranean in 356. The exile allowed him time to master the debate and write a classical defense of the Trinity. He returned to his diocese in 360.

Shortly after his return, Hillary invited Martin to France to assist in the founding of a monastic community at Ligugé, the first in France. He proved a popular leader of the community and in 371 was named bishop of Tours. He resided in the cathedral for a few years and then moved back to his monastic community. When he died more than a quarter of a century later, his tomb became a popular pilgrimage site and generated numerous reports of miracles. In the years before Advent had been firmly set on the church calendar, his feast day was used to mark the beginning of a 40-day period of preparation for the Christmas celebration.

As an early saint in the West, a variety of practices grew up around Martin's person, and he became associated with healings. His reputation grew when Clovis (c. 466–511), the first real king of modern France, attributed his rise to power to Martin. Clovis's successors promoted the veneration of Martin, and his tomb became a site for pilgrims traveling through Europe on their way to Santiago de Compostela.

The medieval church built over the place of Martin's burial was demolished in the wake of the French Revolution, and two streets routed over the site in an attempt to obliterate it. Interest in him, however, revived in the last half of the 19th century, and was tied to the new devotion to the Sacred Heart of Jesus. A new basilica was consecrated in 1925. Modern veneration of Saint Martin had spread throughout the Catholic Church and many local churches are named for him.

Martin of Tours is a French saint, and has been named a patron saint of the country, but is also popular in neighboring Germany, where Martinmas is widely celebrated. German Catholics emphasize Martin's role as a friend of children and patron of the poor. In Dusseldorf, Saint Martin's Eve is a time for a lantern-lit procession centered on the children while the next day is featured a large meal with roast goose as the main entree. It is also appropriate to invite the poor to share in the feast. As Catholics celebrate Martin of Tours, so Protestants may celebrate Martin Luther, who was born on November 10, Saint Martin's Eve. Commemorations of Luther were somewhat stunted after World War II, as many of the sites associated with him, such as his birthplace at Eisleben, were located in Communist East Germany. On Saint Martin's before the war, for example, children would process to the cathedral at Erfurt, where Luther attend the university, and with lighted lanterns form the pattern of a rose, the symbol on the Luther family coat of arms.

J. Gordon Melton

See also Benedict of Nursia, Saint's Day of St.; Calendars, Religious; Dominic, Saint's Day of St.

References

Donaldson, Christopher. *Martin of Tours: The Shaping of Celtic Spirituality*. Norwich, UK: Canterbury Press, 1997.

Pernoud, Regine. *Martin of Tours: Soldier, Bishop, Saint*. Fort Collins, CO: Ignatius Press, 2006.

Spicer, Dorothy Gladys. *Festivals of Western Europe*. New York: H. W. Wilson Company, 1958.

Tille, Alexander. *Yule and Christmas Their Place in the Germanic Year*. London: David Nutt, 1899.

Martyrdom of Guru Arjan

Toward the end of spring each year, Sikhs commemorate the martyrdom of their fifth leader Guru Arjan Dev Ji (1563–1606), which occurred on the fourth day of the light half of the month of Jyaishtha on the Hindu lunar calendar (May 30, 1606 CE). Today, using the new Sikh Nanashahi calendar, the event is celebrated annually on June 16.

Guru Arjan Dev Ji was born on April 15, 1563, as the youngest of the three sons of the Guru Ram Das Ji (1534–1581). He became the new guru following his father's death, though still a teenager. Among the accomplishments for which he is remembered is initiating the compilation of the Sikh holy book, the Guru Granth Sahib. Though he was not an aggressive proselytizer, the Sikh community grew during his tenure in office, many attended upon him at Govindwal, then the center of the Sikh movement.

All was well for the Sikh movement until 1605, when the Mughal emperor Akbar died. His son and successor Jahangir was a fervent Muslim with a vision of turning his land into an Islamic state, which would necessarily include converting the Sikhs. He opened himself to a variety of accusations against Guru Arjan Dev, most significantly to those of Diwan Chandu Shah (whose marriage proposal of the guru's daughter had been refused by Guru Arjun Dev). Arun Dev may have sealed his fate when he showed some kindness to Jahangir's rival Khusrau, who ruled Punjab at the time. In any case, in May, Jahangir ordered Guru Arjan Dev's arrest and transport to Lahore. His possessions were also confiscated. Once in Lahore, he was subject to severe torture for six days, but refused the emperor's demands. On the last day, he died in the river where he had been taken for a bath.

The martyrdom of Guru Arjun Dev is credited with changing the basic character of Sikhism from a passive, peaceable people into a militant group willing to fight for its own survival and to protect its members from persecution. Arjun Dev was succeeded by Guru Har Gobind (r. 1606–1644). He rejected the pacifism and nonviolent stance of previous gurus and organized a small army. He argued that it was necessary to take up the sword in order to protect the weak and the oppressed.

J. Gordon Melton

See also Guru Gobind Singh's Birthday; Guru Granth Sahib, Celebration of the; Makar Sankranti; Martyrdom of Guru Tegh Bahadur.

References

Duggal, K. S. *Sikh Gurus: Their Lives and Teachings*. New Delhi: UBSPD, 2005.

Kapoor, Sukhbor Sing. *Sikh Festivals*. Vero Beach, FL: Rourke Publishing Group, 1989.

Martyrdom of Guru Tegh Bahadur

Guru Tegh Bahadur (1621–1675), the ninth guru of Sikhism, assumed his office on March 20, 1665. He succeeded to the task from his grandnephew, Guru Har Krishan (1656–1664), who had been only five years old when he became the guru and died before his eighth birthday.

Guru Har Krishan did not name a successor, only an ambiguous message that he would be found in Bakala. Several proclaimed themselves the new guru, but eventually, the unassuming Tegh Bahadur was singled out and received the support of the community.

He was named guru during the reign of the emperor Aurangzeb (1618–1707), who had a goal of turning India into a Muslim land. He initiated a program of forced conversion in Kashmir. A group of religious leaders agreed, on the advice of the guru, to tell the Mughal authorities that they would willingly embrace Islam if Guru Tegh Bahadur did the same. Aurangzeb ordered his arrest and before leaving for Delhi, Tegh Bahadur selected his son, Gobind (later Guru Gobind Singh) as his successor, should it be necessary. He was arrested, detained for three months, and then sent on to Delhi in November 1675. He refused to recant his faith under torture, and was eventually beheaded on November 11, 1675. The Gurdwara Sis Ganj Sahib in Delhi was later built over the spot where the execution took place.

The Martyrdom of Guru Tegh Bahadur is now celebrated on Maghar 11 on the Nanakshahi calendar, which was accepted by the administrative authorities of the religion in Amritsar in the 1990. Mughar 11 is equivalent to November 24 on the Common Era calendar. Commemoration of Guru Tegh Bahadur's death is 1 of 12 "Gurpurbs," holidays that recall the birth or death of 1 of the 10 Sikh gurus. Sikhs celebrate the Gurpurbs by performing an *Akhand Path*, a public reading of the Guru Granth Sahib, the Sikh holy scriptures, in gurdwaras (Sikh worship center) around the world. It requires two days to read the entire volume from beginning to end. The reading will thus begin two days before the designated holy day and will end early in the morning of the day of commemoration. Each person chosen to participate will read aloud for two to three hours. The day itself will start early in the morning and include the recitation of prayers, the singing of *kirtans* (holy songs), and speeches on the theme of the day. It will include a communal meal.

Though he was a guru for less than two years, Tegh Bahadur made a significant impact on the movement as a result of his faithfulness under the most severe of circumstances.

J. Gordon Melton

See also Guru Gobind Singh's Birthday; Guru Granth Sahib, Celebration of the; Makar Sankranti; Martyrdom of Guru Arjan.

References

Duggal, K. S. *Sikh Gurus: Their Lives and Teachings*. New Delhi: UBSPD, 2005.

Kapoor, Sukhbor Sing. *Sikh Festivals*. Vero Beach, FL: Rourke Publishing Group, 1989.

Mary—Liturgical Year of the Blessed Virgin (Roman Catholic Church)

Within the Roman Catholic Church, there are several well-recognized liturgical cycles. The two most prominent are a set of fixed holidays surrounding Christmas that begin with Advent and include Epiphany and the Feast of the Annunciation. The second includes a set of movable holidays that surround Easter, beginning with Ash Wednesday and Lent, and including the celebrations of Jesus's Ascension, Pentecost, and Trinity Sunday. Filling out the year are a set of saint's days. Above the major saints known to most church members, there are multiple saints assigned their day, and remembered only locally, for every day of the year, not a major holiday or feast day. With the growth of the veneration of the Blessed Virgin Mary in the church, however, what amounts to a fourth liturgical cycle has emerged around the celebration of the several key dates related to the Virgin in the first two cycles, especially the Feast of the Annunciation and Christmas.

Mary appears in the Christian New Testament only in relation to events in the life of Jesus—beginning with Mary's being informed of her pregnancy even though not married. She subsequently is pictured as giving birth, raising, and being present at the death and resurrection of her son. At the crucifixion, Jesus commends her to the care of his disciple John, but she does not appear as a character of interest in the book of Acts (or writings of Paul) in the post-Pentecost church. In the second and third centuries, some interest is shown in her life both before the birth and after the death of Jesus, and several apocryphal works that circulated in the church attempted to fill out her life. Of these, the second-century *Protoevangelium of James* (a.k.a. *The Nativity of Mary*) is the most important and offers information on the parentage and early life of Mary. It names her parents, Anne and Joachim, and is the sole source of information upon which a set of Marian celebrations would be built.

Crucial to the development of Marian devotion was the definition of Mary as *Theotokos* (Mother or Bearer of God) at the Council of Ephesus in 431. While this affirmation was made as a further statement related to Jesus's status as both human and divine, it supplied the base from which some independent speculation on Mary could build. In both the East and West, as part of the development of attention given to the saints, dates for giving attention to Mary began to appear on the church calendar, beginning with those events mentioned in the New Testament that occurred before Jesus's birth, the Annunciation, by the angel that Mary was

Statue of the Virgin Mary in Hong Kong. (J. Gordon Melton)

to bear Jesus and her visitation to Elizabeth at which she is greeted with some of the most oft-quoted of biblical verses relative to Mary, "Blessed are you among women, and blessed is the fruit of your womb" (Luke 1:42). Once the date of Christmas was set, it was reasoned that Mary would have become pregnant with Jesus nine months earlier, thus the feast of the Annunciation was set on March 25. The feast of the visitation would be set on May 31.

As interest in Mary as the most important of the saints grew, church leaders turned to the *Protoevangelium of James*, which functioned like a host of hagiographical accounts of the apostles and the martyrs of the second and third centuries, and used to build a biography of Mary. She was born to Anne and Joachim, each of whom attained some status as saints, was presented in the temple at the age of three, and subsequently engaged to Joseph. Various traditions developed about the end of Mary's early life, the majority favoring her death in Jerusalem and burial in the Garden of Gethsemane, where Jesus prayed (John 18). Western Christians began to differ from the tradition held in the east and suggested that Mary was, like the prophet Elijah, taken bodily into heaven without experiencing death.

Relatively early feasts celebrating the Nativity of the Virgin (September 8), her Presentation in the Temple (November 21), and her death (August 15) were set in the Eastern Church. It was assumed in the Eastern Church that Mary's soul was immediately assumed into heaven, but that her body was buried in Jerusalem.

In the West, additional speculation on the birth of Mary would lead to a unique doctrine, that she was born without original sin, and thus experienced what became known as the Immaculate Conception. It was further suggested that she had not faced bodily death. Thus, while both East and West celebrate the assumption of the Virgin, they disagree on the content of that belief. In the East, it applied only to Mary's soul, while in the West, it is seen as also applying to Mary's body. Following the split between the Eastern Orthodox churches and the Roman Catholic Church in the 11th century, the West was free to develop its veneration of the virgin in distinctive ways.

Very much affecting the veneration of the Virgin in the West has been a series of apparitions in which the Virgin has appeared to various saintly individuals and initiated new forms of devotion. In the 13th century, for example, she is reputed to have appeared to Dominic de Guzman (1170–1221), the founder of the Dominican order. She suggested the use of the rosary as a form of prayer, and subsequently, it was widely promoted by the growing order. Subsequent apparitions of Mary would suggest additional items, such as the wearing of scapulars of different colors, attention to the Immaculate Heart of Mary, and the circulation of the Miraculous Medal, all of which have become popular practices by groups within the church. With the exception of a few forms of worship that derive from apparitions of Jesus, almost all of the innovative forms of worship introduced into Catholic worship since the 13th century began with an apparition of the Blessed Virgin. The number and frequency of such apparitions has risen notably since the early 19th century.

Coincidental with an apparition of the Virgin to a young Mexican man, a picture of her appeared on his cloak and, as the virgin of Guadalupe, has now become one of the most visible images of the Virgin in the world. Throughout Europe in the 19th and early 20th centuries, apparitions of the virgins to young people in different countries were accepted as genuine and subsequently became the object of widespread attention and pilgrimages to such places as Lourdes, France; Fatima, Portugal; Knock, Ireland; and Medjugorje, Bosnia-Herzegovina.

In addition, the apparitions of the virgin were supplement by the "discovery" of various lost statues or images of the Virgin in the context of some miraculous occurrence that indicated its special status or its desire to be located in a particular place. The discovery of lost statues and their placement in a chapel or other places where believers could gather have become the focus of large pilgrimages and national shrines in many Catholic countries.

The growth of veneration of the Virgin in various guises, the founding of numerous religious orders to perpetuate devotion to her, and the naming of her in her various manifestations as patron saint of countries, cities, and occupations have all contributed to the development of the annual calendar of Marian devotion. This calendar was given added emphasis by the papal declaration of the Immaculate Conception in 1854 and the Assumption of the Virgin in 1950. These were simply two highlights amid a century and a half of papal activity relative to the

January	Feast of the Holy Family
January 1	Solemnity of Mary (Circumcision of the Lord)
January 6	Epiphany
January 8	Our Lady of Prompt Succor
February 2	Feast of the Purification of Mary (a.k.a. the Presentation of Jesus)
February 11	Our Lady of Lourdes
March 25	Annunciation Day
May 31	Feast of the Visitation (of Mary to Elizabeth)
June	Feast of the Immaculate Heart of the Blessed Virgin
June 27	Our Lady of Perpetual Help
July 16	Our Lady of Mount Carmel
July 26	Feast Day of St. Anne (and also of St. Joachim)
August 15	Assumption of the Virgin
August 22	Queenship of Mary
September 8	Nativity of the Virgin (Immaculate Conception)
September 8–15	Festa de Serreta (Azores)
September 12	Most Holy Name of Mary
September 15	Our Lady of Sorrows
September 24	Our Lady of Walsingham (UK)
October 7	Our Lady of the Rosary
October 8	Our Lady of Good Remedy
October 12	Feast of the Virgin of the Pillar (Spain)
October 17	Romeria of Our Lady of Valme (Spain)
November 21	Presentation of Mary
December 8	Immaculate Conception
December 12	Our Lady of Guadalupe
December 25	Christmas

Virgin that included numerous papal encyclicals (open letters to the faithful reflective of the teaching role of the pope), the declaration of Marian years (the first held during 1954), and various actions of notable Marian import, such as visiting a Marian shrine. Pope John Paul II (r. 1978–2005) was particularly notable for his emphasis on Marian devotion punctuated by his several visits to Fatima.

Pope John Paul II's obvious favoring of Marian devotion appeared to many as balancing the seeming de-emphasis on Mary by the Second Vatican Council in the 1960s, which refused to consider Mary as a separate topic, demanding that she be considered under the broader topic of ecclesiology. That action was followed by the reorientation of several Marian feasts around their Christological import as part of the overall reform of the liturgical calendar in 1969.

As it currently stands, the annual cycle of Marian devotion has been abstracted from the liturgical calendar of the Roman Catholic Church, which has remained somewhat stable since 1969. It includes the major holidays celebrated by all Catholics, such as the feasts of the Immaculate Conception, Annunciation, and Assumption, less well-known feasts celebrated by many (such as the Feast of the Presentation of Mary or the saint's day for Saint Anne), and those celebrations that beyond the Marian faithful primarily have more local or regional import, being related to apparition in a particular location.

A variety of countries celebrate the Immaculate Conception in a slightly different manner, with additional content supplied by local events. Most notable of the local variation is in Brazil, where the Feast of the Immaculate Conception is a national holiday devoted to Our Lady of the Aparacita, a statue of the Virgin of the Immaculate Conception now housed in the country's large national Marian shrine. In addition, Marian years were called in 1954 and 1988, and it is difficult to predict when others may be called in the future. The month of May is considered the Month of Mary, while October is set aside as a month for the rosary. Many parishes hold Saturday as a day for Marian devotions.

J. Gordon Melton

See also Anne, Feast Day of St.; Assumption of the Virgin; Christmas; Expectation of the Birth of the Blessed Virgin Mary, Feast of the; Holy Family, Feast of the; Immaculate Conception, Feast of the; Nativity of Mary; Presentation of Mary, Feast of the; Queenship of Mary, Feast of; Solemnity of Mary, Feast of the.

References

Ball, Ann. *Encyclopedia of Catholic Devotions and Practices.* Huntington, IN: Our Sunday Visitor, 2003.

Ball, Ann. *The Other Faces of Mary: Stories, Devotions, and Pictures of the Holy Virgin from Around the World.* Chestnut Ridge, NY: Crossroad Publishing Company, 2004.

Cruz, Joan Carroll. *Miraculous Images of Our Lady: 100 Famous Catholic Statues and Portraits.* Charlotte, NC: TAN Books and Publishers, 2009.

Dodds, Monica, and Bill Dodds. *Encyclopedia of Mary.* Huntington, IN: Our Sunday Visitor, 2007.

Durham, Michael S. *Miracles of Mary: Apparitions, Legends, and Miraculous Works of the Blessed Virgin Mary.* San Francisco, CA: Harper, 1995.

Heintz, Peter. *A Guide to Apparitions of Our Blessed Virgin Mary.* Sacramento, CA: Gabriel Press, 1995.

"The Mary Page." University of Dayton. Posted at http://www.udayton.edu/mary/marypage21.html. Accessed June 15, 2010.

Miravalle, Mark. *Introduction to Mary: The Heart of Marian Doctrine and Devotion.* Goleta, CA: Queenship Publishing Company, 1997.

Zimdars-Swartz, Sandra. *Encountering Mary: From La Salette to Medjugorje.* Princeton, NJ: Princeton University Press, 1991.

Mary Magdalene, Day of the Holy (July 22)

Mary Magdalene (a woman of the city of Magdala) first appears on the scene in the Gospel of Luke where she is identified as one from whom Jesus cast out seven evil spirits and healed of her infirmities. She became a devoted disciple of Jesus and a part of his close circle, and she remained became prominent during his last days on earth. She was present at the crucifixion and burial. She was most notably the first person to see the resurrected Christ and to report her sighting to the unbelieving apostles (Luke 24:1–10). The most detailed scene of Mary's visitation with the resurrected Jesus is found in the Gospel of John (20:11–18). The Roman Catholic Church and the Eastern Orthodox churches considered her a saint and fixed her feast day as July 22. That commemoration was continued by the Anglican and Lutheran churches.

In the Gnostic scriptures, from the Pistis Sophia, one of the few Gnostic texts to survive and be known through the centuries, to the lost works rediscovered in 1945 at Nag Hammadi in Egypt, Mary's role as an important disciple in the early church is made more explicit. In the *Pistis Sophia*, for example, she is described as one "whose heart is raised to the kingdom of heaven more than all thy brethren." In the Gospel of Philip, she is mentioned as one whom Jesus loved more than all the others.

In spite of the place that Mary Magdalene had in the early church, in the opinion of many, her reputation was hurt severely by Pope Gregory the Great (r. 590–604) who identified her with the unnamed sinful woman of Luke 7:37–39. Subsequently, Mary Magdalene was identified as a woman who had committed a range of sexual sins and would later be named the patron saint of penitent women and reformed prostitutes. In the Roman Catholic Church, Saint Mary Magdalene was traditionally celebrated as a penitent.

The discovery and publication of the Gnostic scriptures at Nag Hammadi coincided with the late-20th-century feminist movement. Mary Magdalene became a powerful symbol of both Gnostics and feminists of the patriarchal structures that dominated mainstream Christianity. Even as the Catholic Church implicitly corrected the misidentification of Mary Magdalene as a repentant sinner in their 1969 revision of the Calendar of Saints, by removing any reference to her as a penitent, Gnostic Christians elevated Mary Magdalene to a central role in their liturgical year. She was given particular attention by Bishop Rosamonde Miller, the founder of the Ecclesia Gnostica Mysteriorum based in Palo Alto, California. As with the parent Ecclesia Gnostica, Miller sees the feast day of Mary Magdalene as initiating a season of liturgical reflections of the feminine. Mary Magdalene is viewed as the consort of Jesus, and the one to whom Jesus revealed the fullness of his teaching (that is, Gnosticism).

Mary Magdalene's Day has become a significant festival for contemporary Gnostics as she represents the "archetypal Feminine Principle manifested in humanity." The Gnostics have aligned with contemporary feminism in elevating the status and role of women.

J. Gordon Melton

See also Ecclesia Gnostica—Liturgical Year; Madeleine, Fête de la.

References

Ecclesia Gnostica: Liturgical Calendar. Posted at http://gnosis.org/eghome.htm. Accessed March 15, 2010.

Leloup, Jean-Yves. *The Gospel of Mary Magdalene*. Rochester, VT: Inner Traditions, 2002.

Meyer, Marvin. *The Gospels of Mary: The Secret Tradition of Mary Magdalene, the Companion of Jesus*. New York: HarperOne, 2006.

Schaberg, Jane. *The Resurrection of Mary Magdalene: Legends, Apocrypha, and the Christian*. New York: Continuum, 2002.

Welborn, Amy. *De-coding Mary Magdalene: Truth, Legend, and Lies*. Huntington, IN: Our Sunday Visitor, 2006.

Marymas Fair. *See* Assumption of the Virgin

Mauna Agyaras

Maun Ekadashi, or Mauna Agyaras, is a Jain holy day observed on the 11th day (*ekadashi*) in the month of Magrashirsha (November–December on the Common Era calendar). It is observed as a day for fasting and meditation in an environment of complete silence (*maura*). This day has taken on significance as it is considered the appearance day or birthday of a number of the saints or Tirthankaras that constitute the lineage behind Mahavira, the founder of Jainism. Jains look to this lineage of saints as demonstrating the ideals of the Jain lifestyle.

All of the Tirthankaras are assumed to have attained the highest level of spiritual attainment and exist in the afterlife as arhants (fully enlightened masters). An arhant is assumed to be devoid of all evils. He has destroyed all his enemies, namely the internal enemies of anger, greed, ego, and deceit. The arhants are also said to possess pure knowledge and perception and infinite power, and thus to be in a passionless existence.

The object of one's contemplation on this day is the clerical leadership of the Jain community, those who have taken the path of renunciation of the world, and who exist at various levels of accomplishment. Still in this life are the sadhus, the upadhyayas, and acharyas. Already in a disembodied state are the siddhas and arhants.

Constance A. Jones

See also Akshay Tritiya (Jain); Diwali; Gyana Panchami; Kartika Purnima; Mahavir Jayanti; Navpad Oli; New Year's Day (Jain); Paryushana; Paush Dashami.

References

Jaini, P. S. *The Jaina Path of Purification*. Delhi: Motilal Banarsidass, 1979, 1990.

Singh, Narendra K., ed. *Encyclopedia of Jainism*. 30 vols. New Delhi: Anmol, 2001.

Wiley, Kristi L. *Historical Dictionary of Jainism*. Lanham, MD: Rowman & Littlefield, 2004.

Maundy Thursday

Maundy Thursday, or Holy Thursday, is the Thursday celebration of the last week of Jesus's life on earth, which began with his entrance into Jerusalem and ended with his arrest, death by crucifixion, and resurrection. On that day, Christ held a final supper, the Jewish Passover meal, with his 12 close disciples, the apostles. The event is mentioned in various passages of the New Testament and is featured as an important occurrence toward the end of each of the gospels. The supper is described in the Gospel of Mark 14:17–26:

> And when it was evening he arrived with the twelve. And as they sat and were eating, Jesus said, "Verily I say unto you, One of you shall betray me, even he that eats with me."
>
> They began to be sorrowful, and to say unto him one by one, "Is it I?"
>
> And he said unto them, "It is one of the twelve, he that dips with me in the dish. For the Son of man goes forth, even as it is written of him: but woe unto that man through whom the Son of man is betrayed! Good were it for that man if he had not been born.
>
> And as they were eating, he took bread, and when he had blessed, he brake it, and gave to them, and said, "Take ye: this is my body."
>
> And he took a cup, and when he had given thanks, he gave to them: and they all drank of it. And he said unto them, "This is my blood of the covenant, which is poured out for many. Verily I say unto you, I shall no more drink of the fruit of the vine, until that day when I drink it new in the kingdom of God."
>
> And when they had sung a hymn, they went out unto the Mount of Olives.

From this and the similar accounts elsewhere in the Gospels, the Christian Church developed its celebration of what is termed by various denominations as the Eucharist, the Lord's Supper, or Holy Communion. This rite is regularly repeated by some groups as frequently as every day or as infrequently as once a year. Most Protestant groups do it monthly, a few quarterly. For different groups, it is part of the regular weekly Sunday church service.

Different churches also think differently about the Lord's Supper. Most liturgical churches, including the Roman Catholic, Eastern Orthodox, and most Lutheran and Anglican churches, believe in what is termed the real presence, that Christ is truly present in the bread and the wine once what is termed the words of institution are spoken. These churches have slightly different explanations of the nature of that real presence. Churches out of the Reformed tradition (Presbyterian, Congregational, Methodist) believe in a real spiritual presence, which the believer perceives by faith. This position allows the sacramental element to remain, but reputes and discards any remaining magical element in the liturgical position. Churches out of the free church position have discarded any hint of a sacrament.

They believe that the Lord's Supper is an ordinance to be practiced because Jesus said to keep it in remembrance of Him. In holding the Lord's Supper, they remember what Jesus did.

However, at that meal, Jesus also introduced the sacramental practice of washing feet. Foot washing was a common occurrence, given the dry climate, but was a task assigned to slaves and servants. Jesus took the common practice and transformed its significance:

> Now before the feast of the passover, Jesus knowing that his hour was come that he should depart out of this world unto his Father, having loved his own that were in the world, he loved them unto the end. And during supper, the devil having already put into the heart of Judas Iscariot, Simon's son, to betray him. Jesus, knowing that the Father had given all the things into his hands, and that he came forth from God, and goes unto God, rose from supper, and laid his garments aside; and he took a towel, and girded himself. Then he poured water into the basin, and began to wash the disciples' feet, and to wipe them with the towel wherewith he was girded. So he came to Simon Peter. He said unto him, "Lord, dost thou wash my feet?"
>
> Jesus answered and said unto him, "What I do you do not now know; but you will understand hereafter."
>
> Peter said unto him, "You will never wash my feet."
>
> Jesus answered him, "If I do not wash you, you have no part with me.
>
> Simon Peter said to him, "Lord, not my feet only, but also my hands and my head."
>
> Jesus said to him, "He that is bathed has no need to wash his feet, but is clean every whit: and you are clean, but not everyone."
>
> For he knew him that should betray him; therefore he said, "You are not all clean."
>
> So when he had washed their feet, and taken his garments, and sat down again, he said unto them, "Do you know what I have done to you? You call me, Teacher, and, Lord: and you say well; for so I am. If I then, the Lord and the Teacher, have washed your feet, you also ought to wash one another's feet. For I have given you an example, that ye also should do as I have done to you. Verily, verily, I say unto you, a servant is not greater than his lord; neither one that is sent greater than he that sent him. If ye know these things, blessed are ye if ye do them."

The ritual of sharing bread and wine became a regular occurrence integrated into church life, while the washing of feet became an annual occurrence tied to the celebration of Maundy Thursday. In fact, the name Maundy Thursday derives from the Latin words that open the foot-washing rite. The practice has varied over the years. From the Reformation era to 1955, a rite of foot washing was published for Maundy Thursday as a seratae rite following the Eucharistic service. Since

1955, in the Catholic Church, they have occurred together. The Mass at which the pope washes the feet of a small circle of selected participants is a major event of Holy Week in Rome. A similar practice is also followed in the Eastern churches.

In the free church tradition that began with the Anabaptists, the sacramental natured of the Lord's Supper was discarded, but at the same time, in reading the scriptures, the importance assigned to foot washing was discovered. Foot washing became a third ordinance beside Baptism and the Lord's Supper and was regularly practiced as part of worship. It became a distinguishing element in the life of many Baptist groups. Other Protestants also rediscovered foot washing but did not see it as having the same sacramental nature as the Lord's Supper. They practiced it occasionally, often as part of Maundy Thursday rituals. In the contemporary church, it has been reintroduced periodically as a sign of church renewal with an emphasis on its role as a sign of humility and a means of deepening the level of communion among members.

In the Catholic tradition, after the Maundy Thursday service, all of the cloths are removed from the church altar as a sign of Christ being stripped of his clothes before he was tortured following his arrest.

J. Gordon Melton

See also Easter; Eucharistic Congresses; Good Friday; Holy Week; Liturgical Year—Western Christian; Palm Sunday.

References

Ball, Ann. *Encyclopedia of Catholic Devotions and Practices.* Huntington, IN: Our Sunday Visitor, 2003.

Nocent, Adrian. *The Liturgical Year.* Vol. 3: *The Paschal Triduum, the Easter Season.* Collegeville, MN: Liturgical Press, 1977.

Ramshaw, Gail. *The Three-Day Feast: Maundy Thursday, Good Friday, Easter.* Minneapolis, MN: Augsburg Fortress, 2004.

Stevenson, Kenneth. *Jerusalem Revisited: The Liturgical Meaning of Holy Week.* Washington, DC: Pastoral Press, 1988.

Mauni Amavasya

Mauni Amavasya is a special day during the larger 45-day bathing season known as Magh Mela, a sacred season that many Hindus observe as a time to wash away sins and illnesses. The period takes the whole month of Magha in the Hindu lunar calendar plus two additional weeks, beginning in December and going through the middle of February. Mauni Amavasya is the new moon day in the month of Magha, usually occurring toward the end of the Magh Mela.

The word "mauni" means silence, and those who observe this day do so by keeping complete silence throughout the day. Silence is seen as an essential part of spiritual discipline, as it offers an opportunity for introspection and initiates a dialogue with one's inner self. Silent time allows an individual opportunity to observe how the mind works.

Among the activities that Vaishnava Hindus engage in their silence is circumambulation of the pipal tree (the same tree that the Buddhists revere as the Bodhi Tree). They believe, as related in the Brahma Puran and the Padma Purana, how Vishnu hid in the peepal, and even that he was born under this tree. The aswattha or peepal tree is also linked to Krishna, given his quote in the Bhagavad Gita, "Among trees, I am the ashvattha." Krishna is also believed to have died under this tree.

Celebration of Mauni Amavasya is focused on the ancient city of Prayag, known today as Allahabad, Uttar Pradesh, believed to be the place where Brahma made his initial sacrifice following his creation of the world. It is noteworthy as the site of the confluence of the Ganges and Yamuna rivers. According to Hindu belief, the two very real rivers are also joined here by a third invisible river, the Sarasvat. Allahabad is the site of the Magh Mela every year. Every six years, the Magh Mela is transformed into the Ardh Kumbh Mela, a smaller version of the Kumbha Mela, which is held in Allahabad every 12 years. The Kumbha Mela is held four times every 12 years in four different locations, its location on any specific occasion being determined by the position of the Jupiter in the zodiac.

Constance A. Jones

See also Kumbha Mela.

References

Gour, Neelum. *Allahabad*. Mumbai: Marg Publications, 2010.

Maclean, Kama. *Pilgrimage and Power: The Kumbh Mela in Allahabad, 1765–1954*. New York: Oxford University Press, 2008.

Mawlid an-Nabi

Mawlid an-Nabi is a holiday on which Muslims celebrate the birthday of the Prophet Muhammad (c. 570–632). Muhammad was first visited by the archangel Gabriel (or Jibril) on Mount Hira near Mecca on the 17th night of Ramadan in 610 and to have begun revealing the Qur'an, the Islamic Bible, with what would become chapter (or sura) 96.

1. Read: In the name of thy Lord Who createth,
2. Createth man from a clot.
3. Read: And thy Lord is the Most Bounteous,
4. Who teacheth by the pen,

5. Teacheth man that which he knew not.
6. Nay, but verily man is rebellious
7. That he thinketh himself independent!
8. Lo! unto thy Lord is the return.
9. Hast thou seen him who dissuadeth
10. A slave when he prayeth?
11. Hast thou seen if he relieth on the guidance (of Allah)
12. Or enjoineth piety?
13. Hast thou seen if he denieth (Allah's guidance) and is froward?
14. Is he then unaware that Allah seeth?
15. Nay, but if he cease not, We will seize him by the forelock -
16. The lying, sinful forelock -
17. Then let him call upon his henchmen!
18. We will call the guards of hell.
19. Nay, Obey not thou him. But prostrate thyself, and draw near (unto Allah).

Several years later, he began to reveal the teachings from the revelation, to attack the idolatry that made up the religion of the residents of Mecca (now Saudi Arabia), and call for submission to Allah, the one God. In the year 620, Muhammad experienced a mysterious visit to Jerusalem, with Gabriel riding the winged horse Buraq. From Jerusalem, he was taken into the heavens, where he met some Prophets who in previous centuries had preceded him.

Getting primarily a hostile reception for his new message in Mecca, Muhammad moved to Medina, where what would become Islam was initially organized, distinct from the local practice of both Christianity and Judaism. After a number of years of armed hostilities with Meccans, he finally returned in 629. Muhammad won over the leadership of his own clan and was able to emerge as the authority in Mecca in 630. He ended the idolatry that had been focused at the Kaaba, the main religious shrine in the city, and spent the rest of his life building the movement he founded. In the Qur'an, he is termed the seal of a lineage of prophets (33.40) that began with Adam and continued through Moses to Jesus.

He was not deified by his followers, but has served as the exemplar of the faith and the descriptions of him by those who knew him have been assembled in a collection, the Hadith, that serves as a second holy book, providing much data not touched upon in the Qur'an. While Sunni Muslims share a high view of Muhammad, the smaller Shi'a Muslim community also concluded that only someone related to the Prophet and his descendants could legitimately rule. They traced their lineage from his daughter Fatima and her husband Ali.

Muslims center their celebration of Mawlid an-Nabi on the life and teachings of Muhammad. They sing songs about him and say special prayers. They remember the forgiveness he showed to those who were at one time bitter enemies. It is also a day to share wealth with the less fortunate.

Mawlid an-Nabi began to be celebrated in the 13th century and culminated a month of festivities. The day itself would be a time for large gatherings, gift giving, and feasting. In more recent times, celebrations have been more subdued out of a recognition that Muhammad had urged followers not to make it a matter of special focus. In fact, it was a month in which he tended to fast, not unlike the month of Ramadan. Some Muslims question the legitimacy of any celebration of Muhammad's birthday, while others completely ignore it.

James A. Beverley

See also Ashura; Data Ganj Bakhsh Death Anniversary; Hajj; Id al-Adha; Id al-Fitr; Islam—Annual Festivals and Holy Days; Laylat al-Mir'ag; Laylat al-Qadr; Layalt ul Bara'ah; Ramadan; Urs Festival.

References

Kaptein, M. J. G. *Muhammad's Birthday Festival: Early History in the Central Muslim Lands and Development in the Muslim West until the 10th/16th Century.* Leiden: Brill Academic Publishers, 1997.

Katz, Marian Holmes. *The Birth of the Prophet Muhammad: Devotional Piety in Sunni Islam.* New York: Routledge, 2007.

Kayani, Muhammad Afaq. *Should Muslims Celebrate the Birthday of the Holy Prophet (Sall Allahu Alaihi wa Sallum): A Reply to Hizb ul Tahrir.* Mumbai: Raza Academy, 1996.

Peters, F. E. *Muhammad and the Origins of Islam.* Albany: State University of New York Press, 1994.

Ramadan, Tariq. *In the Footsteps of the Prophet: Lessons from the Life of Muhammad.* New York: Oxford University Press, 2007.

Rubin, Uri., ed. *The Life of Muhammad.* Aldershot: Ashgate, 1998.

Mayan Calendar

In the 1990s, an obscure calendar from ancient Meso-America gained some importance among followers of Western Esotericism. The importance of the Mayan calendar was initially proposed by art historian José Arguelles (b. 1939) in his 1987 book, *The Mayan Factor: Path beyond Technology.* The unexpected success of *The Mayan Factor* among followers of the New Age led him to put out a new calendar for their use, a 13-moon/28-day calendar focused on phases of the moon, which many New Agers had begun to follow. This calendar runs from July 26 to July 24 of the following year, a total of 364 days. July 25 is left as a "Day out of Time." He attempted to synchronize his calendar with the Mayan calendar, while drawing on other non-Mayan sources, and make it available to modern people who otherwise live by the Common Era calendar (the modern revised Gregorian calendar used by most countries as the 21st century begins). His work was highly criticized by his scholarly colleagues, though those criticisms were usually ignored by his New Age audience. Through the several organizations he founded, the Planet Art Network and the Foundation for the Law of Time, he has continued to speculate on the calendar and its modern spiritual and metaphysical implications.

Even before Arguelles, however, speculation concerning the Mayan calendar was made by Michael D. Coe, who in his 1966 book *The Maya* offered the suggestion, in passing, that civilization might end on December 24, 2011. In later editions, he revised the date to the now-familiar December 23, 2012. The idea was discussed by Frank Waters in his *Mexico Mystique: The Coming Sixth Age of Consciousness* (1975) and again mentioned briefly by Arguelles in both *The Transformative Vision* (1975) and *The Mayan Factor* (1987), but the idea was largely forgotten in the 1990s with the New Age movement in sharp decline.

Then, after 20 years of neglect, Daniel Pinchbeck revived speculation about the Mayan calendar and the 2012 date while linking them to a wide variety of beliefs surrounding UFOs, though his best-selling 2006 book *2012: The Return of Quetzalcoatl* was essentially based on his own experiments with mood-altering substances and channeling. He also tempered Coe's original apocalyptic predictions and proposed a shift from materialistic to spiritual consciousness in its stead. By the time Pinchbeck's book appeared, the most popular prophetic Esoteric text of the 1990s, James Redfield's *The Celestine Prophecy*, appeared to have faded in popularity, and within a short time, a host of new books appeared discussing and offering alternative speculation about what, if anything would occur in December 2012.

While the literature on 2012 generally refers to the Mayan calendar, the Mayans actually had three calendars. Two of these calendars were called the Haab' and the Tzolk'in. The Haab' was the 365-day political calendar. It consists of eighteen 20-day divisions, plus a five-day period added at the end of the year. These last five days, having been added to being the year close to the solar year, were to some degree out of the system and viewed as unlucky and unfortunate. The Haab' started at the winter solstice and marked out the planning for an agricultural year.

The Haab' was combined with the Tzolk'in, the 260-day religious ceremonial calendar. At the beginning of the Mayan cycle, the Haab' and Tzolk'in would begin running side by side simultaneously. When the Tzolk'in ran out, it would simply begin again. It took 52 years for the Tzolk'in to once again end and begin at the winter solstice as did the Haab'. The 52-year cycle would operate for most people and most concerns, as very few lived to be more than 52 years old. The combined Haab'-Tzolk'in calendars named but did not number the years.

For the recording of events more than 52 years ago, a third calendar was employed, the so-called Long Count calendar. It is this calendar around which modern prophetic speculation has gathered. The Long Count begins counting years from what most believe to be the Mayans' date for creation, which would be August 11, 3114 BCE in the Common Era calendar used in most countries today. The Long Count calendar runs for 5,125 years and hence will run out in 2012 and start over again.

The 2012 date has been correlated with a variety of facts. Some have suggested, for example, that in 2012, the plane of the solar system will line up exactly with the plane of the Milky Way, thus completing a wobble cycle that that takes five times the 5,125 years of the Mayan calendar, or approximately 26,000 years.

Prophecies concerning 2012 vary from anticipations of catastrophe to hopes for positive social change and large-scale spiritual transformation for individuals. The expected changes vary from the visible and disruptive alternation of social and natural structures to the invisible and hence difficult-to-detect changes in human consciousness.

J. Gordon Melton

See also Common Era Calendar; Winter Solstice.

References

Arguelles, José. *The Mayan Factor: Path beyond Technology*. Rutland, VT: Inner Traditions/Bear & Company, 1987.

Braden, Greg. *The Mystery of 2012: Predictions, Prophecies and Possibilities*. Louisville, CO: Sounds True, Incorporated, 2009.

Coe, Michael D. *The Maya*. Rev. ed. London: Thames & Hudson, 1987 (originally published 1966).

Miller, Mary, and Karl Taube. *The Gods and Symbols of Ancient Mexico and the Maya: An Illustrated Dictionary of Mesoamerican Religion*. London: Thames & Hudson, 1993.

Pinchbeck, Daniel. *2012: The Return of Quetzalcoatl*, Los Angeles: Tarcher, 2006.

Sanderford, Susan K. *What's Up with 2012?* Scotts Valley, CA: CreateSpace, 2008.

Schele, Linda, and David Freidel. *A Forest of Kings: The Untold Story of the Ancient Maya*. New York: William Morrow, 1990.

Schele, Linda, and Ken Jordan, eds. *Toward 2012: Perspectives on the Next Age*. Los Angeles: Tarcher, 2009.

Mazu Festival, Goddess

Mazu (a.k.a. Matzu, Tianhou) is one of the most popular goddess figures in traditional Chinese religion. According to most accounts, she was once a real historical person, born as Lin Moniang in Putian county of Fujian Province, China. She was born in 960 CE on the 23rd day of the 3rd lunar month, which happened to be the first year of the reign of Jianlong of the Song dynasty. She died at a relatively young age on the ninth day of the ninth lunar month. She was only 28 years old, and she never married.

According to the legends that have built up around Lin Muniang, her conception was miraculous, her mother having been assisted by the goddess Guan Yin. Her

Statue of the goddess Mazu in China. (Peng Guang Chen/Dreamstime.com)

name Moniang, or "mute maiden," derived from her reputation for not crying as a child. When she was 16 years old, a spirit gave her a magical charm that allowed her to exercise magical powers and to travel outside her body. She worked many miracles and defeated many demons and monsters. Many of the stories about her involve water. She saved her father who got caught in a storm with his fishing vessel. She provided safe drinking water, ended droughts, and turned back floods.

In the end, she was welcomed to the heaven by the Jade Emperor, who heads the pantheon of deities in traditional Taoism. Mazu experienced her first wave of popularity as a deity during the Song dynasty. She was among a number of new-breed deities who operated somewhat apart from the tradition Taoist hierarchy, much as bodhisattvas in Pure Land Buddhism or angels and saints in Catholicism. Through the centuries, different emperors bestowed elaborate titles on her. After conquering Taiwan, The Kangxi emperor named her empress of Heaven.

The first temple primarily dedicated to Mazu appeared to have been built in 1122 in Fujian. The first in Hong Kong arose in 1266, and worship was established in Taiwan in the 18th century. By the end of the 20th century, there were some 800 Mazu temples noted in Taiwan, and more than 100,000 people traveled annually to Putian to her traditional home. Here annually, on the day of her birth and death in April and October, there is a large festival in her honor.

Festivities may include performances of Chinese opera on stages set up in front of a temple, the movement of processions honoring the deity through the neighborhood, various types of musical performances, and a puppet show for the kids and young at heart. When an important temple has its festival, the lesser temples may send their deity there for a visit. These images from lesser temples are believed to be empowered from passing through the incense smoke of one of the larger temples.

Besides the temple on Meizhou Island in Putian county of Fujian Province, other important pilgrimage sites for Mazu believers are the Chaotian Gong temple in Beigang, Taiwan, which has a statue of Mazu that comes from Meizhou Island; the A-Ma Temple, which is the oldest temple in Macau, constructed in 1488 to commemorate Mazu as the goddess who blesses Macau's fishermen; and the old temples in Kowloon, Wanchai, Stanley, and Joss House Bay in Hong Kong.

J. Gordon Melton

See also Che Kung, Birthday of; Double Ninth Festival; Guan Yin's Birthday; Kwan Tai, Birthday of; Monkey King, Birthday of the; Pak Tai, Birthday of.

References

Bosco, Joseph, and Puay-peng Ho. *Temples to the Empress of Heaven*. Hong Kong: Oxford University Press, 1999.

Dean, Kenneth. *Taoist Ritual and Popular Cults of Southeast China*. Princeton, NJ: Princeton University Press, 1995.

Hatfield, D. J. W. *Taiwanese Pilgrimage to China: Ritual, Complicity, Community*. London: Palgrave Macmillan, 2009.

Meat Fare Sunday. *See* Mardi Gras

Medicine Buddha's Birthday

The Medicine Buddha (Bhaisayja-guru or in Japan, Yakushi-nyorai) is the bodhisattva most known as a healing force in the Mahayana Buddhist tradition. According to Buddhist teachings, prior to attaining enlightenment, Medicine Master made 12 vows to cure all illnesses and lead all people to enlightenment. The circumstances of the making of the vows are revealed in the Medicine Master Sutra, which also speak of the benefits to be offered to believers who invoke Medicine Buddha's name.

Medicine Buddha is charged with healing all diseases in the sick as well as any deficiencies of wisdom we might have. He is often depicted with the attending bodhisattvas Sunlight (on his left) and Moonlight (on his right), who lead the cadre of bodhisattvas that surround Medicine Buddha. His body is transparent, and he is pictured as wearing a monastic robe and seated with the legs crossed. His left hand lies in his lap and usually holds the medicine bowl, while his right hand forms the charity mudra and holds either a branch with fruit, or just the fruit of the myrobalan, a medicinal plant found in India and other tropical countries. His birthday is celebrated on the 22nd day of the 8th lunar month.

J. Gordon Melton

See also Amitabha's Birthday; Guan Yin's Birthday; Mahasthamaprapta's Birthday; Manjushri's Birthday; Mudras.

References

Boheng, Wu, and Cai Zhuozhi. *100 Buddhas in Chinese Buddhism*. Translated by Mu Xin and Yan Zhi. Singapore: Asiapac Books, 1997.

Vessantara. *Meeting the Buddhas: A Guide to Buddhas, Bodhisattvas, and Tantric Deities*. Birmingham, UK: Windhorse Publications, 1998.

Meher Baba, Commemoration Days of (January 31, February 25)

Meher Baba is the religious name of Merwan S. Irani (1894–1969), an Indian spiritual teacher who was believed by his disciples to be the Avatar of the Age (i.e., an incarnation of God). He came to his teaching mission after studying with five teachers from several different religious traditions (each now considered a perfect master by the followers of Meher Baba. In 1921, he began to gather followers, and then in 1925, he moved into a period of silence and taught entirely without speaking. While centering his work on India, he also traveled to the West more than a dozen times. In the United States, he accepted into his following Rabia Martin, a female, who led the Sufi movement initiated by Pir Inayat Khan (1882–1927) which emerged as Sufism Reoriented. He died January 31, 1969, at Meherabad, near his birthplace at Poona, India, and left behind a loosely organized but dedicated following generally referred to as Baba Lovers. His tomb has become a shrine.

Each year, Meherabad hosts two events that specifically commemorate the life of Meher Baba. On February 25, his birth celebration begins at 5:00 a.m. at Meherabad for prayers and songs to celebrate the coming of the Avatar into the world. The festive atmosphere will continue through the day. On January 30, thousands of Baba Lovers will begin to arrive at Meherabad for a several-day commemoration of Amartithi, the remembrance of Meher Baba dropping his body (death). That day, a 48-hour program of film, songs, and dance will begin on a stage near Meher Baba's tomb. The climax of the gathering comes shortly after noon on January 31, in commemoration of Baba's earthly end at 12:15 p.m. The followers gather at the tomb shrine for 15 minutes of silence in recognition of Baba's life of teaching in silence. Those who cannot come to Meherabad will attend a similar gathering at their local center.

J. Gordon Melton

See also Osho (Rajneesh), Birthday of; Sai Baba of Shirdi, Birthday of.

References

Baba, Meher. *God Speaks*. Walnut Creek, CA: Sufism Reoriented, 1973.

Davy, Kitty. *Love Alone Prevails*. Myrtle Beach, SC: Sheriar Press, 1981.
Haynes, Charles. *Meher Baba: The Awakener*. North Myrtle Beach, SC: Avatar Foundation, 1993.

Meskal (September 27)

Meskal, the first major date of the liturgical year of the Ethiopian Orthodox Tewahdo Church, celebrates the finding of the True Cross by Saint Helena (c. 248–c. 329), the mother of the emperor Constantine (r. 306–337). This celebration, which also occurs in the Roman Catholic and Eastern Orthodox churches, has assumed a particular importance in the Ethiopian Church. The most elaborate celebration will occur annually in Mescal Square in the center of Addis Ababa, Ethiopia's capital.

Meskal highlights the physical presence of a fragment of the True Cross that resides at the remote Gishen Mariam monastery in Egziabher Ab, some 300 miles north of Addis Ababa. The fragments of the True Cross were a gift of the Christians of Egypt, who during the Middle Ages were on occasion protected from persecution by the Muslim authorities in Egypt, by the intervention of Ethiopians. When offered gold as a thank-you gift, the Ethiopian emperor Dawit I (1362–1413) asked for some pieces of the True Cross, which at the time were in the custody of the Coptic Patriarch of Alexandria. Since that time, Meskal has commemorated both the discovery of the True Cross by Helena and the transfer of pieces of it to Ethiopia.

Originally, in the fourth century, following the establishment of Christianity throughout the Roman Empire, Helena traveled to the Holy Land, where she discovered a number of objects reputed to be relics of biblical times, none more heralded than the cross upon which, it was claimed, Jesus was crucified. Frustrated at not finding the cross, she is said to have lighted incense and followed the smoke to the site where the three crosses of Jesus and the two thieves crucified with him were buried.

In a ritual reenactment of the events of finding the cross, branches of the meskal plant are decorated with flowers and set ablaze. The celebration begins in the afternoon and may continue through the evening hours. The center of attention is a large pyramid-shaped pyre. Atop the pyramid is a tall cross made from the bright yellow meskal flowers. Around the pyre, a procession of priests in liturgical garb and laypeople dressed elaborately for the occasion circle the centerpiece carrying crosses and wooden torches decorated with olive leaves. As the sun sets, those with torches set the pyre alight.

On the next, with the giant fire having finally burned itself out, people return to the site and use the ash to mark their forehead with the sign of the cross.

J. Gordon Melton

See also Ash Wednesday; Elevation of the True Cross; Ethiopian Church—Liturgical Year; Genna; Holyrood or the Feast of the Triumph of the Holy Cross; Procession of the Cross.

References

Gulilat, Ermias. "The Celebration of Maskal—Finding the True Cross." Posted at http://www.ethioembassy.org.uk/articles/articles/focus%20electronic-00/Ermias%20Gulilat%20-%201.htm. Accessed May 15, 2010.

Pohlsander, Hans A. *Helena: Empress and Saint*. Chicago: Ares Publishers, 1995.

Thiede, Carsten Peter, and Matthew d'Ancona. *The Quest for the True Cross*. New York: Palgrave, 2002.

Michaelmas (September 29)

Michaelmas is a feast day of the Roman Catholic Church that celebrates the role of the archangel Michael and by extension of angels in general in the Christian life. Michael is one of several angels (such as Gabriel) who are singled out and mentioned multiple times in scripture. He first appears in the book of Daniel as an angelic price in the vision Daniel had by the river Hiddekel (Daniel 10:13). He then is named in the book of Jude as one who disputed with the devil, and emerges most notably in the book of Revelation (12:7) where he wars victoriously in heaven fighting a dragon.

Though seen as a warrior who defended first Israel, and later the church, Christians also came to see him as a healer from whom the ill could receive care. Among the healing sites associated with Michael was the Michaelion, a church at Sosthenion, about 50 miles south of Constantinople, where he reportedly appeared to the emperor Constantine. A variety of feast days were kept in the ancient church at different locations. Then, late in the fifth century, on May 8 (the year is uncertain), Michael appeared at Monte Gargano, near Foggia, in southern Italy. Here he appeared not as the healer angel, but in his warrior aspect. Pope Gelasius I (r. 492–496) ordered the erection of a basilica at the site of the apparition. This apparition set the stage for a latter sighting of Michael in 663. In the evening, he was seen standing with a flaming sword in his hand atop the mountain as a storm raged. The next day, May 8, an Italian army from Sipontum was victorious over a Greek army loyal to the Byzantine emperor. After the victory, the church at Sipontum instituted a special feast to Michael to be held annually on May 8. This is the feast that spread throughout the Western Church. Originally commemorating the victory, it gradually was transformed into a commemoration of Michael's apparitions, though with references to his warrior role.

Michael is also said to have appeared to Saint Aubert, the bishop of Avranches, France, in 708 and asked him to build a church on a small island off the coast of Normandy, France, at the mouth of the Couesnon River now known as Mont-Saint-Michel. After several visitations, the reluctant Aubert finally began the work on what would become one of the more famous medieval churches.

Through the centuries, the May 8 date for commemorating Michael vied with September 29, the date of an early church in Rome dedicated to the archangel.

Saint Michael slays the dragon in this woodcutting by Albrecht Durer (1471–1528). (Library of Congress)

By the reign of Pope Pius V (r. 1566–1572) the May 8 date was widespread, but September 29 was also an important day falling close to the fall equinox. In England, it was associated with the withdrawal of herds from their summer pastures, the opening of the hunting season, and the beginning of the school year. It had become ingrained in British culture as one of the "quarter days," a moment every three months set aside for the hiring of servants, the electing of magistrates, and caring for many legal matters. Michaelmas remains an important date in the Anglican calendar. In some parts of northern Europe, celebration includes the consumption of "Saint Michael's Love," a special wine.

In 1969, along with other revisions of the Roman liturgical calendar, the commemoration of the feasts to Gabriel (March 24) and Raphael (October 24) were abandoned and collapsed into Michaelmas.

J. Gordon Melton

See also Annunciation, Feast of the; George, Feast Day of St.; Joan of Arc, Saint's Day of St.

References

Ball, Ann. *Encyclopedia of Catholic Devotions and Practices.* Huntington, IN: Our Sunday Visitor, 2003.

Deceneax, Marc. *The Mont-Saint-Michel Stone by Stone.* Paris: Editions Ouest-France, 1906.

Morrell, Patricia. *Festivals and Customs.* London: Macmillan, 1977.

St. Michael the Archangel. Charlotte, NC: TAN Books and Publishers, 2009.

Mid-Autumn Festival

The Mid-Autumn Festival occurs in the middle of the second of the three lunar months that make up the autumn season in China—the seventh, eighth, and ninth months. As the months are measured from new moon to new moon, the middle of the month is always at a full moon. In a time before electricity, the moon was a more important illuminating force than in recent times, and the coming of a full moon at the time of the year when there were few clouds to obscure it and people were at the end of a long farming season were reasons enough for a pause to celebrate.

Buddhists contributed to this festival oriented on the moon by contributing several legends from India that introduced a connection between the moon and rabbits. According to one popular story, the Buddha summoned animals to him as he was preparing for the end of his earthly existence, but only 12 animals showed up to say goodbye. He acknowledged their presence by naming the years of the 12-year cycle in Chinese astrology after 1 of the 12 animals. Of these, the fourth to arrive before the Buddha was the rabbit. Another story tells of Buddha's prior incarnation as a rabbit. One day while traveling with an ape and a fox, he encountered a hungry beggar. The three left to find some food. The ape and fox returned with some, but the rabbit found nothing. In his determination to be of service, however, the rabbit made a fire and then jumped into it so that he would become food for the beggar. The beggar turned out to be the god Indra, who rewarded the rabbit by sending him to the moon.

Picked up by the Taoists, the rabbit on the moon was pictured as standing under a magical tree making the elixir of immortality. This image would be integrated with another story of Hou Yi and his wife Chang E, who lived in ancient China during the reign of the long-lived emperor Yao (2358–2258 BCE). Hou Yi was a member of the imperial guards known for his skill as an archer. At one point during Emperor Yao's reign, suddenly 10 suns appeared in the sky. Their combined heat made life unbearable and the emperor asked Hou Yi to get rid of them. With his arrows, he was able to get rid of nine of them. As a reward, he was summoned to the throne room of the Queen Mother of the West, who resided in the Kunlun Mountains, a very real set of mountains in western China which in places forms the northern border to Tibet. To the Taoists, this mountain was a heavenly place. Though geographically placed on earth, it was analogous to the Buddhists' Pure Land. When Hou Yi visited there, he was given a pill of immortality, but told to prepare himself with prayer and fasting before taking it. His wife, however, discovered the pill and took it. She found she could fly, and to escape her husband's anger, she flew to the moon.

On the moon, Chang E coughed and part of the pill flew out of her mouth. The pill became a jade rabbit and she a toad. Hou Yi in the meantime erected a new home on the sun. He is reunited with his wife monthly in the full moon.

These legends continue to inform what has become a family holiday in modern Chinese society, both in the People's Republic and the diaspora. It is a time to reunite with friends and family and to enjoy a characteristic Chinese delicacy, the moon cake. Moon cakes come in a variety of shapes and are filled with sweets, meats, or salty fillings.

The primary ritual of the Mid-Autumn Festival is conducted by women on the 15th day of the lunar month as the full moon reigns above. It occurs around an open-air altar decorated with a picture of the moon goddess and some representation of the rabbit. Different food substances would be brought to the altar, a wine glass filled, and incense lit. The culmination of the ritual would see the women of the house bowing, what in Chinese is a kowtow, before the goddess. The ceremony ends with the burning of the moon goddess's picture, the act of burning not being a destructive act but one of communion and communication.

J. Gordon Melton

See also Chinese New Year's Day; Double Ninth Festival; Double Seventh Festival; Spring Dragon Festival.

References

Guoliang, Gai. *Exploring Traditional Chinese Festivals in China.* Singapore: McGraw-Hill, 2009.

Kaulbach, B, and B. Proksch. *Arts and Culture in Taiwan.* Taipei: Southern Materials Center, 1984.

Latsch, Marie-Luise. *Traditional Chinese Festivals.* Singapore: Greaham Brash, 1984.

Liming, Wei. *Chinese Festivals: Traditions, Customs, and Rituals.* Hong Kong: China International Press, 2005.

Windling, Terri. "The Symbolism of Rabbits and Hares." *Journal of Mythical Arts*, Winter 2007. http://www.endicott-studio.com/rdrm/rrRabbits.html. Accessed May 16, 2009.

Mid-Lent. *See* Lent

Mid-Pentecost, Feast of

The feast of mid-Pentecost, one of the lesser feasts of the Eastern Orthodox Church, is celebrated on the Wednesday 25 days after Easter, at the midpoint between Easter and Pentecost. The feast is seen as uniting themes of both Easter and Pentecost. Water is a popular symbol for this worship hour—Jesus representing the Water of Life, and the Holy Spirit of Pentecost pictured as being poured out on the people. As part of the service, there is usually a rite termed the Lesser Blessing of the Waters.

In the Orthodox Church, broad use is made of Holy or Blessed Water, a practice derived from the account of Jesus seeking baptism at the hand of John the Baptist. John preached baptism for repentance of sin, but as Jesus was without sin, his baptism is believed to have sanctified the water. Such sanctified water is an instrument of life-giving power. Each year at the Theophany feast in January, water is blessed to be used by the parish during the coming year. At several additional times, however, water may be blessed—Mid-Pentecost being such an occasion. Traditionally, such water was used to bless the fields in the early stages of the growing season.

In parts of Greece, this day became the occasion of a special ceremony to prayer from deliverance of scarlet fever, once a widespread and highly contagious disease among children. It has now largely been wiped out by penicillin and other antibiotics. On this day, the children of the village would bake rolls, which were consumed at a banquet. One girl, selected for her unique name, would make a special ring-shaped cake. This cake was not eaten, but was divided among the children, taken home, and allowed to dry out. If a child came down with symptoms of scarlet fever, the cake piece would be pounded into powder and sprinkled over the body. It was believed to be a cure.

J. Gordon Melton

See also Easter; Eastern Orthodoxy—Liturgical Year; Pentecost; Theophany.

References

Sanidopolous, John. "Feast of Mid-Pentecost." *Mystagogy*, April 28, 2010. Posted at http://www.johnsanidopoulos.com/2010/04/feast-of-mid-pentecost-and.html. Accessed May 15, 2010.

Thompson, Sue Ellen, and Barbara W. Carlson, comp. *Holidays, Festivals and Celebrations of the World Dictionary*. Detroit, MI: Omnigraphics, 1994.

Midsummer. *See* Summer Solstice

Miracles, Festival of Our Lady of (September)

The Festival of Our Lady of Miracles is the primary annual celebrative event of the Roman Catholic community on the island of Terceira, the Azores. The veneration of the Blessed Virgin as Our Lady of Miracles goes back to 1694, when a priest seeing a secluded place for meditation erected a small chapel on the western coast of the island near the village of Serreta, and inside the chapel, he placed a small statue of the Virgin. The chapel was later abandoned, and the statue moved to a church in another village, Doze Ribeiras.

In 1764, Portuguese military personnel arrived to inspect the island's defenses relative to defending the island from invasion from other European powers. They visited the church in Doze Ribeiras and, in the presence of the statue, vowed that they would honor the Blessed Virgin with an annual celebration if the island was spared any attack upon it. The group making the vow named themselves the Slaves of Our Lady. Eight years later, the Slaves moved to build a new chapel at Serreta. Once in place, the statue was returned to it. In 1797, French forces threatened the island and a plan was initiated to reconstruct the wall around the chapel. The invasion never came, and over the next generation, both the population of Serreta and church membership grew. A new church was completed in 1842, and in 1861, it emerged as a separate independent parish. As the parish grew, so the annual celebration of Mary as Our Lady of Miracles grew, and an increasing number of miracle stories were attached to her.

Through the 20th century, the annual event in Serreta attracted more and more people, not only from the Azores, but Portugal as well. It included a weekend of activities the second weekend in September, the effort to get to the rather out-of-the-way location becoming a pilgrimage in itself. Saturday includes a procession, novenas, and an all-night prayer vigil in the church, which concludes with an early morning Mass on Sunday. The weekend also includes a blessing of the cows, a singing contest, and bull fights. The spontaneous singing is of peculiar conversational style unique to the Azores.

Early in the 20th century, Manuel B. Sousa, a citizen of Terceira, moved to the United States and settled in Gustine, California. There in 1936, he and some fellow Azorans started the practice of holding a festival to Our Lady of Miracles reminiscent of the one on Terceira. He commissioned a copy of the statue at Serreta. A group of local men began to organize an initial celebration at which they attempted to include as many of the events, both sacred and secular, associated with the one in Terceira as possible. Over time, the celebration became a major event in the lives of Portuguese-speaking Americans, who travel to Gustine from around the country to attend the annual event. Today the festival includes bull fights and performers brought in from the Azores and Portugal. The local church hosts a novena, a candlelight procession and a Mass at 4:00 a.m. Sunday morning.

J. Gordon Melton

See also Anne, Feast Day of St.

References

"The Legend of Our Lady of Miracles." Posted at http://kathrynmaffei.tripod.com/index-4.html. Accessed April 15, 2010.

Misa de Gallo (December 24)

Misa de Gallo, or Rooster's Mass, is an early morning Mass or worship service held in the congregations of the Roman Catholic Church in many Spanish-speaking countries during the nine days before Christmas. The name relates to an old belief that a rooster was the logical animal to have witnessed the birth of Christ and at dawn to first to herald the event.

In the Philippines, the Misa de Gallo forms a novena (a devotion done in nine parts) also called the Simbang Gabi (or mass at dawn). The Simbang Gabi Mass is held each day in the early morning hours between December 16 and 24, and time to end at about dawn when the rooster crows. The Cock's crow on December 16 marks the official opening of the Christmas season in the Philippines. During the next nine days, upon arriving at and leaving the church service, the faith will encounter vendors selling some traditional food such as *puto bumbong* (a rice pastry seasoned with coconut and brown sugar and cooked in bamboo) and *bibingka* (small rice cakes), and for the thirsty, *tsokolate* (a hot chocolate-flavored drink) or *salabat* (a ginger tea).

The last Misa de Gallo on the morning of Christmas Eve will be followed in the evening with a feast called *Noche Buena*. The feasting and partying will take up much of the evening into the wee hours of the morning. After a brief rest, the faithful will attend Christmas Mass at around 10:00 a.m. and then participate in another Christmas feast.

The Misa de Gallo is equivalent to the Las Posadas celebration in Latin America.

J. Gordon Melton

See also Advent; Christmas; Posadas, Las.

References

Gochenour, Theodore. *Considering Filipinos*. Yarmouth, ME: Intercultural Press, 1990.

Leandro, Deacon, and Tessie Centenera. "Misaisa de Gallo, a Philippine Christmas tradition." Posted at http://cfc–usa.com/index.php?option=com_content&view=article&id=63:misa-de-gallo-a-philippine-christmas-tradition-&catid=6:feature. Accessed May 15, 2010.

Mokshada Ekadashi

Mokshada Ekadashi is one of the ekadashi dates (the 11th day after the new or full moon) that has gained special significance among Vaishnava Hindus. It is observed during the waxing moon in the month of Agrahayana (November–December in the Common Era calendar).

The story behind this ekadashi is found in the Brahmanda Purana, one of the Hindu holy texts, in which the deity Krishna tell Yudhishtira that fasting and worship on this day destroys all one's sins. This day has gained additional importance from a belief that its observance will assist one's deceased ancestors. This belief is attached to the legend of King Vaikanasa, who dreamed that his father was in the hell realm. He sought the advice of Parvata Muni, a legendary sage in Vaishnava literature, who was known for his ability to fly through spiritual realms and had knowledge of past and future, The sage discovered that the king's father had committed some evils that led to his being sent to hell. He then advised the king to observe Mokshada Ekadashi, which soon led to his father's release.

The most devout and able will fast completely on the ekadashi. Others, unable to reach that austere level, will do a partial fast. They will consume only vegetarian items while avoiding foods made with beans, pulses, and grains, especially rice, and not use onion or garlic in the food preparation. They are left with primarily fruits, milk products, vegetables, and nuts.

Mokshada Ekadashi occurs on the same day that many celebrate as Gita Jayanti, the birthday of the Gita.

Constance A. Jones

The Monkey King stands in Buddha's magic hand. (Shupian/Dreamstime.com)

See also Gita Jayanti; Hari-Shayani Ekadashi; Kamada Ekadashi; Mauna Agyaras; Nirjala Ekadashi; Putrada Ekadashi; Vaikuntha Ekadashi.

References

"Mokshada Ekadashi." Hindu Blog. Posted at http://www.hindu-blog.com/2008/11/moksada-ekadasi-mokshada-ekadashi.html. Accessed June 15, 2010.

Tagare, G. V., ed. *Brahmanda Purana*. Columbia, MO: South Asia Books, 1983 (various editions).

Monkey King, Birthday of the

The Monkey King (God) of China (not to be confused with Hanuman, the monkey god of Hinduism) is the product of fiction, having begun life in a novel, *Pilgrim to the West*, written by Wu Cheng'en (c. 1500–c. 1582), during the Ming dynasty (1368–1644). The novel recounts how Xuan Zang, a Buddhist monk of the Tang dynasty (618–907), endured many obstacles imposed by various supernatural characters and finally gets to the West (i.e., India) assisted by his three disciples—Monkey King, Pig, and Friar Sha. The novel received popular acclaim and subsequently became an integral part of Chinese popular culture.

Monkey King (or Sun Wukong) emerges as possibly the most important figure in the novel. He acts freely and spontaneously, shows courage, and is unyielding in the face of the evil supernatural. He is also the epitome of loyalty to his master.

Pilgrim to the West also created a world with very fuzzy lines between the real and the imaginary. The author described real places, which his imaginary characters visit. He describes real parts of the Chinese religious hierarchy (such as the Jade Emperor) with wholly imaginary characters, such as Monkey King. In popular culture, the distinction between reality and fiction also seemed to have been blurred.

Monkey King is a minor Taoist figure appearing in a Buddhist novel. The novel, however, had the effect of elevating him to a high status, at least relative to popularity. Thus, in the wake of the novel's popularity, Monkey King temples began to appear, and a biography constructed.

Monkey King was especially celebrated on the 16th day of the eighth lunar month of the Chinese calendar (usually September on the Common Era calendar), and celebrations are held at the surviving Monkey King temples in Hong Kong (Kowloon) and Taiwan. The birthday is celebrated with the burning of spirit money and incense. In generations past, the birthday was a time for talented spirit mediums to walk on hot coals and climb a ladder made of sharp blades.

J. Gordon Melton

See also Che Kung, Birthday of; Guan Yin's Birthday; Kwan Tai, Birthday of; Mazu Festival, Goddess; Pak Tai, Birthday of; Third Prince, Birthday of the.

References

"Monkey King Temples." Posted at http://www.monkeykingepic.com/Monkey_King/Day_3.html. Accessed on May 15, 2010.

Wu Cheng'en. *Journey to the West*. Translated by W. J. F. Jenner. Beijing: Foreign Languages Press, 2003.

Monlam, the Great Prayer Festival

Immediately following Losar, the Tibetan New Year, and competing with it in importance for Tibetan Buddhists, Monlam, the Great Prayer Festival, begins on the fourth day of the first month of the Tibetan lunar calendar and continues for a week, through the 11th day. The festival was initiated in 1409 by Tsong Khapa (1357–1419 CE), popularly termed Je Rinpoche (Precious Master). One of the most famous of Tibetan leaders, Tsong Khapa founded the Reformed or Gelugpa School of Tibetan Buddhism, the group later headed by the Dalai Lama, who came to also be the temporal ruler of Tibet. Given the political elements of Losar, Monlam emerges as a more focused religious celebration.

Tsong Khapa initiated the first Monlam festival with a ceremony during which he offered a golden crown to the statue of Gautama Buddha at the Jokhang Temple/Monastery near the Potala Palace in Lhasa. That temple became the focus of the annual prayer festival. The celebration waned in the latter half of the 15th century, but in 1518, Gedun Gyatso (1475–1542), then the abbot of Drepung monastery, posthumously designated the second Dalai Lama, revived it, and called the monks from the two other prominent Gelugpa monasteries at Sera and Gaden, to join with him. These three monasteries were the training grounds for the Gelugpa monks, and their gathering in one place became the occasion for lengthy and lively theological discussions. These discussions allowed them to demonstrate what they had learned and formed part of their final examinations for the Buddhist philosophy degree, the Lharampa Geshe degree. From this time, debates on Buddhist teachings became an integral part of Monlam. Monks would also demonstrate their skills in the elaborate traditional cham dancing.

Monlam occurred, of course, while Tibetans throughout the land continued to celebrate Losar, the New Year. Monasteries across Tibet held special ceremonies and as part of their celebration unfold large thankas, holy pictures of Buddhist deities, on the side of the mountains for the veneration of all. The festival is designed to focus attention on Gautama Buddha's personal victory over the ignorance, anger, and greed, and his subsequent attainment of enlightenment.

Following the Chinese occupation of Tibet in the 1950s, the celebration of Monlam suffered greatly. It was banned altogether during the Cultural Revolution (1966–1976). It was revived in the mid-1980s but again banned in 1990. It has gradually been reintroduced in Tibet and at Tibetan temples across China, but its celebration has been a matter of contention in Lhasa itself as monks have become active in protesting the government and calling for the return of the Dalai Lama. As the majority of Tibetans now reside outside Tibet, some of the larger festivals are held in places such as Tongren, Qinghai Province, and the Labrang monastery in Xiahe, the site of the largest Tibetan monastery outside Tibet.

As the various schools of Tibetan Buddhism were reestablished among the self-imposed exiles in India, and the new monastic centers erected, the Monlam festival was revived in stages. Early on, the Venerable Tarthang Tulku, a Nyingmapa lama who had established himself in California, combined his interest in the further development of the Buddhist shrine at Bodh Gaya (where Gautama Buddha received enlightenment) with his concern for the perpetuation of Tibetan Buddhism in the modern world. Beginning in 1989, he provided sponsorship and support for the Monlam gatherings of the leaders of all four schools for the first World Peace Ceremony, which has continued to be held annually. During the early 1990s, the Tibetan leadership that met at Bodh Gaya began to envision Monlam celebration as each of the important sights connected with Buddha's life, especially Lumbini, Sarnath, and Kusinagara. Thus, for example, in 1993, the Sakyapa and Kagyu schools began sponsoring an annual Monlam celebration at Lumbini (in Nepal), where Gautama Buddha was born. In India and Nepal, the Gelugpa School, headed by the Dalai Lama, sponsors the Monlam gathering at Sarnath, as well as at their headquarters in Dharamsala. Monlam occurs as Hindus are celebrating Diwali, the largest national festival in the two countries.

The Monlam celebration officially ends in the 11th day of the month, but festivities continue until the 15th, the day of the Butter Lamp Festival. During Monlam, huge ritual-offering cakes (called *tormas*) are made, each topped with an elaborate sculpture made from butter (which in Tibet has many uses, including being burned in lamps for light). Traditionally, on the 15th day, the Monlam (and New Year's) festival would culminate in Baektor Square in front of Jokhang Temple. The *tormas* would be on display for all to see and the day's event would conclude with *tormas* being brought together in a bonfire.

J. Gordon Melton

See also Butter Lamp Festival; Diwali; Losar; Sakya Dawa Festival; World Peace Ceremony.

References

Levenson, Claude B. *Symbols of Tibetan Buddhism*. New York: Assouline, 2000.

Osada,Yukiyasu, Gavin Allwright, and Atushi Kanamaru *Mapping the Tibetan World*. Tokyo: Kotan Publishing, 2001.

Rigzin, Tsepak. *Festival of Tibet*. Dharamsala, India: Library of Tibetan Works & Archives, 2006.

Von Buchwaldt-Ernst, Beatrice. *Monlam in Labrang*. Hannover, Germany: Offizin-Verlag, 2005.

The World Peace Ceremony/Bodh Gaya. Berkeley, CA: Dharma Publishing, 1994.

Montségur Day (March 16)

Montségur Day remembers the 13th-century Gnostics from southern France, the Cathars (also called Albigensians, as their community was centered on the city of Albi). The Cathars had roots in both the Paulician movement of Armenia and the Bogomils of the southern Balkans, with a tendency toward dualism that suggested contact with Manichaeanism. The Roman Catholic Church regarded the sect as heretical in the extreme. Initially, it initiated some peaceful efforts at conversion, undertaken by Dominic, an effort that would lead to the formation of the Dominican order. These proved insufficient, however, and eventually, Church leaders called for a military solution, which was led by knights from northern France and Germany.

In the first significant engagement of the war, the town of Béziers was besieged on July 22, 1209, and some 20,000 people killed, including many women and children and the city burned to the ground. The war took 20 years to complete and ended in 1229 with the Treaty of Paris (1229). It ended any support the movement leaders could expect from the local nobility. Meanwhile, in 1215, Pope Innocent III (r. 1198–1216) called the Fourth Council of the Lateran, primarily to combat the Cathar heresy. What is now known as the Inquisition would be established as the war ended in 1229 to finally deal with remnants of the Cathar movement. It operated through southern France for the rest of the century and much of the next. Unrepentant Cathars were hanged or burnt at the stake.

In one of the last military actions, the French army besieged the Cathar fortress of Montségur (from May 1243 to March 1244). After the castle fell, on March 16, 1244, over 200 Cathar prefects were burnt at the stake.

Some historians estimate that at least as many as a quarter of a million Cathars and sympathetic neighbors died in the effort to suppress them. These are the people, not the several hundred massacred at Montségur, who are remembered on Montségur Day. The Ecclesia Gnostica commemorates them and identifies with them by holding a solemn Requiem Eucharist.

J. Gordon Melton

See also Sophia, The Descent and Assumption of Holy; Templars, The Day of the Martyrdom of the Holy; Valentinus, Feast of the Holy.

References

Given, James. *The Inquisition and Medieval Society.* Ithaca, NY: Cornell University Press, 1992.

Peg, Mark Gregory. *A Most Holy War: The Albigensian Crusade and the Battle for Christendom.* Oxford: Oxford University Press, 2008.

Peters, Edward, ed. *Heresy and Authority in Medieval Europe.* Philadelphia: University of Pennsylvania Press, 1980.

Stoyanov, Yuri. *The Other God: Dualist Religions from Antiquity to the Cathar Heresy.* New Haven, CT: Yale University Press, 2000.

Most Holy Name of Mary, Feast of the (September 12)

The Feast of the Most Holy Name of Mary, a moment for believers to contemplate the meaning of Mary and her role in the whole scheme of salvation under her various names and appearances, is a relatively new item in the church calendar. The celebration of such a day of contemplation was assigned to the diocese of Cuenca (Spain) by Pope Julius II in 1513. He also placed it on September 15, a week after the celebration of the Feast of the Nativity of Mary. Later in the century, when the liturgical life of the church was reviewed as part of the Counter-Reformation, Pope Pius V (r. 1566–1572) removed the observation of the day from the calendar, but it was replaced by Pope Sixtus V (1585–1590) though he shifted it to September 17. The celebration spread throughout Spain and southern Italy. Its popularization was assisted by its being picked up by several religious orders.

Then on September 12, 1683, Polish king John Sobieski, a Marian devotee, won an important battle with the Turkish forces that were threatening Vienna. In response to the victory, Pope Innocent XI (r. 1676–1689) both elevated and redefined the "The Feast of the Holy Name of Mary" as a celebration of the whole of the Roman Catholic Church. The feast would continue to be celebrated on the Sunday after the Feast of the Nativity of Mary (September 8) until the 20th century when Pope Pius X (r. 1903–1914) set the celebration on September 12, an emphasis of the day as a remembrance of the 1683 victory at Vienna.

J. Gordon Melton

See also Assumption of the Virgin; Immaculate Conception, Feast of the; Solemnity of Mary, Feast of the.

References

Dodds, Monica, and Bill Dodds. *Encyclopedia of Mary.* Huntington, IN: Our Sunday Visitor, 2007.

Stove, John. *The Siege of Vienna: The Last Great Trial between Cross and Crescent*. New York: Pegasus Books, 2007.

Most Precious Blood, Feast of the (July 1)

The blood of Jesus has for Christians been a symbol of God's healing power since the beginning of the church in the first century. The most ubiquitous event in all Christian churches has been the celebration of the Eucharist, in which wine is consumed as emblematic of Christ's blood. Among Protestants, the 1899 hymn by Lewis E. Jones, "Power in the Blood," remains popular. Among Roman Catholics, relics reputed to be of Christ's blood surfaced as early as the 6th century in the West, the most well known being kept at Bruges, Belgium, in the 12th century.

A special day to acknowledge the salvation brought by the spilling of Jesus's blood on the cross appeared in medieval Spain. That idea gained greater acceptance in 1815 with the foundation of the apostolic association of priests and lay brothers called the Missionaries of the Precious Blood, a Roman Catholic community of priests and brothers by Gaspar del Bufalo (1786–1837). The pope granted the missionaries the privilege of observing the day on the fourth Friday in Lent.

Then in the middle of the 19th century, the future of the celebration of the blood was caught up in the midst of the social unrest that led to the destruction of the Papal States and their incorporation into a unified Italy. Unrest in Rome peaked in 1849 when Pope Pius IX (r. 1846–1878) was driven from Rome into exile at Gaëta, a fortress on Italy's western coast between Naples and Rome. Among those accompanying the pope into exile was Don Giovanni Merlini, who at the time led the Fathers of the Most Precious Blood. Once at the fortress, he suggested that the pope make a vow to extend the feast of the Precious Blood to the entire Church if and when he regained control of the Papal States. After considering the suggestion, he decided against the vow and instead placed the feast on the general church calendar immediately. This event happened to coincide with the French army's moving into Rome and temporarily returning it to papal control. A few weeks later, the pope decreed that the first Sunday of July should be celebrated in remembrance of the Most Precious Blood. The French intervention was but a temporary move that delayed but did not stop the unification of Italy, which culminated in the Italian army seizing control of Rome in 1870 and the Lateran Treaty of 1929 that created the present Vatican City state.

Pope Pius X (r. 1902–1914) moved the feast from the first Sunday in July to its present day, July 1. The call of the Second Vatican Council encouraging Christians to venerate the whole person of Christ has led to the dropping of the feast from the liturgical calendar of the general church.

J. Gordon Melton

See also Easter; Holy Week; Holyrood or the Feast of the Triumph of the Holy Cross.

References

Christopher, Joseph P., Charles E. Spence, and John F. Rowan. *The Raccolta or a Manual of Indulgences, Prayers and Devotions Enriched with Indulgences*. New York: Benziger Brothers, 1957.

Klein, Peter. *The Catholic Sourcebook*. Orlando, FL: Harcourt Religious Publisher, 1999.

Paiano, Mary. *Saint Gaspar del Buffalo—Apostle of the Precious Blood*. Precious Blood Fathers & Brothers, 1984.

Mother, Birthday of the (February 21)

The Mother is the term the followers of Indian spiritual teacher Sri Aurobindo (1872–1950) gave to Mirra Richard (1878–1973), who became Aurobindo's companion, collaborator, and successor as head of the ashram he founded in Pondicherry, India. Richard was born in Paris and seemed destined for a life in the arts as a musician and/or painter. She developed an interest in things spiritual and esoteric, however, and in 1906–1907, she ventured to Algeria to pursue her interests. She emerged as a teacher of Esotericism. In 1914, she first visited India, met Aurobindo, and immediate viewed him as the spiritual guide she had been seeking. She returned to India, where she would remain for the rest of her life.

Through the early 1920s, the number of people who responded to Aurobindo and his approach to yoga and Hinduism grew substantially, and the Sri Aurobindo Ashram emerged as their organization. In 1926, Aurobindo entered a period of seclusion and turned over the administration of the ashram and the regular interaction with the disciples to the Mother. She continued to lead the ashram after Aurobindo's death in 1950, and went on to found Auroville, the utopian community built to demonstrate Aurobindo's vision for the world. During her years of leadership, she acquired the same devoted following that had originally gathered around her teacher.

During the years that Aurobindo lived in seclusion, the two of them gave darshan (allowed the disciples to view them and giving them a blessing) on four occasions each year—their birthdays, the day that Aurobindo experienced the descent of the deity Krishna into him, and the anniversary of the Mother's final arrival in Pondicherry. After Richard's death, her giving darshan on her birthday was continued as a celebration of her life and work.

The living quarters of Aurobindo and the Mother were turned into shrines following their deaths. Today, on the Mother's birthday anniversary, her former living quarters are opened for members of the ashram to visit. It was also the practice of the Mother to give written messages to those who came for darshan. In her memory, the present leadership of the ashram gives message cards with sayings drawn from her writings to those who come to the ashram to remember her on her birthday.

J. Gordon Melton

See also Aurobindo, Birth Anniversary of Sri; Siddha Day.

References

Aurobindo, Sri. *The Mother*. Twin Lakes, WI: Lotus Press, 1990.

Joshi, Kirett. *Sri Aurobindo and the Mother: Glimpses of Their Experiments, Experiences, and Realizations*. New Delhi: Motilal Banarsidass, 1996.

Von Vrekhern, George. *Beyond the Human Species: The Life and Work of Sri Aurobindo and the Mother*. New York: Paragon House Publishers, 1998.

Mothering Sunday

Mothering Sunday, observed through much of Europe, is a day for honoring one's mother (the equivalent of Mother's Day in the United States). This appears to have begun as matronalia, a Pagan holiday in the Roman Empire during which the mother goddess Cybele was honored by baking and offering her cakes made of simila flour. As the church grew and superseded the Pagan faith, it seems to have incorporated the Cybele celebration with the addition of a day for honoring the church as mother. In many places, this took the form of seeking out the local cathedral, the symbolic mother church of a city and its surrounding countryside, or return to the church in which they were baptized and in which they grew to adulthood. The day to visit the mother church was on the fourth Sunday of Lent.

Mothering Sunday gradually changed into a day to honor one's physical mother. In various places, it was a day in which young servants were given a day off to visit their family. Often, they would be allowed to bake a cake or cookies to take home to their mother. It was also a day in which the Lenten fasting regulations were somewhat lifted, that action being tied to Jesus's feeding of the 5,000 (Mark 6:44). In recent centuries, the favored cake was a Simnel cake, a raisin/plum cake with a layer of marzipan (sugar almond paste) on top. It would be decorated with 11 marzipan balls symbolic of Jesus's 12 apostles, minus the one who betrayed him. The cake would often be set aside until Easter so as not to violate the Lenten fast.

J. Gordon Melton

See also Easter; Lent; Mother's Day.

References

Ball, Ann. *Encyclopedia of Catholic Devotions and Practices*. Huntington, IN: Our Sunday Visitor, 2003.

Mother's Day

Mother's Day is a modern holiday, secular in origin and meaning, but widely adopted by religions and now integrated into many religious calendars.

The modern holiday originated from a "Mother's Day Proclamation" written in 1870 by Julia Ward Howe (1819–1910). It grew from her reaction to the many deaths incurred during the American Civil War (1860–1865). Her proclamation sounded more like a call for women to assume power than a call for men to honor them. The major sentiment was stated thusly: "We, the women of one country, will be too tender of those of another country to allow our sons to be trained to injure theirs." The actual call was for an international congress of women to work for the cause of peace. Howe's view of the role of women in the governance of the world would be echoed in the next generation by the likes of Frances Willard (1839–1898) and the Woman's Christian Temperance Union. The idea would bear fruit in the International Women's Day (March 8) that was first celebrated in 1909.

Meanwhile, Anna Jarvis (1864–1948) had reacted to her own mother's death in 1905 by starting a campaign to make "Mother's Day" a recognized holiday in the United States. Her campaign culminated in success in 1914. Over the next decade, the holiday caught on and was celebrated across the country, but she was extremely upset by the superficiality of the celebration and the commercialization of her idea. She moved to incorporate the Mother's Day International Association, and trademarked the phrases "second Sunday in May" and "Mother's Day." However, the day had by this time become larger than anything she could control.

In the United States, most churches celebrate Mother's Day with activities integrated into the worship hour on the second Sunday in May. After worship, it is common for husbands and children to take mothers and grandmothers for a special dinner.

Since World War II, a number of countries have copied the United States in designating an annual Mother's Day. The largest number kept the day largely as it was practiced in the United States and maintained its celebration on the second Sunday of May. Some countries already had such a day; England, for example, had a traditional Mothering Sunday. In Roman Catholic and Orthodox Christian countries, the day may be filled with content from images of Mary as the ideal mother of Jesus and Mother's Day celebrated along with an emphasis on the Blessed Virgin Mary. In Spain and Portugal, Mother's Day coincides with the Feast of the Immaculate Conception (December 8). Islamic countries will most often celebrate Mother's Day on the spring equinox. It was initially celebrated in Egypt and from there spread to other Middle Eastern countries.

J. Gordon Melton

See also Immaculate Conception, Feast of the; Mothering Sunday; Spring Equinox (Thelema); Spring Equinox (Vernal).

References

Bosak, S. V. "The History of Mother's Day." *Legacy Project*. Posted at http://legacyproject.org/guides/mdhistory.html. Accessed May 15, 2010.

Rice, Susan Tracy. *Mother's Day: Its History, Origin, Celebration, Spirit, and Significance as Related in Prose and Verse*. Indianapolis, IN: Dodd, Mead, 1954.

Wolfe, Howard H. *Mother's Day and the Mother's Day Church*. Kingsport, TN: Kingsport Press, 1962.

Mount Carmel, Feast Day of Our Lady of (July 16)

Among the many names given to the Blessed Virgin Mary is Our Lady of Mount Carmel, which originated with her role as the patroness of the Carmelite order. The Carmelites emerged from among a group of Christian hermits that resided on Mount Carmel in Palestine at the end of the 12th century. Mount Carmel was famous as the ancient site of the prophet Elijah's confrontation with the prophets of the god Baal. In the 13th century, the hermits built a chapel to the Virgin on the mountain.

From Carmel, the order spread across Europe. Shortly after the order settled in England, in the mid-13th century, a British Carmelite monk, Simon Stock, was reported to have had an apparition of the Virgin in which she promised special favors to any who wore the brown scapular, which became the distinguishing part of the Carmelite monk's habit. The monks wore a scapular, basically a work apron, over the brown belted tunic that they had adopted as their habit. A smaller stylized form of the scapular would be adopted for supporters of the order to wear.

While the story of the scapular became part of the lore of the order, its historicity was challenged in the 17th century, and in the process of defending it, a Carmelite leader produced a fraudulent document purporting to have recorded the date of the apparition, July 16. Modern Carmelites admit to the lack of documentary evidence of the apparition, but retain its use as a sign of Mary's role as the order's protectress. Its use has survived the criticism and maintains papal approval. The use of the brown scapular is tied to membership in the Carmelite's larger community, as devotion to Our Lady of Mount Carmel is viewed by Rome as devotion as tied to the history and spiritual values of Carmelites.

The feast of Our Lady of Mount Carmel seems to date from the last half of the 14th century in England. It also seems to have emerged quite apart from the use of the scapular. The original date selected was July 17, but since that date conflicted with the feast day of the fifth-century saint Alexis, the feast day of our Lady of Mount Carmel was moved to July 16. As late as 2001, Pope John Paul II (r. 1978–2005), on what would be the 750th anniversary of the reputed vision to Simon Stocks, professed to have worn the brown scapular for many years.

J. Gordon Melton

See also Fatima, Feast Day of Our Lady of; Immaculate Conception, Feast of the; Lourdes, Feast Day of Our Lady of; Rosary, Feast of Our Lady of the.

References

Dodds, Monica, and Bill Dodds. *Encyclopedia of Mary*. Huntington, IN: Our Sunday Visitor, 2007.

The Scapular of Our Lady of Mount Carmel: Catechesis and Ritual. Washington, DC: North American Provincials—Carmelite Orders, 2000.

Smet, Joachim. *The Carmelites: A History of the Brothers of Our Lady of Mount Carmel.* Darien, IL: Carmelite Spiritual Center, 1988.

Thurston, Herbert, S. J., "The Origin of the Scapular—A Criticism." *Irish Ecclesiastical Record* 16 (July–December 1904): 59–75.

Mudras

The word *mudra* derives from a set of words in ancient India that carried ideas of authority, the imprint left in wax from a seal, and the way one artistically positions one's fingers. Those words evolved to designate hand gestures or positions that enhanced the spoken word and conveyed a mystical or occult meaning. In Hindu paintings and statues, the deities were pictured with what appears to outside observers as very unusual or even strained hand gestures. Some appear as if a movement has been caught in the middle or with the fingers entwined in a complicated pattern.

Mudras have had intimate connection to the art of the dance as it developed in India, and the graceful hand gestures so characteristic of much traditional Indian dance are mudras. Mudras have also become a very common element of Hindu pujas (worship), adding content to ritual performance beyond the words spoken. While mudras are not the subject of holidays directly, in both Indian-based holiday celebrations and the worship accompanying Mahayana and Vajrayana Buddhists, the use of mudras and their depiction in the environment where worship occurs supplies essential content of the holiday activity.

In the act of creating mudras, each finger is assigned a relationship to one of the five classical elements:

Thumb	Agni/fire
Forefinger	Vayu/air
Middle finger	Akash/ether
Ring finger	Prithvi/earth
Little finger	Jal/water

Mudras can also be classified as *Aasanyukta* (single-handed mudras) or *Sawyakta* (double-handed).

The oft-seen Abhaya or fearlessness gesture is a good example of an Aasanyukta mudra. It is made simply by lifting the right hand to shoulder height with the palm open and facing forward. It represents benevolence, the absence of fear, and the granting of protection. The Pankaj or Lotus mudra is a simple Sawyata mudra. The two hands are brought together in such a way that the fingers are separated and pointed upward, with the two thumbs and the two little fingers touching each other. The person making the symbol is suggesting that like the lotus is detached from the mud below it, so he or she is detached from the world while in meditation. The Pankaj mudra also emphasizes the fire and water elements represented by the thumb and little finger.

Within Mahayana Buddhism, mudras are popularly used to distinguish the different deities whose bodies and faces are often identical in works of art. Thus in statuary and paintings, the different Buddhas and bodhisattvas may most often be identified, amid dozens of very similar representations, by the mudra he or she assumes (along with the objects held). Within Vajrayana or Esoteric Buddhism, mudras have been assigned additional meanings as symbols of various aspects of Esoteric reality. Mudras are designed to evoke both meaning and power among those who understand their significance.

Of the many mudras, five have become central to the presentation of images of the Buddha and bodhisattvas. The Dharmachakra mudra, for example recalls the Buddha's first sermon at Sarnath. Both hands are pictured with the thumb and forefinger touching to form a circle (the Wheel of the Dharma), and the three remaining fingers extended, to which additional meaning is ascribed. The Bhumisparsha mudra recalls the Buddha's enlightenment, with the right hand touching the earth and the left hand placed flat in the lap. The Varada mudra, emphasizing the Buddha's charity and compassion, shows the left hand, palm up and fingers extended. The Dhyana mudra is made with the left hand placed in the lap, a symbol of wisdom (a feminine virtue). Various symbolic objects may then be placed in the open palm. The Abhaya mudra, usually pictured with a standing figure, shows the right hand raised and the palm facing outward. The left hand is at the side of the body, often with the palm also facing outward.

In Esoteric Buddhism, the five Dhayani Buddhas are key deity figures. They are not thought of as historical figures who have reached enlightenment, but are transcendent beings symbolizing universal principles. Each Dhyani Buddha is associated with a spectrum of attributes and symbols. Each one, for example, represents one of the five basic wisdoms, and thus each one can transform one of the five deadly poisons that afflict humankind into one of the wisdoms. When pictured in Tibetan iconography, the five Buddhas are commonly shown sitting cross-legged in the meditative position and at first glance appear to be exactly the same, especially in statuary where the colors that often distinguishes the five Buddhas has been abandoned. What really distinguishes the five Buddhas, however, are the mudras; each one is always shown with one of the basic mudras traditionally identified with the wisdom they embody. The Buddhas and the mudra they demonstrate are:

Vairocana	Dharma chakra, or wheel-turning mudra
Akshobhya	Bhumisparsa, or witness mudra
Ratnasambhava	Varada, or charity mudra
Amitabha	Dhyana mudra
Amogasiddha	Abhaya, or fearlessness mudra

The most ubiquitous bodhisattva in Asia is Guan Yin (a.k.a. Avalokitesvara), who will be shown with a range of mudras or their variations. In one form, the thousand-armed Guan Yin, many of the hands are arranged to show different mudras.

Those who understand mudras will recognize that the Zen Buddhist practitioner, while engaged in zazen or sitting meditation, places their hands in what is known as the cosmic mudra. One hand rests on top of the other, with palms open and up. The joints of the two middle fingers rest on top of the other, and the tips of the thumbs are touching lightly.

In Esoteric Buddhist practice, unique hand positions indicate to the faithful the nature and the function of the deities, Buddhas, and bodhisattvas on which they gaze. Mudras thus symbolize divine manifestation. Teachers use then in rituals and spiritual exercises as aids to the invocation of the deity. When understood in its magical context, the use of mudras by the practitioner facilitates the flow of the invisible forces within the earthly sphere. Some hypothesize that the sequence of hand postures that manifest in ritual contexts may stand behind their entry and evolution in Indian classical dance. Esoteric Buddhists see mudras as physical movements that alter perception and deepen awareness. Their use can assist the awakening of the chakras (energy centers believed to exist along the spine) and the flow of kundalini (the energy that travels along the spine and accompanying enlightenment).

J. Gordon Melton

See also Guan Yin's Birthday; Wesak/Vesak.

References

Bunce, Frederick W. *Mudras in Buddhist and Hindu Practices: An Iconographic Consideration*. New Delhi: D. K. Printworld. Pvt. Ltd., 2005.

Chandra, Lokesh, *Mudras in Japan*. N.p.: Vedam eBooks, 2001.

De Kleen, Tyra. *Mudras: The Ritual Hand-Poses of the Buddha Priests and the Shiva Priests of Bali*. London: Kegan Paul, Trench, Trubner & Co., 1924. Reprint, New Hyde Park, NY: University Books, 1970.

Hirschi, Gertrud. *Mudras: Yoga in Your Hands*. Weirs Bach, ME: Weiser Books, 2000.

Kumar, Nitin. "Mudras of the Great Buddha: Symbolic Gestures and Postures." Exotic India, August 2001. Posted at http://www.exoticindiaart.com/mudras.htm. Accessed May 15, 2010.

Saunders, E. Dale. *Mudra: A Study of Symbolic Gestures in Japanese Buddhist Sculpture*. London: Routledge & Kegan Paul, 1960.

Thrungpa, Chogyam. *Mudras*. Berkeley, CA: Shambhala, 1972.

Muktananda, Birthday of Swami Paramahansa (May 16)

Swami Muktananda (1908–1982) was a spiritual teacher (guru) from India who built a global following through the 1970s. As a young adult, he adopted the life of a *sadhu*, a wandering mendicant, and launched a search of spiritual enlightenment. Though becoming adept in yoga and meditation, his life was changed after he met Bhagavan Nityananda (c. 1897–1961). Nityananda gave the young sadhu shaktipat initiation, through which his *kundalini* energy, pictured lying latent at the base of the spine, was released to travel up his spinal column and project him into an enlightened state. After nine years under Nityananda's guidance, Muktananda attained the state of God-realization in 1955.

In the 1970s, Swami Muktananda brought Nityananda's tradition to the West and introduced thousands to shaktipat initiation. As the movement around him grew, he established the Gurudev Siddha Peeth in India and the SYDA Foundation in the United States to organize his following. He authored several dozen books.

The SYDA Foundation continues under the leadership of Swami Chidvilasananda, who perpetuates Swami Muktananda's spiritual legacy to the world. In honor of Muktananda's birthday each May, Siddha Yogis meet together in their local ashrams for what is termed the Global Siddha Yoga Audio Satsang, an international gathering tied together by modern Internet communications. Via the Internet, individuals may participate in the meditation, chanting, and teachings at their local center or in their home.

The foundation sponsors three such Global Siddha Yoga Audio Satsangs annually, on Muktananda's Birthday, the anniversary of his Mahasamadhi (October 16), and New Year's.

J. Gordon Melton

See also Lahiri Mahasaya, Commemoration Days for; Prasadji Paramahansa, Birthday of Swami Guru; Yogananda, Birthday of Paramahansa.

References

Brook, Douglas Renfrew et al. *Meditation Revolution: A History and Theology of the Siddha Yoga Lineage*. South Fallsburg, NY: Agama Press, 1997.

Muktananda, Swami. *Guru*. New York: Harper & Row, 1981.

Simpson, Margaret. *A Perfect Life: The Story of Swami Muktananda Paramahamsa*. South Fallsburg, NY: Siddha Yoga Publications, 1996.

"Welcome to the Siddha Yoga Path." Posted at http://www.siddhayoga.org/. Accessed April 15, 2010.

Munmyo Ceremony

Munmyo is a Confucian shrine located in Seoul and constructed (1398) during the reign of King Taejo (r. 1392–1398), the founder of the Choson kingdom (1392–1910). It has been destroyed on several occasions, but always rebuilt and restored, the last time in 1869. The shrine houses tablets to Confucius and other famous Confucian scholars, most notably Choe Chiwon (who lived at the beginning of the 10th century) and Seoul Chong (8th century). It is located on the campus of Sungkyunkwan University.

Twice annually, in the spring and fall, a ritual ceremony honoring Confucius and the ether enshrined scholars is held at Munmyo. The Seokjeonje ritual features the formalized line dancing called *ilmu* that was introduced into Korea in the 12th century from China. Ilmu is used to honor people of high status, especially Confucius and people considered like him. The accompanying music at Munmyo is delivered by a spectrum of traditional instruments including flutes, zithers, stone chimes, bronze bells, drums, and wooden clappers (*bak*).

J. Gordon Melton

See also Chinese Religion; Confucius's Birthday; Chongmyo Cherye.

References

"The Characteristics of Korean Dance." *The Taekando Bible*. Posted at http://tkdbible.com/korculture/dance/korean-dance02.html. Accessed July 15, 2010.

"The Enduring Spirit of Confucianism." *JoongAng Daily*, December 1, 2008. Posted at http://joongangdaily.joins.com/article/view.asp?aid=2897973. Accessed July 15, 2010.

N

Nagapanchami

Nagapanchami, a serpent-worshipping festival, is celebrated on the fifth day of the waning half of the Hindu lunar month of Shravana (July–August in the Common Era calendar). The snake, especially the cobra, has had an important role in Hindu thought and iconography since ancient times and is now seen in association with the foremost personages and divinities of not only Hinduism, but Buddhism and Jainism as well. The Hindu deity Shiva is pictured with a serpent around his neck as a necklace, while Vishnu rests on the divine serpent Adishesha, who in turn rests on the primordial Ocean of Milk. One story of the Buddha as he sat in meditation seeking enlightenment under the Bodhi Tree tells of the serpent king Mucalinda rising up beneath the earth to envelope the Buddha in his coils for seven days to protect the Buddha to allow his meditation to be undisturbed by an approaching storm. The Jain Tirthankara (saint) Parshvanath is also pictured in iconography as protected by a huge multi-headed cobra.

At different locations across India, shrines have been constructed at abandoned anthills where snakes reside and where people make offerings and feed the snakes with milk. In southwestern India, people often keep a Naga grove in the corner of their garden. Most often, the snakes are seen as a protective presence, but they are also valued for their associations with immortality and fertility.

Worship most often is directed toward the cobra, which often is seen as a being that can move between this mundane world and the all-powerful underworld. People both offer thanks to the snake for its auspicious presence and attempt to pacify the serpent world so that the snake will not bite the believer or his or her loved ones. Most Hindu temples will have one or more representations of nagas, either in their own right or by their association with the temple's main deity.

On Nagapanchami, the serpents such as Vasuki, considered a great king of the nagas, are worshipped, and offerings of milk, considered among their favorite foods, are presented to their images. Milk is also, of course, given to cobras on a daily basis by villagers throughout India. Snake charmers may be invited to perform on this day, and in certain areas, there are huge processions of men (and some women) who handle cobras in fulfillment of vows.

Constance A. Jones

See also Anant Chaturdashi.

References

Handa, O. C. *Naga Cults and Traditions in the Western Himalaya*. New Delhi: Indus Publications, 2004.

Mundkar, Balaji. *The Cult of the Serpent: An Interdisciplinary Survey of Its Manifestations and Origins*. Albany, NY: State University of New York Press, 1983.

Sinha, Binod Chandra. *Serpent Worship in Ancient India*. New Delhi: Books Today, 1979.

Vogel, Jean Philippe. *Indian Serpent Lore or the Nagas in Hindu Legend and Art*. London: Arthur Probsthain, 1926.

Nagasaki Kunchi (October 7–9)

The Autumn Kunchi (or festival) is the largest annual celebration in the city of Nagasaki. It emerged as a simple autumn festival in the 16th century but took on added importance as a shrine-center festival after the emergence of the Tokugawa Shogunate early in the 17th century and the construction of the new Suwa Shrine in 1642. The shrine in Nagasaki is one of many Suwa shrines, all of which are dedicated to Suwa-no-Kami, a kami of valor and duty. It is also home to two additional kami, Morisaki and Sumiyoshi, and the three together are seen as facilitating contact with the principal Shinto deity, Amaterasu. This shrine is also connected to Suwa Taisha, the head shrine of Suwa-no-Kami worship, located at Suwa, Japan. The festival at Nagasaki celebrates the three Shinto deities enshrined there.

While the Nagasaki Kunchi is a Shinto festival, its origin is intimately connected with Christianity. In 1614, The Shogun Tokugawa Ieyasu issued the Christian Expulsion Edict, which banned Christianity in Japan, expelled all Christians and foreigners, and forbade Japanese-convert Christians from practicing their faith. The largest Christian community in Japan was in Nagasaki, and prior to 1614, it had been the site of a major annual Easter celebration that included a public procession.

That same year, the Shogun initiated construction of the Suwa Shrine, which was designed to replace some of the shrines that the Christians had destroyed. The shrine was a first step in forcing the reconversion of the Christians back to Shinto and Buddhism. The new shrine became a focus of Christian resistance. In 1634, a further edict was issued that required all Nagasaki citizens to register at the shrine. That fall, a great festival was organized to celebrate the shrine's deities, to encourage local participation in the shrine, and to discover any remaining secret Christians in the community. Those who refused to register were assumed to be Christians, and were subject to arrest and possible execution.

To expand the annual festival, the Shogunate supported the development of Nagasaki as a center for Noh drama, a form of classical Japanese musical drama that includes elaborate costumes and is especially known for the expensive masks worn by the performers. Noh remained the main attraction of the growing festival until a fire in 1857 destroyed the costumes and masks. Replacement was prohibitively expensive, and the city altered the format. It invited different neighborhoods to compete with each other in creating performances. The result was a spectrum of new and different presentations that have come to represent the cosmopolitan nature of the contemporary city and often portray its colorful past, and the international heritage of different segments of the population.

Preparation for the October festival will begin in the summer months. The neighborhood performers will start rehearsals, and as the festival approaches, a large viewing stand will be built in front of the Suwa Shrine, the major presentation area. In spite of the official religious intent and the location of the primary festival events adjacent to the shrine, the presentations and the overall celebration has largely lost any religious content and tends more to reflect the historical and cultural past. Besides the stage at the shrine, two other larger staging areas are also constructed and many smaller ones are also present, so that the celebration permeates the city.

J. Gordon Melton

See also Aki Matsuri; Chichibu Yomatsuri; Hadaka Matsuri; Haru Matsuri; Kaijin Matsuri; Natsu Matsuri; New Year's Day; Sakura Matsuri.

References

Littleton, Scott. *Shinto: Origins, Rituals, Festivals, Spirits, Sacred Places*. New York: Oxford University Press, 2002.

Nelson, John K. *A Year in the Life of a Shinto Shrine*. Seattle: University of Washington Press, 1996.

Telkamp, Thomas. "Nagasaki Kunchi Festival." Posted at http://www.ltcm.net/~telkamp/japan/kunchi/kunchi.html. Accessed June 15, 2010.

Nanak's Birthday, Guru

Guru Nanak (1469–1539) was the founder of Sikhism, which he created by merging what he felt was the best of Islam and Hinduism. The religion and its community steadily evolved over the next several hundred years under the leadership of nine gurus who in turn succeed Nanak. The last of the gurus decreed that from that time forward, the Guru Granth Sahib, the book of writings of Nanak and the several gurus, would from that time forward be the community's new guru. Through the book, Guru Nanak's teachings have remained uppermost in the development of Sikhism.

Nanak was born in Talwandi, now known as Nankana Sahib, a village near Lahore, in what is now Pakistan. His birth occurred, according to the Hindu lunar calendar then in effect, on the third day of the light half of the month of Baisakh of the year 1469 CE. This date has now been calculated to be on or about Saturday, April 15, 1469, on the Common Era calendar.

The Sikh community is in a transition concerning its celebration of Nanak's birthday. Until the 1990s, it was celebrated in November. However, in the 1990s, a new Sikh calendar was adopted. The calendar is a solar calendar, named the Nanakshahi calendar after Guru Nanak and based somewhat on the Common Era calendar. March 14 on the Common Era calendar is the first day of the New Year on the Nanakshahi calendar. The new calendar places Guru Nanak's birthday on Vaisakh 1 (or April 14). Most Sikhs now acknowledge that day.

Guru Nanak's birthday is one of 12 "Gurpurbs," holidays that commemorate the birth or death of one of the 10 Sikh gurus. Sikhs will celebrate the Gurpurb for Guru Nanak by performing an *Akhand Path*, a public reading of the Sikh holy scriptures, at both the Golden Temple in Amritsar, the main Sikh temple, and in gurdwaras (Sikh worship centers) around the world. To read the entire Guru Granth Sahib from beginning to end requires two days. The reading will begin two days before the holiday to be commemorated and will end early in the morning of the holy day. Each person chosen to participate will read aloud for two to three hours.

Where possible, on the day prior to the actual birthday celebration, a procession may be held. It will include singers and musicians, and five men who dress to represent the *Panj Piare* (or Five Beloved Ones), the first five members to be formally initiated into the Sikh community.

On the day of the celebration, Sikhs will gather at the gurdwara, which will be decorated for a time of prayer, talks on various aspects of Sikhism, and the singing of *kirtans* (holy songs, in this case from the Guru Granth Sahib) followed by a communal meal. Activities for all ages may continue all day.

J. Gordon Melton

See also Guru Gobind Singh's Birthday; Guru Granth Sahib, Celebration of the; Makar Sankranti; Martyrdom of Guru Arjan; Martyrdom of Guru Tegh Bahadur.

References

Dhillon, Haresh. *The First Sikh Spiritual Master: Timeless Wisdom from the Life and Techniques of Guru Nanak*. Woodstock, VT: Skylight Paths Publishing, 2006.

Duggal, K. S. *Sikh Gurus: Their Lives and Teachings*. New Delhi: UBSPD, 2005.

Kapoor, Sukhbor Sing. *Sikh Festivals*. Vero Beach, FL: Rourke Publishing Group, 1989.

Khalsa, Parmatma S. *Guru for the Aquarian Age: The Life and Teachings of Guru Nanak*. Santa Cruz, NM: Yogiji Press, 1997.

Narak Chaturdashi

Yama is the Indian god of death and the underworld of the dead. He is the son of Visvasvat (or Surya), the sun. In the Vedas, he is seen as the first mortal to die and thereby becomes king of the world of the dead. In the Vedic context, the realm of the dead is quite unlike hell, but more like an afterworld of satisfaction and pleasures; but in later Puranic descriptions, Naraka, Yama's realm, is depicted as a hell realm where sometimes even karmic retributions are meted out. Unlike the Christian hell, it is not a place of eternal torment, but of temporary punishment between incarnations.

Each year in parts of India, on the 14th day of the second half of the Hindu month of Kartika (in November on the Common Era calendar), Narak Chaturdashi is dedicated to Yama and celebrated with a ritual bath early in the morning before sunrise. Following the bath, believers offer three libations to Yama in the hope that it will please him, who will then spare the faithful any time in Naraka. During the day, a fast will be observed, and in the evening, lamps will be lit and offered to Yama.

Yama in his role as guardian of the realm of the dead appears in many contexts in Indian tradition. In the Katha Upanishad, he offers three boons to the young Nachiketas whom he had neglected. In the *Mahabharata*, he assumes an important role in the account of Savitri and Satyavan.

Constance A. Jones

See also Chaitra Purnima; Hanuman Jayanti; Makar Sankranti.

References

Dosson, John. *A Classical Dictionary of Hindu Mythology and Religion, Geography, History, and Literature*. 12th ed. Ludhiana: Lyall Book Depot, 1974.

Hillebrandt, Alfred. *Vedic Mythology*. 2 vols. Delhi: Motilal Banarsidass, 1990.

Merh, Kusum P. *Yama, the Glorious Lord of the Other World*. New Delhi: D. K. Printworld, 1996.

Wilkins, W. J. *Hindu Mythology, Vedic and Puranic*. 2nd ed. Calcutta: Rupa & Co., 1973.

Narasimha Jayanti

Narasimha (or Narsimha) is the fourth incarnation of the deity Vishnu. He appears as half man, half lion, with a human torso and lower body and a lion-like face and claws. The primary story concerning Narasimha appears in the *Bhagavata Purana*, an Indian holy book primarily associated with Vaishnava bhakti yoga or devotional traditions.

The ancient sage Kashyap married two women, Aditi and Diti. Diti became the mother of two sons, Hirnyakasha and Hirneykasipu. The latter, in order to take revenge on the one who slew his brother, underwent severe austerities and obtained a boon from the deity Brahma. The boom granted virtual immortality as it decreed that he could not be killed by any man or animal, either in the day or night, neither inside nor outside, nor by arms or by scriptures.

Statue of Narasimha Jayanti. (J. Gordon Melton)

Meanwhile, Hirneykasipu had a son, Prahalad, whose intent was to undertake devotion (bhakti) to Vishnu. Prahalad refused to quit his devotion in spite of his father's orders, as Hirneykasipu had come to hate Vishnu. One day, as Prahalad was lost in meditation, Hirneykasipu approached his son and pulled his sword. Because of his worshiping Vishnu, Hirneykasipu now saw Prahalad as his enemy, and threatened his life. In reaction to his son's refusal to stop his devotions, Hirneykasipu became outraged and struck the pillar of the temple with his sword. Suddenly, Narasimha appeared. The rare conditions existed at that moment when Hirneykasipu could be killed, and the half man–half lion placed Hirneykasipu on his knees at the threshold of the temple and tore open his stomach.

Prahalad is now honored as an exemplar of bhakti devotion. His story is offered as a motivation to continue devotion even in the face of intense anger. Those who oppose the bhakti practitioner will be slain. Vishnu is seen as having incarnated on this occasion just to acknowledge Prahalad's devotion.

Narasimha Jayanti, the appearance day of Narasimha, is observed with fasting. Believers will take a ritual bath and purification, after which Vedic hymns will be chanted and the image of Narasimha venerated by the offering of donations and alms. At sunset, the time that is neither day nor night, aarti (offering light produced by burning wicks soaked in ghee or camphor) is done at the local temple. Observation of Narasimha is believed to lead to freedom from earthly difficulties.

Observation of Narasimha Jayanti, mostly by Vaishnava Hindus, occurs on the 14th day in the bright half of the Hindu month of Vaishakh. The story of Barsimha is also an integral part of Holi. Members of the International Society for Krishna Consciousness maintain a fast through the daylight hours.

Constance A. Jones

See also Holi; Janmashtami; Onam; Parshurama Jayanti; Rama Navani; Vamana Jayanti.

References

Krishna, Nandita. *The Book of Vishnu*. London: Penguin Global, 2001.

Menon, Ramesh. *The Bhagavata Purana*. New Delhi: Rupa & Co., 2006.

"Narasimha Jayanthi Festival Celebration India." Festivals in India. Posted at http://www.festivalsindia.com/narasimha-jayanthi-festival-celebration-india/. Accessed April 15, 2010.

Narieli Purnima

In western India (Gujarat and Maharashtra), sailors, fishermen, and those who reside on the coast (primarily of Sindhi heritage) celebrate the full moon day of the Hindu month of Sharavana as Narieli Purnima. The intent of the observance is to stave off the fury of the sea god Varuna, a prominent deity in the ancient Hindu holy book, the Rig Veda.

Believers offer coconuts, a popular food to bring to the temple for gods, to Varuna's abode, the sea, of if the sea is located at some distance, a local body of water that substitutes for it.

Constance A. Jones

See also Balarama, Appearance Day of Lord; Guru Purnima; Sharad Purnima.

References

Chouddhuri, Usha. *Indra and Varuna in Indian Mythology.* Delhi: Nag Publishers, 1981.

Griswold, Hervey De Witt. *The God Varuna in the Rig Veda.* Lansing: University of Michigan Library, 2009.

National Bible Week

National Bible Week is a celebration during the week of Thanksgiving in the United States to encourage the reading and study of the Christian Bible. It is sponsored and promoted by the National Bible Association, an interdenominational organization created in 1940 by a group of Christian business and professional people in New York City. The group's original purpose was to strengthen the United States spiritually, given the war that had broken out in Europe the year before, and it appeared that the United States would be drawn into it. They reached an agreement that the since the Bible was a proven source of hope and encouragement, it should be the focus of their efforts.

The idea of National Bible Week was initially proposed in 1941. The first National Bible Week was to be observed December 8–15, 1941. They received time to make an initial nationwide broadcast on NBC Radio on the evening of December 7. That day, the Japanese bombed Pearl Harbor. The idea behind the founding of the organization had happened in a most dramatic fashion.

The work of the small organization continued, and they began to contact the offices of mayors and governors across the country annually, asking them to proclaim the week of Thanksgiving (the fourth week of November) as National Bible

Week in their city or state. The organization also annually communicated with the White House, and regularly received words of encouragement from sitting U.S. presidents, beginning with Franklin D. Roosevelt. Though not receiving any national proclamations, they regularly received letters of personal support on White House stationary. In 1990, George Bush accepted the post of honorary chairman of the event on the occasion of its 50th anniversary. President Clinton also served in that capacity for several years. In recent years, approximately 30 governors and 500 mayors issue National Bible Week proclamations annually.

A similar National Bible Week celebration was inaugurated in the Philippines in 1979 with a presidential proclamation on Ferdinand E. Marcos. His successors in office have followed his precedent and issued similar proclamations.

J. Gordon Melton

See also Bible Sunday.

References

National Bible Association. http://www.nationalbible.org/home/. Accessed July 15, 2010.

National Brotherhood Week (February)

The National Conference of Christians and Jews (NCCJ) was founded in 1928, the occasion for its organization being the anti-Catholic bigotry expressed during the run of Al Smith, the governor of New York and a Roman Catholic, for president. A variety of religious leaders representing the Catholic, Protestant, and Jewish communities felt the time had arrived to attack religious prejudices and misunderstandings head on. The Jewish community had felt the prejudice most critically, and had already organized the Anti-Defamation League to counter it. Through the 20th century, the NCCJ carried on a variety of programs to foster its goals.

In 1931, the Rt. Rev. Hugh L. McMenain, a Catholic priest and rector of the cathedral of the Immaculate Conception in Denver, put forth the idea to his colleagues active in the NCCJ of a week each year that would focus the need for greater brotherhood. Eventually, the national organization agreed to sponsor the idea, and for half a century, promoted it.

By the end of the 1960s, the issues before the NCCJ had shifted radically. The civil rights movement had pushed the role of African Americans to the forefront, while Vatican II gave a boost to interfaith contact, especially among Catholics and Jews. The 1970s brought a much wider interfaith scene with the growth of the Buddhist, Hindu, and Muslim communities in the United States. The continuing crises in the Middle East demanded that Islam be brought into the dialogue. Finally, the rise of the feminist movement challenged the idea of brotherhood, women seeing it as more exclusionary that inclusive.

These many changes in the culture led in the 1980s to the NCCJ abandoning its program of the National Brotherhood Week, which had been generally held during the third week of February since the 1940s. Even more radical changes occurred in the 1990s, when the NCCJ went through a complete reorganization, even emerging with a new name—the National Conference for Community and Justice.

J. Gordon Melton

See also Yom HaShoah.

References

"Brotherhood Week: A Time Of Rededication." *Georgia Bulletin*, February 25, 1965. Posted at http://www.georgiabulletin.org/local/1965/02/25/c/. Accessed May 15, 2010.

"History." National Conference for Community and Justice. Posted at http://www.nccjctwma.org/whoweare/history.html. Accessed May 15, 2010.

National Day (July 28)

Eastern Orthodox Christians throughout Russia and the lands of the modern Russian diaspora celebrated 1988 as a holy year. A thousand years earlier, in 988, Prince (and now Saint) Vladimir I, the grand prince of Kiev, announced his formal conversion and symbolically led in the baptism of the people of Russia into the church. That event is marked as the beginning of the Russian Orthodox Church. That event is especially remembered in Ukraine, where Kiev is located. Ukrainians think of Vladimir's action as leading to the Christianization of the whole of Eastern Europe.

The Kievan church began as an outpost of the Patriarchate of Constantinople (the Ecumenical Patriarchate). Through the ups and downs of history, Kiev lost much of its political significance in the 13th century and the Metropolitan moved first to Vladimir (1299) and then to Moscow (1325). The present Moscow Patriarchate thus continues the original Kiev Metropolitanate, and Russians see the medieval Kievan state as the predecessor to modern Russia, as much as it preceded modern Ukraine and Belarus.

The millennium year occurred in the last years of the Soviet Union. Since the fall of Soviet Russia in 1991, the vastly weakened Orthodox Church has made considerable progress in reestablishing itself as the primary religious organization of the contemporary nation (which operates under a secular constitution with provisions to maintain the separation between the state and the now-numerous religious organizations operating within it. Officials of the Russian Orthodox Church have made no secret of their desire to return it to its former position as Russia's official state-supported religion. Russian political leaders have repeatedly spoken kindly of the Russian Orthodox Church and acknowledged its contributions to Russian life and culture. They have also indicated it as being the country's main faith.

In June 2010, the government took a significant step in recognizing the Orthodox Church by creating National Day, a new official holiday that will annually celebrate Russia's conversion to Christianity in 988. The legislation creating the new holiday was signed by President Dmitry Medvedev on June 1, 2010. In response, Muslims asked that a similar national holiday be proclaimed to mark the arrival of Islam in the land that constitutes contemporary Russia. Islam arrived in the area around the Caspian Sea even before the actions of Saint Vladimir.

J. Gordon Melton

See also Cyril and Methodius, Saint's Day for Sts.; Vladimir, Saint's Day of St.

References

House, Francis. *Millennium of Faith: Christianity in Russia AD 988–1988*. Yonkers, NY: St. Vladimir's Seminary Press, 1988.

"New Russia Holiday Marked as Kremlin Boosts Church." *Reuters*, July 28, 2010. Posted at http://www.reuters.com/article/idUSTRE66R2DC20100728. Accessed July 28, 2010.

Oholensky, Alexander P. *From the First to Third Millennium: The Social Christianity of St. Vladimir of Kiev*. New York: Association of Religion and Intellectual Life, 1993.

National Day of Prayer

During the years of the Truman administration, the idea of a National Day of Prayer emerged in the U.S. Congress as a means of affirming the religious life of the nation. Originally suggested by evangelist Billy Graham, it gained traction when it was related to national goals opposing "godless" Communism. It was also promoted as a means for people, across their denominational and even religious boundaries, to participate in a single spiritual activity. As the idea found wide acceptance, the Congress began to annually designate a day when people were asked to come together and pray, with some attention to intercession with God on behalf of the country. The date varied from year to year until 1968, when President Ronald Reagan fixed it on the first Thursday in May.

It is of some interest that as an argument against those who saw the idea as an infringement of the separation of church and state, some argued that prayers were held during the Constitutional Convention (1781). When later investigated, the claim was found to have been erroneous. Historians discovered that no less a personage than Benjamin Franklin had suggested prayer, but found little support. It was never seriously considered. That consideration did not block the enactment of a national day of prayer, which President Truman signed shortly before completing his last term in office in 1952.

The idea of a National Day of Prayer backed by the government has continued to raise opposition, and different presidents have varied considerably in their attention to it. President Reagan and the first President Bush hosted only one event related to the day, and President Clinton none, while the second President Bush hosted a prayer event at the White House annually throughout his term.

The main focus of the National Day of Prayer, however, was not to be in Washington, but in numerous events across the United States. As the religious right emerged during the Reagan years, a nongovernmental, nonprofit organization was formed, the National Day of Prayer Task Force. It was led by a group of evangelical Christians, most notably James Dobson and his organization Focus on the Family, that had expressed the most interest in promoting the celebration. The task force has annually printed literature advocating a variety of events in observance of the day, while at the same time emphasizing a belief that America is a Christian nation and thus tending to limit leadership in task force–sponsored events to conservative Christians. The task force maintains a web presence at http://www.nationaldayofprayer.org/.

In recent years, the observance of the National Day of Prayer has largely been limited to those evangelical Christians who see no problem with its observance relative to church-state considerations. The primary opposition to the day of prayer has come from atheist and Freethought groups. In 2008, one group, the Freedom from Religion Foundation based in Madison, Wisconsin, filed a suit against the Bush administration and the National Day of Prayer task force, later amended to include the Obama administration, to do away with the National Day of Prayer on constitutional grounds. The suit is ongoing as this encyclopedia goes to press. At the same time, various atheist groups have joined together to promote a National Day of Reason as an alternative to the National Day of Prayer.

J. Gordon Melton

See also National Day of Reason; Week of Prayer for Christian Unity; World Day of Prayer.

References

"National Day of Prayer Challenge Proceeds." *Freethought Today* 26, no. 10 (December 2009). Posted at http://www.ffrf.org/publications/freethought-today/articles/national-day-of-prayer-challenge-proceeds/. Accessed February 15, 2010.

"The National Day of Prayer in the U.S." Ontario Consultants on Religious Tolerance. Posted at http://www.religioustolerance.org/day_pray.htm. Accessed February 15, 2010.

National Day of Reason

The National Day of Reason can be traced to 2003, when a variety of leadership in the community of Unbelief—secularists, atheists, humanists, Freethinkers—began to call for an response to the federally supported National Day of Prayer, which they viewed as both discriminatory and in violation of the establishment clause of the U.S. Constitution, which prohibits the federal government from passing any legislation that tends to support the establishment of a religion. Over the years, observance of the Day of Prayer has been limited to the evangelical Christian community. Especially during the years of the second Bush Administration, the promotion of the day largely fell to the National Day of Prayer Task Force, a non-governmental organization which was widely perceived to be working closely with cooperating government leadership.

The National Day of Reason was promoted as an alternative to the National Day of Prayer, and its observance is held on the same day. It is projected as a day to celebrate rational thinking by both the religious and nonreligious, regardless of their individual worldview. Operating from a much smaller base of operation in the community of Unbelief, advocates of the National Day of Reason have been less successful in inspiring events for its observance. Where observances are organized, however, leaders are encouraged to make them active events that involve service to the local community. Meanwhile, advocates want to communicate to the larger public the possibility of an inclusive and constitutional alternative to the National Day of Prayer, which they view as exclusionary.

In 2005, the Freedom from Religion Foundation, an atheist organization based in Madison, Wisconsin, petitioned the 50 state governors and other government officials to issue a proclamation declaring a day of reason to balance the proclamation supportive of a day of prayer. Though none of the governors responded positively, the mayor of the city of New Orleans, which had been devastated by Hurricane Katrina (2005), did issue such a proclamation.

J. Gordon Melton

See also Darwin Day; Freethought Day; Indivisible Day; National Day of Prayer.

References

"Govs Asked to Balance 'Day of Prayer.' " *Freethought Today* 22, no. 4 (May 2005). Posted at http://www.ffrf.org/publications/freethought-today/articles/Govs-Asked-to-Balance-Day-of-Prayer/. Accessed February 15, 2010.

"Rational Day of Thought—National Day of Reason." Secular Seasons. Posted at http://www.secularseasons.org/may/day_of_reason.html. Accessed on February 15, 2010.

National Founding Day (Scientology)

Through the late 20th century to the present, the Church of Scientology spread from its founding in the United States to more than 70 countries, beginning with England, New Zealand, South Africa, and Canada. It then spread out across Europe and to the rest of the world. This global effort was increasingly fueled by the translation of founder L. Ron Hubbard's Scientology writings into the world's languages. An effort was made to accelerate the number of languages in which *Dianetics: The Modern Science of Mental Health* was available for the celebration of the 50th anniversary of its publication (2000).

As the church spread, each occasion of the opening of the first local church center in each country was duly noted by the international leadership and became the occasion for celebration. That day would subsequently be declared the National Founding Day for each country. It occurs on a different day of the year for each national organization, for example, Belgium (March 13), Denmark (June 3), Zimbabwe (September 18), and Japan (December 31). Commemoration of the date is also carried out as is locally appropriate.

J. Gordon Melton

See also Hubbard, Birthday of L. Ron; Scientology, Holidays of the Church of.

References

What Is Scientology? Los Angeles: Bridge Publications, 1998.

Native Establishment beyond East and West (October 23)

Adidam is a spiritual community founded by Adavita Vedanta teacher Franklin Jones (1939–2008), better known by his religious name, Avatar Adi Da Samraj, believed by his followers to have been a fully enlightened guru (teacher). Each year in October, they begin a three-month period punctuated by the commemoration of the most significant events in a three-month holiday cycle that begins with the celebration of Adi Da's receiving citizenship from Fiji on October 23.

This event was the culmination of a process that had begun some five years earlier when he had announced his role as a human Incarnation of the Invisible Divine and subsequently initiated a small group of his devotees into an esoteric order. The formation of the ordered community led to his announcing that he would begin to work with these few for the sake of all. He also began an intense search for a Hermitage, which led him to Hawaii and then in 1983 to Fiji. He initially set foot on the Fijian island of Naitauba on October 27, 1983.

Once settled on Fiji, he began to speak about his role not just in the West, but in the whole world. He also began to see Fiji as the seat of his Divine Spiritual Power. Over the next decade, he would take steps to ensure that this Hermitage would be secure for him to continue his spiritual work forever. To secure the island, he applied for Fijian citizenship. On October 3, 1993, a representative of the government arrived on Naitauba and presented him with his passport. The island, located on the International Date Line, is symbolically neither East nor West. He interpreted the reception of his passport and the granting of citizenship as a sign of his having completed his work in the West and the beginning of his blessing the world. Four days later, on the 10th anniversary of his initially setting foot on the island, he conducted a ceremony to further empower the island.

October 27 is commemorated by Adi Da's disciples today as marking the point of a significant further expansion of his work and influence. It is also a time to gather and discuss their own roles in making their guru's message more broadly known.

J. Gordon Melton

See also Adi Da Samrajashram, Anniversary of Adi Da's First Footstep on; Avataric Divine Self-Emergence, Day of.

References

"An Introduction to the Sacred History of Adi Da Samraj's Divine Work." The Beezone. Posted at http://www.beezone.com/AdiDa/adidam/introsacredhistoryadidam.html. Accessed March 15, 2010.

Jones, Franklin (as Adi Da Samaj). *See My Brightness Face to Face: A Celebration of the Ruchira Buddha, Avatar Adi Da Samraj, and the First 25 Years of His Divine Revelation Work*. Middleton, CA: Dawn Horse Press, 1997.

Lee, Carolyn. *The Promised God-Man Is Here: The Extraordinary Life-Story, The "Crazy" Teaching Work, and The Divinely "Emerging" World-Blessing Work of the Divine World-Teacher of the "Last-Time," Ruchira Avatar Adi Da Samraj*. Middleton, CA: Dawn Horse Press, 1998.

Nativity of Mary (September 8)

In the biblical material on Mary, she is introduced as a young adult woman engaged to marry the carpenter Joseph. The Bible says nothing of her parents or birth. Mary's early life was discussed, however, in several extra-canonical works that circulated in the early church though not included in the Bible. Written in the mid-second century, the *Protoevangelium of James* (also known as *The Nativity of Mary* or the *Infancy Gospel of James*), names Mary's parents as Anne and Joachim and describes the visit by an angel who informed them that they were to become parents.

In the fifth century, a church was constructed in Jerusalem where many had come to be believed to be the site of Anne and Joachim's home. That church was destroyed and rebuilt in the sixth century, the consecration of the new building, named for Saint Anne, being the occasion for the development of a liturgical celebration of the birth of Mary, who was being increasingly honored as the *Theotokos*, or the Mother of God. In the flow of monks from East to West, the Feast of Mary's nativity was introduced to Rome. As the celebration grew, it was introduced with a fast and stretched to eight days (called an octave). At the end of the seventh century, Pope Sergius I (687–701) began to lead a procession from the Roman forum to Santa Maria Maggiore.

Various dates were celebrated as Mary's birthday, but September 8, a week (or octave) after the beginning of the year in the Byzantine calendar, became the most common. In later centuries, when a date was sought for the Immaculate Conception, the date of Mary's original conception in Anne's womb, the date chosen was nine months before her reputed birth date, or December 8.

The Nativity of Mary is celebrated by the Eastern Orthodox, Anglican, and Catholic churches, all of which assign it a high level of importance at least as a liturgical event, though the Eastern and Anglican churches do not adhere to the Roman pronouncements on the Immaculate Conception nor recognize it on their liturgical calendars.

J. Gordon Melton

See also Anne, Feast Day of St; Annunciation, Feast of the; Christmas; Expectation of the Birth of the Blessed Virgin Mary, Feast of; Immaculate Conception, Feast of the.

References

Dodds, Monica, and Bill Dodds. *Encyclopedia of Mary*. Huntington, IN: Our Sunday Visitor, 2007.

Hock, Ronald F. *The Life of Mary and Birth of Jesus: The Ancient Infancy Gospel of James*. Berkeley, CA: Ulysses Press, 1997.

Natsu Matsuri

Natsu Matsuri is a type of festival held in the Shinto shrines of Japan to honor the gods during the summer. As spring festivals are designed to pray from a good planting season leading to an abundant harvest, and autumn festivals offer thanks for the harvest, so summer festivals tend to be dedicated either to fishermen and those who make their living from the waters (Kaijin Matsuri), or for farmers who must contend with the various hazards to which their crops might fall victim—most notably pestilences, insects, and bad weather. During natsu matsuris, believers find their way to the Shinto shrines to entreat the deities (*kami*) for protection against such disasters. In the cities, where disease often broke out during the humid summers, the festival became a time to pray for the end of epidemics.

In Japan, summer festivals are a ubiquitous item, but the festival in Kyoto, the Gian Matsuri, has turned into a monthlong celebration. While originally built around the Yasaka Shrine, the other shrines such as Kitano Tenman-gū and the Iwashimizu Hachiman Shrine participate fully. In the modern world, with the possibility of limiting damage from disease and natural calamities, the summer festivals have become highly secularized and are now more about finding ways to escape the heat and have a good time than about paying attention to the source of the original festival.

One version of the summer festival known as Taue no Matsuri celebrates the transplanting of the young rice seedling into the ground.

J. Gordon Melton

See also Aki Matsuri; Hadaka Matsuri; Kaijin Matsuri; Kaza-Matsuri; Natsu Matsuri; Sakura Matsuri.

References

Plutschow, Herbert. *Matsuri: The Festivals of Japan*. Richmond, Surrey, UK: Curzon Press, 1996.

Festival participants perform the Garba, a traditional folk dance, in a public square during Navaratri. (*Hinduism Today* Magazine)

Navaratri

The Navaratri (Navaratra) or "Nine Nights" festival (also known as Durga Puja, Dussehra, and in Nepal as Dasain) is celebrated in September–October (during the waxing moon half of the Hindu lunar month of Ashvina) for nine nights (and 10 days). This is a pan-Indian festival, which, as Holi welcomes the spring, welcomes the autumn season. Also, like Holi, it takes very different forms in different regions. In neighboring Nepal, as the national holiday, Dasain, it is the largest festival of the year, involving both Hindu and non-Hindu Nepalis alike in celebration.

In most Hindi-speaking areas of North India, Navaratri is centered on Rama, like Krishna an incarnation of the deity Vishnu. It is celebrated with a drama, the Rama Lila (the mysterious divine magic of Lord Rama), drawn from the *Ramayana* epic story. Here there are recitations every day from the medieval Hindi *Tulsidas Ramayana*, and in most places, plays that depict scenes from the *Ramayana* story are presented in smaller or grander scale.

The largest of the Rama Lila play is staged across the river from Benares, where the king (maharajah) of Benares established an immense ground that represents the *Ramayana* story. Actors go from station to station on different days as the story develops. On Vijayadashami—variously described as the culminating day of

Statue of the Hindu Goddess Durga. (J. Gordon Melton)

Navaratri or the day after Navaratri—the effigies of Rama's enemy the demon king Ravana, along with his son Meghanada and his brother Kumbhakarna, are burned to celebrate the victory of Rama over the forces of the demons or Rakshasas.

In Bihar, Bengal, and Assam, the Navaratri festival, and in Nepal, Dasain, is celebrated as a Durga festival. Durga pujas or worship services are done for her on the last three days of the festival. The festival begins by awakening Durga, who is asleep, and continues by manufacturing a temporary image of her which is enlivened for the purpose of the festival.

On Vijayadashami, the image of Durga will be taken in a great procession to be immersed in the local body of water, be it a river or the ocean or a large tank. Lively festivities follow. In southern India, the goddess Sarasvati, the goddess or learning and the arts, is worshipped on the seventh day of the festival, and Durga only on the eighth day. On the ninth day, there is a worship of instruments and implements of livelihood, which are taken out to be honored with mantras and small offerings.

An additional tradition surrounding Durga and Navaratri concerns the Pandava brothers, important characters in the great Indian epic, the *Mahabharata*. Great warriors, all five brothers were married to one woman named Draupadi. At one point, they lived through a 14-year exile followed by a one-year period of incognito during which time they had to put away their distinctive weaponry. They hid it in a "Shami" tree near their residence. When their incognito year was finished, they went to the tree and retrieved their weaponry. For its safe preservation, they offered worship and thanksgiving both to the Shami tree and the goddess Durga, the deity of strength and victory. Meanwhile, their rivals, the Kauravas, had invaded the region looking for them. After completing their devotions, the Pandavas went directly to engage in the Battle of Kurukshetra, at which they won a decisive victory. That day subsequently became known as "Vijayadashami" ("Vijaya" is Sanskrit for "Victory"). Today, on Vijayadashami, people give *Shami* leaves with a wish that the recipient have victory in their efforts.

While the most celebrated Navaratri festival is in the fall, there is also another Navaratri festival that is celebrated in the spring, during the waxing moon half of the Indian month of Chaitra (March–April). This spring event does not attain the level of the fall festival. The Jain festival of Navpad Oli overlaps the spring and fall celebrations of Navaratri.

Constance A. Jones

See also Dasain; Diwali; Holi; Navpad Oli.

References

Eck, Diana L. *Banaras, City of Light*. New York: Columbia University Press, 1999.

Harshananda, Swami. *Hindu Festivals and Sacred Days*. Bangalore: Ramakrishna Math, 1994.

Mukuncharandas, Sadhu. *Hindu Festivals (Origin Sentiments and Rituals)*. Amdavad, India: Swaminarayan Aksharpith, 2005.

Sharma, Nath. *Festivals of India*. New Delhi: Abhinav Publications, 1978.

Shekar, H. V. *Festivals of India: Significance of the Celebrations*. Louisville, KY: Insight Books, 2000.

Welbon, Guy, and Glenn Yocum, eds. *Religious Festivals in South India and Sri Lanka*. Delhi: Manohar, 1982.

Navpad Oli

Navpad Oli is a nine-day festival observed by Jains twice a year in the spring and fall, the former in the waxing moon of the Indian month of Chaitra (March–April on the Common Era calendar) and then during the waxing moon of Ashwina (September–October). Navpad Oli is designed to end on the day of the full moon, known as purnima. It is also set to begin close to, if not exactly on, the spring and fall equinoxes. Navpad Oli starts during the middle of Navaratri, the Hindu Durga Puja ritual, also held twice annually.

During Navpad Oli, the observant Jain will engage in a particular kind of fast termed Ayambil Tapa, in which a single meal of boiled grains without seasonings like salt are eaten. The devotions shown are seen as keeping one mentally healthy and the fast as energizing the body to fight disease.

Navpad Oli is set aside to worship the nine "posts" or essential realities that uphold the universe, which are termed Arihant, Siddha, Acharya, Upadhyaya, Sadhu, Samyag Darshan, Samyag Jnyana, Samyag Charitra, and Samyag Tapa. The first five of these are equivalent to five posts to which the religious may climb and upon whom the universe depends. According to Jain teachings, anyone may attain any of these supreme posts (position) through the various disciplines of inner self-development. In reaching the first two "posts," the aspirant passes beyond the point of physical embodiment. The next three posts are held by leaders in the present Jain community. The last four posts represent major virtues which anyone may attain and which lead to salvation (*moksha*). During Navpad Oli, each day is set aside to focus upon one of the nine posts.

1. The Arihant has attained freedom from all earthly attachments and hatreds.
2. The Siddha has attained and lives in perfect equilibrium, eternal peace, and joy, while remaining in perfect motionless rest.
3. The Archarya is the supreme authority in all the matters related to the Jain Sangha (the community of monks and nuns) and the interpretation of the Jain scriptures.
4. The Upadhyaya is the guru (teacher) who is responsible for educational activities in the Sangha, and who teaches the Jain monks and nuns.
5. The Sadhu is the renunciate who had begun the path to Arihanthood and devotes himself or herself to the path that leads to *moksha* (salvation). He had begun to practice the four sacred virtues.
6. Samyag Darshan, or right view.
7. Samyag Jnyana, or right knowledge.
8. Samyag Charitra, or right action or conduct.
9. Samyag Tapa, or austerity in abstaining from lusts and desires with the goal of reaching equilibrium and tranquility.

The nine posts are often represented symbolically in the Siddha Charka, a three-dimensional version of the yantra diagram. On a square base, the first five posts are represented as five men sitting in a meditative position, with one (the Arihant) in the center and the other four facing inward, each with their back to one of the four sides. The four virtues are then represented with symbols inside the four corners.

On the last day of the observance, the day of the full moon, Navpad Oli, Jain householders join the monks and nuns in the worship of Samyag Tapa. They will join in the Ayambil fast by eating the meal of boiled rice only, and will pray to attain to the virtue. They will also join the larger local community for the Navpad Mandal Puja.

J. Gordon Melton

See also Akshay Tritiya (Jain); Diwali; Gyana Panchami; Kartika Purnima; Mauna Agyaras; Mahavir Jayanti; New Year's Day (Jain); Paryushana; Paush Dashami.

References

Jaini, P. S. *The Jaina Path of Purification*. Delhi: Motilal Banarsidass, 1979, 1990.

Kothari, Jyoti. "Festival of India: Navpad Oli in Jainism." Posted at http://hubpages.com/hub/Festival-of-India-Navpad-Oli-jain-festivalnavapad-navapada-siddhachakra-ayambil-jainism. Accessed June 15, 2010.

Singh, Narendra K., ed. *Encyclopedia of Jainism*. 30 vols. New Delhi: Anmol, 2001.

Naw-Rúz, Festival of (March 21)

The Festival of the Naw-Rúz is one of five Bahá'í festivals and one of the nine Bahá'í holy days on which work is to be suspended.

On March 21, 2010, the United Nations marked the first "International Day for Nowruz" (Persian, "New Day"), an ancient spring festival of Persian origin (and the Zoroastrian New Year's Day) celebrated for over 3,000 years and enjoyed today by more than 300 million people worldwide as the beginning of the new year. Mary Boyce notes that it "seems a reasonable surmise that Nowrūz, the holiest of them all [Zoroastrian holy days], with deep doctrinal significance, was founded by Zoroaster himself" (Boyce, *Encyclopædia Iranica*). Naw-Rúz may be sacred or secular, depending on the setting. For Bahá'ís, Naw-Rúz is sacred, imbued with the symbolism of spiritual renewal.

As the first day of the Bahá'í New Year, Naw-Rúz coincides with the spring equinox in the Northern Hemisphere, which typically occurs on March 21. However, since Bahá'u'lláh (1817–1892, prophet-founder of the Bahá'í Faith) enjoined that this festival be celebrated on whatever day the sun passes into the constellation of Aries—that is, the vernal equinox—Naw-Rúz could fall on March 19, 20, 21, or 22, depending on the precise time of the equinox (even should this occur one minute before sunset). It is expected that the precise timing of Naw-Rúz will require a designated spot on earth—to be decided by the Universal House of Justice (the governing international Bahá'í council) in the future—to serve as the standard for astronomically determining the spring equinox. Since Naw-Rúz also falls on the first day of a Bahá'í month, it coincides with the day on which a Nineteen-Day Feast is to be observed, but the two events must be kept separate.

Bahá'í communities typically observe Naw-Rúz and meetings that combine prayerful devotions with joyous fellowship. "Naw-Rúz is our New Year, a Feast of hospitality and rejoicing" (Shoghi Effendi, *Directives from the Guardian*, 30). Bahá'ís from Iranian backgrounds may follow some traditions associated with the ancient Persian festival, but these cultural practices are kept distinct from the religious observance itself. To augment the festive joy, signal events are often scheduled to take place on Naw-Rúz, being an ideal time for momentous announcements as well.

The Báb (1819–1850), precursor and herald of Bahá'u'lláh, created a new calendar—called the Badí' ("Wondrous"/"New") calendar—which consists of 19 months of 19 days each, with four intercalary days (five in leap years) to round out the solar year. The only religious festival that the Báb had instituted was Naw-Rúz. The first day of the new year (i.e., the day of "Bahá' ") was Naw-Rúz (March 21), which the Báb specifically set apart in honor of "Him Whom God shall make manifest," whose advent the Báb foretold and whose appearance, as Bahá'u'lláh, the majority of the Báb's followers accepted. The Báb wrote:

> God hath called that month the month of Bahá' (Splendour, Glory), meaning that therein lieth the splendour and glory of all months, and He hath singled it out for Him Whom God shall make manifest. (The Báb, *Persian Bayán* 5:3; provisional translation by Saiedi, *Gate of the Heart*, 328)

Because this day was "singled it out for Him Whom God shall make manifest," Naw-Rúz was highly symbolic and its observance pointed forward to that messianic figure for whose imminent advent it was the Báb's professed mission to prepare the world (and whom the majority of Bábís recognized as Bahá'u'lláh later on). The Báb described Naw-Rúz as the Day of God on which goodly acts performed would receive the recompense for same acts as though performed for an entire year, while those who recite a special verse 361 times would be preserved from anything ill-fated during the course of the coming year (The Báb, *Persian Bayán* 5:3). The Báb's laws, which were scarcely put into practice during the time of the Báb, were primarily intended to prepare his followers for the coming of "Him Whom God shall make manifest" and would be abrogated, except as accepted, at his advent. Such laws, as Nader Saiedi points out, were "not meant to be taken literally but instead perform a symbolic and profoundly transformative function" (Saiedi, *Gate of the Heart*, 343).

Even so, Bahá'u'lláh preserved and adapted several of the Báb's major laws to be observed by the Bahá'ís. Bahá'u'lláh formally ordained Naw-Rúz as a festival unto those who have observed the period of fasting that precedes Naw-Rúz:

> O Pen of the Most High! Say: O people of the world! We have enjoined upon you fasting during a brief period, and at its close have designated for you Naw-Rúz as a feast. Thus hath the Day-Star of Utterance shone forth above the horizon of the Book as decreed by Him Who is the Lord of the beginning and the end. (Bahá'u'lláh, *The Kitáb-i-Aqdas*, 25)

This Bahá'í law refers to the nineteen-day Fast (March 2–20), a period of spiritual discipline and purification, during which Bahá'ís abstain from food and drink from sunrise to sunset. (Bahá'í days begin and end at sunset.) Since the Fast ends on the sunset on which Naw-Rúz begins, Naw-Rúz celebrations are often combined with a dinner.

Unlike the other Bahá'í holy days, which commemorate historic events in Bahá'í history, Naw-Rúz has religious significance primarily due to its symbolism of renewal. As an Indo-European language, Persian is distantly related to English, which explains why the word "naw" (pronounced "no") in Persian is similar to the English word "new." Naw-Rúz not only heralds the advent of spring, but is also symbolic of a "spiritual springtime." On a personal level, the Festival of Naw-Rúz is a time for renewal. On the occasion of Naw-Rúz in 1906, 'Abdu'l-Bahá (1844–1921), the successor to Bahá'u'lláh, wrote to the American Bahá'ís saying, in part:

> It is New Year; . . . now is the beginning of a cycle of Reality, a New Cycle, a New Age, a New Century, a New Time and a New Year. . . . I wish this blessing to appear and become manifest in the faces and characteristics of the believers, so that they, too, may become a new people, and . . . may make the world a new world, to the end that . . . the sword be turned into the olive branch; the flash of hatred become the flame of the love of God . . . all races as one race; and all national anthems harmonized into one melody. ('Abdu'l-Bahá, *Tablets of Abdul-Baha Abbas*, 38–40)

Thus, this ancient Zoroastrian holy day and Persian springtime festival has been transformed into a Bahá'í holy day, which has, as its animating purpose, the creation of a new world in which a new era of peace and prosperity may be brought about through the universal Bahá'í principles of unity through diversity, famously expressed by Bahá'u'lláh in 1890 in a historic visit by Cambridge orientalist Edward G. Browne (*A Traveller's Narrative*, xl), in these oft-quoted words:

> That all nations should become one in faith and all men as brothers; that the bonds of affection and unity between the sons of men should be strengthened; that diversity of religion should cease, and differences of race be annulled—what harm is there in this? . . . Yet so it shall be; these fruitless strifes, these ruinous wars shall pass away, and the "Most Great Peace" shall come.

Bahá'ís see this "New Day" as having transformed the vernal equinox into a universal celebration of the oneness of humankind.

Christopher Buck

See also 'Abdu'l-Bahá, Ascension of; Ayyám-i-Há (Bahá'í Intercalary Days); Báb, Festival of the Birth of the; Báb, Festival of the Declaration of the; Báb, Martyrdom of the; Bahá'í Calendar and Rhythms of Worship; Bahá'í Faith; Bahá'í Fast; Bahá'u'lláh, Ascension of; Bahá'u'lláh, Festival of the Birth of; Covenant, Day of the; Nineteen-Day Feast (Bahá'í); Race Unity Day; Riḍván, Festival of; World Religion Day.

References

'Abdu'l-Bahá, *Tablets of Abdul-Baha Abbas*. Chicago: Bahá'í Publishing Committee, 1909.

Bahá'u'lláh, *The Kitáb-i-Aqdas*. Haifa: Bahá'í World Centre, 1992.

Boyce, Mary. "Festivals: Zoroastrian." In *Encyclopædia Iranica*, edited by Ehsan Yarshater. Vol. 9 (1999). Posted at http://www.iranica.com/articles/festivals-vi-vii-viii. Accessed July 15, 2010.

Browne, Edward G. *A Traveller's Narrative*. Vol. 1. Cambridge: Cambridge University Press, 1891.

Momen, Moojan. "Festivals, vi. Bahai." In *Encyclopædia Iranica*, edited by Ehsan Yarshater. Vol. 9 (1999). Posted at http://www.iranica.com/articles/festivals-vi-vii-viii. Accessed July 15, 2010.

Saiedi, Nader. *Gate of the Heart: Understanding the Writings of the Báb*. Ottawa and Waterloo, Ontario, Canada: Association for Bahá'í Studies/Wilfrid Laurier University Press, 2008.

Shoghi Effendi. *Directives from the Guardian*. New Delhi: Bahá'í Publishing Trust, 1973.

Walbridge, John. "Naw-Rúz: The Bahá'í New Year." In *Sacred Acts, Sacred Space, Sacred Time*, 213–16. Oxford: George Ronald, 1996.

Nehan

Many Buddhists believe that the birth, the day of enlightenment (at the age of 35), and death (in his 80s) of Gautama Buddha, the founder of the Buddhist movement, occurred on the same day of the year. That day, usually called Wesak, is the night of the full moon of the Hindu month of Vaisakha (usually in May on the Common Era calendar). Tibetans call it Sakya Dawa.

Other Buddhists, most notably those in Japan, hold their commemorations of those three events on separate days. Nehan, February 15, is the day Japanese Buddhists believe that Gautama Buddha died near the town of Kushinagara, almost due north of Calcutta near the border with Nepal, on the banks of the Hiranyavati River. The Buddha is often pictured in a reclining state, using his right hand as a pillow, calling to memory the moments before his death. Early accounts of his death suggest that he was sleeping on a bed between two sala trees whose white flowers fell continuously during his last day.

In his last discourse, called the Yuikyogyo, the Last Teaching of Shakyamuni Buddha, he discussed the transitory state of life, noting that the physical body (even his) dies, and that it is the Dharma (the teaching) that is eternal. He also noted that he had withheld nothing from his teachings, that there were no secret teachings, nor any teachings with a hidden meaning, He closed by saying that "In a moment, I shall be passing into Nirvana." His death is popularly referred to as the Mahanirvana or Parinirvana. In Japan, there are a variety of ways to

This painting on silk depicts Buddha's death. Followers show respect as Buddha achieves enlightenment and reaches Nirvana. (Corel)

celebrate Nehan, some peculiar to one group or another, some to different parts of the country.

One commemoration of Nehan at a contemporary Zen center "focuses on a moment when someone goes up to the altar and blows out all the candles and turns off the altar lamp. A statue of the dying Buddha, reclining on his side and surrounded by animals, has been placed on the altar for this ceremony. This is called a Parinirvana statue, indicating that it depicts the Buddha entering his final or complete nirvana (cessation), which comes only with physical death. Behind the statue is a small screen, and behind the screen is a single candle that remains lit. At the end of the ceremony, another person goes up and relights the altar from that single, hidden source."

Among Buddhists in North America, the exact date of the celebration of Nehan may vary both to hold the celebration on the weekend and to facilitate the schedules of officials and guests who might make themselves available to several related local centers.

Japanese Buddhists celebrate the birth of the Buddha on April 8 (Hana Matsuri), of his enlightenment on December 8 (Bodhi Day), and the death on February 15.

J. Gordon Melton

See also Bodhi Day; Hana Matsuri, Sakya Dawa Festival; Wesak/Vesak.

References

Bagchee, Moni. *Our Buddha*. Kuala Lumpur, Malaysia: Buddhist Missionary Society, 1999.

Kashima, Tetsuden. *Buddhism in America: The Social Organization of an Ethnic Religious Institution*. Westport, CT: Greenwood Press, 1977.

"The Last Teaching of the Buddha." Posted at http://www.amidabuddha.org/lastteaching.html.

Nehan—Commemorating the Buddha's Death." Dharma Rain Zen Center. Posted at http://www.dharma-rain.org/index.php?p=ds-manual_cer3-nehan. Accessed March 15, 2010.

Neri-kuyo

The Neri-kuyo is a Buddhist ceremony built around a procession in honor of Amida Buddha (or Amitabha). At this time, Amitabha descends to this world followed by 25 bodhisattvas to save the devout, most often the dying people, and lead them to the Pure Land. Amida is the Buddha of the Sukhavati, the Western Paradise that gives Pure Land Buddhism its popular designation. Pure Land forms of Buddhism (in Japan, the Jodo-shu and Jodo Shinshu sects) honor Amida above all the Mahayana Buddhist bodhisattvas and believe that merely by calling on his name, one can be saved and brought to the Pure Land after death.

The word *kuhon* in Pure Land usage refers to the belief that deeds can be grouped on a goodness/badness scale of one to nine (*ku*), and what part of the Pure Land we will be assigned will be judged according to this scale. It is also the case that in statuary Amida's hands will be positioned in one of nine mudras.

Two Neri-kuyo celebrations are best known in Japan. One occurs in mid-October at Kamakura. The priest and members of Dairisan Ryogaku-in Kuhonji, a Jodo-shu temple, will process to Tenshozan Renge-in Komyoji, the largest of the dozen Kamakura Jodo-shu temples. The Neri-kuyo procession is occasioned by the annual Juya, or Ten Days of Prayer, festival that begins on October 13 every year at Komyoji. Even better known is the Neri-kuyo at Taima-dera in Nara, which occurs on May 14 every year. Officials at the temple dress as various bodhisattvas and lead a process through the temple grounds. Taima-dera was originally established in 612 at what is now Osaka, but in 681, it was moved to Nara. It is famous for a painting that depicts Amitabha, Kannon (Guan Yin, the goddess of mercy), and Manjushri, the bodhisattva of wisdom, together in the Pure Land.

J. Gordon Melton

See also Amitabha's Birthday; Guan Yin's Birthday; Harikuyo; Manjushri's Birthday; Mudras.

References

"Kuhonji." Posted at http://www.asahi-net.or.jp/~qm9t-kndu/kuhonji.htm. Accessed on July 15, 2010.

Mutsu, Iso. *Kamakura Fact and Legend*. Rutland, VT: Charles E. Tuttle Company, 1995.

New Church Day (June 19)

New Church Day celebrates the formal beginning of the Church of the New Jerusalem, the new movement that looks to the revelations received by Emanuel Swedenborg (1688–1772) and his new perspective on the Christian religion. The "official" beginning of the New Church occurred in 1770 and its largely invisible initiation was recorded in Swedenborg's book, *The True Christian Religion*.

A scientist of note in his Swedish homeland after writing a number of works on a spectrum of scientific topics, in the mid-1740s, Swedenborg abandoned his career as the result of a vision of Jesus, and spent much of the rest of his life in conversations with the angelic world, from which he received a constant stream of revelations that led to his extensive "spiritual" commentaries on the Bible and his new interpretation of the true meaning of Christianity. He was 83 when in his last work, *The True Christian Religion*, he summarized his thought in a most succinct manner.

In what amounts to an afterword to *The True Christian Religion*, Swedenborg tells of the events in the heavenly realm that constituted the founding of the new Church:

> After the completion of this book, the Lord called together His twelve disciples, who had followed Him in the world; and a day later He sent them all forth throughout the spiritual world to preach the Gospel, that the Lord God Jesus Christ is king, and His kingdom shall be for ever and ever, as foretold by Daniel (7:13, 14) and in Revelation (11:15): Blessed are they who come to the wedding supper of the Lamb Rev. 19:9. This happened on the nineteenth of June in the year 1770. This was meant by the Lord's saying: He will send his angels, and they will gather together His chosen people from the bounds of the heavens on one side as far as the bounds of the heavens on the other. Matt. 24:31.

This new calling and commissioning of the original 12 apostles is the event from which the members of the several ecclesiastical organizations that follow Swedenborg's teachings now date their beginning. A visible Church of the New Jerusalem would not be formed until after Swedenborg's death, when some followers in England came together. From the original organization, the movement would spread internationally and eventually be organized in Sweden. The Church of the New Jerusalem was the first new church to be organized in the United States after the American Revolution.

Swedenborgians also consider June 19, 1770, to be the culmination of the Lord's Second Coming (as represented in the revelations given to Swedenborg), his judgment on the fallen Christian Church, and the initiation of a church that will become the crown of all the Christian denominations that have previously appeared.

Different New Church congregations will celebrate June 19 more or less elaborately. Some will have programs that feature drama, music, and one or more of the films that have been made about Swedenborg and spread events out over several days, or simply remember the founding events with a worship service.

J. Gordon Melton

See also Festival of Light (Rosicrucian); White Lotus Day (Theosophy).

References

Ayers, David W. "A New Church Day Mystery." *The New Church Newsletter* (Hurstville, NSW, Aust.), June 2001. Posted at http://www.newchurch.org/societies/Hurstville/newsletters/June01.pdf. Accessed July 15, 2010.

Benz, Ernst. *Emanuel Swedenborg: Visionary Savant in the Age of Reason*. West Chester, PA: Swedenborg Foundation, 2002.

Rose, Jonathan S., Stuart Shotwell, and Mary Lou Bertucci, eds. *Scribe of Heaven: Swedenborg's Life, Work, and Impact*. West Chester, PA: Swedenborg Foundation, 2005.

Woofenden, William Ross. *Swedenborg Researcher's Manual*. Bryn Athyn, PA: Swedenborg Scientific Association, 1988.

New Year's Day

Most contemporary religions operate on a calendar based on the annual circulation of the Earth around the sun (Islam being a prominent exception), have designated a beginning point from which to measure that circulation, and acknowledge a New Year's Day (Christianity being a prominent exception). For most religious communities, the New Year begins on either January 1 of the Common Era calendar or the vernal or spring equinox. In the ancient world, the winter and summer solstices and the spring and fall equinoxes were among the most well-known astronomical events.

Some ancient calendars, such as the Babylonian, used the vernal equinox to mark the New Year. The Babylonians invented the zodiac and calculated the movement of the sun through its 12 signs. They passed this system to the Chadeans and Assyrians and on to Egypt. The Hebrews were influenced by the Babylonian calendar during the years of captivity when they picked up the Babylonian days of the months and moved their New Year's celebration (Rosh Hashanah) to the fall. Rosh Hashanah actually falls on Tishri 1, the first day of the seventh month in the Hebrew calendar, the first month (Nissan) coming in the spring. Rosh Hashanah is a prescribed day of rest, like the Sabbath. Its exact date relative to the Common Era calendar varies from year to year, and also must not fall on a Sunday, Wednesday, or Friday.

Julius Caesar (100–44 BCE) revised the Roman calendar as a strictly solar calendar, established January 1 as the beginning of the New Year and ensured the beginning of spring (i.e., the spring equinox) always occurs in March. These strictures were carried forward in the Gregorian reforms and are maintained in our Common Era calendar today.

The Christian Church adopted the Julian calendar as its official calendar at the Council of Nicea in 324 CE. January 1 was not a particularly significant date on the annual liturgical calendar, though once the date of Jesus's birth was set as December 25, the New Year was acknowledged as the date of the Feast of the Circumcision. It was assumed that in Hebrew society, the circumcision of males would be held on the eighth day after birth. The Feast of the Circumcision (now known as the Feast of the Solemnity of Mary) is somewhat lost, falling as it does between Christmas and Epiphany (January 6). That fact, along with the downplaying of the liturgical calendar in general in Protestant circles, has contributed greatly to the almost complete secularization of New Year's Day in the Christian West. One exception is the festival to Bom Jesus dos Navegantes (Good Jesus of Boatmen) that occurs in Salvador, Bahia, Brazil. Jesus is honored with a New Year's Day Catholic Mass and maritime procession in which the seafaring families of the town ask for divine protection.

New Year's Day in Ethiopia is called Enkutatash, and is celebrated on Meskerem 1, the first day of the first month of the Ethiopian calendar (either September 11 or 12 on the Common Era calendar). Enkutatash celebrates the return of the queen of Sheba from her journey to Jerusalem to visit the Hebrew king Solomon (I Kings 10). Her courtiers in Ethiopia welcomed her home by making an offering of jewels to replenish her spent treasury. This day also marks the end of the rainy season in the country. It is celebrated throughout the country, though most notably on Mount Entoto. Here, Emperor Menelik II (1844–1913) erected his palace, looking out over his new capital, Addis Ababa. Mount Entoto is also home to many monasteries, and is considered a sacred mountain by members of the Ethiopian Orthodox Church.

Chinese New Year's Day

While as in the West, the Chinese New Year's celebration has largely become a secular affair, it still retails elements of its religious past in Chinese traditional religion. It is celebrated on the first day of the first month of the Chinese lunar year and has always been a joyful event marking the end of winter and the beginning of spring. That date appears to have been largely set during the Han dynasty (221–206 BCE), which adopted the Taichu calendar that set the first day of the year across the land. Some elements of the festival—staying up all night on New Year's Eve, the lighting of lanterns and fireworks, the drinking of wine—also began to spread at this time. During the Tang dynasty (618–907), the focus of the festival gradually shifted from protecting one's self from ghosts and demons, to enjoying life and expecting good in the year ahead. The celebration took on a lighter, more joyful tone. In later dynasties, more ritualized aspects of the celebration were added, and the variety of entertainments—including lion dancing, dragon dancing, and boat races—were significantly increased. In many places, visits to the temple of the local deity became part of the day's activity.

The New Year's Day festivities have become the most important and celebrated holiday in both China and the Chinese diaspora. Preparation will begin as much as a week ahead of time. Those who have moved to the city in the last few decades will return to their rural home and extended family. The celebration that begins on New Year's Eve may last for a few days or stretch for as long as two weeks. In fact, preparation will have begun during the 12th month of the lunar year with the Laba (Lantern) and New Year Preliminary Festivals (Small New Year), built around the Kitchen God. It was also a time for spring cleaning.

On New Year's Eve, the family will gather and seal the door of their home with red paper, to prevent their good fortune from escaping. They will offer food to the deities on their home altar and pay respects to their ancestors. They will rise early on New Year's Day and remove the paper around the door as it is time to welcome the good fortune of the New Year into their homes. The welcoming is accompanied by firecrackers.

At this time, one would encounter a variety of decorations carrying various forms of well wishes for the coming year. Written on strips of paper, they would be displayed in front of shops and on the doors of homes. The front gates of homes might also have pictures of two guardians and a tiger. This practice is derived from an old Taoist story in which two brothers fought demons and fed them to the tigers, believed to be the enemy of evil spirits and any who would harm the deceased.

New Year's Day is also a time to indulge in food. Enough for everyone for several days will have been prepared ahead of time. One popular practice was to place coins in dumplings (amid the meat dumplings), and being served such a dumpling would be considered a sign of coming good luck. Presents may be exchanged.

In both China and Taiwan, the secularization of the holiday and the following of practices of the traditional culture without taking note of the spiritual reasons that lie behind them has become the norm. A most important sign of the transformation is the opening of retail businesses so that holiday goers may spend New Year's Day shopping.

Islamic New Year's

Islam follows a lunar calendar of 354 days, which means that relative to the Common Era calendar, the next year will begin 11 days earlier each year. The Islamic New Year (Maal Hijra) is celebrated on the first day of Muharram (the first month of the Islamic calendar).

New Year's is approached as a time for quiet and sober reflection. There are special prayers for the occasion, which will be repeated by those who gather at a mosque. For Sunni Muslims, possibly the most important activity is to repeat the story of the Prophet Muhammad's *hijra* (the flight from Mecca to Medina in 622), and to reflect upon one's life and moral state.

For Shi'a Muslims, New Year's Day has a completely different meaning. It marks the beginning of the 10-day Remembrance of Muharram, when Shi'a Muslims recall the Battle of Karbala and mourn the death of Imam Ḥusayn ibn Ali, Muhammad's grandson, at the hands of the army of the Sunni Muslim caliph Yazid I. The time of mourning culminates on the 10th day, the holy day called Ashura, the anniversary of the actual day of the battle. During this period, people will gather in mosques for the reenactment of scenes of the Battle of Karbala. Women will wear black. Groups will begin to construct a replica of Ḥusayn's tomb that will later be carried through the street in a procession led by a horse, recalling Ḥusayn's horse, Dul Dul.

Bahá'í New Year's

The Bahá'í Faith has published its own calendar, which operates within its community for scheduling religious events. It is built around 19 months of 19 days each, plus additional days to keep it aligned to the Common Era calendar. The first day of the year on the Bahá'í calendar is always March 21, thus placing it on the spring equinox, even if in any given year, the exact equinox occurs on March 20 or 22. Traditionally, the Persian (Zoroastrian) calendar begins the year on March 21.

The Bahá'í New Year's Day is termed Naw-Rúz (a name meaning "new day" taken from the same day in the Persian calendar). It marks the end of the annual 19-day month of Alá, which is a time for fasting, and is celebrated with a banquet feast. It is also one of the nine holy days of the year when work and school are suspended.

Indian New Year's

In 1957, the Indian government introduced the new Saka calendar, a solar calendar that corresponds in many ways with the Common Era calendar, but begins on the day after the vernal equinox, on the first day of the month of Chaitra. That day is usually March 22, but will be March 21 during a leap year. Many Hindus focus upon Brahma, the Creator, on this day as they believe that he began creating the world on this day.

India is a relatively new country, having been created by the British as it brought the many states of the Indian subcontinent under a single colonial regime. The various states retain ancient languages and customs, and, in places, their own calendars. In most states of modern India, there are local celebrations of New Year's Day, and the majority of these fall on the first day of the month of Chaitra. Among the different New Year's Days is Puthandu, celebrated as New Year's Day in Tamil Nadu. Puthandu is observed on the first day of the month of Chithirai in the Tamil calendar (April 13 or 14). Celebrating New Year's on April 13–14 is also the traditional way in Nepal and the Indian states of Kerala, Orissa, and West Bengal.

Sikh New Year's Day

Among the Sikhs, New Year's Day continues an old harvest festival in the Punjab called Baisakhi or Vasakhi, which happens to fall on April 13–14 in the Common Era calendar. This day attained a heightened meaning for Sikhs as one of their gurus, Gobind Singh, created the Khalsa, the collective body of all Sikhs, on this day by performing the Amrit (baptism) ceremony in 1699. Traditionally, for 48 hours prior to the beginning of the day, a continuous reading of Guru Granth Sahib is held, and the morning of Baisakhi begins with a completion ceremony. The gathered congregation then sings divine hymns and listened to discourses on the importance of Baisakhi. It is a day for those wish to identify with the Sikh community to take Amrit. Following the activities at the gurdwara, all will engage in a wide variety of *sewa* (religious work).

Other Religions

Most newer religions, those formed in the 19th and 20th centuries, have adopted the dominant calendar in the place of their origin, and only a few have engaged in any attempt to create a new calendar for the special use their group. For most new religions, January 1 on the Common Era calendar is their New Year's Day, though they might attempt to give the day new significance or involve members in special activities. Various religious groups will take advantage of the general holiday spirit during the period (including released time from work and suspension of school activities) from Christmas to New Year's Day in many Western countries to hold retreats, seminars, and other events for their members. Every year, a few days before New Year's Day, the Church of Scientology organizes a gathering of church member in a large auditorium in the Los Angeles area at which the year, especially the accomplishments of the organization, are reviewed and celebrated, and goals for the future projected. This event is recorded and then sent to all the churches worldwide so that it might be shown as gatherings to be held on New Year's Eve.

Among the groups proposing a different New Year's Day are the Wiccans and Neo-Pagans. They build their year around eight evenly placed high holidays—the summer and winter solstices, the spring and fall equinoxes, and four holidays halfway between the equinoxes and solstices. Samhain (summer's end) occurs on October 31, halfway between the fall equinox and winter solstice. It traditionally marks the end of the harvest season, though few modern Wiccans/Pagans engage in agriculture or even reside in rural areas, and hence they have come to emphasize the day as a festival for the deceased. In Samhain gatherings, those who have died in the year previous are acknowledged, and contact with the spirit world is attempted. It is believed that the veil between this world and the next is thinnest on the evening of Samhain.

Many scholars believe that Samhain was the beginning of the Celtic year, and modern Wiccan/Pagans have picked up that idea, along with the convergence of Samhain with the Christian celebration of All Saints Day (November 1) and All Saints Eve or Halloween (October 31).

J. Gordon Melton

See also All Saints Day; Ashura; Bahá'í Calendar and Rhythms of Worship; Calendars, Religious; Chinese New Year's (Preliminary tsagaan Festival); Chinese New Year's Day; Christmas; Epiphany; Fall Equinox; Halloween; Naw-Rúz, Festival of; New Year's Day (India); New Year's Day (Jain); New Year's Eve (Scientology); Nowruz; Rosh Hashanah; Samhain; Solemnity of Mary, Feast of the; Spring Equinox (Thelema); Spring Equinox (Vernal); Summer Solstice; Tsagaan Sar; Wicca/Neo-Paganism Liturgical Calendar; Winter Solstice; Zoroastrianism.

References

Algül, Hüseytinj. *The Blessed Days and Nights of the Islamic Year.* Somerset, NJ: Light, 2005.

Gregory, Ruth W. *Anniversaries and Holidays*. Chicago: American Library Association, 1983.

Latsch, Marie-Luise. *Traditional Chinese Festivals*. Singapore: Graham Brash, 1984.

Liming, Wei. *Chinese Festivals: Traditions, Customs, and Rituals*. Hong Kong: China International Press, 2005.

Mukundcharandas, Sadhu. *Hindu Festivals (Origin, Sentiments and Rituals)*. Amdavad, India: Swaminarayan Aksharpith, 2005.

Mukundcharandas, Sadhu. *Hindu Rites and Rituals (Sentiments, Sacraments and Symbols)*. Amdavad, India: Swaminarayan Aksharpith, 2007.

Parise, Frank, ed. *The Book of Calendars*. New York: Facts on File, 1982.

Plunket, Emmeline. *Calendars and Constellations of the Ancient World*. New York: Cosimo Classics, 2005.

Richards, E. G. *Mapping Time: The Calendar and Its History*. New York: Oxford University Press, 2000.

Talley, Thomas J. *The Origins of the Liturgical Year*. Collegeville, MN: Liturgical Press, 1991.

New Year's Day (India)

Following the gaining of independence in India in 1947, the new government encountered the variety of local calendars that continued in use from the distant past through the era of both Muslim rule and British colonialism. India subsequently established a program of calendar reform that led to the production and promulgation of a modern solar calendar that in many ways followed the Common Era calendar, but differs at two significant points.

The new calendar, called the Saka calendar, places New Year's Day on the vernal (spring) equinox—Chaitra 1 (March 21 or 22 on the Common Era calendar). This day, however, is not an important date in the annual cycle of festival in the country, as the celebration of New Year's Day continues to be marked by the various religious calendars still in use at the local levels. The Saka calendar also chose a uniquely Indian date to begin its numbering of years.

The Saka calendar remains the official calendar for all government business in India and the several official Indian holidays such as Independence Day and Mahatma Gandhi's birthday. News media usually operate from both the Saka calendar and the Common Era calendar. The 12 months of the Saka calendar are: (1) Chaitra, (2) Vaishakh, (3) Jyaishtha, (4) Ashadha, (5) Shravana, (6) Bhadrapad, (7) Ashwin, (8) Kartik, (9) Agrahayana, (10) Paush, (11) Magh, and (12) Phalgun.

Along with the Saka calendar, the Indian calendar reform committee also introduced a new religious calendar by which Hindu festival days could be calculated in a way both related to and separate from the new secular Saka calendar. The religious calendar includes twelve 30-day lunar months (that have the same names as the solar-based Saka calendar. The month is named for the solar month in which the new moon occurs. Should two new moons occur in the same solar month, a 13th month is added and the name of the previous month is repeated. Previously, lunar months were reckoned from new moon to new moon in southern India and from full moon to full moon elsewhere. In the reformed calendar, lunar months are measured from new moon to new moon. Days also begin at sunrise rather than midnight.

A factor in the calculation of the religious calendar over against the Saka calendar is Hindu astrology. Astrologers generally begin the year on the vernal equinox, which is also the date that the sun is deemed to enter into the constellation of Aries. Because of a phenomenon known as the procession of the equinoxes, the sun's entry into Aries has drifted as millennia have passed. It is also calculated differently in Western and Hindu astrology. Thus in Hindu astrology, the vernal equinox is now calculated to fall on April 14. As the beginning of the new year, this day is celebrated under a number of names (and with a variety of local customs) such as Gudhi Padwa (Maharashtra), Samvatsar Padvo (Goa), Yugadi (Karnataka, Kerala, Andhra Pradesh), Nav Varsha Samvat (across North India in Uttar Pradesh, Himachal Pradesh, Haryana, Madhya Pradesh, Rajasthan, Uttarakhand, Bihar and Chhattisgarh), Nau Roz (Kashmir), Naba Barsha (Bengal), Goru Bihu (Assam), Puthandu (Tamil Nadu), and Vishu (Kerala). Baisakhi, the Sikh New Year, is celebrated in the Punjab on April 13.

Puthandu, the Tamil New Year's Day, falls on April 14. It is celebrated in Tamil Nadu, and by the many Tamils now residing in Pondicherry, Sri Lanka, in Malaysia, Singapore, Reunion Island, and Mauritius. Traditionally, New Year's Day is a time for feasting and for a car festival. The name does not refer to top modern automobiles, but to the large, highly decorated chariots used as platforms to pull the statues of deities from the local temples through the streets in a procession. Most of the larger temples throughout the region own chariots and bring them out each New Year's Day.

The government of Tamil Nadu created considerable controversy in 2008 by passing a measure that would change New Year's Day to January, a date coinciding with the harvest festival of Pongal. This proposal met with considerable resistance and had no effect outside of Tamil Nadu, where it had been ignored. Responding to the resistance, the government proposed to continue the April 14 celebration under the name "Chithirai Tirunal" (or the festival of Chithirai), and has been continued as a public holiday to honor B. R. Ambedkar (1891–1956), an Indian statesman known for his fighting the Hindu caste system, who happened to be born on April 14.

Bengalis also acknowledge April 14 as Poyela Boishakh, the first day of the Bengali, which is widely celebrated across the Indian states of Bengal, West Bengal, Assam, and Tripura, the country of Bangladesh, and among the Bengali diaspora worldwide. The Bengali holiday is tied to the advent of Muslim rule and the imposition of the lunar calendar. The day for tax collection would vary annually and soon moved out of synchronization with the harvest season. To accommodate farmers, the ruler Akbar (1542–1605) commissioned a new calendar that began on April 14. Introduced in 1584, it was backdated to commemorate Akbar's ascension to the throne in 1556.

The people of south central India, namely the states of Andhra Pradesh, Karnataka, Goa, and Maharashtra (which are located between the Vindhyas and Kaveri rivers) follow a lunar calendar that begins with the new moon of the Indian month of Chaitra (and hence will vary through late March and early April from year to year). Called Yugadi or Ugadi, the celebration usually includes a gathering of extended families and a large feast. Among the Telugu-speaking peoples, the day begins with a ritual bath followed by prayers. The meal includes the eating of six foods that have six distinct tastes, each representative of the different realities experienced through life (sadness, happiness, anger, fear, disgust, surprise). This is also a day for reading from the *panchangam*, a Hindu astrological text that offers reflections on the future, specifically the coming year. Entertainment is provided by performances of the traditional Carnatic music of the region commonly held in the evenings.

The Telugu-speaking people of Andhra Pradesh see Ugadi as the day that Brahma created the world as well as the day that Vishnu incarnated as Matsya (in the form of a fish).

Holding a vastly different New Year's Day celebration are the people of Gujarat in western India. Here, Nutan Varsh or New Year's Day is celebrated on the day after Diwali, the first day of the month of Kartika, generally in late October or early November on the Common Era calendar. This day is also the first day of the year for members of the Swaminarayan movement.

Among the tales told during the celebration of New Year's Day in the month of Kartika is a story of the god Vishnu, who during his incarnation as Lord Vaman requested the equivalent of three strides of land from the demon Bali Raja. Bali Raja responded by offering everything he had. Lord Vaman was pleased by his devotion and designated the day as Balipratipada. It is therefore a day to offer worship (pujas) to Bali Raja.

Another story relates Nutan Varsh to the harvest time. The story is told that the deity Krishna, during his earthly incarnation at Gokul, questioned the offering of food to Indra, the king of the gods and lord of Heaven, since he sent the rain. Krishna observed that both human happiness and misery are really based on the accumulation of karmas. The Supreme Soul, or Brahman, gives the fruits of the lands according to one's karmas. Krishna advised offering the food previously given to Indra to the cows and the local mountain, Govardhan (or Annahut). Enraged, Indra poured rain on the people of Gokul. Krishna responded by raising the mountain to protect the people.

Swaminarayan adherents celebrate this day by preparing elaborate vegetarian feasts as an offering to Annahut. The largest of these are held at the temple in London.

Constance A. Jones

See also Common Era Calendar; Diwali; Kartika Purnima; New Year's Day; New Year's Day (Jain).

References

Mukundcharandas, Sadhu. *Hindu Festivals (Origin Sentiments and Rituals)*. Amdavad, India: Swaminarayan Aksharpith, 2005.

Parise, Frank, ed. *The Book of Calendars*. New York: Facts on File, 1982.

Seshayya. A. K. *Festivals and Ceremonies*. Kelang, Selangor, Malaysia: KSN Print, n.d.

Sivananda, Swami. *Hindu Fasts and Festivals*. Shivanandanagar: Divine Life Society, 1997. Posted at http://www.dlshq.org/download/hindufest.htm#_VPID_19. Accessed April 15, 2010.

New Year's Day (Jain)

For Jains, the New Year begins on the first day of the Hindu month of Kartika (October–November on the Common Era calendar). This day occurs in the midst of the Hindu celebration of Diwali, which many Hindus think of as the beginning of the new year, although their calendar now begins on the spring equinox. For Jains, Diwali is celebrated on the last day of the month of Ashwin (September–October) and marks the day that Mahavira, their founder, achieved *moksha* or salvation (and passed from his earthly life). The Jain New Year's Day celebration occurs on the following day (still during the Hindu Diwali celebration).

On New Year's Day, Jains will gather in the temple and, following their standard purification ritual, will perform the Snatra Puja ritual, the purpose being to comprehend and worship the virtuous attributes of the Jineshwar (the 24 Tirthankars or saints who are seen as the founders of the religion). The last in the lineage of Tirthankars was Mahavira.

Their ritual also directs the believer to remember to conduct their daily life with the same virtuous attributes, which may be summarized as holding a right view, having right knowledge, following right action or conduct, and attaining austerity in abstaining from lusts and desires with the goal of reaching equilibrium and tranquility. Gaining these attributes will lead to salvation. While they form the essential path adopted by a Jain nun or monk, they may also be integrated into the life of the average Jain lay believer.

J. Gordon Melton

See also Akshay Tritiya (Jain); Diwali; Gyana Panchami; Kartika Purnima; Mauna Agyaras; Mahavir Jayanti; Navpad Oli; New Year's Day; New Year's Day (India); Paryushana; Paush Dashami.

References

Jaini, P. S. *The Jaina Path of Purification*. Delhi: Motilal Banarsidass, 1979, 1990.

Singh, Narendra K., ed. *Encyclopedia of Jainism*. 30 vols. New Delhi: Anmol, 2001.

"Snatra/ Ashta Prakari Puja." *Jainsamaj*. Posted at http://jainsamaj.org/rpg_site/literature2.php?id=1269&cat=42. Accessed June 15, 2010.

New Year's Eve (Scientology) (December 31)

New Year's Eve has emerged as a major point of celebration for Scientologists, and all of its local churches hold festive New Year's Eve celebrations. The celebration will actually begin a few days after Christmas, when a large New Year's Eve gathering will be held in Los Angeles, California, where many of the church's international leadership resides. This gathering will review and celebrate the accomplishments of the past year and project goals and dreams for the next year.

This will be a time to release new editions (often in new formats) of the writings of church founder L. Ron Hubbard (1911–1986), and church leaders will acknowledge individuals especially noteworthy for assisting new church members progress with their appropriation of Scientology.

The event in Los Angeles is then recorded, duplicated, and disseminated to all of the local Scientology churches around the world, each of which organizes a New Year's Eve gathering to which all members of the church are invited and at which the DVD of the Los Angeles gathering is shared. The local New Year's Eve events are actually on December 31.

J. Gordon Melton

See also Hubbard, Birthday of L. Ron; Scientology, Holidays of the Church of.

References

What Is Scientology? Los Angeles: Bridge Publications, 1998.

Nichiren's Birthday (February 12)

Nichiren was a Japanese Buddhist prophet whose career led to the formation of a set of Buddhist groups based on the teachings of the Lotus Sutra, considered to be the epitome of Buddhist scriptures. Members of the several groups practice the regular daily chanting of the phrase "Nam-myoho-renge-kyo" (Myoho-renge-kyo being the title of the Lotus Sutra) out of the belief that the phrase represents the essence of the teaching of the sutra. Nichiren also embodied that essence in a mandala called the Gohonzon. Chanting the title of the Lotus Sutra with faith in the Gohonzon is believed to enable people in the present age to attain Buddhahood.

Nichiren was born in 1222. In 1233, he entered a Tendai Buddhist temple and began a broad study of the Buddhist sutra (holy texts believed to have been authored by the Buddha). Over the years, he became convinced that the highest of the Buddha's teachings were to be found in the Lotus Sutra, and he assigned himself the task of declare the sutra's supremacy and exposing the misconceptions of the various existing Buddhist schools. He adopted the name by which he is now known, Nichiren or Sun Lotus.

His direct and forceful style brought him followers but also opposition from both other Buddhist groups and the secular authorities. He was on several occasions attacked and exiled from his home in Kamakura, then the capital of the Shogunate. On several occasions, he predicted evils falling on Japan unless the country aligned itself with his correct Buddhist teachings. During one of his periods in exile, he wrote most of the books he left for his disciples. He spent the last period of his life at Mount Minobu in Kai Province, lecturing on the Lotus Sutra and training his core disciples.

Shortly before his death, he assigned six senior priests the task of the propagation of what would be known as Nichiren Buddhism after his death. They would soon divide into two camps—the Nichiren-shu and the Nichiren Shoshu, the two primary Nichiren groups. Early in the 20th century, a lay educational organization called Soka Gakkai developed within the larger Nichiren Shoshu movement. It grew significantly in the decades immediately after World War II, spreading to every part of Japan and even building an affiliated political party. It followed the Japanese diaspora around the world, and though it eventually became independent of the Nichiren Shoshu organization, it would become a global organization and the single largest Buddhist group in many Western countries.

Nichiren's birthday is celebrated on February 16. Thought observed by all Nichiren Buddhists, its most visible celebration has been in the Soka Gakkai movement. Each year, Soka Gakkai centers in Japan and around the world hold special services commemorating Nichiren's life and work, expressing gratitude for his propagating of the true highest teachings of Buddhism. Such services are occasions for group chanting of "Nam-myoho-renge-kyo," talks on the significance of Nichiren, testimonies of benefits derived from chanting, and entertainment. In addition to commemorating Nichiren, the Soka Gakkai also sponsor a two-day fall event held on November 20–22, called Nichiren Daishōnin Gotai-e (or more informally, *Oeshiki*), memorial services that commemoration the life and teachings of Nichiren.

J. Gordon Melton

See also Oeshiki.

References

Anesaki, Masaharu. *Nichiren: The Buddhist Prophet*. Cambridge, MA: Harvard University Press, 1949.

The Liturgy of Nichiren Shoshu. Etiwanda, CA: Nichiren Shoshu Temple, 1979.

Murano, Senchu. *An Outline of the Lotus Sutra*. Minobu-San, Japan: Kuonji Temple, 1969.

Nichiren-Buddhist Service Companion. Chicago: Headquarters of the Nichiren Buddhist Temple of North America, 1968.

Nicholas, Saint's Day of St. (December 6)

As with many saints, we know very little of Saint Nicholas (d. 343?). Modern scholars are even hesitant about the few biographical details accepted by many Eastern Orthodox scholars. They see him as having been born during the third century CE in the village of Patara, in what was a Greek area on the southern coast of what is now Turkey. From well-to-do Christian parents, he was orphaned as a youth. He dedicated his life to serving God and was made while still a young man. He studied for the priesthood, was ordained, and due to his piety, was selected as the bishop of Myra. This would have been at a time when the church was still a somewhat clandestine organization, and in the persecution of the church under the emperor Diocletian (303–304 CE), he was forced into exile. He seems to have survived and attended the Council of Nicea in 324 and to have died several decades later. December 6, 343 CE is generally accepted as his death date.

Legends and stories of miracles related to Bishop Nicholas emerged almost immediately. It was claimed, for example, that an unknown substance had condensed on his gravesite in the cathedral. The most repeated story tells of a poor man with three daughters. Without a dowry, the women's future seemed in jeopardy. Their father was tempted to sell them into slavery or prostitution. Then, mysteriously, on three different occasions, a bag of gold was tossed through an open window, the man eventually learned that Nicholas had given him the gold, but was sworn to secrecy. This story became but one of those told that associated Nicholas with gift giving. This led to the custom of children hanging stockings or putting out shoes, eagerly awaiting gifts from Saint Nicholas. Sometimes the story is told with gold balls instead of bags of gold. That is why three gold balls, sometimes represented as oranges, are one of the symbols for Saint Nicholas, and why Saint Nicholas is a gift giver. So many miracles were attributed to him that the Eastern churches began to refer to him as Saint Nicholas the Wonder Worker.

In 1087, for more or less altruistic reasons, the remains and relics of Nicholas were removed from his resting place in Myra, and taken to Bari, in southern Italy. Generally, the rationale for the movement of the saint's relics was based on the instability of the region and the fears that Christian pilgrims would be blocked from visiting Myra. Meanwhile, back in Bari, a huge basilica in Nicholas's honor was constructed.

The move to Bari did nothing to slow down the spread of the legend of Saint Nicholas, nor of the traditions of giving gifts on his feast day (December 6) that developed in hundreds of variations. Saint Nicholas' Day would become November 19 on the Gregorian calendar and then the gift giving transferred to Christmas (December 25) and Epiphany (January 6) and tied to the gifts brought by the Three Magi to the Christ child.

Today, Saint Nicholas, the fourth-century bishop, is most honored by the Greek Orthodox Church, where its annual celebration merges with the recognition of him as the patron saint of the country. There is an equal intensity in celebrating his life in Russia, where he is also been designated the patron saint of the country, and where his name appears frequently in the liturgy quite apart from the special mention on December 6 (or December 19 according to the Gregorian calendar).

A Bulgarian woman places flowers on an image of Saint Nicholas during mass in Sofia, Bulgaria, on the saint's feast day of December 6. (AP/Wide World Photos)

In Bari, Saint Nicholas is considered the city's patron, and an annual celebration, the *Festa di San Nicola*, is held there on May 7–9. As a part of that celebration, on May 8, a boat parade before the city is organized with the saint's relics being carried in the lead vessel. As part of the celebration, it is common for young brides in need of help before getting married to be given gifts.

There is a lesser tradition in Ireland that suggests that Saint Nicholas is actually buried in Jerpoint Abbey in Kilkenny. It is claimed by a few that after a stopover in Bari, the body was taken on to Ireland by one Nicholas de Frainet, a distant relative. The family then constructed a Cistercian abbey, appropriately named the church of Saint Nicholas. Today, residents show visitors the grave which they suggest holds the saint's remains. Celebration of this tradition is largely limited to an annual special Mass on the saint's day.

The celebration of Saint Nicholas' Day in the Netherlands, including Saint Nicholas' Eve (December 5), believed to be his birthday, has become important for the influence it has exerted. The celebration starts when Saint Nicholas (known as Sinterklaas) arrives in the Netherlands on a steamboat in late November. Young children put their shoes in front of the chimneys and look for a present the next morning. Then on the evening of December 5, brings presents to all. Sinterklass seems to be the direct ancestor of the North American Santa Claus.

J. Gordon Melton

See also Advent; Christmas; Epiphany; World Peace Ceremony.

References

DeChant, Dell. *The Sacred Santa: Religious Dimensions of Consumer Culture*. Cleveland, OH: Pilgrim Press, 2002.

Federer, William J. *There Really Is a Santa Claus: The History of St. Nicholas and Christmas Holiday Traditions*. St. Louis, MO: Amerisearch, 2002.

Jones, Charles W. *Saint Nicholas of Myra, Bari, and Manhattan: Biography of a Legend*. Chicago: University of Chicago Press, 1978.

Kelly, Joseph F. *The Origins of Christmas*. Collegeville, MN: Liturgical Press, 2004.

Semanitsky, John L. *The Holy Days of the Russian Orthodox Church*. N.p.: Russian Orthodox Layman's League of Connecticut, 1966.

Nine Emperor Gods, Festival of the

Among followers of traditional Chinese religion, the story is recounted of the Mother of the Big Dipper (*Dou Mu Yuan Jun*), who gave birth to nine children, each one identified as one of the seven stars of the constellation popularly known as the Big Dipper, plus two faint nearby stars. The Dipper mother is pictured as a woman with 16 arms in which she holds the sun and moon and a number of implements and weapons.

These nine deities were especially worshipped in the first nine days of the ninth month of the old Chinese lunar calendar (usually October on the Common Era calendar). This is a time for personal cleansing from any evil accumulated through the past year. Believers dressed in white and carrying candles and incense with them will launch the festival with a procession to the local body of water (river, lake, or ocean) to meet the deities and bring them back to their temple.

In Thailand, this time is called the Vegetarian Festival, and the primary rule for observance of the nine days is the adoption of a vegetarian diet. Meat is usually removed from the meals eaten by believers several days before the festival begins. The more energetic also climb local mountains. The nine days are filled with various rituals at the temple, during which some become possessed with the gods, and different forms of entertainment, all leading to the major celebration on the last day.

On the ninth day, the deities, which are said to reside on an urn with burning incense, are brought from the temple and the urn placed on a sedan chair. A great procession then begins back to the water. Leading the process are a group of boys, each carrying a banner. Then come a variety of performers—lion dancers, stilt walkers, and musicians playing gongs, drums, and cymbals. The believers will join in the procession carrying incense.

On the way to the water, the procession will pause for a priest and nun to bid the deities a proper farewell. Then the chair containing the urn is escorted to the water and placed on a boat, which the priest launches out to sea. Then the gods depart to return from whence they had come.

In China, this festival peaked in popularity during the Ming dynasty (1368–1644), and today mainly survives in Southeast Asia—in the Chinese communities of Thailand, Malaysia, and Singapore—where temples to the Mother of the Dipper and her nine star sons are still popular. The Dipper Mother is still worshipped in a few places in China, most notably at the White Cloud Temple in Beijing, but the most impressive festivals for her sons are found at such places as Phuket Island (Thailand); Penang, Butterworth, and Ampang (Malaysia); and Singapore.

J. Gordon Melton

See also Double Ninth Festival; Pure Brightness Festival; Spring Dragon Festival.

References

Heinze, Ruth-Inge. "The Nine Imperial Gods in Singapore." *Asian Folklore Studies* 40, no. 1 (1981): 151–65.

Tong, Cheu Hock. "The Festival of the Nine Emperor Gods in Malaysia: Myth, Ritual, and Symbol." *Asian Folklore Studies* 55 (1996). Posted at http://www.questia.com/googleScholar.qst;jsessionid=LgTTjFXp1PGfXpc3s6SsQhDkTqh2kmvMFcszJL4pLJZbpn722KTK!555708061!-1331918248?docId=5000374131. Accessed May 15, 2010.

Nineteen-Day Feast (Bahá'í)

Bahá'ís gather together once every 19 days to participate in their local communities' "Nineteen-Day Feast." To those unfamiliar with the Bahá'í Faith, this might seem like odd timing, but it is perfectly in keeping with the seasonal rhythm of the Bahá'í calendar of 19 months of 19 days. In the Bahá'í calendar, each day, month, year and cycle of years is named after a godly attribute that can be expressed as a goodly virtue. The Nineteen-Day Feast is at the heart of Bahá'í community life and is an essential feature of the "community building" that takes place in each local Bahá'í faith-community, which is typically defined by city/town boundaries. Unlike those religious "congregations," where believers choose the particular group with whom they wish to affiliate, Bahá'ís in a given town must learn to function together not as a congregation but as a community, both socially and for purposes of local administration. This structure is itself conducive to achieving the purposes of the Bahá'í Faith—to eliminate barriers and prejudices of all kinds, and to bring about unity through concerted action.

An integral part of the Bahá'í calendar, the first day of each Bahá'í month is often referred to as the "Feast Day." While the Nineteen-Day Feast is not one of the nine Bahá'í holy days on which work is suspended, the Bahá'í Feast, informally at least, functions as though it were a "monthly" Bahá'í holy day. It is a time of worship, deliberation, and fellowship, as reflected in the three formal phases (i.e., devotional, consultative, and social) of each Bahá'í Feast comprising its spiritual, administrative, and unitive functions.

Historically, the Nineteen-Day Feast has its origins in the religion of the Báb (1819–1850), the herald and precursor of Bahá'u'lláh (1819–1892), the prophet-founder of the Bahá'í Faith. In the *Arabic Bayán*, the Báb commanded his followers to invite 19 people every 19 days, even if one is able to offer only water in this offer of hospitality. Bahá'u'lláh ratified this practice in the Most Holy Book: "Verily, it is enjoined upon you to offer a feast, once in every month, though only water be served; for God hath purposed to bind hearts together, albeit through both earthly and heavenly means" (Bahá'u'lláh, *The Kitáb-i-Aqdas*, 40). Here, the primary purpose of the Feast is "to bind hearts together"—that is, to produce unity among the believers.

The term, "Feast" (Arabic, *ḍíyáfat*) primarily means "hospitality" and has been used in connection with sacred events, such as the Lord's Supper, portrayed in the Qur'an (Q. 5:112–15) as a banquet table descending from heaven, from which the disciples ate. "Feast" includes "both earthly and heavenly" food, with spiritual sustenance being the latter meaning. Thus, in current practice, refreshments are commonly served in the social portion of the Feast, after the spiritual enrichment of the devotional portion of Feast, consisting primarily of prayers and readings from the Bahá'í scriptures. In some Bahá'í communities, there may on occasion be a dinner (whether a "potluck" or provided by the host) that takes place before the formal Feast program begins.

The Nineteen-Day Feast was further developed by 'Abdu'l-Bahá and Shoghi Effendi. During the time of the Báb and Baha'u'llah, the Feast was individually observed as the offer of hospitality to guests invited to the home. During the ministry of 'Abdu'l-Bahá, however, the Feast became communal in character and was essentially institutionalized. Of this development, Bahá'í historian Robert Stockman wrote:

> In early 1905 Howard and Mary MacNutt and Julia Grundy attended a Feast hosted by 'Abdu'l-Bahá in Akka. The celebration included Bahá'ís from many parts of the world and was especially moving . . . The next morning at breakfast 'Abdu'l-Bahá praised the Feast, adding, "You must meet together in this way in America." The three pilgrims took His exhortation as a commandment. After returning home Howard MacNutt consulted with the New York Board of Counsel and it organized the first real Feast known to have been held in North America. It occurred on 23 May 1905 in New York City. . . . Isabella Brittingham took the Feast to the rest of the United States. . . . In early 1906 she visited Johnstown, New York; Chicago; Kenosha; Racine; Milwaukee; Minneapolis; and Cleveland. In all of these cities she inaugurated the Feast as a formal community event. (Stockman, *The Bahá'í Faith in America: Early Expansion, 1900–1912*)

'Abdu'l-Bahá stressed the devotional character of these gatherings and their unitive function in providing greater social cohesion among the Bahá'í faithful, and promised that "all its mystic meanings" would unfold in the faithful observance of the Bahá'í Feast (*Selections from the Writings of 'Abdu'l-Bahá*, 91).

Perhaps one of the mystical dimensions of Feast is the very real sense that the spirit of 'Abdu'l-Bahá may be present when true unity is experienced:

> On that night thy house was the nest and the shelter of the birds of God. The divine melodies and the celestial lyres made that place a feast of heaven and an assembly of the Kingdom. 'Abdu'l-Bahá was present there in heart and soul and was joyful and happy. ('Abdu'l-Bahá, *Tablets of Abdul-Baha Abbas*, 216)

Although no sacramental importance attaches to the Bahá'í Feast, 'Abdu'l-Bahá attached great importance to it and, in doing so, compared the Bahá'í Feast to the "Lord's Supper" among Christians:

> Thou hast written concerning the Feast. This festivity, which is held on a day of the nineteen-day month, was established by His Holiness the Báb, and the Blessed Beauty directed, confirmed and warmly encouraged the holding of it. It is, therefore, of the utmost importance. You should unquestionably see to it with the greatest care, and make its value known, so that it may become solidly established on a permanent basis. Let the beloved of God gather together and associate most lovingly and spiritually and happily with one another, conducting themselves with the greatest courtesy and self-restraint. Let them read the holy verses, as well as essays which are of benefit, and the letters of 'Abdu'l-Bahá; encourage and inspire one another to love each and all; chant the prayers with serenity and joy; give eloquent talks, and praise the matchless Lord.
>
> The host, with complete self-effacement, showing kindness to all, must be a comfort to each one, and serve the friends with his own hands.
>
> If the Feast is befittingly held, in the manner described, then this supper will verily be the Lord's Supper, for its fruits will be the very fruits of that Supper, and its influence the same. ('Abdu'l-Bahá, from a Tablet to an individual believer, translated from the Persian, *The Nineteen Day Feast*, 425.)

The devotional portion of the Feast is often themed by the name of that particular Bahá'í month (i.e., "Honor," "Loftiness," "Power," "Mercy," etc.), although there is no requirement to do so. The devotions will consist of selected readings from Bahá'í sacred texts and the recitation or chanting of Bahá'í prayers (from memory or reading a Bahá'í prayer book). Music and singing may be included, and following the Bahá'í readings and prayers, creative or performative expressions of Bahá'í devotion may be integrated into the observance. Occasionally, passages from the scriptures of other world religions may be included in the Feast program. The Feast is the only Bahá'í event intended for the Bahá'í community alone other than elections, and thus not generally open, except that non-Bahá'ís who may be present will be treated cordially as guests, and consultation on sensitive community matters will be deferred.

Shoghi Effendi developed the administrative component by integrating into the institution of the Feast a period of consultation on the affairs of the Bahá'í community.

Thus the consultative part of the Feast is when announcements of upcoming events are made, community affairs are discussed, consultation on topics of special concern is facilitated, where ideas and recommendations for consideration by the local Bahá'í council (i.e., the annually elected, nine-member "Local Spiritual Assembly" or "LSA") are offered and recorded. Such consultation gives every member a voice in community affairs and thus makes the Feast an "arena of democracy at the very root of society" (Letter from the Universal House of Justice to the Bahá'ís of the World, August 27, 1989). Study topics of particular relevance may be presented for brief discussion for the community's edification, and the Bahá'í youth and children may be invited to perform or make special presentations. Thus, the consultative portion has an educative function in addition to its administrative purpose. It is also a venue in which the LSA may report its recent decisions to the Bahá'í community.

The social time of the Feast, which is typically at the end, is vital for promoting unity among the "Bahá'í friends" (as Bahá'ís are often called). Strength and vibrancy of the Bahá'í community is, after all, coefficient with its unity and solidarity. The vitality of social cohesion often manifests itself in the percentage of the enrolled Bahá'í members who participate in their community Feasts, and this, in turn, may have a direct impact on the level of giving to the Bahá'í Fund, to which only Bahá'ís may contribute.

The Bahá'í Faith has been established in every country except for the Vatican and North Korea, thus making it the second-most widespread religion in the world, next to Christianity. Today, the majority of the estimated six million Bahá'ís observe the Nineteen-Day Feast, which is an integral feature of Bahá'í community life. In some Muslim states in the Middle East, this practice has become restricted. For example, the Islamic Republic of Iran has banned the practice as part of a systematic campaign, since the Islamic Revolution of 1979 (and in earlier regimes), to eradicate the Bahá'í Faith in Iran.

The Nineteen-Day Feast is adaptable to a wide array of cultural contexts, which is an important feature, considering the fact that societies are becoming increasingly diverse. Music is often featured in the Feast program and typically reflects the Feast's geographic and cultural milieu. In the United States, for instance, the Feast might well feature upbeat gospel-style music, while Feasts in Bahá'í communities that are predominantly Native American, Native Canadian, or indigenous in Central and South America often incorporate cultural traditions as well; songs might be pentatonic in Bahá'í feasts in Asia. The Feast experience is further enriched by Bahá'í musicians around the world who, working in every genre and style and mixing them as well, set the Bahá'í writings to music, becoming a robust source of music not only for Feast, but for other Bahá'í devotional activities as well.

Ideally, the Nineteen-Day Feast operates to make each local Bahá'í community more tight-knit. This requires that the Bahá'ís themselves make it a priority and attach great importance to it. Although attendance at the Feast is not "obligatory" in the sense of being a Bahá'í law, and no one is pressured to attend, every Bahá'í should consider it a duty and privilege to be present at Feast. As 'Abdu'l-Bahá has said: "As to the Nineteen Day Feast, it rejoiceth mind and heart. If this feast be held in the proper fashion, the friends will, once in nineteen days, find themselves spiritually restored, and endued with a power that is not of this world" (*Selections from the Writings of 'Abdu'l-Bahá*, 91).

Christopher Buck

See also 'Abdu'l-Bahá, Ascension of; Ayyám-i-Há (Bahá'í Intercalary Days); Báb, Festival of the Birth of the; Báb, Festival of the Declaration of the; Báb, Martyrdom of the; Bahá'í Calendar and Rhythms of Worship; Bahá'í Faith; Bahá'í Fast; Bahá'u'lláh, Ascension of; Bahá'u'lláh, Festival of the Birth of; Covenant, Day of the; Naw-Rúz, Festival of; Race Unity Day; Riḍván, Festival of; World Religion Day.

References

'Abdu'l-Bahá. *Selections from the Writings of 'Abdu'l-Bahá*. Haifa: Bahá'í World Centre, 1982.

'Abdu'l-Bahá. *Tablets of Abdul-Baha Abbas*. Chicago: Bahá'í Publishing Committee, 1909.

Bahá'u'lláh, *The Kitáb-i-Aqdas*. Haifa: Bahá'í World Centre, 1992.

Research Department of the Universal House of Justice, comp. *The Nineteen Day Feast*. Vol. 1, *Compilation of Compilations*, 425–58. Haifa: Bahá'í World Centre, 1989.

Stockman, Robert H. *The Bahá'í Faith in America: Early Expansion, 1900–1912*, chap. 2. Oxford: George Ronald, 1996.

Walbridge, John. "The Nineteen-Day Feast." In *Sacred Acts, Sacred Space, Sacred Time*, 206–13. Oxford: George Ronald, 1996.

Watanabe, Joyce, comp. *A Feast for the Soul: Meditations on the Attributes of God and of Humanity*. Los Angeles: Kalimát Press, 2006.

Nino, Saint's Day of St. (January 14)

Nino (c. 296–c. 338), is part of a distinct minority of saints. She was a woman, she was an active missionary for the Christian movement, and she died of natural causes. She is also among the very few Orthodox saints remembered as "*isapostolos*" or equal to the apostles.

Nino, according to most traditional accounts, was from Cappadocia, an area now in central Turkey, and was a relative of George, the Roman soldier who became a Christian martyr and saint. It has been claimed that she was the daughter of the Roman general Zabulon and, on her mother's side, the niece of Houbnal I, the Christian patriarch of Jerusalem. He facilitated her trip to Rome during which she had a vision of the Blessed Virgin Mary in which she was told to go to Iberia (i.e., ancient Georgia) and given a cross as a protective spiritual shield.

While on her way to Iberia, she became part of a community of 37 virgins that the beautiful Armenian Hripsime (or Rhipsime, d. c. 290 CE). They lived together under the leadership of a man named Gayane. When the Armenian king Tiridates III took notice of them, all were killed save Nino. She escaped, some say due to the Virgin's protection, and went on to Georgia. Hripsime, who appears to have died a quite torturous death, would later be canonized as the first Armenian Christian martyr. Linking Nino to the story of Hripsime has a major problem in that the death of Gayane, Hripsime, and the other virgin occurred in the 290s, when if born, Nino would have been an infant.

Better documented is her entering Georgia around 320 CE, and making her way to Mtskheta (then the capital of Iberia). Iberians followed a Pagan religion heavily influenced by Persia. Upon hearing of Nino's arrival, Iberian queen Nana requested an audience with her.

Queen Nana, who at the time was quite ill, had her health restored under Nino's ministrations. She and some of the courtiers who were aware of her healing converted. These conversions brought a heated reaction from King Mirian who attempted to suppress the new faith in his realm. Then, as the story goes, he was struck blind during a hunting trip. He said a prayer to his wife's god, and his sight was restored. The miracle occasioned his conversion and he was subsequently baptized. In 327, he made Christianity the official religion of his kingdom. Georgians count their nation as the world's second Christian kingdom. King Miriam subsequently developed relations with the Byzantine Empire, and Constantine I sent priests and a bishop to Georgia. In 334 CE, the king ordered the construction of the first Christian church in Iberia on the site of the present Svetitskhoveli Cathedral in Mstkheta.

After the king's conversion and the national establishment of Christianity, Nino retired to a remote mountainous area at Bodbe, where she lived out her life as a hermit. A monastery was built at Bodbe, and her body was entombed there. A grapevine cross, a copy of the one given to Nino by the Virgin Mary, is now the symbol of the Georgian Orthodox Church. Saint Nino is also a saint recognized within the Armenian Apostolic Church (where she is known as Saint Nune). Roman Catholics list her feast day as December 15.

J. Gordon Melton

See also George, Feast Day of St.; Lucy, Saint's Day of St.

References

Dowling, Theodore E. *Sketches of Georgian Church History*. London: Adamant Media, 2003.

"The Life of St. Nina—Equal to the Apostles." *St. Nina Quarterly*. Posted at http://www.stnina.org/st-nina/her-life/life-st-nina-equal-apostles. Accessed March 15, 2010.

The Life of St. Nina Equal to the Apostles and Enlightener of Georgia with the Service. Jordanville, NY: Holy Trinity Monastery, 1988.

Wardrop, Margery, and Oliver Waldrop. *The Life of Saint Nino*. London: Clarendon Press, 1900. Reprint, Piscataway, NJ: Gorgias Press, 2006.

Nirjala Ekadashi

The 12 months of the Indian Hindu lunar calendar is divided into halves relative to the waxing and waning moon. The 11th day of the 24 half months is considered by Vaishnava Hindus as a day for fasting and offering puja worship to Lord Vishnu in the local temple. The most severe, and hence most holy, of the Ekadashi fast occurs during the waxing phase of the moon in the month of Jyestha (June on the Common Era calendar) It is thought to be the most beneficial of fasting days, and its proper observation is said to provide the fruits of all 24 fasts observed throughout the year.

This day is unique in that the fast includes refraining even from the consumption of water. It is a 24-hour fast, from sunrise to sunrise, and on the day before Nirjala Ekadashi, evening prayer is offered and only one meal is consumed. Vaishnava Hindus extol the fast, and note that observing it is considered equal to going on a pilgrimage. Vaishnavas also believe that after death, those who have observed Nirjala Ekadashi are received by messengers from Vaikunta, the mythical abode of Vishnu, rather than by Yama, the god of death.

Nirjala Ekadashi is one of the most popular and toughest Ekadashi fasting days. In 2010, the date of Nirjala Ekadashi is June 22. Ekadashi fasting is dedicated to Lord Vishnu and is observed on the 11th day of a fortnight in a traditional Hindu calendar. Nirjala Ekadashi is also known as Pandav Bhim Ekadashi fast. The difference from other Ekadashis and Nirjala is that devotees do not drink water on the day.

The Pandava brothers, the sons of Pandu, appear in the Hindu epic *Mahabharata*. The five brothers—Yudhishtira, Bhima, Arjuna, Nakula, and Sahadeva—were each married to the same woman, Draupadi. They also fought together and won the Battle of Kurukshetra. According to the story, Bhima, the second of the Pandava brothers, wanted to observe the Ekadashi fasting but still eat food, a seeming contradiction. But fasting and eating were not possible. So the Sage Vyasa (the legendary author of the *Mahabharata*) advised Bhima to observe the Nirjala Ekadashi in the month of Jyeshta since it has the benefit of observing all 24 ekadashis. Thus, Bhima attained the benefits of all the fasts from just observing the Nirjala (without water) Ekadashi.

Constance A. Jones

See also Hari-Shayani Ekadashi; Kamada Ekadashi; Mokshada Ekadashi; Putrada Ekadashi; Vaikuntha Ekadashi.

References

"Pandava Nirjala Ekadasi." Hare Krishna Temple Portal. Posted at http://www.harekrsna.de/artikel/nirjala-ekadasi.htm. Accessed April 15, 2010.

Narasimhan, Chakravarti V. *The Mahabharata*. New York: Columbia University Press, 1965.

Seeger, Elizabeth. *The Five Sons of King Pandu: The Story of the Mahabharata*. New York: W. R. Scott, 1967.

Nirvana Day. *See* Nehan

Nityananda Trayodasi

Nityananda Trayodasi is the appearance day (or birthday) of Sri Nityananda Prabhu (b. c. 1474), the close associate of Chaitanya Mahaprabhu (1486–1534), a 16th-century Bengalee saint revered for his effect in reviving bhakti yoga in eastern India. Chaitanya is considered to have been an incarnation of Krishna. Nityananda was such a close devotee of Chaitanya that he has been seen as an incarnation of Balarama, Krishna's brother.

Nityananda was born in Ekacakra, a small village in what is now West Bengal. His birthplace, where a temple has been constructed, remains a popular pilgrimage site. As a child, he showed an unusual devotion to the deities and, at the age of 13, became a traveling companion of the sannyasin Lakshmipati Tirtha, which allowed him to meet a wide circle of Krishna devotees. He met Caitanya in 1506, their first greeting transforming into an intense spiritual encounter. He later became a major instrument in the revival movement through Bengal and Orissa that formed around Chaitanya.

Nityananda Trayodasi is celebrated during the waxing moon of the Hindu lunar month of Magha (January–February on the Common Era calendar). Members of the International Society for Krishna Consciousness will fast until noon on this day, and their temples will be open for celebrants who wish to acknowledge Nityananda. Temple rituals will focus upon care for the statues of Chaitanya and Nityananda, song in their praise, and talks on their virtues.

Constance A. Jones

See also Bhaktivinoda Thakura, Appearance Day of; Gaura Purnima; Holi.

References

Rosen, Rosen (a.k.a. Satyaraja Dasa). *India's Spiritual Renaissance: The Life and Times of Lord Chaitanya*. New York: Folk Books, 1989.

Thakur, Bhaktivinode. *Sri Chaitanya: His Life and Precepts*. San Rafael, CA: Mandala Publishing, 1998.

Verma, Vanish. *Fasts and Festivals of India*. New Delhi: Diamond Pocket Books, 2002.

Niwano, Nikkyo, Centennial of (2006)

Nikkyo Niwano, the cofounder and first president the Japanese Buddhist group Rissho Kosei Kai, was born in 1906. He moved from his childhood home in rural Japan to Tokyo as a young man and there encountered the Lotus Sutra, a Buddhist scripture believed to be a discourse of Gautama Buddha. Many Buddhists, especially those of the Nichiren tradition of Buddhism, believe the Lotus Sutra to be the epitome of the many writings attributed to the Buddha. In 1938, Niwano and

Mrs. Myoko Baganuma established Rissho Kosei Kai as a lay-led Buddhist organization devoted to serving people and promoting the teachings of the Lotus Sutra. In the decades after World War II, the organization grew to include more than six million members spread across Japan, and developed followings throughout the Japanese diaspora communities around the world. Niwano led Rissho Kosei Kai for more than half a century, retiring in 1991. He passed away in 1999.

Though a firm believer in the Lotus Sutra, Niwano had concluded that all religions have a common root. He became active in interfaith work, throwing his energy into cooperative interreligious activities whose goal was world peace. He was one of the founders of the World Conference on Religion and Peace and the Asian Conference on Religion and Peace. The many awards he received for his work included the 1979 Templeton Foundation Prize for Progress in Religion and the 1993 Interfaith Medallion from the International Council of Christians and Jews.

In 1906, Rissho Kosei Kai devoted the year to a celebration of the centennial of their founder's birth. They engaged in a variety of activities including the renovation of the Great Sacred Hall and the opening of the Nikkyo Niwano Memorial Museum in the Horin-kaku Guest Hall, both in Tokyo, and both targets of a variety of group pilgrimages. Growing out of the celebrations of Niwano's life, in 2007, Rissho Kosei Kai founded Kosei-kai International to launch a new long-term effort of the propagation of the teachings of the Lotus Sutra. Local chapters of the organization worldwide organized numerous activities built around either the Lotus Sutra or the cause of world peace. The Sri Lankan chapter, where a civil war has raged for several decades, for example, marked Niwano's birth centennial by holding an Inter Faith Peace Seminar. The New York Rissho Kosei Kai joined with the World Conference of Religions for Peace organized a symposium on the theme "A Life of Compassion and Peace."

J. Gordon Melton

See also Founders' Day, the Church of Perfect Liberty; World Peace and Prayer Day; World Peace Ceremony.

References

"Creating the World of the One Vehicle: The Centennial of the Birth of Rev. Nikkyo Niwano." Special issue of *Dharma World Magazine* 33 (April–June 2006). Posted at http://rk-world.org/dharmaworld/dk_backissues.aspx. Accessed March 15, 2010.

Guthrie, Stewart. *A Japanese New Religion: Rissho Kosei-Kai in a Mountain Hamlet*. Ann Arbor: University of Michigan Press, 1988.

Niwano, Nikkyo. *Buddhism for Today: A Modern Interpretation of the Threefold Lotus Sutra*. Tokyo: Kosei Publishing Co., 1978.

Niwano, Nikkyo. *Lifetime Beginner: An Autobiography*. Tokyo: Kosei Publishing Company, 1989.

Nossa Senhora dos Remédios, Pilgrimage of (September 8)

Among Portuguese-speaking Roman Catholics, devotion to the Virgin Mary as Nossa Senhora dos Remédios (Our Lady of Cures) is most popular, and prominent churches devoted to her may be found not only throughout Portugal, but in the Azores, Brazil, and even Gao, India. The faith will especially be found at these churches on January 6 (the feast of the Three Magi, or Epiphany) and September 8 (the feast of the nativity of Mary).

The most elaborate celebration of Our Lady of Cures occurs annually on September 7 and 8 at the Church of Nossa Senhora dos Remédios in Lamego, Portugal. The church is located on the Monte de Santo Estêvao, a hill adjacent to the town, and is reached by a staircase with almost 700 steps flanked by the Stations of the Cross representing Jesus's journey from his prison to his crucifixion.

As might be expected, pilgrims repair to Our Lady of Cures in search of healing and consolation. The Feast of the Nativity of Mary each fall provides the occasion for large numbers to engage in a set of activities celebrating the miracles that have come in answer to prayers directed to the Blessed Virgin.

Romaria de Nossa Senhora dos Remédios is an annual pilgrimage that makes its way to the shrine of Our Lady of Cures in Lamego, attracting those seeking cures for illness. For some, the staircase will be their primary vehicle for demonstrating their devotion, and many will move up the entire set of steps on their knees. The ascent is dotted with smaller devotional chapels, statues and fountains where people can rest. The highlight of the two days is the Triumph Processional that occurs on September 8. Led by a statue of Mary, it includes many different floats displaying scenes from the Bible and pulled along by oxen.

Other churches dedicated to Nossa Senhora dos Remédios also have pilgrimages and festivals. The church in Serta, Portugal, for example has a two-day festival on August 14 and 15. It grew out of the story of a nobleman who, after calling upon the Virgin, killed a large serpent. The meter-long jaw of the "serpent" is on display at the church. The church in Goa has a nine-day celebration each year that concludes on January 6 with a procession to the church and Mass.

J. Gordon Melton

See also Epiphany; Good Remedy, Feast of Our Lady of; Miracles, Feast of Our Lady of; Peace and Good Voyage, Feast of Our Lady of.

References

"Romaria de Nossa Senhora dos Remedios." Fromme's whatsonwhen. Posted at http://www.whatsonwhen.com/sisp/index.htm?fx=event&event_id=15729. Accessed May 15, 2010.

Nowruz (March 21)

Nowruz, the Zoroastrian (ancient Persian/Iranian) New Year's Day, also begins the year for the people of Afghanistan, Azerbaijan, and Tajikistan. It is also recognized by many in adjacent central Asian countries and the Kurdish people of Georgia, Iraq, Syria, and Turkey. The Iranian calendar originated with the development of a settled agricultural life in the region in the ancient past. Zoroastrians credit their founder Zarathrustra (or Zoroaster) with improving the older calendar along with proclaiming the truths of the faith they profess. As the calendar finally evolved, it emerged as a strictly solar calendar with 12 months of 30 days, with an intercalation of five days, and a further addition of one day every four years. The calendar was supremely accurate for the time, as it was based on the regular reoccurrence of an annual astronomical event, the vernal equinox.

The spring equinox was an important celebrative occasion, as it signaled the change from winter to spring, with the cattle delivering their calves and plants springing forth. It brought the promise of future prosperity. The day coincided with New Year's on the Jewish and Babylonian calendars.

In the court of the Achaemenian king Darius the Great, who established his capital at Percepolis in 487 BCE, Nowruz was a great occasion opening two weeks of celebration. In the preceding month, 12 pillars representing the 12 months were erected. Seed were planted on the top of each pillar and over the next weeks created a green bonnet on each pillar.

On Nowruz, the king held a public audience that began with the High Priest presenting himself and bringing a formal greeting, to be followed by other officials, both secular and priestly. As each approached, presents were exchanged. The audience continued for five days and culminated on the sixth day, the Greater Nowruz, when the king formally received the royal family and the courtiers. Nowruz also included an amnesty for many held in the jails.

With the rise of Muslim rule in Iran and surrounding countries, the celebration of Nowruz has been simplified and is, of course, no longer tied to the activity of the ruler. Attention to it begins in the month preceding, with each Zoroastrian home receiving a thorough cleaning. Some 10 days prior to Nowruz, seeds of different plants are soaked and planted in various containers. In the next 10 days, they will sprout and grow to several inches.

In the home as Nowruz approached, a table is prepared with a copy of the Avesta, the Zoroastrian sacred text, a picture of Zarathustra, a mirror, candles, incense burner, bowl of water with live goldfish, colorfully painted boiled eggs, and the containers with the plant sprouts. There are also seven articles, each of which has a name that begins with an "s," and seven more that begin with an "sh" in the Persian language. The articles are prominently exhibited in small bowls on the table. The table is covered with a white cloth.

The table arrangement symbolizes the message, the messenger, and all the good things given by God to the people. As a part of the celebration, the children will repeat a recitation explaining the significance of each of the 14 "s" and "sh" objects. Thanksgiving is a theme running through the whole event. At the time of the vernal equinox, a special set of prayers are repeated and initial Happy Nowruz greetings offered to all, along with presents for the younger ones present.

Nowruz launches a week of visits with family and friends. The celebration culminates in March 26, when the birthday of the prophet Zarathustra is celebrated. Because of calendar differences, and the drift of New Year's from the actual vernal equinox, many Zoroastrians now begin each New Year's in August. They do, however, maintain a celebration around the vernal equinox, which allows the whole Zoroastrian community to maintain a certain unity.

J. Gordon Melton

See also Fravardegan; Gahambars; Zarathustra, Commemorative Days of; Zoroastrianism.

References

Boyce, Mary. *Zoroastrians: Their Religious Beliefs and Practices*. London: Routledge, 2001.

Hinnells, John R. *Zoroastrians in Britain*. Oxford: Clarendon, 1996.

Jafarey, Ali A. "Nowruz: The Zarathushtrian New Year." Posted at http://www.zoroastrian.org/articles/nowruz.htm. Accessed May 15, 2010.

Nigosian, S. A. *The Zoroastrian Faith: Tradition and Modern Research*. Montreal, QC: McGill-Queen's University Press, 1993.

Nyepi

The Indonesian island of Bali is unique, an enclave of Hinduism in a country that is predominantly Muslim. It survives as a remnant of the old Hindu kingdom that once dominated Java and had its roots in the ancient faith of southern India. While much of Bali now operates out of the Common Era calendar, the religious community continues to use an older religious calendar that, unlike those found in India, begins at the spring equinox each year and includes 12 lunar months used to calculate holidays and celebrations of the various deities through the year.

Among the more unique holidays on Bali is Nyepi, the Balinese New Year, popularly known as the day of silence. It occurs on the new moon after the spring equinox. Nyepi day is based on an account of King Kaniska I of India, the beginning of whose reign in 78 CE is the base date for the ritual calendar. It was at this time that Aji Saka did and a missionary journey that led to the spread of Hinduism to Indonesia. Aji Saka also introduced the calendar that is still used.

People prepare for Nyepi day with the three days of Melasti to clean the deity statues, which will be taken in procession to a nearby source of water and lovingly bathed before being returned to the temples. The day before Nyepi, there will be an exorcism ceremony at the main crossroads (where demons are known to gather) in the village. Participants will make images of monsters from bamboo, and these spirits will be exorcised to the accompaniment of Bleganjur, a Balinese gamelan music, and many expressions of delight. At the climax of the ceremony in the evening, the monsters are burned.

Nyepi day itself is observed by ceasing all normal activity and keeping a quiet day at home. Men especially appointed to keep the village secure, Pecalangs, will wander around the village to stop any activities that would disturb people during the day. Traffic is at a minimum, the television is turned down, and no work is done. Sexual activity is discouraged. It is a day of contemplation. (While the tourist centers are exempt from the expectations of Nyepi celebration, even they will show a marked reduction in their activity levels.)

Ngembak Geni (the day after Nyepi) is a time for starting the New Year on a right course, visiting with family and friends, and asking and granting forgiveness where needed, and the reading of religious texts.

J. Gordon Melton

See also New Year's Day; New Year's Day (India); Spring Equinox (Thelema); Spring Equinox (Vernal).

References

Bakan, Michael B. *Music of Death and New Creation: Experiences in the World of Balinese Gamelan Beleganjur.* Chicago: University of Chicago Press, 1999.

"Bali's Day of Silence." Bali and Indonesia on the Net. Posted at http://www.indo.com/culture/nyepi.html. Accessed May 15, 2010.

Howe, Leo. *Hinduism and Hierarchy in Bali*. Oxford: James Currey, 2002.

Obon Festival(s)

Obon is a Japanese Buddhist festival designed to honor one's deceased relatives. It is an additional holiday, along with Higan, at the time of the spring and fall equinoxes, and is similar to the Tomb-Sweeping Day (Pure Brightness Festival) in Chinese culture. Obon resonates with the older Chinese understanding of the seventh month of the lunar calendar as the month of the Hungry Ghosts, during which the spirits of the dead can wander the earth and interfere with human plans. As the seventh month climaxed, they celebrated a festival to placate the Hungry Ghosts, the spirits trapped in the hell realms.

The celebration of Obon was disrupted by the adoption of a Western calendar by the Shinto-based Meiji government in the 1870s. Obon had always been set by the lunar calendar, on the 15th day of the seventh month, which would place it in July or August on the Common Era calendar. Some people, primarily in rural areas, still follow the older calendar and celebrate the three days of what is known as Old Obon (or Kyu Bon) beginning on that day. The majority of the country celebrate Obon beginning on August 15 (or the week closest to that date), called Hachugatsu Bon. The remainder, which includes the residents of Tokyo, celebrate Shichigatsu Bon (or Bon in July) in the middle of July.

Obon is a time to reconnect with family, and many people will travel to the homes of relatives. One's own home will be cleaned and made presentable, in the understanding that the spirits of the deceased may visit during this time. Lights or lit lanterns may be placed near the entrance to one's home. Lanterns, placed near one's family shrine or at gravesites or placed on small boats and floated on local waterways, have given Obon a popular designation as the Lantern Festival.

Many Buddhists believe that spirits of the deceased may inhabit any of a number of heavenly or hellish realms, but may at various times return and make contact with the living. The Obon festival affirms the interdependence of the living with their ancestors, and offers appreciation for all that those who have gone before did for those now living. Its celebration aims at building a sense of gratitude in those still alive for all the contributions of one's ancestors. The Urabon service at the temple includes offerings to the Three Treasures (the Buddha, the Dharma, and the Sangha) for the benefit of the deceased. That service is derived from the Urabon, or Service for the Deceased Sutra, in which Buddha advises one of his disciples to make an offering to the monks on behalf of his mother on the 15th day of the seventh month (which is toward the end of the Indian rainy season).

Awa Odori dancers perform during the Buddhist festival of Obon. (Willy Setiadi/Dreamstime.com)

In the modern world, Obon has become a time for large-scale celebrative activities. People will gather at Buddhist temples for daylong programs, one regular activity being the performances of a particular dance called the Bon Odori. Bon Odori appears to have been introduced in Hawaii in the first decade of the 20th century, and to have spread along the West Coast in the 1930s, after its introduction by a Jodo Shin-shu minister, Yoshio Iwanaga. In the West, Obon has become a popular time for a public festival to which non-Buddhist visitors are invited and the temple or other sponsor puts Japanese culture—art, folk dancing, music, food, sumo wrestling, martial disciplines, etc.—on display.

In the decades following World War II, American Jodo Shinshu temples, most of which are connected with the Buddhist Churches of America, included performances of Bon Odori (seen as folk dancing) in their Obon programs, while other temples and "churches" did not. This situation reverses what is found in Japan, where the various Jodo Shinshu groups have largely rejected Bon Odori as they reject the notion of spirits being able to return during Obon. By connecting Bon Odori with traditional culture, it has lost its significance as a statement about the souls of one's ancestors for American believers.

J. Gordon Melton

See also Buddhist Churches of America Founding Day; Calendars, Religious; Higan; Pure Brightness Festival; Shinran Shonin, Birthday of; Spring Equinox (Vernal).

References

"Gathering of Joy: A History of Japanese American Obon Festivals and Bon Odori." Japanese American National Museum. Posted at http://janmstore.com/jaobonfestival.html. Accessed July 15, 2010.

The Soka Gakkai Dictionary of Buddhism. Tokyo: Soka Gakkai, 2002.

Yoshika, Eiyu. "O-bon: The time to remember and appreciate our ancestors." *Nichiren-shu News* 22 (July 1998). Posted at http://www.nichiren-shu.org/newsletter/nichirenshu_news/summer98.html. Accessed July 15, 2010.

Oeshiki (October)

Oeshiki is a commemoration of the completion of the earthly life of Japanese Buddhist prophet Nichiren Shonin (1222–1282). He passed away in the residence of the Ikegami family, the lord of Ikegami, now in the Ota ward of Tokyo, on October 13, 1282. Soon afterward, Nikegami Honmon-ji Temple was established as a memorial. Nichiren is considered the founder of both the Nichiren-shu and Nichiren Shoshu sects of Japanese Buddhism. Oeshiki is celebrated across Japan and internationally by members of the spectrum of sects who trace their lineage to Nichiren, including Soka Gakkai International, the largest Nichiren group outside of Japan.

The most elaborate Oeshiki celebration is held at the Ikegami Honmon-ji Temple. It begins relatively calmly on October 11, with a simple memorial service. It then peaks on October 12 with the massive Mando-neri-kuyo parade, a procession through the streets from Ikegami Station to Honmon-ji Temple, which often attracts up to 300,000 observers. The parade itself includes some 3,000 participants, a number of whom pull the large floats, or *mandos*, pagoda-like structures decorated with lanterns and covered with paper cherry blossoms, which represent the oft-repeated Nichiren mantra "Namu-Myoho-Rrenge-Kyo." The event ends on October 13, with ringing of the temple bell, the method of originally announcing Nichiren's death in 1282.

J. Gordon Melton

See also Higan; Nichiren's Birthday.

References

Anesaki, Masaharu. *Nichiren: The Buddhist Prophet*. Cambridge, MA: Harvard University Press, 1949.

"Ikegami Honmon-ji Temple's *Oeshiki* Festival." Posted at http://tcvb.or.jp/en/event/200910a.html. Accessed July 15, 2010.

The Liturgy of Nichiren Shoshu. Etiwanda, CA: Nichiren Shoshu Temple, 1979.

Nichiren-Buddhist Service Companion. Chicago: Headquarters of the Nichiren Buddhist Temple of North America, 1968.

Olaf, Saint's Day of St. (July 29)

Norwegian king Olaf Haraldsson (995–1030) emerged out of obscurity in 1015, when he returned to Norway from England where he had led forces fighting the Danes. Gaining the support of a group of nobles, he declared himself king. He had some success in consolidating his kingdom, fighting off Danish forces and negotiating a treaty with the Swedes. He also continued the spread of Christianity in Norway begun by a predecessor, King Olaf Tryggvason (r. 995–1000). He brought bishops from England and Germany and funded the spread of the faith from the seaport cities to the interior. He also established the church as a legal entity and dictated its organization.

Olaf's kingship was brought to an end as a result of his losing the Battle of the Helgeå (1026). In 1029, the Norwegian nobles allied themselves to Cnut the Great, who invaded from Denmark. Olaf fled and, in spite of several attempts, was unable to regain his throne. He died in battle in 1030. The next year, one of the bishops Olaf had brought from England, Grimkel, declared him a saint. Grimkel also spread the veneration of Saint Olaf in England. Beginning with the rule of Olaf's illegitimate son Magnus (r. 1035–1047), subsequent Norwegian rulers played up the veneration of Olaf, in part to establish their own right to the throne. He was formally confirmed as a saint in Rome in 1888.

Olaf's remains now reside in the Nidaros Cathedral located in Trondheim, Norway, the country's most prominent pilgrimage site. Those wishing to make the pilgrimage may travel along Saint Olav's Way, which covers some 400 miles beginning in Oslo.

The veneration of Olaf was spread in the Eastern Church through the Varangians, a group of Scandinavians residing in Constantinople who served as the bodyguard of the Byzantine emperor. Their chapel was located near the church of Hagia Irene. Saint Olaf became the last saint whose veneration was common to both the Western and Eastern churches prior to the Great Schism of 1054. His feast day, also called Olsok Eve, is July 29. He is considered the patron saint of Norway, though the Faeroes Islands is the only nation that keeps his feast day as a national holiday.

J. Gordon Melton

See also Ansgar, Saint's Day of St.

References

Larsen, Karen. *A History of Norway*. Princeton, NJ: Princeton University Press, 1948.

Phelpstead, Carl. *Passion and Miracles of the Blessed Olafr*. UK: Viking Society for Northern Research, 2001.

Olsok Eve. *See* Olaf, Saint's Day of St.

Omizutori. *See* Shuni-e (Omizutori)

See Shuni-e (Omizutori)

Onam

Onam is the largest annual festival in the south Indian state of Kerala. It occurs during the month of Shravana on the Hindu lunar calendar (August or September on the Common Era calendar), though its observance is actually set annually on the local calendar of the Malayali people of Kerala.

Onam, an ancient rice harvest festival, is now tied to the story of King Mahabali as recounted in the epic Indian tale, the *Mahabharata*. Mahabali was a descendant of Kashyapa. Kashyapa fathered two sons, one of whom, Hiranyakashipu, attempted to kill his own son Prahalad. As he was attempting the evil deed, Vishnu, in his incarnation as Narasimha, stepped in and killed Hiranyakashipu. Mahabali was the grandson of Prahalad.

Meanwhile, Kashyapa's two wives had become the mothers of two rival sets of subdeities, known in Hinduism as the Asuras and Devas. The former are generally thought of in negative terms, but not always. Mahabali was an Asura and in his rise to power had defeated the Devas and taken possession of the three worlds over which they ruled. The Devas approached the deity Vishnu to seek his help in their ongoing battle with Mahabali. Vishnu refused to assist them in light of all the good things Mahabali had done since taking power.

Vishnu decided, however, to test Mahabali, who had established his capital in what is now Kerala. He chose a time when Mahabali was performing the sacrificial rites, during which Mahabali had declared he would grant all wishes presented to him. A small boy visited Mahabali at this time and asked for a piece of land measured by his taking three paces. The king immediately agreed. Unfortunately, when Vishnu took the first two paces he had already covered all the realms over which Mahabali ruled. Mahabali offered himself for the third pace, and the effect was his banishment into a land far away. Vishnu, impressed with Mahabali's devotion, granted him the boon of being able to revisit his former subjects once a year.

The time of Mahabali's rule in Kerala is remembered as a Golden Age; hence, his annual return visit, the subject of the Onam festival, is a time for widespread celebration. Highlights of the 10-day festival include the Onasadya feast, prepared on Thiruonam, the last day when the spirit of the king is believed to be present. It is a large nine-course vegetarian meal that includes a number of prescribed dishes. The meal is served on banana leaves as celebrants sit on the floor on a mat.

The sacred Pampa River, considered by locals as their equivalent of the Ganges River, is the site of the annual Vallamkali, the Snake Boat Race, featuring large boats pulled by oarsmen whose activity in the water is observed by spectators on the river's banks cheering them on. On other days, men engage in a range of sports, while women test their grace in a range of dances.

Constance A. Jones

See also Narasimha Jayanti; Vamana Jayanti.

References

Krishna, Nandita. *The Book of Vishnu*. London: Penguin Global, 2001.

Nambiar, Aruna, and Saibal Das. *Portrait Kerala*. Kerala, India: Stark World, 2007.

Narasimhan, Chakravarti V. *The Mahabharata*. New York: Columbia University Press, 1965.

Pushpanth, Salim. *Romancing Kerala*. Kottayam, Kerala, India: Dee Bee Info Publications, 2003.

Onbashira

Onbashira is a festival held at Suwa, Nagano, Japan, in order to symbolically renew Suwa Taisha, the Suwa Grand Shrine, the main temple in Japan dedicated to Suwa-no-Kami, a kami of valor and duty, a major deity in the Shinto divine hierarchy. The site is some 1,200 years old and now stands as one of the oldest shrines of Japanese Shinto. It is mentioned in the Kojiki, one of the Shinto holy books. The large shrine complex has four parts—the Kamisha (upper shrine), the Shimosha (lower shrine), the Harumiya (spring shrine), and the Akimiya (autumn shrine).

The Onbashira festival occurs every six years and appears to have been celebrated uninterrupted for as long as the shrine has existed. The festival takes place during the years of the Monkey and the Tiger, according to Chinese astrology. The festival takes several months, with the main parts being held in what is April and May on the Common Era calendar. There are essentially three stages to the event.

First, in the weeks leading up to the festival proper, 16 large trees are felled in a forest on the mountain above the shrine, using axes and other tools especially created for this event. Once on the ground, the trees are decorated with red and white ornaments, the traditional colors associated with Shinto, and ropes are attached to them. In April, the festival proper then begins. This segment, called Yamadashi, finds teams of loggers riding the logs down the mountainside to the shrine site. The trip not only strips the logs of their bark and branches, but the ride becomes a text of bravery for the men who ride the logs down what are often quite steep slopes.

In May, the last part of the festival, termed Satobiki, is centered on the placement of the new logs at the four corners of the four parts of the Suwa shrine, They are erected upright and are seen as pillars that serve as the foundational supports of the shrine. This placement is done with all due ceremony and ritual with a group of men who are atop each log as it is lifted into place and who celebrate its successful placement with songs. The completion of Onbashira is marked with a closing ritual called "Building of Hoden."

Onbashira elicits heavy participation in its different stages from the people of Suwa and the surrounding region. Since the lifting of the pillars was integrated into the opening ceremony of the Nagano Winter Olympic Games in 1998, hundreds of thousands of visitors have flocked to Suwa for subsequent staging of Onbashira.

J. Gordon Melton

See also Aki Matsuri; Hakada Matsuri; Haru Matsuri; Kaijin Matsuri; Kyoto Gion Matsuri; Nagasaki Kunchi; Natsu Matsuri; Sakura Matsuri.

References

Littleton, Scott. *Shinto: Origins, Rituals, Festivals, Spirits, Sacred Places*. New York: Oxford University Press, 2002.

Rambelli, Fabio. *Vegetal Buddhas—Ideological Effects of Japanese Buddhist Doctrines on the Salvation of Inanimate Beings*. Occasional Papers 9. Kyoto: Italian School of East Asian Studies, 2001.

Yoda, Hiroko. "Onbashira-sai Festival: The Log Surfers of Lake Suwa." CNNGO. Posted at http://www.cnngo.com/tokyo/play/onbashirasai-festival-holy-log-rollers-023914. Accessed June 15, 2010.

One Great Hour of Sharing

One Great Hour of Sharing is a Protestant Christian commemoration that traces its roots to the various efforts launched after World War II for the reconstruction of Europe. Many church leaders took note of the 1946 call made by the newly elected presiding bishop of the Episcopal Church, Henry Knox Sherrill (1890–1980), to build the Presiding Bishop's Fund for World Relief. Speaking on a nationwide radio hookup, he challenged church members to raise one million dollars in one hour.

In 1949, church leaders from several denominations created an ad hoc committee to support the separate relief campaigns of their various churches. This united effort would serve not only to raise money, but to provide a witness to the effect of Christians uniting around a common cause. An initial effort was made around a dramatic radio presentation that involved several Hollywood stars, most notably Gregory Peck and Ida Lupino, and a greeting contributed by President Harry Truman. The program aired at 10 p.m. on Saturday evening, March 26. Listeners were asked to attend their local church the next day and make a contribution to the churches' relief efforts. Some 75,000 local churches participated. A similar effort was made annually.

Meanwhile, in 1946, a number of the leading denominations united their relief efforts in forming Church World Service, which in 1950 would affiliate with the new National Council of Churches in the USA. As of 2010, 36 Protestant and Orthodox denominations cooperate through Church World Service, and each has its own relief appeal relative to the One Great Hour of Sharing. Of these, nine currently serve on the One Great Hour of Sharing committee and use the One Great

Hour of Sharing event to raise funds for their mutual relief efforts: American Baptist Churches USA, African Methodist Episcopal Zion Church, Church of the Brethren, Christian Church (Disciples of Christ), Cumberland Presbyterian Church, Presbyterian Church (USA), Reformed Church in America, United Church of Christ, and Church World Service. The Christian Church (Disciples of Christ) calls its offering the Week of Compassion. In various ways, all work in cooperation with Church World Service, the relief, development and refugee assistance arm of the National Council of the Churches of Christ in the USA.

United Methodists, who support a massive relief program called the United Methodist Committee on Overseas Relief (UMCOR), use the One Great Hour of Sharing as the occasion to raise funds for their overhead, so that money given to appeals for special needs go entirely to the relief effort. The Presbyterian Church (USA) divides its One Great Hour of Sharing between three funds—The Presbyterian Hunger Program, the Self-Development of People, and the Presbyterian Disaster Assistance.

Today, the different denominations celebrate the One Great Hour of Sharing on a variety of days and issue the funds raised in slightly different ways, though all designate their ultimate use to back efforts at disaster relief, refugee assistance, and development aid. Participating churches along with Church World Service have moved into the forefront as first responders to natural disasters.

J. Gordon Melton

See also World Communion Sunday.

References

"The History of One Great Hour of Sharing." *One Great Hour of Sharing*. Posted at http://www.onegreathourofsharing.org/. Accessed April 15, 2010. Most of the participating churches maintain separate "One Great Hour of Sharing" Web sites for their members and constituency.

Orthodoxy, Feast of

The Feast of Orthodoxy is a celebration of the Eastern Orthodox churches and the Eastern Rite Catholic churches that emerged out of the iconoclasm controversy of the eighth and ninth centuries. At various times in the Middle East, voices have appeared who take the command against graven images to mean any kind of human representational art in the church context. Such iconoclasm became institutionalized in Islam. In the fourth century, the use of icons began to expand in the Christian Church in the Eastern Mediterranean.

Then, toward the end of the 820s, Leo III the Isaurian (r. 717–741), the Roman emperor in Constantinople, set of an empire-wide controversy by having an image of Jesus removed from the entrance to his palace. His action provoked a controversy that would last for a generation.

Finally, in 780, Empress Irene, who held power while her son, Emperor Constantine VI, was still a minor, directed a request to Pope Hadrian I (772–795) to convene a church council to deal with the issue. The council finally met at Nicea in 787. The assembled church leaders defended icons and other representational art as being true to the incarnation. They also drew the distinction between worship, whose only object is God, and the salutation and respectful veneration, which could be directed to the saints and to images such as icons.

The Nicean Council appeared to have definitively dealt with the issue. However, in the next century, a series of Roman emperors favored the iconoclasts, including Nikephoros I (r. 802–811), Leo V (r. 813–820), Michael II (r. 820–829), and Theophilos (r. 829–842). Finally, the young Michael III (842–867), again operating through his mother Theodora, who acted as the regent from 842 to 855, conferred with the future Patriarch Methodios (r. 843–847) to summon the Synod of Constantinople in 842. That synod reaffirmed the use of icons and culminated with a massive procession to the Hagia Sophia, the monumental Orthodox church in Constantinople, to restore them to their proper place in the church.

Before the Synod was dismissed, it further decreed that a feast should be celebrated each year on the anniversary of the restoration of the icons, and that feast should be named the Sunday of Orthodoxy. It continues to be celebrated on the first Sunday of Lent. The veneration of icons has subsequently become one of the most identifying characteristics of the Orthodox churches and from them was passed to the several Eastern-rite Catholic churches.

The Day or Feast of Orthodoxy continues to recall the victory over the iconoclasts, but as the iconoclasm controversy receded into the past, the days became a time to reaffirm the Orthodox position against the range of heresies that had been defined by the Seven Ecumenical Councils between 324 and 787. Most groups that have deviated from the Orthodox position in subsequent centuries have adopted and restated one of the early positions that were defined as heretical by the councils.

J. Gordon Melton

See also Czestochowa, Feast Day of Our Lady of; Eastern Orthodoxy—Liturgical Year.

References

Barnard, Leslie William. *The Graeco-Roman and Oriental Background of the Iconoclastic Controversy*. Leyden: Brill Academic, 1997.

Besançon, Alain. *The Forbidden Image: An Intellectual History of Iconoclasm*. Chicago: University of Chicago Press, 2009.

Hussey, J. M., and Andrew Louth. *The Orthodox Church in the Byzantine Empire*. New York: Oxford University Press, 1990.

Osho (Rajneesh), Birthday of (December 11)

Osho (1931–1990), known for most of his teaching career as Acharya Rajneesh, was an Indian spiritual teacher who lived in the United States through the 1980s and 1990s. He developed a loyal following in the West that grew even as he became the subject of increasing controversy.

Osho was born Chandra Mohan Jain. He completed his advanced degrees and became a professor of philosophy. He then dropped his academic career in favor of becoming a roving teacher of an eclectic and revisionist form of Hinduism. He absorbed elements of the Western Human Potential movement and became known for his attacks on traditional institutionalized religion and his advocacy of liberal sexual mores. These came together as he initiated people into the renounced life (as sannyasins), traditionally a path that includes celibacy. His *neo-sannyasins* offended the Indians with their public displays of affection. In 1974, he settled in Poona and established an ashram where he often made news with his outrageous statements.

As tensions grew in India, in 1981, Rajneesh, as he was then known, moved to the United States and soon established the community of Rajneeshpuram, in rural Oregon. Controversy mounted over conflicts with the area's previous residents, soon outnumbered by the Rajneesh disciples; the guru's ostentation demonstrated in a collection of Rolls-Royce cars given to him by disciples; and the plan to build the community's population by inviting homeless people to move there.

The Rajneesh experiment came to an end when it became known that some of the leadership had been involved in a plot to poison the water in Portland, Oregon. Though he claimed ignorance about the plan, Osho (the name he adopted in the 1990s) was eventually arrested and deported. Denied entry in a number of countries, he reluctantly returned to India, where he died a short time later.

His following remained largely loyal to him. They have kept many of his books in print, continued to nurture an effort to reestablish his reputation as a forward-thinking teacher innocent of the crimes committed by some of his followers, and to maintain a global network of ashrams. The movement is not as strong as it was at its height in the mid-1990s, but it is far from defunct as some have reported.

Ocho's followers honor their teacher on his birthday, December 11, every year, a practice that began while he was still alive (and accounted for many of the Rolls-Royces he owned). The many Osho centers and ashrams will hold a gathering that includes Osho meditations, lessons, dancing, and music. Attendees will also share a meal.

As early as 2002, the movement indicated that the celebration of the birthday may be coming to an end. No celebration was held at the movement's headquarters commune in Poona, India, following a decision to ignore it. This action followed removal of all the pictures of Osho that had previously been prominently displayed, and reflections by the leadership that they wished neither to make Osho an object of veneration nor to institutionalize the movement into an organized religion.

J. Gordon Melton

See also Hubbard, Birthday of L. Ron; Prabhupada, Appearance Day of A. C. Bhaktivedanta Swami.

References

Aveling, Harry. *Osho Rajneesh and His Disciples: Some Western Perceptions*. Flushing, NY: Asia Book Corporation of America, 1999.

Carter, Lewis F. *Charisma and Control in Rajneeshpuram: A Community without Shared Values*. Cambridge: Cambridge University Press, 1990.

Urban, Hugh B. "Osho, from Sex Guru to Guru of the Rich: The Spiritual Logic of Late Capitalism." In *Gurus in America*, edited by Thomas A. Forsthoefel and Cynthia Ann Humes. Albany: State University of New York Press, 2005.

Vaidya, Abhay. "Osho or No, Each Day Is a Celebration at Commune!" *Times of India*, December 13, 2003. Posted at http://www.sannyasworld.com/modules.php?op=modload&name=News&file=article&sid=381. Accessed April 15, 2010.

P

Pak Tai, Birthday of

Pak Tai is a deity of traditional Chinese religion with a strong following in southeastern China, including Hong Kong and Macau. There are at least seven Pak Tai temples in Hong Kong. He is also known as Yuen Tin Sheung Tai (Supreme Emperor of the Dark Heaven).

Pak Tai was a real person, reputedly a prince of the Shang dynasty (c. 1600–1046 BCE) who became a learned Taoist. The story of his life is, however, thoroughly infused with mythological elements. It seems that a demon was loose on the land. The Jade Emperor, a high Taoist deity, appointed Pak Tai the commander of 12 heavenly legions to defeat the demon, which had sought the assistance of a large tortoise and an even larger serpent in the battle. When he defeated the demon and returned to heaven, the Jade Emperor named him the Supreme Emperor of the Dark Heaven. His birthday is celebrated at the Pak Tai Festival, which falls on the third day of the third month of the Chinese lunar calendar (March–April on the Common Era calendar).

Veneration of Pak Tai emphasizes his power, courage, and devotion, but in Hong Kong he is primarily known as someone who can help avert disaster. He is usually portrayed in a sitting position with a serpent and tortoise under his feet. His presence in Hong Kong relates to his ascribed ability to stop the plague.

The largest temple to Pak Tai is found in the Wanchai section on Hong Kong Island, but the most famous temple is on the nearby island of Cheung Chau. Pak Tai was brought to Cheung Chau in the 18th century at a moment when the residents, mostly from the Huizhou area of Guangdong Province, were doubly beset by pirates and an epidemic of the plague. The community of fishermen brought a statue of Pak Tai they had found floating in the sea to the island and held a procession through the streets of the main village. In addition, residents dressed as different deities and walked around the island to drive away the spirits of the dead killed and buried on the island by the pirates. Their actions seem to have relieved the problems. The statue of Pak Tai stayed, and a temple was erected as its home.

Today, in addition to the celebration of Pak Tai's birthday, the temple on Cheung Chau holds a second festival one the eighth day of the fourth lunar month (April–May). It has grown into a weeklong event featuring a large process/parade with a number of floats, and a variety of productions of Cantonese opera. The three central days of the festival begin in front of the Pak Tai temple, where the priests hold their opening ritual and call for the residents to adopt a vegetarian diet in the days ahead. The whole island joins in the spirit of the celebration, and even restaurants that normally serve meat conform to the vegetarian requirements.

The highlight of the festival is the celebration around the towers of buns held in Tung Wan, in the open space outside the temple. At the time that the ghosts of the deceased victims of the pirates were being dealt with, they were offered the buns, a traditional food to placate ghosts. Bakers prepare the buns and add a red-stamp message of good fortune. Humans are supposed to avoid eating the buns themselves until the ghosts have had their fill.

Today, three island associations share responsibility for planning the annual festival, and among themselves have a friendly competition to build a high tower, which will be covered in buns. On the third day of the festival, young people will climb the towers and retrieve the buns, which are distributed to the gathered festivalgoers.

J. Gordon Melton

See also Che Kung, Birthday of; Guan Yin's Birthday; Kwan Tai, Birthday of; Monkey King, Birthday of the; Tam Kung Festival; Third Prince, Birthday of the.

References

"Pak Tai Temple: Wan Chai." Chinese Temples Committee. Posted at http://www.ctc.org.hk/en/directcontrol/temple10.asp. Accessed July 15, 2010.

Savidge, Joyce. *This Is Hong Kong: Temples*. Hong Kong: Department of Government Information Services, 1977.

Palm Sunday

Palm Sunday, the Sunday before Easter in the Christian liturgical calendar, celebrates Jesus's entry into Jerusalem which initiates the events of the last week of his life. It is an ambiguous day in the Christian year. On the one hand, it is celebrated as a time that Jesus was publically acknowledged as someone of importance, while on the other hand, the scene turns dark with his being challenged by Jewish leaders, his overthrowing the money changers in the temple, his cursing a fig tree, and his weeping for the city.

As the Gospel of Luke briefly recounts the story, the disciples are asked to locate a donkey on which Christ would ride.

> And it came to pass, when he drew nigh unto Bethphage and Bethany, at the mount that is called Olivet, he sent two of the disciples, saying, "Go your way into the village over against you; in which as ye enter ye shall find a colt tied, whereon no man ever yet sat: loose him, and bring him. And if any one ask you, 'Why do ye loose him?' you will say, The Lord has need of him."
>
> And they that were sent went away, and found even as he had said unto them. And as they were loosing the colt, the owners thereof said unto them, "Why do you loose the colt?"

And they said, "The Lord has need of him."

And they brought him to Jesus: and they threw their garments upon the colt, and set Jesus thereon. And as he went, they spread their garments in the way. And as he was now drawing nigh, even at the descent of the mount of Olives, the whole multitude of the disciples began to rejoice and praise God with a loud voice for all the mighty works which they had seen; saying, "Blessed is the King that comes in the name of the Lord: peace in heaven, and glory in the highest." (Luke 19:29–38)

Believers and clergymen participate in a Palm Sunday procession in Portugal. (Graça Victoria/Dreamstime.com)

Palm Sunday was celebrated in the church during its early centuries, and became an open-air procession in the fourth century in Constantinople after the church attained legality and developed its ritual in the freedom provided by its being favored by the emperor. By the eighth century, the celebration had permeated the Christian community, both East and West. By the ninth century, in Rome, Palm Sunday had become a festive occasion that included the ritual blessing of the palms, and it continued to evolve through the Middle Ages, a high point being the wheeling of a statue of Jesus astride a donkey around the streets of the city.

In many ways, Palm Sunday is simply another Sunday in Lent for Western Christians, and it is followed by several days in which little is done liturgically. Observation of Holy Week then continues with Maundy Thursday, Good Friday, and Easter, during which Jesus observed the Last Supper, instituted the sacred meal later to become the Eucharist; was arrested; put through a mock trial; and executed by crucifixion. On the next Sunday, he was said to have risen from the grave by his followers.

In the Eastern Church, Palm Sunday is preceded by Lazarus Saturday, a day that celebrates the resurrection of Lazarus of Bethany, which occurred just before he headed for Jerusalem for Passover (John 11:1–45). Lazarus Saturday is a celebrative occasion that marks the transition from lent to Holy Week, and one of the very few occasions in which the resurrection is the focus of worship on a day other than Sunday.

In the West, it has been the tradition to save the palms used on Palm Sunday, to bless them with holy water, and then to burn them. The ashes thus produced are then stored until Ash Wednesday (the first day of Lent) the next year, when they are used to mark the forehead of the attendees at that service.

Palm Sunday is among the most celebrated liturgical events among Protestant Christians, most of whom will emphasize it in their worship on the Sunday before Easter. There are a few denominations that do not observe any of the major Christian holidays, believing them to be later manmade traditions not called for in the Bible.

J. Gordon Melton

See also Easter; Good Friday; Holy Week; Lazarus Saturday; Lent; Liturgical Calendar—Western Christian; Maundy Thursday.

References

Ball, Ann. *Encyclopedia of Catholic Devotions and Practices.* Huntington, IN: Our Sunday Visitor, 2003.

The Liturgy of Holy Week: Celebrating the Eucharist: Palm Sunday to Easter Sunday. Collegeville, MN: Liturgical Press, 2001.

Wallace, Robin Knowles. *Palm Sunday and Holy Week Services.* Nashville, TN: Abingdon Press, 2006.

Ward, Benedicta. *In the Company of Christ: Through Lent, Palm Sunday, Good Friday and Easter to Pentecost.* Harrisburg, PA: Church Publishing, 2005.

Paranirvana Day. *See* Nehan

Parents Day

Parents Day is the first holy day to be celebrated in the Unification Church, founded by Sun Myung Moon (b. 1920) in Korea in 1954. Parents Day was established on March 1, 1960 (and is now set annually by reference to the traditional Korean lunar calendar). It celebrates the establishment of Moon and his wife Hak Ja Han as the True Parents of humanity. Moon is known as True Father and his wife as True Mother.

Their parental role is based on a modification of traditional Christian doctrines about the fall and salvation of humans. According to Moon, the fall of Adam and Eve involved sexual transgression, first Eve with Lucifer and then Eve with her husband. This fall stained the human bloodline and brought ruination to the human family. God has been looking to restore humanity through a new Adam. Jesus was supposed to fulfill that role, but his own failings and those of his parents and John the Baptist led to a path of secondary salvation through Jesus's death on the Cross.

Unificationists believe that Jesus appeared to Sun Myung Moon in 1935 and asked him to complete the liberation of the family. Moon claims to have achieved this as a result of his sinless life, persecution for righteousness, and choice of a new Eve to form the first True Parents in history. According to Unification theology, Moon's wedding in 1960 represents the Marriage Supper of the Lamb and the restoration of True Family.

Moon's children are known as True Children, and those who join the Unification Church are grafted into Moon's family so that his sinless lineage can form the proper base for a new world order. Moon said this of Parents Day in a 1963 sermon: "Parents Day is the first time since God created all things and humankind that there is one balanced man, one balanced woman, balanced in love, to whom God can descend and with whom He can truly be. For the first time in human history this original state of matrimony, the original trinity, has come into existence upon the earth."

Unificationists believe that Moon's children are born without sin. However, they have free will and can choose a path of rebellion against God. The same applies for any followers of True Parents: spiritual birth into the Moon family cleanses from sin, but the capacity for freedom to rebel remains. Obedience to Moon's teaching and example assures a path to earthly blessing and heavenly reward.

James A. Beverley

See also Children's Day; Day of All Things; True Parents' Birthday; Unification Church, Holidays of the.

References

Fichter, Joseph H. *The Holy Family of Father Moon*. Kansas City, KS: Leaven Press, 1985.

Introvigne, Massimo. *The Unification Church*. Salt Lake City, UT: Signature, 2000.

Kwak, Chung Hwan. *The Tradition: Book One*. New York: Holy Spirit Association for the Unification of World Christianity, 1985. Posted at http://www.unification.org/ucbooks/TT1/index.html. Accessed June 15, 2010.

Moon, Sun Myung. "Happy Golden Wedding Anniversary." Posted at http://www.tparents.org/Moon-Talks/SunMyungMoon10/SunMyungMoon-100429.pdf. Accessed June 18, 2011.

Parshurama Jayanti

Vaishnava Hindus who focus their religious life around the deity Vishnu tell the stories of his various incarnations—as for example, Rama or Krishna—and celebrate various important events relative to these incarnations. One of the lesser-known incarnations (for non-Hindus) is Vishnu's appearance as Parashurama, who is said to have appeared at one point as an axe-wielding man to correct the destruction being wrought by members of the warrior caste that had wrongfully usurped power over the Brahmins, the priestly leaders of the social order. At the moment of his birth, Parashurama was given his axe by the deity Shiva.

Many of the stories about Parashurama concern his father, Jamadagni. At one point, for example, Jamadagni, doubting the chastity of his wife, ordered his sons, one by one, to kill her. They refused, and the enraged Jamadagni slew them. He then turned to Parashurama, who obeyed his father. Pleased with his son's action, Jamadagni granted Parashurama any wish, and he asked that all who had been slain be returned to life, which was granted. Parashurama is thus seen as one demonstrating traditional obedience and affection.

The more famous story of Parashurama concerns his attack on the warrior caste. Kartavirya, a powerful king, coveted a cow possessed by Jamadagni and, at a time when Jamadagni was away from his home, took it. Jamadagni and his son pursued Kartavirya and retrieved the cow, and in the process killed the king. Upon hearing of their father's death, the king's sons killed Jamadagni. Ever the loving son, Parashurama swore death on all Kshatryas (the name generally given the warrior caste). This vow he fulfilled in a series of battles that followed.

As a result of Parashurama's action, in the future, the new warrior caste would all be descendants of the Brahmins, a status that manifested the superiority of the priestly caste over that of the warrior caste. The role of Parashurama in stabilizing the caste system and hence the Hindu social order is celebrated on what is designated as his birthday (jayanti), the third day of the waxing moon in the Hindu month of Vaisakha (which occurs in April or May of the Common Era calendar).

Those who fast, practice austerities, and/or offer pujas (worship) on this day are said to be granted Parashurama's virtues. Worship of Parashurama is especially found in Malabar and Konkan, where it is believed that he at one time saved these coastal regions by preventing the ocean from destroying them.

Constance A. Jones

See also Anant Chaturdashi; Janmashtami; Jhulan Yatra; Kartika Purnima; Rama Navani; Vamana Jayanti; Varaha Jayanti.

References

Kelly, Aidan, Peter Dresser, and Linda Ross. *Religious Holidays and Calendars*. Detroit, MI: Omnigraphics, 1993.

Patel, Sushil Kumar. *Hinduism in India: A Study of Vishnu Worship*. Delhi: Amar Prakashan, 1992.

Seshayya. A. K. *Fasts, Festivals and Ceremonies*. Kelang, Selangor, Malaysia: KSN Print, n.d.

Paryushana

Paryushana, also known as Daslakshan Parva or the Festival of Ten Virtues, is a primary festival among the Jains of India. Its origin lies in the beginning of Jainism itself, which emerged as an order of monks. Practicing a form of nonattachment, the monks traveled about living from day to day on what was offered them. India has a rainy season (roughly June to September on the Common Era calendar) in which travel is difficult, and it became common for monks to settle down in one place, usually at the edge of a city, for several months (a minimum of 70 days).

In the old Indian lunar calendar, Paryushana would begin on the fifth day of the waxing moon (*shukla-paksha*) half of the month of Bhadrapad. It would last from 8 to 10 days, depending upon which of the two main divisions of the Jains were holding it. The Swetambaras hold an 8-day festival and the Digambaras a 10-day event.

The festival is a time for reflection on one's life and actions during the past year, and a time to renew one's focus on what are considered the 10 cardinal virtues: forgiveness, charity, simplicity, contentment, truthfulness, self-restraint, fasting, detachment, humility, and continence. These virtues are embedded in a game that is played during the week called Gyanbazi, a game of chance in which morality is taught and the goal becomes enlightenment. The game was observed by the British and brought back to the West where it was secularized and marketed as "snakes-and-ladders" and in the United States as "Chutes and Ladders."

The festival is marked by several events, including recitation of the text of the Kalpa Sutra, the book that includes the earliest accounts of the Tirthankaras, the enlightened masters from whose teachings Jainism derives. Fasting is common among the monks during this time, and many lay people, who already are vegetarians, deny themselves specific food items (much like Christians during Lent). The evening is spent in the in the practice of Pratikraman, a form of meditation that allows for stringent introspection, a review of one's life, a means of repentance for negative thoughts and actions, and a reminder not to repeat them.

There are several types of Pratikraman, one form of which is practiced daily by devout Jains. Other forms are undertaken once every 15 days or once every four months. Samvatsari Pratikraman is done once per year—on the last day of the Paryushana festival. In a sense, the first days of the Paryushana are meant to lead up to the last, during which a most unique practice accompanies the Pratikraman. Those at the event ask forgiveness of every individual they may have offended during the past year. This practice becomes a time to forget old differences and renew the community. It is accomplished by folding one's hands before the person and requesting "Micchamidukadam" (May my bad deeds toward you be fruitless).

A form of Paryushana has been imported to the West, though there are relatively few monks, and the Indian rainy session does not exist. Westerners attending the event have been especially impressed by the acts of forgiveness on its final day.

Constance A. Jones

See also Mahavir Jayanti; Mauna Agyaras; Navpad Oli; New Year's Day (Jain); Paush Dashami.

References

Hynson, Colin. *Discover Jainism*. Edited by Mehool Sanghrajka. London: Institute of Jainology, 2007.

Jain, Duli Chandra, ed. *Studies in Jainism*. 3 vols. New York: Jain Stucy Circle, 2004.

Rankin, Aidan. *The Jain Path: Ancient Wisdom for the West*. Washington, DC: O Books, 2006.

Passover

Passover is the English name of Pesach, the Jewish Feast of Unleavened Bread (discussed in a separate entry under Pesach). Pesach was commanded to be an annual memorial festival among the Jewish people in Exodus 12 recalling God's deliverance of the Jewish people from slavery in Egypt. A key event in that deliverance was the plague in which God killed the firstborn of each Egyptian household, while passing over the homes of the Hebrews whose house had been marked with the blood of a freshly slaughtered lamb. This event was marked by a meal that included a lamb slaughtered in the Jewish temple and unleavened bread, bread taken on the trip out of Egypt prepared in haste with no time for the leaven to act. Each year, Jews would make a pilgrimage to Jerusalem to celebrate Pesach.

The Christian appropriation began simultaneously with the formation of the Christian community. Among the early memories of the life of Jesus was a trip he made to Jerusalem with his parents to celebrate Pesach when he was but 12 years old. While in the city, he wandered from the family and was found in the temple speaking to the elders (Luke 2:40–52). Then, during his adult ministry, he would spend much of the year traveling through the countryside but always returned to Jerusalem for Passover. Traditionally, the length of his ministry was set at three years, as the New Testament accounts of his life placed him at three different Passovers in Jerusalem (John 2, John 5, and Mark 7), prior to the one during which time he is arrested and executed.

On the last visit to Jerusalem, he celebrated the Passover meal with his disciples, the account of which become the basis of the future remembrances of that, as the Eucharist or the Lord's Supper, are regularly celebrated by Christians today (though in a variety of forms and occasions that range from daily to weekly to monthly to quarterly to annually). Following that last Passover supper, he was arrested, tried, and executed. As he died, it was reported that the veil separating the most holy space from the rest of the temple was rent in two.

That year, Passover was on Thursday. Christ was executed on Friday, and remained dead through the Sabbath. Christianity emerged after Jesus was reported to have risen from the dead on the first day of the new week, Sunday, and subsequently appeared to his disciples at various times and places.

The celebration of Easter (i.e., Christ's resurrection) superseded Passover in the Christian church. However, it was tied to Passover in that the events of Christ's death and resurrection began with a Passover Seder (Luke 22:15–16) and were concluded during the Passover week. Jesus was likened to a Passover lamb sacrificed by God for the deliverance of humanity—the lamb of God who takes away the sins of the world. Jesus as the Passover lamb continues as one of the most central and powerful symbols within Christianity.

Beginning early in the fourth century, as the church moved from its outlaw status in the Roman Empire and began to hold church councils for deciding basic questions, the question of dating Easter came to the fore. A method was adopted that followed the Jewish methods of determining the date of Passover, which, due to the use of the lunar calendar, fell on a different day each year on the Julian calendar used throughout the Roman Empire at the time. Easter was set as the first Sunday after the first full moon following the spring equinox (March 21). Passover/Pesach fell on Nissan 15, the first full moon after the spring equinox.

Because of the inaccuracy in the Julian calendar, the actual spring equinox began to drift away from March 21. A reformed Julian calendar continues to be used among Eastern Orthodox (a few even continuing to use the unreformed calendar), and their Easter celebration has become separated from that of the Western church, which adopted the Gregorian calendar that returned the spring equinox to March 21. That congruence remains in effect in the Common Era calendar.

Toward a Christian Passover

In the 19th century, following the Great Disappointment, when Adventist Christians were questioning the nonappearance of Christ as William Miller (1782–1849) had proclaimed would occur in 1843–1844, some Adventist leaders turned to the Bible for new insights. Ellen G. White (1827–1915) was introduced to the sabbatarianism, which she accepted. The practice led to a new appreciation of Jewish law and undergirded her interest in health and diet reform. Among Adventist sabbatarians not connected to White and the Seventh-day Adventist Church she founded, speculation led toward a new appreciation of the Jewish festivals, a celebration of which developed among some of the splinter groups of the Church of God (Seventh-day). The renewed interest in the Jewish festivals was also related to a critique of the celebration of Christmas and Easter as surviving Paganism.

From the sabbatarian Church of God groups, the celebration of the Jewish festivals, especially the Passover and Feast of Unleavened Bread, passed to Herbert W. Armstrong (1892–1986), the founder of the Worldwide Church of God. He tied the celebration of the Jewish feasts to a broad critique of holidays in general, both the uniquely Christian holidays and a number of widely celebrated secular holidays (Valentine's Day, Halloween) along with the idea of celebrating birthdays. Armstrong also believed in the practice of tithing and suggested that along with tithing a tenth of one's income to the Worldwide Church of God that members tithe a second 10 percent to be dedicated to celebrating Passover.

Still other Adventist groups, most notably the Jehovah's Witnesses, recognizing the Lord's Supper as having originated in a Passover seder, adopted the practice of an annual memorial meal, sometimes called the Lord's Evening Meal, which is held on the first evening of Passover/Pesach each year. Witnesses do not use the modern Jewish calendar, and their dating will on occasion correspond more with the same full moon as the Jewish festival of Purim, which is celebrated on the 14th day of the Hebrew month of Adar (and hence usually occurs in mid-March on the Common Era calendar).

Jewish Christians

Over the centuries, many Jews have converted to Christianity, but in the 20th century, a number of Jews who became Christians have consciously decided to keep much of their Jewish culture, some to the point of founding and maintaining synagogues in which worship resembles that in a Jewish synagogue, as much as is possible without directly denying basic Christian affirmations concerning Jesus's divinity and his actions that bring salvation. Most Messianic synagogues continue to celebrate Passover but have poured new content into it. While adhering to many of the forms of the traditional Pesach meal, the Messianic practice centers on the concept that Jesus (whom they call in Hebrew Yeshua) was the sacrificial Passover lamb.

The Jews for Jesus, a group of Christians of Jewish background that originated at the same time as the Messianic movement, but do not believe in separate Christian synagogues, have developed a program for informing congregations of Christian believers about the Jewish background of their practices, especially Passover. Each spring, representatives of the movement will visit Christian congregations and offer a program demonstrating and explaining the Pesach meal and its role as background for the Christian communion service.

J. Gordon Melton

See also Calendars, Religious; Common Era Calendar; Easter; Pesach; Spring Equinox (Thelema); Spring Equinox (Vernal).

References

Boston, Stephen. *The Essential Teachings of Herbert W. Armstrong: His Teachings Focused on the Incredible Human Potential. Did He Solve the Mystery of the Ages?* Lincoln, NB: iUniverse, 2002.

Lipson, Eric. *Passover Haggadah: A Messianic Celebration*. San Francisco: Purple Pomegranate Productions, 1986.

Sampson, Robin, and Linda Pierce. *A Family Guide to the Biblical Holidays*. Stafford, VA: Heart of Wisdom Publishing, 2001.

Stallings, Joseph M. *Rediscovering Passover: A Complete Guide for Christians*. Searcy, AK: Resource Publications, 1994.

Patotsav

Patotsav is a Hindu festival celebrating the anniversaries of the installation of the murtis (statues of the deities) at the temple. It is primarily a festival within the

Swaminarayan movement. Since murtis may be installed at various points during the year, the celebration for any given murti may occur on any given day.

Swaminarayan devotees see Patotsav as a re-consecration ceremony. The practice was begun out of a widespread belief that murtis lose their divinity to some degree simply from the volume of *maya* (illusion) they must deal with in their assisting devotees. Swaminarayan leaders have emphasized that such is not the case; the divinity of the murtis is never dissipated. It is the devotion of followers that often decreases. Patotsav is intended to revive the sentiments that devotees have for the murtis and for their guru.

Besides the annual Patotsav festival for the murtis, in Swaminarayan temples, there is a daily bhakti (devotional) observance that begins with a washing to the murtis first with a mixture of milk yogurt, ghee, honey, and saffon water (*abbishek*) and then with water. Then the deities are dressed in their appropriate clothing for public viewing. The bahishek is later made available to devotees for their consumption. A similar daily occurrence is found in Krishna temples of the Gaudiya Math tradition (including those of the International Society for Krishna Consciousness).

Constance A. Jones

See also Guru Purnima.

References

Mukuncharandas, Sadhu. *Hindu Festivals (Origin Sentiments & Rituals)*. Amdavad, India: Swaminarayan Aksharpith, 2005.

Paush Dashami

Paush Dashami is a Jain holy day celebrated as the birthday of the 23rd Tirthankara (saint). Jains believe that their faith was established by a lineage of 24 saints, the last one being Mahavira, generally considered the founder of the community. The Tirthankara immediately prior to Mahavira was Lord Parshvanath, who is said to have taken human birth on the 10th day of the Indian month of Pausha (December–January on the Common Era calendar). During Pausha, observant Jains join in three days of fasting, the reciting of Jain hymns, and meditation.

Among the places where Paush Dashami is most observed is Shankheswar, a village in the Indian state of Gujarat, in the midst of which a famous Jain temple is located. It has become a site for pilgrimages in that it is especially associated with the 23rd Tirthankara. Pilgrims arrive to both participate in the fast and to attend the large carnival organized for this celebration. The Paush Dashami pilgrimage is known for the fulfillment of those wishes made in an unselfish way with a right faith. The particular fast in which they engage, known as Aththam, is deemed to protect the believer from peril and to promote happiness and prosperity.

J. Gordon Melton

See also Akshay Tritiya (Jain); Gyana Panchami; Kartika Purnima; Mauna Agyaras; Mahavir Jayanti; Navpad Oli; New Year's Day (Jain); Paryushana.

References

Group C-2 Study Class of Jain Society of Greater Detroit. *Jain Tirthas of India*, Detroit: Jain Society of Detroit, 2007. Posted at http://www.jain-temple.org/documents/Tirth-ProjectBook%2009-24-09.pdf. Accessed July 15, 2010.

Jaini, P. S. *The Jaina Path of Purification*. Delhi: Motilal Banarsidass, 1979, 1990.

Singh, Narendra K., ed. *Encyclopedia of Jainism*. 30 vols. New Delhi: Anmol, 2001.

Wiley, Kristi L. *Historical Dictionary of Jainism*. Lanham, MD: Rowman & Littlefield, 2004.

Pavarana Day. *See* Boun Ok Phansa

Peace and Good Voyage, Feast of Our Lady of (May)

The Philippines is home to two large annual celebrations focused upon veneration of the Blessed Virgin Mary. The older of the two occurs in Antipolo, a suburb of Manila, where veneration is directed to a wooden statue of the Virgin originally carved and blessed in Acapulco, Mexico. It was carried aboard a Spanish galleon that moved back and forth from Mexico to the Philippines, and during its several voyages, it was credited with the ship's safely surviving threats from pirates and the ships of hostile competing nations. It finally arrived in the Philippines permanently in the care of the new governor general of the islands, Niño de Tabora (d. 1632), in 1626. He in turn delivered it into the care of the Jesuit priests, who placed it in their church of San Ignacio.

Because of its role in traveling the seas, the sailors had come to refer to the statue as Our Lady of Peace and Good Voyage. Eventually, the statue was taken to the Jesuit church in Santa Cruz. According to the story told about the statue, on two occasions, it disappeared from the Santa Cruz church only to be found high in the branches of a local breadfruit tree. Taking this occurrence as a sign, a new church was built adjacent to the tree, and the tree itself was cut down and the wood used to make the pedestal upon which the statue was then placed. The breadfruit tree's local name, *tipilo*, gave its name to the area of the new church, Antipolo.

The statue would remain in the church until World War II, when it was taken into hiding from the ravages of the war. It was returned when peace was restored; however, the original church in which it had been housed was severely damaged during the war and was pulled down. A new church was completed and, in 1950, the bishops of the Philippines proclaimed the church at Antipolo to be the national shrine of the country.

Our Lady of Antipolo is the subject of a national festival that lasts the entire month of May. It begins with an all-night vigil from 8:00 p.m. to dawn on May

Eve in commemoration of the statue's safe return after the war. Many who visit the statue do so to dedicate their new car or to prayer for safety on a long journey.

In 1997, an oratory to Our Lady of Peace and good voyage was dedicated by the late James Cardinal Hickey (1920–2004) of the Archdiocese of Washington and the Most Reverend Protacio Gungon, Bishop of Antipolo, in services at the Shrine of the Immaculate Conception in Washington, D.C.

J. Gordon Melton

See also Divino Rostro, Devotion to; Immaculate Conception, Feast of the; Peñafrancia, Feast of Our Lady of.

References

"Antipolo." Bohandi: The Philippine Heritage Site. Posted at http://www.lakbay.net/bahandi/antipolo.html. Accessed April 15, 2010.

Dodds, Monica, and Bill Dodds. *Encyclopedia of Mary*. Huntington, IN: Our Sunday Visitor, 2007.

Peñafrancia, Feast of Our Lady of (September)

The Feast of Our Lady of Peñafrancia, the largest annual celebrative event in the Philippines, is a nine-day festival in Naga City, the capital of the province of Camarines Sur, the Philippines, culminating on the actual feast day, the third Saturday of September. The story of the festival begins in the 15th century in Spain. Based on an apparition of the Virgin, a young Frenchman named Simon launched a search for a place he only knew by name, Peña de Francia. It was on no map he could find, so he left Paris and wandered the countryside. Several years later his quest took him to Salamanca, Spain, were he learned of a mountain by that name. In cave in the mountain, prompted by another apparition, he discovered a buried image of the Virgin holding the infant Jesus. That image later became a valued relic for the people of the area.

Three hundred years later, a young seminarian in Manila, the Philippines, from a family that came from Peñafrancia, Spain, became ill. He prayed to the Blessed Virgin, Our Lady of Peñafrancia, whose picture he carried with him everywhere he went. He made a vow to the virgin that if cured, he would build a chapel for her on the bank of the river that flowed through Manila. He was cured and eventually ordained as the first diocesan priest in Naga City (then known as Ciudad de Nueva Caceres), the capital of the province of Camarines Sur, far from Manila. To fulfill his vow, he mobilized a team of men to build a chapel on the banks of the Bikol River that flowed through his new hometown.

Equally important, he also commissioned a local artisan to carve an image of Our Lady of Peñafrancia, based on the ever-present picture of her he carried with him. Even before the statue was completed, reports of miracles credited to the Virgin began to circulate through the town. As the chapel was finished and the image installed, many miracles spread among the people as did devotion to Nuestra Senora de Peñafrancia, from Naga throughout the Diocese of Nueva Caceres. Today, as many as six million people will head to Camarines Sur in September each year.

The annual festival begins on the second Friday of the month when the image of the Virgin is brought from its shrine, now housed at the new Our Lady of Peñafrancia Basilica, the successor to that chapel originally constructed early in the 18th century, to the Naga Cathedral, where it will rest for the next week. For this transfer of the image, the faithful will line the river bank or take to a boat as the route from the shrine to cathedral follows the river through the city, and the virgin will ride on a flatboat decorated for the occasion. During the nine days in the cathedral, each evening will be the occasion of a special nine-day service of prayer (what is termed a novena). The country's elite compete for the privilege of sponsoring one of the evening prayer sessions.

After nine days as the focus of attention in town, Our Lady of Peñafrancia is returned to her shrine, again using the river as her highway. This evening procession will be lit by thousands of candles from followers along the shore and in their own boats following the Virgin's vessel. As the Virgin passes cries of "Viva la Virgen" ("Long live the Virgin!") will echo through the city. Once it reaches the shrine, a group of selected parishioners will lovingly carry it from the riverbank to the shrine, where it will be formally received with a liturgy led by high-ranking church officials from around the country.

In September 2010, the Shrine of Our Lady of Peñafrancia celebrated its 300th year as the place of devotion to the Virgin. The celebration at Peñafrancia is one of two main festivals to the virgin, the other being the Feast of Our Lady of Peace and Good Voyage held annually in May in Antiplolo, in suburban Manila.

In the 19th century, the devotion to Our Lady of Peñafrancia was bolstered by the donation of a cloth image of Jesus, the Divino Rostro, to the chapel of Peñafrancia. That image subsequently has become a secondary focus of devotion, and it accompanies the Virgin as she moves about during the festival.

J. Gordon Melton

See also Devotion to; Divino Rostro; Peace and Good Voyage, Feast of Our Lady of.

References

"The Image of Our Lady of Peñafrancia." Our Lady of Peñafrancia Basilica. Posted at http://www.penafrancia.net/about.html. Accessed on April 15, 2010.

Penitentes

The Penitentes, or Los Hermanos Penitentes, is an association of American Roman Catholics whose members reside in northern New Mexico and southern Colorado, and who have become well known for their realistic reenactment of the events surrounding the crucifixion of Jesus each year during Holy Week. This rather extreme practice of penance is performed in an effort to make reparation for their sins. Their observance of Holy Week includes various forms of bodily mortification, especially flagellation.

The practices of the Penitentes have been traced back to the medieval flagellants, specifically to the Third Order of Franciscans founded by Saint Francis of Assisi in the 13th century. Unlike the brothers and sisters of the first and second orders of Franciscans, the Third Order were lay believers who continued to live a secular life but showed their commitments to Christ through a set of strict disciplines. That the group was early on called the Order of Penitents indicates the priority assigned to various penitential actions as vital elements in the discipline. The Order of Penitents was but one of a number of penitential groups to emerge in this era and who have continued to operate, though their current practices are considerable less extreme than those recorded in medieval times.

Meanwhile, in New Mexico beginning in the 16th century, the Franciscans emerged as a powerful force in the expansion and maintenance of the Catholic Church for three centuries. However, through the early 19th century, as the territory passed from Spanish to Mexican and then American hands, the Franciscan leadership lost much of its power, and its presence was considerably reduced. The Penitentes arose, in part, to fill the vacuum of leadership, especially in areas with little or no pastoral care.

The Penitentes were organized as a decentralized association of a set of locally autonomous groups. Each local fraternity selects its own officers, with the *hermano mayor* or elder brother given extensive authority. The elder brother usually holds office until his death. A very few women have been admitted to a female auxiliary; however, the group remains basically an all-male association.

Penitence is practiced year-round, but activity peaks during Holy Week each year. It is during this time, for example, that new members are admitted to the group. The initiation ceremony occurs in the *morada* or council house. After satisfactorily answering a set of questions, the candidate proceeds to wash the feet of the other members, receives lashes from any members whom he may have offended in the past, and finally receives an incision in the shape of the cross on his lower back.

The most important events occur on Good Friday (the day commemorating Christ's death in the Christian calendar), during which members reenact Christ's march to Golgotha, where he was crucified. In the Penitente process, most members would flagellate themselves. Leading their procession would be one or more people carrying a heavy cross. The procession culminates in planting of the cross (es) in the ground and the lashing of one of the members to it. Though this part of the ceremonies was usually conducted in private, over the years, nonmembers have been present and observed it. In more recent years, the event was photographed and even a documentary film made of it.

The Catholic Church officially distanced itself from the Penitentes and, on several occasions, attempted to suppress it. As early as 1886, the archbishop of Santa

Fe, for example, ordered the groups to stop flagellation and the carrying of the crosses. He distributed copies of the contemporary rules of the Franciscan Third Order and requested them to reformulate their activity in accordance with it. The members of the groups largely ignored him. More recent attempts to disband or reform the movement have not worked, and it continues to operate to the present day. In recent years, large crowds have gathered at sites where the group observes its Holy Week activities to observe the processions.

J. Gordon Melton

See also Easter; Elevation of the True Cross; Good Friday; Holy Week; Maundy Thursday; Procession de la Penitencia, La (Spain); Procession of Penitents; Procession of the Fujenti.

References

Ahlborn, Richard E. *The Penitente Moradas of Abiquiú*. Washington, DC: Smithsonian Institution Press, 1986.

Carroll, Michael P. *The Penitente Brotherhood: Patriarchy and Hispano-Catholicism in New Mexico*. Baltimore: Johns Hopkins University Press, 2002.

Henderson, Alice Corbin. *Brothers of Light: The Penitentes of the Southwest*. New York: Harcourt, Brace & Company, 1937.

Weigle, Marta. *Brothers of Light, Brothers of Blood: The Penitentes of the Southwest*. Albuquerque: University of New Mexico Press, 1976.

Weigle, Marta. *A Penitente Bibliography*. Albuquerque: University of New Mexico Press, 1976.

Pentecost

Pentecost is the festival that marks the birth of the Christian church by the power of the Holy Spirit as recorded in the biblical book of the Acts of the Apostles 2:1–41. The word "Pentecost" means "50th day" and is celebrated 50 days after Easter. Because the timing of Pentecost is tied to the moveable date of Easter, it can occur as early as May 10 and as late as June 13.

The Christian feast of Pentecost originated in the Jewish festival that began on the 50th day after the beginning of Passover (Pesach). It is called the Feast of Weeks (Shavuot) and was originally an agricultural festival celebrating and giving thanks for the "first fruits" of the early spring harvest (Leviticus 23 and Exodus 23, 34). By the early New Testament period, it had gradually lost its association with agriculture and became associated with the celebration of God's creation of his people and their religious history. By the destruction of Jerusalem in 70 CE, the festival focused exclusively on God's gift of *Torah* (the "Law") on Mount Sinai.

According to the account in Acts, 10 days after Jesus ascended into heaven, the apostles gathered together in Jerusalem for the Jewish harvest festival. The day has significance in the history of the Christian church, whose members began to see the events of the day as the time God sent the outpouring of the Holy Spirit promised through the prophet Joel (Joel 2:28–29).

Pope Benedict XVI sprinkles holy water during the Pentecost Mass at Saint Peter's Basilica in Rome on May 23, 2010. (AP/Wide World Photos)

Pentecost is also called "Whitsunday" because in ancient times, it was customary to baptize adult converts on Pentecost. The catechumens would wear white robes on that day, so Pentecost was often called "Whitsunday" or "White Sunday." Consequently, the present-day rite of confirmation is still often celebrated on Pentecost.

The feast of Pentecost is universally celebrated in the Christian church, though the liturgical practices are not as extensive and well-known as the greater feasts of Easter and Christmas, for example. The church fathers Iraneaus and Tertullian attest to its celebration in apostolic times.

In Italy, it is customary to scatter rose leaves from the ceiling of the churches to recall the miracle of the fiery tongues. In France, celebrants will blow trumpets during the service to recall the sound of the mighty wind, which accompanied the giving of the Spirit. The Eastern Orthodox carries flowers and green branches in their hands to mark the day.

Red is the liturgical color for Pentecost. Red recalls the tongues of flame in which the Holy Spirit descended on the first Pentecost. The color red also signifies the blood of the martyrs who, by the power of the Holy Spirit, held firm to the true faith even at the cost of their lives.

Pentecost represents God's gracious, enabling presence actively at work among his people, calling and enabling them to live out in dynamic ways their witness. For Christians, Pentecost Sunday is a day to celebrate hope evoked by the knowledge that God through his Holy Spirit is at work among his people. It is a celebration of newness, of recreation, of renewal of purpose, mission, and calling as God's people. It is a celebration of God's ongoing work in the world. Yet, it is also a recognition that his work is done through his people as he pours out his presence upon them.

Kevin Quast

See also Christmas; Easter; Pesach; Shavuot.

References

Adam, Adolf. *The Liturgical Year: Its History and Its Meaning after the Reform of the Liturgy*. New York: Pueblo, 1981.

Harrington, Daniel J. "Pentecost Past and Present." *America*, May 29, 2006.

Holweck, Frederick. "Pentecost (Whitsunday)." *The Catholic Encyclopedia*, Vol. 15. New York: Robert Appleton Company, 1912.

Stookey, Laurence Hull. *Calendar: Christ's Time for the Church*. Nashville, TN: Abingdon, 1996.

Talley, Thomas J. *The Origins of the Liturgical Year*. 2nd ed. Collegeville, MN: Liturgical Press, 1991.

Perpetual Help, Feast of Our Lady of

In contrast to Eastern Orthodox churches, icons are not among more common items in the Roman Catholic Church, though not unknown. It is also the case that the most well-known icon among Roman Catholics has an Eastern Orthodox origin, having originated on the island of Crete. As the story goes, a merchant stole the icon from a church around 1495 and brought it with him to Rome. He was not able to enjoy the picture for long, as he became ill; and as he was dying, he forced a promise from a friend to return the painting to its original home. The friend's wife rejected that notion as she liked the beautiful painting.

Eventually, the six-year-old daughter of the merchant's friend experienced an apparition of the Virgin who told her that the icon should be given to the Church of Saint Matthew the Apostle, located between the churches of Santa Maria Maggiore and Saint John Lateran, and placed on public view. Most importantly, as she spoke to the young girl, she identified herself as Holy Mary of Perpetual Help.

The picture was formally installed at Saint Matthew's on March 27, 1499. It remained under the care of the Augustinian priests in charge of the church until 1798, when the French invaded Rome. Saint Matthew's was one of the buildings destroyed by the invading forces. Fortunately, the icon was taken out of the church before the army arrived and quietly hidden away at an Augustinian chapel away from the city. There it remained for the next six decades, largely forgotten.

Little thought was given to the icon until 1863, when Fr. Francis Blosi, a Jesuit priest, raised the issue. His words reached the ears of Fr. Michael Marchi, a Redemptorist priest, who happened to have visited the chapel then housing the icon. It was also the case that the Redemptorist order had purchased the land upon which Saint Matthew's was previously located and erected a new building, the Church of the Most Holy Redeemer and of Saint Alphonsus. The story of the missing icon was presented to Pope Pius IX (r. 1846–1878), who ordered the Augustinians to turn the icon over to the Redemptorists so it could be installed in the new Church of Saint Alphonsus.

The icon was returned to Rome in 1866 and formally crowned the next year. June 27 was designated as the feast day of Our Lady of Perpetual Help. A confraternity was formed and soon elevated to archconfraternity status. The piety surrounding the icon had grown steadily through the 20th century to the present. Both a litany and novena to Our Lady of Perpetual Help are widely circulated. Among the many churches now dedicated to Our Lady of Perpetual Help are the cathedrals in Oklahoma City, Oklahoma, and in Rapid City, South Dakota.

J. Gordon Melton

See also Czestochowa, Feast of Our Lady of; Image Not-Made-by-Hands, Feast of the.

References

Connell, Francis J. *Our Lady of Perpetual Help*. Pamphlet, Loreto Publications, 2006.

Dodds, Monica, and Bill Dodds. *Encyclopedia of Mary*. Huntington, IN: Our Sunday Visitor, 2007.

Londono, Noel, ed. *Our Lady of Perpetual Help: The Icon, Favors, and Shrines*. Liguori, MO: Liguori Publications, 1998.

Pitzer, Raymond J. *The Miraculous Image of Our Mother of Perpetual Help*. Brooklyn, NY: Perpetual Help Redemptorist Fathers, 1954.

Pesach

Pesach, the Hebrew name of what in English is termed Passover, is a major festival in the Jewish ritual year. Pesach calls to memory major events in the Exodus of the Hebrew people from Egypt and the establishment of Judaism. The events are recorded in the opening chapters of the book of Exodus in the Jewish Bible (the Christian Old Testament), but especially chapter 12. According to the story, Moses, who had escaped Egypt after killing a brutal Egyptian slave master, returned to Pharaoh's court with a demand that the Hebrews be allowed to leave Israel. When Pharaoh refused, he threatened calamities, and successively a set of plagues hit the land.

Unmoved by the plagues, the still-stubborn Pharaoh was hit with one final plague. God threatened to move among the Egyptians and strike the firstborn in each house with death, including the heir to the throne. Speaking on God's behalf, Moses then instructed the Hebrews to take a lamb free of blemishes and on the appointed day kill it. He then instructed that:

> [T]hey shall take of the blood, and put it on the two side-posts and on the lintel, upon the houses wherein they shall eat it. And they shall eat the flesh in that night, roast with fire, and unleavened bread; with bitter herbs they shall eat it. Eat not of it raw, nor sodden at all with water, but roast with fire; its head with its legs and with the inwards thereof. And ye shall let nothing of

> it remain until the morning; but that which remaineth of it until the morning ye shall burn with fire. And thus shall ye eat it: with your loins girded, your shoes on your feet, and your staff in your hand; and ye shall eat it in haste—it is the LORD'S passover. For I will go through the land of Egypt in that night, and will smite all the first-born in the land of Egypt, both man and beast; and against all the gods of Egypt I will execute judgments: I am the LORD. And the blood shall be to you for a token upon the houses where ye are; and when I see the blood, I will pass over you, and there shall no plague be upon you to destroy you, when I smite the land of Egypt. (Exodus 12:7–13)

In the wake of the deaths, Pharaoh relented and the Hebrew left Egypt, crossed the Red Sea, and found their way to Mount Sinai, where God gave them the law. Pharaoh's army being destroyed when it attempted to pursue the Hebrew, there was no attempt to return them to Egypt in the years ahead in the Sinai.

In the giving of the instructions for the Hebrews to kill the lamb, mark their homes with blood, cook the lamb, and consume it, Moses also underscored the importance of the events by telling the Hebrew to set up their calendar with these events marking the first month, to prepare to repeat the events annually forever as a means of remembering what had happened. After the Exodus had begun, the Hebrews were told that the annual remembrance of Pesach would be for seven days (Exodus 13:6). Further details would be added later.

Through the centuries, the events would be remembered. Throughout the Jewish Bible, God would be spoken of as the "the LORD your God, who brought you up out of Egypt." The events of the Exodus are recalled in the daily morning and evening prayers and tied to the prayer shawl and the *tefillin* worn on the Sabbath.

The celebration of Pesach carried with it the setting of the Jewish calendar to begin in the spring, in what is now termed the month of Nissan. However, in the sixth century BCE, during the Babylonia exile, New Year's was moved to the fall. Today, some speak of the religious year beginning Nissan 1 and the civil year beginning Tishri 1. In either case, should Nissan 1 occur too early (before the spring equinox), an intercalary year is added immediately before the month of Nissan. Passover is a weeklong festival (seven days for Reformed Jews and eight days for Conservative and Orthodox Jews) that begins on Nissan 14.

Pesach, along with Shavuot and Sukkot, was one of the three pilgrim festivals during which the entire Jewish community made a pilgrimage to Jerusalem where access to the temple was available. The destruction of the temple and the scattering of the Jewish people thus had a marked effect upon the way that the three festivals can and are celebrated. The Samaritans, a sect with Jewish origins, still make pilgrimages for these festivals to Mount Gerizim, though only males engage in public worship.

In celebrating Pesach, the Jewish attempt both to remember the events and to symbolically reenact them, and thus come from the festival feeling as if they had just been delivered from bondage. In preparation for the Pesach, houses will be cleaned to make sure that no leavening is in the home. During the week, only matzah bread, unleavened bread made simply and quickly, is an acceptable form of grain product for consumption. When the Exodus began, there was no time to wait for the bread to rise. For this reason, Pesach is often called the Feast of Unleavened Bread. Orthodox Jews will have a separate set of dishes for use during Pesach. Products for Pesach will be especially designated in stores that serve or sell Jewish "kosher" foods.

On the first two evenings of Passover (Nissan 15 and 16), a special ritual feast, the Seder, is held in the home. Guests are invited and included in the celebration where possible. The ritual for the occasion consists primarily of retelling the Exodus deliverance story, especially for the children, recalling Exodus 12:26–27: "And it shall come to pass, when your children shall say unto you: What mean ye by this service? that ye shall say: It is the sacrifice of the LORD'S passover, for that He passed over the houses of the children of Israel in Egypt, when He smote the Egyptians, and delivered our houses." At key pints in the story, the children and youth take the lead in directing the story, and as it begins, the youngest child asks, "Why is this night different from all other nights of the year?"

The Seder service also includes the blessing and consumption of wine—four cups symbolic of the fourfold redemption recounted in Exodus 6:6: "I am the LORD, and I will *bring you out* from under the burdens of the Egyptians, and I will *deliver you* from their bondage, and I will *redeem you* with an outstretched arm, and with great judgments; **7** and I will *take you to Me* for a people." Also, a fifth cup is poured, symbolizing that God's promise of returning his people to their homeland remains unfulfilled. Traditionally, the wine in this cup is not drunk. It is often called Elijah's cup, as the prophet Elijah is supposed to usher in the messianic age. Since the founding of the state of Israel, many Jews look upon the cup as symbolic of a promise that is beginning to be fulfilled, and will sip from Elijah's cup.

As recounted in the instructions instituting Pesach, bitter herbs are eaten with the meal, symbolic of the bitterness of slavery. A mixture of chopped nuts, apple, cinnamon, and wine symbolizes the mortar used in the building projects of the Pharaoh at which the Hebrews labored. A roasted shank bone is placed on the Seder table, but not eaten. It is a reminder of the temple, now destroyed, where the paschal lamb for the Passover meal was sacrificed. Since the destruction of the temple, no paschal lamb can be sacrificed. Thus the Seder ends with the proclamation, "Next year in Jerusalem!"

Contemporary Jews see the liberation-from-bondage theme of Pesach as having great relevance for the Jewish presence in the larger social realm. Jews have been prominent through the 20th century in the struggles to free the Jewish community from the effects of prejudice, and in the struggle have generalized their condition to other groups with whom they share a history of slavery, persecution, and discrimination.

In Israel, Passover is observed as a seven-day holiday. The first and last days are recognized as legal holidays. Within the religious community, these days are considered holy days that should be marked by abstention from work and religious services, especially those surrounding the Seder meals. The middle days of Pesach are known as Chol HaMoed, or festival days.

Passover and Christianity

Of all the Jewish holy days, Pesach has had the most effect on Christianity. Jesus's death was associated with Passover, and Christ was described as the pascal lamb. The setting of the dates of the Christian holy week culminating in Easter is based on the date of Passover. In the 20th century, some Christian groups, primarily out of the Adventist tradition, began to celebrate the Feast of Unleavened Bread as a primary Christian festival. In a different vein, Messianic Jews, consisting of Jews and others who follow Jewish culture, have also instituted the practice of celebrating a Christian Passover. The Christian relation to Pesach is discussed in a separate entry on Passover.

J. Gordon Melton

See also Calendars, Religious; Passover; Shavuot; Spring Equinox (Thelema); Spring Equinox (Vernal); Sukkot.

References

Bloch, Abraham P. *The Biblical and Historical Background of Jewish Customs and Ceremonies*. New York: KTAV Publishing House, Inc., 1980.

Eckstein, Yecheil. *What You Should Know about Jews and Judaism*. Waco, TX: Word Books, 1984.

Greenberg, Irving. *The Jewish Way: Living the Holidays*. New York: Jason Aronson, 1998.

Posner, Raphael, Uri Kaploun, and Sherman Cohen, eds. *Jewish Liturgy: Prayer and Synagogue Service through the Ages*. New York: Leon Amiel Publisher; Jerusalem: Keter Publishing House, 1975.

Schauss, Hayyim. *The Jewish Festivals: A Guide to Their History and Observance*. New York: Schocken, 1996.

Peter and Paul, Saint's Day of Sts. (July 29)

Among the earliest of commemorations known to have been celebrated in the ancient church was a commemoration of what were acknowledged to be the two most important of the apostles. To quell any bickering over which one of the two was more worthy, and in the belief that each was martyred on the same day (July 29)—and some say the same year (67 CE)—their feast day was established on the same day. Thus, they were proclaimed to be equal in the eyes of the church.

Peter, one of the first called, had emerged as the leader of the 12 apostles that gathered around Jesus. He is also the person to whom Jesus spoke in the face of Peter's affirmation of Jesus as the Messiah:

He said unto them, "But who say ye that I am?" And Simon Peter answered and said, "You are the Christ, the Son of the living God."

And Jesus answered and said unto him, "Blessed are you, Simon Bar-jonah: for flesh and blood hath not revealed it unto you, but my Father who is in heaven. And I also say unto you, that you are Peter, and upon this rock I will build my church; and the gates of Hades shall not prevail against it. I will give unto you the keys of the kingdom of heaven: and whatsoever you shall bind on earth shall be bound in heaven; and whatsoever you shall loose on earth shall be loosed in heaven." Then he charged the disciples that they should tell no man that he was the Christ. (Matthew 16:15–20)

Jesus Christ gives the keys to the Kingdom of Heaven to Saint Peter. (Library of Congress)

Peter was believed to have been martyred in Rome, and this charge to Peter and the apostles would later become the basis of asserting the primacy of the Diocese of Rome, which cites Peter as its first bishop. Peter is also believed to be buried under what is now Saint Peter's Basilica.

Paul emerged after Jesus's death and resurrection as an "apostle out of season," having not known Jesus after the flesh. He asserted his place among the apostles as a result of his encounter on the road to Damascus, as recounted in the ninth chapter of the New Testament Book of the Acts of the Apostles. Following his dramatic conversion to Christianity, he was responsible for the spread of the church around the Mediterranean Basin. The many epistles that he wrote to the churches he founded and the people associated with him form a major block of the New Testament writings.

While the Book of Acts ends before describing his death, tradition has placed his death in Rome and his burial just outside the old city. The present Basilica of Saint Paul Outside the Walls rests on what is believed to be his burial site. It is the successor building to the original basilica erected by the emperor Constantine. The heads of both Peter and Paul are said to be preserved at the church of Saint John Lateran in Rome.

The church commemorated the martyrdom of Peter and Paul by the third century. In the Eastern Orthodox churches, the day concludes a several-week fast that began on the second Monday after Pentecost, The Apostles' fast concludes with an all-night prayer vigil on evening of June 28. In recent years, the day has been a time of ecumenical contact between Roman Catholic leadership and that of the Ecumenical Patriarchate.

Each year on the Feast of Saint Agnes (January 21), the Trappist monastery in Rome selects two lambs which are taken to the Basilica of Saint Agnes for a blessing ceremony. The lambs are then taken for an appearance before the pope and then given to the Benedictine nuns at the church dedicated to the martyr Santa Cecilia in Rome. The nuns care for the lambs until Maundy Thursday, during Holy Week, when the lambs are sheared of their wool. Their wool is then used to make a pallium, a unique of ecclesiastical garb which only the pope and archbishops (and on rare occasion, a bishop) are allowed to wear them. The pallium is a sign of episcopal authority, and until he receives his pallium from the pope, an archbishop cannot exercise jurisdiction over his assigned territory. Each year on the day commemorating the martyrdom of Peter and Paul, the pope presents the pallium to the Roman Catholic Church's new archbishops (as well as to those who might be changing jurisdictions).

The Doukhobors, a Russian free church movement, saw the Feast of Saint Peter and Saint Paul as a day of celebration. At the same time, through the 19th century, the group was the target of constant persecution due to its pacifism and refusal to bear arms on behalf of the Russian army. The increased pressure on the group in the 1890s led them, on the evening of Saints Peter and Paul Day in 1895 to conduct a symbolic destruction of all the weapons they had among them. This event of the "Burning of the Arms" is currently celebrated as Peter's Day, sometimes called Doukhobor Peace Day.

J. Gordon Melton

See also Chair of St. Peter, Feast of the; Conversion of St. Paul, Feast of the; Peter and Paul, Saint's Day of Sts.

References

Barnes, Arthur Stapylton. *St. Peter in Rome and His Tomb on the Vatican Hill.* Whitefish, MT: Kessinger Publishing, 1900, 2007.

Peter Baptist and Companions, Saint's Day of St. (February 6)

Sometimes overshadowed by Francis Xavier, who was the first Roman Catholic priest to visit Japan, Peter Baptist (1542–1597) was a pioneering Franciscan missionary who followed up on the work Francis had initiated. Peter Baptist Blasquez, born to a noble Spanish family, joined the Franciscans in 1567. Caught up in the 16th-century international expansion of the order, he was initially sent to Mexico and then assigned to work in the Philippine Islands, which set him in place in

1592 when Philip II of Spain (r. 1554–1598), who also at the time ruled Portugal, needed someone to negotiate a peace agreement with Taiko Toyotomi Hideyoshi, the ruler of Japan.

After working out the peace treaty, Peter Baptist and several colleagues stayed in Japan to spread Christianity. Their success, which included establishing both churches and hospitals, threatened Hideyoshi to the point that in December 1596, he moved against the missionaries. Peter Baptist and 25 others, both Franciscans and Jesuits, were tossed into prison. In January 1597, they were condemned to death. They were subsequently moved to Nagasaki, where they were executed by crucifixion on February 5. During the process, each had had an ear cut off and was stabbed with a spear in a parody of events during Jesus's final week as recounted in the Christian New Testament.

Peter Baptist was beatified in 1627, and he and his companions were canonized as a group in 1862. He is among the patron saints of Japan.

J. Gordon Melton

See also Forty Martyrs' Day; Francis Xavier, Saint's Day of St.; Jogues, John de Brébeuf and Companions, Saint's Day of St. Isaac.

References

Cary, Otis. *A History of Christianity in Japan: Roman Catholic. Greek Orthodox, and Protestant Missions*. Rutland, VT: Charles E. Tuttle, 1987.

Fujita, Neil S. *Japan's Encounter with Christianity: The Catholic Mission in Pre-Modern Japan*. Mahwah, NJ: Paulist Press, 1991.

Peter Chanel, Saint's Day of St. (April 28)

Pierre Louis Marie Chanel (1803–1841), born in La Potière, France, grew up in a pious environment and became a Roman Catholic priest. He developed a desire to become a foreign missionary but, following his ordination in 1827, seemed continually channeled in other directions. In 1831, he learned of a group of parish priests who were planning a new religious order dedicated to the Blessed Virgin Mary. He aligned with them and became a founding member of the Society of Mary (popularly known as the Marists). Six years later, when the new order received papal approval, he was finally commissioned as a missionary to the South Pacific. The trip to the Pacific took him to Gambier, then Tahiti, with the goal of setting up work in the Wallis and Futuna islands. Chanel settled on Futuna Island, along with a French lay brother, Marie-Nizier Delorme.

Warmly received initially by the island's king, Niuliki, Chanel went about the task of learning the language and establishing a small mission. As the king learned about Christianity, rather than being attracted to it, he came to see it as a challenge to his political and religious authority as the leader of the island's people. The crisis came several years after Chanel settled on Futura. The king's son, Meitala, converted and sought baptism. On learning of his son's intention, Niuliki sent his son-in-law, Musumusu, to attempt to resolve the issue. Musumusu got into a fight with Meitala and was injured. On April 28, 1841, he went to Chanel for medical attention, but while there, he took an axe and killed Chanel and dismembered his body.

In January of the following year, it taking some months for word to circulate of Chanel's death, French authorities retrieved his remains, and they were taken to New Zealand. In 1850, they were returned to France, to the Society of Mary's motherhouse in Lyon. Meanwhile, the majority of Futura residents became Roman Catholics, and it remains the majority religion. After converting, the people of Futura created a penitential dance called the *eke*, in Chanel's memory.

Chanel was beatified in 1889 and canonized in 1954. His feast day is April 28. In 1977, his relics were returned to Futuna. He was named the patron saint of Oceania.

J. Gordon Melton

See also White Sunday.

References

Chanel, Peter. *Ever Your Poor Brother Peter Chanel: Surviving Letters and Futuna Journal*. Translated by William Joseph Stuart. Rome: APM, 1991.

Gilmore, Florence. *The Martyr of Futuna: Blessed Peter Chanel of the Society of Mary.* Maryknoll, NY: Catholic Foreign Mission Society of America, 1917.

Symes, W. J. *The Life of St. Peter Chanel: 1803–1841*. Bolton: Catholic Printing Co., 1963.

Peter Claver, Saint's Day of St. (September 9)

Saint Peter Claver (1581–1654) was born and raised in Spain, and as a young man joined the Society of Jesus (the Jesuits). He was still in his 20s when in 1610 he left Europe for the Americas. He settled in Cartagena (Colombia), and there completed his studies and was ordained as a Roman Catholic priest (1615). Cartagena was a center for the slave trade, and Claver was among those who responded to Pope Paul III's (r. 1534–1549) bull against slavery in 1537. Similarly, his predecessor, Alfonso de Sandoval, also a Jesuit, had worked with the slaves for four decades prior to Claver's arrival in Cartagena. Claver became known for his own self-identification as "the slave of the Negroes forever." Claver moved among the slaves, especially those on the waterfront, and brought them food and medicines. By both word and deed, he attempted to bring them the church's teachings and an understanding of their status as people of dignity and worth. During his several decades of activity, it is estimated that he baptized some 300,000 Africans. His fellow Spaniards came to know him as the person who would visit the plantations developing in the interior and stay with the slaves in their quarters rather than the lodging offered by the owners.

His health declined as the 1850s began, and he was forced into inactivity for the last years of his life. He died on September 8, 1654. He was rediscovered amid the slaver debates of the 19th century, beatified in 1850, and canonized in 1888. Pope Leo XIII (r. 1878–1903) declared him the worldwide patron of missionary work among black slaves. Today he is one of the patron saints of Colombia and of African Americans.

J. Gordon Melton

See also Benedict the African, Saint's Day of St.; Martin de Porres, Saint's Day of St.

References

Cassidy, J. F. *St. Peter Claver.* Langley, Slough, Bucks, UK: St. Paul Publications, 1968.

Lunn, Arnold. *A Saint in the Slave Trade: Peter Claver (1581–1654).* New York: Sheed and Ward, 1935.

Valtierra, Angel. *Peter Claver: Saint of the Slaves.* Westminster, MD: Newman Press, 1960.

Peter of Alcantara, Saint's Day of St. (October 19)

Peter of Alcantara (1499–1562) was a Spanish Franciscan friar born at Alcantara, Spain, into a well-to-do noble family. He was given a good education at the University of Salamanca, after which he joined the Franciscans of the Stricter Observance (1515). In 1521, he founded a new community of the Stricter Observance at Badajoz, near the border with Portugal. He was ordained two years later. His career was now marked by his own strict practice of the stricter observance, the severity under which he lived and attempted to communicate to other proving continued opposition. Named a superior of a Franciscan province in 1538, he resigned from that position two years later. He retired to a mountain retreat in Portugal. Over the next years, a number of friars were attracted to him and small communities began to emerge. They emerged as a new Province of Arrábida in 1560.

In 1555, he walked to Rome barefooted to gain the permission of Pope Julius III (r. 1550–1555) to found some new centers in Spain. Several emerged in the next year and became the basis of a new Province of Saint Joseph. The extreme rules spread to other Franciscan centers in Spain and Portugal leading to their reformation (this at the time that Protestantism was thriving in northern Europe). At this time, Peter made common cause with Theresa of Avila, who was working a similar reformation among the Carmelites. It appears that a letter from Peter (dated April 14, 1562) occasioned the founding of her convent at Avila that year. In fact, it is from Saint Teresa's autobiography that we know of much of Peter's life.

Peter led an extremely austere life and made his home in a room with a floor area of only four and a half square feet. He was often seen in prayer and ecstasies, and on occasion was reported to have levitated. He died October 18, 1562, in a monastery at Arenas, not far from Avila.

Peter of Alcantara was beatified in 1622 and canonized in 1669. His feast day is October 19, the day of his death being already assigned to Saint Luke the Evangelist. He is one of the patron saints of Brazil, but that status did not prevent his name from being removed from the list of saints acknowledged by the general church in 1969, meaning that his veneration is now a matter that is optional and local.

J. Gordon Melton

See also Anthony of Padua, Saint's Day of St.; Benedict the African, Saint's Day of St.

References

Muller, Gerald. *Peter Laughed at Pain: A Story of St. Peter of Alcantara.* Notre Dame, IN: Dujarie Press, 1956.

Peter of Alcantara, Saint. *Treatise on Prayer and Meditation.* Charlotte, NC: Tan Books and Publishers, 2008.

Theresa of Avila. *The Autobiography of St. Teresa of Avila.* New York: Image, 1960.

Phagwa. *See* Holi

Phang Lhabsol

Phang Lhabsol is a Buddhist festival unique to Sikkim, a formerly independent state now a part of modern India and adjacent to Tibet. The Buddhism practiced there closely resembles the Vajrayana Buddhism of Tibet. This festival focuses on Mount Khangchendzonga, a spectacular multi-peaked mountain that is regarded as the protective guardian deity of Sikkim. In the festival, supplication is made to the mountain for continued protection from a variety of possible natural calamities, and the necessities for a good harvest.

The celebration of Phang Lhabsol is traced to a treaty signed by Thekong Tek, a priest of the Lepcha people of Sikkim (who shared ancestry with the Tibetans), and Kaye Bhumsa, who ruled the Kham region of Tibet. According to the story, Kaye Bhumsa and his wife Chomo Guru were childless. The lama priests of Kham advised his seeking out Thekong Tek and his wife Nekong Ngyal and receive their blessing, which he did. Over the next few years, three male children were born by his wife. Kaye Bhumsa made a return visit to Sikkim to thank Thekong and his wife for their blessing and offered his pledge that their two peoples would remain brothers forever. A document embodying this agreement was signed at Kabi Longstok, at the foot of Mount Khangchendzonga, some 10 miles from Gangtok. The annual celebration of Phang Lhabsol acknowledges the mountain as the only witness to the signing of the agreement. A large stone marked the spot, and a Statue of Unity was erected in commemoration of this brotherhood treaty, which remains in force to the present.

Highlighting the celebration are the many dances, including the tradition Tibetan chaam dancing by the monks. There is, for example, a warrior dance distinguished by its intricate steps and leaping dancers shouting out war cries. The joy of the occasion is portrayed in a dance in which one monk dresses as Mount Khangchendzonga and another as Mahakala, a Dharma protector deity. Around 1700, the then-king of Sikkim Chogyal Chakdor Namgyal had a dream in which an angel visited him and he learned a new form of dance.

The Phang Lhabsol celebration is held on the 15th day of the seventh month according to Tibetan lunar calendar, which is late August or early September on the Common Era calendar. The celebration was originally held at Rabdenste, the first capital of Sikkim but shifted to the Tsuglakhang Palace at Gangtok, which became the capital in 1894. After the country was absorbed into India, the celebration spread to different locations throughout Sikkim.

J. Gordon Melton

See also Butter Lamp Festival; Chokhor Duchen; Dalai Lama's Birthday; Losar; Monlam, the Great Prayer Festival.

References

"Pang Lhabsol." SikkimOnline. Posted at http://sikkimonline.info/sikkim/Phang_Lhabsol. Accessed March 15, 2010.

Pilgrimage of Sainte Anne d'Auray (July 26)

Sainte Anne d'Auray is a small village in the department of Morbihan in Brittany (France). As Christianity moved into the area, the residents reputedly built a chapel to Saint Anne, the mother of the Blessed Virgin Mary. That chapel was destroyed in the seventh century and it was never rebuilt. Only a passing memory of the chapel remained.

Early in the 17th century, the village's connection to Saint Anne was renewed when a village resident, Yves Nicolazic, reported multiple apparitions of Saint Anne during which, on July 25, 1624, he was instructed to rebuild the chapel. On March 7, 1625, Nicolazic and some companions miraculously discovered what they believed to be the statue from the original chapel. Sebastien de Rosmadec, the bishop of Vannes, in whose diocese the village is located, became convinced of the genuineness of the apparitions and allowed the chapel project to go forward. Once completed, both Anne of Austria (1601–1666) and Louis XIII (1601–1643) contributed to the embellishing of the sanctuary. Included in their gifts was a reputed relic of Saint Anne acquired in the 13th century from Jerusalem.

As the chapel gained in statue, pilgrimages to Sainte Anne d'Auray began, the most important being at Pentecost and on July 26, the Feast Day of Saint Anne. At the time of the French Revolution, the sanctuary was plundered and the Carmelites, into whose care the chapel had been placed, were driven away. In 1793, the old statue of Saint Anne, to which numerous accounts of miracles had been attributed, was burned. In spite of the desecration, the chapel still attracted the faithful.

Once the fury of the revolution died out, some recovery was possible. The Carmelite convent was reoccupied and became a seminary. A new statue of Saint Anne with the Virgin Mary replaced the one that had been destroyed. In 1866, a new basilica began to rise, and in 1868, Pope Pius IX (r. 1846–1878) granted permission for the new statue of Saint Anne to be crowned, a practice he had earlier proposed for statues of the virgin. He also donated the marble for the high altar. The Basilica of Saint Anne has remained the most popular pilgrimage destination in Brittany to the present, more than a half million annually. Pope John Paul II (r. 1978–2005) visited the site in 1996.

Those who come to Sainte Anne D'Auray on pilgrimage plan to spend the entire day of the pilgrimage at the church. They will attend Mass in the early morning and participate in a procession around the church afterwards. This procession will include many who attribute a miraculous escape and hence their life to the saint.

One outgrowth of the pilgrimage to Saint Anne's in Brittany was a pilgrimage gathering that emerged in the late 19th century in western Canada. In 1844, a Catholic mission was established on the shore of a lake in central Alberta, Canada, by Frs. Jean-Baptiste Thibault and Joseph Bourassa. Fr. Thibault named the lake Lac Sainte Anne. The mission was the first permanent Catholic work west of Winnipeg. Later supplied by the Oblates of Mary Immaculate, the mission thrived for a generation but in the 1880s suffered as the buffalo dwindled and the population declined. As the lake seemed no longer to function as a gathering place, by 1887, the decision had been made to close the mission.

At this time, the priest at the mission, a Father Lestanc took a trip back home to France and while there visited the Shrine of Sainte Anne d'Auray. While there, he felt God telling him not to close the mission. Upon his return to Canada, he built a shrine to Saint Anne at the lake and turned it into a place of pilgrimage. The first pilgrimage was scheduled for the summer of 1889. Several hundred attended. Today the shrine continues to draw people each summer for a pilgrimage and gathering for several days in July as close as possible to the feast day on July 26, with as many as 30,000 in attendance, many camping out in tents. It is the largest annual gathering of Native people in Canada.

J. Gordon Melton

See also Anne, Feast Day of St.; Pentecost.

References

Lorenz, Caroline, and Rod Lorenz. "Pilgrimage to Lac Ste. Anne." Posted at http://www.peace.mb.ca/00.Native/nlrnz07.htm. Accessed April 15, 2010.

Nixon, Virginia. *Mary's Mother: Saint Anne in Late Medieval Europe*. University Park: Pennsylvania State University Press, 2004.

Pilgrimage of the Dew

The Romeria del Rocio, or Pilgrimage of the Dew, is a Marian festival over the weekend of Pentecost in the Almonte region of Andalusia, Spain. It focuses upon a relatively modest statue (now almost invisible beneath the elaborate gold covering) of the Blessed Virgin Mary known as La Blanca Paloma, the White Dove, which is found in the Sanctuary of El Rocio, in Almonte. The festival originated in the 15th century after a hunter from the village of Villamanrique came upon a statue of the Virgin in a tree trunk amid the marshes of the Guadalquivir adjacent to what is now the national park of the Coto Donana. For several centuries, the celebration was a purely local affair, but participation slowly grew to become regional and national.

During the week before Pentecost, the roads throughout the region will be clogged with people and ox-drawn wagons. The wagons carry men and women dressed in their finest clothes, and groups of wagons will represent a local brotherhood led by a cart with a banner picturing the Virgin and identifying the group's home base. The walk to Almonte is a time for visiting, self-reflection, and a public demonstration of piety. As evening approaches, a filed or other convenient location will be found to camp out for the evening and celebrate the pilgrimage. The pilgrimage is planned to arrive at their destination on Pentecost, where the crowds will file past the church and pay their initial homage to the Virgin. In the evening, there will be fireworks and celebration into the wee hours.

The climax of the festival occurs on the Monday following Pentecost. The primary event is a massive procession of the statue of the Virgin, which leaves the sanctuary and shrine and is marched through the streets of Almonte. The most privileged of the pilgrims are selected to carry the statue on their shoulders, an honor sought by those hoping for special assistance from the Virgin in the coming year. A cadre of priests lead the procession amid cries of "Viva la Blanca Paloma" heard everywhere. The procession ends with the return of the Virgin to the church's altar. After one more evening of celebration, the pilgrims return to their mundane routines.

J. Gordon Melton

See also Pentecost; Romeria of La Virgen de Valme.

References

"Huelva—The Rocio Pilgrimage." Posted at http://www.andalucia.com/magazine/english/ed2/rocio.htm. Accessed May 15, 2010.

Spicer, Dorothy Gladys. *Festivals of Western Europe*. New York: H. W. Wilson Company, 1958.

Pitra Paksha

Pitra Paksha, observed during the fortnight of the waning moon during the Hindu month of Ashwin (September–October on the Common Era calendar) provides an opportunity for honoring one's recently deceased ancestors. Some Hindus believe that the deceased enter a state of restless wandering in a ghost-like existence without a body. Only after the sacrifice (shraddha) offered during Pitra Paksha do they attain a status among the Divine Father (the Pitris) and a place in the blissful abode known as Pitri-Loka, where they abide for a time before reincarnating. If one's ancestor is in Naraka, the hell realm, the performance of the sacrifice ameliorates their condition.

The offerings and accompanying ritual pujas for one's ancestor is done on the particular day of their death as correlated to a day during the fortnight of the Pitra Paksha. While anyone may do the ritual, it is deemed most proper and efficacious if the eldest son of the family performs it. The puja is followed by a traditional feast offered to the pandits or priest who performs the puja. The puja is normally accompanied by a donation of food, clothing, and/or money to the pandits.

The Pitra Paksha concludes on "Mahalaya Amavasya," the night of the new moon. Ceremonies performed on this day are thought to be of the most benefit to the ancestors. The action initiated during the Pitra Paksha is carried forward on the new moon of each month with a simple ritual called the *pitra tarpan*, a ceremony built around the chanting of mantras seeking peace for the departed souls and accompanying oblation of water.

Constance A. Jones

See also All Saints Day; Chaitra Purnima; Higan; Narak Chaturdashi; Obon Festival(s); Pure Brightness Festival; Samhain; Ullam-bana.

References

Kelly, Aidan, Peter Dresser, and Linda Ross. *Religious Holidays and Calendars*. Detroit, MI: Omnigraphics, 1993.

Sivananda, Swami. *What Becomes of the Soul after Death*. Shivanandanagar, Uttar Pradesh, India: Divine Life Trust Society, 1997.

Pleureuses, Ceremony of. *See* Good Friday

Ploughing Day

Ploughing Day, a Buddhist holiday unique to Thailand, derives from an ancient Hindu Indian day to look forward to a good harvest as the planting season begins.

From India it spread to other Asian countries, including Thailand. However, in Thailand, during the reign of King Rama IV (1804–1868), who also instituted the Magha Puja celebration, reformed the Ploughing Ceremony to align it with Buddhist practice. His new format for the old day also became a two-day ceremony held at the royal grounds (Sanam Luang) in Bangkok. Since the 1960s, the day has again been collapsed into a one-day ceremony held each year in May at the beginning of the rainy season.

The Royal Ploughing Ceremony is designed to encourage all the farmers to do their best for the country as a whole in the production of the rice, which is so vital to the diet. The ceremony begins with a procession led by a high-ranking official of the Ministry of Agriculture and two oxen dressed with golden cloaks and carrying the plough that will be used to perform the ceremony.

A high point in the ceremony is a divination process built around the selection of one of three sarongs, which will indicate factors such as the abundance of water and fertility of the ground. The day proceeds with the symbolic ploughing of three furrows and the planting of rice seeds that are then gathered by the farmer spectators as signs of a coming good harvest. The ceremony culminates with the two oxen being led to a pavilion where they will be offered seven foods. The particular food chosen becomes part of the information to be used by the priests in their formal prediction of the coming harvest. That prediction will, at a later time, be presented to the ruler and to the public.

While obviously a celebration of the agricultural cycle, the Ploughing Ceremony has a peculiarly Buddhist connotation. Most Buddhists think of the Buddha as having been enlightened in his 35th year while sitting under the Bodhi Tree at Bodh Gaya, but there is a quite separate tradition that pictures him as having become enlightened when he was seven years old. At the time, he was watching someone plough a field. It is this tradition, which is alive and well in Thailand, that ties the Ploughing Ceremony to the country's Buddhist community.

J. Gordon Melton

See also Elephant Festival; Kathina Ceremony; Wesak/Vesak.

References

Bagchee, Moni. *Our Buddha*. Kuala Lumpur, Malaysia: Buddhist Missionary Society, 1999.

Irons, Edward A. *Encyclopedia of Buddhism*. New York: Facts on File, 2008.

"Royal Ploughing Ceremony at Sanam Luang." Thai Trave Online. Posted at http://www.thailand-travelonline.com/thailand-activities/culture-of-thailand/royal-ploughing-ceremony-day-at-sanam-luang-bangkok/1049/. Accessed March 15, 2010.

Pongal. *See* Makar Sankranti

Pooram

Pooram is a unique festival of the Indian state of Kerala. Kerala is in turn one of the more unique states of India, having been the place where Christianity first manifested in strength and in which no single form of Hinduism dominates. Bosth Saivite (centered on the deity Shiva) and Vaishnava (centered on the deity Vishnu) are strong, but worship of the Mother Goddess as a manifestation of shakti energy is popular and there are numerous places for worship of the nagas, snake gods. Many have sacred snake groves near to their homes.

Pooram is an annual temple festival held in various locations in Kerala following the summer harvest. The festivals have come to be characterized by the presence of elephants, but on a spiritual level amount to a gathering of the many gods of the thousands of temples in a significant show of Hindu ecumenicity.

The largest and most famous of all Pooram celebrations is held at Thrissur, though this was not always the case. In centuries past, the largest such gathering was at Arattupuzha, some 14 kilometers away. At some point in the later 18th century, however, the participants of the Arattupuzha Pooram were late in arriving for the celebration due to heavy rains that delayed their trip. They were denied entrance to the festival. Offended, the local ruler of Thrissur organized a separate celebration. In 1790, His Highness Ramavarma Raja, popularly known as Sakthan Thampuran (1751–1805) became the Maharaja of Kochi, and he proceeded to put his weight behind the Thrissur Pooram and built it into a mass festival. He organized the festival in its present form in front of Vadakkumnathan, the oldest temple in the area, with the primary participants being the people of the 10 major temples in the area. Over the years, especially since Indian independence, the festival has grown and secularized with professional artists and the use of a cadre of elephants.

The Thrissur Pooram is centered on the Vadakkumnathan Temple, located in the middle of Thrissur and celebrated in the month of Medom on the local calendar (April–May on the Common Era calendar). The 10 temples that officially participate each send several elaborately decorated elephants on processions accompanied by drummers and musicians from their temple to the assembly point at the Vadakkumnathan temple. The 36-hour festival includes parasol displays, dramatic productions, concerts, and a fireworks show that lasts for several hours. Interest in the festival is built by the friendly rivalry of the temples, which are divided geographically into two competing divisions that vie in creating the most spectacular fireworks and the most colorful decoration for the elephants.

Each group may display up to 15 elephants, and the temples attempt to secure the best animals available in southern India for the event. The elephants are in turn richly decorated to serve as the transportation of the deities to be assembled for the festival. The festival reaches its climax at 2:30 in the early morning, with the final fireworks show and the display of the 30 elephants.

There are a number of Pooram celebrations in Kerala, but none match the display of the one at Thrissur.

Constance A. Jones

See also Elephant Festival.

References

Pushpanth, Salim. *Romancing Kerala*. Kottayam, Kerala, India: Dee Bee Info Publications, 2003.

Seth, Pepita. *The Divine Frenzy-Hindu Myths and Rituals of Kerala*. London: Westzone Publishing, 2001.

"Thrissur Pooram." Posted at http://thrissurpooramfestival.com/thrissur_pooram.html. Accessed June 15, 2010.

Posadas, Las

Las Posadas (the Inns) is a nine-day Advent celebration most popularly celebrated in Mexico, which has also spread throughout Latin America and among Spanish-speaking communities in North America. It occurs the nine days immediately before Christmas (December 16–24) and dramatizes the trials faced by Jesus's parents Mary and Joseph in traveling to his birthplace in Bethlehem and locating a place to stay. The celebration is based on the New Testament Gospel of Luke (2:1–7):

> Now it came to pass in those days, there went out a decree from Caesar Augustus, that all the world should be enrolled. This was the first enrolment made when Quirinius was governor of Syria. And all went to enroll themselves, every one to his own city. And Joseph also went up from Galilee, out of the city of Nazareth, into Judaea, to the city of David, which is called Bethlehem, because he was of the house and family of David; to enroll himself with Mary, who was betrothed to him, being great with child. And it came to pass, while they were there, the days were fulfilled that she should be delivered. And she brought forth her firstborn son; and she wrapped him in swaddling clothes, and laid him in a manger, because there was no room for them in the inn.

In this celebration built around the children, the attempt by Mary and Joseph to find a space to stay in Bethlehem is acted out with the children going from house to house while singing an appropriate seasonal song and asking the residents of neighboring houses (who act as innkeepers) for a place to stay. The children carry candles and small statues of Mary, Joseph, and a donkey. Each innkeeper refuses lodging until the children arrive at a prearranged home where they are welcomed in, and a party follows. Once inside, they gather around a nativity scene and offer prayer. The party that follows includes time to break open the colorful paper-maché piñatas.

In any given location, there will be multiple Posadas parties each evening, with each family choosing a night to host the party at their home. On December 24, the festivities will end in time for all to attend the midnight Mass at the local church.

J. Gordon Melton

See also Advent; Christmas.

References

Hoyt-Goldsmith, Diane. *Las Posadas: An Hispanic Christmas Celebration*. New York: Holiday House, 2000 (juvenile text).

Nusom, Lynn. *Christmas in New Mexico: Recipes, Traditions, and Folklore for the Holiday Season*. Phoenix, AZ: Golden West Publishers, 1991.

Poson

Poson is a Buddhist holiday unique to Sri Lanka that commemorates the arrival of Buddhism in the island nation. Prior to the time of King Ashoka's (c. 304–232 BCE) uniting of much of India under his rule, Buddhism had been a relatively small religious movement. Following Asoka's conversion, however, it began a period of rapid expansion. A key event in that expansion, toward the middle of the third century BCE, Asoka sent his son Mahinda, accompanied by a cadre of Buddhist monks, to Sri Lanka. The holiday is celebrated on the full moon near the summer solstice, during what is now the month of June in the Western calendar.

Mahinda is said to have delivered his first discourse to King Devanampiyatissa (c. 250–210 BCE) at Mihintale (the present Missaka Pawwa), located some eight miles from the ancient capital at Anuradhapura. The year 247 BCE is generally accepted as the date of the king's conversion, which came after Mahinda satisfied himself that Devanampiyatissa had mastered the teaching of Buddhism and was a wise ruler. Mahinda would subsequently spend the rest of his life establishing the faith and overseeing the construction of temples across the island. Theravada Buddhism became wedded to Sri Lankan politics and culture. Today, the Sri Lankan constitution requires that the head of state be a Buddhist.

Mahinda was soon joined by his sister Sanghamitta (280–220 BCE). According to the story, Queen Anula, the wife of one of the island's sub-kings, requested Mahinda to accept a nun (a bhiksuni). Since he lacked the power to receive her into the religious life, he requested that his father send Sanghamitta to Sri Lanka, and that she bring with her a branch of the Bodhi Tree, under which Gautama Buddha had received enlightenment. As recorded in the *Mahavamsa*, Sri Lanka's ancient chronicle, Sanghamitta arrived, accompanied by several sister bhiksunis, at Jambukolapattana (today called Point Pedro), and joined in a formal procession to Anuradhapura, where the Bodhi Tree would be planted in a previously prepared spot. In due time, Sanghamitta ordained Anula and a group of 500 women, an important event in the history of Buddhist women. Sri Lankan nuns would later become the source of the movement in China.

Poson is celebrated across Sri Lanka (and among Sri Lankans abroad) with a variety of cultural and religious events, including processions and carnivals. Mihintale and Anuradhapura, where Mahinda is buried, remain the focal points of Buddhist pilgrimage and devotion during Poson time. In addition, Sanghamitta is also honored with her own separate celebration, Sanghamitta Day, celebrated on the full moon in the month of December. Though Buddhism dates its beginning in Sri Lanka with the arrival of Mahinda, according to Sri Lankan tradition, Buddha himself had also visited the island during his earthly lifetime on three occasions—during the fifth month, the fifth year, and eighth year of his enlightenment—and among the country's proudest processions are some relics of the Buddha, especially a tooth kept in a golden stupa at the capital, Kandy, a popular site for celebratory gatherings.

J. Gordon Melton

See also Duruthu Poya; Festival of the Tooth; Sanghamitta Day; Summer Solstice; Wesak/Vesak.

References

Bullis, Douglas, and Thera Mahanama-Sthivara. *The Mahavamsa: The Great Chronicle of Sri Lanka*. Fremont, CA: Asian Humanities Press, 1999.

Geiger, Wilhelm. *The Culavamsa: Being the More Recent Part of the Mahavamsa*. 2 vols. Colombo: Ceylon Government Information Department, 1953.

Gunasekara, Kalasuri Wilfred M. "An Arahat Meets a King." *Sri Lanka Daily News*. 2003. Posted at http://what-buddha-said.net/drops/III/Poson_Poya_artikel1.htm. Accessed March 15, 2010.

Swearer, Donald K. *The Buddhist World of Southeast Asia*. Albany: State University of New York Press, 1995.

Potlatch

The Potlatch is an essential ceremony of the religious life of the Native peoples of the Northwest of the United States, British Columbia, and Alaska. The term "potlatch" is from a word of the Chinook people of Washington State, meaning "to give away." The ceremony serves a spectrum of purposes among the many different people who utilize it. Among the Athabascan people of Alaska, it provides a means of fellowship among the often isolated small groups in which they live and a way of memorializing those who have died. In Washington, it is a means of manifesting wealth in the act of giving it away and thereby of redistributing it.

Those throwing the potlatch will prepare a feast for the attendees and, as the party atmosphere continues, will distribute the majority of their possessions, with some understanding that they will be on the receiving end as each of the attendees in turn throw their own potlatch.

While the giving aspect of potlatches initially attracted the attention of outside observers, the event is a time for a variety of ritualized behavior. Young girls reaching puberty will go through a name-giving ceremony after which they assume a new adult status indicated by their new name. The gathering may also be a time to acknowledge marriages and hold funerals, erect a totem pole or even a new building, or name an heir. The chiefs who attend potlatches would also allow themselves to be possessed by the spirit whose name they bore and, while entranced, offer dances appropriate to that spirit entity.

When a chief (the head of a clan) died, a cycle of potlatches would be initiated. Following the death, there would be eight days of mourning, in the midst of which the body would be cremated. The clan who had lost their chief would be the host, with the members of the other clans attending as guests. The week would be filled with words, songs, and music, and acts of mourning, all of which culminated in a great feast and gift giving by the hosts to those in attendance. At some point in the next year, a new grave house or mortuary pole would be constructed, and a year after the first mourning event, a second one would be held at which representatives of the other clans would officiate at services formally placing the deceased chief's ashes in its new permanent resting place. The immediate kin of the chief would provide the food and gifts for the event, with other clan members assisting in the arrangements. The original clan would again prepare a feast and offer presents for the officiates' services.

These two connected services became a time to affirm the solidarity of all the clans with each other, and their ancestors, whom they believed would be in attendance in spirit. At the second event, the new chief would be recognized, and all would witness the formal name-title transfer to him. This event would also mark the end of the period of formal mourning by the chief's family.

When initially encountered by European explorers, the potlatches were often elaborate affairs lasting several days, but as governmental authority was extended in the region, potlatches were discouraged. The Canadian Indian Act of 1885, passed in part to assist missionaries attempting to eradicate Indian religious practices, included a provision outlawing potlatches and allowing for imprisonment up to two years if convicted. Potlatches became clandestine affairs always conducted under the threat of police intervention. That law remained in force until 1951.

Among the Athabascan people of Alaska, an essential element of potlatches was the supplying of moose meat by the host for the feast. A provision of the Alaska National Interest Lands Conservation Act of 1980 aimed at protecting the moose limited hunting it to specified hunting seasons. In spite of a court ruling placing the hunting of moose for funerary and memorial potlatches under

Indian dancers dress in full costume for a potlatch in Chilkat, Alaska, in 1895. (Library of Congress)

constitutional protections of religious freedom, the authorities have periodically prosecuted and jailed people who killed moose for a potlatch feast.

Today, potlatches continue to be held among groups from Oregon to central Alaska, but are usually small one-day affairs.

J. Gordon Melton

See also Acorn Feast; First Salmon Rites; World Peace and Prayer Day.

References

Barnet, H. G. *The Nature and Function of the Potlatch*. Eugene: University of Oregon, Department of Anthropology, 1968.

Beck, Mary Giraudo. *Potlatch: Native Ceremony and Myth on the Northwest Coast*. Portland, OR: Alaska Northwest Books, 1993.

Hirschfelder, Arlene, and Paulette Molin. *Encyclopedia of Native American Religions*. New York: Facts on File, 2000.

Simone, William E. *Rifles, Blankets and Beads: Identity, History, and the Northern Athapaskan Potlatch*. Norman: University of Oklahoma Press, 2002.

Prabhupada, Appearance Day of A. C. Bhaktivedanta Swami

A. C. Bhaktivedanta Swami Prabhupada (1896–1977) founded the International Society for Krishna Consciousness, which in the last half of the 20th century emerged as the primary organization bringing devotional (bhakti) Vaishnavaism to the Western world.

He was born in Calcutta, India, on what on the Western calendar was September 1, 1896. He later attended the University of Calcutta. Though inclined to the religious life, he bowed to his father's wishes and married and began life as a businessman. Meanwhile, he became a lay follower of the Gaudiya Vaishnava Society and practiced the Bhakti ("devotional") worship of Vishnu's incarnation as Krishna, in the form by Chaitanya Mahaprabhu (1486–1534), a Bengali saint of the 16th century. Krishna's life is described in the Hindu scriptural texts Bhagavad Gita and the Srimad-Bhagavatam.

At the age of 58, Prabhupada became a swami, and in 1965, he immigrated to the United States, where he began to accept devotees and to distribute his translation of the Bhagavad Gita. He also worked on completing a translation and commentary on the Srimad-Bhagavatam, the second main text for Krishna devotion. In the next 12 years, he circled the globe 14 times, initiated over 10,000 disciples, and established 108 Krishna temples.

As he taught his devotees, he spent much time chanting the Hare Krishna mantra, and his devotees saw in him a perfect exemplar of what he was teaching them. He passed away of heart failure on November 14, 1977, at the age of 81, at Vrindavana, India, in the heart of the region where Krishna spent his early years. The movement that he founded, primarily represented by the International Society for Krishna Consciousness, continued to grow after his death and is currently in more than 70 countries.

Annually, those who see themselves in Prabhupada's lineage honor him. He was born on September 1 on the Common Era calendar, but within the movement he built, his appearance day (or birthday) is kept on the Indian Hindu lunar calendar. In that year of his birth, September 1 was the day after Janmashtami, celebrated by Vaishnava Hindus across India as the Appearance Day of Lord Krishna. That day also happens to be a lesser Vaishnava holiday, the day of Nandotsava, which honors Nanda, Krishna's second father. When Krishna was born, he was sought by his uncle the king, who wanted to kill him. Thus, his real father placed him in the care of Nanda the cow-herder to be raised. He grew to manhood in Nanda's family.

Nandotsava is, relative to the Common Era calendar, a moveable date, being on the ninth day of the waning moon during the Hindu month of Bhadrapad, and thus may occur in the latter part of August or early September. Each year in honor of his appearance day, his disciples publish a *Vyasa-Puja* volume of remembrances. It is also a fast day.

J. Gordon Melton

See also Bhaktisiddhanta Sarasvati Thakura, Appearance Day of; Bhaktivinoda Thakura, Appearance Day of; Janmashtami; Prabhupada, Disappearance Day of A. C. Bhaktivedanta Swami.

References

Goswami, Satsvarupa dasa. *Prabhupada Nectar: Anecdotes from the Life of His Divine Grace A. C. Bhaktivedanta Swami Prabhupada.* Port Royal, PA: Gita Nagari Press, 2004.

Goswami, Satsvarupa dasa. *Srila Prabhupada-lilamrta*. 6 vols. Los Angeles: Bhaktivedanta Book Trust, 1980–1983.

Prabhupada, A. C. *KRSHA: The Supreme Personality of Godhead*. 3 vols. New York: Bhaktivedanta Book Trust, 1970.

Prabhupada, A. C. *Letters from Srila Prabhupada*. 5 vols. Culver City, CA: Vaishnava Institute, 1987.

Prabhupada, Disappearance Day of A. C. Bhaktivedanta Swami

In the 12 years that he worked in the West (1965–1977), A. C. Bhaktivedanta Swami Prabhupada (1896–1977), the Founder-Acharya of the International Society of Krishna Consciousness, made a deep impression on those who became his disciples. Amid the many gurus who came to the West in the 1970s, amid the controversy that adhered to his organization, he was among the few who was free from even the accusation of any personal wrongdoing or moral turpitude. Amid the disagreements about leadership in the movement in later years, all agreed that he was the genuine teacher that he called his disciples to find and follow.

In the aftermath of his passing, his disciples came not only to remember him on his birthday, but his day of passing as well. He died, according to the Common Era calendar, on November 14, 1977, in Vrindavan, in the middle of the holy land of Krishna's birth. But as with their other commemorative dates, the organization he founded keeps their remembrance according to the Indian Hindu calendar. According to that calendar, he died on the fourth day of the waxing moon of the month of Kartika.

This day is primarily for a time for those who knew Swami Prabhupada to share memories of him with each other and with those who did not have the opportunity of knowing him. It occurs on a different date in late October or early November.

J. Gordon Melton

See also Prabhupada, Appearance Day of A. C. Bhaktivedanta Swami.

References

Goswami, Satsvarupa dasa. *Prabhupada Nectar: Anecdotes from the Life of His Divine Grace A. C. Bhaktivedanta Swami Prabhupada*. Port Royal, PA: Gita Nagari Press, 2004.

Goswami, Satsvarupa dasa. *Srila Prabhupada-lilamrta*. 6 vols. Los Angeles: Bhaktivedanta Book Trust, 1980–1983.

Prasadji Paramahansa, Birthday of Swami Guru (January 6)

Swami Guru Prasadji Paramahansa (b. 1966) is the current leader and fourth guru in the lineage of the Ajapa Yoga Society. He has led the movement since the death of his father, Swami Guru Janardanji Paramahansa (1888–1980), who adopted him shortly after his birth. He was raised in the atmosphere of the society and, as a youth, learned and mastered the teachings and practice of the Ajapa breathing and meditation. He was only 14 when his father died and left the movement in his care.

Each year on January 6, members of the various ashrams and centers of the society, found in India, Bangladesh, Europe, and North America, gather to celebrate Guru Prasadji's birthday. On each occasion, attendees enjoy a feast and then join in with a time of meditation and prayers. They are asked to bring a flower to place on the altar in the meditation hall, and a dish to share during the meal.

J. Gordon Melton

See also Bhumanandaji Paramahansa, Birthday of Swami Guru; Janardanji Paramahansa, Commemoration Days of Swami Guru; Purnanandaji Paramahansa, Commemoration Day for Swami Guru.

References

"Ajapa Yoga" Ajapa Yoga Society. Posted at http://www.ajapa.org/index_eng.htm. Accessed April 15, 2010.

Bhumananda Paramahansa, Guru, Guru Janardan Paramaha, and Guru Purnananda Paramahansa. *Tattwa Katha: A Tale of Truth*. New York: Ajapa Yoga Society, 1976, 1979.

Presentation of Jesus in the Temple, Feast of the (February 2)

In 1969, when the Roman Catholic Church revised its liturgical calendar in conformity to the suggestions of the second Vatican Council (1962–1965), a new feast appeared for February 2, the feast of the Presentation of Jesus in the Temple. This change gave a direction for a variety of celebrations that have occurred on this day going back to the pre-Christian era, when Pagan culture in Europe celebrated the day as the beginning of spring. This day was, for example, called Oimblc in Ireland. In the fourth century, following the legalization and privileging of Christianity, discussions were held on how the Christian movement might commemorate the events of Luke 2:22–33:

> And when the days of their purification according to the law of Moses were fulfilled, they brought him up to Jerusalem, to present him to the Lord (as it is written in the law of the Lord, Every male that opens the womb shall be called holy to the Lord), and to offer a sacrifice according to that which is said in the law of the Lord, A pair of turtledoves, or two young pigeons. And behold, there was a man in Jerusalem whose name was Simeon; and this man was righteous and devout, looking for the consolation of Israel: and the Holy Spirit was upon him. And it had been revealed unto him by the Holy Spirit, that he should not see death, before he had seen the Lord's Christ.

> And he came in the Spirit into the temple: and when the parents brought in the child Jesus, that they might do concerning him after the custom of the law, then he received him into his arms, and blessed God, and said, "Now let your servant depart, Lord, According to thy word, in peace; For mine eyes have seen your salvation, Which you have prepared before the face of all peoples; A light for revelation to the Gentiles, And the glory of thy people Israel." And his father and his mother were marveling at the things which were spoken concerning him.

According to Jewish law, following childbirth, the new mother must wait 40 days before visiting temple, and must before joining in worship present sacrifices in the form of a two pigeons (a provision that allowed the poor, who could not afford a lamb, to meet the demands of the law). The important happening during this event concerned a man named Simeon, who had been told by the Holy Spirit that he would not die before seeing the Promised Messiah. Upon meeting the Blessed Virgin and her child, he took Jesus in his arms and said, "Lord, now let your servant depart in peace, according to your word, For my eyes have seen your salvation" (v. 29–30). There was also an elderly woman, a prophetess, named Anna who, upon seeing the child, offered prayers of thanks to God for Jesus and addressed the other temple goers concerning him (v. 36–38).

Given that the residence of Jesus's family was in Nazareth, a trip to the temple in Jerusalem was a major event in their life. The many details in Luke's account elevated the event, which is presented as another prophecy of Jesus's coming activity for human salvation.

It was already an established observance in the Eastern Mediterranean, celebrated some 40 days after Christmas, when the church attained legal status in the Roman Empire under Constantine. At the time, many Christians in the East celebrated the birth of Jesus on January 6 (now Epiphany, a celebration of the Three Magi) and thus celebrated Jesus's entrance into the temple on February 14. In the discussion over the dating of Christmas late in the fourth century, December 25 was chosen, and the feast of the Presentation was moved to February 2. As the liturgical calendar developed in the West, the focus of the feast was transformed and the emphasis placed on Mary's purification. In 701, Pope Sergius I (r. 687–701) prescribed a candlelit procession as part of each of the Marian festivals then observed in Rome. Later in the century, priests in Carolingian France introduced the practice of blessing candles on this day. The use of candles in the worship service on this day placed a focus on Simeon's terming Jesus "A light for revelation to the Gentiles." As this practice grew and evolved, the day came to be called Candlemas, and the blessing of the new candles for the new year was a primary activity. Some people would keep a blessed candle to use when a storm arose or when they confronted a particularly frightening situation in the dark.

In Ireland, where the ancient Celtic goddess Brigid had been honored on February 2, her place would be taken by Saint Brigid of Ireland (c. 452–c. 524), who founded an early Irish monastery over a Pagan temple site. Saint Brigid's feast day is now set for February 1, and its observation now flows into Candlemas.

With the 1969 changes in the Roman liturgical calendar, the Western church realigns with the Eastern churches, which have continued to focus the day on Jesus rather than Mary. In the Greek and Syrian churches, for example, the emphasis has been on Simeon's taking Jesus in his arms and proclaiming him the Light unto the Gentiles.

J. Gordon Melton

See also Brigid of Kildare, Saint's Day of St.; Christmas; Epiphany; Imbolc.

References

Ball, Ann. *Encyclopedia of Catholic Devotions and Practices*. Huntington, IN: Our Sunday Visitor, 2003.

Connell, Martin. *Eternity Today: On the Liturgical Year: On God and Time, Advent, Christmas, Epiphany, Candlemas*. New York: Continuum, 2006.

Dodds, Monica and Bill Dodds. *Encyclopedia of Mary*. Huntington, IN: Our Sunday Visitor, 2007.

Presentation of Mary, Feast of the (November 21)

The feast of the Presentation of Mary commemorates an event in the life of the Blessed Virgin Mary not recorded in the Bible, but mentioned in several extra-biblical texts, most notably the *Protoevangelium of James* (also known as *The Nativity of Mary* or the *Infancy Gospel of James*). This apocryphal gospel tells of a couple, Joachim and Anne, who, finding themselves childless after some years of marriage, received a revelation that they would finally become parents. In due time, a female child, whom they named Mary, was born. In gratitude, they took her to the temple in Jerusalem and consecrated her to God. That act included their leaving her at the temple, where she was raised in a manner that prepared her for her later role as the mother of Jesus. After reaching puberty, she was assigned to Joseph as her new guardian. This story is also recounted, with some variations, in such writings as the Gospel of Pseudo-Matthew (also known as *The Book about the Origin of the Blessed Mary and the Childhood of the Savior*).

The status of Mary within church thinking was significantly increased by the declaration of her as *Theotokos*, or Mother of God, by a church council in 431. The celebration of this particular moment in her life was occasioned by the dedication of the Basilica of Saint Mary the New, erected in Jerusalem in 543 during the lengthy reign of Byzantine emperor Justinian I (r. 527–565). From Jerusalem, it spread rather quickly through the Eastern Church and was able to survive the destruction of the basilica following the Persian capturing of Jerusalem in 614.

The feast was slow to gain favor in the West, but in 1372, Pope Gregory XI (r. 1370–1378), then residing in Avignon, France, introduced the feast into the annual celebration at his papal chapel. The feast would then be suppressed in 1372 by Pope Pius V (r. 1566–1572), as part of the liturgical revision during the Catholic Counter-Reformation. It disappeared for only a few years, however, as Pope Sixtus V (r. 1585–1590) reintroduced it on to the Roman calendar among a variety of revisions he made to his predecessor's work. More recently, the feast survived the post-Vatican changes in the Roman calendar made by Pope Paul VI (r. 1963–1978) in 1969.

In 1775, Nano Nagle (1718–1784), a young woman from a well-to-do Irish family, led in the founding of a new order of Catholic sisters, devoted to serving the needy children of the city of Cork. Originally named the Society of Charitable Instruction of the Sacred Heart of Jesus, it would later be renamed as the Sisters of the Presentation of the Blessed Virgin Mary. Several years later in France, where religious activity was also suspect, a woman named Marie Rivier (1768–1838) assembled a small group of women who, on the feast day of the Presentation of Mary in 1976, formed themselves into a new religious order later to be known as the Sisters of the Presentation of Mary.

J. Gordon Melton

See also Anne, Feast Day of St.; Annunciation, Feast of the; Christmas; Expectation of the Birth of the Blessed Virgin Mary, Feast of; Immaculate Conception, Feast of the; Mary—Liturgical Year of the Blessed Virgin; Presentation of Jesus in the Temple, Feast of the.

References

Dodds, Monica, and Bill Dodds. *Encyclopedia of Mary*. Huntington, IN: Our Sunday Visitor, 2007.

Hock, Ronald F. *The Life of Mary and Birth of Jesus: The Ancient Infancy Gospel of James*. Berkeley, CA: Ulysses Press, 1997.

Rey-Mermet, Theodule. *In the Strength of Her Vision; Anne-Marie Rivier, 1768–1838*. Manchester, NH: Presentation of Mary Provincial House, 1975.

Procession de la Penitencia, La (Spain)

The Procession of the Penitents (La Procession de al Penitencia) is an annual event at Roncesvalles, a town in northern Spain in the Pyrenees Mountains, near the French border. Roncesvalle has for centuries been a site on the path of pilgrims to Santiago de Compostela in northwest Spain.

The procession at Roncesvalles is reenacted on each of five days immediately before Pentecost Sunday each year. The procession's beginning has been lost to history, but is tied to some 23 families in the distant past who wished to find a means of atoning for their sins in the previous year. In the mountains above the town, at the end of a steep pathway, lies the monastery of Roncesvalles. The families decided on a penitential trek up the pathway to the monastery as the solution to their problem. Over the years, they were joined by others wishing to make the walk with them.

Today, the procession is carried out by people from each of five nearby villages, with villagers from a single village making the trip each day. The penitents dress in black robes, with hoods covering their head. They have a large cross tied to their back. The crosses are large enough that the person has to stretch out his arms to help carry it. The trek is about two miles in length, and once at the monastery, they attend a Mass led by the brothers.

J. Gordon Melton

See also James the Greater, Feast Day of St.; Procession of the Fujenti; Procession of the Holy Blood.

References

"Pilgrimages to Roncesvalles." Posted at http://www.roncesvalles.es/interior.asp?sec=6&sub=i&lg=eng. Accessed March 15, 2010.

Spicer, Dorothy Gladys. *Festivals of Western Europe*. New York: H. W. Wilson Company, 1958.

Procession of Penitents (July)

On the last Sunday in July, the small Belgian town of Veurne is the site of an annual Procession of Penitents that recalls the country's many years under Spanish control. The procession traces its history to 1637 and to Jacob Clou, a monk of the Order of Canons Regular of Prémontré (popularly called the Norbertines). Clou founded a religious fraternity called a soldarity, whose members in 1644 marched in a procession that had been organized to protect the area from war and the plague. In the procession, Clou and his associates wore hoods and carried crosses (some weighing 50 pounds or more). The original procession has been continued annually. While at most times it has been focused on personal penitence issues, at different times through the years, it has found a focus in larger cultural issues that have most affected the church—the French Revolution, two world wars, and modern secularism, to name a few.

The modern procession moves through the streets of Beurne from Saint Walburga Church on one side of town to Saint Nicholas Church on the other. It includes two distinct elements. Leading the procession is a set of living Bible scenes. Each scene is introduced by a person dressed as an angel carrying a sign naming the scene to be enacted. Penitents pull a stage on which costumed actors offer their interpretation of the particular occurrence from the Bible. In the 1960s, the artist Arno Brys was commissioned to create new costumes, which were created slowly over the next two decades. In 1987, on the occasion of the 350th anniversary of Fr. Clou's Soldarity, the new costumes were worm by the actors.

The rather lighthearted first part of the procession eventually gives way to the more sober second part, in which the penitents, all of whom had made formal application to march, come by, their face covered with a hood and carrying a large cross. On any given year, as many as 400 will make the long walk between the two churches.

The Procession of Penitents occurs in the afternoon and lasts for several hours.

J. Gordon Melton

See also Procession de la Penitencia, La (Spain); Procession of the Cross; Procession of the Fujenti.

References

Devreaux, Anne Shapiro. "Belgium's Procession of Penitents." *New York Times*, June 19, 1988. Posted at http://www.nytimes.com/1988/06/19/travel/belgium-s-procession-of-penitents.html. Accessed May 15, 2010.

Ormond, George W. T. Bruges and West Flanders. N,p.: 1906. Posted at http://www.gutenberg.org/files/18670/18670-h/18670-h.htm. Accessed May 15, 2010.

Procession of the Cross (August 1)

August 1 (on the Julian calendar; August 14 on the Common Era calendar) has been a date of some importance in the Eastern Orthodox churches. In the years after discovery of the True Cross by Saint Helena (c. 248–c. 329), the mother of the emperor Constantine (r. 306–337), part of that cross was kept in Constantinople. As August was a season in which it appeared that the number of illnesses in the city would noticeably increase, a custom was evolved of carrying the Cross through the city in hopes of sanctifying the city and finding relief from all illnesses. On July 31, the wooden relic was taken from the imperial treasury and placed on the altar at the Hagia Sophia church. Beginning on August 1, it would daily be paraded through the city for the next two weeks.

August 1 took on additional meaning in Russia, as on that day in 988, Prince Vladimir and the people were formally baptized into the Christian faith. Then on this day during the reign of the Russian ruler, Prince Andrei I (later known as Saint Andrey Bogolyubsky or Andrey the God-Loving, c. 1111–1174), prince of Vladimir-Suzdal, successfully fought a battle against the Bulgarians. Vladimir-Suzdal was a successor state to Kievan Rus and evolved into the Grand Duchy of Moscow. Prince Andrei built a number of monasteries and churches in Vladimir, his capital city, including Assumption Cathedral, which functioned as the mother church of Russia through the 13th century.

The story is told that at one point he went to war with the Pagan forces in Bulgaria. As the decisive battle approached, he prayed to the Blessed Virgin Mary and then order the troops to carry the Cross and some icons before the troops as they marched into the fight. Shortly thereafter, around 1168, the commemoration of the victory was added to the church calendar.

Thus, within the Russian Church, the celebration of the Procession of the Cross has been combined into a day to remind the faithful that the pioneers of the faith received Christianity by the by the water of baptism and the assurance of salvation by the cross. Thus, believers are called to a rededication to the faith received from the founders of Christianity.

On this day, the cross will be brought into the center of the sanctuary and, where appropriate after the service, will lead a procession through the streets of the town. The priest will at the same time bless the people with holy water that was consecrated just prior to the beginning of the worship time.

J. Gordon Melton

See also Holyrood or the Feast of the Triumph of the Holy Cross; Procession of Penitents.

References

Borgehammar, Stephen. *How the Holy Cross Was Found: From Event to Medieval Legend.* Stockholm: Almqvist & Wiksell, 1991.

Semanitzky, John L. *The Holy Days of the Russian Orthodox Church.* N.p.: Russian Orthodox Layman's League of Connecticut, 1966.

Thiede, Carsten Peter, and Matthew d'Ancona. *The Quest for the True Cross.* New York: Palgrave, 2002.

Procession of the Fujenti

Every year, on Easter Monday (the day after Easter), as many as 100,000 Italian pilgrims make their way to the Church of Saint Anastasia and its sanctuary to the Madonna dell'Arco, the virgin with the wounded face. The most devoted of the pilgrims are called the *fujenti* (people who run). They will walk the 12 kilometers from Naples, many with bare feet, and actually run the last leg of the pilgrimage.

The story is told that on Easter Monday in the year 1500, a mallet player upset with his poor performance assaulted the image of the Virgin with a wooden ball. In response, the image of the Virgin began to bleed, the mallet player ran away in fright, but the bleeding was received by others as miraculous, and the image soon became the object of a growing devotion. It is believed that the barefoot running of the *fujenti* originated as a means of recalling the action of the mallet player.

The *fujenti* are members of associations of devotees that are active across Italy. They dress all in white to signify purity. They then place a blue strip of cloth across their chest (blue being the color most associated with Mary) and a red strip on their hips (signifying blood). Every association selects a group who together carry a *tosello*, a heavy festival display with a statue of the Madonna dell'Arco on her throne. The association will enter the procession as a group led by a banner with their name on it, the *tosello*, and then the uniformly clad members.

The procession begins at sunrise in Naples. When they reach the sanctuary, many are observed in a state of trance or ecstasy. Many *ex voto* offerings are delivered to the image.

J. Gordon Melton

See also Easter Monday; Procession de la Penitencia, La (Spain); Procession of the Holy Blood.

References

"The Outcasts' Madonna." Posted at http://www.oltremarephoto.com/pages/arco.html. Accessed April 15, 2010.

"Processione dei Fujenti al Santuario della Madonna dell' Arco." Posted at http://unisob.erpx.it/show.cfm?id=53. Accessed April 15, 2010.

Procession of the Holy Blood (May)

On Ascension Day (the sixth Thursday after Easter) each May, visitors to and citizens of the city of Bruges, Belgium, participate in an annual pageant in which a bottle believed to contain the blood of Jesus Christ is carried through the city. According to tradition, Derrick of Alsace, a.k.a. Thierry d'Alsace (1099–1168), count of Flanders, brought some drops of Jesus's blood with him after the Second Crusade. Derrick was reputedly given the relic because of his heroic fighting during the crusade. The gift came from his brother-in-law, Baldwin III of Anjou, king of Jerusalem, in 1150 who had received the approval of the patriarch of Jerusalem. Derrick arrived home in Bruges on April 7, 1150, and placed the relic to the chapel in the city that he himself had built.

The earliest mention of an annual procession in Bruges is from a charter of the Unloaders' Guild 1291. The oldest document concerning a relic of the Holy Blood being in Bruges dates only to 1256. This document raises the possibility for another origin of the blood. In 1203, Constantinople, where numerous Christian relics had been accumulated, became the target of frustrated crusaders unable to reach Jerusalem. They sacked the city in 1204. Baldwin IX, count of Flanders (1172–1205), assumed the emperor's throne. Though only in power a year, he had ample time to locate some important relics and have them shipped to Europe, with Bruges as a final destination. There is every reason to believe the relic of the Holy Blood reached Bruges through Baldwin's actions.

It is also the case that bottle that contains the substance, which is believed to be blood, is made of crystal that seems to date to the 11th or 12th century. In all likelihood, it too probably originated in Constantinople (modern-day Istanbul) as a container for perfume.

The modern procession begins at the Chapelle du Saint Sang and heads through the city to the Cathedral of Saint Sauveur. There are many floats in the procession, each relating to a biblical story or historical event (such as the traditional scene of the count of Flanders delivering the blood relic in the 12th century. Accompanying the floats are marchers on foot and horsemen who weave in and out of the scenes in the floats giving the appearance of engaging in historical reenactments. Also, many pilgrims join in the procession.

The high point of the procession is the vial of blood itself, which is contained in a gold reliquary. When the procession reaches the cathedral, the reliquary is placed on the altar and a Pontifical Mass is celebrated. The service culminates in the bishop lifting the blood for all to see. It is then returned to the chapel.

Through the year, the vial of blood is kept in the Chapelle du Saint Sang located on the central square in Bruges. The church, originally built in the 12th century, had a second story added in the 15th century. The blood, originally kept on what is now the ground level, currently rests on a silver altar in the church's upper level. It is on public view each Friday and every day from May 3 through May 17. Adjacent to the church is a museum that details the story of the Holy Blood.

Today, not only is the story of the vial of blood arriving in the 12th century doubted, but many have challenged the idea that a relic such as the blood of Jesus exists, and find no evidence to back up any tradition that Joseph of Arimathea, the person mentioned in the Bible as facilitating the burial of Jesus after the crucifixion, wiped blood spilled by Jesus at the crucifixion on a cloth that he saved and passed it on to be preserved through the centuries.

J. Gordon Melton

See also Procession of the Fujenti; Procession de la Penitencia, La (Spain).

References

"The Holy Blood." http://www.holyblood.com/EN/0.asp. Accessed February 7, 2011.

Spicer, Dorothy Gladys. *Festivals of Western Europe*. New York: H. W. Wilson Company, 1958.

Prompt Succor, Feast Day of Our Lady of (January 8)

The Feast Day of Our Lady of Prompt Succor is one of the important days on the annual calendar of commemoration of the Blessed Virgin Mary within the Roman Catholic Church. Our Lady of Prompt Succor is a title for Mary that originated in New Orleans at the beginning of the 19th century. The 1763 Treaty of Paris ceded Louisiana to Spain. Responding to the change of civil authorities, the Ursuline Sisters from Spain moved to New Orleans to assist in the work initially founded by the French Ursulines. When France resumed control of New Orleans under Napoleon in 1800, the Spanish sisters moved to Cuba.

With only a few sisters left in New Orleans, the work was in trouble, and with the antipapal policies of Napoleon in effect, the possibilities of getting authorization for more sisters to move from France was in doubt. The mother superior in New Orleans wrote a friend in France, Mother Saint Michel for help. Mother Saint Michel was at the time running a board school, having been driven from her convent by the French Revolution. As she wished to move to Louisiana to assist the Ursuline mission, Mother Saint Michel appealed to Mary, promising to establish veneration of her in New Orleans under the name of Our Lady of Prompt Succor. She put her promise into effect after arriving in 1810. While preparing for her move, she had a statue of Mary commissioned and brought it with her. The statue would soon be credited with saving the convent from damage during the fire that swept the French Quarter in 1812 and from the effects of the Battle of New Orleans fought in 1815. In 1828, a shrine for the statue was built in New Orleans.

Acknowledgment of Our Lady of Prompt Succor spread back to Europe, and in 1851, just three years before his defining of the Immaculate Conception of Mary as church dogma, Pope Pius IX (r. 1846–1878) authorized the feast of Our Lady of Prompt Succor. His successor, Pope Leo XIII (r. 1878–1903), authorized the formal crowning of the statue.

Today, the Feast Day of Our Lady of Succor is celebrated on January 8 with a special thanksgiving Mass. A number of churches across the United States and around the world are named in her honor.

J. Gordon Melton

See also Good Remedy, Feast of Our Lady of; Immaculate Conception, Feast of the; Mary—Liturgical Year of the Blessed Virgin; Perpetual Help, Feast of Our Lady of; Rosary, Feast of our Lady of the.

References

Dodds, Monica, and Bill Dodds. *Encyclopedia of Mary*. Huntington, IN: Our Sunday Visitor, 2007.

Freze, Michael. *Voices Visions and Apparitions*. Huntington, IN: Our Sunday Visitor, 1993.

Hogan, J. A. *The Pilgrimage of Our Lady of Prompt Succor*. Kessinger Publishing, 1907, 2008.

Muller, Gerald F. *Our Lady Comes to New Orleans*. Notre Dame, IN: Dujarie Press, 1957.

Pure Brightness Festival

The Pure Brightness Festival is one of the minority of Chinese festivals tied to the solar year rather than to the lunar calendar. It is held 107 days after the winter solstice (and 15 days after the spring equinox, hence it is always April 4 or 5 on the Western or Common Era calendar. It is preceded by what is designated Cold Food Day. As practiced, it has become another day to especially honor one's ancestors.

A man walks past decorated headstones during Qingming, a Chinese grave-sweeping festival organized to honor deceased relatives. (AP/Wide World Photos)

As the story told of Pure Brightness Day goes, a prince of the state of Jin, a power province in the feudal world of northern China's Spring and Autumn Period (722–403 BCE), neglected to reward one of the men who had stood by him in a time of exile prior to his attaining the throne. The man, Jie Zitui, had retired to live quietly on Mian Mountain. Realizing his lack of gratitude, the prince sought out his former companion, but was unable to locate him. A courtier suggested burning the mountainside to force him out, but no Jie Zitui appeared. Further searching found him, and his mother, dead beneath a willow tree. To commemorate his former companion, the prince ordered that the day would henceforth be remembered as the Hanshi Festival and order that no fires be kindled on that day—hence, the eating of cold food. The tree under which Jie Zitui was found was named Pure Bright Willow, and the day after the Hanshi Festival named the Pure Bright Day.

In China, including Taiwan, the Hanshi Festival has largely been neglected, but the Pure Bright Festival is widely celebrated and acknowledged as the first day of the year when one can leave the confinement to the house during the winter and enjoy the outdoors. It is also a popular time to acknowledge one's ancestors by going to their tombs, making necessary repairs, and cleaning then of any clutter or trash accumulated through the winter. Thus, Pure Brightness Day is often termed Tomb Sweeping Day. Before leaving, people will also commonly burn what is called spirit money. Such money is printed especially for burning, hence sending into the spirit world, for the use of the spirits of the dead. It is also a day to think about willow trees. Some plant new willow trees. Others decorate them with model birds made of flour and dates, and called Zitui swallows.

J. Gordon Melton

See also Chinese New Year's Day; Obon Festival(s); Spring Equinox (Thelema); Spring Equinox (Vernal); Winter Solstice.

References

Guoliang, Gai. *Exploring Traditional Chinese Festivals in China*. Singapore: McGraw-Hill, 2009.

Kaulbach, B., and B. Proksch. *Arts and Culture in Taiwan*. Taipei: Southern Materials Center, 1984.

Latsch, Marie-Luise. *Traditional Chinese Festivals*. Singapore: Greaham Brash, 1984.

Liming, Wei. *Chinese Festivals: Traditions, Customs, and Rituals*. Hong Kong: China International Press, 2005.

Purification of Mary, Feast of the. *See* Presentation of Jesus in the Temple, Feast of the

Purim

Purim is an annual Jewish festival that celebrates the deliverance of the Jewish people of the ancient Persian Empire from a plot to annihilate them. The story is recorded in the Hebrew Bible (the Christian Old Testament) in the Book of Esther. In the past, the king Ahasuerus described in the story was believed to be either Ataxerxes I (r. 465–424 BCE) or Ataxerxes II (r. 404–358). More recently, scholars have been more skeptical of the historicity of the story and have seen it more as a legendary tale.

The Book of Esther begins with the account of a feast given by King Ahasuerus at which alcohol flowed freely. In a drunken state, the king ordered his wife Vashti, wearing her crown, to "display her beauty" before those in attendance. Her refusal to do so caused Ahasuerus to put her away and to choose a new wife and queen. He chose a young woman at the court named Esther, unaware that she was, in fact, a Jewish orphan named Hassassah now in the care of her cousin Mordecai. Soon afterward, Mordecai discovered a plot by several courtiers to kill Ahasuerus. He made the plot public.

Haman, the king's highest official, came to despise Mordecai, for he refused to bow down to Haman. Haman discovered that Mordecai was Jewish and hatched a plot to kill not only him, but the entire Jewish minority in the Persian Empire. After obtaining Ahasuerus's permission to go ahead with his plan, Haman cast lots (*purim*) to choose the date for executing it. The lot fell on the 13th day of the month of Adar. When Mordecai discovered Haman's plan, he informed Esther. She asked the Jewish community to engage in three days of fasting and prayer, and then requested an audience with Ahasuerus, even though to do so, without the king having summoned her, could have caused her death. But Esther found favor when the king saw her, and she invited the king and Haman to a feast. At this feast, she invited them to a second feast the next day.

On the night between the two feasts, Ahasuerus had trouble sleeping, and he asked that the annals be read to him. Learning that Mordecai had foiled a plot against him and that he had received no honor in return, the king asked Haman how properly to reward a man the king wished to honor. Thinking it was he himself of whom the king spoke, Haman replied that the man should be dressed in a kingly fashion and paraded on the king's horse. Haman, to his great despair, had then to do these things for Mordecai.

That evening, at the feast, Esther revealed that she was a Jew and informed the king of Haman's plot. She pointed out that if his plot were carried out, she would be executed. Ahasuerus then turned on Haman and ordered him hung. But a problem remained. The decree allowing Haman's action against the Jews had been signed; thus it could not be simply annulled—but it could be countered. Ahasuerus gave Esther and Mordecai leave to write a new decree allowing the Jews to defend themselves. When attacked on Adar 13, the Jewish community fought and triumphed over its enemies. Mordecai subsequently was given a prominent position in Ahasuerus's court. He initiated the annual commemoration of the Jewish people's deliverance.

Purim is celebrated on the 14th day of the Hebrew month of Adar (usually in mid-March on the Common Era calendar). In leap years, when a second month of Adar is added to the Hebrew lunar calendar (seven times in a 19-year cycle), so that holidays stay in their appointed seasons, Purim is celebrated during Adar II. This is the most unequivocally joyous of Jewish festivals, though it begins on Adar 13 with, *Taanit Esther*, a fast (as Esther had asked the Jews to fast before she went to the king). If Adar 13 falls on a Sabbath, there will be further adjustment of the date.

Ritually, the service at the synagogue will feature a reading of the biblical book of Esther. This occurs twice, first after sunset when the new day begins on the Hebrew calendar, and a second time the next morning. In contrast to the quiet demeanor during the scripture readings at Sabbath services, during the reading of the Book of Esther, the congregation shouts and makes noise whenever Haman's name is read so as to blot out the sound of his name. Central to the day is a feast, which has been preceded by the sharing of gifts of food with others and the giving of money to the poor, with the understanding that joy is complete only when shared with the less fortunate. Additional customs have also developed above and beyond the guidelines of the biblical story, including the making of a particular dessert called *hamantaschen* (or "Haman's pockets"), a fruit-filled pastry. Purim is one day in which the drinking of alcohol in excess is acceptable.

The story of Esther is also commemorated as a teaching event. It reminds believers of the capricious nature of evil in the world and the need for action when it arises. It also builds confidence that God does not neglect his people.

From the Middle Ages to the present, Purim has, on occasion, been used, usually as part of a larger anti-Semitic attack, to charge the Jews either with the excessive use of violence or, on occasion, with the inability to respond to violence directed at them (as occurred in the Holocaust). Historic persecutions of the Jews and ongoing tensions with the Arab world since the founding of the state of Israel continue to provide occasions for Jews to construe anew the meaning of Purim and the tyranny of new Hamans who seek their destruction.

Purim is an official holiday in Israel.

J. Gordon Melton

See also Common Era Calendar; Hanukkah; Pesach.

References

Eckstein, Yecheil. *What You Should Know about Jews and Judaism*. Waco, TX: Word Books, 1984.

Greenberg, Irving. *The Jewish Way: Living the Holidays*. New York: Jason Aronson, 1998.

Horowitz, Elliott. *Reckless Rites: Purim and the Legacy of Jewish Violence*. Princeton, NJ: Princeton University Press, 2008.

Posner, Raphael, Uri Kaploun, and Sherman Cohen, eds. *Jewish Liturgy: Prayer and Synagogue Service through the Ages*. New York: Leon Amiel Publisher; Jerusalem: Keter Publishing House, 1975.

Schauss, Hayyim. *The Jewish Festivals: A Guide to Their History and Observance*. New York: Schocken, 1996.

Purnanandaji Paramahansa, Commemoration Day for Swami Guru (September 14)

Swami Guru Purnanandaji Paramahansa (1834–1928) began the modern tradition of teaching Ajapa yoga, an ancient secret yoga system that members of the Ajapa Yoga Society believed was preserved over the centuries at a hidden monastery in Tibet. In the 1860s, he made his way to Tibet and learned the techniques of the system based in breathing and meditation and upon his return to India began to teach it to his followers. He died in 1928, but was succeeded by Swami Guru Bhumanandaji Paramahansa (1873–1958), who passed the lineage to the successive leaders of the Ajapa Yoga Society.

Members of the society remember Swami Guru Purnanandaji on September 14 each year at their various ashrams and centers, of which there were (in 2010) three ashrams in India, one in Bangladesh, and one in California. There are also Ajapa centers located in New York, Honolulu, Montreal, Germany, and Poland. Disciples and friends of the society are invited to the celebration, which will include a feast and then a time of meditation and prayers. Attendees are asked to bring a flower, which will be placed on the altar in the meditation hall, and a dish to share during the meal.

J. Gordon Melton

See also Bhumanandaji Paramahansa, Birthday of Swami Guru; Janardanji Paramahansa, Commemoration Days of Swami Guru; Prasadji Paramahansa, Birthday of Swami Guru.

References

"Ajapa Yoga." Ajapa Yoga Society. Posted at http://www.ajapa.org/index_eng.htm. Accessed April 15, 2010.

Bhumananda Paramahansa, Guru, Guru Janardan Paramaha, and Guru Purnananda Paramahansa. *Tattwa Katha: A Tale of Truth*. New York: Ajapa Yoga Society, 1976, 1979.

Puthandu. *See* New Year's Day (India)

Putrada Ekadashi

The 12 months of the Indian Hindu lunar calendar is divided into halves relative to the waxing and waning moon. The 11th day of the 24 half months is considered by Vaishnava Hindus as a day for fasting and offering puja worship to Lord Vishnu in the local temple. The Putrada Ekadashi is the fast day that occurs during the waxing moon in the month of Shrāvan (December–January on the Common Era calendar). The primary story recounting its importance is found in one of the Hindu holy texts, the Bhavisya Uttara Purana, in a conversation between Lord Krishna and Maharaj Udhister.

Krishna told of an ancient king named Suketumana who ruled a city called Bhadravati. He and his queen Saivya had produced no sons, a matter that became extremely distressful. They had no one to whom they could leave their kingdom, and feared that upon their deaths there would be no one who would continue to offer oblations to their ancestors. Both were deeply religious, which left them wondering about the value of their piety.

Eventually, the depression into which the king fell led to his quitting the palace and going to the nearby forest. In his self-pity, he found his way to a beautiful lake. He found a small group of sages, and to each he offered obeisance. They in returned asked if he sought a blessing. They noted that the day was a fasting day, the auspicious Putrada Ekadashi. If anyone desiring a son will fast on this day, they will be blessed with a male child. The king immediately observed the fast and the next day after again offering obeisance to each of the sages returned home. A short time later, the queen became pregnant and bore a son. Krishna's point in telling the story was to assert that through observing Putrada Ekadashi, one can get a son and attain other rewards.

The Putrada Ekadashi includes a 24-hour abstinence from all grains, beans, cereals, and certain vegetables and spices. It is not as severe as the Nirjala Ekadashi, which requires abstinence also from liquids, even water. Observance of the Putrada Ekadashi is primarily among Vaishnava Hindus.

Constance A. Jones

See also Amalaka Ekadashi; Hari-Shayani Ekadashi; Kamada Ekadashi; Mokshada Ekadashi; Nirjala Ekadashi; Vaikuntha Ekadashi.

References

Aroro, Raj Kumar. *Historical and Cultural Data from the Bhavisya Purana*. New Delhi: Sterling Publishers, 1972.

Balaram Swami, Krsna. *EKADASI: The Day of Lord Hari*. Denver, CO: Bhaktivedanta Institude, 1986.

Wilkins, William Joseph. *Hindu Mythology, Vedic and Purânic*. Calcutta: Thacker, Spink & Co., 1882. Reprint, Adamant Media Corporation, 2001.

Qing Ming Festival. *See* Pure Brightness Festival

Queenship of Mary, Feast of

The elevation of the Blessed Virgin Mary to the role of importance now given her within both the Roman Catholic and Eastern Orthodox churches began in the fourth century, at the beginning of which Christianity was decriminalized and made the privileged religion throughout the Roman Empire. At this time, decision making in the church was focused on the new capital at Constantinople (now Istanbul, Turkey). In the wake of the changed status of the Christian church, church leaders devoted increased amounts of time to the defining of Christian doctrine. Much of the effort came at working out the problem of how it might speak of Jesus as divine without taking away from its affirmation of a strict monotheism. The result was the doctrine of the Trinity, which affirmed God's threefold nature, and dual nature of Jesus Christ as both fully human and divine.

If Jesus was born both human and divine, some reasoned that Mary could correctly be spoken of as *Theotokos*, the Mother of God, the instrument by which God incarnated in Jesus. This concept was accepted by the church's bishop at the council held at Ephesus in 451 CE. That the doctrine was proclaimed at Ephesus was not lost on the local population, as Ephesus was the site of the magnificent temple to the Greek goddess Diana (one of the wonders of the ancient world). The designation by an Ecumenical Council of Mary as *Theotokus* would be the foundation upon which future speculation on the role of Mary in God's plan of human salvation would rest.

The idea of the Blessed Virgin as Queen of Heaven is a direct extension of her designation as *Theotokos*. In earthly kingdoms, the mother of the ruler is honored as the queen, so given Jesus's kingship in heaven, Mary should be honored as queen. This line of development in the understanding of the role of Mary was initially developed in the East, and often expressed with the placement of a gold crown in icons picturing the Virgin. In the West, this practice often took the form of crowning statues of Mary.

The doctrine of Mary's Queenship took a leap forward in the 16th century with the circulation of the Litany of the Blessed Virgin Mary (a.k.a. Litany of Loreto), a worship format initially used at Loretto, where many Catholics believe the house in which Mary bore Jesus was transported to Italy by angels in 1291 to protect it from the emergent Ottoman Turks. It was given formal approval by Pope

Sixtus V (r. 1585–1590) in 1587. The litany makes various references to Mary as Queen and began the extension of the title Queen, for example, to Mary as Queen of the Angels and Queen of Peace.

Mary as Queen was a widely believed and utilized title for Mary that was integrated into the revived interest in mariology in the late 20th century. It was closely associated with the doctrine of the bodily Assumption of the Virgin into heaven. Further consideration of Mary's status culminated in 1954 with the issuance of the encyclical *Ad caeli reginam* by Pope Pius XII (r. 1939–1968) on October 11, the feast of the Maternity of the Blessed Virgin Mary. He proclaimed the doctrine of Queenship of Mary as a teaching of the church (though not a dogma) and established the established the feast day of the Queenship of Mary.

The feast of Mary as Queen of Heaven was first celebrated on May 31, 1955, but in 1969, Pope Paul VI (r. 1963–1978) changed the feast day to August 22, the Feast of the Visitation (of Mary with Elizabeth) having been moved to May 31. The feast day is celebrated with special prayers in the liturgy and opportunity for personal contemplation of the meaning of Mary's Queenship in the salvation of the world. August 22 and the Sunday closest to it will be especially celebrated in the many local churches named for Mary Queen of Heaven. Pope Pius XII related the role of Mary as Queen of Heaven to the cause of those persecuted for their faith and deprived of the freedom to practice their faith.

J. Gordon Melton

See also Fatima, Feast Day of Our Lady of; Mary—Liturgical Year of the Blessed Virgin; Solemnity of Mary, Feast of the; Visitation, Feast of the.

References

Dodds, Monica, and Bill Dodds. *Encyclopedia of Mary*. Huntington, IN: Our Sunday Visitor, 2007.

Graef, Hilda. *Mary: A History of Doctrine and Devotion*. London: Sheed & Ward, 1985.

Pelikan, Jaroslav. *Mary through the Centuries: Her Place in the History of Culture*. New Haven, CT: Yale University Press, 1998.

Steep, Peg. *Mary, Queen of Heaven*. Book-of-the-Month Club, 1997.

R

Race Unity Day

Race Unity Day (called "Race Amity Day" until 1965) was inaugurated in 1957 by the National Spiritual Assembly of the Bahá'ís of the United States (US-NSA), the annually elected governing council of the American Bahá'í community, to promote racial harmony and understanding. While it is a Bahá'í-sponsored occasion, it is not a Bahá'í holy day (nor is it even a "religious" event), yet is observed worldwide as an outgrowth of Bahá'í principles of interracial harmony and as an outreach to the wider community to foster a warm embrace of the social fact of ever-increasing diversity. For instance, a "National Race Amity Conference" was held on June 10–12, 2011, at Wheelock College in Boston, culminating in the first Boston Race Amity Day Celebration on Rose Fitzgerald Kennedy Greenway on June 12. William "Smitty" Smith, EdD, executive director of Wheelock's National Center for Race Amity, has sent to all members of the U.S. Congress a proposed Joint Resolution of Congress to "[d]eclare the 2nd Sunday in June annually be designated as National Race Amity Day."

Although not a "holy day" in the formal sense, Race Unity Day may be seen as contributing to what some scholars call "civil religion" as part of shared cultural values that progress over time. Although the term "civil religion" is commonplace among scholars of religion, the term "civil religious holy day" may be an apt neologism by which to characterize Race Unity Day as a cultural event, in which the sacred Bahá'í values of unity are secularized and thereby transposed into the civic sphere.

Like World Religion Day, another observance conceived and "invented" by the US-NSA, as it were, this community event is universal in that it is not specifically a "Bahá'í" observance, but can be more widely appreciated and participated in. As an US-NSA-inspired "civil religious holy day" (to use the author's term), Race Unity Day has apparently provided a model that appears to have inspired its secular namesake, sponsored by the government of New Zealand.

Usually celebrated annually on the second Sunday in June in the United States, Race Unity Day events have, not infrequently, been accompanied by mayoral proclamations. One of the early observances of Race Amity Day was in San Antonio, Texas, where the event was reported by the *San Antonio Register* on June 6, 1958. Today, Race Unity Day events in the United States are typically the product of local community initiatives, rather than a response to direct encouragement from the National Spiritual Assembly of the Bahá'ís of the United States.

On June 6, 2010, for instance, Bahá'ís in Springfield, Illinois, cosponsored the 13th annual "Race Unity Rally" at the state capitol. This celebration included performances by the Kuumba Dancers, Bahá'í African American drummers, and other musicians. Children were publicly recognized as winners in the sixth annual Vision of Race Unity Art and Poetry Contest. The 2010 event was cosponsored "by Frontiers International Club of Springfield, Women's International League for Peace and Freedom, the Greater Springfield Baha'i community, the First Presbyterian Church of Springfield, the Dominican Sisters of Springfield, and Springfield's Lincoln Library."

The 32nd Annual Race Unity Day, sponsored by the Spiritual Assembly of the Bahá'ís of Harrisburg, Pennsylvania, was held on June 13, 2010, at the City Island Pavilion to "promote religious, racial, and cultural harmony." In Burke, Virginia, the 14th annual "Race for Race Unity 5M" took place that Sunday in Burke Lake Park in order to raise funds for "Health for Humanity" (a humanitarian organization that provides training for health professionals in emerging and developing countries through partnerships with existing health institutions around the world).

The Blount County Race Unity Day was held at the Everett Center in Maryville, Tennessee. The Bahá'ís of Savannah, Georgia, had their annual Race Unity Picnic on June 13, 2010. In Erie, Pennsylvania, the "Race Unity Picnic" at Presque Isle State Park was cosponsored "by members of the Baha'i Faith in the Erie area along with the Race Unity Dialogue Group and Amerimasala Committee." The same day, the Bahá'ís of Rapid City, South Dakota, had their annual "Oneness of Humanity–Race Unity Day" potluck picnic at Canyon Lake Park, while the Bahá'ís of Fargo, North Dakota, hosted their annual Race Unity Day at Rabanus Park. These are some of the reported Race Unity Day events across the United States.

As previously stated, Race Unity Day was called "Race Amity Day" from 1957 to 1965. "Race amity" was a general expression, during the Jim Crow era, for harmonious race relations. The early American Bahá'ís took a leadership role in promoting "race amity" to the fullest extent possible, including advocating interracial marriage for those who wished to so marry. This was quite radical at that time, since antimiscegenation laws prohibiting interracial marriage existed in many states until they were declared unconstitutional by the Supreme Court in 1967.

The first Bahá'í-sponsored "Race Amity Conference" was organized by Agnes S. Parsons (a white woman prominent in Washington, D.C., high society) at the instruction of 'Abdu'l-Bahá (1844–1921; successor to, interpreter, and exemplar of the teachings of the prophet-founder of the Bahá'í Faith, Bahá'u'lláh [1817–1892]), who, in 1920, said to her: "I want you to arrange in Washington a convention for unity between the white and colored people." This came as a shock to Mrs. Parsons, who had no prior experience in race relations.

'Abdu'l-Bahá advised Parsons not to undertake this activity alone. Accordingly, Parsons consulted with the Washington, D.C. Bahá'í Assembly for advice and called upon several of her friends to form an ad hoc race amity convention committee. Among those whose help she solicited were Howard University professor Alain Locke (1885–1954), who joined the "Bahá'í Cause" (as the Bahá'í Faith was then known) in 1918, and Louis G. Gregory (1874–1951), a law graduate of Howard University, who was widely known as a lecturer and writer on Bahá'í topics.

The historic "Convention for Amity Between the Colored and White Races Based on Heavenly Teachings" took place on May 19–21, 1921, at the First Congregational Church in Washington, D.C. Alain Locke chaired the Friday evening, May 20, session, and Louis Gregory was one of a number of speakers—of both races and varied religious backgrounds—who addressed the convention.

Although Locke was not widely known as a professing Bahá'í, he contributed significantly to the Bahá'í "race amity" efforts. Of Locke, Dr. Martin Luther King, Jr. said, in his speech at the Poor People's Campaign Rally on March 19, 1968 in Clarksdale, Mississippi: "We're going to let our children know that the only philosophers that lived were not Plato and Aristotle, but W. E. B. Du Bois and Alain Locke came through the universe."

Locke, who devoted his life and career to fostering interracial unity, wrote in 1933: "If they will but see it, because of their complementary qualities, the two racial groups [black and white] have great spiritual need, one of the other." As Locke said in a speech in 1944: "Just as world-mindedness must dominate and remould [*sic*] nationmindedness, so we must transform eventually race-mindedness into humanmindedness" (see Locke, "Stretching Our Social Mind," *World Order* 38, no. 3 [2006–2007]: 30). These statements fairly characterize the Bahá'í perspective on interracial unity, more broadly stressed as the "consciousness of the oneness of humankind."

The success of the Race Amity Convention in Washington led to a series of similar events over the next several years in Springfield, Massachusetts; New York City; and Philadelphia. Beginning in 1927, Bahá'í-sponsored events promoting interracial harmony proliferated, spreading to many cities, large and small, and to other regions of the United States, and sometimes involving collaboration with the Urban League or the NAACP. Louis Gregory came to play a central role in organizing these events in the period from 1927 to 1947. He set a standard that Bahá'ís continued to emulate throughout the last half of the 20th century.

"The Vision of Race Unity: America's Most Challenging Issue," the 1991 statement by the National Spiritual Assembly of the Bahá'ís of the United States on what Bahá'ís call "America's most challenging issue" (i.e., racial discrimination), together with the video *The Power of Race Unity* broadcast on the Black Entertainment Network and across the country in 1997, has its roots in early Bahá'í race–relations endeavors.

In a letter dated January 14, 1987, to the National Spiritual Assembly of the Bahá'ís of the United States, the Universal House of Justice (international governing council of the Bahá'í Faith, first elected in April 1963 and elected every five years by NSA members worldwide) called for a continuation of the "race amity" efforts which, after all, were called for by none other than 'Abdu'l-Bahá:

> [T]he House of Justice appreciates the attention you are attempting to give to this situation by your appointment each year of a Race Unity Committee;

> however, it has noticed that 'Abdu'l-Bahá's advice concerning the holding of Race Amity Conferences is not being systematically followed. You are asked, therefore, to give the most careful consideration to reviving the Race Amity Conferences as a regular feature among the activities of your national community. (Taylor, *Pupil of the Eye*, 178–79)

In its letter of April 10, 2011, the Universal House of Justice (administrative authority, elected every five years, of the worldwide Bahá'í community), has emphasized the altered dynamics of prejudice today: "The expressions of racial prejudice have transmuted into forms that are multifaceted, less blatant and more intricate, and thus more intractable." Because the current Bahá'í emphasis is on neighborhood outreach with devotional meetings, study circles, children's classes, and junior youth events, Race Unity Day is not presently promoted in Bahá'í communities in the United States, although the U.S. NSA was a major sponsor (along with the *Boston Globe*) of the June 2011 National Race Amity Conference in Boston. Consequently, Race Unity Day may take on a life of its own in the secular sphere, much like World Religion Day, but with continued Bahá'í support at the local level. Although observance of Race Unity Day in the United States has often been replaced by a variety of activities aimed at promoting social unity with a broader focus, it is flourishing now in New Zealand, where it takes place annually in March. This "Race Unity Day," however, is a New Zealand cultural event rather than a Bahá'í-sponsored event, although local Bahá'í communities certainly involve themselves with local Race Unity Day events as promoters and providers of activities. This includes Bahá'í cosponsorship of the annual "Race Unity Speech Awards," popular among secondary school students, a competition that is now a joint venture between the Bahá'ís and the New Zealand Police (who furnish the awards money).

"Race Unity Day 2010," held in Nelson, New Zealand, on March 21, is a notable instance of the practice of the Race Unity Day model. Officially sponsored by the Nelson Multicultural Council, it was a hugely successful event that enjoyed official and popular support. Bahá'í involvement is formally seen in the "2010 Race Unity Speech Award," which is "sponsored by the New Zealand Bahá'í Community and proudly supported by the Human Rights Commission, the New Zealand Police and the Office of Ethnic Affairs."

Race Unity Day events in New Zealand, although government-sponsored, are openly cosponsored by the Bahá'ís, among other groups, in what appears to be a phenomenon of joint community efforts. For instance, the Race Unity Day in Whangarei, New Zealand, on March 21, 2009, was "a successful Race Unity Day organised by Settlement Support, the Baha'i community and English for Speakers of Other Languages (ESOL) home tutors Northland at Hurupaki Primary School" (Ali, "Why Whangarei Enjoys a Degree of Racial Tolerance").

Whatever the future may hold for Bahá'í-sponsored "Race Unity Day" events or "Race Amity Conferences," the emphasis on the oneness of humankind will continue to animate Bahá'í efforts to bridge the racial divide in bringing about harmony among races, nations and religions. As in the case of New Zealand, the model that the Bahá'ís pioneered is taking root across the globe, as racial reconciliation emerges as a self-evident social imperative. As such, the trajectory of Race Unity Day phenomenologically maps the transition from sacred to secular values.

Race Unity Day is not only about promoting racial amity, but "[i]t's about empowering people," according to a Bahá'í organizer of the 2008 event in San Antonio, Texas, where a diverse mix of entertainment included traditional East Indian dance, a "Christian praise dance," Negro spirituals and country music, following San Antonio city council's proclamation declaring Saturday, March 21, 2008, "Race Unity Day." (Ayo, "Race Unity Day Empowers People Personally, Socially.") As a Bahá'í-inspired "civil religious holy day," Race Unity Day quickens the civic heart by fostering the social empowerment that interracial harmony engenders.

Christopher Buck

See also 'Abdu'l-Bahá, Ascension of; Ayyám-i-Há (Bahá'í Intercalary Days); Báb, Festival of the Birth of the; Báb, Festival of the Declaration of the; Báb, Martyrdom of the; Bahá'í Calendar and Rhythms of Worship; Bahá'í Faith; Bahá'í Fast; Bahá'u'lláh, Ascension of; Bahá'u'lláh, Festival of the Birth of; Covenant, Day of the; Martin Luther King Jr., Birthday of; Naw-Rúz, Festival of; Nineteen-Day Feast (Bahá'í); Riḍván, Festival of; World Religion Day.

References

Note: The present writer acknowledges the valuable assistance of Gayle Morrison, for her input in reading a prepublication draft of this entry.

Ali, Imran. "Why Whangarei Enjoys a Degree of Racial Tolerance." *Northern Advocate* (Whangarei, New Zealand), March 23, 2009, 4.

Ayo, Elaine. "Race Unity Day empowers people personally, socially." San *Antonio Express-News* (July 13, 2008), B4.

Buck, Christopher. *Alain Locke: Faith and Philosophy*. Los Angeles: Kalimát Press, 2005.

Locke, Alain. "Alain Locke: Four Talks Redefining Democracy, Education, and World Citizenship." Edited and introduced by Christopher Buck and Betty J. Fisher. *World Order* 38, no. 3 (2006–2007): 21–41. (Features four previously unpublished speeches by Alain Locke: "The Preservation of the Democratic Ideal" [1938 or 1939]; "Stretching Our Social Mind" [1944]; "On Becoming World Citizens" [1946]; and "Creative Democracy" [1946 or 1947].)

McMullen, Michael. *The Baha'i: The Religious Construction of a Global Identity*. Piscataway, NJ: Rutgers University Press, 2000.

Morrison, Gayle. *To Move the World: Louis Gregory and the Advancement of Racial Unity in America*. Wilmette, IL: Bahá'í Publishing Trust, 1982.

National Spiritual Assembly of the Bahá'ís of the United States. "The Vision of Race Unity: America's Most Challenging Issue." Wilmette, IL: Bahá'í Publishing Trust, 1991.

Taylor, Bonnie J., ed. *Pupil of the Eye: The African Americans in the World Order of Bahá'u'lláh*. Rivera Beach, FL: Palabra Publications, 1998.

"Race Unity Day," posted at http://www.nelsonmulticultural.co.nz/EVENTS/Race+Unity+Day+March+2010.html, accessed January 31, 2011; and film footage on "Asia Down Under," posted at http://www.youtube.com/watch?v=PkV8AUMzxsI, accessed January 31, 2011.

Regional Bahá'í Council of the Southern States. " 'Abdu'l-Baha's Initiative on Race from 1921: Race Amity Conferences: A Documentary Video and User's Guide." n.d.

Thomas, Richard W. *Racial Unity: An Imperative for Social Progress*. Ottawa, ON: Association for Bahá'í Studies, 1991.

Radhashtami

The Radhashtami festival is a Vaishnava Hindu celebration of the birthday of the deity Radha, the consort of Krishna. She is a major character in the Bhagavada opurana and the Gita Govinda (or Song of Govinda), a work composed by the 12th-century poet Jayadeva, She is most often pictured standing beside Krishna.

In the story of Krishna, as related, for example, in the *Mahabharata*, he spends much of his youth in the village of Vrindavan in northern India, in the company of gopis, young girls who herd cows. These times are described in some detail in Bhagavata Purana. Radha is not mentioned by name in the Bhagavata Purana, though it seemingly alludes to her. Her story is focused upon later in the Gita Govinda, where her life is related in more detail. Krishna is seen as an incarnation of the deity Vishnu and Radha of Lakshmi.

Krishna was born at a time when his uncle King Kamsa sought his death, as Krishna (the eighth son born to Kamsa's sister) was predicted to kill him. In the process of Kamsa's searching out the baby Krishna, Radha and the other gopis were taken by the Putana demon. Krishna killed the demon, and the gopis were retrieved and placed in various homes. Radha was given to Brishabanu Maharaja and subsequently grew up in his palace in Barshana.

Within the Vaishnava tradition, Radha is held up for her unconditioned love for Krishna. The 13th-century Vaishnava theologian Nimbarka advocated a form of piety built around the devotion to and worship of Krishna and Radha, pictured as surrounded by thousands of gopis in a celestial Vrindavan. This devotion would be developed by the Bengali saint Chaitanya Mahaprabhu (1486–1534) in the 16th century. Chaitanya is believed by the followers of Gaudiya Vaishnavism, best known in the West from the International Society for Krishna Consciousness, to be the full incarnation of both Lord Krishna and Radha.

Vaishnavas celebrate Radha on Radhashtami, which is held on the eighth day of the waning moon of the Hindu lunar month of Bhadrapad (August–September on the Common Era calendar). It is a fast day that begins with a ritual bath. At the temple, Radha's statue will be bathed with panchamrita—a food mix, made of honey, sugar, milk, yogurt, and ghee, that has a variety of uses in Hindu worship—and then richly clothed in fresh attire. She will then be offered food (called prasadam) and worshipped with sacred song.

Constance A. Jones

See also Gaura Purnima; Janmashtami.

References

Jayadeva. *Gitagovinda: Love Songs of Radha and Krishna*. Translated by Lee Siegal. New York: New York University Press, 2009.

Prabhupada, A. C. Bhaktivedanta Swami. *Songs of the Vaisnava Acaryas: Hymns and Mantras for the Glorification of Radha and Krsna*. Australia: Chakra Press, 1989.

Valpey, Kenneth Russell. *Attending Krishna's Image: Chaitanya Vaishnava Murti-seva as Devotional Truth*. London: Routledge, 2006.

Raksha Bandhan

Raksha Bandhan is primarily a north Indian festival carried out on the full moon of the month of Shravana, hence it is also known as Shravana Purnima. It is one of several occasions in which family ties are affirmed ritually, in this case, the bonds of affection and duty that tie together brothers and their sisters. On the day of the Raksha festival, the ritualized activity is initiated by a female sibling who will tie a Rakhi, a woven bracelet, on the wrist of her brother. The bracelet has traditionally been multicolored and with a protective amulet integrated into it. More recently, a wrist watch has become a more-than-acceptable alternative.

After the wristband is put in place, the brother and sister engage in prayer for the well-being of the other. The woman will then perform "aarti," a ritual in which light from wicks soaked in ghee or camphor is offered to a favorite deity, and apply tilak (a mark made with kumkum powder) on the forehead of her brother. In return, brothers pledge to take care of his sister under all circumstances. Traditionally, men will present their sister with a gift as a sign of the pledge.

This ritual is done in the presence of the whole family, which has begun preparation for the key ritual early in the morning. Integral to the event are sweets that have been prepared for everyone's consumption. The activity is also accompanied by a ritual wishing the major participants a long life. The most serious part of the ritual is the vocalizing of the responsibility of the male children of the family to protect the females.

In recent years, women without siblings have brought cousins and more distant relatives and male friends of the family into the family circle for Raksha Bandhan and to have a male to present the Raski bracelet.

The authority for the Raksha Bandhan ritual is derived from many stories of males coming to the rescue of females in the ancient Indian sacred books. One popular story concerns Lord Krishna, the incarnation of the god Vishnu, who developed a relationship with the five Pandava brothers, all of whom were married to one woman, Draupathi. At one point, Krishna was hurt during a battle. Draupathi tore a strip of cloth from her sari, which was used to stop the bleeding. Krishna saw her concern for him in terms of sisterly love, and in return acknowledged that he was now bound to her as a brother.

Many years later, the Pandavas lost their wife in a game of dice. The winners began to remove her sari. Krishna used his divine powers to protect her virtue by elongating her sari to the extent that it could never be removed.

Another story concerns the demon king Mahabali, a great devotee of the god Vishnu. In response to Mahabali's devotion, Vishnu devoted time to protecting his kingdom and, in the process, being absent from his usual haunts and his wife, the goddess Lakshmi. Lakshmi disguised herself as a brahmin woman and went to Mirabali to discuss the situation with him. In the process, on Raksha Bandran, she placed a Rakhi bracelet on King Mahabali's wrist. She then revealed her true identity. The king was moved by her presentation and immediately requested Lord Vishnu to return to his family and home. From this story, Raksha Bandran is sometimes referred to as Baleva, a reference to Mahabali's devotion to Vishnu.

Constance A. Jones

See also Chaitra Purnima; Guru Purnima; Kartika Purnima; Magha Purnima; Narieli Purnima; Sharad Purnima.

References

"Rakska Bandran." Society for the Confluence of Festivals in India. Posted at: http://www.raksha-bandhan.com/rakhi-traditions-and-customs.html. Accessed April 15, 2010.

Ramadan

According to numerous accounts of the Prophet Muhammad, fasting was a regular part of his practice, and he admonished his followers to follow his example as they were able. For him, a normal routine was to fast during the daylight hours and pray during the evening (his prayer time taking from his sleeping hours). For followers, these days of fasting through the years were seen as supererogatory acts, above and beyond the basic requirements of the faith. The fasting done by Muhammad, though not required of the faithful, set the pattern to be followed in the required month of fasting known as Ramadan.

One of the five pillars of Islam, Ramadan is an annual fast named for the ninth month of the Islamic calendar when it occurs. As the Islamic calendar is a strictly lunar calendar, Ramadan occurs at a different point in the Common Era calendar each year. Ramadan recalls the beginning of Muhammad's writing down the Qur'an. It is a requirement of all, and those who because of illness cannot fast, are required to make up the days once they again attain their health.

Fasting begins at daybreak, defined as the moment one can discern the first streak of dawn against the black horizon (usually an hour and a half before sunrise). The fast continues until sunset. The day of fasting begins with a predawn meal (*sahur*) and ends with a light fast-breaking meal (*iftar*) which is followed by a time of prayer. People may gather at the mosque at the end of the day to share the *iftar* and hold communal prayers (*tarawih*). Muhammad advised people to break the fast each day quickly, thus it became common to prepare food ahead of time and have it ready as soon as the sun descended beyond the horizon.

The practice of fasting is seen as one of the ways, if not the best way, to please God, though it is meant as a means of teaching self-discipline not only about food and the body, but about life in general and relationships with others. Thus, during the fast, one takes pains not to use questionable language or show anger, and one responds to any screaming or shouting with the simple observation that they are fasting. Those who have taken up bad habits (such as the consumption of tobacco or alcohol) have Ramadan as a time to drop such practices.

Ramadan is also a time for additional prayer, the reading of the Qur'an, and the showing of generosity. Muslims are also required to pay a percentage of their income for the care of the poor (another pillar of the faith), and Ramadan is often chosen as the time to fulfill that obligation.

While Ramadan as a whole is considered a remembrance of the giving of the Qur'an, one night in particular, called Laylat al-Qadr, the Night of Power, is commemorated as the anniversary of the actual day that the Qur'an first began to be revealed to Muhammad by the angel Gabriel.

The Night of Power is usually observed on the 27th day of Ramadan, but it also carries with a certain element of mystery. It is a night marked by the descent of angels from the heavens to the earthly realm. For those engaged in prayer, it is a time to receive mercy and protection from every bad thing. Muhammad requested his followers to search for it and attempt to discern when it occurred, noting only that it was one night in the last 10 of the 30-day month, and that the time of receiving its benefits lasted until dawn. Appropriate actions for the night include prayer, self-examination, the asking of forgiveness for oneself and all Muslims, listening to sermons and engaging in discussion concerning the Night of Power, and remembering Allah.

Ramadan is immediately followed by Id al-Fitr, the Festival of Breaking the Fast, a feast day that marks the end of the fasting period. It is the 1st day of the 10th month in the Islamic calendar (months being marked from new moon to new moon). The day is a truly festive occasion, being seen as a sign of God's blessing following the time of testing and discipline, and is marked by donning fresh (and/or new) clothes, donating food to the poor ("Zakat al-Fitr"), and visiting family, friends, and neighbors. The day begins early in the morning with prayers in the local mosque.

In countries in which Islam is the predominant religion, the society is organized to accommodate Ramadan. Muslims living in other countries have imported the practice and accommodate their lives so as to participate fully in the fast and other activities.

James A. Beverley

See also Baha'i Fast; Id al-Fitr; Islam—Annual Festivals and Holy Days; Jainism; Laylat al-Qadr.

References

Algül, Hüseyin. *The Blessed Days and Nights of the Islamic Year.* Somerset, NJ: Light, 2005.

Al-Jibouri, Yasin T. *Fast of the Month of Ramadan: Philosophy and Ahkam.* Falls Church, VA: International Islamic Society of Virginia, 1994.

Budak, Ali. *Fasting In Islam and the Month of Ramadan.* Somerset, NJ: The Light, 2005.

Robinson, Neal. *Islam: A Concise Introduction.* Washington, DC: Georgetown University Press, 1999.

Ramakrishna, Birthday of Sri (February 18)

Sri Ramakrishna (1836–1886) was an Indian spiritual teacher who became widely known in the West when his students became central to the first generation of the spread of Hinduism in the West. He was born in a small town near Calcutta, West Bengal. Raised in a religious environment, as a young man he showed a tendency to experiences of spiritual reverie and even temporary loss of consciousness. With little interest in formal schooling or common practicalities, in 1866, he became a priest at a temple located on the Ganges River near Calcutta that was dedicated to the Goddess Kali (a popular deity in Bengal). He fervently meditated upon Kali, and eventually she appeared to him.

Ramakrishna's erratic behavior was ascribed to what was termed "spiritual madness" not unlike that experienced by the Bengali saint Sri Caitanya (1486–1534). He found several teachers who understood what was happening to him and mentored him. He began to emerge as a mystic. He also began to find himself encircled by a group of young disciples. He taught a Vedantist philosophy in which God is described in impersonal terms but juxtaposed his teachings with the practice of devotion to the Hindu deities. He also adopted practices and ideas from a spectrum of religions and found in his mysticism a unifying core, which led him to an understanding that all religions bring people to the same end.

Swami Vivekananda, his most famous student, attended the World Parliament of Religions meeting in Chicago in 1893, and emerged as one of the most popular speakers. He would later found the Vedanta Societies, a loose network of centers in North America, and upon his return to India, he founded the Ramakrishna Math (monastery). By this time, Ramakrishna had died of cancer of the throat. His wife Sarada Devi, much honored by Ramakrishna's disciples, assumed leadership responsibilities in the movement. The Ramakrishna-Vivekananda Vedanta Society became a global network of centers, many established among the Indian diaspora.

Ramakrishna is remembered on his birthday by the Ramakrishna Math and mission and the Vedanta societies around the world. At many locations, there will be special programs to reflect upon his teachings and examples and the world that has derived from his life. Disciples are encouraged to read and study his writings, to take his sayings as their guiding principles, and engage in some of the charitable activities maintained by the movement. Possibly the largest celebration is held annually at the Belur Math, the headquarters of the Ramakrishna Math and mission, located along the Hooghly River (a branch of the Ganges) in West Bengal. Thousands will gather at the math for a full day of lectures, pujas, and other gatherings.

J. Gordon Melton

The teachings of Hindu spiritual leader Ramakrishna Paramahansa are largely reponsible for the spread of Hinduism in the West. (Library of Congress)

See also Gaura Purnima; Sarada Devi, Birthday of; Vivekananda, Birthday of Swami.

References

Gambhrananda, Swami. *History of the Ramakrishna Math and Mission*. Calcutta: Advaita Ashrama, 1957.

Isherwood, Christopher. *Ramakrishna and His Disciples*. New York: Simon and Schuster, 1965.

Müller, Max. *Ramakrishna: His Life and Sayings*. London: Longmans, Greem & Co., 1898.,

Nikhilananda, Swami. *The Gospel of Sri Ramakrishna*. New York: Ramakrishna -Vivekananda Center, 1942.

Ramana Maharshi, Birthday of (December)

Ramana Maharshi (1879–1950) was an Indian spiritual teacher from south India. At the age of 16, he attained a state of self-realization in what was described as a swift and spontaneous act of self-inquiry and left him in a state of total abidance in "God," which in Indian thought is often identified, as Maharshi did, with the true "Self" He then his left home to take up residence on the slopes of the Arunchala Mountain, a sacred place of pilgrimage in southern India. Arunchala is believed by many to be a manifestation of the god Shiva, and there Marharshi was to remain for the rest of his life. He lived what others saw as a pure life that included his never touching money, and wearing only a simple loin cloth.

His disciples understood his most important teachings were imparted in the midst of the silence that pervaded his presence. In that silence mature souls came to apprehend the peace of self-realization. When he spoke, he taught a path of self-inquiry and self-surrender. He asked those who approached him to inquire from where their "I-consciousness" originates, to return to that source, and to abide there. To inquire "Who am I?" is the path of self-knowledge with which he became identified. He also taught seekers to throw all the burdens of life upon the divine and to rest in perfect peace in the heart. Though he was obviously from a Hindu background, he never questioned the outward religious practices or beliefs of those who came to see him. Rather, he taught each person to seek his or her own source. He believed that there was only one source for all, the Supreme Self or God.

Once on Arunachala, Maharshi lived in a cave and maintained a discipline of silence. Very slowly, disciples gathered, buildings began to appear, and an ashram emerged. The central building was the simple meditation hall, in midst of which was a couch, upon which he sat in the daytime and slept at night. During teaching sessions, devotees sat before him on the floor. Following his death, he was buried at the ashram, which has continued as a spiritual center perpetuating the teaching and methods espoused by Maharshi.

The Ashram observed two major celebrations each year in commemoration of the birthday and mahasamadhi (death) of Maharshi. The Jayanti or birthday of Sri Maharshi is celebrated every year during the Indian month of Marga on the day on which the moon is in the constellation known as Punarvasu (late December or early January on the Common Era calendar) and close to the winter solstice. The Aradhana, or day of his passing, is celebrated on the 13th day of the dark half of the solar month of Chaitra, (April–May on the Common Era calendar). This date is relatively close to the spring equinox.

On both dates, devotees arrive at the ashram where elaborate pujas (worship) are led by the priests at Sri Maharshi's shrine. Afterwards they will share a feast especially provided for them. Both Maharshi's mother and brother (Sri Niranjananda Swami) lived for many years and died at the ashram. Their mahasamadhi days are also observed, though on a small scale. The centers led by disciples of Maharshi, now found in many countries worldwide, observances of his birth and death dates are also held.

J. Gordon Melton

See also Ramakrishna, Birthday of Sri; Spring Equinox (Thelema); Spring Equinox (Vernal); Vivekananda, Birthday of Swami; Yogananda, Birthday of Paramahansa.

References

Mahadevan, T. M. P. *Ramana Maharshi, the Sage of Arunchala*. London: George Allen & Unwin, 1977.

Osborne, Arthur. *Ramana Maharshi and the Path of Self-Knowledge*. New York: Samuel Weiser, 1970.

"A Visit to Sri Ramanasramam." Sri Ramanasramam. Posted at http://www.sriramanamaharshi.org/index.html. Accessed May 15, 2010.

Rama Navami

Rama Navami, or the appearance day of Lord Ramachandra, is a popular Indian holiday celebrated on the ninth day of the Hindu month of Chaitra, the first month of the year, As the New Year's Day celebration generally lasts for a week or more, Rama Navami is often seen as the close of the New Year's celebrations. As it concerns the incarnation of the deity Vishnu as Rama, it is especially celebrated by Vaishnava Hindus, including the International Society for Krishna Consciousness.

Rama, or Lord Ramachandra, is a primary character in the *Ramayana*, the ancient Hindu epic. According to the story, his father Dasharatha was the emperor of Ayodhya, an ancient city of India located in Uttar Pradesh. He had three wives—Kausalya, Sumitra, and Kaikeyi. Following instructions given to him, Dasharatha brought in a prominent sage to perform a ritual. The god Yagneshwara then appeared to the king and gave him a bowl of divine pudding with instructions to give this food to his wives. They ate the pudding, and within a very short time, all were pregnant. The eldest wife gave birth to Rama. Sumitra bore twin boys, Lakshmana and Shatrughna.

Vishnu incarnated as Rama in order to slay the demon Ravana. As he grew to adulthood, he married his wife Sita Devi, and lived with her in the forest, where they were joined by his brother Lakshmana. Ravana kidnapped his wife, which became the occasion of Rama assisted by the monkey-headed deity Hanuman, killing the demon. Hanuman's devoted activity on behalf of Ramachandra led to his being seen as the epitome of Vaishnava devotion. Rama is said to have crossed the river Godavari in Andhra Pradesh on his way to rescue Sita at the spot where the Bhadrachalam temple now stands.

An altar is prepared in honor of the Hindu god Rama. Rama Navami is the celebration of Lord Rama's birthday. (*Hinduism Today* Magazine)

Rama Navami is seen as a day to celebrate the marriage of Rama and

Sita Devi, and in both temples and private homes, devotees will reenact their wedding. Toward the end of the day, statues will be taken out into the streets and lively processions occur as crowds gather to celebrate the day. Hare Krishna devotees will also fast through the daylight hours. Rituals of Rama Navami also center on Surya, the sun god, who assisted Rama in defeating Ravana.

The Bhadrachalam Temple located on the northern side of the river Godavari in Andhra Pradesh, India, is one of the more famous locations for the celebrations of Rama Navami. There is also a set of temples in Ayodhya, India, on sites hallowed by Rama's presence.

In southern India, the whole nine days from the beginning of the year are celebrated as Rama Navami. It is a time to retell and dramatize the stories of the *Ramayana*. Japa yoga (the repetition of mantras) calling upon Rama will be continuously heard through the day. Some will carry on a fast through the whole nine days, others just on the ninth day. Temples will organize teaching sessions for people each evening.

Constance A. Jones

See also Gaura Purnima.

References

Menon, Ramesh. *The Ramayana: A Modern Retelling of the Great Indian Epic*. New York: North Point Press, 2004.

Mukundcharandas, Sadhu. *Hindu Festivals (Origin Sentiments and Rituals)*. Amdavad, India: Swaminarayan Aksharpith, 2005.

Pauwels, Heidi R. M. *The Goddess as Role Model: Sita and Radha in Scripture and on Screen*. New York: Oxford University Press, 2008.

Sivananda, Swami. *Hindu Fasts and Festivals*. Shivanandanagar: Divine Life Society, 1997. Posted at http://www.dlshq.org/download/hindufest.htm#_VPID_19. Accessed April 15, 2010.

Ratha Yatra

The Ratha Yatra Festival is the main annual celebrative event at the Jagannath temple in Puri, a coastal city in the state of Orissa in eastern India. Lord Jagannath is an incarnation of the Hindu deity Vishnu. While the festival has its main center in Puri, it is celebrated by Vaishnava Hindus worldwide. It has been celebrated annually in the United States since the 1970s, the primary site being Venice Beach in Los Angeles, and sponsored by the International Society for Krishna Consciousness (ISKCON). Vaishnava Hindus believe that Lord Jagannath was responsible for the creation of the whole universe. Jagannath is closely associated with his sister Subhadra and his brother Balabhadra.

The Jagannath Temple was built by Raja (or King) Ananta Varman Chodaganga Dev in the 12th century CE, and subsequently maintained and expanded by successive Hindu rulers through the next four centuries. Then in 1558, the state of Orissa was conquered by Afghan Muslims who had previously conquered neighboring Bengal. The Afghans suppressed worship at Puri through the rest of the century. They were finally driven out in 1592, the main statues were reinstalled in the sanctuary in the rear of the temple, and worship of Lord Jagannath resumed.

Worship is regularly conducted before the statues in the temple, the daily ritual beginning at 5:00 a.m. It consists of several meals (the presentation of food offerings, called *prasadam*), several dressings (costume changes) of the statues, and the later distribution of the *prasadam* to the people, with no care taken to observe caste lines in the distribution.

The major event each year is the annual Jagannath festival that occurs in midsummer on the second day of the waxing moon of the Indian Hindu lunar month of Ashadha. Lord Jagannath and his two siblings are placed in three large carts and carried from the temple to their "summer temple," the Gundicha Mandir, a little over a mile from the main Jagannath temple. The cart upon which Lord Jagannath rides is a massive wooden structure constructed from hundreds of logs cut from the sacred *phasi* trees, a forest of which is kept in cultivation just for this annual event. Two slightly smaller carts carry Subhadra and Balabhadra. Lord Jagannath's cart requires 4,000 men to pull it, and once it is moving, it is extremely difficult to stop (this fact being the origin of the popular war term *juggernaut*). Devotees in the tens of thousands gather to watch Lord Jagannath take the short trip. He will stay in the summer temple only seven days, after which they are returned to the main temple.

The Jagannath festival, though held in smaller versions in several other Indian cities, was largely unknown in the West until the advent of ISKCON, the Hare Krishna movement, in the United States in the 1960s. Very soon after organizing, ISKCON began to hold Jagannath festivals in different American cities, and their annual reenactment of the trip to the summer temple has become a popular attraction. It is currently held each summer in the major cities throughout the West where the movement has established temples.

Constance A. Jones

See also Balarama, Appearance Day of Lord; Gaura Purnima; Janmashtami.

References

Das Goswami, Satsvarupa. *A Visit to Jagannath Puri*. La Crosse, FL: Gita-nagari Press, 1987.

Deo, Jitamitra Prasad Singh. *Origin of Jagannath Deity*. New Delhi: Gyan, 2003.

Eschmann, Ann, Hermann Kulke, and Gaya C. Tripathi, eds. *The Cult of Jagannath and the Regional Tradition of Orissa*. New Delhi: Manohar Press, 1978.

Schnepal, Burkhard, and Herman Kulke. *Jagannath Revisited: Studying Society, Religion and the State in Orissa*. New Delhi: Manohar, 2001.

Reformation Sunday (October)

Reformation Day is a celebration of the beginning of the Protestant Reformation in the 16th century. Of all of the dates suggested for the beginning of the Reformation and the emergence of the resulting Protestant Christian movement, none has gained the acceptance as the dramatic act of Martin Luther (1483–1546) in nailing his "95 Theses" (points of debate concerning contemporary Roman Catholic practice) on the door of the main church in Wittenberg, Germany, on October 31, 1517. Although the actual date for the observance of Reformation Day is October 31, most churches actually celebrate it on the last Sunday in October. October 31 competes with the growing popularity of Halloween (especially in North America) and All Saint's Eve.

The 95 Theses laid out in some detail Luther's criticism of the practice of selling indulgences for the remission of the punishment of sins in purgatory and the theological affirmations that undergirded indulgences. The debate on this issue would lead Luther to question the authority of the pope as opposed to that of the biblical text, and the role of the church as the sole interpreter of the meaning of the text and the author of ideas that went beyond the text. Eventually, Luther and the Protestants would come to believe in the primal authority of the Bible and to champion the ability of the average believer to read and understand its meaning.

Every 50 or 100 years, large celebrations of the beginning of the reformation will be organized, but annually, most Protestant churches will recognize the anniversary of the Protestant movement on the last Sunday in October with sermons dedicated to the theme and the singing of Luther's hymn, "A Mighty Fortress Is Our God," frequently referred to as the "Battle Hymn of the Reformation." It is a public holiday in Slovenia and Chile and several of the German states

With the transformation of the relationship of the Roman Catholic Church and Protestantism in the post–Vatican II era, emphasis on the Reformation and celebrating the separateness of Protestantism has waned considerably. Many Protestant churches have marginalized the celebration of Reformation Sunday (which has traditionally been used to emphasize protestant differences with Roman Catholicism) while many of the newer denominations have distanced themselves from the history of the movement that gave them birth. At the same time, Roman Catholics have gained a new appreciation for Luther and have added "A Mighty Fortress Is Our God" to their hymnals. Conservative Protestants have used the day to emphasize their differences with the more theologically liberal and ecumenically minded Protestants, often claiming that they have given away their heritage.

J. Gordon Melton

See also Aldersgate Day; Bartholomew's Day, Saint; Martinmas; World Communion Sunday; World Day of Prayer.

References

Bainton, Roland. *Here I Stand*. New York: Abingdon-Cokesbury, 1950.

Chadwick, Owen. *The Reformation*. Harmondsworth, UK: Penguin, 1991.

Ferm, Vergilius. *Pictorial History of Protestantism*. New York Philosophical Library, 1957.

Hilderbrand, Hans J. *Encyclopedia of Protestantism*. New York: Routledge, 2003.

Hilderbrand, Hans J., ed. *The Oxford Encyclopedia of the Reformation*. 4 vols. Oxford: Oxford University Press, 1996.

Religious Freedom Day

Religious Freedom Day is a national observance in the United States that was initially proclaimed by President George Bush in 1993. It is celebrated on January 16, the anniversary of the 1786 passage of the Statue on Religious Freedom by the Commonwealth of Virginia, one of the building blocks of American emphasis on religious liberty. The Virginia legislation led directly to the First Amendment in the U.S. Constitution that guarantees that "Congress shall make no law respecting an establishment of religion, or prohibiting the free exercise thereof." Each year since 1993, the president has issued a new proclamation concerning the day.

The First Amendment of the Constitution has been an active force in the United States. Increasingly so, as the country moved in the 19th century as a land in which Christianity had a virtual monopoly on the religious life of the nation, though only a small percentage of the public were church members, into one that at the beginning of the 21st century that shows Christianity holds the allegiance of a clear majority of the American public (though the Christian community is divided into a number of denominations) but also finds a strong minority presence by groups of the Jewish, Buddhist, Hindu, Muslim, and Western Esoteric traditions. There is also a vocal atheistic community. As the pluralistic nature of the American religious community has become evident, the courts have regularly been asked to rule on a variety of issues relative to religious freedoms. In doing so, the courts are often asked to judge questions as to whether the specific issue before it relates to free exercise or the limitations of government in favoring one religion over another. Smaller groups tend to raise questions involving their ability to exercise their freedoms, while larger groups tend to be involved in questions of expressions of religion in government-supported institutions—schools, government offices, the armed services, and legislatures. Religious Freedom Day appears to have been prompted by a 1992 ruling by the Supreme Court that declared unconstitutional the offering of nonsectarian prayers at public school graduation ceremonies, suggesting that they tended to support the government establishment of religion.

Religious Freedom Day does not speak to the issues so much as it emphasizes the importance of the freedom to American life and calls upon the citizenry to reflect on its importance. This calls attention to the fact that religious freedom was the first item mentioned in the Bill of Rights, added to the Constitution to protect a spectrum of freedoms in the different states. In protecting the freedoms, the government chose to limit its own power.

There are no specifics mandated for celebrating the day, but in 2005, for example, President George W. Bush called upon the citizens to "observe this day through appropriate events and activities in homes, schools, and places of worship." Schools, often a focus of religious freedom issues, have been especially called upon to organize events emphasizing the civil rights issues around religious freedom. The U.S. Department of Education has issued a set of guidelines summarizing the religious liberties of students in the public school system.

A coalition of organizations representing a spectrum of approaches to religious freedom has joined to promote Religious Freedom Day. They include the Association of American Educators, the Beckett Fund, the Council for America's First Freedom, Gateways to Better Education, the Institute on Religion and Democracy, and the Providence Forum.

J. Gordon Melton

See also Human Rights Day; International Religious Freedom Day; World Religion Day.

References

Religious Freedom Day. Posted at http://religiousfreedomday.com/. Accessed on July 15, 2010.

Riḍván, Festival of (April 20–May 2)

The Festival of Riḍván is a 12-day festival. The 1st, 9th, and 12th days of Riḍván are three of the nine Bahá'í holy days on which work is to be suspended. Among the Báhá'í holy days, the Festival of Riḍván ("Paradise") is preeminent, for it marks the inception of the Bahá'í Faith as a distinct religion. Observed from sunset on April 20 (marking the onset of April 21 in the Bahá'í calendar) to sunset on May 2, the Festival of Paradise comprises three Holy Days. On the 1st (April 21), 9th (April 29), and 12th (May 2) days of Riḍván, Bahá'í communities will gather to commemorate the signal events of that historic occasion.

The Bahá'í Faith, one of the youngest world religions, was founded by Mírzá ḥusayn-'Alí Núrí (1817–1892), a Persian nobleman known by his spiritual title, Bahá'u'lláh ("Glory/Splendor of God"). The Bahá'í religion is also regarded as having been cofounded by Bahá'u'lláh's predecessor and harbinger, Sayyid 'Alí-Muḥammad of Shiraz (1819–1850), known as the Báb ("the Gate").

The unfolding of Bahá'u'lláh's prophetic mission was gradual, progressively revealed in a series of disclosures. The "Festival of Paradise" commemorates Bahá'u'lláh's private disclosure of his eschatological identity to a handful of his companions—around four years prior to his public proclamation to the rulers and religious leaders of the world (c. 1867–1873). To a select few Bábís, Bahá'u'lláh announced that he was the "Promised One" foretold by the Báb. To a select group of the world's most powerful potentates and clerics, Bahá'u'lláh sent open epistles, proclaiming himself to be the "Promised One" foretold by the prophets of all past religions. In these "Tablets" (as the epistles were called), together with general Tablets addressed to kings and ecclesiastics collectively, Bahá'u'lláh stated that he was, *inter alia*, the long-awaited "World Reformer" who came to unify the world—a transformation that would, in the course of time, come about through the power of his universal principles and laws adapted to the needs of this day and age.

Briefly, the history of Riḍván began on the afternoon of April 21, 1863 (around 3:00 p.m.). Bahá'u'lláh arrived in the Najíbíyyih Garden, subsequently designated as the "Garden of Riḍván." Located on the east bank of the Tigris in Baghdad, Najíbiyyih was once a wooded garden, where Muḥammad-Najíb Páshá (Turkish: Mehmed Necib, d. May 1851), governor of Baghdad (r. 1842–1847), had built a palace and placed a wall around the garden. It is now the site of "Baghdad Medical City" (formerly known as Saddam Medical City), a large modern teaching hospital in Baghdad.

Bahá'u'lláh's entrance into the Garden of Riḍván signalized the commencement of his momentous announcement, first to his companions, and eventually to the world at large. Exactly what transpired is shrouded in mystery, and accounts vary. Prior to this time, Bahá'u'lláh had concealed his mission for 10 years (1853–1863). This period of "messianic secrecy" has been referred to as the "Days of Concealment" (*ayyám-i-buṭun*—a term that connotes the image of embryonic development), although Bahá'u'lláh's writings in Baghdad during this period are rife with hints about his prophetic mission, especially in his preeminent doctrinal text, the *Book of Certitude* (*Kitáb-i-Íqán*), which was revealed in two days and two nights in January 1861.

In 1869, as part of the subsequent public proclamation of his mission to the world's political and religious leaders, Bahá'u'lláh dispatched his second epistle (c. 1869) to Napoleon III (d. 1873). In this "Tablet" (spirited out of Bahá'u'lláh's prison cell by a Bahá'í pilgrim, who concealed the letter in the brim of his hat) to the emperor of France, Bahá'u'lláh announced: "All feasts have attained their consummation in the two Most Great Festivals, and in two other Festivals that fall on the twin days." Here, the two "Most Great Festivals" are the Festival of Riḍván and the Declaration of the Báb (evening of May 22, 1844). The "twin days" refer to the Birth of the Báb (October 20, 1819) and the Birth of Bahá'u'lláh (November 12, 1817).

The purport of what Bahá'u'lláh proclaimed on that momentous first day of Riḍván, beyond the declaration that he was "He Whom God will make manifest," involves matters of great import in that Bahá'u'lláh had decreed three of his most far-reaching laws, by (1) abrogating holy war, (2) asserting that no independent Messenger of God (literally, "Manifestation of God") after Bahá'u'lláh would appear for at least a full 1,000 years, and (3) dispensing entirely with the Islamic category of ritual impurity or "uncleanness" (*najis*). Bahá'u'lláh later recounted this sweeping pronouncement in the Most Holy Book (the *Kitáb-i-Aqdas*):

> God hath, likewise, as a bounty from His presence, abolished the concept of "uncleanness," whereby divers things and peoples have been held to be impure. He, of a certainty, is the Ever-Forgiving, the Most Generous. Verily, all created things were immersed in the sea of purification when, on that first day of Riḍván, We shed upon the whole of creation the splendours of Our

most excellent Names and Our most exalted Attributes. (Bahá'u'lláh, *The Kitáb-i-Aqdas*, 47)

The Festival of Riḍván is important for yet another reason: most Bahá'í elections take place at this time. On the first day of Riḍván (April 21), all local Bahá'í councils, each known as a Local Spiritual Assembly, is democratically elected, in a "spiritual election" conducted prayerfully and meditatively.

The system of Bahá'í elections is unique, both religiously and politically. Political scientist Arash Abizadeh has observed that Bahá'í elections are governed by formal institutional rules and informal norms that specifically prohibit such familiar features of the political landscape as nominations, competitive campaigns, voting coalitions, or parties. As an alternative model of democratic elections, Bahá'í elections incorporate three core values at the individual, interpersonal, and institutional levels: (1) the inherent dignity of each person; (2) the unity and solidarity of persons collectively; and (3) the intrinsic justice, fairness, and transparency of elected Bahá'í institutions. Bahá'í elections thus serve four primary functions: (1) selection (electing representatives); (2) legitimation (authorizing Bahá'í governing bodies in the eyes of the community at large); (3) education (cultivating the spirit of responsibility in each Bahá'í voter); and (4) integration (fostering solidarity within the community as a whole).

National Bahá'í conventions are also held during the Festival of Riḍván for the purpose of electing national councils, each of which is called a National Spiritual Assembly. An exception to the timing of these conventions occurs once every five years, when the Universal House of Justice, the international governing council of the Bahá'í Faith, is elected during the Festival of Riḍván. The next is scheduled for Riḍván 2013, with national Bahá'í elections rescheduled for May.

The Festival of Riḍván marks the inchoative establishment of the Bahá'í religion as a distinct faith-community through Bahá'u'lláh's disclosure of his divine authority. The Festival of Riḍván also marks the progressive advancement of the Bahá'í Faith as a distinct administrative order through the process of electing the faith-community's governing authorities.

Bahá'ís believe that in a future Golden Age—in which a self-governing world commonwealth emerges as the fruit of social evolution enlightened by Bahá'í sociomoral principles—the Festival of Riḍván is destined to become the greatest celebratory event in the world, according to the teleological Bahá'í vision of the inevitable course of human history.

Christopher Buck

See also 'Abdu'l-Bahá, Ascension of; Ayyám-i-Há (Bahá'í Intercalary Days); Báb, Festival of the Birth of the; Báb, Festival of the Declaration of the; Báb, Martyrdom of the; Bahá'í Calendar and Rhythms of Worship; Bahá'í Faith; Bahá'í Fast; Bahá'u'lláh, Ascension of; Bahá'u'lláh, Festival of the Birth of; Covenant, Day of the; Naw-Rúz, Festival of; Nineteen-Day Feast (Bahá'í); Race Unity Day; World Religion Day.

References

Abizadeh, Arash. "Democratic Elections without Campaigns? Normative Foundations of National Bahá'í Elections." *World Order* 37, no. 1 (2005): 7–49.

Bahá'u'lláh. *The Kitáb-i-Aqdas*. Haifa: Bahá'í World Centre, 1992.

Buck, Christopher. "The Eschatology of Globalization: Bahá'u'lláh's Multiple-Messiahship Revisited." *Studies in Modern Religions, Religious Movements and the Babi-Bahá'í Faiths*, edited by Moshe Sharon, 143–78. Leiden: Brill Academic Publishers, 2004.

Buck, Christopher. *Symbol and Secret: Qur'an Commentary in Bahá'u'lláh's Kitáb-i Íqán*. Los Angeles: Kalimát Press, 2004. First published 1995.

Keil, Gerald. *Time and the Bahá'í Era: A Study of the Badí' Calendar*. Oxford: George Ronald, 2008.

Walbridge, John. "Festival of Ridván." In *Sacred Acts, Sacred Space, Sacred Time*, 232–41. Oxford: George Ronald, 1996.

Rishi Panchami

Rishi Panchami is a Hindu holiday with two related emphases. It is observed on the fifth day after the new moon in the Hindu month of Bhadrapad (August–September on the Common Era calendar), which is the final day of the primary Teej Festival, known as Hartalika Teej, widely celebrated across northern India and Nepal as a women's festival. It is also a day set aside to show respect of the seven legendary sages known as the Sapta Rishis.

Hindu women take turns pouring water on each other while taking a ritual bath in the Bagmati River during Rishi Panchami in Nepal. (Getty Images)

The celebration of Teej is directed to Parvati, the wife of Shiva. She is said to have fasted and practiced various austere practices to win Shiva's affections. Women observe a strict fast dedicated to Shiva on the day of Rishi Panchami. In some regions, the fast is also observed by men. Women begin the day with a special ritual bath and will later in the day visit temples dedicated to Shiva for an appropriate ritual. The fast is usually broken following the Rishi Panchami puja (worship).

Throughout India, homage is also paid to the Sapta Rishis—Kashyapa, Atri, Bharadhvaja, Vishvamitra, Gauthama, Jamadagni and Vashishta. These men are considered the patriarchs of the Vedic religion, and are identified with the seven stars of the Big Dipper constellation. They work to assist every individual return to its divine origin.

The exact list of the seven and the specific tasks they undertake vary over time and among different segments of the Hindu community, although most agree that those sages mentioned in the ancient texts are deserving of honor.

Finally, in Gujarat, this day is also observed as Rushi Pancham.

Constance A. Jones

See also Ahoi Ashtami; Ambuvachi; Dattatreya Jayanti; Rushi Pancham; Teej Festivals.

References

"Rishi Panchami." Hindu Blog. Posted at http://www.hindu-blog.com/2008/08/rishi-panchami.html. Accessed June 15, 2010.

Rogation Days

Rogation Days, in the Roman Catholic Church's calendar, are four days that were established for the holding of solemn processions designed to invoke God's mercy. They took their name from the Latin *rogare*, meaning "to ask." The activities make reference to the biblical admonition. "Ask, and you shall receive" (John 16:24).

The Major Rogation Day is April 25. This day is also set aside for the observation of the saint's day for Saint Mark, but the two have no relation. Should Easter fall on April 25, the Rogation Day is moved to April 27. This day may have arisen to replace the old Roman festival, the Robigalia. The Rogation Day route used in Rome is the same as that for the earlier festival, and there is an obvious similarity of name. The April Rogation Day is quite early, having been inserted into the calendar soon after the Christian rise to power in the fourth century.

Several weeks after the Major Rogation Day, a send set of three days are observed as the Minor or Lesser Rogation Days. Mamertus (d. c. 475). The archbishop of Vienne (Gaul), later canonized for his saintliness, introduced a set of litanies to be used during the week prior to Ascension that called for God's intercession to prevent earthquakes and other natural disasters. These litanies evolved into the Lesser Rogation Days. They are observed on the three days immediately before Ascension Day (the 40th day after Easter, thus always a Thursday).

Rogation Days were observed as a time of fasting, to call attention to the Ascension, a feast day. Farmers would ask the priest to bless their crops. The entirety of Europe was laid out in parishes, one church to a parish. Rogation Days would be a time to process around the boundaries of the parish (called "beating the bounds") during which time the priest would lead in prayers for the general protection and prosperity of the parish during the coming year. Incidentally, the Lesser Rogation

Days introduced a period of weeks (until Trinity Sunday) in which the priest would not perform marriages, an added incentive for scheduling marriages in June.

The wholesale revision of the liturgical calendar by Roman Catholics in 1969 included the elimination of the Rogation Days from an increasingly full calendar. Pope John Paul II (r. 1978–2005) reintroduced Rogation Days as permitted observations, but did not mandate their return. Rogation Days also survived in the Church of England, and are still observed on occasion.

J. Gordon Melton

See also Ember Days.

References

Bain, Ethel M. *Rogation Days across the Years: An Historical Pageant and Prayer Service for Use on Rogation Days*. New York: Division for Rural Work/National Council of the Protestant Episcopal Church, 1930.

Dues, Greg. *Catholic Customs and Traditions: A Popular Guide*. New London, CT: Twenty-Third Publications, 2006.

Valenziano, Mary Jo. *Rogation Days*. Chicago: Catholic Rural Life Department, Archdiocese of Chicago, 1989.

Romeria of La Virgen de Valme (October)

Among the largest annual religious festivals in Spain, the Romeria (pilgrimage) to the town of Dos Hermanas attracts thousands to the town of Los Hemanos, now a suburb of Seville. The celebration dates to the time of the Castilian king Hernando III (1199–1252) who had become king in 1217. Much of Ferdinand's time on the throne was dedicated to reasserting control over the lands to the south that had been occupied by the Muslims since the eighth century. He successfully overran the cities of Úbeda (1233), Córdoba (1236), Jaén (1246), and Seville (1248). He thus united all of Andalusia with the one exception of Granada, from which he received tribute.

When he came to the conquest of Seville, he attributed the inspiration to extend his territory to the motivation and support supplied by the Blessed Virgin in the form of the statue of Our Lady of Valme. Valme is short for *valedme*, Spanish for "be of value to me." According to the story, King Ferdinand had carried a likeness of the Virgin, only seven centimeters in height and carved from wood, with him during the battle and subsequently had sworn an oath to her. After the battle, he transformed the mosque of Seville into a cathedral dedicated to the Virgin, and placed the statue on the hill overlooking Los Hermanos. A shrine was erected to house the statue, which became a subject of local devotion. Ferdinand was buried in the cathedral of Seville before an image of the Virgin, dressed in the attire of a lay Franciscan. He was later canonized as a saint.

Devotion to the Virgen of Valme reached a low point in the 18th century, and the shrine fell into disrepair. It was restored in the 19th century by order of the king of

Spain. The modern Romeria dates from the restoration. In 1894, its administration was placed in the hands of the Brotherhood of Nuestra Señora de Valme.

The annual Romeria is held on the third Sunday in October. A procession begins at eight in the morning at the church of Mary Magdalene in Dos Hermanas (a short distance from Seville) and heads to the Virgin's shrine, Hermitage of the Virgen de Valme. The Virgin leads the parade on a highly decorated cart pulled by oxen, followed by additional floats and numerous people on horseback and on foot. Once at the Hermitage, a Mass is said, and in early evening, the Virgin is returned back to the church of Mary Magdalene. The procession proceeds through the community in the midst of festive atmosphere of music dedicated to the Virgin.

J. Gordon Melton

See also Pilgrimage of the Dew.

References

"Pilgrimage of Nuestra Senora de Valme." Posted at http://www.andalucia.org/eventos/romeria-de-nuestra-senora-de-valme/. Accessed on May 15, 2010.

Rosary, Feast of Our Lady of the (October 7)

The initial phase of establishing and spreading the use of the rosary, a string of beads used to keep count of a prayer that is repeated multiple times, within the Roman Catholic Church is attributed to Saint Dominic (c. 1170–1221) and the first generation of Dominicans. At the more important turning points in the rosary's history, Dominicans were present to promote its cause. A new phase of popularizing its use, for example, began with the efforts of Alain de la Roche (1428–1475), a Dominican who founded the Rosary Confraternity (1470). Pope Leo X (r. 1513–1521) gave his official commendation to the rosary in 1520, just as the Protestant Reformation began and as the expanding Ottoman Empire was threatening Europe from the east. Among the critical events of the 16th century was the battle of Lepanto (1571), at which the large Ottoman fleet was destroyed and the Ottoman approach through the Mediterranean stopped. Within weeks, Pope Pius V (r. 1566–1572), who also was a Dominican and who attributed the victory to the Virgin, instituted a new feast to Mary as "Our Lady of Victory" to celebrate the battle. Two years later, Pius's successor, Pope Gregory XIII (r. 1572–1585) renamed the feast-day as the "Feast of the Holy Rosary."

In 1716, Ottoman forces again suffered a great defeat following their unsuccessful attempt to take the Greek island of Corfu. Immediately after the battle, Pope Clement XI (r. 1700–1721) extended the feast of the Holy Rosary to the entire church. It was placed on the calendar for the first Sunday of October. There it remained until the 20th century. In 1913, Pope Pius X (r. 1903–1914) slightly revised the date of the feast, setting it annually on October 7. Then in 1969, Pope Paul VI (r. 1963-1978) again changed the name to the "Feast to Our Lady of the Rosary."

In addition to her role within the whole of Catholicism, Our Lady of the Rosary is the patron saint of several countries, Guatemala being notable among them. Here, Our Lady of the Rosary has a slightly different reference. In 1592, Friar Lopez de Montoya, a Dominican priest, commissioned a silver statue of the Virgin that would, early in the 19th century, eventually be installed in a Dominican parish church. In 1821, when Guatemalans were fighting for independence from Spain, the revolution's leadership met before the statue and proclaimed the Virgin to be the patroness of the new emerging nation, and pledged that they would not stop until independence was attained.

Subsequently, the Virgin of the Rosary was solemnly declared "Queen of Guatemala" (1833) and in an outdoor ceremony held in front of a large crowd, on January 26, 1934, was formally crowned. The crown includes some 120 emeralds and 44 diamonds among its many jewels. Today, the entire month of October, the month dedicated to the rosary within the Roman Catholic Church, has become a time of religious celebration and activity, including a variety of pilgrimages to the statue of the Virgin.

In 1917, during the apparitions at Fatima, Portugal, the Virgin specifically identified herself as Our Lady of the Rosary.

J. Gordon Melton

See also Fatima, Feast of Our Lady of; Immaculate Conception, Feast of the; Lourdes, Feast Day of our Lady of; Most Holy Name of Mary, Feast of the; Queenship of Mary, Feast of.

References

Dodds, Monica, and Bill Dodds. *Encyclopedia of Mary*. Huntington, IN: Our Sunday Visitor, 2007.

Hopkins, T. C. F. *Confrontation at Lepanto: Christendom vs. Islam*. New York: Forge Books, 2007.

Miller, John D. *Beads and Prayers: The Rosary in History and Devotion*. New York: Continuum, 2001.

Winston-Allen, Anne. *Stories of the Rose: The Making of the Rosary in the Middle Ages*. University Park: Pennsylvania State University Press, 1997.

Rose Monday. *See* Mardi Gras

Rose of Lima, Saint's Day of St. (August 23)

Saint Rose of Lima (1586–1617), canonized in 1671, was the first person in the Americas recognized as a saint by the Roman Catholic Church. She was born Isabel Flores y Oliva in Lima, Peru, on April 20, 1586. He parents were from Spain.

Reportedly, she developed an early tendency to a life of devotion and piety, which set her at odds with her parents, who looked for a favorable marriage for her. She had, however, read of Saint Catherine of Siena, whom she adopted as a role model. Through her teen years, she became known for her veneration of the Blessed Virgin and the Infant Jesus, to which she added fasting thrice weekly and engaging in secret penances.

Isabel took the name Rose at her confirmation. At one point, accused of being vain, she cut her hair and adopted plain clothing. Family opposition simply increased once she announced her decision to live a celibate life. Increasingly, her life revolved around a small grotto that she and her brother had built. The devotion manifest through her teen years led to her becoming a Dominican nun at the age of 20. The new context provided a more welcoming environment for her increased penances, including the wearing of a spiked crown, which she covered from view with roses. She had a variety of mystical encounters with Christ, during which she offered her austerities for the idolatry she perceived to abound in Peru. She also set up a room in her home as a haven for homeless children, the elderly, and the sick.

In the decade following her relatively brief earthly life (she died at age 31), miracles were increasingly attributed to her, thus justifying her beatification by Pope Clement IX (r. 1667–1669) shortly after assuming his office. She is known today as a patroness of the Philippines, Peru, South America, all of Latin America, and of the Western Hemisphere.

J. Gordon Melton

See also Martin de Porres, Saint's Day of St.; Thérèse of Lisieux, Saint's Day of St.

References

Graziano, Frank. *Wounds of Love: The Mystical Marriage of Saint Rose of Lima*. Oxford: Oxford University Press, 2004.

Mary Alphonsus, Sister. *St. Rose of Lima: Patroness of the Americas*. Rockford, IL: TAN Books & Publishers, 1982.

Windeatt, Mary Fabyan. *Angel of the Andes: The Story of Saint Rose of Lima*. Paterson, NJ: Saint Anthony Guild Press, 1956.

Rosh Hashanah

Rosh Hashanah is often referred to as the Jewish New Year, though it is observed on the first day of the month of Tishri, which is the seventh month in the Hebrew calendar. It occurs at some point between September 5 and October 5 on the Common Era calendar. It starts the civil year in the Hebrew calendar, and is considered the New Year for people, animals, and legal contracts. Rosh Hashanah may be adjusted a day as it cannot fall on Sunday, Wednesday, or Friday.

Tradition acknowledges Rosh Hashanah as the point from which new calendar years as well as the sabbatical (*shmita*) and jubilee (*yovel*) years are designated. The dating of Rosh Hashanah was traditionally done by observing the moon, which marked the move from one month to the next. Due to the difficulty in observing the moon in some years, and to getting the word out to the areas farthest from Jerusalem, it became common to celebrate Rosh Hashanah for two days, a practice continued in today's Orthodox and Conservative Jewish communities. The two-day Rosh Hashanah is an official holiday in Israel.

The observance derives from the Torah (the Five Books of Moses in which the Jewish law is laid down), and specifically from Leviticus 23: 23–25, which reads, "And the LORD spoke unto Moses, saying: Speak unto the children of Israel, saying: In the seventh month, in the first day of the month, shall be a solemn rest unto you, a memorial proclaimed with the blast of horns, a holy convocation. Ye shall do no manner of servile work; and ye shall bring an offering made by fire unto the LORD." From this verse comes the practice of the blowing of the *shofar*, a trumpet made from a ram's horn. Its sounding is meant to awaken those within its reach from their soulful slumber. Rosh Hashanah is among the days of rest; hence, many of the prohibitions on activity of the Sabbath are in effect.

The Talmud speculates that Creation began on what would be the 25th day of the Hebrew month of Elul. Six days later, the first day of Tishri, humans were created. Thus Rosh Hashanah, among other things, commemorates the creation of the human race.

Ritually speaking, Rosh Hashanah serves the important function of initiating the High Holidays, the high point in the annual calendar of Jewish observance. The first 10 days of Tishri are a time for self-reflection, confession, and repentance, all leading to the last day, Yom Kippur, the Day of Atonement. The elements for the observance of Rosh Hashanah were spelled out in the Oral Law, which were subsequently written down in the *Mishnah*, a late second-century attempt to commit the Oral Law to written form so it would not be lost in tumultuous times, and which became one of the two main parts of the great body of Jewish law, the Talmud.

On the day of the eve of Rosh Hashanah, the last day of the month of Elul, known as *Erev Rosh Hashanah*, Jews seek to end vows they have made that have not been fulfilled. If one has made a vow to do something, the individual (a male) may gather a small group of cohorts and ask them to nullify the vow. The individual then joins in nullifying the vows of the others. This action is seen as part of starting the New Year with a blank slate.

On Rosh Hashanah, Jews worship together in the synagogue, using a special liturgy that includes Scriptural readings, like on the Sabbath, and that emphasizes God's sovereignty. Worshippers greet each other with good wishes for the coming year. In their homes, they eat festive meals, which typically include apples and honey to symbolize hopes for a sweet year, and many homes display the New Year's cards that modern Jews have come to send to one another. Later in the day, some will walk to a nearby stream and throw in the contents of their pockets, symbolically

Orthodox Jewish men pray at the Western Wall in Jerusalem's Old City in observance of Rosh Hashanah. (Andrea Basile/Dreamstime.com)

casting off the sins of the old year. This ritual, called Tashlikh, points out one of the differences with the Sabbath. For Tashlikh, people carry small pieces of bread in their pockets to cast into the flowing waters. If Rosh Hashanah falls on a Monday, Tuesday, or Thursday, Tashlikh is observed on the afternoon of that day. If, however, it falls on Saturday (the Sabbath), then Tashlikh is observed on the following Sunday afternoon, the second day of Rosh Hashanah, to avoid the prohibition against carrying on the Sabbath, which is considered work.

J. Gordon Melton

See also Days of Awe; New Year's Day; Yom Kippur.

References

Cohen, Jeffrey M. *1,001 Questions and Answers on Rosh HaShanah and Yom Kippur*. New York: Jason Aronson, 1997.

Eckstein, Yecheil. *What You Should Know about Jews and Judaism*. Waco, TX: Word Books, 1984.

Greenberg, Irving. *The Jewish Way: Living the Holidays*. New York: Jason Aronson, 1998.

Posner, Raphael, Uri Kaploun, and Sherman Cohen, eds. *Jewish Liturgy: Prayer and Synagogue Service through the Ages*. New York: Leon Amiel Publisher/Jerusalem: Keter Publishing House, 1975.

Schauss, Hayyim. *The Jewish Festivals: A Guide to Their History and Observance*. New York: Schocken, 1996.

Rukmini Ashtami

Rukmini Ashtami is the birthday of Rukmini, the wife of Krishna. Though Krishna is most often pictured with his consort Radha, one of the gopis who herded cattle in Vrindavan in his youth, he would later marry Rukmini, the daughter of King Bhismaka. The king wanted Rukmini to marry Krishna, but their union was opposed by Rukmimi's brother. To avoid a family division, Krishna kidnapped her and took her to Dwarka, Gujarat, where he then lived, and they were married. She ruled as his queen and bore him a son, Pradyumna.

Today, Vaishnava Hindus worship Rukmini as an incarnation of the goddess Lakshmi. Her birthday is primarily celebrated by women, who venerate her, her husband, and her son. It is a day of fasting. Married women see that honoring Rukmini is a way to ensure conjugal happiness, and they also entreat her assistance in finding a proper spouse for their unwed daughters.

Rukmini Ashtami is observed on the eighth day of the waning moon in the Hindu lunar month of Pausha (December–January on the Common Era calendar). Rukmini is rarely presented in a temple by herself, but always standing beside her husband Krishna. Rukmini Ashtami will be acknowledged with special pujas and rituals in all of the temples dedicated to Lord Krishna, especially those in those parts of India especially associated with him such as Mathura and Vrindavan.

Constance A. Jones

See also Janmasthami.

References

Kelly, Aidan, Peter Dresser, and Linda Ross. *Religious Holidays and Calendars*. Detroit, MI: Omnigraphics, 1993.

Smith, H. Daniel, and M. Narasimhacharya. *Handbook of Hindu Gods, Goddesses and Saints Popular in Contemporary South India*. Columbia, MO: South Asia Books, 1997.

Rushi Pancham

Rushi Pancham is a unique celebration in the state of Gujarat in India observed by farmers and by women on the fifth day of the waxing moon in the Hindu month of Bhadrapad (August–September on the Common Era calendar).

Relative to women, Rushi Pancham speaks to issues of ritual purity. As is true in other traditions, Hindu women should refrain from performing any religious ritual or visiting any temples during their menstrual cycle. In some more conservative rules, the beliefs relative to the menstrual period are much stricter. Should a woman do either, she may perform the Rushi Pancham ritual, which acts to absolve her of any guilt. This day coincides with the last day (called Rishi Panchami) of the women's celebration of the Teej Festival.

For Gujarati farmers, Rushi Pancham serves as a general panacea for any sins such as injuring an animal committed during the previous year. The ritual performed on this day is said to recompense for any sin committed in the past year.

Constance A. Jones

See also Ahoi Ashtami; Ambuvachi; Dattatreya Jayanti; Rishi Panchami; Teej Festivals.

References

"Rushi Pancham in Gujarat." Hindu Blog. Posted at http://www.hindu-blog.com/2009/08/rushi-pancham-in-gujarat.html. Accessed June 15, 2010.

S

Sacred Heart of Jesus, Feast of the

Devotion to the Sacred Heart of Jesus is a popular form of Roman Catholic piety focused in an iconography that pictures Jesus with a body opened to reveal a heart encircled by a crown of thorns symbolic of his sufferings. Above the heart is a cross and flame. Devotion to the Sacred Heart emerged out of contemplation on the suffering of Jesus at his crucifixion. While on the cross, he was stabbed in the side with a spear, a wound that many came to believe must have penetrated his heart. During the Middle Ages, there was a shift in contemplation of the wound in Jesus's side toward a veneration of his heart. Content was added from all of the traditional compassionate attributes associated with the human heart, and drew added connotations from scriptural passages on God's love.

The symbolism of Jesus's loving heart found a new emphasis in the 17th century due to the efforts of Margaret Mary Alacoque (1647–1690). Sister Margaret Mary had experienced apparitions of Jesus for many years prior to her joining the Visitation order in 1671. Then on December 27, 1673, she had another vision of Jesus in which he revealed the secrets heretofore hidden about his Sacred Heart. He also assigned her the task of spreading the message of the Sacred Heart. Her work was given further direction by two additional visions in 1674 and 1675. She began to write about what she had learned in the visions and her sister nuns assisted in the distribution of the message. Soon, all of the chapters of the Visitation order, especially in France, erected an altar to the sacred heart in their chapels.

The devotion to the Sacred Heart grew slowly in France through the 18th century. Doubts had been raised about Sister Margaret Mary and her visions, and it was not until 1765 that these were resolved and the Feast of the Sacred Heart was officially sanctioned throughout the country. In 1856, with the strong urging of the French bishops, the pope approved a feast of the Sacred Heart of Jesus, which was placed on the calendar for the whole Church.

The Basilica of the Sacred Heart on Montmartre in Paris, now one of the most recognizable landmarks in the city, emerged as the great center for the further promotion of the Sacred Heart. Its construction was an outgrowth of the supplication to the Sacred Heart for France made by the faithful during the Franco-Prussian War (1870–1871). Central to the main sanctuary is a mosaic of the Sacred Heart showing Jesus with His arms open wide. In 1899, Pope Leo III (r. 1878–1903) consecrated the human race to the Sacred Heart of Jesus. His successor, Pope Saint Pius X (r. 1903–1914) decreed that a renewal of that consecration be held annually. Later, Pope Pius XI (r. 1922–1929) issued an encyclical that affirmed his belief that Jesus has truly revealed his message to Sister Margaret Mary. Finally, in 1956, on the occasion of the 100th anniversary of the placement of the Feast of the Sacred Heart on the general church's calendar, Pope Pius XII (r. 1939–1958) issued a lengthy letter with instructions of perpetuating worship of Jesus's Sacred Heart.

The feast of the Sacred Heart is celebrated on Friday, 19 days after Pentecost Sunday. Pius XII's 1956 encyclical became the basis upon which an extension of the feast is performed in family homes. Called the Enthronement of the Sacred Heart, the ceremony aims at consecration of a family's member to the Sacred Heart. As part of the ceremony, an image (a statue or a picture) of the Sacred Heart is then formally "enthroned" in the home as a constant reminder of the member's consecration.

Devotion to the Sacred Heart received additional support from the parallel devotion to what is termed the Divine Mercy, a practice initiated by Sister Josefa Menendez (1890–1923), a young Spanish woman who had joined a French religious order.

J. Gordon Melton

See also Divine Mercy Sunday; Immaculate Heart of Mary, Feast of the; Most Precious Blood, Feast of the.

References

Arnoudt, Peter J. *The Imitation of the Sacred Heart of Jesus*. Rockford, IL: Tan Books, 1974.

Haring, Bernard. *The Sacred Heart of Jesus: Yesterday, Today, Forever.* Liguori, MO: Liguori Publications, 1999.

Hume, Ruth Fox. *St. Margaret Mary, Apostle of the Sacred Heart*. New York: Farrar, Straus & Cudahy, 1960.

Saga Dawa Düchen. *See* Wesak/Vesak

Sai Baba of Shirdi, Birthday of

Sai Baba of Shirdi (d. 1918), not to be confused with the contemporary Indian spiritual teacher called Sathya Sai Baba (b. 1926), was a Hindu saint, yogi, and guru who is believed by many to have been an incarnation of a deity, possibly Shiva or Dattatreya (a deity who embodied the three major Hindu deities of Brahma, Vishnu, and Shiva), and/or a Sadguru, a title for the most prominent teachers leading others to the enlightened state. He was honored even in his lifetime in India, and many miracles are ascribed to him. His name draws on both Hindu and Muslim words, and he spent much of his life trying to bring reconciliation to the often-hostile Indian Muslim and Hindu communities, hostilities that would lead to Muslims setting up the nation of Pakistan. While primarily remembered as a saint among the Hindus, who have built a number of temples in his honor, he dressed as a Muslim, often quoted Muslim sources and used Muslim prayers, and engaged in practices identified with the Muslim community, such as eating meat and refraining from the use of alcohol.

Sai Baba's place and date of birth are unknown, an obstacle to those who wish to honor him. Many place his birthday as September 29, but without evidence to support that date. He emerged out of obscurity in his teen years when he settled at Shirdi, Maharashtra, where he was to remain for the rest of his life. He typically dressed and is generally pictured wearing a one-piece robe called a kafni and a cloth cap.

His fame was primarily local until the first decade of the 20th century, when his small band of disciples in Shirdi began to spread the story of their devotion to a modern saint and the miracles that were gathering around him to other parts of India. Pilgrims began to make their way to his town and the mosque in which he resided. Included among the visitors were a few who later became prominent teachers themselves, most notably Meher Baba.

Sai Baba was buried in a Hindu temple in Shirdi. As temples were dedicated to him, murtis (statues) of his likeness were set up for the convenience of disciples wishing to offer veneration. In some locations he sits beside murtis of his mother Easwaramma who has become an honored figure for bearing and raising the future saint. His fame continued to grow through the 20th century, and the contemporary Sathya Sai Baba claims to be his reincarnation.

Most Hindu disciples of Sai Baba of Shirdi celebrate his birthday on the holiday otherwise known as Guru Purnima, on the day of the full moon (purnima) in the Hindu lunar month of Ashadh (which occurs in June or July of the Common Era calendar). This day is set aside for all Hindus to show special veneration to their spiritual teacher, their guru. This date has seemed appropriate given the lack of knowledge of his actual birthday. Sathya Sai Baba, who also has a significant following in India and increasingly around the world, claims that the actual birth date is September 28, and that date is celebrated among his disciples. On his birthday, devotes will gather at the temples dedicated to him for worship (puja) and to share a meal.

J. Gordon Melton

See also Guru Purnima.

References

Kamath, M. V., and V. B. Kher. *Sai Baba of Shirdi: A Unique Saint*. Mumbai: Jaico Publishing House, 2007.

Manual of Sri Sathya Sai Seva Dal and Guidelines for Activities. Bombay: World Council of Sri Sathya Sai Organizations, 1979.

Rigapoulos, Antonio. *The Life and Teachings of Sai Baba of Shirdi*. Albany: State University of New York Press, 1993.

Saint John Lateran, Feast of the Dedication of (November 9)

The fame and hence importance of the Church of Saint John Lateran, more properly the Patriarchal Basilica of the Most Holy Savior and Saint John the Baptist at the Lateran, has been somewhat eclipsed by the role assumed by Saint Peter's Basilica, by far the most well-known Roman Catholic Church. However, officially, Saint John Lateran is the pope's cathedral or principal church of the Diocese of Rome and its bishop. After centuries as the leading church in Western Christendom (the Lateran Palace was, for example, the sight of five all-church councils between the 12th and 16th centuries), it gradually fell into relative obscurity as it was increasingly left to the care of a cardinal vicar named by the pope to administer the Diocese of Rome in his name so he could focus his attention on the global Church. The feast day recalls the church's former glory.

The Lateran Basilica emerges in the fourth century when it served as a palace belonging to Fausta, the wife of the emperor Constantine. After Constantine's conversion to Christianity in 313, he gave the palace to the Pope Miltiades (r. 311–314). It was dedicated to Christ as Savior by Pope Silvester I (r. 314–335) on November 9, 324. The first basilica was destroyed and rebuilt in the 10th century by Pope Sergius III (r. 904–911). At this time, a large baptistery in the rear of the church was added and named for John the Baptist. Pope Sergius then rededicated the church, adding John's name to it. Two centuries later, Pope Lucius II (r. 1144–1145) rededicated the basilica in the name of John the Evangelists. The popular designation as Saint John Lateran relates to it having both Johns as its patron saints.

The centrality of Saint John Lateran began its decline in the 14th century when papal headquarters moved to Avignon, France. In the pope's absence, maintenance at the Lateran basilica was neglected, and it was damaged by several earthquakes. When the popes returned, they tended to stay on the Vatican Hill rather than at the Lateran, located on the Coelian Hill. Then in the 16th century, the present Saint Peter's was erected, and attention was largely moved away from Saint John, though it continues to house the offices of the diocese of and thus functions as the "chancery" of the diocese.

Historically, Saint John Lateran was the sight of the 1929 signing of the Lateran Treaty, three agreements between the Kingdom of Italy and the Holy See that resolved a set of continuing issues that remained from the 19th-century unification of Italy and destruction of the former Papal States in central Italy.

One bit of continuing recognition given Saint John's Lateran, as the practice of holding Jubilee years in Rome emerged, the church was included as one of the four churches that were to be visited during the believer's pilgrimage to Rome. It is also the oldest of the four, and as such, lays some claim to being the mother church of Western Christendom.

J. Gordon Melton

See also Chair of St. Peter, Feast of the; Jubilee Year.

References

Caruana, Edmund. *The Jubilee Guide to Rome: The Four Basilicas, the Great Pilgrimage*. Collegeville, MN: Liturgical Press, 1998.

De Toth, John Baptist. *The Archbasilica of St. John Lateran: Brief Historic and Artistic Guide*. Rome: Tipografia Poliglotta Vaticana, 1967.

Hagstrom, Aurelie A., and Irena Vaisvilaite. *A Pilgrim's Guide to Rome and the Holyland*. Notre Dame, IN: Ave Maria Press, 1999.

Thornton, Francis B. *St. John Lateran in Rome*. St. Paul, MN: Catholic Digest, 1958.

Saint John's Eve/Day. *See* Summer Solstice.

Saint Patrick's Day (March 17)

Saint Patrick's Day, although celebrated by many as simply a secular holiday to honor the Irish, is primarily a commemoration of a most renowned and popular Roman Catholic saint, the patron saint of Ireland, and also incidentally of Nigeria. He was born Maewyn Succat in what is now Scotland late in the fourth century (c. 390–c. 461). He grew up in a Christian home, but during his teen years was captured by pirates and sold as a slave in northern Ireland. He eventually escaped and, after a time in Gaul (modern France), made his way back to Scotland.

Saint Patrick is the patron saint of Ireland and Nigeria. Using the shamrock to teach the holy trinity, he became the first bishop of Ireland. (Library of Congress)

At some point after reestablishing himself in Scotland, possibly toward the end of the 420s, he had a visionary experience that included an admonition to return to Ireland and assist its people. His life begins to take on more detail once he arrived in what would be his new home early in the 430s. A charismatic apostle, he is remembered as a gentle man. He would write two works, an autobiography, the *Confessio*, and his open *Letter to Coroticus*, in which he protested the continuing slave trade.

Though not a monk, Patrick operated out of a monastery he founded at Armaugh, later to become the site of his chair as the first bishop of Ireland. Accounts of the origination of Ireland as a Catholic country usually begin with Patrick, who also became the subject of numerous legendary stories. He is credited with ridding Ireland of snakes and of using the ubiquitous shamrocks as teaching tools—their three leaves becoming symbolic of the Christian Trinity. Biologists have suggested that, in fact, there were never any snakes in Ireland.

He died in 461, at Saul, the site of the first church built by Patrick. His feast day, March 17, is the day of his death. In the wake of the widespread movement around the world in the 19th century, and the role that many Irish came to have in the church, numerous churches and even cathedrals were named for Patrick, most notably the cathedrals in New York City, Chicago, Melbourne, and Auckland, In Ireland, Saint Patrick's cathedral in Dublin is considered the country's national church.

Saint Patrick's Day is celebrated with a special Mass at Catholic churches, especially those with a significant Irish membership, but has become better known as a day in which the Irish and their non-Irish friends dress in green and retire to the local pubs to see how much alcohol can be consumed. Chicago has become known for its attempts to pour green dye into the Chicago River.

J. Gordon Melton

See also Brigid of Kildare, Saint's Day of St.; Willibrord, Saint's Day of St.

References

Bury, J. B. *The Life of St. Patrick and His Place in History.* London: Macmillan, 1905.

Kenney, James F. *The Sources for the Early History of Ireland.* New York: Columbia University Press, 1929.

O'Loughlin, Thomas. *Discovering Saint Patrick.* Maryknoll, NY: Orbis Books, 2005.

Todd, James Henthorn. *St. Patrick: Apostle of Ireland: A Memoir of His Life and Mission.* London: Wipf & Stock, 2003.

Saint Stephen's Day (December 26)

Saint Stephen's Day (the feast of Saint Stephen's) calls attention to the role of martyrdom of Christians throughout Christian history who have died for their profession of faith by recalling the first Christian martyr. Stephen was stoned to death.

Stephen appeared in the church at Jerusalem during its growth phase after the day of Pentecost, when the church members chose him as one of the first seven deacons to assist the apostles in some of the practical matters of running the church. He came to be known as a man of great faith and power around whom numerous miracles were reported. Eventually, he was accused of blasphemy against Moses and God and hauled before the council of Jewish leaders, the Sanhedrin. In his speech to the council, Stephen accused the leaders of being stiff-necked and uncircumcised of heart, and spoke as if he expected them to continue a history he recounted of each generation's killing of its prophets. He ended the speech as a visionary who was seeing the heavens open and himself as a servant of God also ascending on high.

The council reacted emotionally. They sent Stephen from the city where he was stoned (Acts 7:59). His clothes were given to a young Jewish intellectual named Saul who at the time also engaged in activity aimed at suppressing Christianity. Saul would later, following his conversion, become a Christian missionary and the primary subject of the New Testament book of Acts of the Apostles. His martyrdom was witnessed by a Jewish leader, the future Paul the Apostle, who was at the time engaged in activity designed to persecute the church.

Stephen was especially honored in the church during its years of its clandestine existence and repeated persecution prior to being legalized by the emperor Constantine (272–337 CE) in the fourth century. Historians in general see the death of Stephen as occasioning the church's moving from Jerusalem to Antioch and other locations throughout the Middle East.

Over the centuries, Saint Stephen was identified with the wren. The Irish, for example, had a legend that he was in hiding and was betrayed by the sounds of a bird chattering away. In Ireland, where it is celebrated as a national holiday, small boys would hunt a wren, and if caught, the wren was tied to the top of a decorated pole or holly bush. The day is also important in Wales and Catalonia, and Serbia has adopted Saint Stephen as their patron saint. Elsewhere, throughout the Roman Catholic Church and Eastern Orthodoxy, Saint Stephen's Day is celebrated with a special Mass. The Orthodox Church celebrates the day on December 27.

Celebrated on December 26, Saint Stephen's Day often merges into Christmas celebrations, as occurs in John Mason Neale's lively carol, "Good King Wenceslas looked out/On the feast of Stephen," which includes the lines, "Joy that martyrs won their crown,/opened heaven's bright portal,/when they laid the mortal down/for the life immortal" (http://www.carols.org.uk/good_king_wenceslas.htm). Stephen was also designated the patron stain of horses. In central Europe on this day, farmers would decorate their horses and bring to the parish church for a blessing.

J. Gordon Melton

See also George, Feast Day of St.; Peter and Paul, Saint's Day of Sts.

References

Foxe, John. *The New Foxe's Book of Martyrs*. Rewritten and updated by Harold J. Chadwick. Gainesville, FL: Bridge-Logos Publishers, 2001.

Gonzales, Justo. *The Story of Christianity, Volume 1, The Early Church to the Dawn of the Reformation*. San Francisco: Harper, 1984.

Watson, Alan. *The Trial of Stephen: The First Christian Martyr*. Athens: University of Georgia Press, 1996.

Weins, Delbert L. *Stephen's Sermon and the Structure of Luke-Acts*. North Richland Hills, TX: D. & F. Scott Publishing, 1998.

Saint Stephen's Day (Hungary) (August 20)

While most of Christendom celebrates December 26 as the feast of Saint Stephen, a reference to Stephen the first Christian martyr, Hungarians celebrate Saint Stephen's Day in August, but as a remembrance of another Stephen (c. 967–1038), the first Hungarian king (r. 1000–1038), who is recognized for his role in establishing Christianity in Hungary and the surrounding region. He is crediting with organizing the Archdiocese of Esztergom, which had the effect of severing the dependence of the Hungarian church on the German archbishops. He ordered the building of numerous churches and funded the evangelization of the more rural areas of his kingdom.

After his death, his body was mummified. He was canonized in 1083. Some years later, his tomb was opened and his hand removed. Now known as "The Holy Right," it is venerated as a relic. Of the rest of the body, only some bone fragments have survived, and these now have been distributed to churches across Hungary. His life is celebrated by Hungarians on August 20, the day when his relics were formally moved to Budapest. In recent years, Hungarians celebrate Saint Stephen's Day with a procession and exhibition of the "Holy Right," which during the rest of the year is kept in Saint Stephen's Basilica, Budapest, a church completed in 1905.

Ecumenical Patriarch Bartholomew I, the leader of Eastern Orthodoxy, recognized the canonization of Stephen in the year 2000. That same year, U.S. president Jimmy Carter ordered the return of the Holy Crown, believed to have been worn by King Stephen, returned to Hungary. The crown had been entrusted to the U.S. government in 1945 (at the end of World War II) and was subsequently placed in a vault at Fort Knox, Kentucky.

In 1687, the Roman Catholic Church moved the day for the veneration of Saint Stephen to September 2. Then in 1969, when the calendar of saints was significantly revised, September 16, the day after his death, became open, and it was moved. It is still celebrated on that day throughout the church outside of Hungary.

J. Gordon Melton

See also Casimir, Saint's Day of St.; Saint Stephen's Day.

References

Engel, Pal. *Realm of St. Stephen: A History of Medieval Hungary, 895–1526*. London: I. B. Tauris, 2001.

Gyoffry, Gyorgy. *King Saint Stephen of Hungary*. New York: Columbia University/Eastern European Monographs, 1994.

Horvath, Michael J. *An Annotated Bibliography of Stephen I, King of Hungary: His Reign and His Era*. College Park: University of Maryland Library, 1969.

Saints (Roman Catholic Tradition)

The word saint is derived from the Latin *sanctus* (Greek *hagios*), literally meaning holy. In Christianity, it refers to someone who has manifested a holiness of life or someone who has been martyred for the faith, and whom the church believes is now enjoying eternal life with God. In Roman Catholicism, holiness of life is spoken of in terms of "heroic virtue." A saint is someone who has "heroically," or to an exceptional degree, exhibited the supernatural virtues (since they are gifts of God's grace) of faith, hope, and charity and the moral virtues of prudence, justice, fortitude, and temperance.

In its broader meaning, saint can be used to corporately designate all the faithful, both the living and the dead, particularly when describing the church as a "communion of saints." The Second Vatican Council uses similar language in describing the church as a "holy nation" in its theology of sainthood (cf. *Dogmatic Constitution on the Church*, n. 50). In such a theology of holiness, the church recognizes that God alone is holy. God calls all persons to a life of holiness with a hope of sharing in eternal divine life. Holiness or sanctity is not something the church bestows on the individual, but is a gift given freely by God, which the church subsequently formally recognizes in the individual. All the faithful are called to a life of imitation of these saints, and through a special devotion, or veneration, of such saints can seek their intercessions through prayer, since saints enjoy a more perfect relationship, in heaven, with God. A distinction is drawn between the veneration of, or devotion to, saints and the worship which is due to God alone.

History

In the early church, the term saint was most commonly used to describe those who believed in Christ and who were called to follow him (1 Cor. 1:2; Romans 1:7). The Church preeminently recognizes the sanctity of the apostles of Christ and the Blessed Virgin Mary, the mother of Jesus Christ. The term saint was also used describe those who were martyred for their faith during the persecutions of the first three centuries. The memory of these martyrs, their date of martyrdom, place of burial, and relics were venerated in this early period. The term saint was later also applied to monastics, who renounced the world and lived lives of asceticism and prayer; to early theologians, who defended and explicated the faith; and to those who were zealous in their preaching of the faith (like missionaries). Miracles were often attributed to such saints.

In its modern usage, canonization refers to the culmination of a process in which someone is declared a saint and is added to the canon, or list, of saints. However, in the early church period, the declaration of sainthood could be effected in a number of different ways, the most common being by popular acclamation by the people, or later, by the declaration of a bishop, pope, or synod (or council) of bishops. The synodal process has remained the normal avenue for canonization in the Eastern Orthodox churches. The Roman Catholic tradition gradually developed a more formal process, beginning around the 13th century. Various revisions to the process of canonization followed, with the most recent protocols being announced in 1983. These recent changes were in part occasioned by the demands of modern historical and scientific inquiry.

Canonization in the Roman Catholic Tradition

In 1983, in the Apostolic Constitution, *The Divine Teacher and Model of Perfection*, Pope John Paul II established new procedures for canonization. There are two phases on the path toward canonization: the diocesan and the Roman. Normally, the process of initiating a case for the canonization of a person is done at a local level by a diocesan bishop, either Roman Catholic or Eastern Catholic, or by the bishop through a request of an individual or group of faithful. The local bishop appoints a postulator, who directs the investigation process at the local diocesan level. In the language of the constitution, those for whom canonization is sought are initially referred to as "venerable servants of God." Local bishops are to inquire about the life of this person, their heroic virtues, orthodoxy or, in certain cases, their martyrdom. An examination is also done of any published or unpublished writings (such as diaries or letters), and any living witnesses are interviewed. The bishop is also to submit a declaration that no cult around the postulant has arisen. These reports and eyewitness accounts (the "acts") are then gathered and submitted to the Sacred Congregation for the Causes of Saints, which then initiates the Roman phase of the investigation.

In the *New Laws for the Causes of Saints* (1983), the Congregation distinguished between ancient cases and recent cases, with the major difference being whether or not witnesses can give an oral deposition. Recent cases are normally not brought before the Congregation until at least five years after the death of the person, although the pope may unilaterally expedite this process by dispensing with the waiting period. For the latter case, the two most recent examples under consideration are Mother Theresa (1999, by Pope John Paul II), and Pope John Paul II (in 2005, by Pope Benedict XVI).

Within this Congregation exists a College of Relators, who are specifically entrusted with studying the cases for canonization, and preparing reports (or "positions") of their findings and their reviews of the diocesan reports. This College of Relators can also draw upon consultors, that is, other experts in history, theology, and spirituality. A promoter of the faith oversees this process in its various phases.

Miracles

Miracles are seen as divine interventions by God, and thus by extension as confirmations of the sanctity of an individual. The revised constitution makes clear that an inquiry into alleged miracles is conducted separately from the examination of the life of holiness or martyrdom of a servant of God. The Sacred Congregation has a board of medical experts or physicians, who discuss cases of alleged miracles dealing with healing. These experts do not produce a theological judgment that a miracle has occurred, but are only asked whether or not there exists a medical or scientific reason for a miracle or physical cure. No miracles are required for a martyr to be declared a saint.

During this process, relics (such as hair, bone fragments, or pieces of clothing) of the servant of God may be collected. The authenticity and preservation of relics is relegated to the Congregation. Relics are used in the church as a means of remembrance and devotion to a particular saint, and are especially kept in places of pilgrimage or as part of an altar.

At the culmination of the entire examination process, the Sacred Congregation, with its member bishops and cardinals, examines the final reports or votes of the relators, expert consultors, physicians and the promoter of the faith, and issues a report to the pope.

There are two distinct levels, the one preceding the other, of the formal recognition of the sanctity of an individual: beatification and canonization. Beatification requires the verification (or "instruction") of one miracle attributed to the servant of God. If authentic, then the pope can declare the person as "Blessed," wherein the church recognizes that this person is a model of heroic virtue. The person is given the title of Blessed, and a limited cult of veneration of this person is permitted at the local level, in a region or in a religious community. The process from beatification to canonization requires the authentication of a second miracle. Once a second report is submitted and a second miracle verified, the pope can proceed to a declaration of sainthood. This is a definitive declaration by the pope that the saint is enjoying eternal life in God and that a cult of veneration is to be extended to the universal church. Both beatification and canonization normally take place in Saint Peter's Basilica in Rome, during a Pontifical Mass, and are done solely through a decree of the pope. Those designated with the title Saint are assigned a particular feast day, which is commemorated by special prayers in the church's liturgical calendar.

Jaroslav Skira

See also Saints, Celebrating the Lives of (Protestant Tradition); Saints, Veneration of (Roman Catholic Tradition).

References

Cunningham, Lawrence S. *The Meaning of Saints*. San Francisco: Harper & Row, 1980.

Hawley, John Stratton, ed. *Saints and Virtues*. Berkeley: University of California Press, 1987.

Woodward, Kenneth. *Making Saints: How the Catholic Church Determines Who Becomes a Saint, Who Doesn't and Why*. New York: Touchstone/Simon & Schuster, 1996.

Saints, Celebrating the Lives of (Protestant Tradition)

By the time of the Protestant Reformation in the 16th century, the veneration of saints had become a firmly established element in the piety expressed within the Roman Catholic Church, and the veneration of saints had been integrated into the church's life from the use of relics and pilgrimages to the daily worship in which various saints were acknowledged and held up as exemplars for the faithful.

The new authority assigned to the Bible by Protestant leaders meant that the question of saints quickly became an issue, and the different role adopted for saints manifested a division of approaching the Reformation between Lutherans and Anglicans on the one hand and the Reformed and Presbyterians on the other. The Protestant attitude toward saints was initially affected by their rejection of the cult of relics. Protestants found the veneration and use of relics as unbiblical, while simultaneously calling the factual basis of some of the most prominent relics into question. Then, they rejected the veneration of saints, especially the Blessed Virgin Mary, as detracting from the worship of God. The distinction between worship (due only to God) and veneration (offered to a saint) was at best vague, and on the practical level, they were almost indistinguishable. With the abandoning of any doctrine of purgatory, the afterlife place of punishment for final purification before entering heaven, the need of saints to assist souls in purgatory was also abandoned.

Lutherans and Anglicans tended to approach the Reformation from the principle of keeping everything of the medieval Western church that the Bible did not directly condemn. The Reformed church worked to keep only that which the Bible supported. The cult of saints seemed to fall in the middle ground, being neither condemned by the Bible nor advocated by it. The Bible certainly called people to a holy life and seemed to make a place for those who led by example. At the same time, Protestants emphasized God's role in sanctifying people by his grace, as opposed to the effort and pious activity of the individual in gaining saintly status.

Anglican and Lutherans, who most clearly affirmed their connections to the traditions of Western Christianity and who most clearly saw themselves as a reforming force and hence wished to keep alive their communications with Roman Catholics, found in the continued nurturing of the liturgical calendar and the acknowledgment of saints as helpful in that regard. Both revised the liturgical calendar, jettisoned some peculiarly Roman Catholic saints, and adapted it to their own needs. Both discarded the many dates associated specifically with the Virgin Mary, especially those developed primarily for extra biblical sources. Over time, they both added particularly Anglican and Lutheran saints to the observances.

Those churches in the Reformed/Presbyterian tradition (as well as in what became the Mennonite tradition) tended to rid themselves of any acknowledgment of saints in the Roman Catholic sense of that term altogether. They found no biblical basis for the cult of saints. In looking at the biblical use of the term, they found that the New Testament tended to use it to refer to all church members. Paul addressed his letter to the saints or members of a particular church. They saw the saints as all who had been called by God to be a Christian, and who had as a result had their sins forgiven and their life sanctified by the action of God and his grace. One acted to become saintly not to attain sainthood, but out of gratitude for God salvation. Thus, even the practice of citing particular people as saints was abandoned, much less the idea of venerating them in particular form. Biblical passages for developing a position on saints would begin with passages such as Ephesians 3:7–8 and Matthew 11:11, in which Paul and John the Baptist are cited as less than an average Christian.

Apart from those churches in the Lutheran and Anglican tradition, those churches that developed over the centuries within the Protestant world—Baptists, Congregationalists, Methodists, Adventists, Pentecostals—simply never engaged in any discussion of the issue of saints. At best, they offered negative reflections on the idea of saints as part of a general anti-Catholic polemic that distinguished them from Roman Catholics. At best, they used the term in an informal manner to refer to people who exemplified the faith or was a hero missionary activity. In a similar manner, New Testament figures might be referred to as saints—particularly Paul and the gospel writers. United Methodists, for example, have frequently named churches after prominent church leaders, but also have a regulation limiting the designating of a person memorialized in the name of a church with the appellation "saint" to Saints Matthew, Mark, Luke, John, or Paul.

Amid the new relations that have developed within the 20th-century Ecumenical Movement, those Protestants who had abandoned any discussion of saints have learned of the Lutheran and Anglican retention of a calendar of saints and have also gained a new appreciation of the role of saints in the Eastern Orthodox and Non-Chalcedonian Orthodox churches, some of whom became charter members of the World Council of churches and various national church councils. In the changing relationship between Protestants and Catholics in the post–Vatican II era, Protestants have found another motivation to reopen the issue of saints and especially of those saints named by the church prior to the split between the Eastern and Western churches.

The attempt to develop a new appreciation of saints was preceded by a new attention to the liturgical year, which spread among the Protestant churches of the Reformed, Presbyterian, and Methodist traditions. By the end of the 20th century, most of the larger denominations that participated in the World Council of Churches and its affiliated national and regional councils had adopted a liturgical calendar that included the major traditional feast days (Christmas, Epiphany, Ash Wednesday, Palm Sunday, Easter, and Pentecost) and seasons (Advent, Lent, Holy Week, Eastertide, etc.). This new emphasis on liturgical worship was championed among Methodists by the Order of Saint Luke (not to be confused with a similarly named group in the Episcopal Church that concentrates on spiritual healing).

The spread of the acknowledgment of the liturgical year set the stage for a new discussion of a calendar of saints. Again, the Anglicans and Lutherans led the way. In the 1970s, new editions of liturgical materials began to appear that expanded the calendar of saints to include people from a more broadly Protestant community. As expected, among Methodists, the Order of Saint Luke published a volume, *For All the Saints: A Calendar of Commemorations for United Methodists*, issued in 1995, though this book has yet to receive any widespread circulation, much less implementation.

The development of an operative calendar of saints among Protestants is still in a preliminary stage, with many Anglican and Lutheran parishes ignoring any commemoration of saints. In anticipation of possible future interest in developing a calendar of saints as the larger Protestant churches grow more cooperative and familiar with each other and as they continue to dialogue with Eastern Orthodoxy and Roman Catholicism, ecumenically oriented liturgists have proposed calendars of saints that include figures from the ancient and early medieval church, Protestant heroes and martyrs, and modern figures who exemplify more recent themes in social activism and ecumenical endeavors, all set within an acceptable Protestant theological context for the consideration of Christian exemplars. Among the more notable of such pioneering reconsiderations of saints is *A New Book of Festivals and Commemorations: A Proposed Common Calendar of Saints*, compiled by Philip H. Pfatteicher, an American Lutheran. A new openness to considering the idea of saints has been assisted greatly as a result of widespread circulation of information concerning 20th-century martyrs of Christianity, most from the mission fields in non-Western countries.

J. Gordon Melton

See also Saints (Roman Catholic Tradition); Saints, Veneration of (Roman Catholic Tradition).

References

Attwater, Donald, and Catherine Rachel John. *The Penguin Dictionary of Saints*. 3rd ed. New York: Penguin Books, 1993.

Bentley, James. *A Calendar of Saints: The Lives of the Principal Saints of the Christian Year*. New York: Time Warner Books, 2006.

Farmer, David Hugh. *The Oxford Dictionary of Saints*. New York: Oxford University Press, 2004.

Guthrie, Clifton F. *For All the Saints: A Calendar of Commemorations for United Methodists*. Akron, OH: Order of Saint Luke, 1995.

Kolb, Robert. *For All the Saints: Changing Perceptions of Martyrdom and Sainthood in the Lutheran Reformation*. St. Louis, MO: Concordia, 1987.

Perham, Michael. *The Communion of Saints*. London: SPCK, 1982.

Pfatteicher, Philip H. *A New Book of Festivals and Commemorations: A Proposed Common Calendar of Saints*. Minneapolis, MN: Fortress Press, 2008.

Sweeney, Jon M. *The Lure of Saints: A Protestant Experience of Catholic Tradition*. Orleans, MA: Paraclete Press, 2006.

Saints, Veneration of (Roman Catholic Tradition)

The celebration and honoring of saints emerged out of the first three centuries of the church, when it existed as a somewhat clandestine organization within the Roman

Empire and was subject to periodic waves of severe persecution. It saw many of the founding apostles martyred, and over the succeeding decades, bishops, priests, and lay people distinguished themselves by their willingness to maintain their profession of faith through a range of torture and executions. The fourth century opened with one of the more memorable waves of persecution under the emperor Diocletian (r. 284–305 CE) that brought to the fore stories of numerous martyrs. The severe persecutions were followed by an amazing two decades during which time the church was successively decriminalized, officially tolerated, legalized, and them elevated to a privileged position as the favored religion by the emperor Constantine (r. 306–337).

The natural desire to honor the martyrs of the Diocletian persecution was significantly bolstered by the search for items of those associated with the founding events of the Christian movement by Constantine's mother Helena (c. 246–330). As the church expanded, it provided space for the acknowledgment of those who had lived exemplary lives and especially for those who had given their life for the cause of Christianity either by a lifetime of service or martyrdom, or both.

Through the centuries, the list of those who had for various reasons risen above the common norms of Christian living grew, attempts were made to understand the nature of the honor that were properly due to people designated as saints, and to provide some structure in which the veneration of the saints could be given. Within the Roman Catholic Church, efforts to perfect the practice of acknowledging the saints continue even as times change and the number of saints known to the church as a whole steadily grows.

The process of acknowledging an individual as a saint begins with a petition that nominated a person's saintly character to be examined, which may initiate a process of examination, which leads to two major steps when and individual is first beatified and then canonized. When canonized—that is, recognized by the church as a saint—the new saint is assigned a feast day, usually the day of their death, which is assumed to be the day of their rebirth in heaven. The new day may be venerated anywhere within the Catholic Church, but overwhelmingly, most saints are not known beyond the local area in which they lived and worked. In addition, a parish church may be built/named in their honor. The process of canonization is not seen as making anyone a saint, but as a process of recognition of a person's sainthood.

Items associated with a saint, first of all their body, and secondarily things they wore or used, came to be seem as bearers of their sanctity. A saint's relics were seen as inherently sacred and possessed of spiritual power. As Jesus was believed to have ascended bodily into heaven, there were no bodily remains; but there was the possibility of locating significant items associated with him, for example, the cloak he wore, the burial shroud in which his body was laid to rest following the crucifixion, and the wooden cross upon which he was crucified. In like measure, the Blessed Virgin Mary was assumed to have been translated into heaven, and thus only items she had worn or used would be possible relics.

With the martyrs of the first three centuries, their bodily remains were the most valued items associated with them. Beginning with the apostles, the burial places of martyrs would become sites at which shrines and later churches would be built. Churches in Rome were built over the burial sites of the Apostles Peter and Paul, and a church in northwest Spain came to house the body of what was believed to be the Apostle James. After the third century, the relics of martyrs would be transported to already-existing churches and there entombed. The relics of particularly famous martyrs could be divided among multiple locations. In the post-Constantinian church, the martyrs would be joined by the saintly confessors, that is, those who lived a faithful and holy life but died a natural death.

The church grew in large part due to the effort of saintly and holy people who existed as exemplars of the faith and were willing to give their life for their faith if required. These people were rightly honored by the church's membership as a whole. The emphasis given to the veneration of saints at times led to a level of subversion and corruption to enter, in that people desirous of relics to venerate were open to accepting fraudulent and questionable claims about objects presented as relics. Such questionable claims proliferated in the Middle Ages and became an issue at the time of the Protestant Reformation.

At the present time, the veneration of saints within the Roman Catholic Church is widespread; it is conducted within the context of a sophisticated theological structure that begins with distinguishing the veneration (dulia) that is proper to saints from the worship (latria) that is due only to the Holy Trinity. In between the two is the elevated veneration (hyperdulia) that is proper to the Blessed Virgin due to her special role in birthing Jesus and hence in the salvation of humanity. The respect and interaction with saints is distinct from worship, but should lead to the worship of God.

Veneration can include the honoring of saints through pilgrimages to sites identified with them and where their relics are enshrined. On the date assigned for their commemoration, they may be mentioned and/or otherwise acknowledged in the Mass said that day. There may be additional celebratory activities planned, including processions, musical performances, or efforts to educate the public about the saint. The saint's day is an opportune time for pilgrimages to their shrine or relics. On rare occasions, the relics of an especially prominent saint may be taken from their permanent resting place for viewing elsewhere.

Where relics are unavailable, a saint may be venerated through the use of an image—a picture, icon, or statue. Those saints popular enough to have their picture circulated also usually have prayers written for use in their veneration. Some saints have been especially identified with a particular form of devotion, and joining in that devotion is also a means of venerating the saint.

Saints are believed to be in heaven, in the presence of God, and thus immediately available to intercede with God on the behalf of the average believer. Seeking intercession with a saint for a particular need is one of the most popular forms of veneration. Many saints have been named patron saints of particular geographical areas (a country, a city, a district within a country), a particular occupation, or a particular need. People in a particular location or that follow an occupation or that

Calendar of Selected Saints

January 12/14	Sava, Saint's Day of St.
January 20	San Sebastian Day
January 21	Agnes, Feast Day of St.
February 1	Brigid of Kildare, Saint's Day of St.
February 3	Ansgar, Saint's Day of St.
February 6	Peter Baptist and Companions, Saint's Day of St.
March 6	Casimir, Saint's Day of St.
March 17	Saint Patrick's Day
March 19	Joseph, Saint's Day of St.
April 3	Benedict the African, Saint's Day of
April 11	Stanislaus, Saint's Day of St.
April 23	George, Feast Day of St.
	Adalbert of Prague, Saint's Day of St.
April 28	Peter Chanel, Saint's Day of St.
April 29	Catherine of Siena, Saint's Day of St.
May 4	Florian, Saint's Day of St.
May 27	Augustine of Canterbury, Saint's Day of St.
June 1	Boniface of Germany, Saint's Day of St.
June 9	Columba, Saint's Day of St.
June 10	Margaret of Scotland, Saint's Day of St.
June 13	Anthony of Padua, Saint's Day of St.
July 11	Benedict of Nursia, Saint's Day of St.
July 23	Bridget, Saint's Day of St.
July 25	James the Greater, Feast Day of St.
July 26	Anne, Feast Day of St.
July 29	Olaf, Saint's Day of St.
August 1	Alphonse de Ligouri, Saint's Day of St.
August 8	Dominic, Saint's Day of St.
August 23	Rose of Lima, Saint's Day of St.
August 28	Augustine of Hippo, Saint's Day of St.
September 3	Gregory the Great, Saint's Day of St. (September 3)
September 8	Peter Claver, Saint's Day of St.
September 16	Cyprian, Saint's Day of St.
October 1	Thérèse of Lisieux, Saint's Day of St.
October 31	All Hallows Eve
November 1	All Saints Day
November 2	All Souls Day
November 7	Willibrord, Saint's Day of St.
November 11	Martinmas
November 30	Andrew, Saint's Day of St.
December 3	Francis Xavier, Saint's Day of St.
December 6	Nicholas, Saint's Day of St.
December 26	Saint Stephen's Day
December 27	John the Evangelist, Day of St.

have a particular need may immediately identify a saint who has already identified with their particular concern.

Over the years, Mary has appeared to many individuals and been identified with many locations and concerns, and as such, has come to be seen under many titles that offer more specialized introductions to what Roman Catholics believe to be her larger role in human salvation. Those wishing to offer veneration to the Blessed Virgin may do so in any one of her varied images such as Our Lady of Lourdes (healing), Our Lady of Prompt Succor, or Our Lady of Japan, to name just a few.

During the Middle Ages and the early modern period, the Roman Catholic calendar of saints became quite clogged. The saints' commemoration also aligned in an ever-more-complicated ranking system, which interacted with the annual cycle of worship that followed the events in the life of Christ from Mary's pregnancy to his resurrection, ascension, and sending of the Holy Spirit (Pentecost). In the 20th century, the system for laying out the liturgical year, including the days for acknowledging particular saints, was reformed on several occasions, most notably by Pope Pius X (1911), Pope Pius XII (1955), Pope John XXIII (1962), and Pope Paul VI (1969). In 1960, Pope John XXIII introduced a new simplified system of ranking all liturgical days, as first, second, third and fourth class days. In 1969, Pope Paul VI named the top three classes as "solemnities," "feasts," and "memorials," and divided memorial into obligatory and optional. Overwhelmingly, the commemoration of most saints would fall under the heading of optional memorials. The more important days celebrating the events in the life of the Virgin rank as solemnities, while those of the saints who appeared in the biblical record (the apostles, for example) are feasts. Some of the other more prominent saint's days are obligatory memorials.

On a day to which no obligatory celebration is assigned, the Mass may acknowledge any saint mentioned in the Roman martyrology for that day. All Saints Day, November 1, was set aside to honor all saints, all who have made it to heaven, who are unknown, otherwise unrecognized, and have no special feasts.

The Calendar of Selected Saints table in this entry provides a list of saint's days discussed elsewhere in this encyclopedia. Only a few of the more prominent saints could be selected for individual consideration. Those whose celebration had become international, includes activities in the public sphere, or who have been designated as patrons of a country were chosen for inclusion in this particular volume.

J. Gordon Melton

See also Saints, Celebrating the Lives of (Protestant Tradition). Saints (Roman Catholic Tradition).

References

Attwater, Donald, and Catherine Rachel John. *The Penguin Dictionary of Saints*. 3rd ed. New York: Penguin Books, 1993.

Ball, Ann. *Encyclopedia of Catholic Devotions and Practices*. Huntington, IN: Our Sunday Visitor, 2003.

Bentley, James. *A Calendar of Saints: The Lives of the Principal Saints of the Christian Year*. New York: Time Warner Books, 2006.

Farmer, David Hugh. *The Oxford Dictionary of Saints*. New York: Oxford University Press, 2004.

Sakata Chauth. *See* Ganesh Chaturthi

Sakura Matsuri

Possibly the best known of all Japanese festivals, The Sakura Matsuri, or Cherry Blossom Festival, is held each spring as the cherry trees, indigenous to Japan, put out an effusive display of pink and white to the delight of all. The date of the Sakura festival varies each year relative to the weather and the part of Japan in which one lives. The Sakura festival, as most spring events among believers, was directed to entreating the kamis (deities) for a good harvest in the fall. The blossoming of the cherry trees was a good omen of the coming abundance. At the same time, the public nature of trees' display has tended to drive people from the shrines to the outdoors and certainly put everyone, whether Shinto or Buddhist or other, in a festive mood.

The particular tree that is the subject of the festival, the Yoshino cherry tree, is peculiar in several ways. It produces an amazing amount of blossoms, but very few seeds, and must be propagated from cuttings. Its blossom is also very short lived, and this contributed to its symbolic nature as a sign of the brevity of life. This element was used during World War II to motivate the armed forces, especially pilots. It was often used to decorate war planes, including those assigned to suicide missions.

A young girl, balanced on her father's shoulders, reaches up to touch the cherry blossoms at Ueno Park in Tokyo on April 5, 2009. (Yoshikazu Tsuno/AFP/Getty Images)

Apart from the strict religious significance of the cherry blossom in Japan, the government has used it as a positive force in foreign relations. In 1912, for example, it gave 3,020 cherry blossom trees to the United States, the gift being occasioned by the need to destroy Washington's previously existing trees due to a disease that had infested them. The gift was also meant as a sign of friendship between the two countries, and those trees still line the capital's Tidal Basin and remain a major Washington tourist site.

In 1915, the U.S. government gave Japan a number of flowering dogwood trees. In 1926, the Japanese government made a similar gift to

Philadelphia on the occasion of the 150th anniversary of the Declaration of Independence. As part of her beautification program, Lady Bird Johnson, the wife of president Lyndon B. Johnson, accepted a further 3,800 trees in 1965. This latter gift proved fortuitous, as Japan suffered a major loss of trees in due to a flood, and in 1981, the American tress provided cutting for their recovery. Meanwhile, in 1957, a group from the U.S. State Department worked with some officials at the Japanese Embassy in Washington to found the Japan-America Society of Washington, which has worked on Japanese-American relations in nondiplomatic channels and now sponsors many Sakura Matsuri events in the nation's capital.

While the Washington Cherry Blossom Festival is the most heralded in the United States, it is by no means the only one. Besides Philadelphia, other celebrations are found in, for example, Macon, Georgia; Brooklyn, New York; and Newark, New Jersey.

J. Gordon Melton

See also Aizen Summer Festival; Aki Matsuri; Haru Matsuri; Koshogatsu; Nagasaki Kunchi; Natsu Matsuri; Onbashira.

References

Plutschow, Herbert. *Matsuri: The Festivals of Japan*. Richmond, Surrey, UK: Curzon Press, 1996.

Takenaka, Yo. "The Origins of the Yoshino Cherry Tree." *Journal of Heredity* 54, no. 5 (1963): 207–11. Posted at http://www2.odn.ne.jp/~had26900/topics_&_items2/takenaka5.htm. Accessed June 15, 2010.

"Washington, DC Cherry Blossoms." Posted at http://www.dcpages.com/Tourism/Cherry_Blossoms/. Accessed June 15, 2010.

Sakya Dawa Festival

The Sakya Dawa, which occurs on the 15th day (full moon) of the 4th lunar month of the Tibetan calendar, is the Tibetan celebration of what is elsewhere known as Wesak (or Vesak), the combined celebration of the Buddha's birthday, enlightenment day, and death day. Gautama Buddha was born at Lumbini (in what is now Nepal). He attained enlightenment some 35 years later at Bodh Gaya, India, and died in his 80s at Kusinagara, India. Following indications in some of the early Buddhist texts, Tibetans have, as most Theravada Buddhists, adopted the position that Gautama Buddha was born, found enlightenment, and died on the same day of the year. On the Common Era calendar, this day usually falls in May or June. For Tibetans, this day also marked the transition from spring to summer and the beginning of the several months of pleasant weather when they could relax in the outdoors.

For Buddhists, this day was the most holy of commemorative days. It was a fitting occasion for the reading/chanting of the sutras (books believed to be records of the Buddha's discourses) and a variety of actions symbolic of veneration of and devotion to the Buddha's teachings. Among the more notable celebrations of Sakya Dawa occurs in Gangtok, Sikkim, India. The local monks carry the sutras containing the discourses of Gautama Buddha from the Tsuk-La-Khang Monastery, where the Sikkim royal family worships, in a procession around the town. In Lhasa, believers will join in a procession circling the old city (a practice termed circumambulation) ending up at a part at the foot of the Potala Palace for a picnic. Believers who find themselves in Dharamsala will also walk around the Dalai Lama's residence/temple complex, often making repeated prostration as they make their pilgrimage. Thousands of pilgrims find their way to one of the sacred mountains of Tibet, where they could, for example, climb Gephel Ri, the peak behind Drepung Monastery, to burn juniper incense, or travel to Mount Kailash to circumambulate it.

J. Gordon Melton

See also Chokhor Duchen; Lingka Woods Festival; Losar; Nehan; Wesak/Vesak.

References

Glogowski, Dieter. *Buddhism: Eight Steps to Happiness*. Munich: Bucher-Lounge, 2008.

Samantabadhara's Birthday

Samantabadhara (also known as the bodhisattva Universal Worthy or in Japan as Fugen-bosatsu and in China as Puxian) is one of the primary bodhisattvas in the Mahayana tradition and appears as one of the prime characters in the Avataṃsaka or Flower Garland (Adornment) Sutra, along with Guatama Buddha and Manjushri. Toward the end of the sutra, he makes the 10 vows common to the bodhisattva path:

1. To worship and pay respect to all Buddhas.
2. To praise all the Buddhas.
3. To make abundant offerings (i.e., give generously).
4. To repent of all karmic hindrances.
5. To rejoice in others' merits and virtue.
6. To request that the Dharma Wheel continue to be turned (i.e., that teaching activity continue).

7. To request the Buddhas to remain in the world.
8. To follow the teachings of the Buddhas at all times.
9. To accommodate and benefit all living beings.
10. To constantly transfer all merits and virtues to benefit all beings.

From these vows, Samantabadhara is often associated with Dharma practice, most notably, the effort and focus required to follow one's religious obligations. He is often pictured seated on a white elephant with six tusks, and is said to reside on Mount Emei in Sichuan Province, one of the four sacred mountains of Chinese Buddhism, and noted as its patron. Veneration of Samantabadhara/Puxian dates to the third century, when the Chinese monk Huichi built the Puxian Temple (now known as Wannian Temple) there. Then in 964 CE, the Song emperor Taizi (927–976) sent a large Buddhist mission of some 300 people under the leadership of a monk named Jiye to India. Upon their return, the emperor authorized Jiye to construct several temples on Mount Emei, and to cast a bronze statue, some 62 tons in weight and 28 feet high, of Puxian. The statue now resides in the Wannian Temple.

Samantabadhara has a special role in the groups of the Nichiren tradition who privilege the Lotus Sutra above all Buddhist writings. In the 28th chapter of the Lotus Sutra, he emerges as the protector of its and its disciples. He tells the Buddha, "if there is someone who accepts and upholds this sutra, I will guard and protect him, free him from decline and harm, see that he attains peace and tranquility, and make certain that no one can spy out and take advantage of his shortcomings." He emphasizes this vow with another: "I now therefore employ my transcendental powers to guard and protect this sutra. And after the Thus Come One [the Buddha] has entered extinction, I will cause it to be widely propagated throughout Jambudvipa [a continent surrounding the mythical mountain Sumeru] and will see that it never comes to an end."

The Universal Worthy Sutra, seen by Nichiren Buddhists as an epilogue to the Lotus Sutra, describes Samantabadhara's beneficence and power, how believers can meditate on him, and the benefit they gain from their meditations.

In the Chinese tradition, Samantabadhara's birthday is celebrated on the 21st of the second month, two days after Guan Yin's birthday. Because of Samantabadhara's association with Mount Emei, it is one focus of celebrations.

J. Gordon Melton

See also Amitabha's Birthday; Guan Yin's Birthday; Mahasthamaprapta's Birthday; Manjushri's Birthday.

References

Boheng, Wu, and Cai Zhuozhi. *100 Buddhas in Chinese Buddhism.* Translated by Mu Xin and Yan Zhi. Singapore: Asiapac books, 1997.

"Emei Shan." Sacred Destinations. Posted at http://www.sacred-destinations.com/china/emei-shan.htm. Accessed May 15, 2009.

The Flower Adornment Sutra. Posted at http://www.cttbusa.org/avatamsaka/avatamsaka_contents.asp. Accessed May 15, 2009.

The Seeker's Glossary of Buddhism. New York: Sutra Translation Committee of the United States and Canada, 1998.

The Soka Gakkai Dictionary of Buddhism. Tokyo: Soka Gakkai, 2002.

Vessantara. *Meeting the Buddhas: A Guide to Buddhas, Bodhisattvas, and Tantric Deities*. Birmingham, UK: Windhorse Publications, 1998.

Samhain (October 31)

Samhain is considered by most Wiccans and Neo-Pagans as the beginning of the ritual year (based on a belief that it was the Celtic New Year), though some treat Imbolc, the start of the new agricultural season, as the beginning. Traditionally, it was a time to consider death—the end of summer and a time to kill animals and prepare them as food to be stored for the coming winter. Today, it is celebrated primarily by the community of Pagans and Witches (Wiccans) that has been generated from the effort to revive Witchcraft by Gerald B. Gardner (1884–1964). While Gardnerian Wicca is but one strain of modern neo-Pagan and Wiccan belief and practice, the new community shares many of the practices, such as the celebration of Samhain, which Gardner initially presented to the contemporary world. Beginning with Gardner's insights, modern Wiccans and Pagans have expanded consideration of the meaning of the holidays, while maintaining (often without acknowledgment) most of Gardner's original perspectives.

For modern Wiccans and Pagans, Samhain is a time to consider the dead, especially those who have died in the previous 12 months. Pagans meet in small groups (termed covens, groves, nests, etc.) and at Samhain, members or loved ones of members who might have died will become the focus of remembrance rituals. If there is a mediumistic member, attempts might be made to contact the deceased for a word of greeting, there being an underlying belief that the veil between living and dead is the thinnest on this evening. It is also a time to lay to rest the negative events in the member's lives (i.e., things that died or were lost during the year, such as relationships, a job, or valued possessions), and to refocus on the coming year.

After the evening's ritual, it is time to celebrate with food and drink. Apple bobbing is also a popular activity. Apples have notable connotations for Pagans. Cut in half, the center of an apple presents a pentagram, an important symbol for Wiccans. The apple may also be used for divination. It can be peeled in one continuous effort and the peeling tossed over one's shoulder. The letter formed by the peel is believed to be an initial of a future lover or spouse.

Halloween is a modern Christian holiday that appropriated many elements from the European Pagan religions it supplanted. The image of the Christian Satan was borrowed from the Pagan's Horned God, and many of the associations of Halloween with witches and spirits, though now highly secularized, reflect the Church's distorted memory of Paganism and the struggle to eradicate it. (Modern Pagans are still very insistent of separating themselves from any hint of Satan or Satanism.)

J. Gordon Melton

See also All Saints Day; All Souls Day; Beltane; Eostara; Fall Equinox; Halloween; Imbolc; Lammas; Presentation of Jesus in the Temple, Feast of the; Spring Equinox (Thelema); Spring Equinox (Vernal); Summer Solstice; Wicca/Neo-Paganism Liturgical Calendar; Winter Solstice; Yule.

References

Benson, Christine. *Wiccan Holidays—A Celebration of the Wiccan Year: 365 Days in the Witches Year.* Southfield, MI: Equity Press, 2008.

Cabot, Laurie, with Jean Mills. *Celebrate the Earth: A Year of Holidays in the Pagan Tradition.* New York: Delta, 1994.

Crowley, Vivianne. *Principles of Paganism.* London: Thorsons, 1996.

Harvey, Graham. *Contemporary Paganism: Listening People, Speaking Earth.* New York: New York University Press, 1997.

Nock, Judy Ann. *Provenance Press's Guide to the Wiccan Year: A Year Round Guide to Spells, Rituals, and Holiday Celebrations.* Avon, MA: Adams Media, 2007.

Sanghamitta Day

Sanghamitta Day is a unique Sri Lankan Buddhist holiday that celebrates the arrival of Arahat Sanghamitta Therani (280–220 BCE) in the country in 245 BCE. This event was important in the conversion of the country to Buddhism and became significant for the spread of the ordered community of Buddhist nuns internationally. Sanghamitta was the daughter of the Indian king Ashoka (c. 304–232 BCE), who united much of the subcontinent in a series of wars, the horror of warfare becoming the occasion of his becoming a devout Buddhist. He subsequently spent his life spreading Buddhism internationally. His children Mahinda and Sanghamitta joined the Buddhist monastic orders.

Around 247 BCE, Mahinda introduced Buddhism to Sri Lanka. As the faith spread, the wife of one of the sub-kings on the island indicated her desire to become a nun. Mahinda, being a male, could not honor her request, but did ask his father to send Sanghamitta to the island. She arrived a short time later at Jambukolapattana (today called Point Pedro) bearing as a gift a branch of the Bodhi Tree, under which Gautama Buddha (563–483 BCE) was sitting when he reached the enlightened state. His enlightenment was the founding event of Buddhism.

As recorded in the Mahavamsa, the national chronicle of Sri Lankan history, she was met upon her arrival by Mahinda and an entourage from the capital. Together, they made a formal procession to Anuradhapura, where their first act was the planting of the Bodhi Tree at a previously prepared site.

Next, a short time later, Sanghamitta led in the ordination of Queen Anula and a group of 500 women, thus establishing the Buddhist monastic order for women (the Bhikkhunii Sa'ngha) in Sri Lanka. From Sri Lanka, the order would spread to China and from there to other countries. Sanghamitta remained in Sri Lanka with her brother, working with him to establish Buddhism among the population.

Sanghamitta Day is celebrated in Sri Lanka and among Sri Lankans abroad on the full moon near the winter solstice (in what is the month of December on the Western calendar). This day is a time of pilgrimage to Anuradhapura and the Bodhi Tree site. The original Bodhi Tree would not survive the ravages of changing religious rule in India, and cuttings from the Sri Lankan tree were returned to India to become the basis of the present Bodhi Tree seen at Bodh Gaya. The Sri Lankan tree has subsequently become the oldest living tree with a known planting date. It is regarded by Sri Lankans as the oldest historically authenticated tree in the world.

Buddhists will also gather for worship services on Sanghamitta Day, a time in which women will assume a prominent leadership role.

J. Gordon Melton

See also Duruthu Poya; Festival of the Tooth; Poson; Winter Solstice.

References

Bullis, Douglas, and Thera Mahanama-Sthivara. *The Mahavamsa: The Great Chronicle of Sri Lanka.* Fremont, CA: Asian Humanities Press, 1999.

Dewaraja, Lorna. "Sanghamitta Theri: A Liberated Woman." *Daily News*, December 29, 2001. Posted at http://www.dailynews.lk/2001/12/29/fea06.html. Accessed February 15, 2010.

Kariyawasan, G. S. *Buddhist Ceremonies and Rituals of Sri Lanka.* Kandy, Sri Lanka: Buddhist Publication Society, 1995.

Rahula, Walpola. *History of Buddhism in Ceylon: The Anuradhapura Period, 3rd Century B.C.–10th Century A.D.* Colombo: M. D. Gunasena, 1966.

Tsomo, Karma Lekshe, ed. *Innovative Buddhist Women: Swimming against the Stream.* Richmond, Surrey, UK: Curzon, 2000.

Sankt Placidusfest (July 11)

The festival of Saint Placidus, held annually on July 11 at Disentis in the canton of Grisons in Switzerland, celebrates the life and death of one of several saints named Placidus associated with the Benedictines. One Saint Placidus was a companion of Saint Benedict and the son of the man who gave Benedict the Abbey at Monte Casino, Italy. A second Plasidus emerged in Switzerland a century later. A wealthy land owner, when still a young man, he met the monk Sigisbert, and in 614 CE, turned over the land for an abbey, and then professed vows and joined the abbey he had help found. As the story goes, in 670, the abbey was attacked, and both Sigisbert and Placidus were killed defending it. They were both treated as martyrs.

More critical historical work on the history of the monastery has suggested that it was not founded until early in the eighth century. Recent archaeological investigations have shown the existence of a structure built in or about 700. This structure was destroyed in about 940, an act attributed to raiding Saracens. This later research has not stopped the annual honoring of the two martyr saints whose relics they possess and who are still honored by the current residents.

Each year on July 11, the relic of Saints Placidus and Sigisbert are carried out of the abbey in a procession to the Disentis parish church and back to the abbey through the village. Parishoners join the monks in the procession to chant a very long song about Saint Palcidus.

J. Gordon Melton

See also Benedict of Nursia, Saint's Day of St.

References

"Abbey of Dissentis." *Catholic Encyclopedia*. 1917. Posted at http://www.newadvent.org/cathen/05047a.htm. Accessed March 15, 2010.

Spicer, Dorothy Gladys. *Festivals of Western Europe*. New York: H. W. Wilson Company, 1958.

San Sebastian Day (January 20)

Saint Sebastian (d. c. 288) was a Christian who died in the persecutions unleashed upon the church by the emperor Diocletian (r. 284–305) and went on to become one of the most popular of saints/martyrs in the medieval period. He is usually portrayed with his body tied to a post and penetrated by many arrows. We know little of Sebastian apart from his martyrdom.

What little we can glean of Sebastian's life comes from Saint Ambrose (c. 340–397), the long-term bishop of Milan. In a sermon, he noted that Sebastian had come from Milan and as a young man had been appointed as a captain in the Praetorian Guard. During his stay in prison prior to his death, he was said to have been an encouraging voice to his fellow Christians, the source of several miracles, and the instrument of converting several hundred non-Christian prisoners.

According to the story of Sebastian, he was tied, used for target practice, and left for dead. He was not dead, however, and a woman retrieved his body and nursed him back to health. He later publicly spoke against the emperor, who then had him beaten to death and his body cast in a privy. His body was later recovered by the Christian community, which buried it in the catacombs. Two stories are told of his relics. One claims that they were placed in *Basilica Apostolorum*, built by Pope Damasus I in Rome in

367, That church is now known as the church of San Sebastiano fuori le mura. Another account claims that the remains were taken to France, to the Benedictine Abbey of St. Medard, at Soissons, during the renovation and expansion of the abbey under its abbot Hilduin (r. 822–830). Hilduin is said to have obtained them in 826 from Pope Eugene II (r. 824–826) along with the relics of Saint Gregory the Great.

Saint Sebastian's Day is January 20 on the Roman Catholic calendar. He was among a group of soldier saints who became very important in the Middle Ages and were called upon in times when armies threatened. He was also associated with protection from the plague. As such, he became part of what were termed the Fourteen Holy Helpers, a group of saints often venerated because of their reputation as protectors form different diseases. While most of the 14 saints, including Sebastian, remain on the current Roman Catholic calendar of saints individually, the practice of calling upon the 14 as a group was strongly discouraged amid the revisions of the calendar in 1969, following the Second Vatican Council.

Sebastian is the patron saint of Rio de Janeiro, Brazil (whose official name is *São Sebastião do Rio de Janeiro*), and his feast day is a public holiday in the city. Around Brazil and all of Latin America, places named for San Sebastian hold both religious and public celebrations. In San Sebastián, Spain, an annual festival called the Tamborrada has been held since the 19th century. It featured a procession from the Santa Maria Church in the old part of town to the San Sebastián Church. The event concluded with the people dancing to the accompaniment of a military band's flutes and drums. Today, the festival has been highly secularized, with people dressed as cooks and soldiers, marching around the city and the sounds of drums filling the air.

In the Eastern Orthodox churches, Sebastian's feast day is December 18.

J. Gordon Melton

See also Agnes, Feast Day of St.; Florian, Saint's Day of St.; George, Feast Day of St.; Lucy, Saint's Day of St.

References

Farmer, David Hugh. *The Oxford Dictionary of Saints*. New York: Oxford University Press, 2004.

Ferrua, Antonio. *Guide to the Basilica and the Catacomb of Saint Sebastian*. Rome: Pontifical Commission of Sacred Archaeology, 1983.

Sarada Devi, Birthday of (December 22)

Sarada Devi (1853–1920) was the wife of Indian spiritual teacher Ramakrishna Paramahamsa, the guru of Swami Vivekananda (1863–1902), who founded the Ramakrishna Mission and Math and the Vedanta societies, the first Hindu organizations in the West.

When only five, Sarada Devi was betrothed to Ramakrishna, and during her late teens she joined him at the Kali temple as Dakshineswar. As Ramakrishna had taken the vows of the renounced life and become a sannyasin, the marriage was never consummated. He had also become a mystic and contemplative, and had come to view the Kali as his mother and the mother of the universe. He focused attention on his wife as the incarnation of Divine Mother (an incarnation of the goddess Durga as Kali) and his disciples accepted her as such.

Unassuming and in the background, she gained a few disciples prior to Ramakrishna's death, and then assumed a role as a spiritual adviser to the Ramakrishna disciples through the last three decades of her life. She continued to be revered as an incarnation of the goddess. Following her death on July 20, 1920, her body was cremated at the monastery in Belur, India.

After her death, Sarada Devi remained the focus of many females who had come to associate with the Ramakrishna Math and its all-male leadership. She would inspire the formation of the Ananda Ashrama in the United States, an offshoot of the Vedanta Society with all-female leadership. Then in 1954, Swami Shankarananda (1880–1962), the head of the Ramakrishna Math, led in the founding of the Sri Sarada Math and the Ramakrishna Sarada Mission, two monastic organizations for the nuns previously associated with the Ramakrishna Math, to both honor Sarada Devi and respond to the new role being assumed by women in Indian society.

Today, the birthday of Sarada Devi is celebrated at all the centers throughout the spectrum of organizations that grew from the work of Swami Vivekananda as inspired by Ramakrishna. The celebration will take the form of a gathering that will include meditation, chanting, and inspirational talks on the spirituality and accomplishments of Sarada Devi. The celebration may last a few hours or all day at different locations. In 2004, a variety of celebrations were held occasioned by the 150th anniversary of Sarada Devi.

J. Gordon Melton

See also Ramakrishna, Birthday of Sri; Vivekananda, Birthday of Swami.

References

Jackson, Carl T. *Vedanta for the West*. Bloomington: Indiana University Press, 1994.

Kindler, Babaji Bob. *Sri Sarada Vijnanagita: Her Teachings, Selected and Arranged in Verse Form*. Greenville, NY: SRV Association, 2000.

Nikhilananda, Swami. *Gospel of the Holy Mother Sri Sarada Devi*. Belur, India: Sri Ramakrishna Math Printing Press, 1984.

Nikhilananda, Swami. *Holy Mother: Being the Life of Sri Sarada Devi, Wife of Sri Ramakrishna and Helpmate in His Mission*. New York: Ramakrishna-Vivekananda Center, 1982.

Satchidananda, Birthday of Swami (December 22)

Swami Satchidananda (1914–2002), a disciple of Indian spiritual teacher Swami Sivananda Saraswati (1887–1963), brought the teachings of the Divine Life

Society to the United States. Satchidananda went on to establish himself as a major teacher of hatha yoga and the founder of Integral Yoga International, the organization of his disciples.

Though raised in a very devout atmosphere, as a young man, he married and began a business career. His wife, however, died only a few years into the marriage, and the future swami began a period of spiritual quest that led him in 1949 to Swami Sivananda and the Divine Life Society, in Rishikesh, which he headed. Sivananda accepted him into the vows of the renounced life as a sannyasin. At that time, he took the spiritual name by which he became known. He became a field representative for the society, and came to the United States in the 1960s at the insistence of some American students. He founded an Intergal Yoga Institute in New York, the base from which a network of additional centers developed, all of which became focused at the Satchidananda Ashram in Yogaville, Virginia.

At Yogaville, his belief in interfaith work came to the fore under the motto, "Truth is One, Paths are Many." He oversaw the building of the Light of Truth Universal Shrine (LOTUS) at Yogaville, which included altars for each of the major world religions, dedicated in 1986.

Satchidananda built a large following in the West and a large network of religious leaders from various religious communities who accepted his approach concerning the basic unity of religions as different expressions of a single truth. By the 1980s, Satchidananda's disciples began organizing annual birthday celebrations at which they would gather, and various religious leaders would be invited to speak and lead in worship. In addition, a group of his disciples founded the Lifelights Network into which they invited anyone from around the world who have felt that his or her life had been enriched by contact with Swami Satchidananda. Members of the network are invited to honor him by doing acts of kindness and service in their community on the 22nd day of each month (thus memorializing Satchidananda's birthday on December 22).

J. Gordon Melton

See also Sivananda Saraswati, Birthday of Swami.

References

Bordow, Sita, et al. *Sri Swami Satchidananda: Apostle of Peace*. Yogaville, VA: Integral Yoga Publications, 1986.

"Life Lights Network." Posted at http://swamisatchidananda.org/docs2/lifelights.htm. Accessed May 15, 2010.

Satchidananda, Sri Swami. *A Decade of Service*. Pomfret Center, CT: Satchidananda Ashram-Yogaville, 1976.

Weiner, Sita. *Swami Satchidananda*. New York: Bantam Books, 1972.

Sava, Saint's Day of St. (January 12 or 14)

The Serbian Orthodox Church traces its roots to the initial efforts of missionaries based in Constantinople in the last half of the ninth century CE. When Serbia became independent of Constantinople toward the end of the 10th century, under its first ruler, Steven Nemanja (1168–1196), Christianity was still a minority religion. The transformation of Christianity into a majority religion is largely credited to Steven's son Prince Rastko Nemanjic (c. 1176–1235), later to be known as Saint Sava.

As a young man, Rastko moved to Greece and joined the monastic community on Mount Athos, where he received his religious name Sava (after a fifth-century Palestinian saint named Sabbas). Steven joined him for a period, and they restored an abandoned monastery as a new center for Serbians in the monastic life. Steven eventually became a monk and took the name Simeon, under which he would later be canonized. Sava remained at Athos until 1207. He returned to find Serbia split between his rival brothers.

Sava brought his father's body with him, and called his fighting brothers to join him in a proper funeral service. At the funeral, the casket was opened, and a sweet smell flowed outward. Steven has since been known as Saint Simeon the Myrrh-flowing. Shortly thereafter, the schism was healed, and Sava could turn to evangelizing the nation.

Saint Sava then persuaded the Ecumenical Patriarchate to establish the Serbian Church as an autonomous entity. In doing so, the patriarch consecrated Sava as the church's first archbishop, on the feast day of Saint Nicholas, December 6. Among his first acts was to consecrate his brother as the first king of Serbia.

Sava worked through the remainder of the decade to build the Serbian Church. In 1229, he left for a pilgrimage to Jerusalem, only to have his brothers again divide the land and go to war. The war was short, with the younger brother winning and assuming the throne. Sava abdicated in 1233 and appointed a pupil to succeed him. The next year, he returned for an even more extended tour of the Holy Land. On his return, he stopped in Bulgaria and was participating in a worship service when he developed a cough. He contracted pneumonia and died January 14, 1235, without reaching Serbia.

He was initially buried in Bulgaria, but his body was returned to Serbia in 1237 and buried at a monastery in southern Serbia. In 1253, the Serbian Orthodox Church officially canonized their deceased archbishop as Saint Sava. After the Ottoman Turks overran Serbia, they dug up Sava's relics and publicly burned them in Belgrade. April 27 (May 10 on the Common Era calendar) is commemorated throughout the Serbian Church. In 2004, the Serbian Church dedicated the Saint Sava Church in Belgrade on the spot where his bones were burned. The church is currently hailed as the largest active Orthodox Church structure in the world, rivaling the Cathedral of the Savior in Moscow.

Meanwhile, a variety of healings had been attached to the relics. He became the patron saint of the nation he helped create. On Saint Sava Day, January 14 (Julian) or January 27 (Common Era calendar), it has become common since the 19th century for schoolchildren in Serbia to have musical recitals in nearby churches.

J. Gordon Melton

See also Cyril and Methodius, Saint's Day for Sts.; Evtimiy of Bulgaria, Saint's Day of Patriarch; Saint Stephen's Day (Hungary).

References

"Celebration of St. Sava's Day." ERP KIM Info-service, January 27, 2005. Posted at http://www.kosovo.net/news/archive/2005/January_27/2.html. Accessed March 15, 2010.

Pavlovich, Paul. *The History of the Serbian Orthodox Church.* Toronto: Serbian Heritage Books 1989.

Velimirovich, Nicholai. *The Life of St. Sava.* Libertyville, IL: Serbian Eastern Orthodox Diocese for United States of America and Canada, 1951.

Schaferlauf. *See* Bartholomew's Day, Saint

Schneerson, Anniversary of the Death of Rabbi Menachem Mendal

Rabbi Menachem Mendel Schneerson (1902–1994) headed the Chabad-Lubavitcher Hasidic movement for over four decades during the crucial years after World War II and the Jewish Holocaust. He was born in the Ukraine, and lived in various places in Europe. He escaped from France in 1941 and made his way to the United States.

In 1928, Schneerson married Chaya Mushka, the daughter of Yosef Yitzchok Schneersohn (1880–1950), the Chabad-Lubavitcher Hasidic leader or rebbe. The elder Schneersohn arrived in New York in 1940. He died in 1950 leaving no sons behind, and thus his son-in-law, Rabbi Menachem Mendel Schneerson, was chosen as his successor. Over the next 40 years, the charismatic Schneerson led in the development of the Lubavitcher community as a global Hasidic movement.

During the 1990s, Messianic themes became prominent among the Lubavitcher membership, initially as a concern to hasten the arrival of what was felt to be an imminent Messianic age and then the accumulation of images and ideas around Schneerson personally as the Messiah or Anointed One. These considerations were peaking when Schneerson died on June 12, 1994 (or Tammuz 3, 5754, on the Jewish calendar). He was buried next to his father-in-law at Montefiore Cemetery in Queens, Long Island, New York, within the previously built shrine (or *ohel*).

Views of Schneerson among the Lubavitch vary widely. All respect him for his 40 years of leadership and service. Many believe him to be the Messiah and await his return. Some ascribe miraculous and divine powers to him, and consult his writings for various hidden messages, on occasion using them for divinatory purposes. Many, especially those residing in the New York City area, will make a pilgrimage to his grave site on the anniversary of his death, Tammuz 3, which usually occurs in May or June on the Common Era calendar. Some 50,000 gathered in 2010 for the 24-hour observance. Those who are able to approach the tomb will leave write prayer requests on small bits of paper and leave them as the tomb. Most will spend time in prayer, remembrance, and look for inspiration from what is believed the continuing spirit of the late rabbi.

J. Gordon Melton

See also Confucius, Anniversary of the Death of; Data Ganj Bakhsh Death Anniversary.

References

Fendel, Hillal. "16th Annual Memorial of Lubavitcher Rebbe to Be Marked." *Arutz Sheva—Israel National News*. Posted at http://www.israelnationalnews.com/News/News.aspx/138057. Accessed June 15, 2010.

Heilman, Samuel, and Menachem Friedman. *The Rebbe: The Life and Afterlife of Menachem Mendel Schneerson*. Princeton, NJ: Princeton University Press, 2010.

Wolfson, Elliot R. *Open Secret: Postmessianic Messianism and the Mystical Revision of Menahem Mendel Schneerson*. New York: Columbia University Press, 2009.

Schutzengelfest (July)

Schutzengelfest, or the Festival of the Guardian Angel, is an annual observance that occurs on the second Sunday in July at the Wildkirchli, a cave in the Alpstein Mountain range in the Appenzell Innerrhoden canton of Switzerland. The cave has been the site of numerous prehistoric discoveries. The event dates to 1621, when a Capuchin monk concluded that the cave was an ideal place for a mountain worship service. He tried out the idea, but changed his residence after a few years, and the practice was dropped. Then an Appenzell priest named Paulus Ulmann revived the idea. In 1679, he established a foundation to provide financial support for the continued annual observance, and that foundation continues to exist.

Thus, on the second Sunday of July, a priest and those who wish to join him will make the trek to the cave and join in a worship service that concludes with a concert by the yodelers' choir. Afterward, attendees return to the nearby villages of Ebenalp and Aescher to continue the celebration with food, drink, and dancing.

J. Gordon Melton

See also Agua, La Fiesta de.

References

Thonpsson, Sue Ellen, and Barbara W. Carlson, comp. *Holidays, Festivals, and Celebrations of the World Dictionary*. Detroit, MI: Omnigraphics, 1994.

Schwenkfelder Thanksgiving (September 24)

The Schwenkfelder Church is a small Christian group that was formed by people attracted to the mystical teachings of Caspar Schwenckfeld (1489–1561). Schwenckfeld was a well-to-do German nobleman at the time of the Protestant Reformation. He took the Protestant protest in a mystical direction, having come to believe that external things, though people might use them, were manifestations of the perishable material world. He came to value the spiritual imperishable reality behind the material. He discovered what he sought in the inner word, faith, liberty, an invisible spiritual sacrament, and a fellowship of those he considered redeemed and called.

The small group found all of the major Reformation groups refused to accept them, and through the 18th century, they remained a persecuted minority. Thus, in 1734, as a group they decided to leave Silicia and migrate to the United States. On September 24, just prior to their departure, the group gathered to offer thanks for the deliverance from years of persecution and discrimination. Once in the New World, the several thousand members of the six remaining Schwenkfelder churches have continued to gather annually for a thanksgiving service, now held on the Sunday closest to September 24.

J. Gordon Melton

See also Reformation Sunday.

References

Erb, Peter C. *Schwenckfeld in His Reformation Setting*. Valley Forge, PA: Judson Press, 1978.

Kriebel, Howard Wiegner. *The Schwenkfelders in Pennsylvania*. Lancaster, PA: Pennsylvania-German Society, 1904.

Schultz, Selina Gerhard. *A Course of Study in the Life and Teachings of Caspar Schwenckfeld von Ossig (1489–1561) and the History of the Schwenkfelder Religious Movement (1518–1964)*. Pennsburg, PA: Board of Publication of the Schwenkfelder Church, 1964.

Scientology, Holidays of the Church of

The Church of Scientology was founded by L. Ron Hubbard (1911–1986) as his consideration of the human situation and most importantly, the nature of the human individual as a body, mind, and spirit matured. Hubbard, a writer, former U.S. Navy officer, and explorer, began intense consideration of the plight of humankind as early as the 1930s and initially published his early conclusions in the 1940s. His work reached a significant plateau with the 1950 publication, *Dianetics: The Modern Science of Mental Health*, which presented his alternative conclusions relative to contemporary psychology about the human mind and the way to health and wholeness. Further work on the exploration of the inner self led him to reorient his perspective around the human spirit, which he termed the "Thetan." By 1952, he had begun to articulate the basics of Scientology, and the first local Scientology church was founded in Los Angeles, California, in 1954.

Scientology is a Gnostic-Western Esoteric religion. It posits the Thetan as the essential eternal self (the soul or spirit), believes that the Thetan is trapped in the body due to its forgetfulness of its own past, and offers the technology of Scientology as the method by which the Thetan can be freed from all encumbrances to realize its full potential. Hubbard is credited with discovering the best and most efficient means of freeing the Thetan, and Scientology is thus seen as having been one of the most important discoveries in human history. In addition, Hubbard is seen as a Renaissance man, accomplished in a variety of fields from music to corporate management and educational theory. Above and beyond Scientology narrowly defined, Scientologists laud Hubbard for his contributions in a variety fields.

Like other Western Esoteric religious bodies, church life in Scientology is organized around the progressive revelation of its teachings as members read through Hubbard's many writings, appropriate the truths received in church instructions, engage in the self-exploration provided by auditing (counseling), and demonstrate mastery of the material covered. At the higher levels, the instructional material is confidential and not available to either nonmembers or members in the more elementary and intermediate levels of church life. In this manner, the church follows the precedents set by other esoteric religions that preceded it.

As the church of Scientology has grown and developed, it has designated a variety of events as worthy of commemoration, the most important by far being the birthday of the church's founder, L. Ron Hubbard (1911–1986), the first major event of the calendar year. It is followed by six major holidays and a variety of lesser ones.

The seven major holidays on the Scientologist's calendar are:

Hubbard, Birthday of L. Ron Hubbard (March 13)
Anniversary of *Dianetics* (May 9)
Anniversary of the Maiden Voyage of the *Freewinds* (June 6)
Sea Org Day (August 12)
Auditor's Day (Second Sunday in September)
International Association of Scientologists Anniversary (October 7)
New Year's Eve (December 31)

These holidays celebrate major events in Scientology's relatively brief history, beginning with Hubbard's birth (1911), the publication of *Dianetics* in 1950, the development of the church's elite fraternity, the Sea Organization, and the opening of the new center for the highest level of Scientology's religious life, the oceangoing vessel *Freewinds*. The church completes each year with a gathering to celebrate its accomplishments and project future goals.

Among the many lesser commemorations are the National Founding Day that is celebrated by the Scientology church in each country to remember its own unique beginning, and/or its official recognition by local authorities as a new ecclesiastical body. The anniversaries of the founding of the different upper level organizations of the church and the release of different higher levels of church teachings.

While a major holiday celebrates the church-wide organization fighting for religious freedom, the International Association of Scientologists, there are also celebrations for those working in other church-sponsored programs—for example, Narconon (February 19) and Criminon (January 25), which constitute the church's direct effort against the international plague of narcotics. CCHR Day (March 5) celebrates the work of the Citizens Commission on Human Rights to fight what the church views as abuses in the psychiatric field. Most of the celebrations of these lesser holidays do not involve the larger membership at the local church level.

J. Gordon Melton

See also Auditor's Day; *Dianetics*, Anniversary of; Hubbard, Birthday of L. Ron; International Association of Scientologists Anniversary; Maiden Voyage Anniversary; National Founding Day (Scientology); New Year's Eve (Scientology); Sea Org Day.

References

We Are the IAS 2009 Calendar. Los Angeles: IAS Administrations, 2008.

What Is Scientology? Los Angeles: Bridge Publications, 1998.

Sea Org Day (August 12)

The Sea Organization (or Sea Org) is an elite corps of dedicated Scientologists. Members lead an ordered life and make vows analogous to monastic vows, though they are allowed to marry if their spouse is also a Sea Org member. Members sign a billion-year covenant (based on their belief in reincarnation), vowing to work full time for the spread of Scientology in future incarnations.

The Sea Org was founded August 12, 1967, and originally assigned the duty to deliver what was the highest levels of Scientology teachings to the membership. The first two of what were termed the OT (Operating Thetan) levels had been released the previous year, and church founder L. Ron Hubbard (1911–1986) had retired from all his administrative positions in the church to spend the rest of his life developing the higher levels of Scientology teachings and training. The Sea Org was formed from people who had been among the first graduates of the course and who were ready to dedicate themselves to Scientology's future. Then, through the 1970s into the 1980s, the Church of Scientology went through a major reorganization at the highest level and the Sea Org's role expanded to include not only the delivery of the new OT levels (currently, OT VIII is the highest level) but the management and administration of the church above the local

Dormitories provide a home for nearly 400 Sea Organization members in San Jacinto, California. Sea Organization members are Scientologists who make a commitment to their faith, similar to monastic vows. (AP/Wide World Photos)

church level. All international offices in the church are currently held by Sea Org members.

The Sea Org has become a focal point of the intense controversy which has surrounded the Church in recent decades. Its members often are seen in naval-style uniforms, and in spite of the lack of any training in firearms or physical self-defense in their training, critics have pictured them as a paramilitary group. There have also been complaints, primarily by ex-members, of excesses within the internal rehabilitation program for Sea Org members who violate church rules or their vows. The church has denied that any such excesses have occurred, and that most of the complaints have derived from a lack of appreciation of the religious commitments made by Sea Org members.

Sea Org members work six and a half days a week on behalf of Scientology. On August 12, each year, they take a holiday. There are gatherings at the Sea Org managed church centers in Los Angeles, Clearwater (Florida), Saint Hill (England), Copenhagen, and Sydney, at which honors and promotions are announced, the history and accomplishments of the organization are acknowledged and celebrated, and commitments are renewed. The rest of the day is spent in a festive atmosphere.

J. Gordon Melton

See also Hubbard, Birthday of L. Ron; Scientology, Holidays of the Church of.

References

What Is Scientology? Los Angeles: Bridge Publications, 1998.

Sechi Festival (January 4–7)

The Sechi Festival is an annual New Year's celebration held at the headquarters of the Tenrikyo religion at Tenri City in Japan. Tenrikyo, one's of Japan's new religions, was founded in 1838 by Miki Nakayama (1798–1887), known by her religious name Oyasama, a farm wife who found herself entering trance states during which she spoke as if God were speaking through her. She subsequently began a teaching phase of her life that lasted some 50 years, and she taught a mystical view of the world that had roots in Shinto. These teachings were later compiled into a book called the Ofudesaki ("Tip of the Writing Brush") that now serves as the Tenrikyo book of scriptures.

The Sechi Festival grew out of the practice of Tenrikyo groups around Japan sending rice cakes to Tenri City at the beginning of the new year for the New Year's Day service at the Jiba, the site that is believed to be the center of creation. On January 4, these rice cakes would be taken from the main sanctuary, cut into small pieces, and mixed into a broth dish called *zoni*, which would be served to people visiting the church facilities at Tenri City on January 5–7.

During Oyasama's life, people who gathered with her for New Year's partook of the rice cakes with her in a merry atmosphere. As years passed, the amount of rice cakes available for consumption grew steadily. The informal New Year's gatherings evolved into the Sechi Festival. It was discontinued during World War II, but revived in 1956, the 70th anniversary of Oyasama's death. It draws more than 100,000 people annually.

J. Gordon Melton

See also Koshogatsu; New Year's Day; Setsubun.

References

Fukaya, YoshiKazu. "Sechi festival (Sechi-e)." Posted at http://www.tenrikyo.or.jp/kaiden/newsletter/html/tt5/osechi.html. Accessed July 15, 2010.

The Life of Oyasama, Foundress of Tenrikyo. Tenri, Japan: Tenrikyo Church Headquarters, 1982.

Nishiyama, Teruo. *Introduction to the Teachings of Tenrikyo*. Tenri, Japan: Tenrikyo Overseas Mission Department, 1981.

Seijin no Hi (January)

Seijin no Hi, or Coming of Age Day, celebrates the transition to adulthood in Japan. Unlike Shichi-Go-San and Kodomo no Hi, similar days for young children,

Seijin no Hi is a national holiday and especially important to those reaching their 20th birthday when they become eligible to vote and to consume alcohol. It is celebrated on the second Monday of January.

Seijin no Hi was officially recognized in 1948, but has a history that reaches back into the period of the Shogunate. Samurai families would hold a ceremony to recognize male children as adults in a ceremony known as "Gempuku." It would include the adoption of an adult name, and the presentation of an adult hairpiece called "Eboshi." After this time, the youth would begin to assume adult duties and become eligible for marriage. The young girls of Samurai families would go through a corresponding ceremony termed "Mogi," normally between the ages of 12 and 16. They would be given a kimono and afterward be allowed to dress as an adult female.

With the Meiji restoration in 1868, this coming-of-age ceremony became common among the general population, aided by a 1876 law setting the age of adulthood at 20 (much higher than in previous centuries). In the modern world, the practice has been highly secularized. The government sponsors gatherings at which speeches are given on the rights and responsibilities of adulthood. The main event, however, is the fashion show, the day providing an opportunity for women to purchase an expensive new kimono and wear traditional clothing. While most men dress up in Western clothes, many will also don traditional male attire.

J. Gordon Melton

See also Doll Festival; Kodomo no Hi; Shichi-Go-San.

References

"Seijin No Hi." TokyoTopia. Posted at http://www.tokyotopia.com/seijin-no-hi.html. Accessed June 15, 2010.

Seton, Saint's Day of Mother Elizabeth (January 4)

Elizabeth Ann Bayley Seton (1774–1821) was the first person born in what is now the United States to be named by the Roman Catholic Church as a saint. Seton was born in New York City and raised as an Episcopalian, one of her grandfathers being an Episcopal priest. She married and became the mother of five children. In 1805, she converted to Catholicism, then very much a minority faith in New York. Four years later, she moved to Emmitsburg, Maryland, where, in conjunction with some French Sulpicians who had left postrevolutionary France, she established Saint Joseph's Academy and Free School, a school for girls. The school provided the base from which she founded a non-cloistered order of nuns (the first founded in the United States), the Sisters of Charity of Saint Joseph. Its original special mission was to the children of the poor. She devoted the last years of her rather short life to building the order. She died in 1821 in Emmitsburg, and her body now rests in the basilica at what has become the National Shrine of Saint Elizabeth Ann Seton.

A century and a half later, with Catholicism having grown into a large national organization in the United States, Seton began to receive attention for her pioneering effort. She was declared venerable in 1959, beatified by Pope John XXIII (r. 1958–1963) in 1963, and canonized by Pope Paul VI (r. 1963–1978) in 1975. Her feast day was set on January 4. In 2009, in an unusual step, the Episcopal Church (based in the United States) added Seton to its calendar of saints, with her feast day also set on January 4.

The national shrine commemorating Seton's life and work is now one of the most visited pilgrimage sites for American Catholics.

J. Gordon Melton

See also Rose of Lima, Saint's Day of St.; Thérèse of Lisieux, Saint's Day of St.

References

Daughters of St. Paul. *Mother Seton: Wife, Mother, Educator, Foundress, Saint*. Boston: Daughters of St. Paul, 1975.

Fenney, Leonard. *Mother Seton: Saint Elizabeth of New York (1774–1821)*. Boston: Ravengate Press, 1975.

Power-Waters, Alma. *Mother Seton and the Sisters of Charity*. San Francisco: Ignatius Press, 2000.

Setsubun

The Japanese adopted a lunar calendar with 12 months each with two parts related to the new and full moon, thus giving it 24 segments. The end of each segment and the division marking it from the next segment was termed the Setsubun (or seasonal division). Over time, the term Setsubun began to particularly refer to the division at the end of the year and hence immediately before the lunar New Year. The New Year came as winter ended and spring began, which was believed to be the first week of February. Today the Setsubun festival is held in Japan on February 3 or 4, the day before the start of spring. The spring Setsubun festival came to be associated with rituals for chasing away evil spirits.

The practices of the spring Setsubun appear to have originated in folk traditions, but over the centuries were adopted by both Shinto and Buddhist temples. By the 13th century, for example, people attempted to drive away evil spirits by mixing the stench of burning dried sardine heads and wood with the noise of drums. This custom survives in the use of fish head shapes as house decorations, the intention being to keep spirits away from the home.

Today, the most common practice of Setsubun is the throwing of roasted soybeans. They may be thrown around one's house or at temples and shrines, or at people. The act of throwing is accompanied by shouts of "Oni wa soto! Fuku wa uchi!" ("Devils out, happiness in").

Tied to the tossing of the beans is another custom, eating the number of beans corresponding to your age. This is particularly a practice of people whose age is a multiple of 12, meaning that the year is the same as the year in which they were born (according to the Chinese zodiac). Local news coverage will feature stories on celebrities at different temples consuming beans. In the home, one person, usually the male head of the household (or a male who was celebrating one of his 12th-anniversary birthdays), will put on a demon mask, and the other family members will toss soybeans at him as they chant the traditional *oni wa soto fuku wa uchi.*

In a secularized culture such as Japan, variant celebrations of Setsubun are widespread. Disbelief in the existence of evil spirits is widespread, and many Buddhists offer demythologized explanations for Setsubun celebrations. At the same time, both Shinto shrines and Buddhist temples will sponsor ritualized bean-tossing events.

J. Gordon Melton

See also Higan; Nehan; New Year's Day; Obon Festival(s); Spring Equinox (Thelema); Spring Equinox (Vernal).

References

Carlquist, Helen, and Sherwin Bauer. *Japanese Festivals*. Rutland, VT: Charles E. Tuttle, 1965.

Erskine, William Hugh. *Japanese Festivals and Calendar Lore*. Tokyo: Kyo Bun Kwan, 1933.

Seven Sisters Festival. *See* Double Seventh Festival

Shankaracharya Jayanti

Shankaracharya Jayanti is celebrated as the appearance day (birthday) of Jagad Guru Adi Shankaracharya (788–820 CE). It is celebrated on the fifth day of the waxing moon in the Indian month of Vaisakha (May–June on the Common Era calendar) in South India. It is celebrated five days later in northern India. Shankaracharya was one of India's most famous theologian-philosophers and an advocate of what today is known as Advaita Vedanta, a stream of Saivite Hinduism. Advaita Vedanta is a nondualistic worldview that identifies the individual's essential self (*atman*) with the limitless divine human (*Brahman*).

Shankaracharya was born in the village of Kalady in central Kerala, in southern India (now a pilgrimage site). As a young man, he studied with Govinda Bhagavatpāda and then became a teacher himself. In his quest to propagate Advaita Vedanta, with an entourage of disciples, he traveled around every part of India teaching and debating with various religious leaders. He settled in Kashmir at

Śārada Pīṭhaṃ, and while there, bested the other scholars in debate and assumed authority by ascending the throne of transcendent wisdom of that temple.

Shankaracharya went on to found four monasteries placed at strategic points around the Indian subcontinent to guide the people toward the approach to Hinduism he expounded. The head of each of these four monasteries, or mathas, takes the title of Shankaracharya. These four monasteries are located at Sringeri in Karnataka (south), Dwaraka in Gujarat (west), Puri in Orissa (east), and Jyotirmath in Uttarakhand (north). The abbots of these monasteries are among the most respected religious leaders in India. Each traces his authority to one the four men originally appointed by Shankaracharya.

Little is known of either the first or last days of Shankaracharya; even his birth and death dates remain a matter of scholarly discussion. While most place him in the early eighth century, an alternate tradition places him in the fifth century BCE. Irrespective of these discussions, his appearance day is celebrated in the spring each year. Though a prolific author and movement organizer, he died a relatively young man at the age of 32.

Shankaracharya placed his theological work in a Saivite context. One popular legend concerning his birth suggests that his parents received a vision of Lord Shiva in which he promised that he would incarnate in the form of their child. Shankaracharya is also claimed by the Smarta tradition, which emphasizes the centrality and efficacy of temple worship for believers. This tradition looks to Shankaracharya as the founder of the Shanmata system of worship, which builds on Shankaracharya's nondualism to create temples with worship of the six primary (and often competing) deities of Hinduism—Shiva, Vishnu, Shakti, Ganesha, Surya, and Skanda—based on the belief in the essential oneness of all deities as various manifestations of Brahman, the single divine power.

Shankaracharya is respected at all levels of the Hindu community, and the festival in his honor finds scholars organizing learned discourse on his legacy, especially those residing at the four mathas Shankaracharya founded and their satellite mathas, while temples will organize worshipful events to pay homage. Among Saivites, he is acknowledged as an incarnation of Shiva, and among the Smartas as one who made their distinctive style of temple worship possible. In Kerala, pilgrimages to places associated with him are popular, including his birthplace in Kalady; the shrine of the goddess Mookambika, Mother of the Universe, in Kollur, Karnataka, where he resided for a time; or the Vadakkunnathan Temple, an ancient Shiva temple at Thrissur, Kerala, where it is claimed he passed his last days.

Constance A. Jones

See also Ashokashtami; Mahashivaratri.

References

Isayeva, Natalia. *Shankara and Indian Philosophy.* Albany: State University of New York Press, 1993.

Mudgal, S. G. *Advaita of Shankara: A Reappraisal.* New Delhi: Motilal Banarsidass, 1975.

Pande, Govind Chandra. *Life and Thought of Sankaracarya.* New Delhi: Motilal Banarsidass, 1994.

Prabhavananda, Swami, and Christopher Isherwood. *Shankara's Crest Jewel of Discrimination.* Los Angeles: Vedanta Press, 1970.

Sharad Purnima

Sharad Purnima is a Hindu harvest festival celebrated on evening of the full moon of the Hindu lunar month of Ashwin (September–October). The month of Ashwin comes after the annual rainy season, and the festival's major observances are in rural communities.

The celebration is especially directed to Lakshmi, the goddess of wealth and consort of the god Vishnu, who is said to move around the night asking "Who is awake?" and to those she finds awake, she bestows gifts of wealth. This purnima (full moon) is also known as Kojagara, which translates into "Who is awake?"

The origin of the celebration appears to come from Bihar state where a story is told of a relatively poor brahmin named Valit who left home disgusted with his wife, who was known for her quarrelsome nature. His leaving was occasioned by her disturbing a ritual honoring Valit's ancestors. On his trip, he ran into some young girls who were descendants of Kailiya Nag, the giant venomous snake that Krishna had subdued. Valit began gambling with the girls by the light of the full moon and lost what little money he had with him.

At that moment, however, Lakshmi and Vishnu were passing by. Lakshmi graced Valit with a handsomeness similar to the god of love. The girls with whom he had been gambling now fell in love with him and gave him all their riches. He returned home and lived happily ever after.

On the night of Sharad Purnima, Dudha-Pauva, a mixture of parched rice made from the recently harvested crops and soaked in cold milk, will be offered to Chandra, the moon deity and then passed to gathered devotees. Devotees of Durga think of her as having gone into an extended rest following her nine-day war with Mahishasura. On this night, in Durga temples, she will be awakened with music and drumbeats and taken in a torchlit procession around the temple. Devotees of Krishna look upon this night as the anniversary of Krishna's divine play with Radha and the Gopis (cowgirls).

This festival is also known as Navanna (or new food). After Kojagara, the new grain of the autumn harvest is deemed ready for consumption. This practice indicates the origins of the festival, which combine a celebration of the harvest and the light provided by the full moon in an era prior to modern electrical lighting. The acknowledgment of Lakshmi coincides with an acknowledgment of the fruits of the harvest.

Constance A. Jones

See also Chairta Purnima; Diwali; Gaura Purnima; Guru Purnima; Kartika Purnima; Narieli Purnima; Navaratri.

References

Gavin, Jamila. *Three Indian Goddesses: The Stories of Kali, Sita/Lakshmi and Durga.* London: Egmont Books, 2004.

Mukundcharandas, Sadhu. *Hindu Festivals (Origin Sentiments and Rituals).* Amdavad, India: Swaminarayan Aksharpith, 2005.

Pattanak, Devdutt. *Lakshmi: The Goddess of Wealth and Fortune-An Introduction.* Mumbai: Vakils Feffer & Simons, 2003.

Shavuot

Shavuot is a Jewish holiday that celebrates God's giving of the Torah (or Law), the first five books of the Hebrew Bible. It is also a spring festival that celebrates the first harvest and with it the ripening of the first fruits. Shavuot is known as the Feast of Weeks or of the First Fruits. Christians have an analogous holiday called Pentecost (covered in a separate entry). Shavuot is a two-day holiday that begins at sundown on the fifth day of the Hebrew month of Sivan (usually May or June on the Common Era calendar). It is one of three pilgrimage holy days in the Jewish calendar, when, in the days prior to the destruction of the temple, Jews would normally travel to Jerusalem for the observance. It appears that the shift of emphasis from the harvest to the remembrance of the giving of the Torah occurred at the time of the Jewish exile in Babylon.

A view of Mount Sinai in Egypt. The Sinai desert is significant to the Jewish people. It was there that God gave them the Torah, and it was on Mount Sinai where Moses received the Ten Commandments. (Wrangel/Dreamstime.com)

The date of Shavuot is tied to Pesach, which celebrates God's freeing of the Jewish people from their enslavement to Pharaoh; they traveled into the Sinai desert and on Shavuot, God gave them the Law. The people committed themselves as a group to be loyal to God. Shavuot is a national holiday in Israel, which sets aside one day for its observance. Outside Israel, it is generally a two-day celebration except among Reform Jews, who celebrate only one day. While Pesach and Shavuot acknowledge the Exodus events, their dating was also tied to the harvest cycle in Palestine, which began with the harvesting of the barley around Pesach and ended with the harvesting of wheat around Shavuot. Shavuot was the first opportunity each year to being the *bikkurim* (or first fruits) to the Temple in Jerusalem. The first fruits would include offerings from the seven main plants grown as crops in the region: wheat, barley, grapes, figs, pomegranates, olives, and dates (cf. Deuteronomy 8:8).

There are no specific rituals commanded for Shavuot, but a variety of practices has emerged over the centuries. The main event is a service at the synagogue in which the receiving of the Torah is reenacted. It begins with the chanting of a seventh-century prayer, the *Akdamut* (Introduction), followed by the reading of the account of the events at Mount Sinai. The prayer calls upon the Jewish community to remain loyal to their faith. As the Torah reading concludes, the congregation rises and reaffirms their acceptance of it. An important event on the second day of Shavuot is the reading from the Book of Ruth, which tells a story that took place at harvest time. Ruth was a non-Jew who accepted the faith.

In remembrance that at the time of the events at Sinai, the people did not yet know the soon-to-be-observed laws concerning the ritual process for killing animals for food, milk-based foods are the main foods served at meals during Shavuot.

J. Gordon Melton

See also Pesach; Sukkot; Yom Kippur.

References

Eckstein, Yecheil. *What You Should Know about Jews and Judaism*. Waco, TX: Word Books, 1984.

Greenberg, Irving. *The Jewish Way: Living the Holidays*. New York: Jason Aronson, 1998.

Schauss, Hayyim. *The Jewish Festivals: A Guide to Their History and Observance*. New York: Schocken, 1996.

Sheetala Ashtami

Among the lesser-known Hindu deities is Sheetala (or Shitala), but she is worshipped primarily in the small towns and rural areas of North India, Nepal, Bangladesh, and Pakistan, where she is believed to offer protection against epidemics, especially of smallpox. Some have identified her as an aspect of Parvati, the consort of Shiva, or more often as an aspect of Kali, while in South India, her place in the religious culture is filled by the goddess Mariamman. The festival of Sheetala Ashtami is celebrated with the belief that this would prevent them from the deadly epidemics. In temples, the goddess is often represented by a red stone, but is generally pictured as light-complexioned, riding on a donkey, and multi-handed holding a pitcher filled with water and nectar and a broom that she uses to sprinkle water on the people.

Shestala Mata is celebrated on the eighth day of the waxing half of the Hindu month of Chaitra, usually in early April on the Common Era calendar. The festival is celebrated with great excitement in the small towns and is of the occasion of an accompanying fair in which local artisans show off their work. The day will begin with primarily women going to the shrine and making offerings of food to the goddess—rice, sweets, and holy water mixed with milk. During the day, there will be a variety of entertainment as well as religious rituals in which those in attendance may partake.

Among the more notable sites for the Sheetala Ashtami is Chakshu, Jaipur, Rajastan.

Constance A. Jones

See also: Ashokashtami; Dasain; Navaratri.

References

Bang, B. G. "Current Concepts of the Smallpox Goddess Śītalā in West Bengal." *Man in India* 53, no. 1 (1973): 79–104.

Dimock, E. C., Jr. "A Theology of the Repulsive: The Myth of the Goddess Śītalā." In *The Divine Consort: Rādhā and the Goddesses of India*, edited by J. S. Hawley and D. M. Wulff, 184–203. Berkeley: University of California Press, 1982.

Mukhopadhyay, S. K. *Cult of Goddess Śītalā in Bengal: An Enquiry into Folk Culture*. Calcutta: Firma KLM, 1994.

Stewart, T. K. "Encountering the Smallpox Goddess: The Auspicious Song of Śītalā." In *Religious of India in Practice*, edited by D. S. Lopez Jr., 389–97. Princeton, NJ: Princeton University Press, 1995.

Shemini Atzeret/Simchat Torah

Shemini Atzeret and Simchat Torah are two closely related holidays that follow immediately on the heels of Sukkot. Sukkot is a seven-day celebration in the Hebrew month of Tishri, concluding on Tishri 21. According to Leviticus (23:33–36):

> And the LORD spoke unto Moses, saying: "Speak unto the children of Israel, saying: On the 15th day of this seventh month is the feast of tabernacles for seven days unto the LORD. On the first day shall be a holy convocation; ye shall do no manner of servile work. Seven days ye shall bring an offering made by fire unto the LORD; on the eighth day shall be a holy convocation unto you; and ye shall bring an offering made by fire unto the LORD; it is a day of solemn assembly; ye shall do no manner of servile work."

Shemini Atzeret is the convocation of which Leviticus speaks. Simchat Torah refers to another event that occurs at this same time, the conclusion (and the new beginning) of the annual cycle of reading the Torah (the first five books of the Hebrew Bible), a few chapters of which are read at each Sabbat service through the year.

While the dating of the two holidays are tied to Sukkot, as is the alternate name of Shemini Atzeret, the Assembly of the Eighth Day, the two holidays are standalone celebrations in their own right. In Israel, they are celebrated on the same day. Outside of Israel, they are celebrated over two days, with Shemini Atzeret celebrated on Tishri 22 and Simchat Torah on Tishri 23. Shemini Atzeret is seen as a day in which Israel experiences its special intimate relationship with God. Simchat Torah is a celebration of the Torah. During the worship service, the last verses of Deuteronomy are read, immediately followed by the first chapter of Genesis. The congregation is reminded that the Torah is experienced as a never-ending circle.

As the cycle is completed, however, it is a time for rejoicing. The Torah scrolls are carried around the synagogue in a procession with accompanying singing and dancing. Many of the congregation, including children, will be called forward to offer a prayer over the Torah.

Shemini Atzeret and Simchat Torah are holidays on which work is proscribed, and they are observed as an official holidays in Israel.

J. Gordon Melton

See also Sukkot.

References

Posner, Raphael, Uri Kaploun, and Sherman Cohen, eds. *Jewish Liturgy: Prayer and Synagogue Service through the Ages*. New York: Leon Amiel Publisher; Jerusalem: Keter Publishing House, 1975.

"Shemini Atzeret and Simkhat Torah." Jewish Virtual Library. Posted at http://www.jewishvirtuallibrary.org/jsource/Judaism/holiday6.html. Accessed July 15, 2010.

Shichi-Go-San (November 15)

Shichi-Go-San, or Children's Day, is an unofficial but widely observed festival in the Shinto and Buddhist temples of Japan held annually on November 15 (or the weekend closest to that date). It marks the movement of children into a new stage of childhood, and is centered upon what numerologically are considered lucky years—three, five, and seven. On this day, girls who are three or seven and boys who are three or five will be dressed up for a visit to the local shrine or temple. For female children, it is often their first time to wear a kimona in public, and for the boys, their first time in a hakama. The practice emerged among courtiers at the emperor's court in Kyoto during the Heian period (794–1185) and passed to the samurai during the years of the Shogunate.

During the reassertion of Shinto following the Meiji Restoration in 1868, the celebration became established with the general public, and was associated with a visit to a Shinto shrine (or Buddhist temple) to exorcise any evil spirits and pray for a long healthy life for one's children. The primary development in the post–World War II environment is the designation of the event as a photo opportunity.

Older children have another day in May, Kodomo no Hi, while young adults go through a coming-of-age celebration in January called Seijin no Hi.

J. Gordon Melton

See also Kodomo no Hi; Seijin no Hi.

References

"Shichi-Go-San." Japanese Lifestyle. Posted at http://www.japaneselifestyle.com.au/culture/shichi-go-san.html. Accessed June 15, 2010.

Shikinensengu

Shikinensengu refers to the planned renewal of the Ise Jinju Shrine, which occurs every 20 years. The main steps of the renewal process are the construction of a new shrine, the movement of the enshrined deities into their new home, and the destruction of the former shrine and the assignment of its site as the site of the next renewal.

The shrine is some 2,000 years old, but it was the emperor Temmu (c. 631–686) who first suggested the *sengu* or renewal system. His successor, the empress Jitō (645–702) had the *sengu* ceremony performed for the first time for the Inner Shrine in 690 and for the Outer Shrine two years later. In the 10th century, the renewal process became a matter of national law, and an agency was set up to take charge of the event. The legislation provided for the use of public funds and specified the timing of the ceremony and the transfer of the deity. Due to unrest in the country, the ceremony did not happen for more than a century between 1462 and 1585.

While the renewal of the main shrine occurs within a single year, the total renewal takes years, and means the reconstruction of more than 60 structures including all of the treasure houses, offering halls, sacred fences, *torii* gateways, and the buildings of 14 "auxiliary sanctuaries." In addition, all of the offerings of vestments and sacred treasures that have been presented by the imperial family also have to be replaced.

At each stage of the renewal process, specific appropriate rites and ceremonies are performed, for example, for the cutting and transport of cedar logs used for the main shrines, the preparation of the site, and the actual erection of the shrines.

The actual transfer of the deities occurs during an evening in October. As the deity departs the old shrine, an envoy from the emperor announces the departure. Simultaneously, the emperor (who is located at the Imperial Palace in Tokyo) faces toward Ise and performs an additional ritual. Upon arriving at the new shrine, the newly enshrined deity will receive the first offering of sacred food.

The most recent renewal was in 1993, and the next is scheduled for 2013.

J. Gordon Melton

See also Iwashimizu Matsuri; Kanmiso-sai; Shinto—Cycle of Holidays.

References

The Grand Shrine of Ise. Ise City: Office of the Grand Shrines of Ise, 1990.

Jinju. Posted at http://www.isejingu.or.jp/english/. Accessed June 15, 2010.

Littleton, Scott. *Shinto: Origins, Rituals, Festivals, Spirits, Sacred Places*. New York: Oxford University Press, 2002.

Masayuki, Nakanishi. "Shikinensengu." *Encyclopedia of Shinto*. Posted at http://eos.kokugakuin.ac.jp/modules/xwords/entry.php?entryID=747. Accessed June 15, 2010.

Shinran Shonin, Birthday of

Shinran Shonin (1173–1263) was the founder of the Japanese Jodo Shinshu tradition, the largest branch of Pure Land Buddhism in Japan. Pure Land Buddhism seeks to facilitate the salvation of its members through the simple practice of calling upon the name of Amitabha Buddha (known as Amida Buddha in Japan).

Shinran became a Tendai Buddhist monk in 1181 and lived for some 20 years at their monastic complex on Mount Hiei near Kyoto. He then left Mount Hiei somewhat disenchanted with the monastic life and excited by the relatively new teachings being offered by Honen (1133–1212), who founded the first of the Japanese Pure Land sects, the Jodo-shu. He studied with Honen from 1201 to 1207. The new teachings discounted the necessity for long years of study and practice so characteristic of the monastic life.

The Jodo-shu movement ran into trouble when some followers of Honene violated the prohibition on proselytizing. Both Honen and Shinran were exiled and Shinran lost his status as a monk. Shinran assumed the lay name Fuji'i Yoshizane, but went even further and married. He and his wife Eshinni had six children. In 1214, Shinran and his family settled in Hitachi (present-day Ibaraki prefecture) and built a large following and created Pure Land meeting centers termed *dojos*. In 1234, Shinran turned the *dojos* over to his followers and returned to Kyoto with his family.

Shinran would spend much of the rest of his life putting his understanding of Pure Land teachings into writing. He advocated the centrality of *shinjin*, true or sincere faith, Spiritual release comes when the devotee perceives his or her inadequacies and surrenders to the absolute Other Power (*tariki*) of Amida Buddha, whose compassion is the source of the power that makes salvation possible. Even *shinjin* or faith, the prime condition for birth in the Pure Land, emerges as a gift. The sincere utterance of the *nembutsu*, the mantra calling upon Amida Buddha's name, is ultimately an invocation of gratitude and joy for Amida's compassion.

Jodo Shinshu Buddhists commemorate Shinran's birthday with a special Shinran Shonin (Gotan-E) Day worship service at temples worldwide on or near May 1, his birthday and his death with a Ho-On-Ko service, to remember and express gratitude for Shinran's life and work on or near January 16.

J. Gordon Melton

See also Eshinni-Kakushinni Memorial.

References

Bloom, Alfred, ed. *The Essential Shinran: A Buddhist Path of True Entrusting*. Bloomington, IN: World Wisdom, 2007.

Dobbins, James C. *Jodo Shinshu, Shin Buddhism in Medieval Japan*. Bloomington: Indiana University Press, 1989.

Ueda, Yoshifumi, and Dennis Hirota. *Shinran, an Introduction to His Thought*. Kyoto: Honganji International Center, 1989.

■ Shinto

Shinto (the Divine Way), the traditional religion of Japan, is today represented by a spectrum of religious groups in the land of its birth, the largest segment of the movement being Shrine Shinto, which finds embodiment in the thousands of public shrines that dot the landscape. Shrine Shinto was the state religion of Japan in the decades prior to World War II. Sect Shinto designated the 13 Shinto organizations (Kurozumikyo, Shinto Shuseiha, Izumo Oyashirokyo, Fusokyo, Jikkokyo, Shinshukyo, Shinto Taiseikyo, Ontaki-Kyo, Shintotaikyo, Misogikyo, Shinrikyo, Tenrikyo, and Konkyoko) recognized by the government during that period. In addition, there are more than 100 new Japanese religions that draw primarily on Shinto themes, some founded before 1945 and suppressed by the government, and others founded after 1945.

Early in Japan's history, numerous extended family groups (clans) developed, each of which developed religious practices largely tied to its land. There was no central political structure or unified culture. By the third century CE, an agriculturally based religion had become prominent, and over the next centuries, Japan would come together as a nation around the prominent Yamato clan (the source of the later imperial family). During this formative period, two of what would become leading Shinto shrines, Ise and Izumo, were created.

Crucial to the creation of a national Shinto religion (which incorporated the many local variations) was the introduction of Confucianism and its emphasis on ethics and

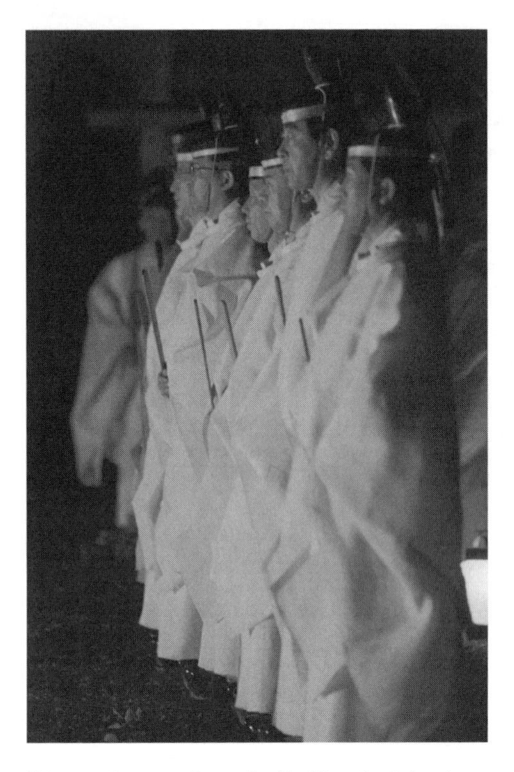

Shinto priests perform the *Tsukinami-sai* ritual at the Ise Shrine in Japan. (AP/Wide World Photos)

social order, the spread of the cosmology that divided the world into ying-yang polarities, and later the arrival of Buddhism. Each challenged the elite elements of Japan to create a uniquely Japanese faith comparable to that of neighboring states. One result was the compilation of the Kojiki (712 CE) and Nihon Shoki (720 CE), the two sacred texts of Shinto that describe the overarching myth out of which the many local cults would operate.

Shinto views the world as alive with divinity. The term *kami* refers to the many deities of heaven and earth, who may include among them some human beings and an array of natural objects (birds, plants, and natural features). Anything above the ordinary or that might awaken a sense of awe or mystery in the human mind may be listed as a kami, including the succession of emperors who have led the country.

Although kami of local significance are acknowledged at different shrines, some kami gained significance as part of the national myth of Japan's origin. The deities Ame-no-mi-naka-nushi-no-Kami (Kami Master of the Center of Heaven), Taka-mi-musubi-no-Kami (High Sacred Creating Kami), and Kami-masubi (Sacred Creating Kami) are seen as the primordial deities who were present when nothing but the primal chaos existed. They were responsible for the formation of the earth and the deities who were later to create Japan and its people.

The High Kami in heaven sent the primal parents—Izanagi (male) and Izanami (female). Their interaction gave birth to numerous islands and other deities. Then Izanami was burned as the fire-god was given birth. She descended into the underworld, where she was trapped after eating of its food. In his attempts to free Izanami, Izanagi bathed in the ocean as a cleansing act. His ablutions also resulted in the appearance of Amaterasu, the goddess who is seen as the ancestress of the Japanese imperial family. While at a festival, another kami held up a mirror for Amaterasu to gaze upon herself. She would later give this mirror to her grandson, who was sent from heaven to establish the Japanese royal lineage. The mirror is now said to be residing hidden in the Ise shrine.

Shinto has an essential communal element, and much of its activity occurs in the many shrines that are found throughout Japan. The shrines, abodes of the kami, are generally located in spots of particular natural beauty or some noteworthy geographical feature. The site itself is marked off with a fence and the entrance with the distinctive gate (*torii*) to which a sacred rope (*shimenawa*) is attached. At the shrine, the kami are invoked on a cycle that follows the agricultural seasons and that affirms the myth of national origins. Many shrines are located at the foot of a mountain, which has the effect of marking the land of death and renewal (the mountain) from the plains, the land of life and activity. Others may be found at the point where two streams merge.

Common elements in Shinto rituals are the offering of foods, which in turn has had a profound influence on the Japanese diet, and purification, harkening back to the baths taken by Izanagi in his attempts to free his wife from the underworld. Food offerings may be classified by type (animal, vegetable, fish), style of preparation (raw or cooked), mode of offering, or whether it is to be viewed by the deities or eaten by them. Frequently the offered food becomes part of a banquet consumed later by the worshippers.

Purification rites have been developed in response to a variety of life's setbacks, from the sickness and death of a loved one to natural calamities and national disasters. They came to include reactions to forms of ritual impurity (from menstruation to sexual activity) and to symbolize the hope of renewal.

After 538 CE, Shinto developed in dialogue with Buddhism, the latter becoming an increasing part of Japanese life. Shinto and Buddhist temples were often constructed adjacent to each other, and they found a common ground in their esoteric element. Buddhists came to accept Shinto as a lesser form of itself, and locally, syncretistic Buddhist/Shinto cults developed that centered on specific shrines and local deities. Shugendo became one of the more interesting new religions drawing deeply from both Buddhist and Shinto sources.

Shinto experienced a revival in the 15th century after many shrines were destroyed in the Onin War (1467–1477). Out of the ashes emerged Yoshida Kanetomo (1435–1511), who dedicated his life to their reconstruction (especially those most associated with his prominent family), the return of Shinto supremacy in the land, and the reestablishment of imperial authority. He recast Shintoism as the original faith and the source of Taoism, Confucianism, and Buddhism. He expounded a new theology built around an exoteric teaching (as found in the Kojiki and Nihon Shoki) and esoteric teachings that he claimed had been revealed by deities to his family (resulting in additional scriptural texts). Kanetomo became the leading figure in Shintoism, and his school would dominate the religion during the next centuries.

The work of Kanetomo and his successors would during the Edo period (1600–1868) lead to a shift in Shinto away from a primary dialogue with Buddhism to one with Confucianism. At the same time, a new scholarly movement, called *kokugaku*

(National Learning), attempted to redefine Japanese tradition and self-identity. Hayashi Razan (1583–1657), who led the new trend, emphasized the immanence of the Absolute as the divine within the inner life of the individual, the divine life expressed in ethical behavior, and, most important for Japan's future, the primary manifestation of divine virtue in the imperial government. During the Edo period, especially in the writings of Yoshikawa Koretari (1616–1694), the deity Kuninoto-kotachi no Mikoto, identified with the primal chaos, emerged as the central figure in the Shinto pantheon.

The continued development of Shinto in the 18th century set the stage for major developments in the 19th century. The variety of Shinto groups, later to constitute Sect Shinto, began to emerge. Most of these new groups were the result of the activity of a creative founder who was also responsible for the composing or receiving by revelation of a distinctive new scripture. These groups were later classified by the major themes they developed. Some emphasized attachment to traditional texts (Kojiki and Nihon Shoki), Confucian ethical principles, or purification rituals. The Fuji and Ontake sects emphasized the long-standing worship at sacred mountains. Spiritual healing, utilizing Shinto rituals, became the center of Tenrikyo and Konkokyo.

A new era for Shinto came in 1868 with the emergence of the Meiji government. The new government brought to the fore a form of Shinto usually referred to as State Shinto. It combined the thought of Hirata Atsutane (1776–1843) with the cult that had grown up around the imperial family. Atsutane had been an effective propagandist of the return of Japan to imperial rule and the establishment of Shinto as the sole religion of the land. State Shinto propagated the belief in the divinity of the emperor and sanctified Japan's national political policies. It proposed as its idea *saisei itchi*, the unity of religion and government. Students of Atsutane were recruited to head a revived Office of Shinto Worship, whose initial mandate was the separation of Shinto from Buddhism and Christianity. As a result, Shinto shrines were stripped of all Buddhist and Christian symbols, and the Imperial Palace was denuded of the heretofore-dominant Buddhist altars and symbols.

In the 1870s, step by step, the government asserted its authority over the Shinto shrines and leadership. The Agency for Spiritual Guidance was given authority over all Shinto priests and designated their place of appointment. The national rituals to be performed at each shrine were also prescribed. The emperor was declared sacred and inviolable in 1889, and, in 1900, Shinto's special place was reemphasized by its being placed under the Bureau of Shrines in the Home Ministry, while Buddhism and Christianity were relegated to a separate Bureau of Religion in the Ministry of Education. In the meantime, Sect Shinto had an intermediary position. The sects were treated much like Buddhism and Christianity, being seen as private religious organizations under the jurisdiction of the Bureau of Religion. Most important, they were allowed neither to create shrines nor to copy shrine architecture in their worship centers, including the use of a torii as a gateway entrance.

Increasingly, Shinto was seen as an arm of the state. In 1911, it ordered all schools (including private religious schools) to take their pupils to shrines for nationally directed ritual events. In 1932, a Catholic school refused to comply with the regulation on grounds of religious freedom. Students at one Catholic school had been asked to visit a shrine particularly associated with Japan's military history. As a result of the protest, the government declared the shrines "nonreligious" sites whose task was to foster national loyalty. Shinto was thus redefined in such a way as to be compatible with any particular religious affiliation; the inclusion of Shinto ritual into both private and public life became a sign of loyalty as Japan went to war. Amulets from the Ise shrine became ubiquitous.

The loss in World War II affected Shinto most of all. The coming of religious freedom gave Sect Shinto a new life, and several sects emerged as popular movements whose adherents numbered into the tens of thousands. Then, on December 15, 1945, General Douglas MacArthur (1880–1964) issued the "Shinto Directive," which ordered the separation of State Shinto from the government. Most important, the government was to end its support of the shrines. This mandate was embodied in the Constitution of 1947.

In the late 1940s, State Shinto evolved into what is today known as Shrine (*jinja*) Shinto. The formerly government-supported shrines were reorganized into a private religious corporation, the Association of Shinto Shrines, with which the great majority of shrines affiliated. There were more than 100,000 such shrines in 1945. By the beginning of the 1980s, some 79,000 shrines were maintained as part of the new system of voluntary support. Two seminaries, one at Kokugakuin University in Tokyo and the other at Kogakukan University in Ise, train Shinto priests. The association represents Shinto in various interfaith activities, including the World Conference on Religion and Peace. It also accepts women into the priesthood.

In spite of the proliferation of Shinto sects, the association includes the majority of the two million to three million Japanese who identify themselves as Shintoists, the number of whom is somewhat difficult to assess, as many people carry dual affiliations, a continuing result of Meiji Era practices. Support for Shinto in Japan pales next to that for Buddhism, which now commands the allegiance of more than half the population. The special Shinto of the Imperial House (*koshitsu*) also survives in a variety of practices associated with the emperor and his family, the shrines at the royal palace, and the Grand Shrine at Ise. The most important rite is Niinamesai, the annual offering of the first fruits of the grain harvest that includes thanksgiving to the deities for their blessing and a sharing of the food with the deities, especially Amaterasu.

The Grand Shrine at Ise, now a popular tourist attraction, includes two shrines. One is dedicated to Amaterasu and, as the shrine of the legendary ancestress of the emperor, has a special relationship to the imperial family. Traditionally, the emperors would make reports to the goddess at the shrine, which was believed to hold the fabled mirror she had passed to her grandson. A second shrine is dedicated to Toyouke, the goddess of food. Every 20 years, new shrines replicating the old ones are erected. Upon their completion, as part of a ceremony of renewal, the ritual objects in the old shrines are transferred to the new ones, and the old shrines are then completely dismantled.

Shinto, as the religion of the Japanese people, has been largely confined to that country. However, early in the 20th century, it was established among Japanese immigrants in Hawaii. Although largely suppressed during World War II, it slowly revived after the war as questions of the loyalties of Japanese Americans were resolved. Shinto has subsequently appeared, in small numbers, in diaspora communities in Canada and South America.

J. Gordon Melton

See also Shinto—Cycle of Holidays.

References

Bocking, Brian. *A Popular Dictionary of Shinto*. New York: McGraw-Hill, 1997.

Breen, John, and Mark Teeuwen, eds. *Shinto in History*. Richmond, UK: Curzon, 2000.

Hardacre, Helen. *Shinto and the State, 1868–1988*. Princeton, NJ: Princeton University Press, 1991.

Kasulis, Thomas P. *Shinto: The Way Home*. Honolulu: University of Hawaii Press, 2004.

Nelson, John K. *A Year in the Life of a Shinto Shrine*. Seattle: University of Washington Press, 1996.

Ono, Sokyo. *Shinto: The Kami Way*. Rutland, VT: Charles E. Tuttle, 1967.

Yamakage, Motohisa. *The Essence of Shinto: Japan's Spiritual Heart*. Tokyo: Kodansha International, 2007.

Shinto—Cycle of Holidays

Shinto is the tradition indigenous religion of Japan, and it was present as a set of local ethno-linguistic religions as Japan emerged out of prehistory into the historical era and written records began to appear. As the islands that make up Japan were united under one ruler, Shinto became identified with the Japanese state and people. It faced several challenges with the introduction of Buddhism in the sixth and seventh centuries from Korea and China and the years of the Tokugawa Shogunate (1603–1868), when Buddhism was favored over Shinto. Shinto came back with a vengeance with the Meiji Restoration in 1868, but suffered significantly with Japan's defeat at the end of World War II and the arrival of religious freedom.

Christianity also posed a challenge to Shinto, but not in the way it did to Buddhism. During its initial period of growth in the 16th century, it was used to balance the power between rival Buddhist and Shinto rivals, but after the union of the country under Tokugawa Ieyasu (1543–1616), the shoguns moved against Christianity. It would not again become a real factor until the 19th century, after the opening of the country to foreign trade.

The Meiji Restoration again placed Shinto at the center of Japanese culture and politics but also brought some important changes, and Japan continued to develop relationships to the outside world. In 1873, the Meiji government allowed the introduction of the Western Gregorian calendar, with its year running from January 1 through December 31, into Japan, although a system of numbering years tied to the reign of the emperor was popularly utilized. Previously, Japan had used a lunar-solar calendar based on the Chinese calendar. Then in 1884, Japan attended the International Meridian Conference held in Washington, D.C., that set the line north and south through Greenwich, England, as the Prime Meridian for the world. That meeting also confirmed the 180-degree meridian (with its several variations) as the International Date Line, important for the growing international shipping market, and set the beginning of the day at midnight. Japan has continued to cooperate with the scientific development of the calendar that has led to the current Common Era calendar now used by almost all governments.

The pervasive adoption of the Common Era calendar has meant that the continued use of other calendars has been primarily by religious communities. The relatively early adoption of the Western calendar by Japan, even as Shinto was attempting to reestablish itself as the national religion of Japan, led to the first steps of the adoption of the Common Era calendar for the holding of Shinto holidays. That move was spurred by the changes at the end of World War II and the growing secularization of Japan. It was assisted by the local nature of many of Shinto holiday festivals, which were always set locally and not coordinated as a national event throughout the country. Many of the local festivals still set their dates by the traditional Japanese calendar, while an equally large number now used the Common Era calendar.

Japan has been the home to numerous local festivals, called *matsuris*, and while any given festival may be celebrated on the same day year after year, if may vary considerably from other similar festivals celebrated elsewhere across the country. This pattern is particularly visible in the seasonal festivals celebrating the spring planting, summer growing, and fall harvest seasons. Most communities hold a festival to mark the beginning of the agricultural year, to hold back threats to their maturing crops, and to give thanks for the harvest, but these would vary from city to city and according to the length of the growing season (which is quite short in the northern parts of the country). In the last half of the 20th century, the business community has thrown its support behind many matsuris, transforming them into significant local tourist attractions. For believers, such festivals become an opportunity for the exercise of their faith, while for the majority, the celebration goes forward with no mention of the religious origins and underpinning.

The Shinto year begins on January 1, with New Year's Day celebrations. New Year's Day is a national holiday in Japan, and for Shinto believers, it is a day to pray for individual health and happiness. The changing calendar means that New Year's will be celebrated at different times by different people. The old-calendar New Year's Day coincided with the Chinese New Year (February–March) and continues as the Setsubun (season-changing) holiday. A setsubun day marks all the season changes; the new year was usually said to begin with the arrival of spring, which in China was in February. Many still observe Setsubun, now set on the solar calendar as February 3, while a lesser lunar New Year's celebration, Koshogatsu, comes in mid-January

The January 1 New Year's celebration in Japan will continue for several days, spurred in part by the celebration of Genshi-sai on January 3. Genshi-sai proclaims the divine origins of the Japanese imperial family, believed to be derived from Ninigi-no-mikoto, grandson of Amaterasu Omikami. In Japanese/Shinto thought, Amaterasu is the child of Izanagi-no-Mikoto and Izanami-no-Mikoto (the details vary), and she then sent her grandson Ninigi-no-Mikoto to bring rice to humankind. Ninigi would become the great-grandfather of Emperor Jimmu, the first emperor of Japan.

The Imperial House of Japan ruled the country through the centuries, and even in the days of the Shogunate, continued as the symbolic head of the country until restored to real power in 1868. Following World War II, the emperor was forced to renounce his status as a divine ruler, the idea (narrowly defined) that he is "divinity in human form," and/or the idea that the Japanese people were superior to other races. The wording of the renunciation left open the question of belief that the emperor and/or the Japanese people are ultimately the descendants of the gods, specifically Amaterasu. The emperor remains in office as the symbol of the Japanese state and the unity of the Japanese people, and various relatives continue to perform a spectrum of ceremonial, social, and specifically religious duties. The place of the emperor in the divine lineage, now in ways that do not contradict the provisions of the Constitution, are affirmed in the ritual of Genshi-sai, which is carried out most importantly at the major site long identified with imperial power at the Ise (near Ise City) and the several shrines in Kyoto.

The high priest(ess) of Ise Shrine is a member of the Japanese imperial family. In 965, the emperor Murakami (926–967) ordered that henceforth, messengers from the imperial throne would be sent to 16 selected shrines around the country to bring reports of important events to Japan's guardian deities (*kami*). Those 16, along with 5 additional shrines added to the list, remain the most important Shinto shrines in the country relative to the continuing relationship between Shinto and the country and the imperial family. Soon after Gensei-sai, these shrines will be the primary sites for the holding of the Shōwa-Tenno-sai-yohai ceremony

(January 7), which remembers the death of the Shōwa emperor Horohito (r. 1926–1989).

Throughout the year, especially at Ise Jinju and the other shrines most tied to the emperor, a series of rites are performed annually that reaffirm the emperor's role in the life of the nation and the familial ties with Amaterasu. Literally hundreds of ceremonies are held through the year, though a few emerge as most important. The more important include:

January 11: Kenkokukinen-sai, celebration of the foundation of the nation.

March 21: Shunki-koreisai-yohai, ceremony remembering the imperial ancestors.

April 3: Jinmu Tenno-sai-yohai, anniversary of the passing of Emperor Jinmu.

May 1: Kanmiso-hoshoku-hajime-sai, ceremony for weaving the sacred silk and the sacred hemp.

May 13: Kanmiso-hoshoku-chinsha-sai, celebration of thanksgiving for the completion of weaving the sacred silk and sacred hemp.

May 14: Kanmiso-sai, offering of the sacred silk and hemp to become the clothing for Amaterasu.

October 1, 13, and 14: The Kanmiso ceremonies of May are repeated.

In addition to the imperial holidays, there are an additional set of celebrations to Amaterasu related to food production. The first of the year occurs on January 11, and is termed Ichigatsu-juichinichi-mike, the purpose being to offer sacred food to Amaterasu (and the other deities). This ceremony leads to the most important spring celebration of Kinen-sai (February 17–23), the spring festival at which prayers are given for a plentiful harvest. Two ceremonies are held, one focused on food, the other on clothing materials. People traditionally dressed in clothing made from silk (the emperor and nobility) and hemp (the great majority of the people). Kinen-sai initiated a set of ceremonies around the weaving of cloth, especially the emperor silk.

Kinen-sai would be reflected across Japan in a number of local spring festivals, with some, such as the one at Takayama, becoming internationally famous. The underlying purpose of all the spring festivals was to pray for the crops that were being planted so that they would take root and eventually produce an abundant harvest. In the modern world, they become an extension of the New Year's celebration in which people see good fortune through the coming year. This emphasis is also reflected in the Shinto celebration of the spring equinox on March 21. Misono-sai is a ceremony is held at Ise Jingu, specifically again to pray for a plentiful harvest.

The transition to the summer season is reflected in the May 14 ceremony of Kazahinomi-sai, at which prayers are offered for good weather and sufficient rain for the all-important rice crop. It also noted that the popular alcoholic drink sake is also made from rice. This ceremony is repeated on August 4, and is reflected in the many summer festivals such as the Aizen Summer Matsuri, at which prayers are given to stave off any disasters that might negatively affect the crops in the field by weather, insects, or disease. The prosperity of the nation as a whole was dependent on the food being raised, symbolized by rice.

Ritual concern for the harvest reaches a climax in October with the celebration of Kanname-sai, at which the first fruits from the rice harvest are offered to Amaterasu. The emperor personally harvests the initial plants and sends them via an imperial envoy to Ise, where they will be offered as part of the ceremony. He also sends samples of silk for the ceremony. This ceremony also coincides with the accepted date of Amaterasu's original enshrinement ceremony at Ise jinju two millennia ago, and has become the single most important ceremony of the year at the shrine.

Kanname-sai is conducted in three steps. The first, the Yukino-omike ceremony, held in the evening, centers on the food offerings. The Hoheisai ceremony then focuses on the offerings of silk and other materials. The final phase is built around ceremonial court music and dance dedicated to all the enshrined kami. This last celebration is held in the evening following the Hoheisai ceremony. Kanname-sai, held over 10 days in October, initiates a series of fall thanksgiving celebrations across Japan that will celebrate the abundance of the harvest.

As the cycles of imperial and agricultural celebrations proceed, on the second Monday of the year, the first of the several coming-of-age ceremonies held in Japan occurs. Seijin no Hi, or Coming of Age Day, also an official holiday throughout Japan, celebrates the transition of teenagers to adulthood, which in Japan occurs when they reach their 20th birthday. It is followed by three widely observed events, to celebrate young boys (Kodomo ni Hi, or Children's Day, May 5) and girls (the Doll Festival, March 3) and the smaller children (aged three, five and seven, Shichi-Go-San or Children's Day, November 15).

J. Gordon Melton

See also Aizen Summer Festival; Doll Festival; Kanmiso-sai; Kodomo no Hi; Koshogatsu; Seijin no Hi; Shikinensengu.

References

Breen, John, and Mark Teeuwen, eds. *Shinto in History: Ways of the Kami*. Honolulu: University of Hawaii Press, 2000.

Jinju. Posted at http://www.isejingu.or.jp/english/. Accessed June 15, 2010.

Littleton, Scott. *Shinto: Origins, Rituals, Festivals, Spirits, Sacred Places*. New York: Oxford University Press, 2002.

Nelson, J. K. *Enduring Identities: The Guise of Shinto in Contemporary Japan*. Honolulu: University of Hawaii Press, 2000.

Picken, Stuart D. B. *Essentials of Shinto: An Analytical Guide to Principal Teachings*. Westport, CT: Greenwood Press, 1994.

Plutschow, Herbert. *Matsuri: The Festivals of Japan*. Richmond, Surrey, UK: Curzon Press, 1996.

Shivaratri. *See* Mahashivaratri

Shravava Mela

The month of Shravana on the Hindu calendar (July–August on the Common Era calendar) is sacred to the deity Shiva. It is believed that it was during this month that the churning of the Ocean of Milk, one of the most famous stores in Hindu thought, occurred during this month. During the churning, some poison was released, and to save humankind from its effects, Shiva drank the poison.

One place where Shiva's saving act is remembered is the Shiva Temple at Deogharh in Jharkhand. During Shrevana, thousands of pilgrims arrive at this temple from across India and neighboring Nepal. Those who wish to make the pilgrimage will first come to Sultanganj, a town on the Ganges River in the state of Bihar. Sultanganj is notable as being located at the only point on the river where it briefly turns and flows north. It is also the location of a monthlong fair during the holy month, the Shravava Mela. Pilgrims to the Shiva Temple will begin their trek with a visit to the fair.

While in Sultanganj, pilgrims will also collect water from the river, which they will carry to the Deoghar Temple. The water will be used to bath the Shiva lingam (a phallic symbol of Shiva) on display there. The pilgrims, called Kanwarias, believe this action will assist in removing ignorance and fulfilling their desires.

In Hindu thought, Mondays are sacred to Shiva, and hence, that day is the heaviest in the month for pilgrims arriving at the temple. Believers also will fast all day on Monday.

Constance A. Jones

See also Amarnath Yatra; Kumbha Mela; Mahashivaratri.

References

"Shravani Mela 2009 at Deoghar Temple." Hindu Blog. Posted at http://www.hindu-blog.com/2009/07/shravani-mela-2009-at-deoghar-temple.html. Accessed June 15, 2010.

"Stage Set for Shravani Mela." *Telegraph* (Calcutta, India), July 4, 2004. Posted at http://www.telegraphindia.com/1040705/asp/jamshedpur/story_3455577.asp. Accessed June 15, 2010.

Shrove Monday *See* Mardi Gras

Shrove Tuesday. *See* Mardi Gras

Shuni-e (Omizutori)

The Shuni-e (or "Second-Month Service") is a Japanese Buddhist ceremony devoted to the bodhisattva Guan Yin (Avalokitesvara), known in Japan as Kannon. It is a two-week celebration held in the second month of the traditional lunar calendar (which falls in February or March on the Common Era calendar) in a few select temples especially dedicated to Kannon, of which there are many in Japan. The best-known celebration is at the old temple at Nara, Todai-ji.

The Todai-ji Shuni-e originated in the early years of Buddhism's presence in Japan, being traced the eighth century and the building of Todai-ji, begun in 745 at the behest of the emperor Shomu (701–756), a staunch Buddhist. Shortly after its completion, however, the emperor fell ill, and his wife, the empress Kōmyō, requested Jitchū, a prominent Kegon monk at Todai-ji, to create a new ritual for his benefit. In response, he developed the Shuni-e ceremony focused upon devotion to and confession before Bodhisattva Kannon. According to the story, the ritual reproduces one that Jitchu experienced in a heavenly vision. It has subsequently remained an annual event since its first observance in 752. Since 772, the ritual has been held at Nigatsu-dō, a hall constructed especially for the conducting of the ritual. Nigatsu-dō is located just east of the hall where the Great Buddha of Todai-ji is housed.

The Shuni-e ritual, which the public may not attend, is conducted by a small group of monks who gather in Nigatsu-dō (or its equivalent in other temples) six times during each 24-hour period. The sessions at which prayers are offered, confessions made, and the name of Kannon invoked (using the Eleven-Faced Avalokitesvara Heart Dharani Sutra), vary in length, though the longest is the late evening session, which lasts three hours.

Although not allowed inside the hall, believers will gather around the hall where the ritual sessions are occurring each evening for a nightly fire ceremony. Each night, a small group of believers are selected to carry torches and run along the balcony of Nigatsu-dō, allowing sparks from the torches to be showered on the gathered assembly. At the same time, the monks will be chanting, performing ritual circumambulation of the hall, and waving swords in the air to ward off evil spirits.

The most important day of Shuni-e is the last. Following the fire ceremony that evening, the monks will retire to a place underneath the ritual hall, where a well is located. Legend suggests that on this day alone, water will spring forth from it, and the monks gather the water in two pots. One pot contains some water from the previous year, and the other water from all previous observances of Shuni-e. The water is then offered to Kannon and subsequently to the general public (which usually occurs around 2:00 a.m.). The water is believed to have miraculous powers.

This water ceremony is known as Omizutori, a name that has come to be used synonymously with Shuni-e as the name of the whole two-week activity. After the ceremony, the remaining water in the two pots is preserved for the following year's celebration.

J. Gordon Melton

See also Guan Yin, Renunciation of; Guan Yin's Birthday; Jizo Bon.

References

Abe, Ryuichi. *The Weaving of Mantra: Kukai and the Construction of Esoteric Buddhist Discourse*. New York: Columbia University Press, 1999.

Blofeld, John. *Bodhisattva of Compassion: The Mystical Tradition of Kuan Yin*. Boulder, CO: Shambhala, 1988.

Martin, John H., and Phyllis G. Martin. *Nara: A Cultural Guide to Japan's Ancient Capital*. Rutland, VT: Charles E. Tuttle Publishing, 1994.

Shunki-Korei-Sai. *See* Higan

Siddha Day (November 24)

Sri Aurobindo (Aravinda Akroyd Ghose, 1872–1950) was an important early-20th-century Indian spiritual teacher who operated from Pondicherry, on India's eastern coast. Having received a good education, Ghose threw himself into the fight for Indian independence, which took much of his time through the first decade of the 20th century. His activity led to his arrest on several occasions. Simultaneously, he had been practicing meditation and yoga, and in 1907, he had a significant experience of inner illumination. During a later period (1909–1910), he had had repeated mystical encounters. In 1910, he dropped his political work to concentrate on his spiritual vision.

He moved to Pondicherry and there he continued his yoga and meditation disciplines, and was joined his work by the person who was to share his vision and eventually become his coworker and successor, Mirra Richard, known more popularly as just the Mother.

On November 24, 1926, the efforts of his spiritual disciplines culminated in and intense experience now remembered as the Siddha event, which he described as the descent of the divine consciousness into the physical. It would later be described as the descent of the Higher Power symbolic of the victory of their mission, that is the Delight consciousness (symbolized by the deity Krishna) in the Overmind (the highest divine realm) descended on this day into the physical, rendering possible the descent of the Supermind into Matter.

Following this event, Aurobindo largely retired from contact with the world. From that point, he communicated to his growing following through the Mother, and as he worked on the spiritual planes, she led in the building of his movement internationally. Over the next years of their lives, the pair offered darshan (opportunities for the ashram members to see them and receive a personal blessing) a few times each year. One of these occasions was the anniversary of the Siddhi event. The annual Siddhi darshan was continued by the Mother in the years following Aurobindo's death. Since her death, the date has become a commemoration date at the ashram for Aurobindo's followers, many coming from around the world to remember their spiritual teachers.

On this day, the living quarters of Aurobindo and the Mother will be opened for viewing by their disciples, and special programming will be offered—some informational and some celebrative. Siddha Day is also the anniversary of the founding of the ashram.

J. Gordon Melton

See also Aurobindo, Birth Anniversary of Sri; Mother, Birthday of the.

References

Aurobindo, Sri. *The Integral Yoga: Sri Aurobindo's Teaching and Method of Practice.* Twin Lakes, WI: Lotus Press, 1993.

Heehs, Peter. *The Lives of Sri Aurobindo.* New York: Columbia University Press, 2008.

Pandit, M. P., comp. *Dictionary of Sri Aurobindo's Yoga.* Twin Lakes, WI: Lotus Press, 1992.

Purani, A. B. "November 24—the Siddhi Day or Day of Victory." Sri Aurobindo Sadhana Peetham. Posted at http://sasp.collaboration.org/Nov24.html. Accessed April 15, 2010.

Sigd

The Sigd is an ancient holiday of Ethiopian Jews (Beta Yisrael) that highlighted their desire to move to the Land of Israel and be reunited with their fellow believers. It was a time to fast, repent, and beseech God concerning their return to Jerusalem. The ritual called those in attendance of the renewal of the covenant by Ezra in the sixth century BCE, when the Jews returned from exile in Babylon. The Book of Nehemiah (9:1–3) states:

> And on the twenty-fourth day of this month the children of Israel assembled with fasting and with sackcloth and earth on them. And the seed of Israel separated themselves from all foreigners and stood and confessed their sins and the iniquities of their fathers . . . and read the Torah . . . and prostrated themselves.

The Sigd is held annually on the 29th day of the Hebrew month of Heshvan, 50 days after Yom Kippur. Jewish leaders in Ethiopia tied the events recounted in Nehemiah that they are emulating to the harvest season, which differs in Ethiopia. Thus, the dating of the Sigd was changed to accommodate the local growing season.

Prior to the immigration of most Ethiopian Jews to Israel in the last generation, the community fasted on the Sigd. In the morning hours, the *kaisim* (spiritual leaders) carried the Orit (the Torah written in Ge'ez) to a nearby mountain with the faithful in a procession behind them. Like Moses, they ascended the mountain. Once at the top, the kaisim would chant special holiday prayers (based on Ezra's prayer), and read passages from the Bible, including the one from Nehemiah concerning the first Sigd. The prayers concern the welfare of the Jewish community as a whole, the rebuilding of the Temple, and for the return of the entire Jewish people to Israel. After the return down the mountain, the Orit is returned to its normal resting place, followed by a meal, with music and dance. A special bread, the Dabu, is also served. The gathering lasts all night, and in the morning, breakfast is served before everyone returned to their homes.

The Sigd celebration has been continued in Israel, with many non-Ethiopian Jews joining the festivities. Instead of going up a mountain, the community visits Jerusalem for a mass meeting at De Haas Promenade in Armon Hanatziv and the Western Wall (of the old temple). The kaisim lead various processions in different parts of the city, and the faithful fast until the meal and the serving of the Dabu bread.

Most Ethiopian Jews regard themselves as the descendants of the lost tribe of Dan. Others suggest that they derive from Jewish immigrants from Egypt or Yemen. Still others hold to the notion that they date from the meeting of the Jewish king Solomon and the Ethiopian queen of Sheba. In either case, they have been welcomed to Israel through the law of return and are being integrated into Israeli society.

J. Gordon Melton

See also Yom HaAatzmaut; Yom HaZikaron; Yom Yerushalayim (Jerusalem Day).

References

"The Sigd." Israel Association for Ethiopian Jews. Posted at http://www.iaej.co.il/newsite/content.asp?pageid=407&lang=en. Accessed July 15, 2010.

Silent Day. *See* Holy week

Simchat Torah. *See* Shemini Alzeret/Simchat Torah

Sivananda Saraswati, Birthday of Swami (September 8)

While birthdays are natural occasions for celebration, they pose some problems for many in the Hindu community. They view birth in human form in a somewhat negative occurrence by a soul trapped by karma in the cycle of reincarnation. The aim of the spiritual quest is to escape this life and the cycle of repeated return. In addition, to those who accept the renounced life, little reference is made to the period before becoming a sannyasin.

Exceptions to the view about birth in a human body comes in the cases of a deity who incarnates or an evolved human who returns to share their spirituality for the benefit of humanity in general. Their incarnation is a blessed event to be remembered and celebrated. Their life and death is an ephemeral affair and remain ever present to help souls find their way back to God. To members of the Divine Life Society, for example, holidays like Christmas or Janmashtami are occasions where believers celebrate the incarnation of a deity. It is in this spirit that they celebrate the anniversary of the birth of Swami Sivananda Saraswati (1887–1963), whom they consider an evolved soul of the highest order.

As a young man, the future swami started on a medical career, which was cut short by the death of his father and his having to assume responsibility for his young siblings. After his responsibilities were fulfilled, he renounced his secular life and took the sannyasin vows. In 1924, he moved to Rishikesh, and emerged as a master of meditation and yoga. As disciples gathered around him, he founded the Divine Life Society and the Yoga-Vedanta Forest Academy. He authored literally hundreds of books and built an international network. Following his death in 1963, a number of his students created new networks of yoga centers throughout the West to perpetuate his teachings.

Sivananda was buried at the academy site in Rishekish, now a shrine to his memory. His birthday is commemorated throughout the world at the many centers in his lineage, though the largest celebration is a Rishekish where the main academy's temple and the Sivanada shrine will be decorated with candles and flowers. The commemoration will begin early in the morning and last all day with pujas, music, chanting, and inspirational talks on the spirituality and accomplishments of Sivananda. The sandals he wore have been kept as a relic, and these are now used as a focus for veneration. Those who remain that remember Sivanada will share their personal experiences of him.

J. Gordon Melton

See also Christmas; Janmashtami; Satchidananda, Birthday of Swami.

References

Sivananda, Swami. *Sadhana*. Sivanandanagar, India: Divine Life Society, 1967.

The Sivananda Yoga Center. *The Sivananda Companion to Yoga*. New York: Simon & Schuster, 1983.

Tawker, K. A. *Sivananda, One World Teacher*. Rishikish, India: Yoga-Vedanta Forest University, 1957.

Venkatesananda, Swami. *Gurudev Sivananda*. Durban, South Africa: Divine Life Society of South Africa, 1961.

Skanda Shashti

Saivite Hindus, especially among Tamils, consider shastri (the sixth day after the new or full moon) sacred to Murugan, much as Vaishnavas considered the 11th

Young boys prepare to celebrate Skanda Shashti. Often a young, unmarried male student is invited to dinner and given gifts as a representative of Lord Skanda. (*Hinduism Today* Magazine)

day (ekadashi) sacred to Vishnu. In Saivite thought, Murugan, also known as Subrahmanya, is the son of Shiva. The sixth day of the waxing moon in the month of Kartika is celebrated as Shanda Shastri by Saivites, Skanda being another of Murugan's names.

Lord Murugan is considered as a symbol of a variety of virtues such as compassion, benevolence, and valor. He commands an army of demigods (Devas) and was born to destroy the demons and protect the demigods. Skanda Shashti celebrates Lord Murugan's destruction of the demon Sura Padman, which occurred at Tiruchendur, one among the six major Saivite sacred sites in Tamil Nadu. In the battle, using a sphere given him by his mother Parvati, Murugan split the demon (who has assumed the form of a tree) into two halves. Murugan then granted each half of the defeated demon a boon. As a result, the halves were transformed into the peacock (who became Murugan's mount) and the rooster, pictured on the flag of his army.

Skanda Shashti is a six-day fast dedicated to Lord Murugan that immediately follows Diwali, the single most celebrated holiday among Hindus worldwide, though many Tamils will only fast on the shashti day. The six days are the first days of the Hindu month of Kartika (October–November on the Common Era calendar) also known as the month of Aippasi on the Tamil calendar. The fast means avoiding non-vegetarian food and, in its more severe form, avoiding the strong seasoning provided by onion and garlic. Some will consume only one meal in 24 hours, with that meal being at either noon or in the evening following a visit to the local temple.

Skanda Shasti is celebrated across Tamil Nadu and nearby Sri Lanka and throughout the Tamil diaspora in places such as Singapore, Malaysia, Guyana, Trinidad, and the United States. One American Hindu group, the Saiva Siddhanta Church, originally known as the Subramuniya Yoga Order, is dedicated to Lord Murugan. It will often include dramatic reenactments of Murugan's destruction of the demon, and climax on the day following with a reenactment of Murugan's visits with his consort Deivanai, commonly known as Tirukalyanam. The observant will end their fast on either the sixth day or with the celebration of the marriage on the seventh day.

Constance A. Jones

See also Diwali; Hala Shashti; Narasimha Jayanti; Surya Shashti; Thaipusam.

References

Geaves, Ron. *Saivism in the Diaspora: Contemporary Forms of Skanda Worship*. London: Equinox Publishing, 2007.

Seshayya. A. K. *Festivals and Ceremonies*. Kelang, Selangor, Malaysia: KSN Print, n.d.

Wood, Michael. *The Smile of Murugan: A South Indian Journey*. London: John Murray Publishers, 2002.

Snan Yatra

Snan Yatra, a special bathing ceremony for Lord Jagannath (an incarnation of the Hindu deity Vishnu) takes place on the purnima (full moon) of the Indian month of Jyestha (May–June in the Common Era calendar). It commemorates the jayanti or appearance day (birthday) of Lord Jagannath.

The festival his held at the Jagannath temple in Puri, a coastal city in the state of Orissa in eastern India, best known as the site of the Rathayatra festival held several weeks later in which the statues of Lord Jagannath, his sister Subhadra, and his brother Balabhadra (or Balarama) are processed through the streets on the large carts that gave the word juggernaut to the English language. Vaishnava Hindus attribute the creation the whole universe to Jagannath (Vishnu), and the bathing ceremony in Puri is duplicated in all other important temples in Orissa and among Vaishnava Hindus now scattered worldwide, including centers of the International Society for Krishna Consciousness in the West.

On the day before the full moon, the statues to be bathed are removed from their resting place in the Puri temple and processed Snana Vedi (or bathing pandal), an elevated, elaborately decorated platform near the temple that allows the gathered crowd to see what is occurring. The deity statues are covered with flowers. The deities are presented with incense and other sweet-smelling substances and entertained with music.

For the bath, water is ceremoniously brought from the Suna Kua (or golden well) in special covered containers made of copper and gold. Once in place, the water is blessed by the priests by adding to it a variety of substances including turmeric, rice, flowers, perfumes, and medicinal herbs. The actual bathing ceremony begins in the morning hours of the purnima. The vessels of holy water are brought by procession to the Snana Vedi.

It being the hottest time of the year in Orissa, the liquids that are now poured over the statues are thought of as being offered to cool the lord's transcendental body. The practical effect of the bath is that the traditional paints used to color the statues tend to be washed away. To deal with this "embarrassing" moment, the statues are redressed and an elephant mask is placed so as to cover their face. For what is now called the Hati Vesha festival, Lord Jagannatha and Lord Balarama wear an elephant dress, and Lady Subhadra a lotus flower costume. The story is told that the elephant mask was occasioned by the visit of a Ganesh scholar to Orissa. He refused the invitation of the king to visit the Snan Yatra event since he worshipped only Ganesh (the elephant-headed deity and son of Shiva) but, in wandering through the city, came upon the festival in any case. To his amazement, Lord Jagannath had assumed Ganesh's appearance just for him. Since that time, the mask has annually been placed on the Jagannath statue by his devotees.

Immediately after the Snan Yatra festivities, the deities are returned to the Puri temple and the daily routine at the temple suspended for the next two weeks. No one is allowed to view the deities. During this time, the statues are repainted and restored to the condition devotees except when offering them worship. On the 16th day after the Snan Yatra, the statues are deemed ready to hold darshan (allow the public to view their divine countenance). This darshan event is termed Netrotsava (festival for the eyes) or Nava Yauvanotsava (festival of the ever new youth). To participate in this event is believed to wash away the devotee's sins. The statues are also now considered ready to participate in the even-larger festival of Rathayatra.

Constance A. Jones

See also Balarama, Appearance Day of Lord; Ganga Dussehra; Kartika Snan; Magha Purnima; Mauni Amavasya; Parshurama Jayanti; Ratha Yatra.

References

Das Goswami, Satsvarupa. *A Visit to Jagannath Puri*. La Crosse, FL: Gita-nagari Press, 1987.

Deo, Jitamitra Prasad Singh. *Origin of Jagannath Deity*. New Delhi: Gyan, 2003.

Eschmann, Ann, Hermann Kulke, and Gaya C. Tripathi, eds. *The Cult of Jagannath and the Regional Tradition of Orissa*. New Delhi: Manohar Press, 1978.

Schnepal, Burkhard, and Herman Kulke. *Jagannath Revisited: Studying Society, Religion and the State in Orissa*. New Delhi: Manohar, 2001.

"Snana Yatra." Posted at http://www.hknet.org.nz/parishad117.htm. Accessed June 15, 2010.

Solemnity of Mary, Feast of the (January 1)

In 1751, Joseph Emmanuel, the king of Portugal, requested a new celebration for the Portuguese branch of the Roman Catholic Church—a feast for the Motherhood of Mary. Pope Benedict XIV (r. 1740–1758) not only approved the idea but wrote the original liturgy for the day. Its celebration was designated for October 11. Pope Pius XI (r. 1922–1939) saw the connection of the celebration to the proclamation of Mary as Theotokos (Mother of God) by the Council of Ephesus in 431 and took the occasion of the 1,500th anniversary of the council's action to make the feast universal throughout the church.

In 1969, in light of the decisions of the Second Vatican Council (1962–1969), a number of changes were made to the church's liturgical calendar. Among the most significant changes related to Mary was the movement of the Feast of the Motherhood of Mary from October 11 to January 1, where it replaced the traditional Feast of the Circumcision of Jesus. Now known as the Solemnity of Mary, the holy Mother of God, Mariologists saw it as emphasizing the part played by Mary in this mystery of salvation. They see Mary as exalted above all angels and all humans and second only to her Son. Both historically and theologically, the assertion of her mission as the Mother of God is the foundation for the additional assertions of the Immaculate Conception, her perpetual virginity, and assumption into heaven.

To the celebration of Mary as the Mother of God, the post-1969 liturgy also celebrates her role as the Mother of the Church. This title of Mary, derived from its usage by Bishop Ambrose of Milan (c. 340–397 CE), was inserted into a talk by Pope Paul VI (r. 1963–1978) at the Second Vatican Council. His successor, Pope John Paul II (r. 1978–2005) subsequently elaborated upon the idea. This new title revived for Mary was seen by many as balancing the seeming denigration of Mariology as a separate field of theology by placing it as a subtopic in ecclesiology, the theology of the church.

J. Gordon Melton

See also Circumcision, Feast of the; Mary—Liturgical Year of the Blessed Virgin; Most Holy Name of Mary, Feast of the.

References

Ball, Ann. *Encyclopedia of Catholic Devotions and Practices.* Huntington, IN: Our Sunday Visitor, 2003.

Dodds, Monica, and Bill Dodds. *Encyclopedia of Mary.* Huntington, IN: Our Sunday Visitor, 2007.

Songkran

Throughout Southeast Asia, the traditional New Year's Day is somewhat related to the spring or vernal equinox, though it has drifted in several cases due to calendar inaccuracies and the neglect of astrological recalculations. The several countries from Burma (Myanmar) and Sri Lanka to Vietnam used a variation of the Buddhist calendar, a lunar calendar that began annually when the full moon arose in the astrological month of Taurus with regular readjustments to keep it in line with the solar year. Each country made the adjustments slightly differently, and thus the day of the celebrations began to differ slightly. The larger event being marked was the annual shift in weather, from the dry to the rainy season. Throughout the region, however, a common feature of the celebration was the dousing of friends, neighbors and passersby with water, and New Year's celebrations are often referred to as the water festival.

In Thailand, being thrust into the modern world changed the celebration significantly. Prior to 1888, the Thai New Year, called Songkran, was the functional New Year throughout the country. Then from 1888 to 1940, April 1 (on the Common Era calendar) became New Year's Day, with January 1 succeeding to the role in 1940. The traditional Thai New Year was transformed into a national holiday, and fixed as a three-day celebration on the Common Era calendar, April 13–15. Cambodia went through a similar process of adjusting its calendar to the Common Era and also now celebrates its traditional New Year's Days, known as Chol Chnam Thmey, beginning on April 13 or 14. In Myanmar, it is called Thingyan, and in Laos as Bpee Mai.

Common to many New Year's celebrations worldwide, as the date approaches, people began a time of general cleaning of their living quarters. The water used in washing homes, or ritually washing Buddhist statues, naturally grades into the water for soaking others, especially ones otherwise in a position of authority, all in good fun. Amid the fun, a certain sign of respect is shown by the addition of flowers and/or perfume fragrances to the water. The perfume is especially used in ritualized settings where the dousing with water becomes an anointing, a way of giving and receiving a blessing to and from Buddhist monks or one's elders. In some countries, young people will also wash the hair of elders in preparation for the larger celebration.

While New Year's is a widespread secular holiday, it has its religious aspect. In Laos, for example, sand brought to the Buddhist temples will be shaped into stupas (generally used for housing relics), decorated, and given to the monks. This practice grew out of a story of one of the country's former kings, King Kabinlaphom. It seems that following Kabinlaphom's death, his daughters placed his head in a cave, which they visited annually to perform a ritual asking for happiness for the Laotian people and good weather for the growing season. The sand stupas represent Phoukao Kailat, the mountain where the cave with the king's head was located. A similar related story is told in other countries.

Also, believers will bring many flowers to the temples to decorate the statues of the Buddha (most Southeast Asian temples having but one statues of Gautama Buddha as the focal point of their worship. In Chiang Mai, Thailand, there is a tradition of removing the statues of the Buddha from the city's monasteries and carrying them around the city on floats in multiple processions. As a procession passes, watchers throw water on the statues, thus providing them with a ritual bath. Meanwhile, in Bangkok, the Phra Buddha Sihing, a well-known and revered image of the Buddha, is marched through the streets to the royal grounds (Sanam Luang), where it will rest for the celebration's duration.

For young boys, the beginning of the new year is an occasion to go through shinbyu ritual, in which they adopt the life of a monk for a short period of time in a monastic setting and the study of Buddhism (analogous to the catechism classes that prepare Christian children for their first communion). Most males in Southeast Asia have spent at least a few months as a monk during their youth.

Buddhists also judge their ethical behavior not just relative to humans, but to all sentient life. Thus, New Year's becomes a time to set animals free, and many small animals, such as birds or fish kept as pets, will be released.

J. Gordon Melton

See also Elephant Festival; New Year's Day; Spring Equinox (Thelema); Spring Equinox (Vernal).

References

"Laos New Year." ThingsAsian. Posted at http://www.thingsasian.com/stories-photos/1731. Accessed March 15, 2010.

Min, Kyaw. "Thingyan: A Festival for All to Enjoy." Posted at http://www.seasite.niu.edu/Burmese/Culture/thingyan.htm. Accessed March 15, 2010.

"Songkran." Posted at http://www.buddhist-tourism.com/buddhist-festivals/songkran.html. Accessed March 15, 2010.

Songkran Thai New Year's Celebrations Happiness on Earth." News Room, Tourist Authority of Thailand. Posted at http://www.tatnews.org/THAILAND_GRAND_EVENTS/2829.asp. Accessed March 15, 2010.

Sophia, The Descent (September 8) and Assumption (August 15) of Holy

An initial appearance of the Sophia (Wisdom) occurs in the biblical Book of Proverbs, which says of her:

> Does not wisdom cry, and understanding put forth her voice? On the top of high places by the way, where the paths meet, she stands; Beside the gates, at the entry of the city, At the coming in at the doors, she cries aloud: "Unto you, O men, I call; And my voice is to the sons of men. O ye simple, understand prudence; And, ye fools, be of an understanding heart. Hear, for I will speak excellent things; And the opening of my lips shall be right things. For my mouth shall utter truth; And wickedness is an abomination to my lips. All

the words of my mouth are in righteousness; There is nothing crooked or perverse in them. They are all plain to him that understands, And right to them that find knowledge. Receive my instruction, and not silver; And knowledge rather than choice gold. For wisdom is better than rubies; And all the things that may be desired are not to be compared unto it." (Proverbs 8:1–11)

This passage from the Jewish Bible found a heightened meaning when Jewish culture encountered Greek culture in the new world created by the conquests of Alexander's culture. Wisdom (Sophia in Greek) was a major concept in Greek thought, and in the learned world of ancient Alexandria, Jewish philosophy speculated on the idea of the divine Sophia as the revelation of God's inward thought-world. This concept subsequent fed into the Gnosticism of the second century CE as represented, for example, in the teachings of Valentinus (c. 100–c. 160 CE), who had been trained at Alexandria.

In Gnostic interpretations, the Sophia resides in the invisible, but becomes the highest ruler over the visible universe, and thus the mediatrix between the higher and lower realms in the layered cosmos of Gnostic thought. Also, important in their thinking, Sophia is a she, and she is the mother. It was also envisioned that there had been a descent of Sophia from her spiritual home into the dark material world. As a feminine figure, Sophia is both analogous to the human soul and seen as a feminine aspect of the transcendent God.

Sophia appears in a number of Gnostic texts, including some of those known through the centuries such as the Pistis Sophia, and those lost and rediscovered in 1945 at Nag Hammadi, Egypt. She has a slightly different role assigned by the authors of the different texts; however, in the contemporary revived Gnostic movement, Sophia's role as a feminine aspect of God has come to the fore.

Some modern Gnostic groups, such as the California-based Ecclesia Gnostica, has responded positively to the concerns raised by the modern feminist movement and attempted to embody significant references to the divine feminine in its liturgies. In its annual liturgical calendar, the Ecclesia Gnostica, in particular, has assigned to Sophia the days normally assigned to the Blessed Virgin Mary in the annual calendar of the Roman Catholic Church. Through the 19th and 20th centuries, the Catholic Church has experienced a visible rise in interest in the role of the Virgin in human salvation and, in the midst of this revived interest, has defined several new dogmas, most notably that of the Immaculate Conception and the Assumption of the Virgin. The former deals with the sinless birth of the Virgin, and the latter addresses her ascent into heaven without first having experienced bodily death.

The Catholic Church observes liturgically a set of significant events in the life of the Virgin, including: her Immaculate Conception (December 8), her Birth or Nativity (September 8), the announcement of her pregnancy with Jesus (March 23), her giving birth to Jesus (December 25) and her Assumption into heaven (August 15).

Corresponding to the Roman Catholic celebration of the Assumption of the Virgin Mary into heaven, on August 15, the Ecclesia Gnostica celebrates the Assumption of the Holy Sophia into the Pleroma (the heavenly realm in Gnostic cosmology). It has developed this celebration from accounts in the various Gnostic writings, which it considers scripture of Sophia wandering out of heaven and getting lost in the lower realms. She sings praises to the Light, and is rescued by the Savior who aids her return to heaven. This story is related to the Gnostic analysis of the individual state of being cast out of the Fullness of Being to become differentiated egos. The Logos (the Word of God) also assists us to return to the state of Wholeness.

Corresponding to the Roman Catholic celebration of the Nativity of the Blessed Virgin, on September 8, the Ecclesia Gnostica celebrates the Descent of the Holy Sophia. The Gnostic literature also tells how part of Sophia returns to her true home, while part of her comes to the lower regions to be with humanity, her children. She became humanity's consolation and the inspiration for love. The image of Sophia is a promise that humans are not left alone in the darkness, but have Sophia's abiding presence in their lives.

J. Gordon Melton

See also Assumption of the Virgin; Christmas; Ecclesia Gnostica—Liturgical Year; Immaculate Conception, Feast of the; Nativity of Mary.

References

Ecclesia Gnostica: Liturgical Calendar. Posted at http://gnosis.org/eghome.htm. Accessed March 15, 2010.

Good, Diedre Joy. *Reconstructing the Tradition of Sophia in Gnostic Literature*. Atlanta, GA: Scholars Press, 1987.

MacDermott, Violet, trans. *The Fall of Sophia: A Gnostic Text on the Redemption of Universal Consciousness*. Hudson, NY: Lindisfarne Books, 2005.

Malachi, Tau. *Living Gnosis: A Practical Guide to Gnostic Christianity*. St. Paul, MN: Llewellyn Publications, 2005.

Sorrows, Feast of Our Lady of (September 15)

As attention was focused on the Blessed Virgin Mary in the early Middle Ages, note was made of different moments in Mary's earthy life that were times of sorrow, to be born with patience. Her going through these moments, each mentioned in the New Testament, came to be seen as primary signs of her saintliness. Four of these moments related to her witnessing the events of the last week of Jesus's earthly life.

In 1239, five years after establishing what would become the Servite order, the seven founders of the order decided to make the seven sorrows the primary devotional format they would follow. As the order grew, the members popularized devotion to Mary as Our Lady of Sorrows. This devotion came before a synod held at Cologne in 1413, called to deal with the Protestantizing followers of John Hus (c. 1369–1415) based in Prague. The synod proposed a feast day to honor Mary as Our Lady of Sorrows, with a focus on those sorrows related to the crucifixion, as a liturgical response to the Hussites who tended to abandon various devotional practices deemed to be unbiblical. It was to be held on the third Sunday after Easter. Over the next century, both the date and the number of sorrows commemorated varied significantly.

Initially, the feast was celebrated through southern Europe, but spread significantly in the wake of the Counter-Reformation in the late 16th century. In 1727, Benedict XIII (r. 1724–1730) placed the feast on the Roman Catholic Church's calendar. Besides the celebration of the Seven Sorrows on September 14, the Servites also hold a second like-feast day on June 9. The feast is especially popular in South America where September 15 is a day of devotional activity at the churches. In the United States, the focus of devotion to the Sorrowful Mother is provided by the Sorrowful Mother Shrine in Bellevue, Ohio.

Berthe Petit (1870–1943), a Belgian visionary and a Franciscan tertiary, who frequently reported apparitions of both Mary and Jesus, proposed a form of devotion to the Sorrows of Mary that combined recognition of the Sorrows with devotion to the Immaculate Heart of Mary.

J. Gordon Melton

See also Immaculate Heart of Mary, Feast of the; Solemnity of Mary, Feast of the.

References

Benassi, Vincenzo. *A Short History of the Servite Order.* Rome: General Secretariat for Servite Missions, 1987.

Dodds, Monica, and Bill Dodds. *Encyclopedia of Mary.* Huntington, IN: Our Sunday Visitor, 2007.

Parker, Elizabeth. *A Crown of Tribulation: Being Meditations on the Seven Sorrows of Our Blessed Lady Mary.* Whitefish, MT: Kessinger Publishing, 1920, 2007.

Rosary of Our Lady of Sorrows. Chicago: Friar Servants of Mary, 1990.

Words of Divine Love to Berthe Petit. N.p.: Secret of the Rosary Publications, 2005.

Spring Dragon Festival

The dragon is a ubiquitous symbol throughout China and traditional Chinese lore. The dragon was seen as positive creature, or more precisely as an auspicious creature, and served as a symbol of the emperor. It is its association with water, as the bringer of rain, that the Spring Dragon Festival is held. It is based upon an ancient belief that on the second day of the second lunar month (generally in early March on the Common Era calendar), the dragon raises its head. In agricultural areas, it

Chinese young men perform the dragon dance during the Spring Dragon Festival in 2010. (Donkeyru/Dreamstime.com)

was hoped that the dragon's action would lead to large barns being full and small ones overflowing.

A popular Taoist legend recounts the coming of Wu Zetian, a Tang dynasty queen to the throne. In his anger, the Jade Emperor ordered the four dragon gods to withhold the rain for three years. One dragon took pity and allowed it to rain. The Jade Emperor punished the dragon by hiding him away in a mountain for a thousand years, or until "golden beans give birth to flowers." The people went searching for the golden beans, which they discovered to be popping corn. When the Jade Emperor saw that the people had in fact met his conditions, he called the dragon back to heaven to oversee the rains for the growing season. Since this time, popped corn is one of the three foods most associated with the festival.

In addition to popped corn, Spring Dragon foods include noodles, symbolic of the dragon's lifting his head, and fry cakes, associated with the dragon's gallbladder, the gallbladder being associated with courage.

The Spring Dragon Festival was celebrated in northern China, where the spring rains (monsoon season) tended to start after the second day of the second lunar month.

J. Gordon Melton

See also Chinese New Year's Day; Double Ninth Festival; Double Seventh Festival; Dragon Boat Festival.

References

Guoliang, Gai. *Exploring Traditional Chinese Festivals in China*. Singapore: McGraw-Hill, 2009.

Latsch, Marie-Luise. *Traditional Chinese Festivals*. Singapore: Greaham Brash, 1984.

Liming, Wei. *Chinese Festivals: Traditions, Customs, and Rituals*. Hong Kong: China International Press, 2005.

Spring Equinox (Thelema) (March 20–23)

To Thelemites, followers of the religion initially articulated by Aleister Crowley in 1904, the spring equinox has become one of the most important of holidays, and is celebrated for four days, March 20–23. First, it allows the members of this small magical religious community a means of identifying with the larger religious community, especially other Esotericists with whom they share common religious roots and who also celebrate the Equinox.

At the same time, Thelemites draw their own inspiration from the changing seasons and the rebirth of life in the Northern Hemisphere. It is seen as a time for individuals to cleanse their body and spirit and prepare for the rebirth. It is a time to celebrate the traditional spring fertility festival and to honor Oestre the fertility goddess and make magic for her fruitfulness. Oestre is ultimately the source of the association of the Christian spring festival (Easter) with both the rabbit and Easter eggs.

The spring equinox has added significance for Thelemites, for on March 20, 1904, Aleister Crowley was in Cairo, Egypt, and made an invocation to the ancient Egyptian deity Horus. The invocation would result several weeks later in the communication to Crowley of the Book of the Law, the sacred scripture of Thelema, dictated to him by the spiritual entity known as Aiwass. Crowley would go one to issues a substantial biannual periodical called the *Equinox* (1909–1913) in March and September of each year. The first issue appeared in March 1909 and publicly announced his new magical order, the Astrum Argentum.

At the equinox, the dull pace of winter is thrown off and a new rhythm to life begins. It becomes a time for spring cleaning of the inner self, one's sacred space (home altar/temple area), and one's inner psyche. Hope for changes springs eternal. The equinox is the beginning of the New Year for Thelemites.

J. Gordon Melton

See also Feast for the Three Days of the Writing of the Book of the Law; First Night of the Prophet and His Bride; Spring Equinox (Vernal).

References

Crowley, Aleister. *The Confessions of Aleister Crowley*. Edited by John Symonds and Kenneth Grant. New York: Hill and Wang, 1970.

Crowley, Aleister. *Liber Al vel Legis* in *The Magical Record of the Beast 666*. Edited by John Symonds and Kenneth Grant. London: Duckworth, 1972 (frequently reproduced).

Sutin, Lawrence. *Do What Thou Wilt: A Life of Aleister Crowley.* New York: St Martin's Press, 2000.

Symonds, John. *The King of the Shadow Realm: Aleister Crowley, His Life and Magic.* London: Duckworth, 1989.

Spring Equinox (Vernal)

The spring or vernal equinox was one of four points in the year (the others being the winter and summer solstices and the fall equinox) discovered and marked by ancient peoples who observed the heavens. At the winter solstice, from the viewpoint of an observer in the Northern Hemisphere, the sun rises at a point farthest to the south and is in the sky the least amount of time. As the days pass, the sun rises at a point slightly further north each day and finally reaches a point, three months later, around March 21, when it is in the sky for 12 hours, and below the horizon for 12 hours. That point is the equinox. Viewed from above earth, the equinox is that point where the center of the sun passes through the plane created by the Earth's equator. (Following the summer solstice, the sun will appear to be moving south and again reach a point where the day and night are equal—the fall equinox. In the Southern Hemisphere, the vernal equinox is September 21.

Both the spring and fall equinoxes were important dates in the ancient calendars, the latter being the time for the end of harvest festival for a wide variety of peoples in the temperate and northern climate zones. As the modern calendar began to be developed, however, the spring equinox assumed a far more important role. First, in the Middle East, as the zodiac was developed, the spring solstice, defined as when the sun moved from the sign of Pisces into Aries, was the beginning of the years and the moment for the annual adjustment of the calendar. As the zodiac was passed from nation to nation, the spring equinox maintained its importance. It then became crucial to Julius Caesar whose new Roman calendar posited two crucial events—the beginning of the year on January 1 and the spring equinox in March. Thus for much of the world, the spring equinox became either the beginning point of the year or a major supplements marker and time for celebration. Among the major calendars that begin on the vernal equinox is the new Saka calendar adopted by the postcolonial government of India. The calendar begins with New Year's Day on the vernal (spring) equinox, March 21 or 22, on the Common Era calendar. The Bahá'í Faith's Bodi calendar also begins on the spring equinox (March 21). The last of the Bahá'ís' 19 months, which occurs just prior to the spring equinox, is a month of fasting.

In the mid-19th century, Persia (Iran), where the Bahá'í Faith originated, extensive use began of the zodiacal or Borji calendar, which begins the new year on March 21 when the sun enters the sign of Aries. Each remaining month was begun on the day the sun entered a new sign. The 12 months had either Arabic or Parsi names. In 1925, the shah of Iran replaced the Borji calendar with an Iranian solar calendar. It also followed the 12 zodiacal signs but gave them their Persian name. Thus, the New Year begins on Farvadin 1 (or March 21 in the Common Era calendar). The years are countered from 622, the year of the Prophet Muhammad's *hegira*. Farvadin 1–4 (March 21–24) is celebrated at the Iranian New Year.

The spring equinox remains an important moment for Western astrology, but has otherwise been a nonentity on the calendars used by Jews, Christians, and Muslims. The major spring festivals of the Jews, namely Passover, is calculated on a lunar calendar and thus moved significantly from year to year, as does the Christian Easter celebration.

The primary groups who celebrate the spring equinox in the West currently are the closely related Neo-Pagans and Wiccans. Both use the modern Common Era calendar and meet for the eight equally spaced dates that include the summer and winter solstices, the spring and fall equinoxes, and the four dates halfway between them. For Wiccans and Pagans, the spring equinox begins the planting season, often for the urbanized, a time to plant flowers or a small garden. It is also seen as a time to plant new seeds symbolically in the sense of planning new projects that will produce results at a later date.

One interesting if obscure religious acknowledgment of the spring equinox originates within the Jewish community. In the Talmud, the volumes of Jewish law, written down in the second century BCE, suggests that an individual should make a special blessing when the sun reaches its "turning point," that is the vernal equinox. Further, it notes that the sun returns to this position every 28 years. Writing in the 11th century, the great French rabbi Rashi (1040–1105), who authored a commentary on the Talmud, taught that the sun, which according to the book of Genesis was created on the fourth day of creation, adds that God placed it in the sky at the exact position it reaches at the vernal equinox. That moment in time every 28 years provides a unique glimpse of the creation, and an opportunity to the one who is thus aware to bless the Creator for his work. This blessing, which a person has the opportunity to offer once every generation, is termed the "Birkat HaHammah." This event most recently occurred on April 8, 2009.

The Japanese observe Higan, a time to remember ones' ancestors, twice annually, at the spring and fall equinoxes. During Higan, people will visit graves and think about those who have died, especially those who have passed away in the last year.

J. Gordon Melton

See also Bahá'í Calendar and Rhythms of Worship; Bahá'í Fast; Common Era Calendar; Easter; Fall Equinox; Higan; Naw-Rúz, Festival of; New Year's Day; New Year's Day (India); Nowruz; Passover; Pesach; Summer Solstice; Winter Solstice.

References

Crowley, Vivianne. *The Principles of Paganism*. London: Thorsons, 1996.

Farrar, Janet, and Stewart Farrar. *A Witches Bible Complete*. New York: Magickal Child, 1984.

Parise, Frank, ed. *The Book of Calendars*. New York: Facts on File, 1982.

Waskow, Arthur. "Blessing the Sun: Looking Backwards." Birkat HaHammah. Posted at http://www.blessthesun.org/tiki-index.php?page=Articles+and+Divrei+Torah. Accessed June 15, 2009.

Spy Wednesday. *See* Holy week

Stanislaus, Saint's Day of St. (April 11)

Stanislaus Szczepanowski (1030–1079) was a nobleman born in southern Poland not far from Krakow. He was educated in Paris, became a priest, and subsequently accepted the appointment as the bishop of Krakow in 1072 from Pope Alexander II (r. 1061–1073). Stanislaus was one of the first native Polish bishops. He subsequently became an adviser to the duke of Poland, who strove to become recognized as the king of Poland by the Holy Roman emperor. Stanislaus assisted with that process by encouraging the appointment of papal legates to Poland by Pope Gregory VII (r. 1073–85).

Boleslaus assisted his own cause by building up the church in Gniezno, which emerged as an important new diocese. Boleslaus was crowned king in 1076. Subsequently, Stanislaus encouraged King Boleslaus to nurture a set of Benedictine monasteries whose residents were a significant factor in the Christianization of Poland.

Unfortunately, the supportive relationship between the king and the bishop did not last. A variety of issues emerged, including the king's unfaithfulness to his wife, which led to a series of denunciations of the king by Stanislaus. The unheeded calls to repent eventuated led to his excommunicating Boleslaus. In the midst of an angry confrontation, the king ordered his soldiers to kill Stanislaus, and when they refused, he personally killed the bishop, reportedly as Stanislaus was celebrating Mass at the church on Skalka hill located outside the walls of Kraków. (Other sources say it occurred at a nearby castle.) The bishop's body was hacked to pieces and thrown into a pool. Sources also disagree on the exact date of Stanislaus's death, either April 11 or May 8, 1079.

The public reaction to the murder forced Boleslaus off his throne. He fled to Hungary and took refuge in a Benedictine abbey. Meanwhile, Stanislaus began to be venerated as a martyr/saint. His bodily remains were moved to the cathedral in Krakow in 1245, and eight years later, Pope Innocent IV (r. 1243–1254) pronounced him a saint. In Poland, his life is commemorated on May 8, the accepted date of his death. It was originally placed on the Roman Catholic Church's Calendar of Saints on May 7, but in 19869, amid the wholesale changes in that listing, it was moved to April 11, the most commonly accepted date of Stanislaus's death. Each year on May 8, the bishop of Kraków leads a procession from the cathedral to the Church on the Rock at Skalka where Stanislaus was killed. The procession took on new significance during the years of Communist rule and was promoted in the last half of the century by Polish primate Stefan Cardinal Wyszyński (r. 1953–1981) and the former archbishop of Kraków who became Pope John Paul II (r. 1978–2005).

As the first native Polish saint, Stanislaus has been named a patron saint of Poland.

J. Gordon Melton

See also Adalbert of Prague, Saint's Day of St.; Casimir, Saint's Day of St.

References

Davies, Norman. *God's Playground: A History of Poland, Vol. 1: The Origins to 1795*. New York: Columbia University Press, 2005.

Gruszins, Tadeusz. *Boleslaus the Bold, Called Also the Bountiful, and Bishop Stanislaus: The Story of a Conflict*. New York: Hippocrene Books, 1987.

Starr, Eliza Allen. *Patron Saints*. Baltimore: John B. Piet & Co., 1883.

Student Day (Russia). *See* Tatiana, Saint's Day of St.

Sukkot

The Festival of Sukkot, or Booths, is a seven-day holiday period that begins on the 15th day of the month of Tishri, only five days after the conclusion of the 10 Days of Awe, which begin with Rosh Hashanah and culminate with Yom Kippur. Sukkot represents quite a drastic transition, from the most solemn holy days in the Jewish year to one of the more joyous. Sukkot is immediately followed by two additional holidays, Shemini Atzeret and Simchat Torah.

Sukkot has a double thrust, in that it functions as a harvest festival but also remembers the 40 years in which the Israelites lived a nomadic life in the Sinai desert after leaving Egypt, but before they made a home for themselves in the Land of Canaan. During this time, believers build a temporary shelter, a booth called a *sukkah* (*Sukkot*, pl.), in which they reside, a shelter that recalls the temporary homes in which the Israelites resided during the wandering.

The basic parameters and timing of the holidays are laid out in the Torah, in the book of Leviticus 23:33–44,

> And the Lord spoke unto Moses, saying: "Speak unto the children of Israel, saying: On the fifteenth day of this seventh month is the feast of tabernacles for seven days unto the Lord. On the first day shall be a holy convocation; ye shall do no manner of servile work. Seven days ye shall bring an offering

An Orthodox Jewish man prepares a roof of palm fronds for his Sukkah. The Sukkah is built for the weeklong celebration of Sukkot. (AP/Wide World Photos)

> made by fire unto the Lord; on the eighth day shall be a holy convocation unto you; and ye shall bring an offering made by fire unto the Lord; it is a day of solemn assembly; ye shall do no manner of servile work. These are the appointed seasons of the Lord, which ye shall proclaim to be holy convocations, to bring an offering made by fire unto the Lord, a burnt-offering, and a meal-offering, a sacrifice, and drink-offerings, each on its own day; beside the sabbaths of the Lord, and beside your gifts, and beside all your vows, and beside all your freewill-offerings, which ye give unto the LORD. Howbeit on the fifteenth day of the seventh month, when ye have gathered in the fruits of the land, ye shall keep the feast of the LORD seven days; on the first day shall be a solemn rest, and on the eighth day shall be a solemn rest. And ye shall take you on the first day the fruit of goodly trees, branches of palm-trees, and boughs of thick trees, and willows of the brook, and ye shall rejoice before the LORD your God seven days. And ye shall keep it a feast unto the LORD seven days in the year; it is a statute forever in your generations; ye shall keep it in the seventh month. Ye shall dwell in booths seven days; all that are home-born in Israel shall dwell in booths; that your generations may know that I made the children of Israel to dwell in booths, when I brought them out of the land of Egypt: I am the LORD your God. And Moses declared unto the children of Israel the appointed seasons of the LORD."

The sukkah may be built in one's yard according to particular specifications. It must be large enough to fulfill the requirements for the week's activity and have no less than two and a half walls made of material that will not blow away in a high wind. The roof or covering must be made of something that has grown in the ground—tree branches, corn stalks, or bamboo reeds are often used. The covering materials should generally make the dwelling shady, but are left loose, neither bundled together nor tied down. They allow rain in, and those inside can see the stars. If it is raining, rainproof material may be put over the booth to protect its inner contents, but it must be removed as soon as the rain ceases.

In the modern world, quickly assembled sukkot are available for purchase, or they may be made from scratch. Canvas is often used for the walls. One should spend as much time as possible in the booth during the seven days. The first two days of the festival are treated as Sabbaths, and no work is allowed. Though the Bible calls for one day of rest, due to the problems inherent in observing the moon (by which the timing of the holiday and getting the word out to people in the countryside was determined) two days would often be observed to make sure the holiday had been observed correctly. Such two-day observances had become a custom among Jews outside the Land of Israel, and continued even after later sages fixed the Hebrew calendar for the future based on mathematical calculations.

The first and last (Hoshana Rabbah) days of Sukkot include gatherings at the synagogue, while the five middle days include special prayers that are read by the family within their booth. The first (and the second day of the festival in the lands of the diaspora) are treated as Sabbath days of rest. The middle days are less than a Sabbath, but distinct from normal workdays. One may engage in work necessary for getting through the days, including food preparation, but nothing that interferes with the holiday spirit. This time is often treated as a vacation and a time to entertain friends, visit with neighbors, and enjoy festive meals.

Integral to Sukkot is the invitation of symbolic guests to the family booth each day. These spiritual guests, or *ushpizin*, are traditionally seven biblical heroes—Abraham, Isaac, Jacob, Moses, Aaron, Joseph, and David. Among the Hasidic Jewish communities, there are seven Hasidid heroic figures who accompany the seven traditional heroes, and in the contemporary postfeminist world, seven women are also included in the invitations. It is thought that one of the traditional heroes of the faith visits the Sukkot each day.

Also integral to the festival are the materials (called the four species) that are held during the Sukkot blessings in synagogue. The four species are an *etrog* (citron), a citrus fruit native to Israel, and three kinds of branches—one palm, two willow, and three myrtle branches—which are bound together and are called the *lulav*. The citron is held in one hand and the *lulav* in the other. As one repeats the blessing over these, the four species are waved in six directions (north, east, south, and west, and up and down), in acknowledgment that the Almighty is everywhere. Some see the four species as four types of Jews, and the Sukkot blessing reminds everyone that all four are important to the community.

Closely associated with Sukkot are two adjacent but quite separate holidays, Shemini Atzeret and Simchat Torah. Because they immediately follow Sukkot, they are often incorrectly thought of as part of Sukkot. Shemini Atzeret is observed on the 22nd day of the month of Tishri, and everywhere but Israel, Simchat Torah is observed the following day. In Israel, Shemini Atzeret and Simchat Torah are observed on the same day, Tishri 22. During the two holidays, one no longer resides in the booths, although outside of the Land of Israel, some continue to reside in the sukkah on Shmini Atzeret, but not on Simchat Torah. Also, the four species are not used on these holidays.

Shemini Atzeret is the "assembly of the eighth day." It is explained as a time for the Jewish people to have a more intimate and exclusive celebration with the Almighty. They think of it as if God has been their host and they the guests through Sukkot. But as the time of visiting comes to an end, God asks the guests to stay an extra day, to extend their time together. The day is observed as a Sabbath, and those observing it do no work.

Simchat Torah is a day for "Rejoicing in the Torah," the first five books of the Hebrew Bible (also known as the Five Books of Moses). Through the year, at synagogue services, one reads through the entire Torah, a few chapters each week. This cycle is completed on Simchat Torah, and on that day, the last chapter of the Torah (in Deuteronomy) is read to be immediately followed by the reading of the first chapter of Genesis. The completion of the cycle is an occasion for rejoicing that occurs as people process around the synagogue carrying Torah scrolls. The service includes spirited singing and dancing in the synagogue with all the Torah scrolls, which are removed from the ark in which they normally rest.

The first day of Sukkot and the joint celebration of Shimin Atzeret and Simchat Torah are official public holidays in Israel. In the days prior to the destruction of the temple and the diaspora of the Jewish people through the Middle East and around the Mediterranean Basin, Sukkot was one of three major holidays (along with Passover and Shavuot or the Festival of Weeks), during which Jews made a pilgrimage to Jerusalem for the celebration.

Christian Appropriation

The Hebrew Bible was incorporated into the Christian Bible as the Old Testament, and is held in high esteem by most Christian denominations. In North America in the 19th century, from their reading of the books of Moses, a new appreciation of the Jewish festival cycle appeared among a small group of Christian denominations, most notably those that had emerged from the disappointed expectation of the Second Coming of Christ announced by William Miller in the 1830s. Initially, some groups adopted the seventh-day Sabbath. In the 20th century, some groups that grew out of the Church of God (Seventh-day) began to follow the Jewish liturgical year, the most notable being the Worldwide Church of God. For these groups, what they termed the Feast of Tabernacles (tabernacle being the common translation of sukkot in English-language Bibles) became the most important event of the year. Members of the Worldwide Church of God would save 10 percent of their income to enjoy a week of feasting with fellow church members at campgrounds around North America and increasingly other countries to which the church spread. The money would be spent on fine camping equipment, fine food, and given in offerings at the church meetings.

In the 1990s, the Worldwide Church of God went through a radical change of belief and practice that included the abandonment of its belief in the Old Testament festival cycle. It lost most of its members to several splinter groups such as the United Church of God and the Philadelphia Church of God, and an uncounted number of smaller groups, which continue this Christianized version of the Feast of Tabernacles.

Sukkot is also celebrated among the different Messianic Jewish groups that emerged in the 1970s. These groups consider themselves to be Jews who have discovered that Jesus Christ (whom they refer to by his Hebrew name Yashua) to be the Messiah, a claim rejected by all mainstream Jewish groups. Messianic Jews continue as much of Jewish culture, including synagogue ritual, that they find compatible with their Christian faith and reinterpret Jewish holidays as heralding Christianity. They also invite Gentile Christians to celebrations as a means of educating them about their Jewish heritage.

J. Gordon Melton

See also Days of Awe; Passover; Pentecost; Pesach; Rosh Hashanah; Shemini Atzeret/Simchat Torah; Yom Kippur.

References

Eckstein, Yecheil. *What You Should Know about Jews and Judaism.* Waco, TX: Word Books, 1984.

Greenberg, Irving. *The Jewish Way: Living the Holidays.* New York: Jason Aronson, 1998.

Posner, Raphael, Uri Kaploun, and Sherman Cohen, eds. *Jewish Liturgy: Prayer and Synagogue Service through the Ages.* New York: Leon Amiel Publisher; Jerusalem: Keter Publishing House, 1975.

Schauss, Hayyim. *The Jewish Festivals: A Guide to Their History and Observance.* New York: Schocken, 1996.

Summer Solstice (June 21)

The longest day of the year, the summer solstice, along with the related winter solstice, was among the earliest astronomical phenomena observed by people observing the sky and relating what they saw to the changing weather and agricultural seasons. In the Northern Hemisphere, if one observed the rising sun in the spring, it appears to rise a little bit further north day by day until it reaches a point in the last half of June where the northern drift stopped. After what appeared to be a pause, it began to rise bit by bit further south each day. In the Southern Hemisphere, of course, the drift is exactly opposite. The summer solstice is the point at which the drift stops and pauses before starting in the opposite direction. The summer solstice, June 21 on the Common Era calendar, occurs in the midst of the northern growing season—after planting has been completed, but prior to the beginning of the harvest.

The summer solstice was celebrated in most ancient cultures. However, most of these celebrations were abandoned as the major world religions spread and absorbed the thousands of indigenous religions. Christianity designated June 24 (the summer solstice on the old Julian calendar, and six months prior to Christmas) as the birthday of John the Baptist, who was believed to have been born six months prior to the birth of Jesus. John's birthday, or Midsummer Day, is observed by the Roman Catholic Church, the Eastern Orthodox churches, and a few Protestant churches. Midsummer Day, blending Christian themes and Pagan practices, is celebrated across Europe and is an official holiday in several countries, such as Latvia and Estonia. In Finland, the summer solstice is known as Juhannus and is seen as the time to begin the celebration of the relatively short number of days with warm weather.

The last half of the 20th century saw the founding of the Neo-Pagan movement, which has as its largest visible segment the Wiccan or Witchcraft movement. This movement was inspired by the ancient Paganism of Northern and Western Europe and posed eight equally positioned holidays that anchored its liturgical year. The summer solstice was one of the eight Pagan/Wiccan festivals. For modern neo-Paganism (and accompanying Pagan revivalist movements in Europe, the summer solstice has become one of its most important holidays and a time for large outdoor gatherings. As relatively little is known about either the practices or the details of belief of the ancient Pagans, a non-literary people, the new Pagans have been able to pour content into their ritual and practice from a variety of sources, most notably Western Esotericism.

In the 18th century, England saw the founding of two organizations that became precursors of the modern neo-Pagan movement, the Druids. As early as 1649, John Aubrey (1626–1697) suggested that the ancient Druids discovered by Julius Caesar when he came to Briton oversaw the building of Stonehenge, a view later championed by William Stukeley (1687–1765), who, it appears, founded the first modern Druid revivalist group in 1717. A more permanent group, the Ancient Order of Druids, was founded in 1781 by Henry Hurle. Over the years, several additional druid groups were formed and died. By 1955, only one group, the British Circle of the Universal Bond, survived. It claimed to be the true descendant of the 18th-century groups, and thus inherited the right to conduct the summer solstice celebrations that had become an annual event at Stonehenge.

The claims of the Druids were caught up in the breakthrough archeological work on Stonehenge in the 1960s, when some scholars discovered that the placement of some of the stones, including those in the very center and the Heel Stones far outside, were arranged in such a way as to point to major astronomical occurrences, most notably the apparent movement of the sun in the sky between the summer and winter solstices. This discovery raised questions of how Stonehenge functioned in the ancient agricultural cycle of the British Isles, and especially how the knowledge of the solstices and equinoxes were integrated into the religious thinking of British Pagans. Druids and Wiccans immediately seized the new archeological insights and began using it as foundational information for their practice. The Druids saw it as further confirmation of their claims to use Stonehenge for religious rituals.

As Stonehenge passed into the care and control of the British government, and Stonehenge was fenced off from visitors to prevent further damage, the Druids have been the only outsiders to gain access to the site, each year on the morning of the summer solstice, when they ritually greet the rising sun. Access to Stonehenge was withdrawn in 1985 when revilers and police clashed, but was reinstituted in 2000. In 2009, some 35,000 people showed up for the summer solstice celebration.

Meanwhile, Neo-Pagans and Wiccans across Europe and North America gather for additional summer solstice celebrations. It is a highly important festival for many Pagans due, for example, to the short summer in northern climes, where this is the first of the festivals in which the weather will allow comfortable outdoor celebration. In North America, It is the first major celebration after the school season and with leisure time to travel to a large solstice gathering away from the city.

J. Gordon Melton

See also Christmas; Fall Equinox; John the Baptist, Nativity of; Juhannus; Spring Equinox (Thelema); Spring Equinox (Vernal); Winter Solstice.

References

Carr-Gomm, Philip. *The Druid Tradition*. Shaftesbury, Dorset, UK: Element, 1991.

Crowley, Vivianne. *The Principles of Paganism*. London: Thorsons, 1996.

Farrar, Janet, and Stewart Farrar. *A Witches Bible Complete*. New York: Magickal Child, 1984.

Hawkins, Gerald S., and John B. White. *Stonehenge Decoded*. New York: Barnes & Noble, 1993.

Matthews, John, ed. *The Druid Sourcebook*. London: Blandford, 1887.

Matthews, John, ed. *The Summer Solstice: Celebrating the Journey of the Sun from May Day to Harvest*. Wheaton, IL: Quest Books, 2002.

Surya Shashti

Surya (also known as Vivasvan), the deified sun, was one of the primary deities in the ancient Vedic texts, and remains a prominent deity in Hinduism. The sun is pictured as crossing the sky each day on a chariot pulled by horses. He is referred to as the son of Aditi, one of the rare female deities mentioned in the Vedas and of Dyaus (the heavens). He is also mentioned as either the son of or occasionally the

Statue of the Hindu god Surya. (J. Gordon Melton)

husband of Ushas, the dawn. In later Puranic writings, Surya is cited as the son of Aditi and the sage Kashyapa.

The sun god is also known as Savitri. It appears that in ancient times, the sun had different names at different times of day, times of year, or for different purposes. Savitri particularly seems to run parallel with the name Surya, with which it at times is used interchangeably. The sun (under the name Savitri) is worshipped each morning by those Hindus who regularly chant the Gayatri Mantra.

Surya Sashti (also called Chhath) is an annual acknowledgment of Surya observed on the sixth day of the waxing moon during the Hindu month of Kartika (and thus shortly after Diwali). It is noteworthy as being one of the few Hindu holy days that does not include the assistance of a priest. It is observed by both men and women, but primarily the latter, as many of the prayers of the day are directed to the well-being of one's family, especially one's husband.

Those planning to observe Chhath will sequester themselves for several days prior to the day, refrain from sexual contact, and sleep on the floor. The sun is worshipped in both the evening and the morning (noting that the life cycle begins with death) and a rather severe fast is kept. Ritual purity is a persistent theme, even in relation to the foods offered to the deity, which is vegetarian and prepared without strong seasoning agents such as salt, onions, or garlic. When the observation day itself arrives, they will rise early for a ritual bath and fast during the day. The fast is broken in the evening after the final ritual. This fast includes liquids, while the offering to the sun god includes water. Once begun in the family, it is important that it is perpetuated year by year, though it is not performed if there has been a death in the immediate family in the past year.

Sun worship has been most observed in the eastern Indian states of Bihar, Jharkhand, and Orissa, but is seen across the country and now throughout the world in the Indian diaspora. Many will gather at the pools on the sun temple grounds or at other bodies of water and replace the distance observed with their family with the community of others engaged in the ritual.

Bihar has a number of sun temples, usually including a sacred pool of the sun, the focal spot for the observant to gather. The largest and single most famous temple to the sun is found at Konaak in Orissa. This 13th-century edifice was constructed in order to represent the chariot that carries the sun across the heavens each day. Pulled by seven fiery maned horses, the chariot has 24 massive wheels.

This temple once had a tower some 200 feet high, decorated with erotic sculpture resembling that at Khajuraho. The tower appears to have fallen, and is no longer present. Other famous sun temples include Arasuvilli Surya Devalayam in Andhra Pradesh and the temple at Modhera in Gujarat.

The worship of the sun on Surya Shastri in northeast India competes with the worship of Shiva and his son Murugan among Saivite Hindus in southern India. Shastri (the sixth day after the new or full moon), is considered sacred to Muragan. The sixth day of the waxing moon in the month of Kartika is celebrated as Skanda Shastri by Saivites.

Constance A. Jones

See also Narak Chaturdashi; Skanda Shashti.

References

Boner, A., S. R. Sarma, and R. P. Das. *New Light on the Sun Temple of Konarka: Four Unpublished Manuscripts Relating to the Construction History and Ritual of the Temple.* Varanasi: Chowkhambha Sanskrit Series Office, 1972.

Gupta, Shakti M. *Surya, the Sun God.* Bombay: Somaiya Publications, 1977.

Hillebrandt, Alfred. *Vedic Mythology.* Delhi: Motilal Banarsidass, 1990.

Pandit, P. *Aditi and Other Deities in the Veda.* Pondicherry: Dipti Publications, 1970.

Wilkins, W. J. *Hindu Mythology, Vedic and Puranic.* Calcutta: Rupa & Co., 1973.

Takayama Matsuri

Takayam is a city in central Japan north of Nagoya. It is home to the Hie Jinja Shinto Shrine, a 12th-century shrine originally built in the Katano section of town but now located on Shiroyama Hill. The principal deity enshrined is Ohyama Kuinokami, viewed as the city's guardian.

In this rather mountainous region known for its forests, winter is long and spring comes late, and is dated from the melting of the snow. When the ground reappears, it is time to celebrate. On April 14–15, the shrine hosts the largest festival in the region, the Sanno Matsuri, the Takayama Spring Festival, which has been dated to the 17th century.

Takayama is a quaint and colorful city through which several small rivers flow, and over these rivers, there are numerous, relatively small, vermillion-colored bridges. The river banks are lined with pine and cherry trees. For the festival, a procession of elaborate floats will traverse an intricate route through town, weaving through the streets and across the bridges. It is the major attraction that brings the thousands to Takayama each April. The floats, some several hundred years old, are decorated with dolls, lacquered wood carvings, and thick woven curtains.

The spring festival is, as with most spring matsuris, devoted to prayers for a good growing season and abundant harvest. An equally well-attended and similar festival is held in Takayama on October 10–11, this time hosted by the Sakurayama Hachiman Shrine. Its purpose is to give thanks for the abundance of the harvest, and signals it is time to prepare for winter.

J. Gordon Melton

See also Aki Matsuri; Iwashimizu Matsuri; Nagasaki Kunchi.

References

Plutschow, Herbert. *Matsuri: The Festivals of Japan*. Richmond, Surrey, UK: Curzon Press, 1996.

"Takayama Festival." Posted at http://www.hidanet.ne.jp/e02/ematsuri/ekigen.htm. Accessed June 15, 2010.

Tam Kung Festival

Tam Kung, one of several patron deities, of fishermen and sailors, was a figure of Chinese legend brought by the Hakka people to the Hong Kong/Macau region toward the end of the 19th century. He was reputedly a real person, born in Waui Dung county of Guangdong Province during the 13th century (during the Qing dynasty). As a youth, he gained a reputation for healing people, for being friendly with tigers, and for controlling weather. As the stories developed around him, he was said to be able to change the weather by throwing things in the air from a cup. He threw peas in the air to stop a typhoon or water in the air to bring a shower to put out a fire. Those who go out in boats invoke him for safety and the protection of their means to a livelihood.

His birthday is celebrated on the eighth day of the fourth lunar month (April). There are a variety of temples to him in Hong Kong and Macau, but the one in Shau Kei Wan (built in 1905) on Hong Kong Island is the focus of the main annual festival. On his birthday, visitors might see a kung fu demonstration, a procession, and a performance called the Dance of the Drunken Dragon.

J. Gordon Melton

See also Che Kung, Birthday of; Guan Yin's Birthday; Kwan Tai, Birthday of; Mazu Festival, Goddess; Monkey King, Birthday of; Third Prince, Birthday of the.

References

Lim, Patricia. *Discovering Hong Kong's Cultural Heritage.* Hong Kong: Oxford University Press, 1997.

Tatiana, Saint's Day of St. (January 12)

Tatiana was child of a prominent Roman family of the third century CE. Her father was a secret Christian who raised her in his faith. As a young woman, she accepted Christianity and decided to remain celibate as the betrothed of Christ. Named as a deaconess in one of the congregations in Rome, she developed a reputation for her piety and her work assisting the sick and needy.

During the reign of the Roman emperor Alexander Severus (222–235 CE), a persecution of the church was active in Rome. Tatiana was taken into custody. She was tortured and, it was later reported, appeared before her torturers each day as if she had never been cut, burned, or mutilated. She was, however, finally killed around 225 CE by beheading (as was her father). January 12 (January 25 on the Common Era calendar) was named her holiday.

Though a Roman saint, Tatiana is primarily remembered and celebrated in Russia. That oddity is due to circumstances surrounding Russian intellectual Ivan Shuvalov (1727–1797), the country's first minister of education. Among his many accomplishments were his participation in the development of Russia's first university, and its academy of arts. He also had an intimate relationship with Empress Elizabeth (1709–1762). On January 12, 1755, the empress took the occasion of the name day of Shuvalov's mother, Tatiana Rodionovna, to formally approve his petition to establish a university in Moscow. A church would be erected on campus and dedicated to Saint Tatiana, while the Russian Orthodox Church declared Saint Tatiana the patron saint of students. To this day, January 12, Tatiana Day, is also celebrated as Russian Students Day. Tatiana Day is a public holiday in Belarus, Russia, and Ukraine.

J. Gordon Melton

See also Alphabet Day; Eastern Orthodoxy—Liturgical Year; Vladimir, Saint's Day of St.

References

Attwater, Donald, and Catherine Rachel John. *The Penguin Dictionary of Saints*. 3rd ed. New York: Penguin Books, 1993.

Bartenev, Pavel. *Ivan Ivanovich Shuvalov: A Biography*. Moscow, 1857.

Coughlan, Robert. *Elizabeth and Catherine: Empresses of All the Russias*. London: Millington, 1974.

Teej Festivals

Teej, a festival for Hindu women, is one of several occasions in which family ties are affirmed ritually—in this case, the bonds of affection and duty that tie husband and wife. It occurs on the third day of the full moon of the Hindu month of Bhadrapad (late August/early September on the Common Era calendar). It also marks the beginning of the monsoon season, following a long summer season and its sometimes oppressive heat. The three-day-long celebration combines hearty feasting with prescribed fasting. The festival is named for a small red insect that tends to appear as the rains start.

Through the year, there are actually three Teej festivals. The main one, celebrated in the month of Bhadrapad, is called Hartalika Teej and is mainly observed in North India and western parts of India. Observed on the third day after the new moon in the month of Shravana, across northern India but especially Rajasthan, is Hariyali Teej. The third, Kajari Teej, is also observed on the third day after the new moon in the month of Shravana, but primarily in Rajasthan, Uttar Pradesh, Madhya Pradesh, Chhattisgarh, Jharkhand, and Bihar.

The primary deity reference on Teej is Parvati, the wife of Shiva (Siva). Parvati is regarded by many as the supreme Divine Mother, with all other goddesses referred as her incarnation. *Shakta* Hindu consider her the Divine Shakti—representing the total energy of the universe. Parvati is considered the second consort of Shiva, though she is not different from his first wife Sati, being her reincarnation. Parvati is also the mother of the deities Ganesha and Skanda, the sister of god Vishnu, and the daughter of the Himalayas.

The ancient Hindu sacred texts, the Puranas, tell of Shiva marrying Sati against the will of her father Daksha. She subsequently committed an act of self-immolation during a fire ritual performed by her father. Shiva was intensely grieved by his loss, but she returned to him in her divine persona and told him that she would return to him. She was reborn as Kali, the dark one. As she grew up, she engaged in austere practices to please Shiva and sought to be reunited with him. He tested her by disguising himself and going to her and using their meeting as a time to criticize himself. She ignored the criticisms. He eventually married her and she moved to his home at the sacred mount Kailash. Parvati's story is told in some detail in an epic poem *Kumarasambhavam* ("Birth of Kumara") written by the poet Kālidāsa.

Celebrations of Teej vary across India, but there are common elements. First, it is a festival of swings. Swings are hung from trees and women dressed in green clothes sing songs in celebration of the advent of the monsoon and the goddess. Parvati is worshipped especially by unmarried young women seeking a mate. For married women, it is a time to visit relatives and to offer prayers for the well-being of their husbands. In Jaipur, on two days, an elaborate procession with the statues of Parvati the main object of attention. For most women, it is a time to dress up, and stalls for saris are regularly held in store in the weeks prior.

In Nepal, Teej is an intense three-day festival. The first day is for feasting and the second for fasting. On both days, the women gather with great frivolity for dancing and singing, and a visit to the local Shiva temple. At the Shiva temple, women circumambulate the Shiva Lingam (a symbolic phallus), where they will also place offering flowers, sweets, and coins. The main puja (worship) is made to Shiva and Parbati, and includes prayer for blessings upon their husband and family. During this time an oil lamp is kept burning, it being a bad omen should its flame become extinguished. On the third day, called Rishi Panchami, the women take a bath with water mixed with leaves of a sacred plant, the datiwan bush. This ritual bath is considered an act that absolves from sins.

Constance A. Jones

See also Ahoi Ashtami; Ambuvachi; Dasain; Rishi Panchami.

References

Bedi, Ashok. *Awaken the Slumbering Goddess: The Latent Code of the Hindu Goddess Archetypes*. Charleston, SC: BookSurge Publishing, 2007.

Dehejia, Harsha. *Parvatidarpana: An Exposition of Kashmir Saivism through the Images of Siva and Parvati*. New Delhi: Motilal Banarsidass, 1997.

"Hartalika Teej Vrat." Hindu Blog. Posted at http://www.hindu-blog.com/2007/09/hartalika-teej-vrat-in-2007.html. Accessed June 15, 2010.

Kinsley, David. *Hindu Goddesses: Visions of the Divine Feminine in the Hindu Religious Tradition*. Berkeley: University of California Press, 1988.

Tejomayananda, Birthday of Swami (June 30)

Swami Tejomayananda (the present head of the more than 250 centers of the international Chinmaya Mission) was born Sudhakar Kaitwade in Madhya

Pradesh in 1950. During his student days, he was attracted to the writings of Swami Vivekananda (1863–1902), and led to his meeting Hindu scripture scholar Swami Chinmayananda (1916–1993) in 1970. He was initiated as a sannyasin (the renounced life) in 1983 and assumed a leadership role in the mission. He came to the United States in 1989 as the head of Chinmaya Mission West. He succeeded to the international leadership of the Chinmaya Mission in 1993. In 2005, *Hinduism Today* named him the "Hindu of the Year." He has followed his own guru as a scholar of the Hindu texts.

Each year, members of the Chinmaya Mission pause to celebrated Swami Tejomayananda's birthday. Celebrations are low key in keeping with the swami's own following of the renounced path, but none the less effusive in its expression of gratitude for his labors on behalf of the mission.

J. Gordon Melton

See also Chinmayananda, Commemoration Days for; Vivekananda Birthday of Swami.

References

Chinmaya Mission UK. http://www.chinmayauk.org/. Accessed January 30, 2011.

Tejomayananda, Swami. *Hindu Culture: An Introduction*. Chinmaya Publications, 1993.

Templars, The Day of the Martyrdom of the Holy (October 13)

Among the more notable events in Western Esoteric history was the sudden end of the Templar Order and the significant role the Templars had played since the time of the Crusades. The Knights Templar, officially the Poor Fellow-Soldiers of Christ and of the Temple of Solomon, had been formed around 1119 to protect pilgrims to the Holy Land, especially on the leg of the journey from Jaffa on the Mediterranean Sea and Jerusalem. It operated as a military monastic order with its headquarters on the Temple Mount in Jerusalem in the Al Aqsa Mosque (hence the reference to the Temple of Solomon in their name). Beginning as a relatively small and poverty-struck organization, the Knights grew into a large and powerful order with centers across southern Europe.

Several factors converged in the early 14th century to bring about the Order's downfall. First, the Holy Land was lost to Muslim forces, significantly reducing their perceived relevance and thus their support. Second, rumors abounded about the Templars' secret initiation ceremony and created a level of hostile speculation about the inner life of the group. Third, and possibly most relevant, the always financially strapped King Philip IV of France (1285–1314), who owed the Order a significant sum, took advantage of the situation. In 1307, Philip ordered the arrest of the Order's members in his domain. They were subsequently tortured, rendered a set of incriminating confessions especially related to their supposed clandestine secrets and ceremonies, and, as a result of the latter, executed by being burned at the stake. Five years later, Pope Clement V (r. 1305–1314) formally disbanded the order.

The abrupt disappearance of the order and the circulation of the confessions (which some people wanted to believe) fueled speculation, and many stories about the Templars and their magical operations emerged, especially after the French Revolution, when a revived Templar Order was founded as a secret magical society. That order would in turn give rise to a host of new Templar groups across Europe. The new Templar groups would take their place in the revived Western Esoteric milieu of the 19th century.

The revived Templar movement and the perceived injustice done the Templars by both French and Catholic forces have given the Templars a place in the history of the Christian Church's persecution of Esoteric movements (and its continued unwillingness to acknowledge them as legitimated religious equals). Among the contemporary Gnostic movements, such as the Ecclesia Gnostica, the Templars are associated with the tradition of chivalry and knighthood, and the element of Gnosticism associated with the tradition through the Middle Ages. They affirm the warrior monastic ideal, noting that individuals must be able to lift either the chalice or the sword depending on circumstances.

The Ecclesia Gnostica remembers the Knights Templar on October 13, the anniversary of the date that King Philip ordered for the arrest of the French Templars. It is observed with a requiem Eucharistic service.

J. Gordon Melton

See also Ecclesia Gnostica—Liturgical year; Montségur Day.

References

Barber, Malcolm. *The New Knighthood: A History of the Order of the Temple*. Cambridge: Cambridge University Press, 1994.

Ecclesia Gnostica: Liturgical Calendar. Posted at http://gnosis.org/eghome.htm. Accessed March 15, 2010.

Haag, Michael. *The Templars: The History and the Myth: From Solomon's Temple to the Freemasons*. New York: Harper, 2009.

Martin, Sean. *The Knights Templar: The History and Myths of the Legendary Military Order*. New York: Thunder's Mouth Press, 2005.

Tenjin Matsuri (July 24–25)

Tenjin Matsuri is the largest annual celebration held in the city of Osaka, Japan. It is built around and dedicated to the Osaka Temmangu Shrine, a 10th-century Shinto shrine. Sugawara no Michizane (846–903) was a famous ninth-century scholar/warrior. At the height of his career, Michizane faced disaster when the new emperor came to believe that Michizane was plotting against him. The scholar died in exile, and subsequent calamities that hit Japan's capital were attributed to his vengeful spirit. His reputation was posthumously revived. In 949 CE, on the orders of Emperor Murakami (926–957) the temple at Osaka was constructed and dedicated to him as Tenjin, a god of scholarship and fine arts, one of many Tenjin temples opened across Japan. The shrine has been destroyed by fire on several occasions. The present main hall and entrance gate were erected in 1845.

Today, the Tenjin Matsuri is held on July 24 and 25 every year and draws hundreds of thousands of spectators, but has reputedly been celebrated for over 1,000 years. According to the story, the festival began after a sacred halberd (a spear-like weapon) was found floating in the water near the shrine. When the halberd was recovered, the people at the shrine organized a feast and held a Shinto purification ceremony. Then as Osaka became a key Japanese marketing center during the early 19th century, the festival emerged as a major summer event.

On the main festival day, the 25th, some 3,000 people wearing traditional clothing make a procession through the streets of Osaka following a portable shrine with the enshrined Sugawara no Michizane. Other shrines are also included in the parade. At Tenjin Bridge, the group boards boats and, as night falls, creates a torchlit process on the Dojimagawa River through Osaka to Enokoshima, a section of the city. The festival climaxes with a grand fireworks display.

J. Gordon Melton

See also Aizen Summer Festival; Aki Matsuri; Chichibu Yomatsuri; Hadaka Matsuri; Haru Matsuri; Kaijin Matsuri; Natsu Matsuri; Sakura Matsuri.

References

"Festivals." Osaka-Info. Posted at http://www.osaka-info.jp/en/culture/2007may/08.html. Accessed June 15, 2010.

Plutschow, Herbert. *Matsuri: The Festivals of Japan*. Richmond, Surrey, UK: Curzon Press, 1996.

Tens of Thousands of Lanterns Ancestral Memorial Service (July 13–15, August 13–15)

Twice annually, members of Agon Shu, a Japanese Vajrayana Buddhist group, gather to honor and prayer for their ancestors, especially the recently deceased. They do so through the Tens of Thousands of Lanterns Ancestral Memorial Service held in Tokyo on July 13–15 and in Kyoto on August 13–15. These events roughly coincide with the national Obon Festival in Japan. Included in the memorial observation in August are visits by members to their ancestors buried at the Agon Shu cemetery at Nara, near Kyoto.

At the Agon Shu cemetery, adjacent to each tomb, there is a "Ho Kyo Into," which contains a small replica of the Busshari (a relic of the Buddha, which was presented to the Agon Shu in 1986) and its casket. It remains there as a constant prayer for Buddha's continued blessing of the deceased.

As people gather for the memorial service, they will light a lantern upon which their prayers and the names of loved ones who have passed on are inscribed. In the mail ritual, the thousands of lanterns and the deceased ancestors they represent are dedicated to the Lord Buddha.

J. Gordon Melton

See also Great Buddha Festival; Higan; Hoshi Matsuri; Obon Festival(s); Pure Brightness Festival.

Reference

Agon Shu. Tokyo: Agon Shu Educational Department, 1995.

Teppotsavam. *See* Magha Purnima

Tet (Vietnam). *See* New Year's Day

Thadingyut. *See* Abhidhamma Day

Thaipusam

Thaipusam is an annual South Indian festival, also known as Magha Purnima, primarily celebrated by the Tamil-speaking Saivite Hindus of Tamil Nadu. The festival gets its name from its occurrence at the full moon (*purnima*) during Thai, the 10th month of the Tamil calendar that runs from the end of January to the beginning of February on the Common Era calendar. Thaipusam is the birthday of Lord Subramaniya (aka Lord Murugan or Karttikeya), who in Hindu mythology is the younger son of Lord Shiva.

Thaipusam includes some austerities and acts of devotion that many Westerners have found both amazing and offensive. The British banned the celebration in India; however, through the 19th century, many Tamils moved to Malaysia, Singapore, and other parts of the world, where the British needed laborers. Today, while one may still find celebrations of Thaipusam in India, for example, at the Periyanayaki temple in Palani, the most well-known celebrations are held in Singapore and on Penang Island, Malaysia.

The festival extends over a week but culminates in an elaborate all-day procession. In Singapore, it begins at one temple and passes by each of the seven Tamil temples in the city. In Kuala Lumpur, it begins at the Sri Mahamariaman Temple in Chinatown and ends at the Batu Caves north of the city. While most in the Tamil community take part in the processional, a few, mostly young adult males, engage in the more memorable part of the procession. Their actions are the result of a belief that the way to salvation includes enduring a time of penance and pain.

The young men who wish to participate will dedicate a month to preparation for the day of the procession. On the full-moon day, they rise early and take a ritual bath and enter into a trance-like state. Then, they allow their bodies to be pierced with a number of fishhooks. Once they are in place, a large round platform, a *kavadi*, is lifted onto each person's shoulders; lines are attached between it and the hooks. The young men undergoing this ritual, then carry the *kavadi* along the processional route. The intriguing event now attracts thousands of devotees and observers.

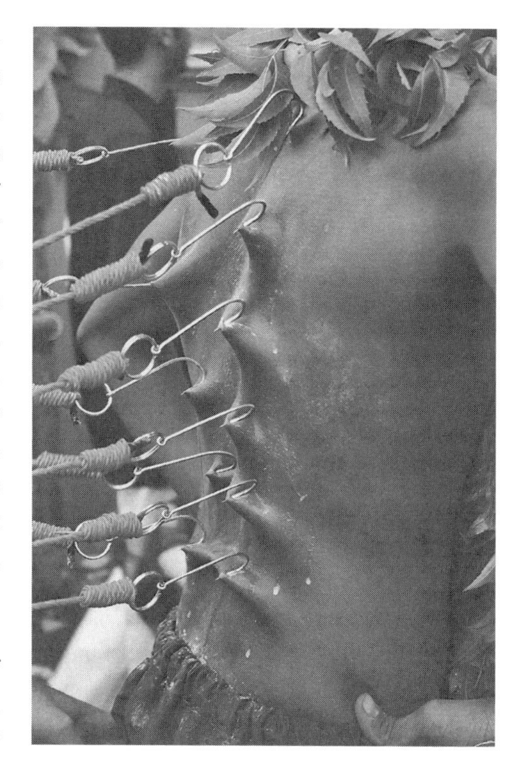

Hindu devotees walk to the Batu Caves temple during the Thaipusam festival in Kuala Lumpur, Malaysia. Participants subject themselves to the painful ritual to demonstrate their faith and penance. (iStockPhoto)

Upon reaching the end of the route, which in Kuala Lumpur is a flight of steps leading to the main Batu Caves temple, the men lay down the *kavadi* and some experienced assistants help with the removal of the hooks while a priest leads the puja chants. The wounds are treated with hot ash. Those who participate in the ritual, surprisingly, suffer minimal scarring from their ordeal.

Constance A. Jones

See also Chittirai Festival; Guru Purnima; Magha Purnima.

References

Collins, Elizabeth Fuller. *Pierced by Murugan's Lance: Ritual, Power, and Moral Redemption among Malaysian Hindus*. DeKalb, IL: Southeast Asia Publications, 1997.

Hullet, Arthur. "Thaipusam and the Cult of Subramaniam." *Orientations* 9 (1978): 27–31.

Ward, Colleen. "Thaipusam in Malaysia: A Psychoanthropological Analysis of Ritual Trance, Ceremonial Possession and Self-Mortification Practices." *Ethos* 12 (1984): 4.

Wilkins, W. J. *Hindu Mythology, Vedic and Puranic*. Calcutta: Rupa, 1973.

Theophany (January 6)

Theophany is the common name to the festival of the manifestation of Jesus as Christ in the Eastern Orthodox churches. In the West, the celebration is usually called Epiphany and is focused on the arrival of the Three Magi in Bethlehem and the presentation of gifts to the infant Jesus. In the East, the day (January 6 on the Julian calendar and January 19 on the Common Era calendar) is focused upon the baptism of Jesus in the Jordan River by John the Baptist.

This event opens the Gospel of Mark, the earliest of the books on Jesus's life and teachings:

> The beginning of the gospel of Jesus Christ, the Son of God. Even as it is written in Isaiah the prophet, "Behold, I send my messenger before thy face, Who shall prepare thy way. The voice of one crying in the wilderness, Make ye ready the way of the Lord, Make his paths straight";
>
> John came, who baptized in the wilderness and preached the baptism of repentance unto remission of sins. And there went out unto him all the country of Judaea, and all they of Jerusalem; And they were baptized of him in the river Jordan, confessing their sins. And John was clothed with camel's hair, and had a leathern girdle about his loins, and did eat locusts and wild honey.
>
> And he preached, saying, "There comes after me he that is mightier than I, the latchet of whose shoes I am not worthy to stoop down and unloose. I baptized you in water; But he shall baptize you in the Holy Spirit."
>
> And it came to pass in those days, that Jesus came from Nazareth of Galilee, and was baptized of John in the Jordan. And straightway coming up out of the water, he saw the heavens rent asunder, and the Spirit as a dove descending upon him: And a voice came out of the heavens, "Thou art my beloved Son, in thee I am well pleased." (Mark 1: 1–11).

In the Orthodox Church, Theophany is a two-day festival. It begins on Theophany Eve, which is a fast day—meaning that no food is eaten during the day until the Holy Supper in the evening. That meal is made without the use of fats, butter, or milk and served without any meat. The food is also blessed with a little holy water, the first blessing of the water of the overall event.

On the day of Theophany itself, a worship service features the blessing of the congregation with water. The priest dips his hand in the holy water and makes the sign of the cross. He breathes on the water three times and prays that God impart to it the grace of redemption, that it might be a fountain of immortality, a remedy for sickness, and effective in destroying demons. He follows with a dipping of the cross into the holy water three times, accompanied by the dipping of a lighted candle. Later in the day, the priest will make the rounds of the parish to bless the homes of the members with the holy water.

Theophany is an important day in Orthodox churches, and even more so in the Ethiopian church where Theophany, called *Timkat*, has been integrated with the belief by church members that it possessed the original Ark of the Covenant that was once housed in the Temple in Jerusalem.

J. Gordon Melton

See also Epiphany; John the Baptist, Nativity of; Timkat.

References

A Monk of the Eastern Orthodox Church. *The Year of Grace of the Lord: A Scriptural and Liturgical Commentary on the Calendar of the Orthodox Church.* Yonkers, NY: St. Vladimir's Seminary Press, 1997.

Semanitzky, John L. *The Holy Days of the Russian Orthodox Church.* N.p.: Russian Orthodox Layman's League of Connecticut, 1966.

Thérèse of Lisieux, Saint's Day of St. (October 1)

Though only canonized in 1925, Thérèse of Lisieux (1873–1897), also known as the Little Flower, quickly became one of the most popular saints in the Catholic Church. She was born at Alençon, France, to a couple who both wanted to follow the religious life. Her mother died when she was but four, and she was raised largely by an aunt. Her father, however, was more than supportive of any children who showed any inclination toward the religious life. Theresa was the fourth of his daughters to become a Carmelite nun and was 15 when she applied for entrance into the convent at Lisieux. She was refused because of her young age.

Shortly after her application was refused, she accompanied her father on a pilgrimage to Rome with the goal of asking his support for her intention. At an audience with Pope Leo XIII (r. 1878–1903) she broke the normal silence and made her intention known. He considered her request and referred it back to the local superior. This time the request was honored, and she was able to join the sisters at the convent in 1888. Though she would live less than a decade and die in her mid-20s, she became noteworthy for her devotion. Her superior asked her to write an account of her experiences and reflect on the holy life.

Two years after her death on September 30, 1897, her autobiography was published as *The Story of a Soul*, with an English edition appearing in 1901. In it she described the devotion as the "Little Way," a path centered upon the love of and trust in God. The story of her life found an immediate response throughout the church. It spurred devotion to her as a saint who had abandoned herself in the service of God, her existence keynoted by accomplishment in mundane duties.

With reports of many miracles attributed to her intercession, a formal investigation of her saintliness began in 1914. She was beatified in 1923 and canonized in 1925. Michael J. Gallagher, the bishop of the Diocese of Detroit, was in Rome and present for the canonization ceremonies. He immediately moved to create the first shrine to the new Saint Thérèse of Lisieux, in suburban Detroit. In 1944, in the midst of World War II, Pope Pius XII (r. 1939–1958) named her a patroness of France. The new basilica in her honor at Lisieux (consecrated in 1954) soon rivaled Lourdes as a popular place of pilgrimage in France. In 1997, Pope John Paul II (r. 1978–2005) named her a doctor of the church. She has also been named a patron saint of France, Russia, and Australia.

Theresa's feast day was originally set for October 3. In 1969, during the wholesale revision of the Calendar of Saints, it was moved to October 1. In 2009, her relics went on tour through England and were placed in display at the Anglican cathedral in York on October 1.

J. Gordon Melton

See also Catherine of Siena, Saint's Day of St.; Rose of Lima, Saint's Day of St.

References

Hollings, Michael, *Therese of Lisieux: An Illustrated Life*. London, W. Collins & Co., 1981.

Nevin, Thomas R. *Thérèse of Lisieux: God's Gentle Warrior*. New York: Oxford University Press, 2006.

Thérèse of Lisieux, Saint, *The Story of a Soul*. Translated by Michael Day. Wheathampstead, Hertfordshire: Anthony Clarke Books, 1973.

Von Balthasar, Hans Urs. *Therese of Lisieux: The Story of a Mission*. New York: Sheed and Ward, 1954.

Thingyan. *See* New Year's Day

Third Prince, Birthday of the

On the eighth and ninth days of the fourth lunar month (usually in May of the Common Era calendar), followers of traditional Chinese religion in Singapore celebrate the birthday of the miracle-working child god Lotos (or Ne Zha) who is pictured riding the wind and holding a magic bracelet and a spear. This deity appears to have originated as an ancient Hindu deity known as Nalakuvara, the third son of the north guardian king Vaisravana. In Chinese mythology, however, he is known as the Jade Emperor's Princely Lord and the Marshal of the Central Altar. Ne Zha was a general for the Jade Emperor (who rules the Chinese pantheon), and incarnated as the third son of Li Jing, the Celestial King Tuota. When he was 10 years old, he fought and killed the son of the dragon king of the Eastern Sea. He subsequently stripped off the flesh from his own bones to keep his parents from being implicated in his deed. Afterwards, his teacher, the Perfected One of Taiyi, used a lotus to reconstitute his scattered souls. In his resurrected state, Ne Zha wields magical weapons given him by Taiyi. He is now believed to be effective in quelling demonic forces.

His birthday is the occasion of a gathering of the many spirit mediums who work within the tradition. It is an occasion for the different mediums to show their competitive spirit in both their spirit-summoning and in acts of personal courage. During the ceremony, they will work themselves into a frenzy and, during their trance state, cut and pierce themselves with swords. Prior to their actions, the floor of the temple space will be covered with sheets of yellow paper, upon which the blood from their wounds is allow to drip. After they finish, the paper will be collected and distributed to the faithful as protective talismans.

A similar event occurs in Taiwan at several temples dedicated to Ne Zha—the Sanfeng Temple in Kaohsiung, as well as Kaichi Temple in Hsinying on the seventh day of the seventh month, at a time most Chinese will be celebrating the Double Seventh Festival.

J. Gordon Melton

See also Double Seventh Festival; Mazu Festival, Goddess.

References

Gao, Pat. "Dancing with the Gods." *Taiwan Review*, January 1, 2010. Posted at http://taiwanreview.nat.gov.tw/ct.asp?xItem=83089&CtNode=1337&mp=1. Accessed March 1, 2010.

Thompson, Sue Ellen, and Barbara W. Carlson, comp. *Holidays, Festivals, and Celebrations of the World Dictionary*. Detroit, MI: Omnigraphics, 1994.

Thomas Paine Day (January 29)

British-born radical journalist Thomas Paine (1737–1809) is most commonly remembered as the author of a short 1776 pamphlet, *Common Sense*, which rallied the American colonists to the cause of revolution. He urged immediate action to declare independence and to establish a republic separate from the British monarchy. As the revolution proceeded, he published essays to keep up the spirits of the troops and the people, and that projected the belief that Britain would soon give up the fight and recognize the new country. He ended the war a hero, but financially in a difficult situation. The government finally gave him a modest award for his efforts. He would later move back to Europe where he penned the *Rights of Man* (1791, 1792) in support of the French Revolution and against the British constitutional monarchy. He fled England, where he was declared an outlaw. Though awarded French citizenship, he alienated his new countrymen by opposing the execution of the former king.

Thomas Paine is the famous author of the pamphlet *Common Sense*. To his credit, he wrote *The Age of Reason*, which was rediscovered by atheists during the 20th century and inspired the celebration of Freethinkers Day on January 25. (Library of Congress)

While sitting in prison in Luxembourg, Paine began writing a new book, which would later be published as *The Age of Reason* (1794–1795). Paine turned from politics to religion and from condemning monarchy to condemning the Christian churches. Reflecting primarily on some writings of Isaac Newton, Paine presented his own version of the Deist universe, in which God established a uniform, immutable, and eternal order and left creation as His only revelation. Paine went further than Newton, however, by rejecting Christianity. He denied the authority of the Bible and condemned specific Old Testament stories as immoral. His attack upon Christianity was marked by a level of bitterness that many could not pass off as simply a difference of opinion. When he finally returned to the United States, Thomas Jefferson was among his few friends. He ended his life in poverty.

His political works survived, though memory of them was lost for a period due to the reaction to his Deism (which church leaders attacked as atheism). Only in the 20th century, as atheism emerged as an organized community, was *The Age of Reason* rediscovered by a larger audience, though writing about Paine still concentrates on his two major political works. Then, in the 1990s, the *Truthseeker*, an atheist periodical, began to call for the celebration of Paine's birthday, January 25, as Freethinkers Day and use the occasion to educate the public on the significant role Thomas Paine played in the history of democracy and human freedom. About the same time, the Thomas Paine Foundation, founded in 1992 by Philadelphian Margaret Downey, began celebrating Thomas Paine Day. The foundation became a standing committee of the Freethought Society of Greater Philadelphia, through which it continues its promotion of Paine both as an American hero and a pioneer of Freethought. Included in its work is support for the Thomas Paine National Historical Museum, located on Paine's former farm in New Rochelle, New York.

The celebration of Thomas Paine's birthday spread from the United States to atheists and humanists internationally. Activities focus upon the promotion of the use of reason over faith, and the rejection of arbitrary authority.

J. Gordon Melton

See also Darwin Day; Freethought Day; Ingersoll Day.

References

Ayer, A. J. *Thomas Paine*. Chicago: University of Chicago Press, 1990.

Hitchens, Christopher. *Thomas Paine's Rights of Man: A Biography*. New York: Atlantic Monthly Press, 2007.

Keane, John. *Tom Paine: A Political Life*. New York: Grove Press, 2003.

King, Ronald E., and Elsie Begler, eds. *Thomas Paine: Common Sense for the Modern Era*. San Diego: SDSU Press, 2007.

Paine, Thomas. *Thomas Paine Collection: Common Sense, Rights of Man, Age of Reason, An Essay on Dreams, Biblical Blasphemy, Examination of the Prophecies*. Charleston, SC: Forgotten Books, 2007.

Three Hierarchs, Day of the (January 30)

The liturgical Christian churches both East and West have saint's days honoring Saints Basil of Caesarea known as the Great (30–379), Gregory of Nazianzus (c. 329–390), and John Chrysostom (c. 347–407), all of whom worked in the fourth century in the wake of the legalization of Christianity and the promulgations of the Council of Nicea (324 CE). However, in the Eastern churches, the three are also remembered collectively on January 30, the celebration of the Day of the Three Hierarchs (or Three Archbishops). The three, all leading intellectuals of their century, have been designated the patron saints of education and culture.

This day came about due to a controversy that arose among some scholars in the Eastern churches in the 11th century, during the reign of Byzantine emperor Alexius Comnenus (1081–1118). Some began to argue that Basil was superior to John, as he demanded the upholding of moral standards, while John tended to emphasize the forgiveness and absolving of the sin of Christians. John's supporters came to his support, while still a third group rose up to champion Gregory over the others. With no clear criteria by which to judge, the arguments persisted, promoting more heat than light.

A solution was proposed in 1084 following the report of a dream experienced by Saint John Mauropus (c. 1000–c. 1075), the archbishop metropolitan of Euchaïta. The three hierarchs appeared to him and declared their equality and lack of discord or division. They asked John to speak to the controversialists and ask them to cease their quarrelling and join together the three commemorations in one feast to be celebrated annually. Most of his colleagues received his word concerning the dream and responding by requesting him to compose the liturgy for the celebration. He chose January 30, as three celebrations for the hierarchs were already on the calendar for that month.

J. Gordon Melton

See also Augustine of Hippo, Saint's Day of St.; Cyprian, Saint's Day of St.

References

"Feast of the Three Holy Fathers, Great Hierarchs and Ecumenical teachers, Basil the Great, Gregory the theologian and John Chrysostom." *Greek Orthodox Archdiocese of America.* Posted at http://www.goarch.org/special/threehierarchs/. Accessed July 15, 2010.

Florovesky, George. *The Eastern Fathers of the Fourth Century.* Posted at http://www.holytrinitymission.org/books/english/fathers_florovsky_1.htm. Accessed July 15, 2010.

Makarios of Simonos Petra, Hieromonk, comp. *The Synaxarion: The Lives of the Saints of the Orthodox Church.* Vol. 3. Translated by Christopher Hookway. Chalkidike, Greece: Holy Convent of the Annunciation of Our Lady, 2001.

Meredith, Anthony. *The Cappadocians.* Crestwood, NY: St. Vladimir's Seminar Press, 1995.

Three Kings Day, Native American Pueblos (January 6)

January 6 is Epiphany on the Western Christian calendar, a day to remember the Three Magi's visit to the Christ child and offer of the gifts of gold, frankincense, and myrrh. Among the Native people of New Mexico, Epiphany has assumed a unique significance under its local designation the Three Kings Day. New Mexico is home to a set of native people distinguished by their construction of villages known as pueblos, and the Pueblo culture not only covered much of what is now New Mexico, but extended into the neighboring states of Arizona and Colorado. There are 19 Pueblos in New Mexico: Acoma, Cochiti, Isleta, Jemez, Laguna, Nambe, Ohkay Owingeh, Picuris, Pojoaque, Sandia, San Felipe. San Ildefonso, Santa Ana, Santa Clara, Santo Domingo, Taos, Tesuque, Zia, and Zuni.

Catholic history among the Pueblo people begins in 1539 with the arrival of Franciscan Friar Marcos de Niza and his African companion Estevanico, who settled in the Zuni pueblo. The first mission was not founded, however, until the 1590s and the establishment of Santa Fe. This work grew through the 17th century, only to be lost when the native population rebelled at the harsh treatment given them by the Spanish authorities. New Mexico was reconquered in the 1690s and Catholic work restarted. Over the following century, most New Mexico Native people became Roman Catholic Christians, and the current celebration of Three Kings Day at the pueblos reflects the synthesis of that new faith with the older Native culture.

January 6 has become the day for the installation of new pueblo officers. Pueblo members gather at their churches for special services during which the new governors and officers begin their term of office. The new pueblo governor receives four canes, the symbol of his authority. Following the service, there is a dance ceremony, in which the governor is honored with a set of religious dances, many inspired by different animals. The religious aspect of the dance, considered an expression of thanksgiving, renewal, and harmony with nature, is punctuated by the respectful silence observed by observers during their performance and the absence of any applause during or following the dances.

The 19 pueblos are each distinctive and each has its own patron saint, unique dances, and native dress. In the post–civil rights era in the United States, the native leadership has asserted a new element of self-determination in their religious life, leading to an even greater integration of Native culture in their celebrations of traditional Christian holidays.

J. Gordon Melton

See also Christmas; Epiphany; Theophany.

References

Kessell, John M. *Pueblos, Spaniards, and the Kingdom of New Mexico*. Norman: University of Oklahoma Press, 2010.

Stewart, Dorothy Newkirk. *Handbook of Indian Dances: I. New Mexico Pueblos*. Santa Fe: Museum of New Mexico, 1952.

Thompson, Sue Ellen, and Barbara W. Carlson, comp. *Holidays, Festivals, and Celebrations of the World Dictionary*. Detroit, MI: Omnigraphics, 1994.

Tihar. *See* Diwali

Timkat (January 20)

The Eastern Orthodox churches celebrate January 6 (January 19 on the Common Era calendar) as Theophany or Epiphany. This day does not commemorate the arrival of the Three Magi to give gifts to Jesus as in parts of the West, but rather the baptism of Jesus in the Jordan by John the Baptist. The Ethiopian celebration has taken on added importance, due in large part to the claims of the Ethiopian Orthodox Tewahedo Church to possess the original Ark of the Covenant that had been placed in the Holy of Holies of the Jewish temple in Jerusalem. An object believed by Ethiopians to be the ark is now kept in the chapel of the Tablet near the Church of Our Lady Mary of Zion in Axum, Ethiopia. Replicas of the ark are placed on the altar of every Ethiopian church.

Timkat is an important celebration in the Ethiopian Orthodox Tewahedo Church whereby people renew their baptismal vows. (Carolyne Pehora/Dreamstime.com)

On Timkat Eve, the congregation's priests and deacons (dressed in their most elaborate liturgical garb) will oversee the removal of the ark replica, the *tabot*, from their parish church and its movement to a local body of water—a lake, pool, or river. The *tabot* is carried by one of the priests atop his head. It is covered in thick cloth to keep away the gaze of impious onlookers. The procession is animated with the sound of ritual bells, and the air is filled with the scent of incense. Once at the site, the tabot is placed in a special tent, as the priests proceed to bless the water in preparation for the next day's events. The priests and the most faithful will spend the night in prayer at the water's edge.

Meanwhile, crowds will begin to gather, many pitching tents close by and partying into the evening. As dawn approaches, the crowd gathers around the water and the tent holding the tabot as the prayers of the evening continue. The high point of the service occurs as the priest dips a golden cross into the water and extinguishes a consecrated candle in a similar manner. Thereafter, the priest takes blessed water and sprinkles it on the assembled group as a remembrance of Christ's baptism. The tabot is then processed back to the church and replaced on the altar, while the congregation disperses to continue the celebration through the rest of the day.

The most elaborate celebration of Timkat is held in Addis Ababa, where the Ethiopian pope, the head of the church, usually officiates, and at Gondar and Lalibela. The annual celebration is a highpoint of Ethiopian church life each year.

J. Gordon Melton

See also Epiphany; Theophany.

References

Bayens, Patrick James. *Journeys in African Zion*. San Francisco: Blurb, 2009.

Grierson, Roderick, and Stuart Munro-Hay. *The Ark of the Covenant*. London: Orion Books Ltd., 2000.

Yesehaq, Archbishop. *The Ethiopian Tewahedo Church: An Integrally African Church*. Nashville, TN: Winston-Derek Publishers, 1997.

Tin Hou, Birthday of. *See* Mazu Festival, Goddess

Tirupati Brahmotsava Festival

The Tirupati Brahmotsava Festival or simple Brahmotsavam is a nine-day Vaishnava Hindu festival that celebrates the deity Venkateshwara, one of the more popular forms of Vishnu. Venkateshwara is commonly known simply as Balaji. He is pictured as having a black complexion. He has four hands. In two hands, he holds a discus (a symbol of power) and a conch shell (a symbol of existence). His lower hands point downward, a gesture that devotees interpret as a request for faith and surrender to the deity's protection. In most temples, his body is covered in elaborate clothing and flowers; thus, the devotee rarely if ever sees the hands gestures (*mudras*).

The most important temple dedicated to Venkateshwara is at Tirupati in Andhra Pradesh, India. The temple located on the top of the hill above Tirupati is considered the abode of Lord Venkateshwara. The temple rests among the famous seven hills of the Sheshacalam Mountain range, which believers relate to the hoods of the divine serpent Adishesha upon which the recumbent Vishnu rests on the Ocean of Milk. The oldest part of the temple dates to the 9th or 10th century. It appears that it was originally a temple dedicated to Shiva (or his son Lord Murugan), but was transformed into a Vaishnava temple by the Acharya Ramanuja in the 12th century. The Titupati temple has become the model for Balaji temples now found in countries around the world.

Brahmotsavam is celebrated in the Hindu month of Ashwin (September–October on the Common Era calendar), which on the Tamil calendar is called Purattasi. Preparation for what is one of the more important festivals in Andhra Pradesh will begin several weeks before the start of the festival, with the prescribed cleaning and decoration of the temple with flowers. On the eve before the formal beginning of the festival, a ritual is performed to Sri Vishvaksena, the leader of Vishnu's army and one considered able to remove obstacles and protect worship.

On the first day, the raising of the Garuda flag signals the beginning of the festival. At this point, the Garuda, an eagle-like creature, flies to Devalokam, the realm of gods and angels, and invites them to attend the festival.

Each day of the festival is marked by fire rituals and processions of the deity statues on elaborately decorated chariots (*vahanas*) through the streets of Tirupati. The main statues in the temple are permanently fixed in their place in the temple, but smaller movable statues, referred to as the *utsava murtis*, are brought from the temple for the processions.

Each evening, the statues will be decorated with elaborate new clothes and a surrounding halo of color. Each procession carries its own particular meaning and brings slightly different blessings to those who participate. Many participate looking for very practical ends, including hopes for children, wealth, or success in education.

On the concluding day, the murti of Sri Balaji is given some special decorations. Also, the last day of the festival builds around the Sudarsana Chakra, a disc-shaped weapon identified with Vishnu. At various locations in the festival area, a representation of the Sudarsana Chakra will be bathed and the power from it transferred by various means to the crowd of devotees that has gathered.

The final action of the celebration is the lowering of the Garuda flag. The priests offer their final greetings to the attending deities by chanting various mantras. They thus signal their return to the Devalokam.

Hundreds of thousands flock to Tirupati each year for the festival, while many unable to make the trip will celebrate at the many other Balaji temples.

Constance A. Jones

See also Anant Chaturdashi; Chittirai Festival; Jhulan Yatra; Kartika Purnima; Parshurama Jayanti.

References

"Brahmotsavam Activities." Tirumala Tirupati Devasthanams. Posted at http://www.tirumala.org/default.htm. Accessed June 15, 2010.

Krishna, Nandith. *Balaji, Venkateshwara, Lord of Tirumala-Tirupati—An Introduction.* Mumbai: Vakils Feffer & Simons, 2000.

Rao, Velcheru Narayana, and David Shulman. *God on the Hill: Temple Poems from Tirupati.* New York: Oxford University Press, 2005.

Sri Venkateshwara. Chennai: Sura Books, 2007.

Tisha B'Av

Tisha B'Av is the culminating day of a three-week fasting/mourning period observed annually within the Jewish community in memory of the destruction of the temple in Jerusalem. Tisha B'Av (literally the ninth day of Av) usually occurs on in August on the Common Era calendar. Tisha B'Av references the destruction of the both the first and second temples that had been constructed in Jerusalem, both of which happened to have been destroyed on this day. In 586 BCE, the first temple was destroyed by the Babylonians, and in 70 BCE, the second temple was razed by the Romans. In the modern world, the commemoration of Tisha B'Av has been expanded to reference a variety of tragedies that had fallen upon the Jewish people in this month, most notably the order to expel the Jews from Spain (1492) and the beginning of World War I (which is tied to the downward slide of Europe toward the Holocaust).

The period of mourning begins on the 17th day of the Hebrew month of Tammuz, the anniversary of the day that the walls of Jerusalem were breached in 586 by the Babylonians. During the next three weeks, observant Jews do not schedule celebrative events such as weddings and parties, nor do they cut their hair. They will not don new clothing and generally refrain from the consumption of meat or wine. On the day of Tisha B'Av, the restrictions become more severe. A complete fast is kept. Water is not used for washing, shaving, bathing, and even drinking for the most observant. Women do not wear cosmetics, and couples refrain from sexual activity. People will act in a mournful manner and avoid lighthearted conversation.

As people gather for prayers in the synagogue, they will find the ark (the cabinet that contains the scroll of the Torah) draped in black, and will hear passages from the biblical book of Lamentations and prayers for mourning read.

J. Gordon Melton

See also Fast of Gedaliah; Yom HaAatzmaut

References

Kaplan, Aryeh. *The Story of Tisha B'Av*. Brooklyn, NY: Moznaim Publishing Corp., 1981.

The Ninth of Av. Posted at http://www.ou.org/yerushalayim/tishabav/. Accessed July 15, 2010.

Solloveitchik, Joseph B. *The Koren Mesorat HaRav Kinot: The Complete Tisha B'Av Service with Commentary by Rabbi Joseph B. Soloveitchik*. Jerusalem: Koren Publishers Jerusalem, 2010.

Tohji-Taisai (December 22)

Tohji-Taisai is a Shinto celebration centered on Amaterasu Omi-Kami, the sun goddess, held on the winter solstice each year. In Shinto thought, Amaterasu was the offspring of Izanagi, as was her brother Susano-o no Mikoto. As the sun goddess, Amaterasu exercised her hegemony over the sky and emerged as the ruler of the other deities. She is represented with a mirror and symbolized in the rising sun that appears on the Japanese flag.

Amaterasu became the subject of a variety of Japanese stories that concern the seasons and the rising of the sun each day. The story told at the winter equinox concerns her brother, the storm god Susano-o Mikoto. At one point, he went about ravaging the Earth and was so noisy that she retreated to a cave, which she closed with a boulder. Unfortunately, her action deprived the Earth of light and life. Demons ruled in her stead.

The other kami (deities) were unable to entice Amaterasu out of the cave. Then Uzume, the goddess of joy and happiness, began to do her comical and obscene dances. The gods laughed so hard and so loud that Amaterasu grew curious of what was happening. She ventured forth from the cave and saw her own brilliant reflection in a mirror that Uzume had hung in a nearby tree. As she gazed in the mirror, the gods grabbed her and removed her from the cave entrance. She returned to the sky, and light returned to the world.

Tohji-Taisai celebrates Amaterasu's leaving the cave and light beginning to return to the world.

J. Gordon Melton

See also Kanmiso-sai; Nagasaki Kunchi; Shinto—Cycle of Holidays.

References

Littleton, C. Scott. *Shinto: Origins, Rituals, Festivals, Spirits, Sacred Places*. New York: Oxford University Press, 2002.

Ono, Sokyo. *Shinto: The Kami Way*. Rutland, VT: Charles E. Tuttle, 1991.

Picken, Stuart D. B. *Historical Dictionary of Shinto*. Metuchen, NJ: Scarecrow Press, 2002.

Tomb Sweeping Day. *See* Pure Brightness Festival

Transfiguration, Feast of the (August 6)

In the Christian New Testament, there is an account of one of the more memorable events in Jesus's life. As reported in the 17th chapter of the Gospel of Matthew:

> After six days Jesus took Peter, James, and John his brother, and led them up a high mountain by themselves. And he was transfigured before them; his face shone like the sun and his clothes became white as light. And behold, Moses and Elijah appeared to them, conversing with him. Then Peter said to Jesus in reply, "Lord, it is good that we are here. If you wish, I will make three tents here, one for you, one for Moses, and one for Elijah." While he was still speaking, behold, a bright cloud cast a shadow over them, then from the cloud came a voice that said, "This is my beloved Son, with whom I am well pleased; listen to him." When the disciples heard this, they fell prostrate and were very much afraid. But Jesus came and touched them, saying, "Rise, and do not be afraid."
>
> And when the disciples raised their eyes, they saw no one else but Jesus alone. As they were coming down from the mountain, Jesus charged them, "Do not tell the vision to anyone until the Son of Man has been raised from the dead."

This event came to be considered both a great miracle and a beginning point for understanding the heavenly state toward which Christians were headed following this earthly life. In the years after the church became a legal entity under Emperor Constantine (272–337 CE), Christians speculated on the exact location at which the transfiguration occurred. Some suggested Mount Hermon, the peak closest to Caesarea Philippi, where the Bible suggests that the Apostles were immediately prior to the Transfiguration event. By the fifth century, however, Mount Tabor, in Galilee, had emerged as the favored site, and a church dedicated to the transfiguration was built there.

Given its biblical basis, the celebration of the Transfiguration has become one of the most ubiquitous of Christian festivals. It is observed on August 6 by the Roman Catholic, Eastern Orthodox, and Anglican churches. Methodists and Lutherans celebrate it on the Sunday immediately preceding Ash Wednesday and the beginning of Lent. In the (Lutheran) churches of Sweden and Finland, Transfiguration Sunday is the seventh Sunday after Trinity Sunday (which is also the eighth Sunday after Pentecost).

The day has become an occasion to preach from the biblical text relative to the Transfiguration event, which lends itself to discussions of a variety of issues from the nature of life after death to the ordering of church authority.

J. Gordon Melton

See also Lent; Liturgical Year—Western Christian; Trinity Sunday.

References

McGuckin, John Alexander. *The Transfiguration of Christ in Scripture and Tradition*. Lewiston, NY: Edwin Mellen Press, 1987.

Nes, Solrunn. *The Uncreated Light: An Iconographical Study of the Transfiguration in the Eastern Church*. Grand Rapids, MI: William B. Eerdmans Publishing Company, 2007.

Perry, John Michael. *Exploring the Transfiguration Story*. New York: Sheed & Ward, 1993.

Trinity Monday

Rarely acknowledged today, Trinity Monday was seen in the Western church as the beginning of the long period between the celebration of events around Easter culminating in Pentecost and Trinity Sunday and the events of the Christmas season beginning with Advent. Whereas most Christian holidays acknowledge a specific event in church history, or the death of a specific hero of the faith, Trinitytide is a period for focus upon the unique concept of the Christian faith that distinguishes it from the other monotheistic traditions, most notably Judaism and Islam. As with Judaism and Islam, Christianity affirms one God, but then declares that God manifests in three distinct and co-equal "persons," the Father, the Son, and the Holy Spirit. Thus, the Sundays after Trinity Sunday have traditionally been a season of instruction in the great truths upon which the faith is constructed, as opposed to remembering the events out of which the church grew.

Trinitytide is carried on the calendars of the Roman Catholic, Anglican, and Lutheran churches and, in recent decades, has been added to the calendar of a variety of Protestant churches that has begun to use a Christian liturgical calendar as a result of their ecumenical contacts. Trinity Monday has, however, dropped in significance in recent centuries. Among the places it retains some significance is at Trinity University in Dublin, Ireland, where it has traditionally been the day upon which, with pomp and pageantry, the election of new Fellows and Scholars was announced.

J. Gordon Melton

See also Easter; Pentecost; Trinity Sunday.

References

Smolarski, Dennis C. *Liturgical Literacy*. Mahwah, NJ: Paulist Press, 1990.

Wilder, Lesley. *The Christian Year*. Oxford: Oxford University Press, 1977.

Trinity Sunday

Trinity Sunday is the Sunday after Pentecost in the Western church (Roman Catholic, Anglican, and most Protestant churches). It is known formally in the

Roman Catholic Church as the Solemnity of the Most Holy Trinity. The day has two purposes. For the church, it is an affirmation of God and the mystery of God's unique essence. For others it is an affirmation of the nature of God as a unity expressed in three persons over against a variety of views that were denounced as heretical.

During the second and third centuries CE, the Christian movement grew into a large international body of believers that was also, in most places, the object of suppression and persecution by the authorities of the Roman Empire. It had inherited a strictly monotheistic view of God from its Jewish background, but had increasingly affirmed the divinity of Jesus. Once legalized and given the backing of the Roman emperor at the beginning of the third century, bishops were able to meet and make decisions about the direction that the church would take. Initially spurred by the challenge of Arius (c. 260–336 CE), church leaders met in council at Nicea in 324 CE and produced what became the orthodox solution to the problem of the nature of God. It promulgated the doctrine of the Trinity, which over the next centuries would be refined and become the unique identifying doctrine of Christian faith.

The essence of the Nicean position concerned the divinity of Jesus Christ, which was affirmed thusly:

> We believe in one Lord, Jesus Christ,
> the only Son of God,
> eternally begotten of the Father,
> God from God, light from light,
> true God from true God,
> begotten, not made,
> of one Being with the Father;
> through him all things were made.
> For us and for our salvation
> he came down from heaven

The full working out of the doctrine of Christ's full divinity and the understanding of the Triune nature of God's existence would engage the church for several centuries after Nicea and the six remaining Ecumenical councils that met through the eighth century. One popular statement of the Trinity in the western church was the Athanasian Creed promulgated in the sixth century, but ascribed to Athanasius (c. 300–373) who championed the Trinitarian position against Arius. It reads:

> And the Catholic Faith is this: That we worship one God in Trinity, and Trinity in Unity; Neither confounding the Persons; nor dividing the Essence. For there is one Person of the Father; another of the Son; and another of the Holy Ghost. But the Godhead of the Father, of the Son, and of the Holy Ghost, is all one; the Glory equal, the Majesty coeternal. Such as the Father

is; such is the Son; and such is the Holy Ghost. The Father uncreated; the Son uncreated; and the Holy Ghost uncreated. The Father unlimited; the Son unlimited; and the Holy Ghost unlimited. The Father eternal; the Son eternal; and the Holy Ghost eternal. And yet they are not three eternals; but one eternal. As also there are not three uncreated; nor three infinites, but one uncreated; and one infinite.

The nature of the affirmation of God as Three in One is at best difficult to understand, the intent of the doctrine being in large part to confirm both the complete humanity and full divinity of Jesus while affirming a strict monotheism. At the same time, the doctrine denies a variety of views that would undermine one of the other of those positions—tritheism (the belief in three gods), Arianism (which denies the divinity of Jesus), and modalism (which also ultimately denies the divinity of Jesus).

Through the early Middle Ages, the idea of the Trinity was integrated into the church's regular lineage. Pope Alexander II (1061–1073) was petitioned to establish a special feast to honor the Holy Trinity, but refused the petition on the grounds that the Church honored the Holy Trinity daily in its worship. John XXII (1316–1334) reversed that position and ordered the feast for the entire Church and set the date as the first Sunday after Pentecost (which is 40 days after Easter). In 1911, Pope Pius X (r. 1903–1914) raised the feast to a celebration of the first order.

Protestants, who were raising issues not dealt with in the traditional creeds of the church, were quick to affirm the creeds and to argue that their position in no way contradicted the position of the early church councils. They professed faith in the Trinity in their confessions of faith, used the ancient creeds in their liturgy, and maintained Trinity Sunday on their church calendars as part of a total affirmation of their orthodoxy.

The Trinitarian understanding of God was, of course, denied by the Socinian movement of the 16th century, and most notably by Spanish physician Michael Servetus (1511–1553), who fled to Protestant territory hoping to escape Catholic authorities. Instead of escaping, however, he was arrested and executed by the Reformed Protestants based at Geneva. Socinians would gain some early support in Poland but survived only in Transylvania. Their ideas would eventually come to England, where they would reemerge in the Unitarian movement.

The doctrine of the Trinity became an issue in the early 20th century when some modern theologians in mainline churches denied the Trinity and/or the full divinity of Jesus. It had remained an issue with Fundamentalist and Evangelical churches claiming that liberal Protestant churches have become slack in discipline and have allowed people who hold a non-trinitarian theology to become pastors, bishops, theologians, and church leaders and to hold responsible positions in spite of their heretical views. Meanwhile, ecumenical organizations such as the National Council of Churches of Christ in the USA and the World Council of Church have designated themselves as fellowships of churches that hold to a trinitarian understanding of God. At the same time, they have welcomed into membership denominations that traditionally rejected the seven ecumenical councils and the "orthodox" view of the Trinity.

While Trinity Sunday is still carried on the calendar of most Protestant churches, it is usually left to local pastors as to whether the churches they lead will celebrate it year after year. Many non-liturgical churches have simply jettisoned any attempt to follow the liturgical calendar and dispense with any attempt to acknowledge the Christian holidays beyond Easter and Christmas.

In the Eastern Orthodox churches, Trinity Sunday is celebrated as part of Pentecost Sunday.

J. Gordon Melton

See also Liturgical Year—Western Christian; Pentecost; Trinity Monday.

References

Duck, Ruth C., and Patricia Wilson-Kastner. *Praising God: The Trinity in Christian Worship*. Louisville, KY: Westminster John Knox Press, 1999.

Durzl, Franz. *A Brief History of the Doctrine of the Trinity in the Early Church*. London: T. & T. Clark Publishers, 2007.

Letham, Robert. *The Holy Trinity: In Scripture, History, Theology and Worship*. Phillipsburg, NJ: P & R Publishing, 2005.

Morneau, Robert F. *Trinity Sunday Revisited: Patterns for Prayer*. Collegeville, MN: Liturgical Press, 1980.

Triumph of the True Cross, Feast of the. *See* Holyrood or the Feast of the Triumph of the Holy Cross

True Parents' Birthday

True Parents' Birthday is a holy day of the Unification Church, the Korean new religious movement founded by Sun Myung Moon (b. 1920) in 1954. It is celebrated on the sixth day of the new year in the first month of the traditional Korean lunar calendar and commemorates the common birthday shared by Moon and his wife Hak Ja Han. Most Unification holy days have been celebrated using the Korean lunar calendar, and in 2010, Moon ruled that all holy days would follow that tradition. The Korean lunar calendar is similar to the traditional Chinese calendar.

Moon was born in 1920, and his wife was born in 1943. Her mother was a famous and long-time follower. Hak Ja Han married Moon in 1960, and their wedding date marks Parents Day, the first holy day of the Church. True Parents' Birthday is one of the five most significant holy days of the Unification church year. Unificationists believe that Moon and his wife are the spiritual True Parents for a human race that fell because of the transgressions of Adam and Eve.

Unification theology teaches that Sun Myung Moon was asked by God to complete the mission of Jesus. Jesus failed to complete the task of becoming a True Parent and finding a Second Eve. Moon is regarded as the fulfillment of the Second Coming of Christ and Hak Ja Han is the restored Eve. These beliefs form the background to the celebration of their birthdays.

As with other holy days, members engage in an early morning worship celebration. Gifts are offered to Moon and his wife, prayers are said in the names of True Parents, and tables are set with food and a cake. Members are also encouraged to arrange parties and special events after official ceremonies are completed.

James A. Beverley

See also Children's Day; Day of All Things; Parents Day; Unification Church, Holidays of the.

References

Introvigne, Massimo. *The Unification Church.* Salt Lake City, UT: Signature, 2000.

Kwak, Chung Hwan. *The Tradition: Book One*. New York: Holy Spirit Association for the Unification of World Christianity, 1985. Posted at http://www.unification.org/ucbooks/TT1/index.html. Accessed July 2, 2010.

Tsagaan Sar

Tsagaan Sar, the traditional New Year's celebration in Mongolia, is held on the first day of the Mongolian lunar calendar, which is similar to the Chinese calendar (generally in February on the Common Era calendar). It generally coincides with other lunar New Year celebrations, like the Chinese, and marks the transition from winter to spring.

Festivities begin on New Year's Eve with a celebration called Bituuleg celebrated with special food, traditional games, and storytelling. The arrival of *Bituun* Baldanlham, a local Buddhist bodhisattva, pictured riding a mule, is imminent. She is believed to make three passes by each home, which is acknowledged by the family making three pieces of ice available outside their residence for the mule to drink.

New Year's Day is an affirmation of the extended family. Children visit their parents and then other members of the family according to prescribed seniority and present gifts, traditionally food and pastries. The most senior are presented with scarves, a sign of respect and honor. In the next days of visiting back and forth, each person publicly affirms their understanding of who constitute their kin.

In the Buddhist monasteries, New Year's Eve is a time to burn rubbish, symbolic of destroying the people's sin of the past year, followed by a ritual focused upon Lhame, a dharma protector. Buddhist families will also display their religious paintings (similar to Tibetan *thankas*) that picture the Buddhas and bodhisattvas. The paintings become the center of devotions that might include the burning of oil lamps and incense and the turning of prayer wheels. Prayers are also said to one's ancestors.

Pre-Buddhist shamanistic beliefs and practices have very much survived in Mongolia. On New Year's Eve, the third day of Tsagaan Sar, people gather for the shaman to make an offering to the sky through a ritual to the Seven Stars, seen as seven old men, and the household spirits. This ritual is conducted around a small table, which serves as an altar in one's yard. On this table will be nine bowls of water and sticks of incense. Nearby, a large fire is kindled. The fire's smoke is pictured rising to heaven and melting the ice accumulated on the whiskers of the dragon. Shortly after the New Year, the shaman will hold a ritual in which mundane water is transformed into holy water. The water is subsequently sprinkled on all present as a purifying and protection ritual.

The Communists tried to suppress the traditional celebrations of New Year's Day, but they came back quickly in the 1990s following the government's fall.

J. Gordon Melton

See also Chinese New Year's (Preliminary Festival); Chinese New Year's Day; New Year's Day.

References

Humphrey, Caroline. *Shamans and Elders: Experience, Knowledge and power among the Daur Mongols*. New York: Oxford University Press, 1996.

Marsh, Peter. *The Horse-Head Fiddle and the Cosmopolitan Reimagination of Tradition of Mongolia*. London: Routledge, 2009.

Verboom, Guido. *A Fire on the Steppes: Religion and Public Celebrations of Greater Mongolia*. Mongoluls.Net. Posted at http://mongoluls.net/shashin/celeb.shtml. Accessed July 15, 2010.

Tsong Khapa Anniversary (December)

Tsong Khapa (1357–1419 CE) was a Tibetan Buddhist reformer recognized as the founder of the Gelugpa school of Tibetan Buddhism. The Gelugpa or Yellow Hat school was the dominant school in Tibetan Buddhism prior to the Chinese occupation of the country in the 1950s, and includes among its leaders the Dalai Lama. Above and beyond the special reverence paid to him by the Gelugpa School, all of the schools and sects of Tibetan Buddhism see him as a foremost exemplar of the shared history. Popularly called "Je Rinpoche" (or Precious Master), he is regarded as an enlightened being and the emanation of two divine personages, the bodhisattvas of compassion and wisdom—Avalokitesvara (a.k.a. Guan Yin) and Manjusri.

Tsong Khapa was born in the Amdo province of eastern Tibet in 1357, but according to his traditional spiritual biography, his life story begins long before

Statue of Buddhist deity Tsong Khapa. (J. Gordon Melton)

his birth. According to his hagiography, in a previous life, Tsong Khapa lived in the time of Gautama Buddha (563–483 BCE), the founder of Buddhism. As a boy, he offered a crystal rosary to the Buddha, who gave him a conch shell in return and prophesied that in a future life, he would be a great teacher born in Tibet named Losang Drakpa—the name given to Tsong Khapa when he took his novice monastic vows at seven years of age. Further, it was reported that Tsong Khapa's birth was heralded by the auspicious dreams of his mother and father.

The Tsong Khapa Anniversary, also called Galdan Namchot or Gahden-Namgye is held in December, on day 25 of the 10th lunar month on the Tibetan calendar. It is generally also seen as the starting point of winter, and people in pre-1950s Tibet would don their winter clothes. Around Lhasa, butter lamps would light up the evening hours. During the day, monks and priests would make their way to the Potala Palace (where the Dalai Lama resided and from which he ruled) and visit the various shrines and stupas therein. Today, the butter lamps will still light up Lhasa, and in the various monasteries, the daily worship hours will include processions holding aloft images of Tsong Khapa.

In the Gelugpa School, it is a practice to set up 1,000 offerings to Tsong Khapa, each offering being a small assemblage of items that relate to the five senses, and then repeat a liturgy called "The Thousand Offerings to Lama Tsong Khapa." The worship extols Tsong Khapa's virtues and attainments and allows time for worshippers to rejoice in their repetition and hope to also make similar spiritual accomplishments.

J. Gordon Melton

See also Butter Lamp Festival; Dalai Lama's Birthday; Guan Yin's Birthday; Losar; Manjushri's Birthday; Mudras.

References

Hopkins, Jeffrey. *Tsong-Kha-Pa's Final Exposition of Wisdom*. Ithaca, NY: Snow Lion Publications, 2008.

Thurman, Robert A. F., ed. *The Life and Teachings of Tsong Khapa*. Dharamsala: Library of Tibetan Works and Archives, 1982.

Zopa Rinpoche, Lama. "Practices for Lama Tsongkhapa Day." Foundation for the Preservation of the Mahayana Tradition. Posted at http://www.fpmt.org/teachers/zopa/advice/lamatsongkhapa.asp. Accessed May 15, 2010.

Tu B'Shevat

Tu B'Shevat, the 15th day of the month of Shevat according to the Jewish calendar (January–February on the Common Era calendar) marks the beginning of a new year for trees, most notably in Israel. It marks the end of the winter and rainy season and the beginning of a new growing season.

For observant Jews, the observance of Tu B'Shevat relates to the tithing of the crop for the support of the priests (Levites) and the poor. The Hebrew calendar was built around seven-year cycles, in which the seventh year was a jubilee year and the land was not tilled so it could be renewed. During the first, second, fourth, and fifth years, the farmers dedicated a first tithe to go to the Levite tribe, and a second tithe to be brought to Jerusalem, where it would be consumed. On the third and sixth year, the second title became a tithe to be given to the poor.

In judging the tithe to be taken from the fruit of the trees, a new year was to begin when a new set of blossoms sprouted, and thus Tu B'Shevat marks the point between the old year and the new. In the first year of the seven-year cycle, the year following the Jubilee year, those fruits that blossomed before Tu B'Shevat were to be considered as belonging to the first year of the cycle, while fruits that blossomed later belonged to the second year.

Tu B'Shevat remains relevant in Israel, but not so much in the Jewish diaspora. Those who continue to celebrate it do so by eating fruit, particularly fruits mentioned in the Jewish Bible—grapes, figs, pomegranates, olives, and dates. In contemporary Israel, the almond tree is especially singled out on Tu B'Shevat, as it produces beautiful blossoms (not unlike the cherry tree blossoms in Japan) at this time of year.

In 1890, a new custom was added to the observance of Tu B'Shevat: tree planting. That year, Rabbi Zeev Yavetz, one of the founders of the Mizrachi (religious

Zionist) movement, initiated the practice Zichron Yaakov, an early Jewish agricultural colony. The practice was later picked up by the Jewish Teachers Union and the Jewish National Fund. Annually, more than a million Israelis now celebrate Ti'Bshevat in this manner.

J. Gordon Melton

See also Counting of the Omer; Jubilee Year; Pesach; Rosh Hashanah; Sakara Matsuri.

References

Steinberg, Paul. *Celebrating the Jewish Year: The Winter Holidays: Hanukkah, Tu B'Shevat, Purim*. Philadelphia: Jewish Publication Society of America, 2007.

Waskow, Arthur Ocean, Naomi M. Hyman, and Ari Elon, eds. *Trees, Earth, and Torah: A Tu B'Shvat Anthology*. Philadelphia: Jewish Publication Society of America, 1999.

Tulsidas Jayanti

Gosvāmī Tulsidas (1532–1623) was a prominent Hindu devotee and philosopher, best known as the author of *Ramacharitamanasa*, an epic poem scripture devoted to the Hindu deity Rama, an incarnation of the Vishnu. He was born in Uttar Pradesh, India, during the reign of the Mughal ruler Akbar (1542–1605), a Muslim whose realm included much of India.

Tulsidas's great accomplishment was the translation and adaptation of the ancient epic *Ramayana* (written in Sanskrit) into the Awadhi language (a dialect of Hindi) and giving it grounding in Bhakti devotion. In this and his other writings, he emphasized the significance of the path of devotion in attaining one's spiritual evolution and advocated the used of the repetition of the name of Rama (and Krishna) as one reached for the final liberation (moksha).

Tulsidas Jayanti (appearance day) is celebrated on the seventh day of the waxing moon in the Hindu lunar month of Shravan (July–August on the Common Era calendar). Orphaned early in life, he was taught by Narhari Das, from whom he developed his devotion to Lord Rama. He eventually took the vows of the renounced life as a sannyasin and moved to Varinasi, where he wrote his magnum opus.

Today, many Vaishnava consider Tulsidas as a reincarnation of Valmiki, who wrote the original *Ramayana*. They celebrate his life and teaching on Tulsidas Jayanti by visiting temples, now located in countries around the world, dedicated to Lord Ram and reciting the *Ramacharitamanasa*, with intensity. They will also arrange a variety of educational and religious programming to discuss and call attention to Tulsidas's teachings.

Constance A. Jones

See also Guru Purnima; Rama Navani.

References

Bahadur, S. P. *Complete Works of Goswami Tulsidas: Ramacharitmanasa*. Columbia, MO: South Asia Books, 1994.

Frawley, David. *Oracle of Rama: An Adaptation of Rama Ajna Prashna of Goswami Tulsidas with Commentary*. Delhi: Motilal Books, 1999.

Hawley, John Stratton, and Mark Juergensmeyer. *Songs of the Saints of India*. New York: Oxford University Press, 1994.

Twelfth Night. *See* Epiphany

Tyvendedagen. *See* Epiphany

Ugadi Parva. *See* New Year's Day (India)

Ullam-bana

Ullam-bana is a Chinese festival celebrated in China, Korea, Japan, and throughout the Chinese diaspora. The Mahayana Buddhist scriptures describe the hell realms to which the evil and otherwise flawed souls go after this life, as various points merge with tradition Chinese beliefs. Though most developed in China, Ullam-bana originated in India, where it was tied to the rainy season. Indian monsoon retreats traditionally lasted from the 16th of the fourth lunar month to the 15th of the seventh month. Buddhist monks ceased their largely wandering life and generally spent the time in company with others. For the monk, the time allowed for growth and regeneration, but popular speculation suggested that the travel restrictions actually provided protection for newly arisen life forms who might be harmed by traveling monks. Ullam-bana derived from the last day of the retreat period, traditionally referred to as the Buddha Happiness Day as the monks would have made progress in their cultivation (practice) from their retreat.

Ullam-bana was transferred to China quite early—the first recorded instance dates to 538 CE, when it was noted that the emperor Liang carried out a fast on the 15th day of the seventh month. Over time, the festival was also conflated with the Taoist Zhong Yuan festival of the 15th of the seventh month, in which officials in the lower realms forgive sins. The combined version of the Taoist and Buddhist celebration meant that the seventh month was the time when the gates of hell would be opened and the suffering ghosts could wander freely in the realm of humans. The souls of those trapped in the underworld, whose descendants have made no offerings for them, would be free to cross the boundaries where the underworld and the visible world meet. These souls are known as pretas (the "hungry ghosts" seen in many Hong Kong "vampire" movies), and if unchecked, may cause a variety of mischief and evil. Thus, Ullam-bana also came to be known as the festival of Hungry Ghosts, and the entire month as the "ghost month."

For the Buddhist, the observance of Ullam-bana derives its content from the *Ullambana Sutra*, a Mahayana text, which tells the story of the arhat (enlightened person) Maudgalyayana (or Mulian). Mulian discovered that his deceased mother was trapped in a realm of pain and suffering most characterized by an inability to eat. He made his way to the netherworld in hopes of ameliorating her situation, but all his efforts proved futile. Finally, he appealed directly to the Buddha, who informed him that by himself he can do nothing to relieve his mother's suffering. The Buddha informed Mulian that he must make offerings of various items to the sangha (the monks and nuns), and then join them in prayers for his mother's liberation from hell. His action will affect his mother, but also will be advantageous for all of his other deceased relatives.

Ullam-bana marks the day on which Mulian performed what the Buddha had told him to do. Today, the Buddhist faithful will offer prayers for the souls of their ancestors going back seven generations, but focus especially on deceased parents. They will also visit local temples with offerings for the monks and nuns. The prayers and offering of the day are believed to alleviate the suffering of ancestors and shorten the time before they are able to enter the heavenly realms. At the same time, those who follow traditional Chinese religion (and there is no strict line demarking them from Buddhists) may burn spirit money for their ancestors to use in their present spirit life, and will attempt to appease the hungry ghosts by offering them food, drink, and entertainment and use the occasion to also imbibe of the same.

In Japan, Ullam-bana is celebrated as Obon and observed at about the same time, though with slightly different emphases.

J. Gordon Melton

See also Chinese New Year's Day; Double Ninth Festival; Double Seventh Festival; Higan; Obon Festival(s).

References

Guoliang, Gai. *Exploring Traditional Chinese Festivals in China.* Singapore: McGraw-Hill, 2009.

Kaulbach, B, and B. Proksch. *Arts and Culture in Taiwan.* Taipei: Southern Materials Center, 1984.

Latsch, Marie-Luise. *Traditional Chinese Festivals.* Singapore: Graham Brash, 1984.

Liming, Wei. *Chinese Festivals: Traditions, Customs, and Rituals.* Hong Kong: China International Press, 2005.

Robinson, Richard H., and Willard L. Johnson. *The Buddhist Religion: A Historical Introduction.* Belmont, CA: Wadsworth Publishing Company, 1997.

Stepanchuk, Carol, and Charles Wong. *Mooncakes and Hungry Ghosts: Festivals of China.* South San Francisco, CA: China Books & Periodicals, 1992.

Thompson, Laurence G. *Chinese Religion.* Belmont, CA: Wadsworth Publishing Company, 1996.

■ Unbelief

The term "unbelief," as used in this encyclopedia, refers directly to the modern community of people and organizations who advocate those philosophical/ideological positions that do not include a belief in God, either in the singular or plural, and have no use for various supernatural realities often seen as the essence of religion, including prayer, miracles (in the sense of divine intervention in the natural order), revelation, or life after death. Such philosophical positions go under a variety of names—atheism, humanism, agnosticism, freethought, rationalism, secularism, and so forth.

Through the centuries, numerous individuals, and even religious groups, have espoused positions that formally could be called Unbelief. In the ancient West, Unbelief has been ascribed to those philosophers who challenged various supernatural assumptions commonly held within Greek society, such as the belief in demonic inspiration and divination. In the East, Jainism and Theravada Buddhism developed extensive religious systems without the need of positing a God as a focus of worship.

However, modern Unbelief does not encompass every form taken by alternatives to theism and polytheism. Rather, it refers to the critical approach taken to Western Christianity that emerged in post-Reformation Europe in which generally in the name of reason, Unbelief was offered as unbelief in Christian theism (and to a lesser extent, Judaism). Attacks upon the belief in God as "irrational" and as lacking evidential support began to be made in the 18th century, but a foundation for these attacks had been laid by the events of the previous centuries, when challenges were made to the specifically Christian idea of the Trinitarian God. Dissent in the form of Unitarianism would be followed in the next century by questioning of the basic ideas of supernatural approaches to religion as doubts were raised about God's interaction with the world, the validity of prayer, and the existence of miracles. As this position matured, it became known as Deism. Deism, its adherents being accused of atheism, would give way to a full-blown atheism in the 19th century. Atheism would initially manifest as the opinion of a group of individuals, the Freethinkers, and only slowly become the basis of organizations as Freethinkers aligned with various social reform movements calling for freedoms from religiously imposed restrictions.

In the 20th century, the tradition of dissent from religion in the name of reason assumed a more communal form as charismatic leaders and groups offering a more complete vision of a nontheistic belief system, morality, and lifestyles in a secularized social order emerged as alternatives to life as a religious believer. New communities of atheists, humanists, and secularists saw themselves as inheriting the tradition of Western unbelief and offering new forms of it as an alternative to life as a Buddhist, Christian, Hindu, Jew, or Muslim. In the context of the religiously pluralistic contemporary world, nontheistic Unbelief groups assumed a dual role of both dissenting from religion and the prophets of belief systems and communal existence that assumed many of the roles traditionally supplied by religion. This new role for Unbelief is clearly manifest in the adoption of holidays specifically designed to commemorate Unbelief heroes and significant events and to celebrate the reasonable alternative to religion.

Portrait of Michael Servetus, a Spanish physician and vocal nonbeliever (1511–1553). He was executed for his views on religion. (Carl Theophilus Odhner, *Michael Servetus: His Life and Teachings*, 1910)

Early Challenges to Western Christianity

At the beginning of the 16th century, Western Europe was united religiously by the Roman Catholic Church. Although its power varied considerably from country to country, the challenges to its hegemony were relatively localized and were dealt with by the power of the state. However, the attack on the Church's power that began with Martin Luther (1483–1546) in the second decade of the new century would by the end of the century remake the religious map of Europe significantly. Different countries would emerge with Lutheran, Reformed-Presbyterian, or Anglican establishments in power, and additional space would be provided for Mennonites, Socinians (nontrinitarians), and various small mystical groups such as the Schwenfelders.

Relative to the time, the champion of Unbelief was Michael Servatus (1511–1553), the Spanish physician who wrote a book comparing the Christian Trinity to the three-headed hound of hell. For this and other opinions expressed in his 1553 work on the restitution of Christianity, he was first imprisoned by the Inquisition. Escaping, he fled to Geneva, where Reformed Church leader John Calvin (1509–1564) saw to his arrest and execution. Although Lutherans, Calvinists, and Anglicans had challenged a set of Roman Catholic beliefs, they did not disagree concerning the doctrine of God (and that unanimity would quickly push the Socinians from their brief ascendancy in Poland).

Protestantism, while still operating within an orthodox Christian world, did begin the process of criticism of popular supernaturalism that had become institutionalized in Roman Catholicism. It challenged the nature of the Eucharist, the central Christian sacrament, and offered alternatives to the Roman Catholic doctrine of transubstantiation, which holds that the bread and the wine once consecrated are transformed in substance into that of the Body and Blood of Christ (although their appearance remains unchanged). Protestants also challenged the use of numerous relics and the doctrine of purgatory (and the accompanying system of rewards and punishments associated with it).

A next step, the challenge to some of the pervasive views shared by both Protestant and Roman Catholic Christians alike, emerged in the 17th century. Deism affirmed the existence of God but generally denied its miraculous or supernatural elements. Such belief generally saw Jesus as a great moral teacher but denied that as the Christ, he was the second person of a Triune God. Deism was often seen as a natural or reasonable religion (as opposed to revealed religion). According to its initial advocate, Edward Herbert, Lord Cherbury (1583–1648), Deism focused on five affirmations: the existence of a supreme being; the need for worship; piety and virtue as the primary forms of worship (rather than prayer and ritual); the need to repent of shortcomings; and a set of rewards and punishments awaiting individuals in the afterlife. The Deist worldview undercut belief in God's activity in the world, apart from maintaining the system through natural law and the validity of prayer.

Deism became popular among the educated elite as science developed. Although affirming the existence of God, it supplied a worldview that did not interfere with scientific experimentation and investigation, and a theology that did not answer scientific questions in a way that blocked further inquiry. Deism tended to adopt the view of God as the watchmaker who created the world, wound it up, and left it to run according to natural laws. Deism also included an anticlerical element, and many Deists attacked the Church and the authority of its priests and ministers in secular matters, and publicized immoral acts attributed to church leaders in centuries past.

While arising in the 17th century, Deism became a significant movement in the 18th century. British Deist leaders included Lord Shaftsbury (1621–1683), Alexander Pope (1688–1744), Anthony Collins (1676–1729), and Thomas Woolston (1669–1732). In France, Voltaire emerged as the leading Deist spokesperson and used his literary abilities to attack religion in general and the Roman Catholic Church in particular. In the British American colonies, Deism emerged as the faith of the most prominent revolutionaries—Thomas Jefferson, Benjamin Franklin, Thomas Paine, John Adams, and George Washington.

Atheism

As Deism was gathering a wide following, a next step was taken away from the dominant religious sentiments in Western society with the development of perspectives that dispensed with the notion of a deity as an ultimate point of reference. Because of the need to establish itself within a society in which the overwhelming majority professes theism, the nontheistic perspective struggled to find space to exist in reference to the larger community; it was commonly perceived as a negative position, simply a denial of God and religion. To the contrary, atheists have generally insisted that their position is not so much a denial of God as the development of a perspective on life after having found no convincing evidence that something called God exists, and of creating a lifestyle in which God is unnecessary either as a moral authority or an object of worship.

Atheism thus includes a variety of belief systems that lack any belief in a God or in multiple gods. Some go even further and say that the very term "God" has no meaning to them. The assertion of such a perspective has put atheists at odds with the mainstream of religious thought as it has existed in the West since the 17th century. Although hinted at in earlier works, atheism was first openly asserted in the modern West in 1772 in the book by Paul Henri Holbach (1723–1789), *The System of Nature*, though his position had been implied in several earlier texts in which he criticized the Church and Christian theology.

As atheism developed, it did so under a variety of names, each indicating a major theme and a slightly different emphasis in thought—Freethought, rationalism, secularism, and humanism being the most popular. The concept of Freethought developed in the 18th century to describe systems of dissent from specific religious propositions. As science was emerging as a relatively secular endeavor, Freethought insisted that science be free from various theological debates and conclusions, and be allowed to develop its own vocabulary and methodology as it pursued its investigation of the world—that scientists be freed to follow the paths opened by the logic of their thoughts. Inasmuch as scientific conclusions offered dissenting views on what most considered religious issues, from the sanctity of the human body to the age of the universe, Freethought became identified with non-Christian views and eventually with atheism.

Rationalism refers to any one of several philosophical positions characterized by the elevation of reason to the level of a dominating metaphysical or epistemological principle. In one sense, rationalism has a significant philosophical history, as in the philosophical school begun by Rene Descartes (1596–1650). In the more popular sense, however, rationalism refers to a position adopted by many Unbelievers suggesting that religious beliefs and practices be subjected to a rational examination and accepted or rejected on the same basis as one would accept or reject other matters. In examining religions, rationalists tended to reject theological supernaturalism and practices such as worship and prayer, which they tended to condemn as "irrational"—that is, contrary to reason as they used it.

Secularism is a perspective on the world that begins with the division of the world into two realms, the sacred and the secular—that is, the realm of the divine and the religious, and those aspects of life that may be considered apart from either. As originally proposed in the mid-19th century, secularism had a special concern for ethics, and the development of ethical systems apart from theology. Secularism thus came to mean the practical process of improving humans and society without reference to religion or religious institutions. Secularism has also taken on special connotations with regard to the single issue of the separation of church and state, in its more absolutist sense—namely that not only should government not interfere with religion, but that religious ideas should not be injected into governmental processes.

Humanism, a term that covers a variety of philosophical perspectives, arose anew in the early 20th century as a renewed attempt to build a human-centered worldview and ethic that by implication rejected supernatural understandings of the operation of the universe and an ethic based upon pragmatic human values and love.

France has been particularly important in the development of Unbelief. The term "atheism" was coined in France, where it was often used in conjunction with the term "libertine" (freed man). The latter term came to be used almost exclusively for sexually liberated individuals, but originally it included those who were intellectually and theologically free. Deism flowered in France in the 18th century, Voltaire (1694–1778) emerging as its champion. Denis Diderot (1713–1974) was possibly the first true French atheist.

A prolific writer and philosophe, Denis Diderot may also have been France's first true atheist. (Helen Clergue, *The Salon, A Study of French Society and Personalities in the Eighteenth Century*, 1907)

The revolution in France, as in the American colonies, was led by Deists but, because of the power exercised by the Catholic Church, included a strong element of anticlericalism. Atheism was present in postrevolutionary France and produced some outstanding lights, such as pioneer sociologist August Comte (1798–1857), but it found its major expression over the next century in various anti-Catholic events, including the secularizing of the schools in the 1880s. Church and state were separated in 1905. French Freemasonry also created a nontheistic form of its esoteric teachings. In the 20th century, atheism has found expression in various Freethought groups (La Libre Pensée being the largest national organization), and atheists have taken to promoting the national policy against minority religions.

In the last half of the 19th century, throughout the Western world, people who identified themselves as atheists, Freethinkers, rationalists, secularists, or humanists began to create organizations and movements to support their various tendencies, now grouped under the umbrella of Unbelief. Among the earliest and most important of the 19th-century organizations were the First Society of Free Enquirers (founded by Abner Kneeland [1774–1844] in Boston in 1834); the Bund freier religiöser Gemeinden Deutschlands (founded in Germany in 1859); and the National Secular Society (founded by Charles Bradlaugh [1833–1891] in England in 1866).

The Issue of Marxism

In the West, Unbelief has generally distinguished itself from what was arguably the most successful nontheistic system to arise in the modern world, Marxism.

Karl Marx was the founder of modern communism. He believed that religion was "the opiate of the people." (Library of Congress)

Marxism has been tied in the public consciousness with totalitarian governments in the Soviet Union and postrevolutionary China.

The philosophy of Karl Marx (1818–1883) was much more anticlerical than atheistic, and he felt that most religion (as experienced in the state-aligned religions of the 19th century) was, as expressed in his most famous quotation, the "opiate of the people": it lulled people into accepting their exploited status in the lower levels of the social order and acquiescing to rule by the few. He had positive views of some Christian movements, but he argued that both Judaism and Christianity were expressions of stages in human development that had to be surpassed if progress were to occur. Marx felt that religions are a human product that, like other human ideologies, reflects the social systems that perpetuate them.

Marx's economic critique of history took form primarily in political parties that went on to participate in the governmental systems of different countries. The atheism that was implicit in his thought became operationalized in the Communist Party. However, it was largely assumed in the 20th century that to be a communist was to be an atheist, and the support for atheism and the resultant disparagement of religion became embedded in the national policies of those countries in which Marxism became the ruling philosophy—the Soviet Union, the People's Republic of China, North Korea, Vietnam, the countries of Eastern Europe. Albania was the only country, however, that formally (in 1967) proclaimed itself an atheist nation and acted on that proposition by outlawing all forms of religion, closing all of its churches and mosques, and imprisoning many of the clergy. Only in 1991 was freedom of religion restored.

In the Soviet Union, atheism became institutionalized in a succession of organizations: the League of the Godless, the League of the Militant Godless, and the Institute of Scientific Atheism (which continues into the post-Soviet era). Initially, the Soviets focused upon efforts to marginalize religion and end the institutional authority of the church. The formation of the League of the Godless, however, represented the emergence of active promotion of atheism through the press, social institutions, and specialized organizations. Through succeeding decades, religious policy periodically shifted its emphases between the promotion of atheism and the forceful suppression of religion.

In China, the critique of what were seen as various systems of exploitation reached out to include religion. Chinese policy led initially to the cutting of the ties between religious groups and any foreign leadership, especially in the case of Christianity, the complete reorganization of the various religious communities into five approved religious organizations, and the imposition of an ideology that was more aligned to the new Marxist Maoist government. While this reorganization was occurring, many government leaders, representing the Chinese community, argued that religion and Marxism were incompatible. Chinese Communist antagonism toward religion reached its zenith during the period of the Cultural Revolution (1966–1976). Since that time, a much more accommodationist policy has been adopted, though government attacks on religion have continued.

As the new century begins, religion in China survives, and an official policy of freedom of religious belief has been written into the law. It is also the case that the Chinese Communist Party is officially atheist, and that membership in the party and belief in religion are considered mutually exclusive. In between those people who are members of officially accepted religions and the party is a mass of unofficial religious activity that is still subject to periodic suppression by the atheist government. It remains the strong belief in those countries still ruled by Marxism that religion and belief in God will eventually pass away. In the world, the spread of Marxism accounts for the great majority of Unbelief, which includes some 55 percent of the North Koreans, 42 percent of the Chinese, 31 percent of the Czechs, and 27 percent of the Russians.

Modern Western Unbelief

Through the 20th century, as Marxism rose and then faced the crisis of the fall of the Soviet Union, non-Marxist forms of Unbelief emerged as a popular movement that competed for the support of the public with religious groups. Groups professing nontheistic philosophies supported many values commonly offered by religious groups, including answers to the three main religious questions: Where did we come from? Why are we here? And, where are we going? Answers to these questions were given without reference to God or the supernatural. Atheist groups also offered moral systems devoid of supernatural authorities and communal fellowship in their various local gatherings, national and international conventions, and even ritual life.

Non-Marxist atheism as a positive philosophy, as opposed to simple irreligion or concern with ultimate questions, enjoyed its greatest response in Europe and European outposts in North America, South Africa, Australia, and New Zealand. It has not fared well in South America, although it found some support in India, where a movement critical of Hinduism attacked many of the supernatural powers ascribed to various Indian spiritual teachers. As early as 1875, the Hindu Freethought Union appeared in Madras. It survived for two decades. Through the 20th century, a succession of Indian organizations appeared, the most successful being the Indian Rationalist Association, founded in 1960.

In the West, organized atheism has proceeded country by country. In the United States, popular leadership was provided by organizations such as the National Liberal League, the Freethinkers of America (Joseph Lewis), the American Association for the Advancement of Atheism, the American Humanist Association, American Atheists (Madalyn Murray O'Hair), and the Council for Secular Humanism (Paul Kurtz). Similarly, across Europe, a number of national rationalist, humanist, Freethought, and atheist groups have been organized.

As early as 1880, the International Federation of Freethinkers (since 1936 the World Union of Freethinkers) was organized. The more substantive International Humanist and Ethical Union was formed in 1952. It now includes member groups from around the world. A specifically Jewish form of Unbelief emerged in the 1960s and eventually gave birth to the International Federation of Secular Humanistic Jews.

Although the different communities of Unbelief have generally reached a consensus on the issues of God and the supernatural, they have disagreed on the issue of religion. Humanists, in particular, have expressed positive approaches to religion and have developed (or continued) religious structures that they feel contribute to ameliorating the human condition or provide a ritual dramatization of the important events of the life cycle—birth, coming of age, marriage, and death. Secular Judaism perpetuates synagogue life under the leadership of rabbis. The American Humanist Association "ordains" celebrants (Humanist ministers) who lead celebration services (analogous to Protestant worship services). Operating in a somewhat different context, the Norwegian Humanist organization Human-Etisk Forbund, one of the largest in Europe, has worked for a secular alternative to Christian confirmation (through which most Norwegian youths have traditionally passed). As the new century begins, these "civil" confirmations are celebrated annually in some 90 locations throughout Norway with some 4,000 young people, approximately 10 percent of the relevant age group, taking part.

In response, many atheist and Freethought groups eschew any form of religious activity. They see themselves as overly against religion rather than providing a nontheistic or nonsupernatural alternative to it. The Council for Secular Humanism is among those groups opposed to associating Unbelief in any way with religion.

In the first decade of the new millennium, neo-atheism, a new, assertive form of atheism, made its appearance in the wake of a rising belief in creationism as a pseudoscientific hypothesis challenging the teaching of evolutionary biology in the public schools in the United States. The leading voice of the new movement, which differs from older non-Marxist forms of atheism more by its aggressive attempts to proselytize for atheism than any content in its stance, is Richard Dawkins (b. 1941), a professor of biology at Oxford University. He has been joined by writers such as Sam Harris and Christopher Hitchens (b. 1949), who lecture widely on evolution and atheism.

Holidays of Unbelief

In the last half of the 20th century as Unbelief communities emerged, its exponents were challenged to go beyond simply critiquing religion and to offer alternatives to the structures they advocated abandoning. Such alternatives first appeared in the form of ethical perspectives. Humanists, in particular, took the lead in championing nontheistic approaches to the ethical life and entering the social conversation on how society should be organized and regulated. While sophisticated ethical systems were presented by nontheist intellectuals, more accessible moral pronouncements were made in the periodic Humanist Manifestos.

The role of public holidays also claimed the attention of humanists and atheists, who came to understand that in the West, many of the opportunities for communal celebration were tied to a reinforcement of theism and religions, especially the pervasive celebration of Christmas gift giving and the civil religion operating through celebrations of patriotism (Independence Day) or community (Thanksgiving Day). One by one, exponents of Unbelief proposed secular alternatives to religious holidays and religiously tinged national holidays. By the beginning of the 21st century, a whole spectrum of secular holidays had been proposed and found support through the communities of Unbelief, most noticeably in North America.

The most notable of the new proposed holidays picked up on the new pluralistic setting of Western religion and the problem faced by all non-Christians due to the pervasiveness of Christmas, whose celebration dominates the month of December. As other groups developed Hanukkah, Kwanzaa, and the winter solstice (the Pagan Yule) as a means to participate in the holiday season, Humanists proposed HumanLight as a holiday alternative. HumanLight allows celebrants to affirm many of the values espoused by the more dominant Christmas, including the emotive desire for light in the midst of darkness, while offering another personal rationale for joining in the larger holiday spirit.

The proposed National Day of Reason celebrates a basic value of nonbelievers, the separation of religion and government, and offers a less-than-subtle critique of what Unbelievers see as the religious subversion of a secular government that should operate for the benefit of all its citizens. The National Day of Reason parodies the National Day of Prayer, which is seen as trying to tie religion to government in ways that assume a privileged position in society and undermine the government's ability to respond to all its citizens.

In celebrating Thomas Paine, Charles Darwin, Robert Ingersoll, and Jean-François Lefevre de la Barre, the community of Unbelief holds up the cultural heroes who have embodied their ideals and goals and who have found a place in history quite apart from their role in challenging religion—patriot, biologist, orator, and victim. Finally, as Unbelief becomes established as a community positing positive values in the culture, that community can affirm its own existence in the celebration of, for example, World Humanist Day and Freethought Day.

J. Gordon Melton

See also Darwin Day; Death of Jean-François Lefevre de la Barre; Festivus; Freethought Day; HumanLight; Hanukkah; Indivisible Day; Ingersoll Day;

National Day of Reason; Thomas Paine Day; Winter Solstice; World Humanist Day; Yule.

References

Angeles, Peter A., ed. *Critiques of God: Making the Case against Belief in God*. Amherst, NY: Prometheus, 1997.

Dawkins, Richard. *The God Delusion*. Boston: Houghton Mifflin Harcourt, 2006.

Flynn, Tom, ed. *The New Encyclopedia of Unbelief*. Amherst, NY: Prometheus books, 2007.

Harris, Sam. *The End of Faith: Religion, Terror, and the Future of Reason*. New York: W. W. Norton, 2005.

Hitchens, Christopher. *God Is Not Great: How Religion Poisons Everything*. Toronto: McClelland & Stewart, 2007.

Howlett, Duncan. *The Critical Way in Religion*. Buffalo, NY: Prometheus, 1980.

Husband, William B. *Godless Communists, Atheism and Society in Soviet Russia, 1917–1932*. DeKalb: Northern Illinois University, 2000.

Johnson, B. C. *The Atheist Debater's Handbook*. Buffalo, NY: Prometheus, 1982.

Kurtz, Paul, ed. *The Humanist Alternative*. Buffalo, NY: Prometheus, 1973.

Lamont, Corliss. *Humanism as a Philosophy*. New York: Philosophical Library, 1949.

Larue, Gerald A. *Freethought across the Centuries: Toward a New Age of Enlightenment*. Amherst, NY: American Humanist Press, 1996.

O'Hair, Madalyn Murray. *Atheist Primer: Did You Know All the Gods Came from the Same Place?* Austin, TX: American Atheist Press, 1978.

Robertson, J. M. *A History of Freethought, Ancient and Modern to the Period of the French Revolution*. 2 vols. London: Watts and Co., 1936.

Shermer, Michael. *Why People Believe Weird Things*. New York: W. H. Freeman and Company, 1997.

Smart, J. J. C., and J. J. Haldane: *Atheism and Theism*. Oxford: Blackwell Publishers, 1997.

Smith, George H. *Atheism: The Case against God*. Amherst, NY: Prometheus, 1989.

Stein, Gordon, ed. *The Encyclopedia of Unbelief*. 2 vols. Buffalo, NY: Prometheus, 1985.

Thrower, James. *Western Atheism: A Short History*. Amherst, NY: Prometheus Books, 1999.

Unification Church, Holidays of the

The Unification Church was founded in 1954 by Sun Myung Moon (b. 1920). The church is known both by its early title, the Holy Spirit Association for the Unification of World Christianity, and by the more recently proposed name, Family Federation for World Peace and Unification. Moon was born in Sangsa-ri (in what is now North Korea) and raised in a Presbyterian family. Unificationists believe that Moon received a visitation by Jesus on April 17, 1935, and that Moon was asked to complete the mission of Jesus. He is also viewed by followers as Lord of the Second Advent (the fulfillment of the Second Coming of Christ).

Moon's first marriage ended in divorce in 1953, and he married Hak Ja Han, his current wife, in 1960, an event regarded as the Marriage Supper of the Lamb. Moon claims to be the True Father of fallen humanity. He is viewed as sinless by most Unificationists. Moon and his wife are also known as True Parents and their children are called True Children, and Unificationists believe that the children were born without original sin. Moon's vision to restore fallen humanity involves redemption of the family unit, symbolized most famously in Moon's mass wedding ceremonies.

Moon settled in the United States in 1971 and received scrutiny for his endorsement of Richard Nixon during the Watergate crisis. The church also garnered media attention through giant rallies at Madison Square Garden (September 18, 1974), Yankee Stadium (June 1, 1976), and at the Washington Monument (September 18, 1976).

Moon served prison time in the mid-1980s for income tax evasion, but this was interpreted by Unificationists and others as proof of U.S. government harassment. Moon held strategic meetings with Mikhail Gorbachev on April 11, 1990, and with North Korean leader Kim Il Sung in November 1991. Moon held these meetings up as demonstrations of his complete supremacy over communism. Moon has also taken credit for the fall of the Berlin Wall in 1989 and for the Allied Forces' victory in the Persian Gulf War in 1991. Along with these political matters, Moon has established significant media enterprises (including the *Washington Times*), various educational institutions (including the University of Bridgeport, Connecticut, and Sun Moon University in Cheonan, Korea, with its associated graduate school of theology), and many cultural organizations.

Moon's youngest son Hyung Jin Moon became the top leader of the international movement in April 2008. His daughter, In Jin Moon, leads the American church movement. However, as of 2010, both Hyung Jin and In Jin are in conflict with Hyun Moon, the oldest surviving son, for control of various Unification properties and assets. Hyun Moon seemed to be on course to succeed his father but lost to his younger brother. This has resulted in major division in the Moon family and the Unification Church. In June 2010, Sun Myung Moon issued a proclamation in favor of Hyung Jin, the youngest son, as the leader of the Unification movement.

The major holy days of the Unification Church are centered on the theme of restoration, involving family (Parents Day, Children's Day), the environment (Day of All Things), and God (God's Day). Another major holy day involves celebration of the birthdays of Reverend and Mrs. Moon (True Parents' Birthday). In prior years, all holy days were celebrated according to the traditional Korean lunar calendar (which is similar to the Chinese calendar), with the exception of God's Day, which took place on January 1 of the Common Era calendar. Starting in 2010, God's Day will also be set by the lunar calendar.

Members also celebrate the founding anniversary of the Church (May 1, 1954), the 1976 rallies at Madison Square Garden and the Washington Monument

(Foundation Day), and a memorial day called the Day of the Victory of Love that relates to the death of Heung Jin Moon, Moon's second son, in 1984. He died from injuries sustained in a car accident but his death is interpreted as a spiritual sacrifice, one greater than the death of Jesus.

The various holy days are celebrated with offerings of food and money. Unificationists gather as early as 7:00 a.m. for the holy day events and often have an earlier Pledge service at 5:00 a.m. Members are expected to dress in holy robes or their best clothing. True Parents receive bows of respect and pledges of blessing even if they are not physically present at local Unification sites. Rev. Moon often delivers a message in relation to the theme of the particular holy day. Holy day services usually close with a dramatic shout of victory.

The Unification holy days further illustrate the Unification Church as a Korean movement that draws on themes from traditional indigenous Korean religion. The motif of Moon as the returned Messiah was also influenced by his early contact with several recently founded Korean religions that taught that Korea would be home base for the Second Coming (of Jesus). Further, the holy days continue the great stress found throughout Asia on the importance of ancestors and family lineage. Unificationists are encouraged to pay for the liberation of ancestors through various ceremonies.

James A. Beverley

See also Children's Day; Day of All Things; God's Day; Parents Day; True Parents' Birthday.

References

Buswell, Robert E., Jr. *Religions of Korea in Practice*. Princeton, NJ: Princeton University Press, 2007.

Introvigne, Massimo. *The Unification Church*. Salt Lake City: Signature, 2000.

Kwak, Chung Hwan. *The Tradition: Book One*. New York: Holy Spirit Association for the Unification of World Christianity, 1985. Posted at http://www.unification.org/ucbooks/TT1/index.html. Accessed July 2, 2010.

Moon, Hyung Jin. "Instructions Regarding the Eight Holy Days." Posted at http://www.tparents.org/Moon-Talks/HyungJinMoon-10/HyungJinMoon-100115.htm. Accessed July 2, 2010.

Universal Week of Prayer. *See* Week of Prayer for Christian Unity

Up Helly Aa (January)

Up Helly Aa refers to a variety of secularized Pagan midwinter holidays celebrated in the Shetland Islands of the northern coast of Scotland. The various celebrations, held at different times in the islands' towns, culminated the winter holiday Yule season and recall a Norse Viking heritage largely lost as the islands were Christianized. Norwegians took control of the islands in the ninth century CE, and Christianity cane to dominate through the next century. They came under Scottish control in the 16th century. The variant dates of the celebrations are related to the changes of the dating of New Year's Day (from September to January) by James VI (1599) and the adoption of the Gregorian calendar by Great Britain (in 1852).

One of the older midwinter events is known as the burning of the *claviie* held each year on January 10 or 11 at Burghead, a town in northern Scotland. It dates to 1689, when the male youth of the town were chastized by the courts for paying superstitious worship to a "burning clavie" and taking too seriously any pre-Christian customs. A clavie is a tar-filled barrel, which is placed on a pole and lit aflame. It is carried around town following a clockwise route by a small group of men. Bits of smoldering embers from the wood mixed with the tar are dispensed for good luck. The procession ends at a hilltop altar, where the small fire in the barrel is built into a large fire, and the final embers are again collected as good luck charms (and talismans against witchcraft). The modern performance has been severely restricted because of the fire hazard it poses.

In the Shetlands, the burning of the clavie was eventually proscribed altogether and the Up Helly Aa emerged in its stead. The largest of the Shetland celebrations occurs annually at Lerwick, where a torchlit procession emerged in the 1870s to replace the tar barrels burning, which had occurred previously on several occasions each winter. The initial torch procession occurred in 1876. The first Up Helly Aa day procession was held in 1881. It grew significantly the next year, occasioned by a visit of the duke of Edinburgh. The burning of a replica of a Viking warship was added in 1889.

The celebration of the Up Helly Aa, held on the last Tuesday in January, is placed in the hands of a group of men, the Jarl, who become Vikings for a day. Individual members of the Jarl are called guizer, their leader being the Worthy Chief Guizer or Guizer Jarl. They will work for a whole year planning the event and creating their costumes.

The day of the celebration begins early with a procession through town by Guizer Jarl and the other Jarl members. They will make several stops on their way to a reception at the town hall. After a toast, Guizer Jarl is given the freedom of the town for the next 24 hours. The main event of the day starts in the early evening as the Guizer Jarl assumes the lead in a procession of the site for the burning of the Viking ship to which, interestingly enough, the public is not invited. After the burning, however, the members of the Jarl move out into the town again for 11 hours of visiting and partying (from 9:00 p.m. until 8:00 a.m.). All the public halls are sites for parties, each of which will have visits from multiple Jarl groups. The following day, Wednesday, is a public holiday to allow everyone to recover from the evening events.

J. Gordon Melton

See also Christmas; Winter Solstice.

References

Up Helly Aa. Up Helly Aa Committee. Posted at http://www.uphellyaa.org/. Accessed May 15, 2010.

Uposattha Observance Day

In the early years of the Buddhist movement, the monks gathered twice a month, on the new and full moons, for a fast. The practice grew out of Gautama Buddha's interaction with King Bimbisara, the head of the ancient Magadhan kingdom. Responding to the king's request for a time when lay people could be instructed in the Buddhist teachings, the Buddha instructed his monks to use the day for fasting, a reaffirmation of the rules under which they live (the Vinaya), and spreading the teachings to the public. Monks were especially to recite the rules, every second uposattha day each month.

The uposattha day would commonly begin with a time for the monks to examine themselves, confess any failings regarding their following of the precepts, and make repentance. Most Theravada Buddhist holidays fall on (or begin on) what for the monks is a fast or uposattha observance day. The monastic community is strongest in Theravada countries.

Over the centuries, in different countries, the designation of uposattha observance days was expanded. For example, the number of uposattha days was doubled and came to include the day halfway between the new and full moons, the day of the waxing and waning moons. On those days, observant lay Buddhists would cease work and visit the temples. It came to function somewhat like the sabbath day in the West. In Mahayana countries such as China, Korea, and Japan, six uposattha observance days were designated by including two days in the new and full moon days. All the major Buddhist holidays fall on the new or full moon.

J. Gordon Melton

See also Kathina Ceremony; Vassa.

References

Van Hien Study Group, eds. *The Seeker's Glossary of Buddhism*. Bronx, NY: Sutra Translation Committee of the United States and Canada, 2003.

Urs Festival

The Urs festival is an annual event at Ajmer, Rajasthan, India, celebrating the life of the Sufi Saint Khwaja Moinuddin Chisti (1141–1230 CE). Khwaja Muin-nddin Chisti was a Sufi leader born in Persia who became an adherent of the Chisti Sufi order, a Muslim devotional order founded in the town of Chisti, Afghanistan, in the 10th century. Having studied the Muslim faith at several schools, the youthful Moinuddin joined the order and became an accomplished leader. After settling at Amjer, he gained a large following because of his attention to the poor and his practice of what was termed the Sulh-e-Kul (peace to all) ideal in an attempt to build understanding and respect between Muslims and non-Muslims. He did not advocate a staunchly sectarian form of Islam. He did not write down his teachings, nor did either he or his immediate students form the order in Amjer. The order would only be founded some years after his death.

In the meantime, he was buried at the Dargah Sharif at Ajmer, and annually on the anniversary of his death, crowds of pilgrims began to gather at his tomb to honor him. The pilgrims would recite poems (*qawwalis*) written in the saint's honor. Various religious assemblies (*mehfils*) would be held at which mass prayers (*fatihas*) would be offered. Professional singers (*qawwals*) gather in groups outside the tomb to sing the praises of the saint. They are noted for the high-pitched sound they deliver.

Over the centuries, thousands became tens of thousands, which today have become hundreds of thousands. During the week of festivities, *kheer* (a milk-based pudding) is cooked in large cauldrons (*degs*) and distributed as blessed food (*tabarruk*).

Many Muslims discourage the honoring of saintly Muslims, especially leaders of the devotion-oriented Sufi orders, but Chisti's disciplined life in service to others earned him a high status in Amjer and led to people making their pilgrimage to the city to pay their respects. They will bring a variety of fragrant objects (flowers, perfumes, incense, sandalwood paste, etc.) which fills the tomb and the space nearby. Devotees who believe that they have been blessed with answered prayers directed to the saint will leave votive offers at the tomb site.

The Urs celebration is begun annually by the leader of the Chisti Order hoisting a white flag. This action is taken on day 25 of the sixth month of the Islamic lunar calendar (hence on a different day annually of the Common Era calendar). Then five days later, on the last day of the month, a site known as the Jannati-Darwaza (or gateway of heaven) is opened, and pilgrims may pass through the gate seven times in the belief that they will henceforth be assured of a place in heaven. On the first day of the new month, Rajab, devotees will perform the ghusal ritual which includes washing the tomb with rose water and sandalwood paste and anointed it with various perfumes. The ritual concludes with the tomb being covered with an embroidered silk cloth.

James A. Beverley

See also Ashura; Hajj; Ramadan.

References

Jaffer, Mahru. *The Book of Muinuddin Chisti*. London: Penguin Books, 2009.

Ram, S. *Chisti Order of Sufism*. New Delhi: Anmol, 2003.

"Urs—Ajmer, Rajasthan." Festivals of India. Posted at http://www.festivalsofindia.in/urs/index.aspx. Accessed May 15, 2010.

Vaikuntha Ekadashi

Vaikuntha Ekadashi is the name given to the two fast days on the 11th day of the two halves of the month of Magha (December and January on the Common Era calendar) for Vaishnava Hindus. The Hindu calendar is divided into 12 months, and each month is divided into two halves between the new and full moons. Vaishnava Hindus fast on the 11th day of each half.

The Vaikuntha Ekadashi is observed with an all-night vigil punctuated with Japa yoga (the repetition of mantras), meditation, and the singing of sacred songs (kirtans). At the temple, a gateway is opened through which devotees pass signifying their aspirations to enter vaikuntha or the heavenly realm. The promise of the day is that if it is observed with dispassion, faith, and devotion, and if one fixes the mind on Hari (Vishnu), one can be freed from the rounds of birth and death (i.e., future reincarnation).

The practices of this day are related to two stories from the Hindu scriptures. One tells of a demon named Mura, the father of 7,000 sons, who harassed the gods. The gods prayed to Vishnu to end the harassments, and he sent his own Shakti, his Yog Maya, to kill the demon and his offspring. His Yog Maya having accomplished the task, he decreed that she (Shakti being a feminine energy) would henceforth be known by the name Ekadashi (11) and that the people would observe a fast on this day as a means of being freed of sin and acquiring an entrance into heaven.

The story is also told of a demon that emerged from the sweat that had appeared on the deity Brahma's brow. Wanting to live far from the god, he was told by Brahma to go live among the rice grains eaten by people on Ekadashi and to become worms in their stomach. Thus, on Vaikuntha Ekadashi, believers attempt especially to avoid eating rice, otherwise a staple in the diet. If unable to do a full fast, fruit and milk are eaten.

Constance A. Jones

See also Amalaka Ekadashi; Hari-Shayani Ekadashi; Kamada Ekadashi; Mokshada Ekadashi; Nirjala Ekadashi; Putrada Ekadashi; Vaitarani.

References

Krishna, Nandita. *The Book of Vishnu*. London: Penguin Global, 2001.

Celebrants gather together in India for a day of fasting and prayer to Lord Vishnu. (*Hinduism Today* Magazine)

Sivananda, Swami. *Hindu Fasts and Festivals*. Shivanandanagar: Divine Life Society, 1997. Posted at http://www.dlshq.org/download/hindufest.htm#_VPID_19. Accessed April 15, 2010.

Vaisakha. *See* Wesak/Vesak

Vaitarani

Vaitarani is the name of the subtle river which, like the river Styx in Greek mythology, divides this earthly realm from the land of the dead. In the great Indian epic, the *Mahabharata*, the story is told of Lord Brahma asking Vishvakarma the divine architect to create a place of judgment. He asked Vishvakarma to build a suitable place within the realm of Yama, the god of death and lord of the infernal regions that all humans must visit after death.

Vishvakarma built a huge palace with four pits to punish the wicked. Brahma subsequently asked the architect to place a trench filled with water around the palace. This trench is the river Vaitarani. Brahma then called upon Agni (the fire god) to go into the river to heat the water to the point of boiling. After death, every person must swim across this river. Good souls pass quickly without pain, while the evil ones suffer in the boiling water. The river is also pictured as being full of a variety of filth and waste materials.

There are a variety of ways to prepare for crossing the river, including the doing of many good deeds in one's life or finding a genuine guru (spiritual teachers) and following him or her across. One method, however, is the worship of a cow on Vaitarani, the 11th day of the waxing moon in the Indian Hindu month of Magha (November–December in the Common Era calendar). One source of the phrase "sacred cow," the cow chosen for Vaitarani is worshiped by being bathed in perfumed water, applying a paste made of the fragrant sandalwood to the horns, and giving it food. It is also a time to make donations or gifts to the priests at the temple.

The cow is worshiped in the belief that a cow is a necessary aid in crossing the river in the afterlife. A cow given to Brahmin priests will later transport weary souls over the river. Thus, it is common when a loved one dies to donate a cow to the temple, a practice described in the Garuda Purana, a Hindu holy text.

Another popular belief in India is that when a person deemed to have been sinful dies, he or she may be helped across the Vaitarani River by descendants chanting "*Shree Gurudev Datta*," a mantra calling upon Dattatreya.

This day occurs on Vaikuntha Ekadashi, a day of fasting for Vaishnava Hindus.

Constance A. Jones

See also Dattatreya Jayanti; Vaikuntha Ekadashi.

References

Chaturvedi, B. K., ed. *Garuda Purana*. New Delhi: Diamond Pocket Books, 2005. (There are a variety of editions.)

Kelly, Aidan, Peter Dresser, and Linda Ross. *Religious Holidays and Calendars*. Detroit, MI: Omnigraphics, 1993.

Verma, Manish. *Fasts and Festivals of India*. New Delhi: Diamond Pocket Books, 2002.

Valentine's Day. *See* Valentinus, Feast of the Holy

Valentinus, Feast of the Holy (February 14)

Valentinus (c. 100–c. 160 CE) was a prominent Christian Gnostic teacher in Rome in the second century. He is best known because his teachings were broadly condemned by Irenaeus (c. 110–c. 220), the bishop of Lyon, and other representatives of the orthodox Christian tradition. Valentinus was for centuries known primarily through the fragments of his writings that were quoted in works critiquing his position. More recently, a text with the same title as one he was known to have written was found among the books of the library uncovered in 1945 in the Egyptian desert at Nag Hammadi. Many scholars have identified this text as that written by Valentinus.

Valentinus was born in Egypt and was educated at Alexandria. He appears to have come to Rome in the late 130s and left for Cyprus around 160. While in Rome, considerable controversy flew around him, and at one point he left the church and organized a competing following. Through the middle of the second century, he developed a large following, and his version of what was termed Gnosticism was among the most successful. After his death, his students could be found around the Mediterranean Basin for several centuries.

Once the *Gospel of Truth* found at Nag Hammadi was translated and published, the pioneers of the modern revived Gnostic movement accepted its validity, integrated it into their sacred literature, and assigned to Valentinus a status analogous to a saint in the Roman Catholic Church. The Ecclesia Gnostica, a sacramental Gnostic church, created a Gnostic liturgical calendar not unlike that developed over the centuries by the Catholic Church, with feast days assigned to the religious heroes who life and work should be remembered. Valentinus was assigned a feast day on February 14.

The assignment of February 14 was done, in part, due to the similarity of Valentinus's name with that of Saint Valentine, whose feast day is February 14, and whose name has been associated with the secular Valentine's Day as a day for lovers. The Gnostic celebration of Valentinus provides an opportunity for presenting an exposition of his own unique spiritual teachings on sexuality. It also provides further opportunity to speculate upon some popular themes among modern Gnostics such as the possible personal relationship between Jesus and Mary Magdalene.

During the celebration of Valentinus's Day, quotes from his writings are injected into the Gnostic liturgy, and a prayer of thanksgiving for the gift of Valentinus to the world is spoken.

J. Gordon Melton

See also Ecclesia Gnostica—Liturgical year; Mani, Commemoration of the Prophet.

References

"Ecclesia Gnostica: Liturgical Calendar." Posted at http://gnosis.org/ecclesia/calendar.htm. Accessed March 15, 2010.

Hoeller, Stephan A. *Gnosticism: New Light on the Ancient Tradition of Inner Knowing*. Wheaton, IL: Quest Books, 2002.

Hoeller, Stephen A. *The Royal Road*. Wheaton, IL: Theosophical Publishing House, 1975.

Lampe, Peter. *From Paul to Valentinus: Christians at Rome in the First Two Centuries*. St. Paul, MN: Fortress Press, 2003.

Pagels, Elaine. *The Gnostic Gospels*. New York: Random House, 2004.

Robinson, James M. *The Nag Hammadi Library*. New York: HarperOne, 1990.

Valmiki Jayanti

Valmiki (also known as *Adi Kavi*) is the fabled author of the Indian epic *Ramayana*. He was a Hindu sage about whom little is known. He is believed to have lived toward the beginning of the 10th century BCE. He was the first to use the "sloka," a verse form utilized in the *Ramayana*, and later by others in the writing of such notable texts as the *Mahabharata* and the *Puranas*.

Though a Brahman (of the highest Indian caste), he grew up within a family of robbers. Along the way, he encountered the *saptarsis* or seven sages, the seven planetary spirits associated with the seven stars of the Big Dipper (Ursa Major). He began to practice japa yoga, repeating the name of God (Rama) for long hours each day and reached enlightenment. His name came from the anthill or *valmika* that had been built over his body as he engaged in austerities during this period of his life.

Valmiki originally learned of Rama, the incarnation of the Hindu deity Vishnu, from the sage Narada. However, Rama was also a contemporary, and Valmiki wrote as one participating in some of the stories about which he wrote. Valmiki resided in a hermitage in the Bundelkhanda district in central India, and there at one point he entertained Rama's wife Sita when she had been banished from his presence.

Valmiki credits the deity Brahma with commanding him to retell the story of Rama in the form of an epic poem in Sanskrit using the new poetic meter Valmiki had discovered. Brahma also gave him visions that revealed all the details of the story as he wrote.

Apart from his writing the *Ramayana*, very little is known about Valmiki. He describes himself briefly as the 10th son of the sage Prachetas. He is remembered as a virtuous man and a great poet.

On his birthday, people will pray to him and will have parades/processions through the streets honoring him.

Constance A. Jones

See also Parshurama Jayanti; Rama Navani.

References

Altekar, G. S. *Studies on Valmiki's Ramayana*. Poona, India: Bhandarkar Oriental Research Institute, 1987.

Kelly, Aidan, Peter Dresser, and Linda Ross. *Religious Holidays and Calendars*. Detroit, MI: Omnigraphics, 1993.

Mudaliar, Subramania. *Valmiki Ramayana and South Indian Sociology and South Indian Castes at the Time of the Ramayana*. New Delhi: Asian Educational Service, 2003.

Rao, I. Panduranga. *Makers of Indian Literature: Valmiki*. New Delhi: Sahitya Akademi, 1994.

Swamigal, Pandrimalai. *The Ten Incarnations: Dasvatara*. Mumbai: Bharatiya Vidya Bhavan, 1982.

Vamana Jayanti

Vamana Jayanti celebrates the appearance (birthday) of Lord Vamana, the fifth incarnation of the deity Vishnu. It is observed by Vaishnava Hindus on the 12th day of the waxing moon during the Hindu month of Bhadrapad (August–September on the Common Era calendar). Much of the Vaishnava sacred literature concerns the 10 lifetimes Vishnu is said to have come to earth in human form. Lord Vamana came on this occasion to deal with a demon named Mahabali.

Mahabali had defeated Indra, the king of the gods (devas) and lord of heaven, who ruled from Amaravati, the capital of Svarga, the heavenly realm where the righteous dead reside awaiting their next reincarnation. It stands at the entrance to Svarga, which is located on the mythical Mt. Meru. Driven from Amaravati, Indra appealed to Vishnu.

As Vamana, Vishnu approached Mahabali, who ignored the warning to have nothing to do with this person. Indeed, he showed his gracious side by requesting that Vamana ask any gift of him. Vamana asked only that he be granted a piece of land equal to what he could cover in three steps. Mahabali ignorantly agreed to the request. At this point, Vamana turned from his dwarfish appearance into a giant, and in two steps covered the heavens and earth. There being no place left to make a third step, Vamana stepped on Mahabali's head, thus sending him to rule in Patala, a region inhabited by good demons.

Those who observe Vamana Jayanti by offering pujas (worship) to Vishnu are said to obtain strength to resist and even destroy their enemies.

It is to be noted that in Hindu thought, Mahabali is not an entirely evil entity. In fact, he is considered by many to have been a benevolent ruler and is looked upon in quite a positive light. Such is the case in Karala. At the end of some accounts of his interaction with Vamana, Mahabali is asked a boon of Vishnu, namely that once a year he be allowed to visit the people he formerly rules. Thus, each year, the people of Kerala celebrate Onam, the day of Mahabali's annual visit. In what has become a four-day festival, women prepare elaborate flower displays called Pookkalam in front of their homes, while the men engage in boat races.

Constance A. Jones

See also Janmashtami; Narasimha Jayanti; Onam; Parshurama Jayanti; Rama Navani; Varaha Jayanti.

References

Patel, Sushil Kumar. *Hinduism in India: A Study of Visnu Worship*. Delhi: Amar Prakashan, 1992.

Seshayya. A. K. *Fasts, Festivals and Ceremonies*. Kelang, Selangor, Malaysia: KSN Print, n.d.

"Vaman Jayanti." *Hindu Blog*. Posted at http://www.hindu-blog.com/2009/08/vaman-jayanti.html. Accessed June 15, 2010.

Varaha Jayanti

Among the 10 incarnations of the Hindu deity Vishnu, in several he appears in a half-human/half-animal form. Such is the case with his incarnation in a boar-like appearance as Varaha. Varaha's story begins at Vaikuntha, the abode of Vishnu, his consort the goddess Lakshmi, and the serpent upon which they rest. At one point, they were visited by some saints who, as they approached the seventh gate of the realm, were stopped by two guards named Jaya and Vijaya. The saints considered their entrance being challenged an act of disrespect, and they cursed the two guards by declaring that they would be reborn on earth.

On earth, they were reborn as the brothers Hiranyaksha and Hiranyakashipu. In their earthly existence, they did a considerable amount of trouble. Hiranyaksha pulled the earth to the bottom of the ocean, prompting Vishnu to incarnate as Varaha, who, after a lengthy battle, slew Hiranyaksha. He then used his boar's tusks to lift the earth out of the watery depths. In another incarnation as Narasimha, he would slay Hiranyakashipu, and the brothers would eventually return to their posts as guards in Vaikuntha.

The dating of Varaha Jayanti is different in different parts of India; for some it is during the month of Chaitra (March–April on the Common Ear calendar), and for others it is in the month of Bhadrapad (August–September). In either case, those who offer their worship on this day are promised Vishnu's blessing, wealth, and good health.

Constance A. Jones

See also Janmashtami; Kartika Purnima; Narasimha Jayanti; Parshurama Jayanti; Rama Navani; Vamana Jayanti.

References

Gupte, Rai Bahadur B. A. *Hindu Holidays and Ceremonials*. Calcutta and Simla: Thacker, Spink & Co., 1919.

Patel, Sushil Kumar. *Hinduism in India: A Study of Visnu Worship*. Delhi: Amar Prakashan, 1992.

Seshayya. A. K. *Fasts, Festivals and Ceremonies*. Kelang, Selangor, Malaysia: KSN Print, n.d.

"Varaha Jayanti." Hindu Blog. Posted at http://www.hindu-blog.com/2008/08/varaha-jayanti.html. Accessed June 15, 2010.

Vartan's Day, St.

Saint Vartan's Day is an Armenian national holiday that recalls the Battle of Avarayr, which occurred on May 26, 451 CE. An Armenian army under the command of General Vartan Mamigonian (d. 451 CE) met an overwhelming force of Persians. The Armenians had formally converted to Christianity at the beginning of the third century CE, but by the middle of the fourth century, they found half their country under Persian hegemony. In the middle of the fifth century, the Persian ruler attempted to establish the Zoroastrian faith throughout his kingdom. The Armenians refused to accept the Persian decrees on religion, and the Persian king sent his army to enforce his will. At the battle of Avarayr, the Armenians were defeated, and Vartan and more than a thousand of his soldiers were killed. The battle did not lead to a complete Persian victory, however, and for the next generation, Armenian forces operated from their mountain homeland to resist Persian rule. The issues were not resolved until 484, when the Treaty of Nuvarsag allowing the Armenians to maintain their Christian faith was signed.

In retrospect, the battle at Avarayr was seen as a defining moment in the emergence of the integrating Christianity into the national self-image of the Armenian people. General Vartan was canonized as a saint, and those lost at Avarayr were designated as martyrs of the faith. The battle and the lengthy set of hostilities that followed are now viewed as assigning the Armenian Apostolic Church a key role in the maintenance of the identity and unity of the Armenian people.

Saint Vartan's Day is celebrated on the Thursday before the beginning of the Lenten season (late January or early February on the Common Era calendar). It has become a time to gather for both patriotic and religious affirmation, a time to recall the often difficult eras in which Armenia was ruled by non-Christian neighbors (including Turks and Russians in recent centuries), and proclaim the continued loyalty of the people to their faith. In the United States, the cathedral of the Primate Archbishop of the American diocese is dedicated to Saint Vartan.

Among those who fell at Avarayr was Leondius the Cleric (or Ghevond, in Armenian) and a set of priests (including the Catholicos, the head of the Armenian church, and his fellow bishops). They are remembered for entering the battle carrying a cross in one hand and a sword in the other. Their role is celebrated on the Tuesday immediately preceding Saint Vartan's Day, designated the Feast of the Ghevondians, which is marked by a gathering of the church's clergy for a commemorative worship service.

J. Gordon Melton

See also Forty Martyrs' Day; Nino, Saint's Day of St.

References

Raymond, Walter. "Vartanants—Armenian National Feast Day/" Ecumenical Pilgrimage. Posted at http://www.epilgrim.org/vartanants.htm. Accessed May 15, 2010.

Russell, James R. *Armenian and Iranian Studies*. Cambridge, MA: Department of Near Eastern Languages and Civilizations, Harvard University, 2005.

Vasant Panchami

Vasant Panchami, also recognized as the first day of spring in India, is a festival focused upon Saraswati, the goddess of knowledge, music, and art. In Bengal, where its observance is among the strongest, it is also called Saraswathi Puja. In Hindu mythology, she is the wife of the creator deity Brahma and closely associated with Kamadeva, the god of love (understanding that desire was the first thing to stir at the dawn of creation). She presides over every form of art and is even said to have invented writing in general and Sanskrit in particular.

Saraswati is especially honored each year on the fifth day of the Indian month of Magha (January–February on the Common Era calendar). She is often pictured dressed in yellow (a color of auspiciousness and spirituality), and on this day, women will don yellow saris or wear yellow accessories to their clothes. They will also distribute yellow sweets to be consumed within their family, and color food by adding saffron.

Vasant Panchami is a day to think about the person one loves, a spouse or special friend. In rural areas, people note that the crops are already in the field and ripening. It has in the modern world developed a reputation as a Hindu form of Valentine's Day. This day is also identified with the day the deity Shiva was struck with an arrow from Kamadeva. The gods had sent Kamadeva to arouse Shiva from his deep meditation, as he was neglecting his duties toward the world. They wished to fall in love and began a sone that could destroy Tarakasura, a wicked demon. As Parvati approached Shiva, Kamadeva hit him with an arrow. Shiva became enraged, opened his third eye, and burned Kamadeva, even though he later fell in love with Parvati and married her.

Believers engage in a variety of activities on this day. In recognition of Saraswati's role as discoverer of writing, children might be taught to write their first words. It is a day to venerate one's ancestor. One might attend a temple to make a special puja to Saraswati. Some will rise in the early morning to bathe and then engage in the worship the Sun, Mother Ganga (the deity of the sacred river Ganges), and the earth.

Constance A. Jones

See also Chinese New Year's Day; Spring Equinox.

References

Kelly, Aidan, Peter Dresser, and Linda Ross. *Religious Holidays and Calendars*. Detroit, MI: Omnigraphics, 1993.

Sivananda, Swami. *Hindu Fasts and Festivals*. Shivanandanagar: Divine Life Society, 1997. Posted at http://www.dlshq.org/download/hindufest.htm#_VPID_19. Accessed April 15, 2010.

"Vasant Panchami." *Pilgrimage India*. Posted at http://www.pilgrimage-india.com/upcoming-festivals/vasant-panchami.html. Accessed April 15, 2010.

Vassa

In the early centuries of the Buddhist movement, and to this day in Southern Asia, much of the life of the Buddhist community revolves around the Vassa or Rains

Retreat. For three months each year, the monks ceased their travels and routines and settled in one spot, as the rainy season made being outside uncomfortable and moving about the countryside difficult. The Buddhist movement began soon after Gautama Buddha found enlightenment as he set under the Bodhi tree and meditated. A short time afterward, he traveled from Bodh Gaya, where the enlightenment event had occurred, to Sarnath, where some of his former cohorts in the search for enlightenment had gone. Not having any faith in the process, the Buddha had ultimately chosen to find Truth. Upon reaching Sarnath, he found the five form colleagues and delivered his first discourse, later written down as the Dhammacakkappavattana Sutra, in which he discussed the basics of his new approach, most importantly the Middle Way, the Noble Eightfold Path, and the Four Noble Truths. This event is remembered and commemorated in the annual Asalha Puja Day celebration.

As a result of the Buddha's discourse, one of the five companions immediately accepted the teachings and attained a level of enlightenment. Shortly thereafter, all five joined together and accepted ordination as monks and by that act created the monastic fraternity, the Sangha. This action occurred just as the rainy season began, and the Buddha and his first converts decided to stay in Sarnath at the Deer Park. Over the next three months, the 5 grew to be 60. Today, the monks will stay in the temples or monasteries to which they may be attached. Once the rains ended, the monks scattered in different directions to spread the teachings, but returned each year to spend the rainy season together in retreat.

This period became a time to exercise discipline within the community, and monks were given the opportunity to confess any deviation in their behavior, find forgiveness, and move forward in their practice. Intense times were spent in meditation. While Buddha was still alive, a set of rules for their common life were established by the Buddha (the Vinaya). Once an order of nuns emerged, they were given some additional rules and joined in the practice of the rainy season retreat. In some monasteries, monks dedicate the Vassa to intensive meditation.

Though a time primarily for those in monastic orders, Buddhist lay people often take the occasion as an opportunity to strengthen their own spiritual life. Some will adopt one or more ascetic practices—for example, giving up meat, alcohol, or smoking for a period. In Thailand, lay believers will often assume temporary monastic vows during Vassa, move in with the monks for a month or more, and then return to their lay existence. Monks generally count the number of years they have been a monk by counting the number of Vassa retreats they have observed.

The end of the Vassa three months later also became an occasion for another widespread celebration, termed Boun Ok Phansa in Thailand and Laos. Those monasteries that have had at least five monks in residence during the Vassa retreat period may also plan a celebration called Kathina in which the eligible monks received gifts of cloth from which new robes may be made.

J. Gordon Melton

See also Asalha Puja Day; Boun Ok Phansa; Kathina Ceremony.

Buddhist monks and believers gather during a ceremony to mark the beginning of Vassa in Bangkok, Thailand on July 27, 2010. Vassa is held during the rainy season and is a time for believers to come together and reaffirm their faith. (AP/Wide World Photos)

References

Bagchee, Moni. *Our Buddha*. Kuala Lumpur, Malaysia: Buddhist Missionary Society, 1999.

St. Ruth, Duane, and Richard St. Ruth. *Theravada Buddhism*. Simple Guides. London: Kuperard, 2008.

Stuart-Fox, Martin, and Somsanouk Mixay. *Festivals of Laos*. Seattle: University of Washington Press, 2010.

Swearer, Donald W. *The Buddhist World of Southeast Asia*. Albany: State University of New York Press, 2010.

Thanissaro Bhikkhu, trans. "Dhammacakkappavattana Sutta: Setting the Wheel of Dhamma in Motion." Posted at http://www.accesstoinsight.org/tipitaka/sn/sn56/sn56.011.than.html. Accessed March 15, 2010.

Vata Savitri

Vata Savitri is a day for married women, the object of the observance being the longevity and well-being of their husbands. It occurs on the 13th day of the dark fortnight of the Hindu month of Jyaishtha (May–June on the Common Era calendar), though in some places it is also observed on Jyaishtha Purnima (the day/evening of the full moon). It appears to be a popular day in Maharashtra.

Vata Savitri is based on a legendary story of Savitri, the daughter of King Aswapati, and her husband Satyavan. According to the scriptures, Savitri married

Satyavan in spite of the fact that she had been warned by a seer that he would only live one year. As it happened, a year later, Satyavan went out to cut wood and fell ill. As he lay dying, Savitri cradled him. A figure approached them and informed Savitri that he was Yama, the god of death, and had come to claim her husband's soul. He took the soul and headed toward his abode.

As her husband and Yama departed, Savitri offered worship at the sacred vata (or banyan) tree and then left immediately to follow Yama to the underworld. Meanwhile, Yama took notice of her piety and devotion and was so pleased that he restored Satyavan's life.

Today, on Vata Savitri, women rise early in the morning, bathe, dress in bright gay clothes, and, having eaten no food, join with their friends and acquaintances at a banyan tree. As they gather, they will retell the story of Satyavan and Savitri among themselves and offer prayers for the prosperity and good health of their husbands. Their activity there will include sprinkling the tree with water and with red powder and wrapping it with cotton threads. They conclude by circumambulating the tree seven times.

When they return home, they will paint a banyan tree on a wall using turmeric powder and sandalwood paste as an object of worship. At the end of the worship, they will break their fast. They will conclude their day by making offerings to the local priests.

Constance A. Jones

See also Ahoi Ashtami; Chaitra Purnima; Teej Festivals.

References

Kelly, Aidan, Peter Dresser, and Linda Ross. *Religious Holidays and Calendars*. Detroit, MI: Omnigraphics, 1993.

Vernal Equinox. *See* Spring Equinox (Thelema); Spring Equinox (Vernal)

Vesak. *See* Wesak/Vesak

Virgen de los Angeles Day (August 2)

Virgen de los Angeles Day, a national holiday in Costa Rica, recalls the discovery in 1635 of a small stone statue of a woman with a child in her arms by a young woman named Juana Pereira. Initially, Pereira considered the statue a new plaything, and she took it home. But then the next day, she found what appeared to be a similar statue at the same spot as the original. She took it home only to discover that the first statue had disappeared. A third time, the statue at home disappeared and repeated at the original site, which prompted Pereira to take it to the local Catholic priest. He immediately recognized the statue as a representation of the Blessed Virgin Mary, and reverently placed it in a chest at the church. It disappeared from the chest, however, and the priest and girl found it again at the original site.

The priest took the occurrence to indicate the Virgin's desire to be at the place where Pereira initially discovered her, and shortly thereafter, a small shrine was erected to house the statue. Veneration of the statue spread during the next decades. A chapel was built and, in 1652, an association was created to care for the chapel, which stood at the edge of Cartago, then the capital of Costa Rica. The area immediately surrounding the chapel was home to native people, Africans, and people of mixed blood rather than the Spanish who formed the ruling elite. That the statue was made of a dark rock was not lost on those who flocked to the chapel.

The statue significance increased in the 18th century when, on two occasions, it was the focus of prayer to protect the people of Cartago from volcanic eruptions (1723) and an epidemic (1737). Then, in 1782, as the Virgen de los Angeles, the Virgin Mary was designated the patron of Cartago. After the capital was moved to San José, she was named the patron saint of the country.

At the beginning of the 20th century, the Basilica de Nuestra Señora de los Angeles replaced the chapel. August 2, the anniversary of the statue's discovery by Juana Pereira, is now a national holiday and a time of pilgrimage to the statue. Annually, on August 3, a procession takes the statue from San José to the main church in Cartago, where it remains until the first Sunday in September, when it is returned to its permanent home. The small statue itself is only three inches in height. It is now richly clothed in gold, and only the face of the Virgin and the Child are visible. It is displayed within a large, gold monstrance that enlarges its appearance. The small image was solemnly crowned in 1926, an action related to proclaiming the Virgin as the Queen of Heaven and Mother of God. The feast of the Queenship of Mary now occurs on August 22, when the statue is in Cartego. In 1835, Pope Pius XI (r. 1846–1878) designated the shrine church as a basilica.

Of additional interest relative to the Virgen de los Angeles, the stone on which the statue was originally discovered is now in the basilica. The stone shows signs of being worn away as thousands of pilgrims pass by and touch it. A spring of water has appeared beneath the stone, and pilgrims may take the water home with them for use in anointing the ill.

J. Gordon Melton

See also Aparecita, Feast of Our Lady of; Mary—Liturgical Year of the Blessed Virgin; Queenship of Mary, Feast of.

References

Fernandez Esquivel, Franco. *Nuestra Señora de los Angeles: Patrona de Costa Rica.* Cartago, Costa Rica: Editorial Cultureal, 1997.

Flores, Dra. "Nuestra Señora de Los Angeles, Patrona de Costa Rica." *María y sus siervos* 25 (1995): 4–12.

Vishwakarma Puja (September 17)

The Vishwakarma Puja (or Jayanti) is a rare Hindu celebration celebrated on the solar rather than the lunar calendar, hence occurring every year on September 17. It is celebrated on Kanya Sankranti Day, the day in Hindu astrology that day when the Sun deity, Surya Bhagwan (or Vivasvan) leaves the astrological sign of Simha rashi (Leo) and enters into Kanya rashi (Virgo), an event that occurs on the same day each year.

Vishwakarma is, in Hindu thought, considered to be the divine engineer of the world. He is, like other deities, assigned a day as a birthday (jayanthi), a fact that raises some interesting issues. He is seen as the original creator of the world, thus having existed before days were created. It seems highly illogical to think of him as having originated on a particular day. He did not incarnate in human history as did, for example, Vishnu. To assign him a day would suggest that he was in turn created by an even older deity. However, most who worship him do not worry about such matters and simply seek a commemorative day to especially acknowledge him.

The few who worship Vishwakarma who have also responded to the problem of his birthday focus their devotion on another day called Rishi Panchami Dinam, or the day of the five rishis. They acknowledge that Vishwakarma had no birthday. Instead, they propose celebrating a commemoration of the day in which his five children (the rishis) declared their solidarity and prayed to their illustrious father. This day is set on the lunar calendar and thus changes each year on the Common Era calendar.

Vishwakarma Jayanthi or Rishi Panchami Dinam is celebrated by industrial workers, artists, craftsman, and weavers. Vishwakarma is also reverenced by the engineering and architectural community and a spectrum of professionals in all fields. Craftsmen will worship their tools in the deity's name. Vishwakarma is seen as the original architect and the one who passed on the rules for constructing buildings.

There are only a few temples at which Vishwakarma is the principal deity, but he often finds a secondary place in Vaishnava temples. He is pictured as a mature man with a full white beard, holding tools in his left hand. He is considered the sculptor of the famous Jagannath Temple in Puri, India, a temple known for its statues (and worship) of Krishna and his siblings. Worship of Vishwakarma is often done at the worshipper's workplace before the tools of the trade rather than at a temple.

Constance A. Jones

See also Chaitra Purnima; Hanuman Jayanti; Makar Sankranti; Narak Chaturdashi; Surya Shashti.

References

Nath, Kailash, and B. K. Chaturvedi. *Gods and Goddesses of India*. New Delhi: Diamond Books, 2005.

Vaze, Arvind P. *Akshay Vastu Arvind*. India: Amarraj Prakashan, 1995.

Visitation, Feast of the (May 31)

In the growing focus on the Blessed Virgin Mary, Roman Catholics, especially members of the Franciscan order, began to define the Joys of Mary, key moments of special happiness in Mary's earthly life as recorded in the Bible. Initially, five events were noted, but their number increased later to seven. The second joyful event, the visitation of Mary to her cousin Elizabeth, is described in the Gospel of Luke 1:37–55. Mary's words in verses 46–55 would become a popular Roman Catholic prayer known as the Magnificat. These verses also make up one source of the even more popular prayer, the Hail Mary.

Liturgical interest in the second joy is traced to the notable Franciscan, Saint Bonaventure (1221–1274), who proposed a special feast day to commemorate the event which called attention to both John the Baptist (Elizabeth's child) and Mary, who had just learned that she would be pregnant with Jesus. Elizabeth was much older than Mary, and, after years of marriage without having a baby, it was believed that she was barren. The Franciscans adopted the celebration and led in its spread internationally. It also became a central feature of Cistercian's worship life.

Drawing on both the Bible and extra-biblical sources, some Marian devotees have made much of the visitation event. The Bible notes that when the two women met, John jumped in his mother's womb and that Elizabeth was filled with the Holy Spirit. Some have suggested that John was also filled with the Holy Spirit and thus born without original sin. As such, John would join Jesus and Mary as a third person since the fall of humanity into sin who was born without original sin. Parallels have also been drawn between the account in Luke's gospel with David's visit to the Ark of the Covenant recounted in I Kings 6 in the Hebrew scripture (the Christian Old Testament). From the likenesses between the two events, Mary is often seen as the New Ark of the Covenant. As the first Ark carried God's Words to Moses, so the second Ark carried the "Christ, the Word of God," to the world.

Pope Urban VI (r. 1378–1389) elevated the festival to a celebration for the whole of the Roman Catholic Church, setting its date on July 2. In 1610, Saint Francis de Sales (1567–1622) and Saint Jane Frances de Chantal (1572–1641) founded a new religious order for women, the Order of the Visitation of Mary, in France. As the order spread, it was commissioned to found and staff a number of schools for girls. In 1969, Pope Paul VI (r. 1963–1978) moved the Feast of the Visitation to May 31, so that it would fall between the remembrance of the

Annunciation (on March 25) and the celebration of the nativity of John the Baptist (on June 24). In making that adjustment, he also moved the date of Feast of the Queenship of Mary from May 31 to August 22. Pre-Vatican Catholics and Anglicans tend to adhere to the July 2 date in their celebration of the Visitation.

J. Gordon Melton

See also Annunciation, Feast of the; John the Baptist, Nativity of; Queenship of Mary, Feast of.

References

Cistercian Chants for the Feast of the Visitation. Collegeville, MN: Liturgical Press, 2003.

Crichton, J. D. *Our Lady in the Liturgy.* Collegeville, MN: Liturgical Press, 1998.

Dodds, Monica, and Bill Dodds. *Encyclopedia of Mary.* Huntington, IN: Our Sunday Visitor, 2007.

Tavard, George H. *The Forthbringer of God: St Bonaventure on the Virgin Mary.* Chicago: Franciscan Herald Press, 1989.

Vivekananda, Birthday of Swami (January 12)

Swami Vivekananda (1863–1902) was an Indian spiritual teacher and disciple of Sri Ramakrishna (1836–1886) who was a pioneer in bringing Hinduism to the West. He graduated from Calcutta University, and it was during his years as a student that he was initially attracted to Sri Ramakrishna, whom he met in 1881. He subsequently became a part of the group of young men who had gathered around the mystic. He emerged as the leader of the group that gradually reformed as a monastic order. They took the vows of the renounced life as sannyasins in 1887, a year after Ramakrishna's passing. They were joined by Sri Sarada Devi, Ramakrishna's widow.

Vivekananda developed a twofold mission emphasis of inspiring people and then teaching them the practical knowledge that will lead to improvement in their lives. To accomplish this mission, he began to plan the establishment of an organization that could carry out the vision he was developing. In the meantime, in 1993, he took the bold step of traveling to the United States to attend the World's Parliament of Religions held in Chicago in the summer of 1893. He received a strong response from his presentations in Chicago and remained for three and a half years in North America, where the first Vedanta centers were set up.

Soon after his return to India in 1897, Vivekananda founded the Ramakrishna Mission, envisioned as a place where monks and lay people would jointly propagate Vedanta and engage in a spectrum of social services, which led to the founding and maintaining of hospitals, schools, colleges, hostels, and rural development centers. The mission also organized to respond to natural disasters. In 1898, he acquired land in West Bengal, where the headquarters of the mission, now known as the Belur Math (monastery), would be established. In the few years remaining, he made one more trip to the United States. He died in India in 1902; he was but 39 years old.

The various organizations Vivekananda founded flourished through the 20th century. The Ramakrishna Math and Mission developed affiliated centers across India and around the world, especially in the lands of the Indian diaspora. Vivekananda is honored as both an outstanding teacher of Vedanta Hinduism and the founder of a large international movement. Each year on his birthday, the many centers of the Ramakrishna-Vivekananda Vedanta Society observe January 12 as a day to gather for programs that praise Vivekananda and discuss his life and teachings. It is a day to read from his many books, engage in meditation, and remember his accomplishments. Possibly the largest celebration occurs annually at the Belur Math of the Ramakrishna Mission in West Bengal.

J. Gordon Melton

See also Ramakrishna's Birthday; Sarada Devi, Birthday of.

References

Nikhilananda, Swami. *Vivekananda: A Biography.* New York: Ramakrishna-Vivekananda Center, 1989.

Rolland, Romain. *The Life of Vivekananda and the Universal Gospel.* Calcutta: Advaita Ashrama, 1970.

Vivekananda, Swami. *Complete Works of Swami Vivekananda.* Los Angeles: Vedanta Press & Bookshop, 1947.

Vladimir, Saint's Day of St. (July 15)

Vladimir Svyatoslavich (958–1015) the Grand Prince of Kiev, is remembered for moving from his own baptism as a Christian to "baptizing" symbolically the whole people of Russian and Ukraine into the church. Among Russian Orthodox believers, he has attained a high status as one of the saints labeled as *isapostolos* or "equal to the Apostles."

Vladimir's grandmother and reputed tutor was Olga (c. 890–969), the first Russian ruler to convert to Christianity. Vladimir's father, Sviatoslav of Kiev (c. 942–972), did not become a Christian, and Vladimir, an illegitimate son, was raised as a Pagan. When in 969, Sviatoslav divided his kingdom and named Vladimir ruler of Novgorod the Great and his brother Yaropolk (c. 960–980) of Kiev, a civil war resulted that led to Vladimir's eventual victory and his brother's death. In the next years, Vladimir was an active Pagan, and at one point, according to the story, he decided to sacrifice a human to a Pagan deity. The human chosen turned

Vladimir I was the grand prince of Kiev from 980 to 1015 CE and is considered to be the founder of Russian Christianity. (John Clark Ridpath, *Ridpath's History of the World*, vol. 4, 1901)

out to a Christian, and his family refused to turn him over for the sacrificial ceremony. The open defiance of the Pagan led to a mob attacking and killing the young man and his father. The incident appears to have caused Vladimir to rethink his own religion and institute a broad inquiry into the religious option in his kingdom.

Ultimately, Vladimir chose Orthodox Christianity, his emissaries being duly impressed with the architecture and vivid worship life of the Orthodox Church in Constantinople. In 988, following his conquest of the town of Cherson in Crimea, he negotiated with the Byzantine emperor Basil II (976–1025) with the goal of marrying his sister Anna. Basil sought support for a war in which he was engaged. These negotiations became the occasion of his receiving Christian baptism and his subsequent marriage to Anna. He took his new faith quite seriously, however, and upon his return to Kiev, he moved against his former Pagan colleagues and worked to build the Christian movement across the lands he ruled. He ordered his subject en masse to go to the Dnieper River and receive baptism. He built the Church of the Dormition of the Virgin, the first stone church building in Kiev.

The last years of Vladimir's life were relatively uneventful. He seems to have lived peacefully with most of his neighbors. After his death, his body was dismembered and passed around as relics to the different churches and religious institutions he had founded. Two of his children also attained sainthood—Boris and Gleb—both of whom were murdered during the internecine wars that broke out after Vladimir's death (1015–1019). They were both named saints in 1071 by Russian church authorities.

Vladimir's sainthood is commemorated by the Russian Orthodox Church on July 15 (July 28 on the Common Era calendar).

J. Gordon Melton

See also Cyril and Methodius, Saint's Day for Sts.

References

Breck, John, John Meyendorff, and E. Silk. *The Legacy of St. Vladimir: Byzantium, Russia, America*. Yonkers, NY: St. Vladimir's Seminary Press, 1997.

Korpela, Jukka. *Prince, Saint, and Apostle: Prince Vladimir Svjatoslavic of Kiev, His Posthumous Life, and the Religious Legitimization of the Russian Great Power.* Wiesbaden, Germany: Harrassowitz, 2001.

Oholensky, Alexander P. *From the First to Third Millennium: The Social Christianity of St. Vladimir of Kiev.* New York: Association of Religion and Intellectual Life, 1993.

Semanitsky. John L. *The Holy Days of the Russian Orthodox Church*. N.p.: Russian Orthodox Layman's League of Connecticut, 1966.

Walpurgisnacht (April 30–May 1)

Walpurgisnacht (or Walpurgis Night) is a day named for Saint Walpurga (c. 710–c. 777), a British nun who went as a missionary to what is now France and Germany. Two of her brothers were also later canonized, and she was the niece of Saint Boniface (d. 754 CE). She died on February 25 and was initially buried at Heidenheim, Bavaria, where she had been abbess of a community of nuns. A hundred years later, following her canonization on May 1, her relics were moved to Eichstätt (also in Bavaria). She was canonized around 870 by Pope Adrian II (r. 867–872).

Saint Walpurga's designated feast day is February 25, but in various places where it has been regularly celebrated in Scandinavia and Germany, especially Bavaria, her feast day commemorates both the movement of her relics to Eichstätt and her canonization, both of which occurred on May 1.

The date of the transfer of Saint Walpurga's relics coincided with an older May Eve festival celebrated in much of northern Europe with a night of dancing by the light of bonfires. The celebration would go on until dawn, and in many places, Walpurga's feast day became associated with May Eve, which was popularly called Walpurgisnacht (or Walpurgis Night) throughout Scandinavia, the Low Countries, and the German-speaking world. In German-speaking lands, a tradition tied Walpurgisnacht to a continuing belief in the presence of witches, and on this night they would hold a large celebration. This belief is amply illustrated in a short story, "Dracula's Guest," originally written as one of the opening chapters for *Dracula*, the novel by Bram Stoker. The story takes place in Munich, Germany, as Jonathan Harker is on his way to Transylvania. In the 1931 film version of *Dracula*, the opening scene, which in the book occurred on Saint George's Eve, has been shifted to Walpurgisnacht.

Across Europe, a variety of pre-Christian festivals had been celebrated at this time (halfway between the spring equinox and summer solstice) under different names, to mark the beginning of summer. These pre-Christian celebrations were revived in the late 20th century by the Wicca/Neo-Pagan movement in the English-speaking world, generally under the name Beltane.

In 1966, Anton LaVey (1930–1997) formally announced the formation of the new Church of Satan in San Francisco, California, on Walpurgisnacht. Though the church never became a large organization, it enjoyed great fame over the next generation. Church members celebrated their own birthday as the main holiday each year, but Walpurgisnacht was the second-most important day in the church

Anton Szandor LaVey, founder of the Church of Satan, poses for a photograph with a female church member. (AP/Wide World Photos)

year, as it combined both a traditional date reputedly celebrated by those who opposed Christianity, and the anniversary of the founding of the Church of Satan. On this date, members would gather for rituals to which nonmembers were not permitted and held parties restricted to church members and close friends.

On this day in contemporary Europe, numerous cities sponsor a variety of secular celebrations featuring music, dancing, and bonfires combined with both a skeptical and satirical approach to the associations of the day with witches and things occult.

J. Gordon Melton

See also Beltane; George, Feast Day of St.; Spring Equinox (Vernal); Summer Solstice.

References

Eighteen-Bisang, Robert, and Elizabeth Miller. *Bram Stoker's Notes for Dracula: A Facsimile Edition*. Jefferson, NC: McFarland & Company, 2008.

Frazer, James G. *The New Golden Bough*. New York: Anchor Books, 1961.

LaVey, Anton Szandor. *The Satanic Bible*. New York: Avon, 1969.

Waso Full Moon. *See* Asalha Puja Day

Water Splashing Festival. *See* Songkran

Week of Prayer for Christian Unity

What came to be known as the ecumenical movement, which had as its goal the reunion of the many Christian denominations into one ecclesiastical body, emerged in stages through the 19th century. Primary support came from the many missions established by European-based churches in the colonies established by their home countries. Missionaries often found the issues that had divided Christians in past centuries back in Europe to be irrelevant and a hindrance to evangelism in the colonial context. Simultaneously, Christians in Europe, for purely theological reasons, called for an end to denominational divisions and began to organize events at which prayer and action to end denominationalism was advocated.

Early in the 20th century, two American Episcopalians, Father Paul James Wattson and Sister Lurana White, cofounded the Franciscan Friars and Sisters of the Atonement, an Anglican religious order. The pair was committed to the reunion of the many different Christian churches with the Roman Catholic Church. They enlisted the aid of a colleague in the Church of England, Rev. Spencer Jones, and together committed themselves and proposed to others a new level of prayer for a reunited church. They offered a plan for an eight-day effort (termed an "octave"). It was held beginning with the Feast of the Chair of Saint Peter (January 18) and the Feast of the Conversion of Saint Paul (January 25). Shortly thereafter, Fr. Wattson and Sister Lurana became Roman Catholics. Pope Pius X (r. 1903–1914) gave his initial blessing to the octave and his successor, Pope Benedict XV (r. 1914–1922) extended its observance to the whole of the Roman Catholic Church.

Seen primarily as a Roman Catholic effort, the Octave for Christian Unity did not catch on widely outside of that church. Then in 1933, Fr. Paul Coutrier, a priest from Lyon, France, recast the Octave as what he termed the Week of Universal Prayer for the Unity of Christians. This new approach led directly to the Decree on Ecumenism promulgated by the Second Vatican Council in 1964, which suggested that it was desirable for Roman Catholics and other Christians to pray together for Christian unity.

Meanwhile, quite apart from the earlier suggestion of Fr. Wattson, Sister Lurana, and Rev. Jones, the Faith and Order ecumenical discussions that would lead to the founding of the World Council of Churches in 1948 had made its own proposals for Christians to pray for Christian Unity. These prayer efforts were continued by the new Council, which also welcomed the Vatican Council's Decree on Ecumenism. The Week of Prayer for Christian Unity subsequently became a joint event cosponsored by the World Council's Commission on Faith and Order and the Pontifical Council for promoting Christian Unity. It is held January 18–25 in the Northern Hemisphere and during the week beginning with Ascension Day and culminating with Pentecost in the Southern Hemisphere.

During the week, Catholic, Protestant, and Orthodox churches will promote daily gatherings that focus on prayers for unity, including widely circulated liturgies. Each year a particular theme is chosen. In 2010, for example, reference was made to the centenary of the important ecumenical gathering at Edinburgh, Scotland, often thought of as the formal beginning of the modern ecumenical movement, whose theme was "Witnessing to Christ Today." The 2010 theme was, "You are witnesses of these things."

J. Gordon Melton

See also Ascension Day; Chair of St. Peter, Feast of the; Conversion of St. Paul, Feast of the; Pentecost; World Communion Sunday.

References

MacDonald, Timothy. "Brief History—Week of Prayer for Christian Unity 2010." Graymoor Ecumenical and Interreligious Institute. Posted at http://www.geii.org/wpcu_brief_history.htm. Accessed January 15, 2010.

"100 Years of the Week of Prayer for Christian Unity." Special issue of the *Ecumenical Review* 59, no. 4 (October 2007).

Wesak/Vesak

Early Buddhist sources (apart from the sutras) suggest that Gautama Buddha's birthday, day of enlightenment, and his paranirvana or death all occurred on the same day of the year. That day, designated Wesak, or Vaisakha, is the night of the full moon of the Hindu month of Vaisakha (usually in May on the Common Ear calendar). Through the centuries, Wesak has primarily been an event commemorated by Theravada Buddhists for whom its celebration emerged as the most important festival of the year. Originally a time to remember the birth and death of Buddha, it evolved primarily into a celebration of his enlightenment. In the 20th century, Wesak has been adopted as a favorite celebration within the Mahayana and Vajrayana Buddhist traditions, especially in the West.

The observance of Wesak usually includes both a formal and an informal aspect. The local temple or monastery will take the lead in the formal part of the celebration, which will include a procession by the monks, the presentation of an offering, and the chanting of sutras. In more recent times, the ceremony might also include a presentation on some aspect of the Buddha's teachings followed by the bathing of a statue of the Buddha. The Buddha's birth is usually acknowledged in the evening of the full moon with a Vaisakha Puja (sacramental offering).

Lay leaders take the lead in the more informal aspect of Wesak, which will occur over several days. Gathering will include liberal amounts of food and drink, various artistic and cultural programming, and even academic discussions of Buddhist history and theology. This more informal program will usually begin immediately after the more formal rituals.

As Buddhism has become a recognized part of the global religious community and as the Buddhist diaspora has taken Buddhists to countries around the world, Wesak has acquired new functions. It is now a popular time for interaction between Buddhists of different sectarian and ethnic backgrounds, and a place to showcase the dialogue between Buddhists and their non-Buddhist neighbors. These functions have attained a high level of importance in the West, where Buddhists often exist as a religious minority.

Wesak is an official holiday in Hong Kong, Singapore, Thailand, Myanmar, Malaysia, Indonesia, India, and, since 1888, in Sri Lanka. Wesak was accepted as the official Buddhist holiday by the United Nations in 1998. In Korea, Wesak is known as the Festival of the Lanterns. Along with the more familiar rituals conducted at Buddhist temples around the world, the Koreans decorate their temples and related structures with paper lanterns, covered with Buddhist symbols and inscribed with wishes for a long life. These lanterns will also be featured in parades through the street. The festival was designated as a Korean national holiday in 1975.

In the 20th century, several Western Esoteric groups have made an interesting appropriation of Wesak. In particular, theosophical teacher Alice A. Bailey (1880–1949) added three holidays that she saw as particularly relevant to the quest for spiritual enlightenment to the calendar of Arcane School, which she founded—Easter (full moon in April), the Day of Goodwill (full moon in June), and Wesak (full moon in May). In the 1970s, as Bailey's thought was integrated into the New Age movement, the celebration of Wesak as a ceremonial occasion spread far beyond the Arcane School and the several groups that had originated from it.

In Tibet, the birth and passing of Gautama Buddha is acknowledged during their Sakya Dawa Festival, held on the 15th day (full moon) of the fourth lunar month of the old Tibetan calendar.

Edward Allen Irons

See also Bodhi Day; Hana Matsuri; Nehan; Sakya Dawa Festival.

References

Bailey, Alice A. "The Wesak Festival." Posted at http://www.lucistrust.org/meetings/wesak2.shtml. Accessed September 15, 2005.

Ganeri, Aneri. *Buddhist Festivals through the Year*. London: Watts Group, 2003.

Ganeri, Aneri. *Wesak*. London: Heinemann Educational Books, 2002.

Snelling, John. *Buddhist Festivals*. Vero Beach, FL: Rourke Enterprises, 1987.

Turpie, David. "Wesak and the Re-Creation of Buddhist Tradition." Posted at http://www.mrsp.mcgill.ca/reports/html/Wesak/. Accessed September 15, 2005.

White Lotus Day (May 8)

White Lotus Day, the primary commemoration shared among the various divisions of the Theosophical movement, remembers the cofounder of the original Theosophical Society, Helena Petrovna Blavatsky (1831–1891). H. P. Blavatsky was born in Ekaterinoslav (now Dnepropetrovsk), Ukraine, and grew up in an affluent Russian family. Her marriage as a teenager to a Russian army general did not work out, and she left her home, traveled widely, and spent much of her time investigating esotericism, especially mediumship and Spiritualism. After moving to the United States, while investigating American Spiritualism in 1873, she met Henry Steel Olcott (1832–1907). Two years later, she, Olcott, and lawyer William Q. Judge (1851–1896) founded the Theosophical Society. Soon afterward, she completed her early summary of occult truth, *Isis Unveiled*, published in 1877. The

Helena Petrovna Blavatsky. (Helena Petrovna Blavatsky, *Isis Unveiled: A Master-Key to the Mysteries of Ancient and Modern Science and Theology*, 1891)

following year, she and Olcott moved to India and, from their base in Madras, grew the Theosophical Society as an international movement.

Here, she also claimed contact with a set of Masters or mahatmas, teachers of occult wisdom from whom she received messages that became the basis of a number of books and led to her reputation as a messenger of the Masters. That reputation would be besmirched in 1885 by charges of fraudulent mediumship brought by Richard Hodgson (1855–1905), an investigator from the Society for Psychical Research based in London. The resulting scandal caused her to leave India and finish her career in Germany and England, where she tried to live down the scandal. In London, she completed her most important work, *The Secret Doctrine* (1989), and she met and converted atheist orator Annie Besant (1847–1933) to Theosophy, and left her legacy to her young disciple. Besant would lead the society through the early decades of the 20th century.

In the years since Blavatsky's death, Theosophists have attempted to rehabilitate her reputation, while acknowledging the role she played in shaping the movement both intellectually and experientially. They will gather each year in small groups to remember her accomplishments and note their debt to her.

Constance A. Jones

See also Festival of Light (Rosicrucian); World Invocation Day.

References

Blavatsky, H. P. *Isis Unveiled*. New York: J. W. Bouton, 1877 (there are numerous editions).

Blavatsky, H. P. *The Secret Doctrine: The Synthesis of Science, Religion and Philosophy*. London: Theosophical Publishing Company, 1888 (there are numerous editions).

Harris, Iverson L. *Mme. Blavatsky Defended*. San Diego, CA: Point Loma Publications, 1971.

Meade, Marion. *Madame Blavatsky: The Woman behind the Myth*. New York: Putnam, 1980.

Murphet, Howard. *When Daylight Comes: A Biography of Helena Petrovna Blavatsky*. Wheaton, IL: Theosophical Publishing House, 1975.

White Sunday (October)

White Sunday, the largest annual event honoring the children in the Samoan Islands, is held on the second Sunday of October. The event celebrating the blessings of children is sponsored by the various Christian churches, from Roman Catholic to the Congregational Christian Church (the largest in the Islands) and the various Protestant churches—Assembly of God, Methodists, Baptists, etc. Traditionally, the children of each congregation dress in white and place a crown of fragrant blossoms on their head. They parade to church, where their parents are already waiting, and present a program consisting of Bible verse recitations, skits, and music. After the church service, they are treated to a large meal in their homes at which their parents do all the serving. It is the one meal each year in which the children are seated and served ahead of the adults. They are also allowed to eat all they want.

In 2009, the White Sunday celebration took on new meaning. It occurred just two weeks after the island suffered a massive earthquake (8.3 on the Richter scale) followed by aftershocks and a tsunami. A significant percentage of the several hundred who died were minors. Church sanctuaries were among the buildings destroyed. Though still reeling from the event, the churches decided to hold the White Sunday celebration as usual. Congregations that had lost their buildings were invited to merge their celebration with neighboring churches.

J. Gordon Melton

See also Week of Prayer for Christian Unity; World Communion Sunday.

References

Mata'afa, Tina. "After the Tsunami, Children Prepare for White Sunday." Samoa News.com, October 9, 2009. Posted at http://www.samoanews.com/viewstory.php?storyid=9770&edition=1255113586. Accessed March 15, 2010.

Thompson, Sue Ellen, and Barbara W. Carlson, comp. *Holidays, Festivals, and Celebrations of the World Dictionary.* Detroit, MI: Omnigraphics, 1994.

Whit-Monday. *See* Pentecost

Whitsunday. *See* Pentecost

■ Wicca/Neo-Paganism Liturgical Calendar

Through the early and mid-20th century, there were a variety of attempts to revive ancient Pagan worship, at times as an individual devotion, and on a few occasions among small groups. These efforts remained quite isolated until the 1950s, when Gerald B. Gardner (1884–1964), a retired British civil servant residing in England,

Gerald Brosseau Gardner traveled around the world learning about various faiths and from his research founded Gardnerian Wicca. (Raymond Buckland/Fortean Picture Library)

responded to the removal of the country's archaic anti-Witchcraft laws that had in the 20th century primarily been used against Spiritualist mediums. Gardner had followed a unique spiritual path that included adherence to Freemasonry and Theosophy, and veneration of a female deity. Back in England after many years in Asia, he began to put together a new religion given form by his attempt to recreate pre-Christian Pagan religion. There being little written record of the actual practices and/or rituals of the ancient Paganism in Western Europe, Gardner assembled bits and pieces of magical lore, more modern magical ritual material and his own writings, to create a new religion that he called Witchcraft and is today commonly called Wicca.

Gardnerian Witchcraft was released to the public in stages, with the initial announcement of its existence coming in several books. As people contacted him and learned the basics of the religion, he initiated priestesses and priests to carry it to North America. Through the remaining decades of the century, it grew into a substantial movement involving tens of thousands (some say hundreds of thousands) of people. Members of the movement met in small groups (congregations) called covens averaging 8 to 15 participants.

As the Gardnerian movement spread, three grouping became noticeable. First, one branch followed Gardner's initial impulse and formed covens linked by a lineage of priestesses (a priestess being essential to worship) and worshipping in the nude. Covens gathered twice monthly at the new and full moons, the meetings being called esbats. Second, new covens and associations of covens appeared, which abandoned the necessary female lineage of leadership and worship in the nude. They also explored a variety of alternate worship rituals apart from those originally passed on by Gardner. Third, a group of people emerged calling themselves Pagans rather than witches and using a variety of names for their local groups. In contrast to the two main types of witches, those groups that met as Pagans tended to not hold the esbat meetings every two weeks.

While a few individual groups claimed pre-Gardnerian beginnings, all three groupings shared a common bond in tracing their emergence to the presence of the new energy given to Pagan traditions by Gardner, a focus of worship on a primary female deity (as the main deity of a pantheon that included both male and female deities), and a worship cycle built around eight evenly placed annual festivals called sabbats.

The eight festivals drew primarily upon what was known of Celtic traditions. They began with the key points in the movements of the sun, the spring and fall equinoxes, and the winter and summer solstices. Halfway between these four days are an additional four days and to which most Witches assign their Celtic names. The equinox and solstice dates are among the most well known in ancient cultures, and the spring equinox especially was unitized as an important benchmark for most ancient calendars. As the Christian church spread into Europe, it tended to adapt Christian worship to Pagan practice both by transforming Pagan festivals into Christian holidays and building Christian churches over the sites of former Pagan worship centers. Many Pagan practices not considered directly antithetical to Christianity were continued either as secular practices in the new Christian societies or even adapted as Christian practices.

In the modern post-Gardnerian revival, the new generation of Wiccans and Pagans adopted a seasonal calendar usually referred to as the wheel of the year. It is built around eight evenly placed holidays:

Samhain (or Hallowe'en), October 31

Yule (Winter Solstice), December 21

Imbolc (or Bridgid or Candlemas), February 2

Eostara (or Lady Day or Spring Equinox), March 21

Beltane (May Day), May 1

Summer Solstice, June 21

Lammas (Lughnasadh), August 1

Mabon (Fall Equinox), September 21

As soon as the movement spread to Australia and New Zealand, where the seasons are reversed, a reworking of the calendar (designed for use in the Northern Hemisphere) had to be made. Different groups made different adjustments to accommodate the opposing seasons and the larger cultural setting.

The year begins at Samhain, on the day when it is believed that the veil between the dead and the living is thin and contact with the dead is easiest. It is a time to remember and celebrate the life of the recently departed and complete their release from earthly ties, and to refocus the living on their plans for the coming year. Because of the larger cultural setting in which the simultaneous Christian celebration of All Hallow's Eve (or Halloween) is tied to medieval images of witches, the days approaching Samhain has been a popular time for Wiccans to make contacts with the media and engage in image building, especially in attempts to distinguish their religion from Christian beliefs about Satan and the practice of Satanism.

Samhain is followed by the winter solstice, in which the dark side on the environment is seen as a metaphor for the dark side (not to be confused with evil) of human experience, while waiting for the coming light. The following holidays are traditionally tied to the agricultural season, but few modern Pagans are farmers or even rural dwellers. The spring and summer holidays have become times for urban and suburban Wiccans and Pagans to gather outdoors, either with trips to the countryside, with gatherings in parks, or just in one's backyard. While Samhain and Yule are usually times for individual covens to gather, a variety of opportunities for larger gatherings are arranged for the spring and summer. The spring equinox is a time for geographically near covens to meet, while the summer holidays are times for larger Pagan gatherings on a regional or even national and international basis.

The highlight of the year is the summer solstice. The most famous Pagan gathering annually is the Solstice gathering at Stonehenge, the megalithic site in western England. Though historians have debunked any ties between Stonehenge and the ancient Druids, 19th-century hypotheses about the monument having been built by the Druids allowed modern Neo-Druids to claim a connection to the site. Once a year, on June 21, they are allowed access to the site for a dawn ritual (there is also a smaller, less well-known gathering for the winter solstice). Other summer Pagan gatherings are held at Glastonbury and at the stone circle at Avebury. Not especially a pagan gathering, many Pagans attend the Summer festival at Glastonbury which is held annually near, but not on the summer solstice. One of the largest in North America occurs at the rural Wisconsin sanctuary of Circle, a large Pagan association that plays host to sabbat gatherings throughout the year.

The Pagan/Wiccan community presents a small presence within the larger predominantly Christian community. As a whole, the culture does not recognize their holidays, which most often fall on what for most are workdays. It is most common, even in the summer, for Wiccans and Pagans to schedule their holidays on the weekend nearest to the actual holiday.

J. Gordon Melton

See also Beltane; Eostara; Fall Equinox; Imbolc; Lammas; Samhain; Spring Equinox (Thelema); Spring Equinox (Vernal); Summer Solstice; Winter Solstice; Yule.

References

Benson, Christine. *Wiccan Holidays—A Celebration of the Wiccan Year: 365 days in the Witches Year.* Southfield, MI: Equity Press, 2008.

Cabot, Laurie, with Jean Mills. *Celebrate the Earth: A Year of Holidays in the Pagan Tradition.* New York: Delta, 1994.

Crowley, Vivianne. *Principles of Paganism.* London: Thorsons, 1996.

Harvey, Graham. *Contemporary Paganism: Listening People, Speaking Earth.* New York: New York University Press, 1997.

Nock, Judy Ann. *Provenance Press's Guide to the Wiccan Year: A Year Round Guide to Spells, Rituals, and Holiday Celebrations.* Avon, MA: Adams Media, 2007.

Wigilla. *See* Epiphany

Willibrord, Saint's Day of St. (November 7)

Willibrord (c. 658–739), a native of Northumbria (northern England just south of Scotland), became a Christian missionary to what is now the Netherlands. He was eventually named the first bishop of Utrecht. His father, a pious man, sent the young Willibrord to the Benediction abbey at Ripon, York, and he later affiliated with the Benedictine Order. Around 678, he moved to the Abbey at Rathmelsig (Ireland). From there, he was commissioned to travel to Frisia, then nominally under the control of the Franks, and attempt to Christianize the local residents.

The Frankish ruler Pepin (c. 635–714) sent Willibrord to Rome twice, and during the second trip in 695, he was consecrated as a bishop. Upon his return to Frisia, he devoted his life to building the church. He opened a monastery at Utrecht, which subsequently became the site of his cathedral church. In 698, Irmina, the daughter of Dagobert II (c. 650–679), the king of the Franks, gave him an old Roman villa at Echternach, Luxembourg, which he transformed into an abbey. In 714, the Frisian Pagan leader Radbod assumed control of much of the land previously under Pepin's rule, and in the process he undid much of Willibrord's work. After Radbod died, Willibrord was able to restart his mission, this time assisted by Saint Boniface (c. 680–754). When he finally passed away, after many years of work, his body was buried at Echternach.

Willibrord was named a saint soon after his death. In the Church of England, and in the Roman Catholic Church outside of England, his commemoration is on November 7, the anniversary of his death. By order of Pope Leo XIII (r. 1878–1903), Roman Catholics in England commemorate Willibrord on November 29. He is called the Apostle to the Frisians and is a patron saint of the Netherlands.

On Whit Tuesday, the Tuesday after Pentecost, a dancing procession honoring Willibrord takes places in Echternach, Luxembourg. The event begins in the morning at the bridge across the river Sauer. The parish priest delivers a message relevant to the theme of the day. The procession itself is made up of musicians and pilgrims, including some who carry the reliquary of Saint Willibrord, who will travel through the town to the church where Willibrord is buried. The musicians play a traditional melody, while the pilgrims engage in a fairly simple dance step that moves them forward at a slow pace, it taking several hours to cover the distance, around a mile. The procession moves into the church where Willibrord's crypt is located. The proceedings conclude with a Eucharistic service. The dancing step of the procession is somewhat related to the hope of some to attend who have diseases affecting their motor skills—epilepsy, Parkinson's disease, etc.

Willibrord's name and reputation became associated with the Old Catholic movement of the 1870s that was opposed to the declaration of papal infallibility, as the Diocese of Utrecht was one of the centers that assumed leadership among the Old Catholics.

J. Gordon Melton

See also Boniface of Germany, Saint's Day of St.; Saint Patrick's Day.

References

Pruter, Karl. *St. Willibrord, 658–739.* Chicago: St. Willibrord's Press, 1982.

Spicer, Doris Gladys. *Festivals of Western Europe.* New York: H. W. Wilson Co., 1973.

Talbot, C. H. *The Anglo-Saxon Missionaries in Germany: Being the Lives of SS. Willibrord, Boniface, Sturm, Leoba and Lebuin.* New York: Sheed & Ward, 1954.

Verbist, C. J. Gabriel H. *Saint Willibrord.* Louvain, Belgium: Bureau du Recueil, 1939.

Winter Solstice

The shortest day of the year, the winter solstice was among the earliest astronomical phenomena observed by human cultures that observed the sky and related it to the weather and agricultural seasons. In the Northern Hemisphere, if one observed the rising sun in the fall, it appears to rise a little bit further south day by day until it reaches a point in the last half of December where the southern drift stops. After what appears to be a pause, it begins to rise bit by bit further north each day. In the Southern Hemisphere, the drift is exactly opposite. The winter solstice is the point at which the drift stops and pauses before starting in the opposite direction.

The Julian calendar, adopted in 45 BCE, established December 25 as the winter solstice throughout the Roman Empire. That calendar was officially adopted by the Christian Church in 324 CE as the calendar of Christianity. Christmas, the celebration of the birth of Jesus Christ, was set on the 25th of December. In the meantime, the winter solstice gradually drifted due to small inaccuracy in the Julian calendar.

In 1582, Pope Gregory XIII (r. 1572–1585) made the changes in the calendar to account for the problem in the Julian calendar. The Gregorian revisions mean the northern winter solstice occurs around December 21.

In ancient Rome, the winter solstice was associated with the deity Saturn, the god of agriculture and the harvest. He was also believed to have had oversight of a mythological Golden Age. Rome's winter solstice festival was the Saturnalia, held in his honor. Originally held on December 17, it was gradually expanded as Rome prospered to a weeklong event, during which time war would not be declared, slaves and masters swapped status, prisoners would not be executed, and people gave gifts. In general, people forgot their problems and enjoyed life. The Romans also tended to conflate Saturn with the deity Cronus, the god associated with calendars, seasons, and harvests.

Though no date for the birth of Jesus is given in the New Testament, biblical scholars have frequently noted that events described in the Gospels in association with Christ's birth, such as shepherds being in the outdoors in the evening, do not support a winter event. Many have suggested that the dating of Christ's birth was affected by the attempt to supplant the Saturnalia with Christmas. Christmas more directly supplanted the Sol Invictus festival, which was added to the calendar in Rome in the later centuries of the empire and was celebrated on December 25. Attributes of the sun god were later applied directly to Jesus.

The winter solstice was celebrated in most ancient cultures, especially in temperate zones. For some it was the middle of winter, and for some the beginning. It would be a time when one batch of wine would have finally fermented, and when some animals would be slaughtered in order to save the food they would consume for human consumption. Most of these celebrations were supplanted by the holy days of the larger world religions, either by absorption or force.

In the modern West, the emergence of Neo-Paganism, a large movement inspired by ancient Pagan practice and belief, has signaled a return of the winter solstice. Neo-Pagans, including their largest segment, the Wiccans, annually celebrate Yule on the winter solstice, and make note of the many practices of ancient Pagans that have been adopted by Christians—Yule logs, Christmas trees, and carol singing.

At the same time, as religious pluralism has increased in predominantly Christian lands, Christmas has developed a prominent secular element, and other religions have emphasized holidays that also occur in close proximity to it. That new emphasis, along with the commercial aspects of Christmas gift giving and the close proximity of New Year's Day the week after Christmas, has contributed to the defining of a winter holiday season in Western society. In this regard, communities of Unbelief, especially Humanists, have revived the winter solstice as an occasion for celebration, and American Humanists have proposed HumanLight Day (December 23) as a day to celebrate humanity and the production of culture with events that include art, music, dancing, storytelling, and candlelight events, and social outreach through developing social awareness, helping the needy, and community involvement. As least one new holiday, Kwanzaa, was created to allow people (in this case, African Americans) who did not want to observe Christmas to have a holiday to celebrate during the winter holiday season.

J. Gordon Melton

See also Christmas; Common Era Calendar; Festival of Light (Rosicrucian); Hanukkah; HumanLight; New Year's Day; Summer Solstice; Up Helly Aa.

References

Crowley, Vivianne. *Principles of Paganism*. London: Thorsons, 1996.

DeChant, Dell. *The Sacred Santa: Religious Dimensions of Consumer Culture*. Cleveland, OH: Pilgrim Press, 2002.

Harvey, Graham. *Contemporary Paganism: Listening People, Speaking Earth*. New York: New York University Press, 1997.

Matthews, John. *The Winter Solstice: The Sacred Traditions of Christmas*. Wheaton, IL: Quest Books, 2003.

Ratsch, Christian, and Claudia Müller-Ebeling. *Pagan Christmas: The Plants, Spirits, and Rituals at the Origins of Yuletide*. Rochester, VT: Inner Traditions, 2006.

World Communion Sunday

World Communion Sunday is celebrated on the first Sunday of the month of October as an act of recognition, primarily within Protestant churches, of the oneness of the Christian community in spite of their denomination divisions. A World Wide Communion Sunday was first proposed and celebrated in several of the larger American Presbyterian denominations (now united in the Presbyterian Church [USA]) in 1936, but had been conceived within the context of the larger ecumenical movement that would soon lead to the formation of the World Council of Churches.

The idea of World Communion Sunday was shared with leaders of other denominations, especially those within the Federal Council of Churches, the major ecumenical organization in the United States at the time, and in 1940, Jesse Bader, the executive secretary of the Council's Department of Evangelism, took the lead in promoting it through the member churches. The celebration was carried on by the National Council of Churches of Christ in the USA, which superseded the Federal Council in 1950. Through its member churches, it was carried to their congregations worldwide and introduced to the member churches of the World Council of Churches.

World Communion Sunday spoke to a prominent problem that had arisen in dialogues on church union. Churches that had some desire to merge were most frequently blocked by differences in their understanding and practice of the Eucharist, frequently termed Holy Communion or the Lord's Supper, in which Christians partake sacramentally of the body and blood of Christ. Some Anglicans and Lutherans had a very high doctrine of the Eucharist, while Methodists and Presbyterians had a more spiritualized understanding of the sacrament, and Baptists and free churches replaced the idea of sacrament entirely and celebrated the Lord's Supper as an ordinance and memorial. These differences even prevented very ecumenically minded Lutherans, Presbyterians, and Baptists from celebrating the Eucharist at ecumenical gatherings.

World Communion Sunday avoided the problems that had arisen in union discussions and ecumenical gatherings by proposing that the common element be the day of the celebration rather than an agreement of doctrine of the manner of celebration. Thus, each congregation carries forward with its regular celebration of Holy Communion while recognizing its oneness at an ideal level, with the whole of the divided Christian community. The day has become a major element in the generation of positive attitudes among members of different churches.

While mainly celebrated in Protestant churches, the recognition of World Communion Day has received limited recognition in Catholic and Orthodox churches.

J. Gordon Melton

See also Week of Prayer for Christian Unity; World Day of Prayer.

References

Note: Each participating Christian denomination will create and circulate ephemeral material each year for its member churches.

"World Communion Sunday, October 4, 2009." National Council of the Churches of Christ in the USA. Posted at http://www.ncccusa.org/unity/worldcommunionsunday .html. Accessed January 15, 2010.

World Community Day (November)

World Community Day was initially observed in 1939 as an occasion for women to pray and work for lasting peace and justice in the global society. It was initially observed by women in a variety of Protestant Christian churches, and in 1941, with the formation of the United Council of Church Women (now known as Church Women United), the council assumed responsibility for its sponsorship. Today, World Community Day is most observed by the 24 member denominations of Church Women United, most of whom are also with the National Council of Churches of Christ in the USA.

World Community Day is generally observed on the first Friday of November, the weekday being assigned so as to not interfere with regular Sunday congregational activities. As the celebration has spread to Jewish women and beyond, the day may be adjusted locally. Each year, the theme of the day is adopted to focus prayerful attention on a major social concern, with an underlying aim of motivating women to action on the selected issue. World Community Day emerged as the opening shots of World War II were heard, and peace has always been uppermost in its agenda.

J. Gordon Melton

See also Human Rights Day.

References

"World Community Day." Church Women United. Posted at http://www.church women.org/community.html. Accessed May 15, 2010.

World Day of Prayer (March)

The World Day of Prayer is a global Christian ecumenical event in which women from a broad spectrum of Christian traditions unite for a day of prayer, reflection on their common bonds, and consideration of their commitment to mission. The event took form in the 1920s, but grew out of the 19th-century struggle of Protestant women to participate in the church's ministry beyond the local church that initially took form in numerous women's auxiliary missionary groups, which raised funds for mission work and brought women together of days of prayer.

By the beginning of the 20th century, women in the United States had become active participants in numerous ecumenical endeavors, and these several trends came together in 1908 with the formation of the Council of Women for Home Missions that assumed responsibility for work with immigrants and organized a joint day of prayer. During 1910 and 1911, women celebrated their decades of missionary activity by organizing a series of speaking engagements across the country that both celebrated and allowed women to experience all that they had achieved in the fields of home and foreign missions and ecumenical endeavors and the manner in which mutual prayer times had empowered them.

World War I and the devastation it wrought further motivated women to action and added the cause of world peace to their agenda. In Canada, some Presbyterian women leaders took the lead in calling for a national Day of Prayer. This led to the formation of the Women's Inter-Church Council of Canada, which in turn sponsored the initial national Day of Prayer in Canada on January 9, 1920.

A parallel effort in the United States led to an initial joint day of prayer for missions on February 20, 1920, the first Friday of Lent. This effort received enthusiastic support across the country and support for the annual event quickly spread through the member churches of the Federal Council of Churches. Within a couple of years, the Canadian women also aligned their prayer day with the first Friday of Lent.

In 1926, the women of North America distributed the outline for the day of prayer to women in countries where their church operated missions. Again, the response seeking participation was enthusiastic, and thus at the beginning of 1927, a national Day of Prayer transformed into the World Day of Prayer for Missions. The next year, at the large International Missionary Conference in Jerusalem, women delegates envisioned the World Day of Prayer as a symbol of their ecumenical bonding. Methodist educator Helen Kim (1899–1970) of Korea was selected to prepare the order of worship for the World Day of Prayer in 1930.

For many years, the administrate duties required to perpetuate the World Day of Prayer was coordinated through Church Women United (and its predecessor organizations) and implemented the Foreign Missions Conference of North America. In 1969, in the wake of the Second Vatican Council, the World Union of Catholic Women's Organizations decided to align their Day of Prayer with that of Protestant women.

In the new century, the World Day of Prayer has become a more globally focused movement, in line with the larger movement of shifting control for global Christianity from exclusively Western hands. In 2005, the World Day of Prayer USA Committee became one of 170 such committees that now coordinates the activity of the World Day of Prayer. It was assigned the task of preparing resources for the day, managing the offering received, and distributing the funds.

J. Gordon Melton

See also Common Prayer Day; National Day of Prayer; Week of Prayer for Christian Unity; World Peace and Prayer Day.

References

"About World Day of Prayer." World Day of Prayer USA Committee. Posted at http://www.wdpusa.org/about.html. Accessed May 15, 2010.

World Day of Prayer. Posted at http://www.worlddayofprayer.net/. Accessed May 15, 2010.

World Day of the Sick. *See* Lourdes, Feast Day of Our Lady of

World Humanist Day (June 21)

In the 1980s, various Humanist groups and individual leaders began promoting the idea of a World Humanist Day as a means of showcasing Humanism as a positive moral worldview that provides benefits to both individual believers and the surrounding society. The suggestions for the celebration emanated from a variety of sources, and as groups began to observe the day, it was done on different days and lacked a central focus. Some saw the day as a time to promote the work of the International Humanist and Ethical Union. By the end of the decade, both the American Humanist Association and the International Humanist and Ethical Union passed resolution declaring the summer solstice as the referred day for observing World Humanist Day. At that time, the summer solstice was just beginning to experience a revival of interest among different religious groups in the West, most notably the Neo-Pagans.

Through the 1990s to the present, several groups beyond the American Humanist Association and the International Humanist and Ethical Union have announced their support of World Humanist Day, including the Council for Secular Humanism, the Campus Freethought Alliance, and the Secular Student Alliance. At the same time, the day has not found widespread support among the larger community, and the majority of local Humanist groups have yet to organize celebrations. Among the reason for the slow acceptance of the day has been the lack of guidance on celebrating the day offered by its supporters.

J. Gordon Melton

See also Darwin Day; Freethought Day; HumanLight.

References

Friedman, Elaine. "Today is World Humanist Day." *Humanist Network News Ezine Archives*, American Humanist Association, June 21, 2006. Posted at http://

www.americanhumanist.org/hnn/archives/index.php?id=248&article=0. Accessed February 15, 2010.

"World Humanist Day." Secular Seasons. Posted at: http://www.secularseasons.org/june/world_humanist.html. Accessed February 15, 2010.

World Invocation Day

World Invocation Day is an annual celebratory event proposed by Alice A. Bailey (1880–1949), cofounder with her husband Foster Bailey (1888–1977), of the Arcane School, an organization that grew out of her work as the channel for an evolved Ascended Master named Koot Hoomi (generally known simply as the Tibetan). The Theosophical Society, which Bailey had joined in her early adult years, had proposed the existence of a hierarchy of spiritually evolved individuals, the Ascended Masters, who guided the course of human history and evolution.

In the course of her work expounding the teachings of the Ascended Masters, Bailey proposed the existence of divine energies of love and light that could be accessed by humans during meditation and diffused in the world for the betterment of all. These energies were most accessible during the time of the full moon, and the Arcane School and the several groups which have emerged from it have regularly held gatherings each month on the day of the full moon.

To facilitate the access to, and the reception and diffusion of the divine energies, Bailey also proposed the use of a brief prayer, which she termed the "Great Invocation."

From the point of Light within the mind of God
Let Light stream forth into the minds of men.
Let Light descend on Earth.

From the point of Love within the Heart of God
Let love stream forth into the hearts of men.
May Christ return to Earth.

From the centre where the Will of God is known
Let purpose guide the little wills of men—
The purpose which the Masters know and serve.

From the centre which we call the race of men
Let the Plan of Love and Light work out
And may it seal the door where evil dwells.

Let Light and Love and Power restore the Plan on Earth. (http://www.lucistrust.org/invocation)

This prayer has been widely distributed, both in pamphlets that offer some basic explanations for its use and on cards with just the simple text printed on them.

While the Great Invocation can be and is used by people at any time, Bailey also proposed three special times when men and women of every spiritual path could together use the Great Invocation to call for light and love and the spiritual direction needed to create a world characterized by justice, unity, and peace. Along with the monthly full moon gatherings of members of the Arcane School, Bailey called for the organization of three major spiritual festivals each spring. The three festivals would occur when the Full Moon was in the astrological sign of Aries (March), Taurus (April), and Gemini (May). The first usually occurs close to the traditional Christian celebration of Easter and the second to the traditional Buddhist celebration of Wesak and are seen as an esoteric celebration of those events. The last has not been associated with a particular holiday of an older faith; it is termed Great Invocation Day.

The theme of the day has been the appeal for the release of the energies that will enable humanity to create a new civilization. The energies released by the intoning of the Great Invocation are for light to illumine the way ahead, love to govern human relationships, and a will to goodness that will guide decision making. The use of the Great Invocation on World Invocation Day is believed to charge the day with deep spiritual significance by building a channel through which spiritual energies can reach the hearts and minds of people globally.

The major gatherings on the evening of the full moon for Great Invocation Day (as well as Easter and Wesak) are held at the three international headquarters of the Arcane School in New York City, London, and Geneva, as wells as the centers of the Arcane School and the several groups that derive from it such as Meditation Mount in Ojai, California.

J. Gordon Melton

See also Easter; Festival of Light (Rosicrucian); Wesak/Vesak.

References

The Great Invocation—The Use and Significance of the Great Invocation. London: World Goodwill, 1990.

Moore, Francis Adams. *The Great Invocation*. Ojai, CA: Meditation Group, Inc., 1990.

Sinclair, John R. *The Alice Bailey Inheritance*. Wellingborough, UK: Turnstone Press, 1984.

"A World Day of Prayer, Invocation and Meditation—An Invitation to Men and Women of Goodwill." Posted at http://www.lucistrust.org/en/meetings_and_events/world_invocation_day/about. Accessed March 15, 2010.

World Peace and Prayer Day (June 21)

World Peace and Prayer Day is a global observance held annually on June 21 (the summer solstice) as a time to pray for peace and the healing of the Earth.

It originated in 1996 from the suggestion of Chief Arvol Looking Horse of the Lakota Nation, a Native American people. Arvol was responding in part to the birth in 1994 of a white buffalo. There was a tradition among the Lakota that a legendary person named White Buffalo Calf Woman had appeared among the Lakota and imparted to them instruction on living in balance with the earth as well as predicting a time of her return. Arvol believed the birth of a white buffalo calf to be the sign that the predicted time had arrived.

Arvol held a series of ceremonies at various sacred sites designed to bring people who shared concerns about peace and the destruction of the Earth together and to share the message of White Buffalo Calf Woman. The first ceremony took place at Gray Horn Butte in Wyoming, near the site where White Buffalo Calf Woman was believed to have initially appeared. Some 2,000 people, mostly Native Americans, participated. Ceremonies were held in Canada and Minnesota in 1997 and 1998, and then moved to Costa Rica, the site of the University for Peace, in 1999.

With the 2000 ceremony on Lakota land in South Dakota, Arvol felt he had completed the original idea, holding four ceremonies representative of the four directions and then a final ceremony in the center. Subsequently, Arvol turned the idea of the Peace Day over to the larger community and asked them to continue it at other sacred sites around the world. Whether each future celebration occurred at a place of worship or at a significant geographical site considered of spiritual significance, the local residents of the community had accepted the responsibility of continuing the prayers and activities on behalf of world peace.

After the 2000 ceremony, two English representatives approached Arvol with a request to conduct a similar series of ceremonies, this time on four continents with a fifth returning to the Americas. Thus, summer solstice celebrations were held in Ireland (2001); Durban, South Africa (2002); Australia (2003); and Mount Fuji, Japan (2003). In 2005, the ceremony returned to the Black Hills of South Dakota. With a large international contingent at the 2005 gathering, attention was directed to creating a global invitation for people to join in a summer solstice united prayer/meditation to heal the Earth. An effort also was launched to have the United Nations recognize the day as "Honoring Sacred Sites Day." This latter effort was on behalf of Native peoples who wished to protect sacred lands from modern development.

The new directions proposed at the 2005 gathering also led to the need for an organization that could raise the funds to keep the vision alive. Thus, the leadership created the Wolakota Foundation. It is charged with continuing the annual celebrations as well as creating a center with programs for sustaining traditional teachings of the Lakota, Dakota, and Nakota nations and researching and demonstrating practices for sustainable, ecologically balanced living. The foundation, based in Eagle Butte, South Dakota, sees its purpose as promoting, protecting, and educating others about the traditional values and wisdom of indigenous people worldwide.

J. Gordon Melton

See also Doukhobor Peace Day; Summer Solstice; World Peace Ceremony.

References

"Wolakota Foundation." http://wolakota.org/menu.html or http://www.worldpeace day.com/. Accessed June 15, 2010.

World Peace Ceremony (Tibetan Buddhist)

The World Peace Ceremony is the annual celebration of Monlam, the Prayer Blessing Festival, among the most important annual holidays observed by Tibetan Buddhists, held at Bodh Gaya, India, under the sponsorship of the Nyingmapa School of Tibetan Buddhism. In the 1950s, the Tibetan Buddhist community experienced a trauma as the People's Republic of China extended its control over the country. Most of its leadership and more than 100,000 lay believers left the country and, through the next decades, slowly began to reestablish themselves in northern India. The exiles engaged in a massive effort to preserve Tibetan culture and religion, build new centers for worship and for the training of monks, and, as much as possible, recreate life as it was in Tibet.

Among the monks who moved into exile was the venerable Tarthang Tulku, a Nyingma lama who moved to Berkeley, California, and founded the Nyingma Meditation Center. By the 1980s, the center had prospered and become an important focus of the preservation of the Tibetan tradition outside of Tibet. Thus, in the 1980s, Tarthang Tulku turned some attention to the situation in Bodh Gaya, an important site for Buddhists as the place where Gautama Buddha had experienced his enlightenment, the seminal event in the origin of the faith. Over the centuries, as Buddhism died out in India, the site had been lost, and through the 20th century, a movement had developed to recover the site and make it into a major Buddhist pilgrimage center. A major step in that regard was taken in 1949 when control of the site was turned over to a new management committee. Though still under Hindu control, Buddhists have remained participants in the committee.

As part of the effort to develop Bodh Gaya, and simultaneously assist the revival of the Tibetan community-in-exile, Tarthung Tulku, in 1989, sponsored the first annual World Peace Ceremony. This event was, to the Tibetan Buddhists who attended a celebration of the annual Monlam or Prayer Blessing festival, an important annual event on the Tibetan Buddhist calendar. The Monlam celebration happened to coincide with the annual Hindu national festival of Diwali, the Festival of Lights, and the largest annual holiday in both India and Nepal. The ceremony brought together exiled leaders from the four major schools of Tibetan Buddhism. The idea of the World Peace Ceremony as an appropriate celebration of Monlam caught on among the attending lamas, and they returned annually and began to envision its expansion to the other sites associated with the Buddha. Thus in 1993, the Sakya and Kagyu Buddhists began to sponsor a Monlam/World

Peace Ceremony at Lumbini, where the Buddha was born, and then the Gelugpa School accepted responsibility for the celebrations at Sarnath, where the Buddha began his public ministry and preached his first sermon.

The development of the World Peace Ceremony celebrations has left the original event at Bodh Gaya as primarily a gathering for the various sub-schools of the Nyingma tradition, though its observance regularly includes a visit from the Dalai Lama, who will make several stops in India throughout the week of Monlam.

J. Gordon Melton

See also Diwali; Doukhobor Peace Day; Monlam, the Great Prayer Festival; Nehan; Wesak/Vesak; World Peace and Prayer Day.

References

The World Peace Ceremony/Bodh Gaya 1994. Berkeley, CA: Dharma Publishing, 1994.

The World Peace Ceremony/Prayers at Holy Places. Berkeley, CA: Dharma Publishing, 1994.

World Religion Day (January)

World Religion Day, observed worldwide on the third Sunday of January each year, is a Bahá'í-inspired idea that has taken on a life of its own. In 2009, for instance, the Halifax (Nova Scotia) Regional Municipality in Canada celebrated its sixth annual World Religion Day in the Cathedral of All Saints, in recognition of which the mayor and councilors of the Halifax Regional Municipality issued a proclamation. In 2007, at the World Religion Day event hosted by the Entebbe Municipal Council of Entebbe, Uganda (situated on the northern shores of Lake Victoria), participating religious leaders signed a joint declaration to establish the Entebbe Inter-Faith Coalition. The signatories pledged to use "the unifying power of religion to instill in the hearts and minds of all people of faith the fundamental facts and spiritual standards that have been laid down by our Creator to bring them together as members of one family."

World Religion Day, now observed internationally, originated among American Bahá'ís. Its history dates back to 1949, when the National Spiritual Assembly of the Bahá'ís of the United States (the national Bahá'í governing council) instituted an annual World Religion Day "to be observed publicly by the Bahá'í Communities wherever possible throughout the United States." The third Sunday of January each year was designated for this celebration, and the first World Religion Day event took place on January 15, 1950.

The Bahá'í Faith, among the younger of the independent world religions, emphasizes unity in the human community, and the inauguration of World Religion Day seemed a natural expression and extension of the Bahá'í focus on the unity of religions, races, and nations. However, this was not the exclusive, nor even the primary original purpose of World Religion Day. In 1968, the Universal

House of Justice, the international Bahá'í governing body established in 1963, wrote:

> Your letter of September 30, with the suggestion that "there should be one day in the year in which all of the religions should agree" is a happy thought, and one which persons of good will throughout the world might well hail. However, this is not the underlying concept of World Religion Day, which is a celebration of the need for and the coming of a world religion for mankind, the Bahá'í Faith itself. Although there have been many ways of expressing the meaning of this celebration in Bahá'í communities in the United States, the Day was not meant primarily to provide a platform for all religions and their emergent ecumenical ideas. In practice, there is no harm in the Bahá'í communities' inviting the persons of other religions to share their platforms on this Day, providing the universality of the Bahá'í Faith as the fulfillment of the hopes of mankind for a universal religion are clearly brought forth. (Lights of Guidance, no. 1710)

On April 2002, the Universal House of Justice issued a letter "To the World's Religious Leaders," in which interfaith dialogue is highly regarded. However, the letter states that the initiatives of the interfaith movement of the previous century "lack both intellectual coherence and spiritual commitment." For its part, "the Bahá'í community has been a vigorous promoter of interfaith activities from the time of their inception" and will continue to assist, valuing the "cherished associations" that these activities create. It continued: "We owe it to our partners in this common effort, however, to state clearly our conviction that interfaith discourse, if it is to contribute meaningfully to healing the ills that afflict a desperate humanity, must now address honestly . . . the implications of the over-arching truth . . . that God is one and that, beyond all diversity of cultural expression and human interpretation, religion is likewise one."

While neither the Universal House of Justice nor the National Spiritual Assembly of the Bahá'ís of the United States currently plays an active role in promoting World Religion Day events, the Bahá'í International Community (an official organ of the Universal House of Justice) has consistently reported on such events, with obvious appreciation. In the United States, the timing of World Religion Day now conflicts with Martin Luther King, Jr., Day (the third Monday in January), observed for the first time on January 20, 1986. While this has led to the discontinuance of World Religion Day in many locales, some Bahá'í communities integrate the two days, while others may hold their World Religion Day events a few days earlier.

This, in brief, is how and why World Religion Day has subsequently taken on a life of its own. There are several outstanding examples of this. On January 20, 2007, in Brazzaville, the Congo Republic became the second country to issue a postage stamp for World Religion Day. Featuring a globe surrounded by the symbols of 11 religions, the stamp bears a French superscription which, translated, reads: "God is the source of all religions." Following a World Religion Day program that drew more than 250 participants from eight faith-communities, agents were present to sell both the stamps and first-day covers. In 1985, Sri Lanka had become the first country to issue a World Religion Day stamp.

The purpose of World Religion Day today is to highlight the essential harmony of the world's religions, to foster their transconfessional affinity through interfaith ecumenism, and to promote the idea and ideal of world unity in which the world's religions can play a potentially significant role. This generalization is based on observations of how World Religion Day is celebrated in events that are sponsored by organizations that are not Bahá'í, whether in concert with local Bahá'í sponsorship or entirely independent of it. (In most cases, the Bahá'ís continue to play a vital role in the orchestration and success of these events.) The day is celebrated with interfaith dialogue, conferences, and other events that advance not only mutual understanding (or what scholars call "spiritual literacy"), but recognition, respect, and reciprocity among the followers of all religions who join together in celebrating World Religion Day.

Where observed, World Religion Day events typically do not attract representatives and participants from all local faith-communities, primarily for religious reasons. As such, World Religion Day provides an insightful social barometer of the extent to which various religious groups are willing to formally associate with each other

While World Religion Day events are still sponsored and cosponsored by local members of the Bahá'í Faith worldwide, an increasing number of World Religion Day events are independently organized by interfaith or multi-faith coalitions. For instance, in Tralee, Ireland, the local World Religion Day observance was organized by the Kerry Diocesan Justice, Peace and Creation Committee, a member organization of Pax Christi International in Ireland. In 2009, the third annual observance of World Religion Day in Greensboro, North Carolina, was organized by FaithAction and the Piedmont Interfaith Council. Also in 2009, World Religion Day was celebrated by Vadamalayan Hospitals and Vadamalayan Institute of Paramedical Sciences, in which a quiz competition was held to mark the occasion.

In certain cases, civic governments, both national and local, have recognized the positive social value of World Religion Day events. In 2004, the House of Representatives of the General Assembly of the Commonwealth of Kentucky proclaimed January 17–18, 2004, as "World Religion Weekend" and went on to "urge the Commonwealth's citizens to participate in the observance of World Religion Weekend." In 2007, the Republic of Ghana's Ghana@50 Secretariat organized a symposium themed "The Unity of the Faiths" on World Religion Day on Sunday, February 18, 2007. In January 2008, the City Council of Duncan, British Columbia, Canada, proclaimed January 20, 2008, as World Religion Day. In a 2009 World Religion Day event in Australia, the parliamentary secretary for multicultural affairs and settlement services, Laurie Ferguson, said: "Interfaith dialogue plays an important role in increasing understanding of our nation's religious and cultural diversity and bringing Australians closer together. The Australian Government supports interfaith dialogue at the highest levels." Many World Religion Day events are associated with mayoral or municipal proclamations.

World Religion Day is self-perpetuating, thanks to the initiatives of progressive individuals and institutions who share a vision of religious confraternity. It is an inspired idea, with widespread appeal and remarkable longevity.

Christopher Buck

See also 'Abdu'l-Bahá, Ascension of; Ayyám-i-Há (Bahá'í Intercalary Days); Báb, Festival of the Birth of the; Báb, Festival of the Declaration of the; Báb, Martyrdom of the; Bahá'í Calendar and Rhythms of Worship; Bahá'í Faith; Bahá'í Fast; Bahá'u'lláh, Ascension of; Bahá'u'lláh, Festival of the Birth of; Covenant, Day of the; Naw-Rúz, Festival of; Nineteen-Day Feast (Bahá'í); Race Unity Day; Riḍván, Festival of.

References

Bahá'í Computer and Communications Association (BCCA). "World Religion Day" ("Sample Press Release"). Posted at http://www.bcca.org/orgs/usnsa/samples.html. Accessed September 30, 2009.

Bahá'í International Community. "Congo Republic Issues Stamp for World Religion Day." *One Country* 18, no. 4 (January–March 2007). Posted at http://www.onecountry.org/e184/e18409as_Congo_Stamp.htm. Accessed July 15, 2010.

Hornby, Helen, comp. *Lights of Guidance: A Bahá'í Reference File*. 6th ed. New Delhi: Bahá'í Publishing Trust, 1999.

National Spiritual Assembly of the Bahá'ís of the United States. "World Religion Day." *Bahá'í News*, no. 226 (December 1949): 5.

Parliamentary Secretary for Multicultural Affairs and Settlement Services. "World Religion Day 2009." Posted at http://www.minister.immi.gov.au/parlsec/media/media-releases/2009/lf09002.htm. Accessed July 15, 2010.

Universal House of Justice, The. Letter to a Local Spiritual Assembly, October 22, 1968. Lights of Guidance, no. 1710.

Universal House of Justice, The. "To the World's Religious Leaders." 2002.

World Religion Day. Posted at http://www.worldreligionday.org. Accessed July 15, 2010.

Yogananda, Birthday of Paramahansa (January 5)

Paramahansa Yogananda was an Indian teacher known as the founder of the Self-Realization Fellowship and a pioneer Hindu teacher in the West. He was born in 1893, in Gorakhpur, Utter Pradesh, India. As a youth, he began a spiritual search that led him to the person who became his teacher (guru), Sri Yukeswar Giri (1855–1936)

Sri Yukteswar initiated Sri Yogananda in 1915 into the renounced life as a sannyasin and introduced him to kriya yoga. In 1920, Paramahansa Yogananda started his mission in the West, coming to the United States at the invitation of the Unitarian-sponsored International Association for Religious Freedom. He remained in the United States and founded what became the Self-Realization Fellowship to disseminate the teachings of Kriya Yoga.

In 1935, Swami Sri Yukteswar recognized his accomplishments and mastery of the tradition by giving the title Paramahanse (literally, "supreme swan") to Yogananda. From his base in southern California, he built a national following through the use of lessons that he mailed out to students. His *Autobiography of a Yogi* (1946) became a classic of Hindu literature in the West. Yogananda died on March 7, 1952, and his living quarters at the fellowship's headquarters in Encinatas, California, were subsequently turned into a shrine to him.

Paramahansa Yogananda's birthday has become an annual event and a time to remember the fellowship's founder. Celebrations are held in the fellowship churches and centers around the world, usually with a gathering of friends and members in the evening. The worship service will include prayers, chants, readings from Yogananda's many writings, and meditation. Those who attend are asked to bring a flower, which is used in a brief ritual as a symbol of devotion to him. Attendees also make an offering as an expression of loyalty to the fellowship.

This tradition is also carried on within the Center for Spiritual Awareness, led by former fellowship minister Roy Eugene Davis, and the Ananda Church of Self-Realization, founded by Swami Kriyananda, formerly a prominent leader in the Self-Realization Fellowship. In recent years, Ananda has also sponsored a two-day event the weekend prior to the actual birthday commemoration that has allowed a more in-depth exploration and appropriation of Yogananda's teachings. The Weekend, held in Nevada City, California, includes movies of Yogananda, a tour of a museum with relics of him and the other masters in his lineage, meditation, chanting, and shared meals. Attendees are invited to turn the time between

Paramahansa Yogananda. (Ananda.org)

the weekend and the actual birthday celebration on January 5 into a personal retreat at the churches mountain facilities.

J. Gordon Melton

See also Babaji Commemoration Day; Yogananda, Mahasamadhi of Paramahansa; Yukteswar, Commemorative Days of Swami Sri.

References

Self-Realization Fellowship Highlights. Los Angeles: Self-Realization Fellowship, 1980.

Self-Realization Fellowship Manual of Services. Los Angeles: Self-Realization Fellowship, 1965.

Yogananda, Paramahansa. *Autobiography of a Yogi.* Los Angeles: Self-Realization Fellowship, 1946.

Yogananda, Mahasamadhi of Paramahansa (March 7)

Paramahansa Yogananda, an Indian spiritual teacher known for founding the Self-Realization Fellowship (SRF), pioneered the development of Hinduism in the West. He was born in 1893, and in 1920, he accepted an invitation from the Unitarian-sponsored International Association for Religious Freedom to come to the United States. He spent the rest of his life in the United States as a teacher, author, and the spiritual head of the Self-Realization Fellowship (SRF).

He spent the last years of his life largely in seclusion. He worked to complete some writings, most notably his commentaries on the Bhagavad Gita and the Christian Gospels in the New Testament, and final revisions of the lessons taken by all SRF members. Yogananda died (spoken of as entering *mahasamadhi*) on March 7, 1952. Subsequently, the fellowship's headquarters in Encinatas, California, preserved his living quarters there as a shrine to him. Members of the SRF note that after his death, his body manifested no signs of physical disintegration, which the morticians noted as a most unusual occurrence.

Yogananda is remembered by the SRF and by a number of other groups which have derived from it, most notably the Ananda Church of Self-Realization. All of the Yogananda-oriented groups gather on March 7, the anniversary of his passing, with a service of commemoration that includes meditation, chanting, messages about and Yogananda, reading from his writings. The Ananda church has made much of Yoganada's promise to return to his disciples, about which he wrote a drama, which is occasionally performed on the anniversary of his mahasamadhi. Attendees are asked to bring a flower and a love offering to the service.

In 1977, on the 25th anniversary of Paramahansa Yogananda's death, the Government of India issued a commemorative stamp in his honor.

J. Gordon Melton

See also Babaji Commemoration Day; Yogananda, Birthday of Paramahansa; Yukteswar, Commemorative Days of Swami Sri.

References

Self-Realization Fellowship Highlights. Los Angeles: Self-Realization Fellowship, 1980.

Self-Realization Fellowship Manual of Services. Los Angeles: Self-Realization Fellowship, 1965.

Yogananda, Paramahansa. *Autobiography of a Yogi.* Los Angeles: Self-Realization Fellowship, 1946.

Yom HaAtzmaut

Yom HaAtzmaut is one of four new holidays (including Yom HaShoah, Yom HaZikaron, and Yom Yerushalayim) proposed for the Jewish community since the founding of the modern state of Israel in 1948. It is celebrated on the fifth of the Hebrew month of Iyar (but occasionally moved if it conflicts with the Sabbath). Yom HaAtzmaut celebrates the founding of Israel and is closely tied to Yom HaZikaron, the memorial day for the soldiers who lost their life in the effort to secure an independent Israel. The official end of Yom HaZikaron and beginning of Yom HaAtzmaut occurs shortly after sundown during a ceremony on Mount Herzl in Jerusalem, in which the flag of Israel that had been set at half-mast in acknowledgment of the fallen soldiers is raised to the top of the flagpole.

Yom HaAtzmaut would appear to be primarily a secular holiday, but given the intimate connection of Jewish religious commitments to and beliefs about Israel, it was inevitable that Yom HaAtzmaut would acquire its religious aspect. The Chief Rabbinate of Israel (which represents the Orthodox community) has declared that Hallel (the psalms of praise found in Psalms 113–118) be read in morning services as is done on other joyous holidays, and including the reading of a special *haftarah* (prophetic portion).

Those ultra-Orthodox Jews who have rejected the general perspective of Zionism and the formation of the state of Israel do not celebrate this day. On the other end of the spectrum, some rabbis have argued for the close association of Yom HaAtzmaut with Hanukkah and Purim, as each of these commemorate a "miraculous" victory of Jewish forces over an enemy of seemingly superior military strength. The Modern Orthodox Kibbutz Movement has, for example, proposed a version of the prayer Al HaNissim ("Concerning the Miracles") to be added to the *Amidah* (the central prayer recited while standing) on Yom HaAtzmaut, as is done on Hanukkah and Purim, and both the Masorti (Conservative) and the Progressive (Reform) congregations in Israel accepted this suggestion.

Most of the Jewish communities in the West have incorporated a celebration of Israel's independence into their annual holiday calendar, but consider it a strictly secular affair, to show solidarity with Israel. Meanwhile, the celebration in Israel has been focused in the events on the evening as the day begins (a new day always begins at sunset on the Israeli calendar). Israel's president address the country's armed forces, whose representatives then march in a parade on Mount Herzl. Following the parade, there is a torch-lighting ceremony acknowledging the country's achievements in all spheres of life. During the next day, the Israel Prize awards are given to individuals for their contributions to the country.

J. Gordon Melton

See also Hanukkah; Purim; Yom HaShoah; Yom HaZikaron; Yom Yerushalayim (Jerusalem Day).

References

Cohen, Michael Joseph. *Palestine to Israel: From Mandate to Independence*. London: Routledge, 1988.

Newman, Aryeh. *Acknowledge the Miracle: Yom Ha'Atzma'ut Israel Independence Day in the Perspectives of Judaism*. Jerusalem: Jewish Agency Torah Department, 1957.

"Yom Ha-Atzmaut: Israeli Independence Day." Jewish Virtual Library. Posted at http://www.jewishvirtuallibrary.org/jsource/Judaism/yomhaatzmaut.html. Accessed July 15, 2010.

Yom HaShoah

Yom HaShoah (Holocaust Remembrance Day) is a Jewish commemoration day dedicated to the remembrance of the Holocaust, the destruction of some six million Jews that began with the rise to power of the National Socialist Party (the Nazis) in Germany in the 1930s and reached its zenith in the last years of World War II with the development of the gas chambers in the several death camps, most notably Auschwitz in Poland. Shoah is a Hebrew word meaning catastrophe or utter destruction.

Yom HaShoah is held on the 27th of Nissan (which occurs in late April or early may on the Common Era calendar) and is an official holiday in Israel. In 2005, the United Nations designated January 27 as the international Holocaust Memorial Day, and that date is acknowledged in most of the countries of the European Union. Neither day is recognized in the United States, but the Jewish community and many in the Christian community hold a commemoration on or near Nissan 27.

As a relatively new day of commemoration, not only has no date been agreed upon by all, but there is not set ritual. Many will light candles, often six candles symbolic of the six million who died, though much more emphasis is placed upon holding some form of commemoration rather than the form that the observance will take. In Israel, a siren will sound at which point everyone stops any activity in which they are engaged. Integral to the day is the retelling the stories of what people experienced. The United Kingdom first celebrated a Holocaust Remembrance Day in 2001, the year following the opening of a permanent Holocaust Exhibition at the Imperial War Museum.

In 1994, following the release of *Schindler's List* (1993), director Steven Spielberg formed the Survivors of the Shoah Visual History Foundation (now the USC Shoah Foundation Institute for Visual History and Education) to record and preserve video testimonies of survivors of the Holocaust. The foundation concentrated on documenting the stories of Jewish survivors, but also interviewed other victims including homosexuals, Jehovah's Witnesses, Gypsies, and a variety of others who had knowledge of the events. By the end of the 1990s, the archive (since 2006 housed at the University of Southern California) included some 52,000 video testimonies offered by people from 56 different countries.

The Holocaust began with a campaign of anti-Semitism by the Nazis and accompanying acts of violence and destruction. Once Adolf Hitler came to power, plans were put in place to eradicate various segments of the population, including homosexuals and Gypsies, but most notably the Jews. In the end, the Nazis adopted a policy, termed the "Final Solution," that looked toward the complete annihilation of the Jews from all of Europe. Systematically, Jews were confined to overcrowded ghettos, then sent to concentration camps, and as additional countries were overrun, sent to death camps. By the time the Nazi regime was brought down, two-thirds of Europe's Jews had been killed.

J. Gordon Melton

See also Common Era Calendar; Yom HaAtzmaut; Yom HaZikaron; Yom Yerushalayim (Jerusalem Day).

References

Berman, Judith E. *Holocaust Remembrance in Australian Jewish Communities*. Perth: University of Western Australia Press, 2002.

Cargas, Harry James. *A Holocaust Commemoration for Days of Remembrance: For Communities, Churches, Centers and for Home Use*. Philadelphia: Holocaust Remembrance Foundation, 1982.

Hornstein, Shelley, and Florence Jacobowitz. *Image and Remembrance: Representation and the Holocaust*. Bloomington: Indiana University Press, 2002.

Miller, Marjorie. "Britain Devotes a Day to Holocaust Victims." *Los Angeles Times*, January 27, 2001.

Smith, Lyn. *Remembering: Voices of the Holocaust: A New History in the Words of the Men and Women Who Survived.* New York: Basic Books, 2007.

Yom HaZikaron

Yom HaZikaron is one of four new holidays proposed to the Jewish community in the wake of the formation of the modern state of Israel (the others being Yom HaShoah, Yom HaAatzmaut, and Yom Yerushalayim). Yom HaZikaron is intimately tied to Yom HaAatzmaut, the celebration of the formation of the state of Israel, and is held the day before on the fourth day of the Hebrew month of Iyer. In contrast to the joyous celebration of Yom HaAatzmaut, Yom HaZikaron is a somber occasion, memorializing those soldiers who have died initially in the battles leading to independence and subsequently to defend it in the years since 1948. For the majority of the Israeli population, Israel's several wars remain a vivid memory.

Within the religious community, special prayers to the evening prayer service have been added for Yom HaZikaron. Also, a special *yizkor* (remembrance) prayer and a memorial prayer for deceased members of the Israeli Defense Forces is included as part of the Yom HaZikaron ceremonies.

For most, the secular patriotic aspect of Yom HaZikaron dominates the day. The most widely recognized commemoration follows the air raid siren that is sounded twice—at the beginning of the day, and immediately prior to the public recitation of prayers in military cemeteries. At these moments, activity ceases, and all pause to acknowledge the sacrifice of those who died defending the country.

Numerous public ceremonies are held throughout Israel, and the day concludes with a national ceremony at the military cemetery on Mount Herzl. The day will officially end there shortly after sundown, when the flag, which had been lowered to half-mast, is raised to the top of the flag pole and the celebration of Independence Day (Yom HaAtzmaut).

Yom HaZikaron is not widely observed outside of Israel.

J. Gordon Melton

See also Tisha B'Av; Yom HaAatzmaut; Yom HaShoah; Yom Yerushalayim (Jerusalem Day).

References

Grunor, Jerry A. *Let My People Go: The Trials and Tribulations of the People of Israel, and the Heroes Who Helped in Their Independence from British Colonization.* Lincoln, NB: iUniverse, 2005.

Hein, Avi. "Yom Ha-Zikaron." Jewish Virtual Library. Posted at http://www.jewishvirtuallibrary.org/jsource/Judaism/yomhazikaron.html. Accessed July 15, 2010.

Mauman, Daniel, and Eyal Ben-Ari, eds. *Military, State, and Society in Israel: Theoretical and Comparative Perspectives.* Piscataway, NJ: Transaction Publishers, 2001.

Yom Kippur

Yom Kippur (the Day of Atonement), possibly the single most observed holy day in the Jewish year, is one of two Jewish holidays not related to a specific historical event in Jewish memory (as are, for example, Passover or Purim). Like Rosh Hashanah, it is related primarily to the commandment of God for an annual act of atonement. It occurs on the 10th day of the month of Tishri in the Jewish calendar and follows over a month of preparation that began on the first day of Elul, the previous month. During the month of Elul, one begins to think about the issues of self-reflection, repentance, and atonement for one's failings, and begins to bring one's consciousness and behavior into a repentant mode. This preparation leads to Rosh Hashanah, the Day of the Shofar Blast or the Jewish New Year, which kicks off the High Holy Days. The High Holy Days are seen as a time of concentrated self-reflection and repentance, and for special acts of charity and forgiveness. Following Rosh Hashanah, the Days of Awe lead to the Day of Atonement in which God seals His judgment for the coming year.

The observance of Yom Kippur is mandated in Leviticus 23: 26–32:

> And the LORD spoke unto Moses, saying: Howbeit on the tenth day of this seventh month is the day of atonement; there shall be a holy convocation unto you, and ye shall afflict your souls; and ye shall bring an offering made by fire unto the LORD. And ye shall do no manner of work in that same day; for it is a day of atonement, to make atonement for you before the LORD your God. For whatsoever soul it be that shall not be afflicted in that same day, he shall be cut off from his people. And whatsoever soul it be that doeth any manner of work in that same day, that soul will I destroy from among his people. Ye shall do no manner of work; it is a statute for ever throughout your generations in all your dwellings. It shall be unto you a sabbath of solemn rest, and ye shall afflict your souls; in the ninth day of the month at even, from even unto even, shall ye keep your sabbath.

On Rosh Hashanah, believers think of God writing a judgment upon them relative to their behavior and motivations over the previous year. The succeeding Days of Awe are a time to reflect upon the past year, seek forgiveness, and make amends. The Day of Atonement represents one last chance to change the judgment of God in one's favor before the day ends, and God seals His judgment for the coming year. That judgment heralds one's prosperity, happiness, and even life or death for the coming year.

Yom Kippur is observed as a Sabbath. One refrains from all work. It is also a day of fasting, with no food or drink beginning shortly before sunset and continuing for the next 25 hours. Additional restrictions punctuating the uniqueness of the day include refraining from washing and bathing, not using cosmetics products such as deodorants, wearing shoes made of something other than leather (like canvas sneakers), and of course, refraining from sexual relations. Many people will dress in white.

Most of Yom Kippur is spent in communal prayer in the synagogue, there being five services. The first service at sundown on the eve of Yom Kippur begins the start of the fast; the last ends at nightfall the next day, and concludes the fast with the *shofar* (ram's horn) sounded in a final long blast. Part of the Yom Kippur liturgy is a lengthy and broadly worded confession of the sins of the community, with an emphasis on sins that were detrimental to one's neighbor, acts of both omission and commission.

Yom Kippur is a public holiday in Israel. Radio and television stations cease broadcasting; airports and other public transportation shut down; and all businesses, including restaurants, close. In Israel, even many, who consider themselves irreligious Jews fast and avoid using prohibited transportation and communication systems. Soldiers seek leave to be with their families for the day.

In 1973, well aware of Israel's vulnerability on this, the most sacred day on the Jewish calendar, Egypt and Syria attacked Israel. As radios, which had been silent, began calling up the reserves and soldiers left their prayers to return to their units, Israel retreated before the advancing Egyptian and Syrian armies. However, within a few days, Israel recovered and fought the war to a point that victory seemed imminent before a cease-fire went into effect.

By 2008, 63 percent of the Israeli public said they planned to fast on Yom Kippur, the great majority for religious reasons. A third, who did not intend to fast, did not plan to flaunt openly the traditional observance of the holy day.

J. Gordon Melton

See also Days of Awe; Rosh Hashanah.

References

Cohen, Jeffrey M. *1,001 Questions and Answers on Rosh HaShanah and Yom Kippur.* New York: Jason Aronson, 1997.

Eckstein, Yecheil. *What You Should Know about Jews and Judaism.* Waco, TX: Word Books, 1984.

Greenberg, Irving. *The Jewish Way: Living the Holidays.* New York: Jason Aronson, 1998.

Posner, Raphael, Uri Kaploun, and Sherman Cohen, eds. *Jewish Liturgy: Prayer and Synagogue Service through the Ages.* New York: Leon Amiel Publisher; Jerusalem: Keter Publishing House, 1975.

Schauss, Hayyim. *The Jewish Festivals: A Guide to Their History and Observance.* New York: Schocken, 1996.

"63% of Israelis Jews plan to fast on Yom Kippur." *Ynet News.* Posted at http://www.ynetnews.com/articles/0,7340,L-3606942,00.html. Accessed June 15, 2009.

Yom Yerushalayim (Jerusalem Day)

In the last half of the 20th century, four holidays were added to the Jewish calendar (Yom HaShoah, Yom HaZikaron, Yom HaAtzmaut, and Yom Yerushalayim). The most recently added date commemorates the unification of Jerusalem under Jewish sovereignty as a result of the Six Day War (1967). Jerusalem Day is observed on the 28th day of the Hebrew month of Iyar, approximately six weeks after Passover and a week before Shavuot.

The Six Day War gained added significance for most Jews in that for the first time in more than 2,000 years, the entire city of Jerusalem was under Jewish sovereignty. The Israeli army assumed control over the eastern part of the city on the third day of the War, and shortly thereafter, an official unification of the two sections of the city took place.

In the wake of the reunification and the declaration of the new holiday, The Chief Rabbinate of Israel (representing Orthodox Jewry) declared that this day should be observed with the recital of Hallel (the recitation of Psalms 113–118) during the morning service. The Progressive or Reform Jews have made a similar suggestion, while the Conservative Jews have made alternative suggestions of additional readings for the day. Some of the ultra-Orthodox Jews, who have maintained an anti-Zionist perspective, have not acknowledged Yom Yerushalayim as a holiday.

For many Israeli Jews, including many secular Jews, Jerusalem Day has become a day to travel to Jerusalem to show their solidarity with the idea of a united city and with the government in charge of it. Given the lack of approval of the unification by much of the international community, demonstrations of approval of the ending of the segregation instituted in 1948 when the Israeli state was formed is important for the government authorities. The government has responded to its own declaration of Jerusalem Day by using the day preceding it as an opportunity to education the population on the city's heritage.

Yom Yerushalayim is not, as of the first decade of the new century, observed by the majority of Jews outside of Israel. Many non-Israeli Jews remain conflicted about the manner in which the city was united and the future of the many Arabs still residing in the city.

J. Gordon Melton

See also Fast of Gedaliah; Yom HaAtzmaut; Yom HaShoah; Yom HaZikaron.

References

Cline, Eric H. *Jerusalem Besieged: From Ancient Canaan to Modern Israel.* Ann Arbor: University of Michigan Press, 2005.

Dumper, Michael. *The Politics of Jerusalem since 1967.* New York: Columbia University Press, 1997.

Heim, Avi. "Yom Yerushalayim - Jerusalem Day." *Jewish Virtual Library*. Posted at http://www.jewishvirtuallibrary.org/jsource/Judaism/yomyerushalayim.html. Accessed on July 15, 2010.

Levine, Lee I. *Jerusalem: Its Sanctity and Centrality to Judaism, Christianity, and Islam*. New York: Continuum International Publishing Group, 1999.

Yukteswar, Commemorative Days of Swami Sri (March 9, May 10)

Swami Sri Yukteswar Giri (1855–1936) was an Indian spiritual teacher who became known in the West initially as the teacher (guru) of Paramahansa Yogananda (1893–1952). He was born Priya Nath Karar near Calcutta and married as a young man. His wife died giving birth to their daughter. Shortly thereafter, in 1883, he was initiated into the practice of kriya yoga by Lahriri Mahasaya. As he mastered the discipline, he authored a book (*The Holy Science*) that appeared in 1894. He was later initiated into the renounced life as a sannyasin.

Yukteswar seems to have met Yogananda about 1912 and, several years later, initiated him as a sannyasin. Yogananda moved to the United States in 1920, and originally set up what was to become the Self-Realization Society as a branch of Sri Yukteswar's organization in India. Yukteswar died in India on March 9, 1936.

Centers of the Self-Realization Fellowship and the several organizations derived from it hold commemorations of both the birthday and death day of Sri Yukteswar. Members and friends will gather in the evening for a special service that will include meditation, chanting, reading form Sri Yukteswar's writings, and a common meal. Attendees are asked to bring a flower and an offering for participation in the ritual.

J. Gordon Melton

See also Yogananda, Birthday of Paramahansa; Yogananda, Mahasamadhi of Paramahansa.

References

Yogananda, Paramahansa. *Autobiography of a Yogi*. Los Angeles: Self-Realization Fellowship, 1946.

Yogananda, Paramahansa. *Man's Eternal Quest*. 2 vols. Los Angeles: Self-Realization Fellowship, 1982.

Yukteswar, Swami Sri. *The Holy Science*. Los Angeles: Self-Realization Fellowship, 1990.

Yule

Yule is the midwinter celebration of the modern Pagan and Wiccan community. That community, though now quite diverse, grew primarily out of the effort of

Gerald B. Gardner (1884–1964) to create a new Goddess-oriented religion, which he saw as a continuation of ancient practice in Europe before the arrival of Christianity. Many of the elements of Yule survived as Christianity became the dominant religion and integrated as much of Pagan practice that did not directly contradict the faith into its life. The contemporary use of a slow-burning Yule log and holly derive from Yule. The holiday was also celebrated for 12 days, and there is some reason to conclude that the Christian calendar's setting 12 days between Christmas and Epiphany reflects earlier Pagan practice.

Yule was primarily a festival among the Germanic people, a time to break the boring patterns of winter's existence and gather for storytelling—hero tales being popular items for retelling—and to dream about life in the coming spring and summer.

In the modern world, in which Pagans and Wiccans remain a small minority, Yule has joined the growing list of midwinter celebrations proposed by those who do not celebrate the dominant Christmas season. Many Pagans draw upon modern historical knowledge of the ancient Roman festival to the sun god, which even many Christians now acknowledge as the rationale for the dating of Christmas near the winter solstice (a date that drifted due to inaccuracies with the Julian calendar). Pagans celebrate Yule on the winter solstice, December 21.

For modern Pagans, Yule comes as the amount of daily sunlight is at its least and weather is cold, with several months of more cold ahead. However, they see it as a time to note that the sun has traveled to the Southern Hemisphere, is now beginning its journey back, and will soon bring the spring and summer. The giving of gifts has been added to Yule, an accommodation to Christmas primarily for the children.

Most Yule celebrations/rituals are done in the small groups (covens, groves, nests) around which Wiccans and Pagans are organized.

J. Gordon Melton

See also Beltane; Christmas; Eostara; Fall Equinox; Festival of Light (Rosicrucian); HumanLight; Imbolc; Lammas; Samhain; Spring Equinox (Vernal); Summer Solstice; Winter Solstice.

References

Benson, Christine. *Wiccan Holidays—A Celebration of the Wiccan Year: 365 Days in the Witches Year.* Southfield, MI: Equity Press, 2008.

Cabot, Laurie, with Jean Mills. *Celebrate the Earth: A Year of Holidays in the Pagan Tradition.* New York: Delta, 1994.

Crowley, Vivianne. *Principles of Paganism.* London: Thorsons, 1996.

Harvey, Graham. *Contemporary Paganism: Listening People, Speaking Earth.* New York: New York University Press, 1997.

Nock, Judy Ann. *Provenance Press's Guide to the Wiccan Year: A Year Round Guide to Spells, Rituals, and Holiday Celebrations.* Avon, MA: Adams Media, 2007.

Z

Zaccheus Sunday

Zaccheus is a New Testament character whom Jesus meets briefly as he traveled through Jericho. He was a wealthy man, largely despised by the Judeans because he collected taxes for the occupying Romans, but he had heard of Jesus and wanted to catch a glimpse of him.

> And he sought to see Jesus who he was; and could not for the crowd, because he was little of stature. And he ran on before, and climbed up into a sycamore tree to see him: for he was to pass that way. And when Jesus came to the place, he looked up, and said unto him, "Zaccheus, make haste, and come down; for to-day I must abide at thy house."
>
> And he made haste, and came down, and received him joyfully. And when they saw it, they all murmured, saying, He is gone in to lodge with a man that is a sinner. And Zaccheus stood, and said unto the Lord, "Behold, Lord, the half of my goods I give to the poor; and if I have wrongfully exacted aught of any man, I restore fourfold."
>
> And Jesus said unto him, "To-day is salvation come to this house, forasmuch as he also is a son of Abraham. For the Son of man came to seek and to save that which was lost." (Luke 19:3–10)

After this brief encounter, Zaccheus dropped out of the biblical text as swiftly as he had entered it. Biblical commentators have seen Zaccheus as someone who went out his way to meet Jesus, who showed humility, and eventually repented of his sins as a result of this encounter.

In the Eastern Orthodox and Eastern Catholic churches, a Lenten fast is held for seven weeks before the celebration of Holy week and Easter. In addition to Lent, there is a three-week preparation for the coming Great Lenten fast. The Sunday prior to that three-week preparation is the Sunday in which the gospel text is Luke 19: 1–10, the story of Zaccheus. Hence the name, Zaccheus Sunday. It begins the annual cycle of worship centered on Easter. It occurs on a different day every year, but is always 11 weeks before Easter.

Though Zaccheus was a relatively minor character in the New Testament, over the centuries, various writers supplied additional biographical details concerning his life. Clement of Alexander (c. 150–c. 215) identified him with Matthius, the person chosen to join the Apostles after Judas committed suicide (Acts 1:21–26).

In other traditions, he was identified as the first bishop of Caesarea, a city located south of present-day Haifa, Israel.

J. Gordon Melton

See also Easter; Lazarus Saturday; Lent.

References

Farley, Lawrence. *Let Us Attend: A Journey through the Orthodox Divine Liturgy.* Ben Lomond, CA: Conciliar Press, 2007.

Stewart, Mary. *A Man Named Zacchaeus: Jesus Miracle Stops and Parables.* Bloomington, IN: AuthorHouse, 2008.

Wybrew, Hugh. *The Orthodox Liturgy: The Development of the Eucharistic Liturgy in the Byzantine Rite.* Yonkers, NY: St. Vladimir's Seminary Press, 1997.

Zarathustra, Commemorative Days of (March 26, December 26)

The Prophet Zarathustra or Zoroaster was the founder of the Zoroastrian faith. One of the earliest religious leaders known to have existed, he is often cited as contemporaneous with Moses. In fact, little is known of Zoroaster's life, which scholars have placed as early as the sixth century BCE and as recently as the 16th century. He is generally associated with Bactria, a land that included parts of present-day Afghanistan, Tajikistan, and Uzbekistan. Many different groups have their own stories of Zarathustra and suggest that he was of their tribe.

He flourished in what is now eastern Iran, Afghanistan, and Turkmenistan and centered his teachings on the existence of one creator God, named Ahura Mazda or "Lord Wisdom." Some speculate on his life from an analysis of the Gathas, holy books incorporated into the Zoroastrian sacred scripture, the Avesta. The Denkard, another part of the Avesta, a part written last, contains a brief biography of Zarathustra, but it appears to be more legendary than historical in content.

Little is also known of the end of Zarathustra's life. Different sources suggest that he died peacefully in his sleep, while others state that he was murdered. Others suggest that he was in the temple, possibly killed there by an invading army.

Contemporary Zoroastrians have commemorated Zoroaster on two dates: his birth on March 26, and his death on December 26. No one knows the date of Zoroaster's birth (known as Khordad Sal) or death, but on March 26 (in late August or early September in India), and December 26 (late May or early June in India), believers will organize gatherings at which prayers are recited and speeches centered on the life and teachings of Zoroaster are delivered. March 26 is just a few days after the Zoroastrian New Year (Nowruz), and revelers will often simply continue the New Year's celebration for several days and conclude it on March 26. On each occasion, Zoroastrians will visit one of their fire temples if possible. Non-Zoroastrians are not invited to these gatherings, as they are not allowed in the temple. Zarthost No Deeso, as Zoroaster's death day is known in India, prompts observances especially in Mumbai and in the state of Gujarat.

J. Gordon Melton

See also Fravardegan; Gahambars; Nowruz; Zoroastrianism.

References

Boyce, Mary. *Zoroastrians: Their Religious Beliefs and Practices*. London: Routledge, 2001.

Hinnells, John R. *Zoroastrians in Britain*. Oxford: Clarendon, 1996.

Kriwaczek, Paul. *In Search of Zarathustra: Across Iran and Central Asia to Find the World's First Prophet*. New York: Vintage, 2004.

Nigosian, S. A. *The Zoroastrian Faith: Tradition and Modern Research*. Montreal, QC: McGill-Queen's University Press, 1993.

Writer, R. *Contemporary Zoroastrians: An Unstructured Nation*. Lanham, MD: University Press of America, 1994.

Zartusht-no-diso (December 26)

The birth and death dates of Zarathustra (or Zoroaster), the founder of the Zoroastrian faith, are a matter of intense debate. While some place his life as early as the fifth millennium BCE, the more commonly accepted date is during the second millennium BCE. It is believed that he came from what is now Kazakhstan, where the modern Iranian people originated. After he influenced a tribal chief named Vishtaspa, the Iranians carried Zarathustra's teachings with them into northeastern Iran around the 12th century BCE. From there, it spread among the Medes and Persians. In the sixth century BCE, during the reign of Cyrus the Great (559–530 BCE), it reached a new zenith as the Persian Empire encompassed a land from Turkey to Afghanistan. Zorastrianism remained a powerful force in the Middle East until the emergence of Islam in the seventh century and the overrunning of those countries previously dominated by Zorastrianism by Muslim forces.

While becoming a minority religion even in Iran, Zorastrianism has survived, primarily in Iran and India; but it has spread to the West, and small communities now exist in Great Britain, Canada, and the United States. The total global community has been reduced to between 100,000 and 200,000.

Zarathustra died at the age of 77, though how he died has been a matter of conjecture. Zoroastrian tradition suggests that he may have been killed while praying in the sanctuary by a foreign enemy of the king in whose court he served. Other traditions believe that he died peacefully.

Zartusht-no-diso is the day in the Zoroastrian sacred calendar designated for worshippers to remember the death of Zarathustra. On that day, special prayers are recited, and believers make a visit to the temple to mark the anniversary.

J. Gordon Melton

Zarathustra, or Zoroaster, is credited with founding Zoroastrianism, though little more is known about him. (Hulton Archive/Getty Images)

See also Zarathustra, Commemoration Day of; Zoroastrianism.

References

Hinnells, John R. *Zoroastrians in Britain*. Oxford: Clarendon Press, 1996.

Modi, Jivanji J. *The Religious Ceremonies and Customs of the Parsees*. New York: Garland, 1979.

"Zarathustra's Life." Parsi Zoroastrian Association of Singapore. Posted at http://www.pza.org.sg/index.html. Accessed June 15, 2010.

■ Zoroastrianism

Zoroastrianism, the ancient religion of Persia (Iran), is most known in the West from the biblical story told of the Magi visiting the child Jesus (Matthew 2). The wise men known for their searching the heavens for signs were Zoroastrians who would take note of a new star. In ancient Persia, large pyramidal structures called ziggurats were erected from which the Zoroastrian priests could make their astronomical/astrological observations.

Zoroastrianism is named for Zarathustra (or Zoroaster). Little is known about Zarathustra, including the years in which he lived. The best estimate is that he came from that area of modern Kazakhstan east of the Volga River from which the Iranian people originated. It is believed that he influenced a tribal chief named Vishtaspa in his favor, and that his faith was then carried among the Iranians when they moved into northeastern Iran around the 12th century BCE. Zarathustra may have lived as early as the 17th century. From that base, Zoroastrianism spread among the Medes and Persians in western Iran.

During the reign of Cyrus the Great (559–530 BCE), an empire was created that extended from Turkey to Afghanistan. Under Cyrus, Zoroastrianism moved from its prehistorical to its historical phase, when Cyrus made it the empire's state religion. By this time, the ziggurats were in place, as were the Magi, originally the priestly class from the Medes. The life of Zoroastrianism was completely disrupted during the conquests of Alexander the Great. Among other actions in subduing the land, Alexander burned Percepolis, the capital, and in the process destroyed many Zoroastrian records and writings. Then, in the name of spreading Hellenistic culture, his successors suppressed Zoroastrianism until a new Persian Empire was finally created toward the end of the second century BCE. The Parthian Empire (c. 129–224) reestablished the primacy of Zoroastrianism, which it enjoyed through successive regimes until the coming of the Arabs and Islam in the seventh century. For the next centuries, Zoroastrianism would battle Islam for the hearts of the people, and by the 10th century, it had become not only the state religion, but also the dominant religion practiced across the Persian lands.

The dislodging of the Zoroastrian leaders from the Persian court became the motivation for some to begin the migration to what was perceived as a less hostile land, and early in the eighth century, migrations to western India began. They became the nucleus of the Parsee (or Persian) Zoroastrian community, which from India has now spread to Africa and the West.

Zarathustra preached a dualistic understanding of the universe. In it, two forces fight for the hearts of humans. Ahura Mazda, the eternal God, is wise, good, and just, but unfortunately, not omnipotent. There also exists a second entity, Angra Mainyu, like Ahura Mazda uncreated, but the embodiment of evil. In order to defeat Angra Mainyu, Ahura Mazda created the world, which exists as a battleground between the good and the bad. To assist him in the creative act, he called upon his Holy Spirit and evoked the Holy Immortals, all emanations of the one God. His emanations are, however, properly seen as divine. and as such are objects of veneration and even worship. Each of these seven emanations represents a high value, such as truth, health, or power. Zoroastrians should invite these Holy Immortals into their lives and make these qualities/values their own.

In the cosmic battle, Angra Mainyu brought evil spirits to oppose the Holy Immortals, some pictured as gods of war. They brought death into the world. The good spirit countered evil by bringing more life into existence to replace those who have died. Individuals are called through their life to align with good or evil, and will be judged at the end by which choices they made.

Humans have an important role in the cosmic battle. Collectively, they have the power to align with good and become the decisive force in the ultimate triumph of goodness. Then, at the end of earthly life, each person will be judged; those who were more good than bad will go to a heavenly existence, and the others are destined for hell and punishment. Although the dominant form of Zoroastrianism looked for the gradual triumph of good over evil and the eventual destruction of the evil order, a second form of understanding the end-time, an apocalyptic system, also developed. In that second presentation, evil would gradually win, with an accompanying increase in chaos, natural disasters, and social ills. The inevitable growth of evil would at the last moment be halted by the appearance of a Saoshyant, a Savior figure who will appear out of the family of Zarathustra to lead a final battle of good people triumphing over the evil one. The dead will then be resurrected and the final judgment will take place. At that time, the evil will be destroyed and the good purged of the remaining evil they possess. The good will enjoy eternal life. The correlations of this form of Zoroastrianism with later Christian perspectives are obvious.

The Zoroastrian cosmology is derived from its scripture, the Avesta, a volume of approximately 1,000 pages. The oldest part of the Avesta consists of the Gathas, the hymns of Zarathustra, which are written in an ancient dialect known as Old Avestan. The original collection of the Avesta, known to have existed in the ninth century (two centuries after the Muslim takeover of Persia), included some 21 books. Much of the text was lost in subsequent years, the present text being the result.

In addition to the Avesta, Zoroastrians recognize a second level of holy writings that were written and compiled in the centuries of the Sassnian Persian Empire (third to seventh centuries CE). They are distinguished by being written in a later Persian dialect called Pahlavi. These texts include commentaries on the Gathas and summaries of the lost Avesta texts. Although the Pahlavi texts have an important role, the Avesta remains the primary sacred text.

Leadership in the Zoroastrian community is supplied by the priests, identified by their all-white clothing, a symbol of the high value placed on purity and cleanliness in Zoroastrian culture. They oversee the temples, at the center of which are the ever-burning fires, which are symbols of righteousness. Fire is a key reality in Zoroastrian life and culture. It symbolizes light and ties the believer to the heavens through the fiery lightning bolt—and acknowledges the importance that fire has had in the daily life of individuals, at least in pretechnological cultures. The Gathas speak of fire as the creation of Ahura Mazda and set fire as the superior symbol of divinity, as opposed to the idols, which it replaced. The primary fire is the Atash Bahram, which is created with special rituals of consecration and remains burning brightly in the primary hall of a temple. Lesser fires, the Atash-I-Aduran and the Dadgah, are used for minor rituals and as the center of space used for daily prayers.

Youth are initiated into the faith by passing through a simple ceremony that begins with learning a set of prayers. On the day of the ceremony, they engage in some purification rituals and don a sacred shirt. Performing ablution rituals will be a standard beginning to all sacred acts in the future. The heart of the rather brief ceremony is the reception of the sacred cord, called a *kusti*, from a priest. The cord is wrapped three times around the waist over the shirt, and then tied with a simple knot. The ceremony is like a wedding, a moment for general celebration by friends and relatives. The full member of the faith is expected to engage in prayer five times daily (similar to Muslim practice) before a fire. During the prayers, the kusti is untied and retied.

The Zoroastrian Calendar

The Zoroastrian calendar has undergone a variety of transformation over the years. The traditional calendar had twelve 30-day months with five days added at the end of each year. By the beginning of the 11th century, the date of the beginning of the year had drifted considerably from the spring equinox, and the celebration of the season no longer fit the time for celebration. A revision was instituted in

2006, with plans for an added month periodically to keep the calendar aligned. This calendar is called the *Shahenshahi* (or imperial) calendar.

The Iranians appear to have made that addition of the needed month in their calendar on one occasion, but the Indian Zoroastrians never did, thus creating a 30-day difference in the two calendars. In succeeding centuries, as the needed changes were neglected, the calendar gradually drifted again.

In 1720, the visit of an Iranian priest among his fellow believers in India resulted in a branch of the Indian Zoroastrians eventually reforming their calendar (in 1745). The new calendar in use in Iran and among the reformists in India came be called the *Kadmi* calendar. The calendar used by most of the Indian Zoroastrians, the Farsis, was called the *Shahenshali* or imperial calendar.

Then in 1906, a calendar reform movement was initiated by the Zarthosti Fasili Sal Mandal, or Zoroastrian Seasonal-Year Society. The *Fasli* calendar, as it became known, included two prominent features: (1) New Year's Day was located on the spring or vernal equinox, and (2) it used an old Egyptian-Zoroastrian format with 12 months of 30 days each, with five days added at the end of the year and a leap year day added every four years.

The Indian Zoroastrians showed indifference to the new calendar, but in Iran quite apart from the Fasli movement, a new calendar, the Bastani calendar, was adopted by the Iranian Parliament. It incorporated the two major features of the Fasli calendar, and retained the Zoroastrian names of the months. Subsequently, the *Bastani* calendar was accepted by the majority of Zoroastrians. Only in Yazd, an important ritual center, did the community resist, and to this day the Zoroastrians of Yazd follow the *Kadmi* calendar.

In the *Fasli/Bastani* variant of the Zoroastrian calendar, Navroz (New Year's Day) is always the day of the vernal equinox (nominally falling on March 21). In the *Shahenshahi* and *Kadmi* calendars, which do not account for leap years, the New Year's Day has drifted ahead and now occurs in August. These latter two variants of the calendar are followed by the Zoroastrians of India and around Yazd in Iran, who celebrate the spring equinox as *Jamshed-i Nouroz*, with their New Year's Day then being celebrated in August.

The Bastani Zoroastrian calendar now begins on the spring equinox (March 21 on the Common Era calendar) with 12 months of 30 days each:

1. Frawardin
2. Ardwahisht
3. Khordad
4. Tir
5. Amurdad
6. Shahrewar
7. Mihr

Iranian Zoroastrians gather and share food during Farvardigan in Tehran on April 8, 2009. (AP/Wide World Photos)

8. Aban
9. Adur
10. Dae
11. Wahman
12. Spendarmad

Zoroastrian Holidays

Among the important rituals to which Zoroastrians must periodically give attention are funerals. Rituals are designed to deal with the uncleanliness of the body of the deceased and to assist the soul on its way. Traditionally, the body is placed on a high tower and its flesh devoured by vultures and the bones bleached by the sun. Today, cremation is more common, especially in the West. The funcral is then directed toward the soul, which is believed to linger close by for three days. The funeral is done the day after the death, but the priests continue the rituals for the deceased for the next several days. The family joins in important good-bye activities on the fourth day. Commemoration of the deceased will continue monthly for the next year and then annually for the next 30 years at the annual ceremony for the dead. The day may be celebrated in the temple or in people's homes.

The last 10 days of the Zoroastrian calendar (which include the last five days of the last month and the five days added to the year before the New Year begins) are known as the *Fravardegan* (also spelled Farvardagân) or *Muktad* days. During these days, believers offer special prayers for the fravashis (the divine essence, not to be confused with the soul) of their departed loved ones. During this period, it is believed that the fravashis of the righteous dead descend from the spiritual realm into the material world in order to bless those who have remembered and prayed for them.

The annual time of special acknowledgment of the deceased is just one holy period ritualized by Zoroastrians. The most important are the seven obligatory holy days that acknowledge the one God Ahura Mazda and the six Holy Immortals, Nowruz, or "New Day" (which celebrates the beginning of the year according to the Zoroastrian calendar), and the six *gahambars*, or days of obligation. The Zoroastrian year has six seasons, with one of the gahambars (festivals) in each season. Celebration of the gahambars is largely limited to the Zoroastrian community, as nonmembers are not invited to Zoroastrian temples.

Nowruz is celebrated on the first day of the Zoroastrian month of Frawardin. The first of the gahambars follows at the end of April, with others approximately every two months. The five-day gahambar festivals are observed with prayers, ritual offerings, and communal feasts designed to give thanks to Ahura Mazda for his many bounties and to acknowledge the change of seasons. The gahambars and their approximate dates (for those following the Bastani calendar) on the Common Era calendar are:

Gahambar Hamaspathmaedem (March 16–20)

Gahambar Maidyozarem (April 30–May 4)

Gahambar Maidyoshem (June 29–July 3)

Gahambar Paitishahem (to celebrate the creation of the earth, September)

Gahambar Ayathrem (to celebrate the creation of plant life, October 12–16)

Gahambar Maidyarem (to celebrate the creation of animals, December)

In addition, there are two holidays celebrating the religion's founder, Zarathustra (or Zoroaster):

Khordad Sal, or the Birth of Zarathustra (March 26)

Death of Zarathustra (December 26); known in India as Zartusht-no-diso or Zarthost No Deeso

Recent History

The movement of Zoroastrians to India beginning in the ninth century created two somewhat separated communities. Given their poverty and existence in a more-or-less hostile climate, there was little contact between them over the next centuries, and each community developed its own distinctive customs while trying to preserve its community and faith. Some changes came to the communities as they began to interact with the British in the 18th and 19th centuries. The rise of British power in India preceded the emergence of the Parsees as a well-to-do trading community. In the 18th century, they had developed trading centers in the Orient (the history of which continues in the small Parsee community still found in Hong Kong).

As the British entered East Africa, Zoroastrians relocated to Zanzibar, Mombassa, and Nairobi, from where they expanded inland. By the mid-20th century, though remaining a somewhat separatist community culturally and religiously, they became prosperous, with members assuming leading roles in the business community and the professions. As decolonization proceeded, the Parsees were among the Asians who were viewed as having secured their position because of colonial advantages, and pressure came to bear on many to leave—especially during the regime of Idi Amin in Uganda. Rather than return to India, many Parsees relocated to the West. The largest community has emerged in London and its immediate environs, but scatted communities have also appeared across the United States and Canada, and more recently in Australia.

Meanwhile in India, the Parsee community had tended to shift from Gujarat southward toward Mumbai and into what is now Pakistan. The largest communities currently are in Mumbai and Karachi. In both countries, Parsees have become prominent business leaders and, on occasion, have served in important political posts.

The Zoroastrian community in Iran almost disappeared at the end of the 19th century, but through the 20th century, it experienced a revival, growing fivefold. Zoroastrians have enjoyed guarantees of religious freedom articulated in the 1906 Constitution of Iran, and toleration under the post-1979 changes wrought by the Islamic Revolution. They are expected to observe Islamic codes of public conduct. They are represented at the Majlis (parliament) and serve in the armed forces. Furthermore, many members of these religions fought side by side with Muslim Iranians in the Constitutional Uprising of the late 19th century that finally resulted in the Constitution of 1906.

A visit by a group of Parsee priests to Iran in the late 1990s found that in spite of the revival, much was still lacking in the Iranian Zoroastrian community. The religion is, to put it bluntly, in shambles. There was no place where the major ritual ceremonies could be performed. None of the priests were holding the *barashoom*, the purification ceremony necessary to perform the "inner" rituals, which can be done only by a priest in the sacred space in the temple. There are fire temples in several cities, but some did not have the fires burning. The priests are largely uneducated, and many do not wear their priestly garb. Many laypeople do not wear the sacred shirt and cord. Although discouraged somewhat by what they had observed, the delegation held out hope for the continued revival and rebuilding of the Iranian community with assistance from India and the West.

Currently, Zoroastrians may be seen as divided into two primary communities, one based in Iran and the other in India, with both communities represented by diaspora communities in Africa and the West. The communities are further divided by what might be seen as traditionalist and modernist wings. The latter group has adapted to life in urban centers and the modern West. Traditionalists adhere with more strictness to older rituals and prayer life, and pay attention to the laws of purity relative to women in their menstrual cycle and the bodies of the dead (traditionally, there were people set apart as unclean, whose job was to handle corpses). They eschew cremation and demand disposal of corpses by carrion birds and the sun. They do not sanction marriage outside the faith, and do not engage in attempts to convert others to Zoroastrianism.

In the West, several organizations have arisen to serve the Zoroastrian community. In 1980, an international group of Zoroastrian leaders founded the World Zoroastrian Organization, based in London, out of an expressed desire especially among diaspora Zoroastrians for an international structure to protect, unite, and sustain what is a very small community, almost invisible in the pluralistic West. In North America, where many Parsees migrated after 1965, a number of local Zoroastrian associations were established. In 1987, a number of these associations came together to create the Federation of Zoroastrian Associations of North America. Many of these associations, representative of the more modernist trends in the Western Zoroastrian community, also support the World Zoroastrian Organization. There are several local associations of Iranian Zoroastrians in North America, primarily along the Canadian and U.S. West coasts.

As early as 1962, a World Zoroastrian Congress was held in Tehran, Iran. Successive congresses have been held irregularly, the ninth meeting having been in Dubai in 2009.

J. Gordon Melton

See also Fravardegan; Gahambars; Now Ruz; Zarathustra, Commemoration days of.

References

Boyce, Mary. *A History of Zoroastrianism.* 3 vols. Leiden: Brill, 1975, 1982, 1991.

Boyce, Mary. *Zoroastrians: Their Religious Beliefs and Practices.* London: Routledge, 2001.

Geldner, K. *Avesta: The Sacred Books of the Parsis.* 3 vols. Stuttgart, Germany: Kohlhammer, 1986.

Hinnells, John R. *Zoroastrians in Britain.* Oxford: Clarendon, 1996.

Kriwaczek, Paul. *In Search of Zarathustra: Across Iran and Central Asia to Find the World's First Prophet.* New York: Vintage, 2004.

Nigosian, S. A. *The Zoroastrian Faith: Tradition and Modern Research.* Montreal, Quebec, Canada: McGill-Queen's University Press, 1993.

Writer, R. *Contemporary Zoroastrians: An Unstructured Nation.* Lanham, MD: University Press of America, 1994.

About the Editor and Contributors

The Editor

J. GORDON MELTON is distinguished professor of American religious history at Baylor University, Waco, TX, and the director of the Institute for the Study of American Religion, located in Waco after many years in Santa Barbara, CA. Melton is the author of more than 40 books, including *American Religions: An Illustrated History*; *Melton's Encyclopedia of American Religions*, now in its eighth edition; and *A Will to Choose: The Origins of African American Methodism.*

The Contributors

MARTIN BAUMANN is professor of the Study of Religions at the University of Lucerne in Switzerland. His research interests focus on religious pluralism and public space, migration and religion, diaspora studies, and Hindu and Buddhist traditions in the West. He has published on these topics in both English and German, and his most recent coedited book is *Eine Schweiz—viele Religionen* (2007).

JAMES A. BEVERLEY is professor of Christian thought and ethics at Tyndale Seminary in Toronto, Canada, and associate director of the Institute for the Study of American Religion. He is a specialist on new religious movements and the relationship of Christianity to other world religions. He is author and editor of 10 books, including *Islam* (2011), *Islamic Faith in America* (2011), and *Nelson's Illustrated Guide to Religions* (2009).

CHRISTOPHER BUCK is a Pennsylvania attorney and independent scholar. He holds a PhD from the University of Toronto (1996) and JD from Cooley Law School (2006). He previously taught at Michigan State University (2000–2004), Quincy University (1999–2000), Millikin University (1997–1999), and Carleton University (1994–1996). His publications include: *Religious Myths and Visions of America: How Minority Faiths Redefined America's World Role* (2009); *Alain Locke: Faith and Philosophy* (2005); *Paradise and Paradigm: Key Symbols in Persian Christianity and the Bahá'í Faith* (1999); *Symbol and Secret: Qur'an Commentary in Bahá'u'lláh's Kitáb-i Íqán* (1995, 2004), various book chapters, encyclopedia articles, and journal articles.

EDWARD ALLEN IRONS is the director of the Hong Kong Institute for Culture, Religion, and Commerce, a religious studies research facility concentrating on Hong Kong and Chinese cultural studies, Chinese religions, and the interaction of cultural and religious issues with commerce in contemporary society.

CONSTANCE A. JONES is a professor of transformative studies at the California Institute of Integral Studies, San Francisco. She received her PhD in sociology from Emory University and was awarded a postdoctoral fellowship at the Center for the Study of New Religious Movements of the Graduate Theological Union in Berkeley, California. Beginning with her doctoral dissertation on the caste system in India, she has pursued a lifelong interest in the cultures and religions of the East. As a Fulbright scholar in India, she taught at Banaras Hindu University and Vasanta College and conducted research at the Krishnamurti Study Center, Varanasi. She is a member of the International Advisory Board for "The Complete Teachings of J. Krishnamurti, 1910–1986." Her publications include: the *Encyclopedia of Hinduism* (with James D. Ryan, 2007); *The Legacy of G. I. Gurdjieff*

(2005); *G. I. Gurdjieff from South Caucasus to Western World: His Influence on Spirituality, Thought and Culture in Italy, Europe, and the U.S.A.* (2007).

PAMELA S. NADELL is the Inaugural Patrick Clendenen Professor of History and director of the Jewish Studies Program at American University. Her books include *Women Who Would Be Rabbis: A History of Women's Ordination, 1889–1985* (1998), which was a finalist for the National Jewish Book Award. She is past chair of the Academic Council of the American Jewish Historical Society, book review editor of the journal *American Jewish History*, and one of four members of the historians' team of the new National Museum of American Jewish History, scheduled to open in Philadelphia in November 2010.

KEVIN QUAST has taught in the area of religious studies at colleges, universities, and seminaries across Canada for the past 25 years. Presently, he teaches part-time for Tyndale Seminary (Toronto) and lives in Edmonton, Alberta, Canada. Dr. Quast has published 3 books and more than 100 articles and chapters in academic and popular journals. In addition to his teaching and writing, he has served as a pastor, chaplain and academic dean.

ELIJAH SIEGLER received his BA from Harvard University and his MA from the University of California at Santa Barbara, both in religious studies. He is currently completing his doctorate at UCSB, writing on the history and practice of Taoism in America. His published works include articles on religion on television police dramas and on New Age channeling groups, and a book, *New Religious Movements* (2006).

ROBERT STOCKMAN has a doctorate in history of religion in the United States from Harvard University. He is the author of *The Bahá'í Faith in America, I* (1985) and *The Bahá'í Faith in America, II* (1994), *Thornton Chase: The First American Bahá'í* (2002), as well as various articles about Bahá'í history and theology. Currently he is Director of the Wilmette Institute, an online Bahá'í educational institution, as well as an instructor in religious studies at DePaul University.

JAROSLAV Z. SKIRA is an associate professor of historical theology and Director of the Eastern Christian Studies Program at Regis College, University of Toronto, Canada.

Index

Note: Page numbers in **bold** indicate main entries in the encyclopedia. i after page number indicates illustrations.

95 Theses, 741–42
2012 (Pinchbeck), 573
"A Mighty Fortress Is Our God," 742
Aasanyukta mudras, 596
'Abbás, 87
Abbey of Fulda, 125
Abbey of Kildare, 128
'Abduh, Muhammad, 438
'Abdu'l-Bahá
  appointed "Centre of the Covenant," 97
  ascension of, **1–4**
  on Bahá'í teachings, 92
  Bahá'u'lláh, Ascension of, 96
  Covenant, Day of the, 225–27
  on fasting, 94–95
  Nineteen-Day Feast, 642–43
  on other religions, 91–92
  Parsons and, 728
  Race Unity Day and, 729–30
  spreading of Bahá'í Faith, 87–88
  succession of, 98
  The Tablets of the Divine Plan, 89
  writings of, 90
'Abdu'l-Bahá, Ascension of, **1–4**
'Abdu'l-Hamíd, Sultán, 96
Abgar, King, 199, 419
Abhaya mudra, 596, 597
Abhidhamma Day, **4–5**, 145
Abizadeh, Arash, 746
Aboakyer Festival, **5–6**
Abraham, Prophet, 417, 475
Abu Bakr, 21
Acorn Feast, **6–7**
Acts of Pilate, 251
Acts of the Apostles, 222, 682–83, 689
Adalbert of Magdeburg, Archbishop, 7
Adalbert of Prague, Saint's
  Day of St., **7–8**
Adams, John, 881
Ad caeli reginam, 726
Addai (Thaddeus), 199
Ad-Din, Khair, 438
Adidam, 8–9, 57–58, 234, 613
Adi Da Samraj, **57–58**, 58i, 234–35, 613
Adi Da Samrajashram, Anniversary of Adi
  Da's First Footstep on, **8–9**
Adi Granth, 355
Adinath, Lord, 19, 495
Adishesha, 364, 601
Aditi, 605
Aditya, 325
The Admirable Heart (Eudes), 423
Adoration, Feast of the, 280
Adrian II, Pope, 230
Adrian VI, Pope, 166
Advaita Vedanta, 57, 796–97
Advent, **9–11**, 526
Advent calendars, 10
Adventist Christians, 675–76, 769
Affan, Uthman ibn, 442
African Methodist Quarterly Meeting Day,
  11–12
African Union Church, 11
African Union Methodist Protestant Church,
  11–12
Agamas, 357
Agency for Spiritual Guidance, 808
The Age of Reason (Paine), 857i, 858

Aggai, 199
Agnes, Feast Day of St., 12i, **12–14**, 690
Agnosticism, 879
Agnostics, 426
Agon Shu, 342–43, 411, 851–52
Agostino de Jesus, Frei, 42
Agua, La Fiesta de, **14–15**
Ahasuerus, King, 719–20
Ahoi Ashtami, **15**
Ahsá'í, Shaykh Ahmad, 68
Ahura Mazda, 957
Airing the Classics, **15–16**
Aiwass, 302, 309
Aizen-Myoo, 16
Aizen Summer Festival, **16–17**
Ajahn Chah, 135
Ajapa Yoga Society, 115, 458, 707, 721
Akaranga Sutra, 357
Akbar, emperor, 383, 558, 634
Akha Teej. *See* Akshay Tritiya (Jain)
Aki Matsuri, **17–18**
Akshay Tritiiya, **18–19**
Akshay Tritiya (Jain), **19–20**, 455
Alacoque, Margaret Mary, 757–58
Al-Afghani, Jamaluddin, 438
Alakar, 195
Alaska National Lands Conservation Act of 1980, 704
Albania, 884
Al-Banna, Hasan, 438
Albany, New York, 62
Albigensians, 258
Aldersgate Day, **20–21**
Alexander I (Yugoslavian ruler), 408, 467
Alexander II, Pope, 834, 869
Alexander Severus, emperor, 846
Alexander the Great, 478, 956
Alexius Comnenus, emperor, **859**
Al-Husayn, 22
Ali, Husayn, 47, 629
Ali ibn Abi Talib, Commemoration Days for, **21–22**
Allah, 431, 432, 434, 435, 516. *See also* Islam
Allahabad, India, 505–6, 570
All Hallow's Eve. *See* Halloween
Alliance for Secular Humanist Societies, 238
All Saints Day, **22–23**, 275, 277, 403, 631, 774
All Saints Eve, 366, 631
All Souls Day, **23–25**, 275, 277
Al-Masjid al-Harām mosque, 433
Alphabet Day, **25–26**
Alphonse de Ligouri, Saint's Day of St., **26–27**
Alphonse II, King, 456
Al Queda, 438
Alsean people, 310
Altan Khan, 139
Amalaka Ekadashi, **27–28**
Amarnath Yatra, **28–29**
Amaterasu, 601, 806, 813–14
Amaterasu Omikami, 492, 865
Ambedkar, B. R., 633
Ambrose, Bishop, 54, 824
Ambrose, Saint, 782
Ambuvachi, **29–30**
Ame-no-mi-naka-nushi-no-Kami, 174, 806
American Association for the Advancement of Atheism, 886
American Atheists, 886
American Humanist Association, 238, 413, 886, 931
Amida Buddha, 625, 804
Amitabha, 543, 625
Amitabha Buddha, 351, 804
Amitabha's Birthday, **30–32**
Ammianus Marcellinus, 285
Anabaptists, 569. *See also* Mennonites
Analects, 182–83, 185
Ananda Ashrama, 784
Ananda Church of Self-Realization, 77, 512, 941, 942–43
Ananda Marga Yoga Society, 385
Anandi Ma, Shri, 248
Anant Chaturdashi, **32–33**
Anapanasati Day, **33–34**
Anapanasati Sutta, 33–34
Ancestor worship, 181–82
Ancient Mystical Order of the Rosae Crucis (AMORC), 303
Ancient Order of Druids, 840
'Andalib, 97–98
Andrei I, Prince, 713
Andrew, Brother, 429
Andrew, Saint's Day of St., **34–36**
Andrey the God-Loving, 713
Angkor Wat, 134i, 135

Anglican Church
All Saints Day, 23
Annunciation, Feast of the, 39
Ascension Day, 45
Ash Wednesday, **49–50**
Augustine of Canterbury, Saint's Day of St., 53
Bartholomew's Day, Saint, 105, 106
Boniface of Germany, Saint's Day of St., **125–26**, 925
Circumcision, Feast of the, 215
Conversion of St. Paul, Feast of the, 223
emergence of, 880
Epiphany, 286
establishment of, 207
Eucharist and, 928
Eucharistic Congresses, 291
George, Feast Day of St., 333
Gregory the Great, Saint, 346
James the Greater, Feast Day of St., 456
John the Baptist, Beheading of, 466
John the Baptist, Nativity of, 468
John the Evangelist, Day of St., **469–70**
Lord's Supper, 567
Mary Magdalene, Day of the Holy, 565
Michaelmas, 580
Nativity of Mary, 614–15
Restoration, 208
Rogation Days, 749
saints and, 768–69
Transfiguration, Feast of the, 866
Trinity Monday, **867**
Trinity Sunday, 867
Angra Mainyu, 957
Animals
Anthony of Padua, St., and, 40–41
Buddha and, 581, 624
Elephant Festival, **279–80**
Pooram, 700
Songkran, 826
zodiac and, 159
Animal sacrifice, 240, 363, 380, 417
Anís, 74–75
Anjana, 372
Anna Koot. *See* Diwali; Govardhan Puja
Anne (mother of Mary), 614
Anne, Feast Day of St., **36–37**
Anne of Austria, 36, 695–96
Annianus of Alexandria, 288
Annunciation, Feast of the, **37–39**, 293, 909–10
Ansgar, Saint's Day of St., **39–40**
Anthony of Padua, Saint's Day of St., **40–41**
Anthony the Abbott, Saint, 41
Anti-Catholic bigotry, 608
Anti-Defamation League, 608
Antiochus IV, king, 478
Antiochus IV Epiphanes, 369–70, 486
Anti-Semitism, 482–83, 608, 945
Anula, Queen, 702, 781
Anuruddha, king, 134
Anusuya, 242–43
Aparecida, Feast of Our Lady of, **41–43**, 564
Apostles (Christian), 197, 198i. *See also specific apostles*
Apostolic Catholic Assyrian Church, 201
Apparitions
of Jesus, 757
of Michael, archangel, 579
of Virgin Mary, 299–300, 562, 595, 684
April celebrations
Adalbert of Prague, Saint's Day of St., **7–8**
Benedict the African, Saint's Day of St., **110–11**
Catherine of Siena, Saint's Day of St., **166–68**
Feast for the Three Days of the Writing of the Book of the Law, **301–3**
George, Feast Day of St., **333–34**
Hana Matsuri, **367–68**
Janardanji Paramahansa, Commemoration Days of Swami Guru, **458–59**
Mani, Commemoration of the Prophet, **549**
Peter Chanel, Saint's Day of St., **691–92**
Riḍván, Festival of, **744–47**
Stanislaus, Saint's Day of St., **834–35**
Walpurgisnacht, 108, **915–16**
Áqásí, Hájí Mírzá, 74
Aquinas, Thomas, 54, 223–24
Arab Muslim kingdom, 203
Arcane School, 919, 932–33
Ardh Kumbh Mela, 570
Arguelles, José, 572–73
Arianism, 200
Arius, 200, 556, 868

Arjan, Guru, 558
Arjuna, 336–37, 388
Ark of the Covenent, 477, 854, 861, 909
Armenia, 645–46, 901–2
Armenian Apostolic Church, 105, 201, 646
Armstrong, Herbert W., 675
Arthur, Chester A., 153
The Art of War (Sunzi), 182
Arya, 56
Aryan people, 378–80
Arya Samaj, 384
Asalha Puja Day ("Dhamma Day"), **43–44**
Asbury United Methodist Church, 11
Ascended Masters, 932
Ascension, 3, 748
Ascension Day, **45–46**, 403, 527
Ascension Sunday, 277
Ashoka, King, 133, 381, 702, 780
Ashokashtami, **46–47**
Ashura, **47–49**, 442
Ash Wednesday, 49i, **49–50**, 521. *See also* Holy Week
Asian Conference on Religion and Peace, 649
Assembly of God, 921
Assembly of the Church of the Universe, 165
Association of Shinto Shrines, 809
Assumption of the Virgin, **50–51**, 403, 562, 726
Astha-Matrikas, 239
Astion, Saint, 283–84
Astrology, Chinese, 660
Astrology, Hindu, 633
Asuras, 541, 659
Ataxerxes I, 719
Ataxerxes II, 719
Athabascan people, 703–4
Athanasian Creed, 868–69
Athanasius, Bishop, 200, 556
Atheism, 611–12, 879, 881–83, 884–85, 886. *See also* Unbelief
Atheists and Other Freethinkers of Sacramento, 320
Atisa, 139
Atlantic coast, of United States, 120
Atri Maharishi, 242–43
Aubert, Saint, 579
Aubrey, John, 840
Auditor's Day, **51–52**
August celebrations
  African Methodist Quarterly Meeting Day, **11–12**
  Alphonse de Ligouri, Saint's Day of St., **26–27**
  Assumption of the Virgin, **50–51**, 403, 562, 726
  Augustine of Hippo, Saint's Day of St., **54–56**
  Aurobindo, Birth Anniversary of Sri, **56–57**
  Bartholomew's Day, Saint, **104–6**
  Celebrity Center International, 168i, **168**
  Clement of Ohrid, Saint's Day of St., **215–16**
  Czestochowa, Feast Day of Our Lady of, **231–32**
  Dhyanyogi's Mahasamadhi, **247–48**
  Dominic, Saint's Day of St., **257–58**
  First Night of the Prophet and His Bride, **309–10**
  Forgiveness, Feast of, **312–13**
  Founders' Day, the Church of Perfect Liberty, **316–17**
  Image Not-Made-by-Hands, Feast of the, **419–20**
  Ingersoll Day, **425–27**
  Lammas, 277, **513–14**
  Procession of the Cross, 281, **713–14**
  Rose of Lima, Saint's Day of St., **751–52**
  Saint Stephen's Day (Hungary), **764**
  Sea Org Day, **791–93**
  Sophia, The Descent and Assumption of Holy, **826–28**
  Tens of Thousands of Lanterns Ancestral Memorial Service, **851–52**
  Transfiguration, Feast of the, **866–67**
  Virgen de los Angeles Day, **906–8**
Augustine of Canterbury, Saint's Day of St., **52–54**
Augustine of Hippo, Saint's Day of St., **54–56**
Aurangzeb, emperor, 559
Aurobindo, Birth Anniversary of Sri, **56–57**
Aurobindo, Shri, 384, 592
Australia
  atheism in, 885
  Buddhism in, 141
  Wicca and pagan religions, 923
  Zoroastrianism in, 962
Autobiography (Darwin), 237
Autobiography of a Yogi (Yogananda), 941
Autumn equinox. *See* Fall equinox
Autumn Kunchi. *See* Nagasaki Kunchi
Avadhuta Gita, 243

Avalokitesvara, 31, 350, 351–52, 543
Avatamsaka Sutra, 777–78
Avatar Adi Da Samraj's Birthday, **57–58**
Avataric Divine Self-Emergence, Day of, **58–59**
Avatar of the Age, 577
Avesta, 319, 651, 958
Awakening of the Dragon, 264
Awa Odori dancers, 656i
Awashima Shrine, 256
Awwal Muharram. *See* New Year's Day
Ayambil Tapa, 618–19
Ayruveda community, 247
Ayyám-i-Há (Bahá'í Intercalary Days), **60–63**
The Ayyám-i-Há Camel, 61

Baal Shem Tov, 482
Báb
  Bábí religion, 65–66, 71, 75, 79
  Badí' calendar, 163
  Bahá'í Calendar and, 79–81
  death of, 71, 75
  establishment of Bahá'í Faith, 86–87, 99–100
  Festival of the Birth of the, **65–67**, 82, 101
  Festival of the Declaration of the, **67–73**, 101, 226
  Islam and, 65, 67–68, 70–71
  Martyrdom of the, 67–68, **73–76**
  Naw-Rúz, Festival of, 621
  Nineteen-Day Feast, 641–43
  Persian Bayán, 70, 74
  Riḍván, Festival of, 744
  Shrine of, 97
  "Tablet of the Eternal Youth," 71–72
  "Tablet of the Youth of Paradise," 72
  view of history, 70
  writings of, 90
Baba, Brahma, 78
Babaji Commemoration Day, **76–78**, 649
Baba Lovers, 577
Baba's Day, **78–79**
Bábí religion, 65–66, 70–71, 73–74, 75, 79
Bábism, 65–66
Babylon, 477, 477i
Babylonians, 627
Bader, Jesse, 928
Badí' calendar. *See* Bahá'í Calendar and Rhythms of Worship
Badr, battle at, 22
Bagdadi, Junaid, 241
Bagmati River, 747i
Bahá, significance of, 80–81
Bahá'í calendar and Rhythms of Worship, 60, **79–86**
  Bahá'í Calendar Table, 83i
  "names of God," 79–81, 83–85
  naming conventions, 82, 83–85
  Naw-Rúz, 81–82
  origins and history in, 82
  seasonal aspect of, 82–83
  solar and lunar holidays, 101
  structure of, 81
  symbolic aspects, 85
  theophoric metamorphosis, 85
Bahá'í Faith, **86–94**. *See also* Báb; Bahá'u'lláh
  'Abdu'l-Bahá, Ascension of, **1–4**
  'Abdu'l-Bahá, succession of, 98
  authoritative texts, 90, 92–93, 98
  Ayyám-i-Há (Bahá'í Intercalary Days), **60–63**
  Báb, Festival of the Birth of the, **65–67**, 82, 101
  Báb, Festival of the Declaration of the, **67–73**, 101, 226
  Báb, Martyrdom of the, 67–68, **73–76**
  Bábí religion and, 65–66, 70–71, 73–74, 75, 79
  Badí' calendar, 163–64
  beliefs and practices, 90–94
  Covenant, Day of the, **225–27**
  devotional life of individuals, 93–94
  elections, 46
  establishment of, 86–87, 99–100
  Hands of the Cause of God, 88–89
  in Latin America, 90
  liturgical calendar, xxi
  manifestation, 90–92
  meditation in, 80, 85
  Naw-Rúz, Festival of, 81–82, 101, **620–23**, 630
  New Year's Day, 630
  Nineteen-Day Feast, 82–83, 620, **641–45**
  in North America, 89
  other religions and, 91
  pilgrimages, 98
  Race Unity Day, **727–32**
  Riḍván, Festival of, **744–47**
  Seven Year Plan, 89

Shoghi Effendi. *See* Shoghi Effendi
spread of, 87–88, 89, 90
spring equinox, 832
"Tablet of Visitation," 3, 75, 96, 98
The Tablets of the Divine Plan, 89
unity in, 91–93
Universal House of Justice, 81, 88–89, 98, 101, 226, 729, 746, 936
World Religion Day, **936–39**
Bahá'í Fast, **94–96**
Bahá'í Feast, 641–45
"Bahá'í Holy Year," 98
Bahá'í Intercalary Days. *See* Ayyám-i-Há (Bahá'í Intercalary Days)
Bahá'í Writings, 60–61
Bahá'u'lláh
Ascension of, **96–99**
Ayyám-i-Há (Bahá'í Intercalary Days), 60
Badí' calendar, 163
Bahá'í Calendar and, 79
on Bahá'í teachings, 92
Covenant of, 225–26
Declaration of the, 101
early life of, 100
establishment of Bahá'í Faith, 86–87, 99–100
on fasting, 94–95
Festival of the Birth of, 82, **99–102**
as founder of faith, 67–68, 74
Gems of Divine Mysteries, 84–85
imprisonment of, 65–66
Kitáb-i-Aqdas, 75
on "Manifestations of God," 83–85
Naw-Rúz, Festival of, 81–82, 620–21
Nineteen-Day Feast, 641–42
on other religions, 91–92
on prayer, 93–94
Riḍván, Festival of, 744–45
Shrine of, 96–97, 98
tablets and, 71–72
on word Bahá, 80–81
writings of, 87, 90–92
Bahíyyih Khánum, 1–2
Bailey, Alice A., 919, 932–33
Bailey, Foster, 932
Baillie, James S., 471i
Baisajya-guru (Medicine Buddha), 30
Baisakhi. *See* Vaisakhi
Baizhang Huaihai, 416
Balaji, 862–64
Balarama, 364–65, 648
Balarama, Appearance Day of Lord, **102–3**
Balarama, Lord, 823
Baldwin II of Constantinople, 419
Baldwin III of Anjou, 715
Baldwin IX, 715–16
Bali, 652–53
Bali Raja, 634
Balyuzi, Hasan M., 226
Bandi Chhor Divas, 163
Bangladesh, 144, 800–801
Baptisimal vows, 861i
Baptism of the Lord, Feast of the, **103–4**
Baptist, Peter, 690–91
Baptist Missionary Society, 208
Baptists, 207, 208, 569, 769, 921, 928
Báqir, Imam Mhuammad, 80
Barsimha, 606
Bartholomew I, Ecumenical Patriarch, 26, 764
Bartholomew's Day, Saint, **104–6**
Basil, Saint, 314
Basilia of Born Jesus, 318
Basilica de Nuestra Señora de los Angeles, 906
Basilica of Guadalupe, 347–50
Basilica of Saint Agnes Outside the Walls, 13
Basilica of Saint Anne, 696
Basilica of Saint Mary the New, 710
Basilica of Saint Paul Outside the Walls, 689
Basilica of Saint Pius X, 534
Basilica of the National Shrine of Our Lady of Aparecida, 42
Basilica of the Sacred Heart, 757
Basil II, emperor, 912
Basil of Caesarea, Saint, 859
Basket Dance, **106–7**
Bastani calendar, 959
"Battle Hymn of the Reformation," 742
Battle of Avarayr, 901
Battle of Kurukshetra, 618
Battle of New Orleans, 717
Battle of the Helgeå, 658
Batu Caves temple, 852–53, 853i
Beatification, 767
Bede the Venerable, Saint, 267
Befana, **107**
Before the Common Era (BCE), 151
Beheading of Saint John the Baptist, 274
Belarus, 231
Belgium, 712–13, 715–16

Belletable, Henri, 403–4
Beltane, **108–9**, 915
Ben & Jerry's Ice Cream, 306
Benedict of Nursia, Saint's Day of St., **109–10**
Benedict the African, Saint's Day of St., **110–11**
Benedict XIII, Pope, 293, 829
Benedict XIV, Pope, 26, 824
Benedict XV, Pope, 404, 462, 917
Benedict XVI, Pope, 291, 301, 473, 683i, 766
Bengal, 19, 29, 113–14, 330–31, 633–34
Bernardine of Siena, 471
Bernini, Gian Lorenzo, 169
Besant, Annie, 920
Bhadrabahu, 450
Bhadrachalam Temple, 740
Bhagavada opurana, 732
Bhagavad Gita, 114, 331, 336–37, 384, 384i, 388, 570, 706
Bhagavata Purana, 331, 605
Bhagiratha, 327
Bhairava Ashtami, **111–12**
Bhaktisiddhanta Sarasvati Thakura, Appearance Day of, **112**, 113
Bhaktivinoda Thakura, Appearance Day of, **112–13**
Bhakti yoga, 103, 112, 331, 460, 605, 648
Bhavisya Uttara Purana, 722
Bhiksu, Acarya, 451
Bhishma, 364
Bhishma Ashtami, **113–14**
Bhole Bhandari Charitable Trust, 29
Bhumanandaji Paramahansa, Birthday of Swami Guru, **115**
Bhumisparsha mudra, 597
Bhutan, 134, 144, 239–41
Bible, 199, 201, 434–35
Bible Society, 115–16
Bible Sunday, **115–16**
Biblical criticism, 209
Bienville, Jean Baptiste Le Moyne de, 551
Bihari, Bipin, 113
Bijl, Andrew van der, 429
Biloxi, Mississippi, 120, 120i
Bimbisara, King, 892
Birth and rebirth, 386
Birthday celebrations
  Amitabha's Birthday, **30–32**
  Aurobindo, Birth Anniversary of Sri, **56–57**
  Avatar Adi Da Samraj's Birthday, **57–58**
  Báb, Festival of the Birth of the, **65–67**, 82, 101
  Bahá'u'lláh, Festival of the Birth of, 82, **99–102**
  Bhumanandaji Paramahansa, Birthday of Swami Guru, **115**
  Che Kung, Birthday of, **173**
  Confucius's Birthday, **220–22**
  Dalai Lama's Birthday, **233–34**
  Guan Yin's Birthday, **351–53**
  Guru Gobind Singh's Birthday, **353–54**
  Haile Selassie I, Birthday of Emperor, **360–61**
  Hubbard, Birthday of L. Ron, **411–13**
  John the Baptist, Nativity of, **467–69**, 910
  Ksitigarbha's Birthday, **504–5**
  Kwan Tai, Birthday of, **507–8**
  Laozi, Birthday of, **515–16**
  Lotus, Birthday of the, **532**
  Mahasthamaprapta's Birthday, **543–44**
  Manjushri's Birthday, **549–51**
  Martin Luther King, Jr., Birthday of, **554–56**
  Medicine Buddha's Birthday, **576–77**
  Monkey King, Birthday of the, **586–87**
  Mother, Birthday of the, **592–93**
  Muktananda, Birthday of Swami Paramahansa, **598–99**
  Nanak's Birthday, Guru, 162, 163, **603–4**
  Nativity of Mary, **614–15**
  Nichiren's Birthday, **636–37**
  Osho (Rajneesh), Birthday of, **664–65**
  Pak Tai, Birthday of, **667–68**
  Ramakrishna, Birthday of Sri, **736–37**
  Ramana Maharshi, Birthday of, **737–39**
  Sai Baba of Shirdi, Birthday of, 399, **758–59**
  Samantabadhara's Birthday, **777–79**
  Sarada Devi, Birthday of, **783–84**
  Satchidananda, Birthday of Swami, **784–85**
  Shinran Shonin, Birthday of, 31, **804–5**
  Sivananda Saraswati, Birthday of Swami, **819–20**
  Tejomayananda, Birthday of Swami, **848–49**
  Third Prince, Birthday of the, **856–57**
  True Parents' Birthday, **870–71**
  Vivekananda, Birthday of Swami, **910–11**
  Yogananda, Birthday of Paramahansa, **941–42**, 942i
Birth of Mary. *See* Nativity of Mary
Black Christ, Festival of the, **116–18**
Black Nazarene Festival, **118–19**

Blajini, Easter of the, **119–20**
Blavatsky, Helena Petrovna, 920i
Bleganjur, 653
"Blessed Assurance" (Crosby), 21
Blessed Water, 582
Blessing of Beans and Grapes, 45
Blessing of the Fleet, 120i, **120–21**
Blood, of Jesus Christ, 715–16
Blosi, Francis, 684
Bodh Gaya, India, 122i, 935
Bodhi Day, **121–22**, 122i
Bodhidharma, 136
Bodhidharma Day, **122–24**
Bodhisattvas, 146, 461, 549–50, 550i, 576, 597–98
Bok Kai Festival, **124–25**
Boleslaus, King, 834
Bomb Day celebration, 124
Bom Jesus dos Navegantes, 628
Bonaventure, Saint, 909
Boniface, Saint, 925
Boniface IV, Pope, 22
Boniface VIII, Pope, 472
Boniface IX, Pope, 127, 473
Boniface of Germany, Saint's Day of St., **125–26**
Bon Matsuri. *See* Obon Festival(s)
The Book about the Origin of the Blessed Mary and the Childhood of the Savior, 710
Book of Certitude (Bahá'u'lláh), 87
Book of Changes, 185
Book of History, 185
Book of Mencius, 185
Book of Rites, 185
Book of Songs, 185
"Book of the Covenant," 98, 226
Book of the Law (Crowley), 302, 309
The Book of the Sacred Magic of Abramelin the Mage, 302
Booth, Catherine Mumford, 314–15
Booth, William, 314–15
Boris-Michael, Prince, 215
Boston University, 555
Boun Kao Phansa. *See* Asalha Puja Day ("Dhamma Day")
Boun Ok Phansa, **126**
Bourassa, Joseph, 696
Boyce, Mary, 620
Bradlaugh, Charles, 883
Brahma
  Bhairava Ashtami, 111
  Dattatreya Jayanti, 242
  Diwali, 253
  Ganga Dussehra, 327
  Hirneykasipu and, 605
  New Year's Day (India), 395
  Ugadi, 634
  Vaikuntha Ekadashi, 895
  Vaitarani, 896–97
  Valmiki and, 899
Brahma Kumaris, 78, 385
Brahma Kumaris World Spriritual University, 78
Brahmanda Purana, 585
Brahmanism, 378–80, 382
Brahma Sutra, 384
Brahmo Samaj, 384
Brahmotsavam. *See* Tirupati Brahmotsava Festival
Brazil
  Aparecida, Feast of Our Lady of, **41–43**, 564
  Bom Jesus dos Navegantes, 628
  Buddhism in, 141
  Burning of Judas, 148
  Divine Holy Spirit Festival, 250
  Rio de Janeiro, 552, 783
  San Sebastian Day, 783
Brébeuf, Jean de, 463–64
Bridget, Saint's Day of St., **127–28**
Bright Monday. *See* Easter Monday
Brigid (Gaelic goddess), 420, 709
Brigid, Saint, 420, 709–10
Brigid of Kildare, Saint's Day of St., 128i, **128–29**
Brigid's Cross. *See* Saint Brigid's Cross.
Brihaspati, 170
Brill, Gary, 413
Brister, Timothy, 276
British and Foreign Bible Society, 115
British Circle of the Universal Bond, 840
British East India Company, 383
British Humanist Association, 238
Brittingham, Isabella, 642
Brotherhood of Nuestra Señora de Valme, 750
Brotherhood of the Holy Spirit, 249, 308
Brotherhood of the Pleroma, 276
Browne, Edward G., 65–66, 73, 97, 622
Bruges, Belgium, 715–16
Bruhaspati, 539

Brys, Arno, 712
Buddha. *See also* Buddhism
Enlightenment of, 121–22
Lha Bab Duchen, 523
magic hand, 586i
Mid-Autumn Festival, 581
Nagapanchami, 601
preaching in Sarnath, 131i
in Sri Lanka, 265
statue at Angkor Wat, 134i
statues of, 353
Buddha Amida, 138
Buddha Amitabha, 136
Buddha Happiness Day, 877
Buddha Lokesvararaja, 30
Buddha of Kamakura, 353
Buddhadasa, 135
Buddha Purnima. *See* Wesak/Vesak
Buddha's Birthday. *See* Wesak/Vesak
Buddha's Enlightenment. *See* Nehan
Buddha Shakyamuni, 129–30
Buddhism, **129–44**. *See also* Mahayana Buddhism
in Australia, 141
Chan Buddhism, 122–23, 136, 137, 138, 184, 416
characteristics of in the West, 141–42
in China, 136, 183–84, 188
Chinese immigrants to United States, 140
in Europe, 139–40
First Turning of the Wheel, 145
Four Noble Truths, 130–31
fundamental principles of, 129
Hinduism and, 133–34, 381
in Israel, 141
Iwashimizu Matsuri, 444
in Japan, 138
Jodo Shinshu, 140
Kagyu Buddhists, 588, 935–36
Khmer Buddhism, 135
in Korea, 137
Laba Festival and, 511
in Laos, 134–36
Lha Bab Duchen, 145
liturgical calendar, xx–xxi
local holidays, 146–47
Mahayana Buddhism, 131, 132
Mid-Autumn Festival, 581
Middle Path, 130
monastic orders, 131, 135, 184, 188, 499–500, 903–4, 905i
mudras, 597
Mulian and, 877–78
Nichiren Buddhism, 376, 648, 778
Noble Eightfold Path, 130–31
in North America, 133, 140
origins of, 133–34
primary traditions, 132–33
Pure Land tradition, 31, 136, 184, 351, 525, 543–44, 625, 804–5
rebirth and depedent origination, 130
in Republic of China (Taiwan), 136–37
Rinzai Zen Buddhism, 138, 416, 525
Sakya Buddhists, 935–36
Shinto and, 806, 807, 811
Shravakayana Buddhism, 132
Sinhalese Buddhist community, 141
Songkran, 825–26
in South Africa, 141
in Southeast Asia, 134–35
spread and local development of, 133–39
teachings, 129–30
Tendai school, 138
Theravada Buddhism. *See* Theravada Buddhism
Tiantai school, 136
in Tibet. *See* Tibetan Buddhism
Vajrayana Buddhism. *See* Vajrayana Buddhism
in Vietnam, 137
Vipassana Buddhism. *See* Vipassana Buddhism
in the West, 139–42
Zen Buddhism. *See* Zen Buddhism
Buddhism cycle of holidays, **144–47**
Abhidhamma Day, **4–5**, 145
Airing the Classics, **15–16**
Aizen Summer Festival, **16–17**
Amitabha's Birthday, **30–32**
Anapanasati Day, **33–34**
Asalha Puja Day ("Dhamma Day"), **43–44**
Bodhi Day, **121–22**, 122i
Bodhidharma Day, **122–24**
Boun Ok Phansa, **126**
Butter Lamp Festival, **149–50**
Chokhor Duchen, **195–96**
Daruma Kuyo, **235–36**
Duruthu Poya (Sri Lanka), **265–66**
Elephant Festival, 279i, **279–80**

Eshinni-Kakushinni Memorial, **287–88**
Festival of the Tooth, **304–6**, 305i
Great Buddha Festival, **342–43**
Guan Yin, Renunciation of, **350–51**
Hana Matsuri, **367–68**
Higan, 296, **375–76**, 833
Hoshi Matsuri, **411**
Jizo Bon, **461–62**
Kathina Ceremony, **499–500**
Kodomo no Hi, 343, **501**
Ksitigarbha's Birthday, **504–5**
Lha Bab Duchen, **523–24**
Lingka Woods Festival, **524–25**
Linji/Rinzai Day Observance, **525**
Magha Puja Day, **538–39**
Mahasthamaprapta's Birthday, **543–44**
Manjushri's Birthday, **549–51**
Medicine Buddha's Birthday, **576–77**
Monlam, the Great Prayer Festival, 149, **587–89**, 935
Nagapanchami, **601–2**
Nehan, **623–24**, 624i
Neri-kuyo, **625**
Nichiren's Birthday, 138, **636–37**
Niwano, Nikkyo, Centennial of, **648–49**
Obon Festival(s), **655–57**, 656i, 878
Oeshiki, **657**
Phang Lhabsol, **694–95**
Ploughing Day, **698–99**
Poson, **702–3**
Sakya Dawa Festival, 144, **776–77**, 919
Samantabadhara's Birthday, **777–79**
Sanghamitta Day, **780–81**
Setsubun, **795–96**
Shichi-Go-San, **802–3**
Shinran Shonin, Birthday of, 31, **804–5**
Shuni-e (Omizutori), **816–17**
Tens of Thousands of Lanterns Ancestral Memorial Service, **851–52**
Tsagaan Sar, **871–72**
Tsong Khapa Anniversary, **872–74**
Ullam-bana, 191, **877–78**
Uposattha Observance Day, **892**
Vassa, **903–5**, 905i
Wesak/Vesak, 144, 162, 623, 776, **918–19**
Buddhist Association of the Republic of China, 136–37
Buddhist Churches of America (BCA), 140, 147–48, 656
Buddhist Churches of America Founding Day, **147–48**
Buddhist Federation of Australia, 141
Buddhist Mission to North America, 140
Buddhist Study Group, 141
Bufalo, Gaspar del, 591
Bulgaria, 25
Bulgarian Orthodox Church, 215–16, **291–92**
Bund freier religiöser Gemeinden Deutschlands, 883
Burma. *See* Myanmar (Burma)
Burning of Judas, **148–49**
Burning of the Arms, 263, 690
Burning of the Moon House, 343–44, 344i
Bus boycott, 555
Bush, George H. W., 555, 608, 743
Bush, George W., 743–44
Bushrú'í, Akhúnd Mullá Husayn, 67
Buta Malik, 29
Butter Lamp Festival, 145, **149–50**, 150i
Buzurg, Mírzá, 100
Byzantine Empire, 200, 203, 284, 646. *See also* Eastern Orthodox Churches

Cairo Declaration on Human Rights in Islam, 414
Caitanya, Sri, 736
Calendars, religious, xx–xxii, **151–65**
alternate religious calendars, 155
Bahá'í calendar, 60, 79–86, 163–64
Chinese calendar, 159–61, 176, 177, 190
Christian adoption of Julian calendar, 152
Common Era calendar, xxii, 154–55, **217–18**, 393, 627, 811
Eastern Orthodox Churches and, 154–55
Egyptian calendar, 151–52
Ethiopian calendar, 288–89, 332
Gregorian calendar, 153–55, 161, 217, 272–73, 393
Haab' calendar, 573
Hebrew calendar, 155–57, 627
Hindu lunar calendar, 394–95
Indian calendars, 161–62, 393–94
Islamic calendar, 157–59, 393, 440–43
in Japan, 161, 811
Julian calendar, 152–53, 154, 202, 217, 272–73, 526
Korean calendar, 161, 244, 343
liturgical year, **526–29**, 560

Long Count calendar, 573–74
move to international political control of calendars, 153–54
Nanakshahi calendar of the Sikhs, 162–63, 604
Roman calendar, 152, 627
Saka calendar, 161–62, 393–94, 395, 630, 632–33
Tibetan calendar, 530
Calixtus I, Pope, 281
Call to prayer (Islam), 435–36
Calvin, John, 207, 880
Cambodia, 134–35
Campus Freethought Alliance, 931
Canada
Bahá'í Faith in, 89
Saint Anne d'Auray, 696
World Day of Prayer, 930
World Religion Day, 936
Zoroastrianism in, 955, 962
Canadian Indian Act of 1885, 704
Candlemas. *See* Bridget, Saint's Day of St.; Imbolc; Presentation of Jesus in the Temple, Feast of the
Candle Mass, 277
Candles, 10, 44
Cannabis Day, **165**
Canonization, 765–67, 771. *See also* Saints, veneration of (Roman Catholic tradition)
Capek, Maja, 312
Capek, Norbert F., 312
Caribbean islands, 208
Carling Sunday, 521
Carmelite order, 595
Carnival. *See* Mardi Gras
Carp fish, 501
Carter, Jimmy, 764
Carthage, 228
Cartherine of Aragon, 207
Casimir, Saint's Day of St., **166**
Casimir II, duke, 311
Casimir IV, King, 166
Cathars, 589
Cathedral of Christ the Savior, 26
Cathedral of Saint Sauveur, 716
Catherine of Siena, Saint, 127
Catherine of Siena, Saint's Day of St., **166–68**
Catherine of Vadstena, 127
Cecilia, Santa, 13
Celebrity Center International, 168i, **168**
The Celestine Prophecy (Redfield), 573
Celibacy, 79
Center for Inquiry and Campus Freethought Alliance, 238
Center for Spiritual Awareness, 941
Central America, 208
Cessatio of Suffering, truth of, 130
Chabad-Lubavitcher Hasidic movement, 787
Chabanel, Noel, 464
Chair of St. Peter, Feast of the, **169**
Chaitanya, 383, 397. *See also* Gaura Purnima
Chaitayna's Birthday. *See* Gaura Purnima
Chaitra Purnima, **170–71**
Chali Mukte, 540
Chan Buddhism, 122–23, 136, 137, 138, 184, 416
Chandan Yatra, **171–72**
Chandogya Upanishad, 387
Chane E, 581
Chanel, Pierre, 691–92
Chantal, Jane Frances de, Saint, 909
Chanukah. *See* Hanukkah
Chaotian Gong temple, 576
Chapelle du Saint Sang, 716
Chapel of Saint Vincent, 249
Chapel of San Lorenzo Ruiz, 529
Chapel of the Rosary, 534
Charlemagne, 229
Charles the Bald, 169
Charles VII, King, 462
Charlotte Atheists and Agnostics, 424
Chaturmas Vrat, **172–73**
Chavez, Hugo, 149
Che Kung, 192
Che Kung, Birthday of, **173**
Chenrezig. *See* Guan Yin, Renunciation of
Cherry Blossom Festival. *See* Sakura Matsuri
Chhath. *See* Surya Shashti
Chichibuhiko-no-mikoto, 174
Chichibu Yomatsuri, **174**
Chidvilasananda, Swami, 599
Children's Day, **175**
Children's Day (Japan). *See* Kodomo no Hi
China, 188. *See also* Buddhism; Buddhism cycle of holidays; Chinese Religion; Confucian tradition; Taoism
Airing the Classics, **15–16**
Amitabha's Birthday, 31
astrology, 660
Bodhi Day, **121–22**, 122i

bodhisattvas in, 146
Buddhism in, 136, 183–84, 188
calendars and, 159–61, 176, 177, 190
Confucius, Anniversary of the Death of, **219–20**
Confucius's Birthday, **220–22**
Double Ninth Festival, 191, **260–61**
Double Seventh Festival, 191, **261–62**
Dragon Boat Festival, 160, 190, 191, **263–64**, 264i
Eastern Zhou dynasty, 182
establishment of, 179–80
Han dynasty, 177, 183, 184, 260, 514, 515, 628
Hundred Schools period, 182
Ksitigarbha's Birthday, **504–5**
Laba Festival, 121–22, 190, **511–12**, 628
Lantern Festival (China), 179, 191, **514–15**
Losar and, 149, 530–31
Lotus, Birthday of the, **532**
Mahasthamaprapta's Birthday, 544
Mahayana Buddhism in, 136, 184
Manjushri's Birthday, **549–51**
Marxism and religion in, 884, 885
Ming dynasty, 136, 187, 586, 640
New Year's Day, 628–29
Nine Emperor Gods, Festival of the, **640–41**
Pak Tai, Birthday of, **667–68**
Qing dynasty, 136
Shang dynasty, 159, 180–81, 667
Song dynasty, 173, 504, 575
Southern Sung dynasty, 187
Spring Dragon Festival, **829–31**, 830i
Sung dynasty, 186, 525
Tang dynasty, 136, 177, 180, 416, 504, 515, 586, 628
Ullam-bana, 191, **877–78**
Unbelief in, 884–85
Uposattha Observance Day, **892**
Warring States period, 182, 263
Western Zhou dynasty, 177
Xia dynasty, 180
Zhou dynasty, 180–82
Chinese calendar, 159–61, 176, 177, 190
Chinese Communist Party, 885
Chinese deities, festivals based on, 191–92
Chinese Exclusion Act, 140
Chinese immigrants, 124, 140, 141
Chinese New Year's (Preliminary Festival), **176–77**
Chinese New Year's Day, **177–79**, 178i, 191, 628–29
Chinese religion, **179–90**, 628–29. *See also* Chinese New Year's Day; Confucian tradition
ancestor worship, 181–82
Buddhism and, 136, 183–84, 188
Chinese cosmology, 183
Corpus Christi, Feast of, **223–24**, 403
current state of, 187–89
divination, 181
earliest dynasties, 180–82
early Confucian tradition and, 182–83
five agents, 183
Guan Yin, Renunciation of, **350–51**
Guan Yin's Birthday, **351–53**
literati and neo-Confucianism, 185–86
Maoism, 189
Mazu Festival, Goddess, **574–76**
Mid-Autumn Festival, 191, **580–82**
Nine Emperor Gods, Festival of the, **640–41**
overview of, 179–80
Pak Tai, Birthday of, **667–68**
popular religion, 186–87
Pure Brightness Festival, 191, **717–19**, 718i
quasi-religious institutions, 188
sacrifice, 181
sectarianism, 187
Spring Dragon Festival, **829–31**, 830i
Taiping rebellion, 187
Tam Kung Festival, **845–46**
Third Prince, Birthday of the, **856–57**
Ullam-bana, 191, **877–78**
Yin-yang, 183, 185, 260
Chinese religion, annual cycle of festivals, **190–93**
Chinmaya Mission, 193–94, 849
Chinmayananda, Commemoration Days for, **193–94**
Chinmayananda, Saint, 849
Chinook people, 310, 703
Chisti, Saint Khwaja Moinuddin, 892–93
Chisti Sufi order, 892–93
Chithirai Tirunal, 633
Chitragupta, 170–71
Chitragupta temple, 170
Chittirai Festival, **194–95**, 398
Chodaganga, King, 740
Choe Chiwon, 599
Choegyal Phagpa, 530

Chogyal Chakdor Namgyal, 695
Chokhor (prayer wheels), 195–96
Chokhor Duchen, **195–96**
Cholera epidemics, 251–52
Chomo Guru, 694
Chongmyo Cherye, **196–97**
Chongmyo Royal Shrine, 196
Chongyangjie. *See* Double Ninth Festival
Choson dynasty (Korea), 137, 196
Chotrul Duchen. *See* Butter Lamp Festival
Christian Expulsion Edict, 601
Christian Gnosticism, 199, 200
Christianity. *See also* Christianity, festivals and holidays; Eastern Orthodox Churches; Martyrs; Protestants; Roman Catholic Church; Saint's days; *specific churches*
  during Age of Exploration, 207–8
  church-state relations, 204
  commemorations, development of, 201–3
  doctrinal development, 200–201
  early challenges to, 879, 880–81. *See also* Unbelief
  eastward spread of, 199–200
  Holy Trinity, doctrine of, 867–70
  in India, 200
  Islam and, 203, 204–5
  in Japan, 808–9
  liturgical calendar, xx–xxi
  martyrdom, theology of, 202
  in the Middle Ages, 203–4
  Nagasaki Kunchi and, 601
  origins of, 197–98
  Pagan religions and, 923
  Paine on, 858
  persecution, 202
  in Persian Empire, 199–200
  Protestant expansion, 208–9
  Protestant Reformation, 206–7
  reform of, 205
  relics. *See* Relics
  sacraments, 205–6
  scriptures, 198–99. *See also* Bible; New Testament, Christian; Old Testament, Christian
  second millennium, 204–5
  Servetus on, 880
  Shinto and, 808–9, 811
  Sukkot and, 838–39
  twentieth century, 209–10
Christianity, festivals and holidays. *See also* Christianity; Saint's days
  Advent, **9–11**, 526
  All Saints Day, **22–23**, 275, 277, 403, 631, 774
  All Souls Day, **23–25**, 275, 277
  Alphabet Day, **25–26**
  Annunciation, Feast of the, **37–39**, 293, 909–10
  Aparecida, Feast of Our Lady of, **41–43**, 564
  Ascension Day, **45–46**, 403, 527
  Ash Wednesday, 49i, **49–50**, 521
  Assumption of the Virgin, **50–51**, 403, 562, 726
  Baptism of the Lord, Feast of the, **103–4**
  Bible Sunday, **115–16**
  Black Christ, Festival of the, **116–18**
  Black Nazarene Festival, **118–19**
  Blajini, Easter of the, **119–20**
  Blessing of the Fleet, 120i, **120–21**
  Burning of Judas, **148–49**
  Chair of St. Peter, Feast of the, **169**
  Christmas, 202, **211–13**, 289, 403, 526, 927
  Christ the King, Feast of, **213–14**
  Circumcision, Feast of the, **214–15**, 627
  Conversion of St. Paul, Feast of the, **222–23**
  Divine Holy Spirit Festival, **249–50**
  Divine Mercy Sunday, **250–51**
  Easter, 39, 152–53, 199, 202, **267–69**, 289, 526–28
  Easter (Ethiopian Church), **269–70**
  Easter Monday, **270–72**, 714
  Elevation of the True Cross, **280–81**
  Ember Days, **281–82**
  Epiphany, 103–4, 107, 211, 274, **284–86**, 285i, 289, 402, 527
  Eucharistic Congresses, **290–91**
  Expectation of the Birth of the Blessed Virgin Mary, Feast of, **293**
  Fasinada, **297**
  Fatima, Feast Day of Our Lady of, **299–301**
  Fiesta dos Tabuleiros, **307–8**
  Forgiveness, Feast of, **312–13**
  Forty Martyrs' Day, **313–14**
  Good Friday, 199, **338–40**, 339i, 410, 521, 682
  Good Remedy, Feast of Our Lady of, **340–41**

Grotto Day, **346–47**
Guadalupe, Feast of Our Lady of, **347–50**
Holy Days of Obligation, **402–3**
Holy Family, Feast of the, **403–4**
Holy Innocents' Day, **404–5**
Holy Maries, Festival of the (La Fête des Saintes Maries), **405–7**, 537
Holyrood or the Feast of the Triumph of the Holy Cross, **407–9**
Holy Week, **409–10**
Image Not-Made-by-Hands, Feast of the, **419–20**
Immaculate Conception, Feast of the, 349, 403, **421–22**, 562, 564
Immaculate Heart of Mary, Feast of the, **422–23**
International Day of Prayer for the Persecuted Church, **429–30**
John the Baptist, Beheading of, 274, **464–67**
John the Baptist, Nativity of, **467–69**, 910
Juhannus, **487–88**
Lazarus Saturday, 274, **519–20**, 669–70
Lent, 39, **520–23**, 527, 551
liturgical year, **526–29**, 560
Lourdes, Feast Day of Our Lady of, **532–35**
Madeleine, Fête de la, **537–38**
Mardi Gras, **551–52**
Martinmas, **556–57**
Mary Magdalene, Day of the Holy, **564–66**
Mary, liturgical year of the Blessed Virgin, **560–64**
Maundy Thursday, 224, 409, 521, **567–69**
Michaelmas, **579–80**
Mid-Pentecost, Feast of, **582–83**
Miracles, Festival of Our Lady of, **583–84**
Misa de Gallo, **584–85**
Most Holy Name of Mary, Feast of the, **590–91**
Most Precious Blood, Feast of the, **591–92**
Mount Carmel, Feast Day of Our Lady of, **595–96**
National Bible Week, **607–8**
National Day, **609–10**
National Day of Prayer, **610–11**, 612
Nativity of Mary, **614–15**
Nossa Senhora dos Remédios, Pilgrimage of, **650**
One Great Hour of Sharing, **661–62**
Orthodoxy, Feast of, **662–63**
Palm Sunday, 198–99, 409, 521, **668–70**, 669i
Passover, 156, 198, 224–25, 267, 485, **674–76**, 688
Peace and Good Voyage, Feast of Our Lady of, **678–79**
Peñafrancia, Feast of Our Lady of, **679–80**
Penitentes, **680–82**
Pentecost, **682–84**
Perpetual Help, Feast of Our Lady of, **684–85**
Pilgrimage of Sainte Anne d'Auray, **695–97**
Pilgrimage of the Dew, **697–98**
Posadas, Las, **701–2**
Presentation of Jesus in the Temple, Feast of the, **708–10**
Presentation of Mary, Feast of the, **710–11**
Procession de la Penitencia, La (Spain), **711–12**
Procession of the Cross, 281, **713–14**
Procession of the Fujenti, 271–72, **714–15**
Procession of the Holy Blood, **715–16**
Procession of the Penitents, **712–13**
Prompt Succor, Feast Day of Our Lady of, **716–17**
Queenship of Mary, Feast of, **725–26**, 910
Reformation Sunday, **741–43**
Rogation Days, **748–49**
Romeria of La Virgen de Valme, **749–50**
Rosary, Feast of Our Lady of the, **750–51**
Sacred Heart of Jesus, Feast of the, 557, **757–58**
Saint John Lateran, Feast of the Dedication of, **760–61**
Saint Patrick's Day, **761–62**
Saints, celebrating the lives of (Protestant tradition), **767–70**
Saints, veneration of (Roman Catholic tradition), **770–74**
Saint Stephen's Day, **762–64**
Saint Stephen's Day (Hungary), **764**
Sankt Placidusfest, **781–82**
San Sebastian Day, **782–83**
Schutzengelfest, **788**
Schwenkfelder Thanksgiving, **789**
Solemnity of Mary, Feast of the, 215, 402, **824**
Sophia, The Descent and Assumption of Holy, **826–28**
Sorrows, Feast of Our Lady of, **828–29**
Theophany, 527, 582, **853–55**

Three Hierarchs, Day of the, **859**
Three Kings Day, Native American Pueblos, **860–61**
Timkat, 289, 861i, **861–62**
Transfiguration, Feast of the, **866–67**
Trinity Monday, **867**
Trinity Sunday, **867–70**
Valentinus, Feast of the Holy, **897–98**
Virgen de los Angeles Day, **906–8**
Visitation, Feast of the, **909–10**
Walpurgisnacht, 108, **915–16**
Week of Prayer for Christian Unity, 169, 223, **916–18**
World Communion Sunday, **928–29**
World Community Day, **929**
World Day of Prayer, **929–31**
Zaccheus Sunday, **953–54**
Christian V, King, 219
Christian VII, King, 219
Christmas, 202, **211–13**, 289, 403, 526, 927
Christ the King, Feast of, **213–14**
Christmas trees, 212
Chroses I, King, 419
Chrysanthemum, 260
Chrysostom, John, 859
Chulalongkorn, King, 135
Chung Yeung Festival. *See* Double Ninth Festival
Churchill, Winston, 1
Church Missionary Society, 208–9
Church of England. *See* Anglican Church
Church of God, 675, 838–39
Church of Nossa Senhora dos Remédios, 650
Church of Notre Dame de la Mer, 406, 537
Church of Perfect Liberty, 316–17
Church of Saint Anastasia, 271, 714
Church of Saint Bartholomew of the Armenians, 419
Church of Saint George, 334
Church of Saint John Lateran, 760
Church of Saint John the Baptist, 307–8
Church of San Silvestro, 419
Church of Santa Maria Antiqua, 314
Church of Satan, 915–16
Church of Scotland, 209
Church of the Dormition of the Virgin, 912
Church of the East, 199
Church of the Holy Sepulchre, 269, 280–81, 339, 408
Church of the Incarnation (Episcopal), 552
Church of the New Jerusalem, 625–26
Church-state relations, 204
Church Women United, 415, 929, 930
Church World Service, 661
Circumcision, Feast of the, **214–15**, 627
Citizens Commission on Human Rights, 791
The City of God (St. Augustine), 55
Civil Rights Movement, 554–56
Civil War, U.S., 594
Ci Xi, Dowager, 260
Classical Hinduism, 380–82
Claver, Saint Peter, 692–93
Claviie, burning of, 891
Clean Monday, 521
Clement IX, Pope, 752
Clement of Alexander, 953
Clement of Ohrid, Saint's Day of St., **215–16**
Clement V, Pope, 307, 850
Clement VIII, Pope, 169
Clement XI, Pope, 231, 750
Clement XIII, Pope, 554
Clinton, Bill, 608
Clou, Jacob, 712
Clovis, King, 557
Cnut the Great, 658
Coe, Michael D., 573
Cofradia de Santo Cristo Jesús Nazareno, 118
Cold Food Day, 717
Collins, Anthony, 881
Colonialism, 383–86
Columba, Saint's Day of St., **216–17**
Coming of Age Day. *See* Seijin no Hi
Commemoration of the Faithful Departed, 23
Commemorations
Ali ibn Abi Talib, Commemoration Days for, **21–22**
Ashura, **47–49**
Babaji Commemoration Day, **76–78**
in Bahá'í Faith, 80
Chinmayananda, Commemoration Days for, **193–94**
Christianity, development in, 201–3
Commemoration of the Faithful Departed, 23
Confucius, Anniversary of the Death of, **219–20**
Data Ganj Bakhsh Death Anniversary, **241–42**
Death of Jean-François Lefevre de la Barre, **245–46**
Janardanji Paramahansa, Commemoration Days of Swami Guru, **458–59**

of Jesus Christ, 201–2
Lahiri Mahasaya, Commemoration Days for, **512–13**
Mani, Commemoration of the Prophet, **549**
Mass in Commemoration of the Dead, 45
Meher Baba, Commemoration Days of, **577–78**
Menon, Balakrishnan. *See* Chinmayananda, Commemoration Days for
Purnanandaji Paramahansa, Commemoration Day for Swami Guru, **721–22**
Schneerson, Anniversary of the Death of Rabbi Menachem Mendal, **787–88**
True Cross, commemoration of, 408
Zechariah and Elizabeth, Commemoration of Saints, 468
Commercial fishing fleet, 120–21
Common Era (CE), 151
Common Era calendar, xxii, 154–55, **217–18**, 393, 627, 811
Common Prayer Day, **218–19**
Common Sense (Paine), 857
Communism, 884, 884i. *See also* Marxism
Comte, August, 883
Confessio (St. Patrick), 762
Confessions (St. Augustine), 54
Confucian tradition
Chongmyo Cherye, **196–97**
currently, 188
early years, 182–83
Munmyo Ceremony, **599–600**
Shinto and, 805–6, 807
Confucius, 182, 220
Confucius, Anniversary of the Death of, **219–20**
"The Confucius Forest," 219
Confucius's Birthday, **220–22**
Confucius Temple, 221
Congregational Church, 208, 567, 769, 921
Congregation of the Holy Cross, 408
Congregation of the Holy Redeemer, 26
Congress, U.S., 610
Conservative Judaism, 482, 949
Constantine, Emperor, 12, 200, 202, 280, 313–14, 408, 760, 771, 866
Constantine Porphyrogenitus, 419
Constantine VI, Emperor, 663
Constantinople, 203–4, 280–81, 419, 466, 713
Constitution, U.S., 611
Constitutional Convention, 610
"Convention for Amity Between the Colored and White Races Based on Heavenly Teachings," 729
Convent of Saint-Gildard, 534
Conversion of St. Paul, Feast of the, **222–23**
Coptic Orthodox Church, 201, 270
Cordero, Gil, 347
Cornelius, Pope, 228
Corporation for National and Community Service, 555–56
Corpus Christi, Feast of, **223–24**, 403
Cosmology, 183
Costa Rica, 49i, 906–8
Council for Secular Humanism, 238, 426, 886, 931
Council of Basel, 127
Council of Chalcedon, 201
Council of Contance, 127
Council of Ephesus, 55, 200–201, 203, 560, 725, 824
Council of Nicea, 152–53, 155, 200, 202, 267, 627, 638, 663, 859, 868
Council of Trent, 153, 421
Council of Women for Home Missions, 930
Counter-Reformation, 405, 590, 711, 829
Counting of the Omer, **224–25**, 485
Coutrier, Paul, 917
Couture, M. l'abbé Daniel, 37
Covenant, Day of the, **225–27**
Creationism, 238
Cromwell, Oliver, 208
Cronus, 926
Crosby, Fannie J., 21
Crowley, Aleister E., 301–2, 309, 831
Crozier Theological Seminary, 554
Crucifixion, of Jesus Christ, 338–40
Crusades, 204–5, 438, 715
Cultural Revolution, 136, 176, 188, 189, 192, 221, 588, 885
Cybele, 593
Cyprian, Saint's Day of St., **228–29**
Cyprus, 148, 499
Cyril and Methodius, Saint's Day for Sts., 25, **229–31**
Cyrillic alphabet, 25–26, 229
Cyrus, king, 478, 485
Czechoslovakia, **312**, 885
Czestochowa, Feast Day of Our Lady of, **231–32**

Dadu, 383
Dahi Handi. *See* Janmashtami
Dairisan Ryogaku-in Kuhonji, 625
Daksha, 847–48
Dalai Lamas, 139, 233–34, 234i, 530–31, 587–88, 872. *See also* Tibetan Buddhism
Dalai Lama's Birthday, **233–34**
Damasus I, Pope, 782
Da Mo. *See* Bodhidharma Day
Danavira Mela, **234–35**
Dance
  Bon Odori, 656, 656i
  Garba, 616i
  Line dancing (Ilmu), 196–97
  mudras and, 596
  Phang Lhabsol, 695
  Potlatch, 705i
Dancers, 305i
Dandapani, 111
Daniel, Anthony, 464
Daniel, Book of, 579
Daodejing (Tao-te ching), 515
Darius the Great, 651
Daruma Daishi. *See* Bodhidharma Day
Daruma Kuyo, **235–36**
Darwin, Charles, 236–39, 887
Darwin Day, **236–39**
Dasain, **239–41**
Dasharatha, 739
Daslakshan Parva. *See* Paryushana
Dass, Rajaram, 141
Data Ganj Bakhsh Death Anniversary, **241–42**
Dattatreya Jayanti, **242–43**, 540
Dattatreya Temple, 243
David, King, 477
Davis, Roy Eugene, 941
Dawit I, emperor, 578
Dawkins, Richard, 886
The Dawn-Breakers, 72
Dawn Horse Community, 57, 59
"Day of Accession," 227
Day of All Things, **243–44**
Day of Atonement. *See* Yom Kippur
Day of Slavic Culture and Literature. *See* Alphabet Day
"Day of the Covenant," 227
Day of the Dead (Día de los Muertos). *See* All Souls Day
The Day of the Victory of Love, 890
Days of Awe, **244–45**, 485
"Days of God," 61
Days of Sacrifice. *See* Id al-Adha
Death commemorations. *See* Commemorations
Death of Jean-François Lefevre de la Barre, **245–46**
Deceased, honoring, 319, 655–57, **698**, **851–52**
December celebrations
  Bhumanandaji Paramahansa, Birthday of Swami Guru, **115**
  Bodhi Day, **121–22**, 122i
  Danavira Mela, **234–35**
  Expectation of the Birth of the Blessed Virgin Mary, Feast of, **293**
  Festival of Light (Rosicrucian), **303–4**
  Festivus, **306–7**
  Francis Xavier, Saint's Day of St., **317–19**
  Giant Lantern Festival, 335i, **335–36**
  Guadalupe, Feast of Our Lady of, **347–50**
  Harikuyo, **373**
  HumanLight, **413–14**, 887
  Human Rights Day, **414–15**, 415i
  Immaculate Conception, Feast of the, 349, 403, **421–22**, 562, 564
  Janardanji Paramahansa, Commemoration Days of Swami Guru, **458–59**
  John the Evangelist, Day of St., **469–70**
  Lucy, Saint's Day of St., **535–36**
  Misa de Gallo, **584–85**
  New Year's Eve (Scientology), **636**
  Nicholas, Saint's Day of St., **638–40**
  Osho (Rajneesh), Birthday of, **664–65**
  Ramana Maharshi, Birthday of, **737–39**
  Saint Stephen's Day, **762–64**
  Sarada Devi, Birthday of, **783–84**
  Satchidananda, Birthday of Swami, **784–85**
  Tohji-Taisai, **865**
  Tsong Khapa Anniversary, **872–74**
  Zarathustra, Commemorative Days of, **954–55**
  Zartusht-no-diso, **955–56**
Decius, emperor, 202, 228
Delhi Sultanate, 383
Degree on Ecumenism, 917
Deir al-Sultan monastery, 269–70
Deism, 237, 858, 879, 880–81, 883
Deities. *See also specific deities*
  Chinese, 191–92
  Hindu, 806
  Shinto, 806

De Leon, Moses, 480–81, 482
Denmark, 39–40, 218–19
Derrick of Alsace, 715
Descartes, Rene, 882
The Descent of Man (Darwin), 237
Dev, Arjun, 354–55
Devaki, 102, 364
Devanampiyatissa, King, 702
Devas, 659
Devathani Ekadashi. *See* Kartika Snan
Devi. *See* Mother Goddess Devi
Devi, Sarada, 736, 783–84
Devi Bhagavatam, 29–30
Devnampiya Tissa, 265
Dexter Avenue Baptist Church, 555
Dhammacakkappavattana Sutra, 44, 195
"Dhamma Day." *See* Asalha Puja Day ("Dhamma Day")
Dhammakaya, 135
Dhammayuttika, 135
Dhanvantari, 246–47, 253, 542
Dhan Teras, **246–47**, 254
Dharma, 4, 386
Dharmachakra mudra, 597
Dharmakara, 30
Dharmapala, Anagarika, 140
Dhayani Buddhas, 597
Dhritarashtra, King, 336
Dhundhi, 401
Dhyana mudra, 597
Dhyanyogi's Mahasamadhi, **247–48**
Dia de los Muertos. *See* All Souls Day
Dianetics, Anniversary of, **248–49**
Dianetics: The Modern Science of Mental Health (Hubbard), 248–49, 411, 612, 789, 790
Diatessaron, 199
Diaz, Erno, 529
Diderot, Denis, 883, 883i
Diego, Juan, 347–49
Digambaras, 448, 450, 544–45
Dinh dynasty (Vietnam), 137
Diocletian, Emperor, 12, 202, 311, 333, 535, 638, 771, 782
Dionysius Exiguus, 288
Distaff Day, 286
Diti, 605
Divination, 181
Divine Holy Spirit Festival, **249–50**
Divine Life Society, 784–85, 820
Divine Light Mission, 385
Divine Mercy Sunday, **250–51**
Divine Shakti, 847
The Divine Teacher and Model of Perfection (John Paul II), 766
Divinity, of Jesus Christ, 200–201, 202, 725, 868–69
Divino Rostro, Devotion to, **251–52**
Diwali, 162, 173, **252–55**, 254i, 394, 398, 502
Diwali (Jain), 254, **255–56**, 455, 635
Dnyaneshwar, 374
Dobson, James, 611
Doctrine of the Mean, 185
Dogen, 138
Dogwood, 260
Doinel du Val-Michel, Jules-Benoit, 276
Doll Festival, **256–57**, 257i
Dolls, 235–36, 256–57, 257i
Dol Purnima. *See* Gaura Purnima; Holi
Dome of the Rock, 433, 440
Dominic, Saint, 750
Dominic, Saint's Day of St., **257–58**
Dominican Order, 257, 553, 589
Dominican Third Order, 167
Domitian, 469
Donatism, 54–55
Donatus, 54
Doré, Gustave, 522i
Dormition of the Theotokos, 274
Dosojin Matsuri, **259–60**
Dos Santos, Lucia, 299, 301
Double Ninth Festival, 191, **260–61**
Double Seventh Festival, 191, **261–62**
Double Sixth, 15
Doukhobor Peace Day, **262–63**
Doukhobors, 690
Downey, Margaret, 858
Doze Ribeiras, 583
Dracula (film), 915
Dracula (Stoker), 915
"Dracula's Guest" (Stoker), 915
Dragon, killing of, 333, 334i
Dragon Boat Festival, 160, 190, 191, **263–64**, 264i
Dragon dance, 830i
Draupadi, 617
Draupathi, 734

Dreidels, 369i, 370
Druids, 296i, 840–41, 924
Duc de Palatine, Richard, 276
Dungus Monday, 271
Dunkley, Archibald, 360
Dunpanloup, Felix-Antoine-Philibert, 462
Duran, Roberto, 117
Durer, Albrecht, 580i
Durga, 46, 239, 240i, 398, 425, 540, 617i, 617–18
Durga Puja. *See* Navaratri
Duruthu Poya (Sri Lanka), **265–66**
Duryodhan, King, 114
Duryodhana, 364
Dussehra. *See* Navaratri
Dussera, 162
Dyngus Day, 271

East Africa, 962
Easter, **267–69**
  Annunciation, Feast of the, and, 39
  Ethiopian Church, 289
  in liturgical year, 526, 527–28
  setting the date for, 152–53, 202
  story of, 199
Easter (Ethiopian Church), **269–70**
Easter Monday, **270–72**, 714
Eastern Byzantine Empire, 200
Eastern Europe, 141, 271, 884
Eastern Orthodox Churches
  Advent, 10
  All Souls Day, 25
  Alphabet Day, **25–26**
  Ascension Day, 45
  Assumption of the Virgin, 50
  Augustine of Canterbury, Saint's Day of St., 53
  Augustine of Hippo, Saint, and, 55
  Baptism of the Lord, Feast of the, 104
  Calendar of Saints, 274–75
  canonization, 765
  Circumcision, Feast of the, **214–15**, 627
  Clement of Ohrid, Saint's Day of St., **215–16**
  Conversion of St. Paul, Feast of the, 223
  Cyril and Methodius, Saint's Day for Sts., 25, **229–31**
  Elevation of the True Cross, **280–81**
  Epiphany, **284–86**. *See also* Epiphany
  Eucharistic Congresses, 291
  expansion of, 204
  foot washing, 569
  Gregorian calendar and, 154
  Gregory the Great, Saint, 345–46
  Holy Days of Obligation, 403
  Holy Innocents' Day, **404–5**
  Holy Week, 410
  Image Not-Made-by-Hands, Feast of the, **419–20**
  Immaculate Conception and, 421
  James the Greater, Feast Day of St., 456
  John the Baptist, Beheading of, 466
  John the Baptist, Nativity of, 468
  Julian calendar, revised, 154
  Lazarus Saturday, 274, **519–20**, 669–70
  Lent, 521
  liturgical year, 526
  Lord's Supper, 567
  Mary Magdalene, Day of the Holy, 565
  Meskal, 578
  Mid-Pentecost, Feast of, **582–83**
  Midsummer Day, 840
  Mother's Day, 594
  National Day, **609–10**
  Nativity of Mary, 614–15
  Nino, Saint's Day of St., **645–46**
  Olaf, Saint's Day of St., 658
  Old Calendarists, 155
  Orthodoxy, Feast of, **662–63**
  Palm Sunday, 669–70
  Pentecost, 683
  Peter and Paul, Saint's Day of Sts., 689–90
  Procession of the Cross, 281, **713–14**
  Queenship of Mary, Feast of, **725–26**, 910
  relationship with other Christian churches, 201
  Roman Catholic Church and, 203–4, 272, 290
  Saint Stephen's Day, 763
  Saint Stephen's Day (Hungary), **764**
  San Sebastian Day, 783
  Theophany, 527, 582, **853–55**
  Three Hierarchs, Day of the, **859**
  Transfiguration, Feast of the, 866
  Trinity Sunday, 870
  Universal Exaltation of the Precious and Life-creating Cross, 408
  Virgin Mary and, 421, 561–62
  World Communion Sunday, 929
  Zaccheus Sunday, 953

Eastern Orthodoxy, liturgical year, **272–76**
Eastern Rite Catholic churches, 662–63
Eastern Zhou dynasty (China), 182
Easter Procession, 268i
"Eastertide," 267
"Easter Triduum," 409
Easter Vigil, 268, 527
Ecclesia Gnostica, 549, 565, 589, 827–28, 850, 898
Ecclesia Gnostica Mysteriorum, 276, 277
Ecclesia Gnostica, liturgical year, **276–79**
Ecclesiastical History (Eusebius), 105
Ecumenical movement, 769, 916
Ecumenical Patriarchate, 273, 292
Ecumenism, 209–10
Edessa, 419
Edo period (Japan), 138, 508, 807–8
Edward VI, King, 207
Effutufo people, 5–6
Eglise Gnostique Catholique Apostolique, 276
Egypt, 151–52, 948
Egypt, Israelites exodus from, 475, 476i, 484, 485, 685–86
Egyptian Coptic Church, 105
Eisai, 138
Eisenberger, Fred, 60
Ekadashi fasting, 647
Elephant Festival, 279i, **279–80**
Elevation of the Holy Cross, Feast of, 274
Elevation of the True Cross, **280–81**
Eliezer, Israel ben, 482
Elizabeth (mother of John the Baptist), 909
Elizabeth, Empress, 846
Elizabeth I, Queen, 207
Elizabeth of Portugal, Saint, 308
Elzéar-Alexandre Cardinal Taschereau, 37
Ember Days, **281–82**
Emerson, Ralph W., 140
E-meter, 51
England. *See also* Anglican Church
  Age of Exploration, 208
  Aldersgate Day, 21
  Augustine of Canterbury, Saint's Day of St., **52–54**
  Buddhism in, 139–40
  Druids, 296i, 840–41, 924
  Ember Days, 282
  Epiphany, 286
  George, Saint, 333
  Gregory the Great, Saint, 346
  Grotto Day, **346–47**
  Holocaust Remembrance Day, 945
  Indian and, 383–86
  James the Greater, Saint, 346–47
  Lady Day in, 38
  Mothering Sunday, 594
  Mount Carmel, Feast Day of Our Lady of, 595
  Pagan religions in, 53
  Protestant expansion, 208–9
  Protestant Reformation, 207
  Restoration, 208
  Roman Catholic Church in, 290–91
  rule of India, 383–86
  Zoroastrianism in, 955
Engrams, 52
Engraving, 313i
Enkutatash, 289, 628
Enlightenment, 209, 481
Entrance of Jesus into Jerusalem, Feast of the, 274
Entry of the Most Holy Theotokos into the Temple. *See* Presentation of Mary, Feast of the
Eostara, **282–83**
Eostre. *See* Eostara; Spring equinox (Thelema); Spring equinox (vernal)
Epictetus, Saint, 283–84
Epictetus the Presbyter and Astion, Saints Day of Sts., **283–84**
Epiphanius, 50
Epiphany, **284–86**
  Befana, 107
  Christmas and, 211
  Ethiopian Church, 289
  fasting and, 274
  as Holy Day of Obligation, 402
  in Kiev, 285i
  in liturgical year, 527
  Magi, visit of, 103–4
Episcopal Church
  Gregory the Great, Saint, 346
  Martin de Porres, Saint's Day of St., 554
  Martin Luther King, Jr., Birthday of, 555
  One Great Hour of Sharing, **661–62**
  Order of the Holy Cross, 408
  Seton, Saint's Day of Mother Elizabeth, 795
Episcopal Church of Scotland, 553
Equinox, 831
Equinox. *See* Fall equinox; Spring equinox (Thelema); Spring equinox (vernal)

Esala Perehera. *See* Festival of the Tooth
Eschraghi, Armin, 65, 70, 74
Eshinni, 287
Eshinni-Kakushinni Memorial, **287–88**
Esoteric Buddhism, 597–98
Esoteric Buddhists, 411
Esotericists, 831
Estanislao, Francisco, 335
Estevanico, 860
Esther (Hassassah), 719–20
Esther, Book of, 719–20
Esther, Queen, 486
Ethelbert, King, 53
Ethiopia
  Easter, **269–70**
  Enkutatash, 628
  Genna (Christmas, Ethiopia), 213, **332**
  Haile Selassie I, Birthday of Emperor, **360–61**
  Jewish people and, 818–19
  Sigd, **818–19**
Ethiopian calendar, 288–89, 332
Ethiopian Church, 105, 854
Ethiopian Church, liturgical year, **288–90**
Ethiopian Orthodox Tawahdo Church, 289, 332, 578–79, 628, 861i, 861–62
Eucharist, 205–6, 223–24, 567
Eucharistic Congresses, **290–91**
Eudes, Jean, 423
Eugene II, Pope, 345, 783
Europe
  atheism in, 885
  Buddhism in, 139–40
  Islam in, 204–5
  Judaism in, 481
  Mardi Gras, 551
  Midsummer Day, 840
  Mothering Sunday, **593**
  pagan religions, 780
  Roman Catholic Church and, 203–4
  Walpurgisnacht, 108, **915–16**
  Zen Buddhism in, 140, 142
Eusebius, 35, 105
Evangelical Awakening, 208
Evangelical churches, 429, 430, 611–12, 869
Evangelical Lutheran Church, 346
"The Eve of Saint Agnes" (Keats), 13
Evergreens, use of in Advent, 10
Evidence on Man's Place in Nature (Huxley), 237
Evlavios, 419
Evolution, 236–39
Evtimiy of Bulgaria, Saint's Day of Patriarch, **291–92**
Exodus, Book of, 485
Exodus from Egypt, Israelites, 475, 476i, 484, 485, 685–86
Expectation of the Birth of the Blessed Virgin Mary, Feast of, 38, **293**. *See also* Annunciation, Feast of the
Exxon, 149
Ezion Methodist Church, 11
Ezra, 485
Fage, Antoinette, 51
Falcoia, Bishop Tommaso, 26
Fall equinox, **295–96**, 296i
Falsi calendar, 959
Falun Gong, 188
Family Federation for World Peace and Unification. *See* Unification Church
"Farewell Pilgrimage," 363
Farvardigan, 960i. *See also* Zoroastrianism
Fasching. *See* Mardi Gras
Fasinada, **297**
Fasting
  Akshay Tritiya (Jain), 19
  Amalaka Ekadashi, **27–28**
  Anant Chaturdashi, 32
  Ashura, 47
  Bahá'í Fast, **94–96**
  Eastern Orthodox Churches, 274
  Ethiopian Church, 289
  Genna (Christmas, Ethiopia), 332
  in Islam, 436
  Karwa Chauth, 497–98
  Lent, 274, 521
  Narasimha Jayanti, 606
  Navpad Oli, 618
  Nineteen-Day Fast, 621
  Nirjala Ekadashi, 647
  Ramadan, **734–36**
  Yom Kippur, 948
Fast of Gedaliah, **297–98**
Fast of the Apostles, 274
Fast of the First Born, **298–99**
Fatima (Muhammad's daughter), 21, 518
Fatima, Feast Day of Our Lady of, **299–301**
Fatima, Our Lady of, 423
Fatima Sanctuary, 300i
Fat Tuesday, 551–52. *See also* Mardi Gras

Feast Days
Agnes, Feast Day of St., **12–14**, 690
Anne, Feast Day of St., **36–37**
Annunciation, Feast of the, **37–39**, 293, 909–10
Aparecida, Feast of Our Lady of, **41–43**, 564
Baptism of the Lord, Feast of the, **103–4**
Chair of St. Peter, Feast of the, **169**
Christ the King, Feast of, **213–14**
Circumcision, Feast of the, **214–15**, 627
Conversion of St. Paul, Feast of the, **222–23**
Corpus Christi, Feast of, **223–24**, 403
Czestochowa, Feast Day of Our Lady of, **231–32**
Expectation of the Birth of the Blessed Virgin Mary, Feast of, 38, **293**
Fatima, Feast Day of Our Lady of, **299–301**
Forgiveness, Feast of, **312–13**
George, Feast Day of St., **333–34**
Good Remedy, Feast of Our Lady of, **340–41**
Guadalupe, Feast of Our Lady of, **347–50**
Holy Family, Feast of the, **403–4**
Holyrood or the Feast of the Triumph of the Holy Cross, **407–9**
Image Not-Made-by-Hands, Feast of the, **419–20**
Immaculate Conception, Feast of the, **421–22**
Immaculate Heart of Mary, Feast of the, **422–23**
James the Greater, Feast Day of St., 349, 403, **455–57**, 562, 564
Joseph, Feast Day of St., **470–72**
Lourdes, Feast Day of Our Lady of, **532–35**
Mid-Pentecost, Feast of, **582–83**
Most Holy Name of Mary, Feast of the, **590–91**
Most Precious Blood, Feast of the, **591–92**
Mount Carmel, Feast Day of Our Lady of, **595–96**
Orthodoxy, Feast of, **662–63**
Peace and Good Voyage, Feast of Our Lady of, **678–79**
Peñafrancia, Feast of Our Lady of, **679–80**
Perpetual Help, Feast of Our Lady of, **684–85**
Presentation of Jesus in the Temple, Feast of the, **708–10**
Presentation of Mary, Feast of the, **710–11**
Prompt Succor, Feast Day of Our Lady of, **716–17**
Queenship of Mary, Feast of, **725–26**, 910
Rosary, Feast of Our Lady of the, **750–51**
Sacred Heart of Jesus, Feast of the, 557, **757–58**
Saint John Lateran, Feast of the Dedication of, **760–61**
Solemnity of Mary, Feast of the, 215, 402, **824**
Sorrows, Feast of Our Lady of, **828–29**
Transfiguration, Feast of the, **866–67**
Visitation, Feast of the, **909–10**
Feast for the Three Days of the Writing of the Book of the Law, **301–3**
Feast of Fast-Breaking. *See* Id al-Fitr
Feast of Tabernacles, 838
February celebrations
Ansgar, Saint's Day of St., **39–40**
Ayyám-i-Há (Bahá'í Intercalary Days), **60–63**
Brigid of Kildare, Saint's Day of St., 128i, **128–29**
Chair of St. Peter, Feast of the, **169**
Daruma Kuyo, **235–36**
Darwin Day, **236–39**
Data Ganj Bakhsh Death Anniversary, **241–42**
Harikuyo, **373**
Hoshi Matsuri, **411**
Imbolc, **420–21**
Lourdes, Feast Day of Our Lady of, **532–35**
Meher Baba, Commemoration Days of, **577–78**
National Brotherhood Week, **608–9**
Nichiren's Birthday, **636–37**
Peter Baptist and Companions, Saint's Day of St., **690–91**
Presentation of Jesus in the Temple, Feast of the, **708–10**
Ramakrishna, Birthday of Sri, **736–37**
Federal Council of Churches, 928, 930
Federation of Jain Associations in North America, 452
Federation of Zoroastrian Associations of North America, 963
Feminism, 565, 827
Ferguson, Laurie, 938
Ferrata, Ercole, 13
Festa di San Nicola, 639

Festival of Light (Rosicrucian), **303–4**
Festival of Lights. *See* Hanukkah
Festival of Lights (Diwali), **252–55**
Festival of Riḍván, 67–68
Festival of the Guardian Angel. *See* Schutzengelfest
Festival of the Tooth, **304–6**, 305i
Festivals and holiday celebrations, importance of, xxii–xxiii
Festivus, **306–7**
Fiesta dos Tabuleiros, **307–8**
Fiji, 8–9, 613
Finland, **487–88**, 840, 866
Fiqh Council of North America (FCNA), 443
First Amendment, U.S., 742–43
First Night of the Prophet and His Bride, **309–10**
First Salmon Rites, 6, **310–11**
First Society of Free Enquirers, 883
First Turning of the Wheel, 145
Five agents, 183, 260
Five Beloved Ones, 604
Five Classics (Wu Jing), 185
Five Precepts (Panca Sila), 5
Flag Service Organizations, 52
Fleury Abbey, 109
The Flight into Egypt (Baillie), 471i
Floating Lantern Ceremony (Honolulu). *See* Obon Festival(s)
Florian, Saint's Day of St., **311**
Flower Communion, **312**
Flower Garland Sutra, 549
Focus on the Family, 611
Fogaça, Donna Maria, 308
Foguangshan order, 141
Foot washing, 568–69
For All the Saints, 769–70
Forgiveness, Feast of, **312–13**
Forty Immortals, 540
Forty Martyrs' Day, **313–14**
Foundation for the Law of Time, 573
Founders' Day (Salvation Army), **314–16**
Founders' Day, the Church of Perfect Liberty, **316–17**
Four Books (Se Shu), 185
Four Noble Truths, 130–31, 195
Fourteen Holy Helpers, 783
Fourth Council of the Lateran, 589
Fox, Joseph, 413
Frainet, Nicholas de, 639
France
  Age of Exploration, 208
  Death of Jean-François Lefevre de la Barre, **245–46**
  Deism in, 883
  Madeleine, Fête de la, **537–38**
  Martinmas, 557
  Protestant Reformation, 207
  Unbelief in, 883
Franciscan Friars and Sisters of the Atonement, 917
Franciscan order, 40–41, 909
Franciscans of the Stricter Observance, 693
Francis of Assisi, Saint, 212, 277, 312–13, 313i, 471, 681
Francis Xavier, Saint, 318i
Francis Xavier, Saint's Day of St., **317–19**
Francoz, Father, 404
Frankel, Zacharias, 482
Franklin, Benjamin, 610, 881
Fravardegan, **319–20**
Fravardin Yasht, 319
Frawadigan. *See* Zoroastrianism
Free church tradition, 568, 569
Free Daist Communion, 57, 58
Freedom from Religion Foundation, 238, 611, 612
Freemasons, 470, 883
Freethinkers, 425–26, 611–12, 857i, 879, 882, 887
Freethinkers Day. *See* Thomas Paine Day
Freethinkers of America, 886
Freethought, 246
Freethought Day, **320–21**, 887
Freethought Soceity of Greater Philadelphia, 858
Freewinds, 546
Friends (Quakers), 208, 262–63
Friends of the Western Buddhist Order, 142
Fundamentalists, 238, 869
Fu Xi, 180
Fyodorovna, Empress Maria, 467

Gabriel, Angel, 37–38, 432–33, 434, 440, 516, 570–71
Gahambars, **323–24**
Gahden-Namgye. *See* Tsong Khapa Anniversary
Galapagos Islands, 236

Galdan Namchot. *See* Tsong Khapa Anniversary
Gallagher, Michael U., 855
Ganden Ngamcho. *See* Tsong Khapa Anniversary
Gandhi, Mahatma, 384–85, 554
Gandhi, Virchand, 452
Ganesh, 18–19, 29, 324–27, 325i, 823
Ganesh Chaturdashi, 397
Ganesh Chaturthi, **324–27**, 325i
Ganga Dussehra, **327–29**, 328i
Gangaur, **329–30**
Ganges River, 327, 328i, 570
Ganjitsu (Japan). *See* New Year's Day
Garba dance, 616i
The Garden of the Martyrs (Kashifi), 48
Gardner, Gerald B., 108, 282, 513, 779, 921–22, 922i, 951
Garnier, Charles, 464
Garuda Purana, 897
Garvey, Marcus, 360
Gathemangal, **330**
Gaudentius, Saint, 314
Gaudiya Math, 112
Gaudiya Vaishnava *sampradaya*, 383
Gaura Purnima, **330–32**
Gauri, 329
Gautama Buddha
  Avatamsaka Sutra, 777–78
  Bodhi Day, **121–22**
  death of, 624i
  Hana Matsuri, **367–68**
  historical Buddha, 30
  King Bimbisara and, 892
  Magha Puja Day, **538–39**
  meditative Buddhism and, 43, 123
  Monlam, the Great Prayer Festival, 149, 587
  Nehan, **623–24**
  relics and, 304
  Sakya Dawa Festival, 776
  Tsong Khapa and, 873
  Vassa, 904
  Wesak/Vesak, 918
Gayane, 645–46
Gayatri Mantra, 547
Gedaliah, 297–98
Gedko of Kraków, Bishop, 311
Gedun Gyatso, 587
Geiger, Abraham, 481i, 482
Gelasius I, Pope, 579
Gelugpa School, 587, 588, 872–73, 936
Gelukpa order, 139
Gems of Divine Mysteries, 84–85
Genkoji Temple, 367
Genna (Christmas, Ethiopia), 213, **332**
Genoa, Italy, 419
Genshi-sai, 812
George, Feast Day of St., **333–34**
George, Saint, 334i
Georgia, 646
Georgian Orthodox Church, 334, 646
Germany, 125–26, 139, 207, 482–83, 557
Ghana, Africa, 5–6, 141
Ghantakarna, 330
Ghatasthapana, 239
Ghose, Aravinda Akroyd. *See* Aurobindo, Birth Anniversary of Sri
Ghost Festival. *See* Ullam-bana
Gian Matsuri, 615
Giant Buddha at Kamakura, 31
Giant Lantern Festival, 335i, **335–36**
Gilles, James, 553
Giri, Sri Yukteswar, 512
Gishen Mariam monastery, 578
Gita Govinda, 732
Gita Jayanti, **336–37**
Global Country of World Peace, 385
Global Siddha Yoga Audio Satsang, 599
The Glories of Mary (Ligouri), 27
Gniezno, Poland, 8
Gnosticism
  Ecclesia Gnostica, liturgical year, **276–79**
  Mani, Commemoration of the Prophet, **549**
  Mary Magdalene and, 565
  Montségur Day, **589–90**
  Sophia, The Descent and Assumption of Holy, **826–28**
  Templars and, 850
  Valentinus, Feast of the Holy, **897–98**
Gnostic scriptures, 565
Gnostic Society, 276
Gnostic-Western Esoteric religion. *See* Scientology, Church of
Gobind Singh, Guru, 354–55, 540–41, 559, 630
God's Day, **337–38**
Gohonzon, 636
Golden Boy, 501
Golden Friday, 282
Golden Temple, 355
Good Friday, 199, **338–40**, 339i, 410, 521, 682. *See also* Holy Week

"Good King Wenceslas" (Kiefer), 763
Good Remedy, Feast of Our Lady of, **340–41**
Good Tidings, Feast of the. *See* Annunciation, Feast of the
Gorbachev, Mikhail, 889
Gordon, Charles George, 340
Gosala, Makkhali, 545
Gospel of Truth, 898
Gospels, Christian, 198–99
Govardhan Puja, **341–42**
Gozo Tenno, 508
Graham, Billy, 610
Grand Shrine at Ise, 806i, 809–10, 812
Granth Sahib, Guru, 353, 558, 559, 603–4, 630
Great Britain. *See* England
Great Buddha Festival, **342–43**
Great Fire Festival. *See* Hoshi Matsuri
Great Full Moon Festival, **343–44**, 344i
Great Invocation, 932–33
Great Learning, 185
Great Mosque at Damascus, 467
Great Persecution of Diocletian, 54
Great Schism of 1054, 658
"Great Vehicle," 132
Greece, 148, 154, 582–83, 879
Greek mythology, 295
Greek Orthodox Church, 638–39
Greek Orthodox Patriarchate of Alexandria and All Africa, 204, 273
Greek Orthodox Patriarchate of Antopch and All the East, 204, 273
Greek Orthodox Patriarchate of Jerusalem, 204, 273
Greenwich, England, 153
Greenwich Mean Time, 218, 443
Gregorian calendar, 153–55, 161, 217, 272–73, 393. *See also* Common Era calendar
Gregory, Louis, 29, 92
Gregory I, Pope, 52, 203
Gregory II, Pope, 125
Gregory IV, Pope, 22, 366
Gregory VII, Pope, 834
Gregory IX, Pope, 40, 258
Gregory XI, Pope, 167, 710–11
Gregory XII, Pope, 554
Gregory XIII, Pope, 106, 153, 217, 272, 750, 926
Gregory XV, Pope, 318
Gregory of Nazianzus, 285, 859
Gregory the Great, 345i
Gregory the Great, Pope, 565
Gregory the Great, Saint, 783
Gregory the Great, Saint's Day of St., **344–46**
Grotto Day, **346–47**
Ground Hog Day. *See* Presentation of Jesus in the Temple, Feast of the
Grundy, Julia, 642
Guadalupe, Feast of Our Lady of, **347–50**
Guadalupe, Our Lady of, 562
Guadalupe, Shrine of Our Lady of, 348i, 349
Guan Yin, 124, 191–92, 351i, 574, 598, 816–17
Guan Yin, Renunciation of, **350–51**
Guan Yin's Birthday, **351–53**
Guatemala, 751
Gulf coast, of United States, 120–21
Gupta dynasty (India), 381
Gurdwara Sis Ganj Sahib, 559
Gurudev Siddha Peeth, 599
Guru Gobind Singh's Birthday, **353–54**
Guru Granth Sahib, Celebration of the, **354–55**
Guru Purnima, **355–57**
Gusri Khan, 139
Guzman, Dominic de, 562
Gyana Panchami, **357**, 454
Gyatso, Losang, 139
Gyatso, Sönam, 139
Gyatso, Tenzin, 139, 233–34, 234i
Gyatso, Tupden, 139
Gyokyo, 444
Gypsies. *See* Romany people

Haab' calendar, 573
Hachiman, 17, 444–45
Hadaka Matsuri, **359–60**
Hadith, 417, 517–18, 571
Hadrian I, Pope, 663
Hagar, 363, 417
Hagia Sophia, 713
Haile Selassie I, Birthday of Emperor, **360–61**
Hajj, 158, **361–64**, 417, 436, 442, 443
Hakka people, 845–46
Halahala, 172
Hala Shashti, **364–65**
Halloween, 277, **365–67**, 366i, 631, 780
Haman, 719–20
Hamburg, Germany, 39–40
Han, Hak Ja, 175, 870–71, 889
Hana Matsuri, **367–68**
Hands of the Cause of God, 88–89

Han dynasty (China), 177, 183, 184, 260, 514, 515, 628
Hanshi Festival. *See* Pure Brightness Festival
Hanukkah, **368–71**, 369i, 371i, 486
Hanuman, Lord, 170, 371–73, 739
Hanuman Dhoka, 425
Hanuman Jayanti, **371–73**
Haraldsson, Olaf, 658
Harappa culture, 378
Hare Krishna movement, 331, 740, 741
Har Gobind, Guru, 558
Har Gobind Ji, Guru, 254
Hari, 27
Haridwar, India, 505
Harikuyo, **373**
Hari-Shayani Ekadashi, **373–74**
Haritalika Teej. *See* Teej Festivals
Hariyali Teej. *See* Teej Festivals
Har Krishan, Guru, 559
Harris, Sam, 886
Haru Matsuri, **374–75**
Hasan, Siyyid, 74
Hasidism, 481, 482, 787
Hatha yoga, 785
Hayagriva, 494
Hayashi, Razan, 808
Heavenly Stems, 159
Hebrew Bible, 434–35, 475, 719
Hebrew Calendar, 155–57, 627
Heian period (Japan), 138, 375, 802
Helena, Saint, 231, 280, 280i, 289, 407–8, 578, 713, 771
Hell, 877
Hemecandra, 448
Hemis Festival. *See* Padmasambhava
Hemp, 492–93
Henry I, King, 53
Henry VIII, King, 207
Henry of Navarre, 106
Henslow, John Stevens, 236
Heraclius, emperor, 281
Herbert, Edward, 881
Hererra, Casimiro, 252
Heriga, 157
Heritage Day, 21. *See also* Aldersgate Day
Hermetic Order of the Golden Dawn, 301
Hermitage of the Virgen de Valme, 750
Hernando III, King, 749
Herodius, 466
Herod the Great, 218, 404, 464–65
Herzl, Theodore, 483
Hibbert, Joseph, 360
Hickey, James Cardinal, 679
The Hidden Words (Bahá'u'lláh), 87
Hie Jinja Shinto Shrine, 845
Higan, 296, **375–76**, 833
High Holy Days (Jewish), 485, 753, 947. *See also* Days of Awe
High Kami, 806
Hijra, 433
Hilduin, 345, 783
Hillary of Poitiers, 556
Hina-Ningyo, 256
Hinds, Robert, 360
Hindu Freethought Union, 885
Hinduism, **377–92**. *See also* Hinduism festivals and holidays; India; *specific deities*
  Amaterasu, 601, 806, 813–14
  astrology, 633
  birth and rebirth, 386
  Brahmanism, 378–80, 382
  British rule and independence, 383–86
  Buddhism and, 133–34, 381
  classical Hinduism, 380–82
  deities, 806.
  See also specific deities
  dharma, concept of, 4, 386
  diaspora, 399
  diversity of, 377–78
  Harappa culture, 378
  Indra Jatra, **425**
  Islamic rule and, 383
  Jainism and, 381, 447–53
  Kazahinomi-sai, 813–14
  Kinen-sai, 813
  liturgical calendars, xx, xxii
  Neo-Hinduism, 383–86
  origins of the term, 377–78
  postclassical Hinduism, 383
  principal concepts and practice, 386–90
  Saivite Hindus. *See* Saivite Hindus
  six orthodox systems, 388–89
  spread of, 382
  Vaishnava Hindu. *See* Vaishnava Hindu
  Veda, 378–80, 604–5
  Vedanta Hinduism, 910–11
Hinduism, festivals and holidays, **392–400**. *See also* Hinduism
  Ahoi Ashtami, **15**

Akshay Tritiya, **18–19**
Amalaka Ekadashi, **27–28**
Amarnath Yatra, **28–29**
Ambuvachi, **29–30**
Anant Chaturdashi, **32–33**
Ashokashtami, **46–47**
Avatar Adi Da Samraj's Birthday, **57–58**
Avataric Divine Self-Emergence, Day of, **58–59**
Babaji Commemoration Day, **76–78**
Baba's Day, **78–79**
Balarama, Appearance Day of Lord, **102–3**
Bhairava Ashtami, **111–12**
Bhaktisiddhanta Sarasvati Thakura, Appearance Day of, **112**, 113
Bhaktivinoda Thakura, Appearance Day of, **112–13**
Bhishma Ashtami, **113–14**
Bhumanandaji Paramahansa, Birthday of Swami Guru, **115**
calendars, 393–95
Chaitra Purnima, **170–71**
Chandan Yatra, **171–72**
Chaturmas Vrat, **172–73**
Chinmayananda, Commemoration Days for, **193–94**
Chittirai Festival, **194–95**, 398
Danavira Mela, **234–35**
Dasain, **239–41**
Dattatreya Jayanti, **242–43**, 540
Dhan Teras, **246–47**, 254
Dhyanyogi's Mahasamadhi, **247–48**
Diwali, 162, 173, **252–55**, 254i, 394, 398, 502
Ganesh Chaturthi, **324–27**, 325i
Ganga Dussehra, **327–29**, 328i
Gangaur, **329–30**
Gathemangal, **330**
Gaura Purnima, **330–32**
Gita Jayanti, **336–37**
Govardhan Puja, **341–42**
Guru Purnima, **355–57**
Hala Shashti, **364–65**
Hanuman Jayanti, **371–73**
Hari-Shayani Ekadashi, **373–74**
Holi, 162, 395, **400–402**, 401i
Janaki Navami, **457–58**
Janmashtami, 162, **459–60**
Jhulan Yatra, 103, **460–61**
Kamada Ekadashi, **490–91**
Kartika Purnima, **493–95**
Kartika Snan, **495–97**
Karwa Chauth, **497–99**, 498i
Kojagara, **502–3**
Kumbha Mela, **505–7**
Magha Purnima, **539–40**
Mahashivaratri, 162, 397, **541–43**, 542i
Makar Sankranti, **547–48**, 548i
Mauni Amavasya, **569–70**
Mokshada Ekadashi, **585–86**
Mother, Birthday of the, **592–93**
Mother Goddess Devi, 398–99
Mudras, **596–98**
Muktananda, Birthday of Swami Paramahansa, **598–99**
Nagapanchami, **601–2**
Narak Chaturdashi, **604–5**
Narieli Purnima, **607**
Narasimha Jayanti, **605–7**, 606i
Navaratri, 162, 395, 398, 616i, **616–18**
New Year's Day (India), 395–96
Nirjala Ekadashi, **647**
Nityananda Trayodasi, **648**
Nyepi, **652–53**
Onam, **659–60**
Osho (Rajneesh), Birthday of, **664–65**
Patotsav, **676–77**
Pitra Paksha, **698**
Pooram, **700–701**
Prabhupada, Appearance Day of A. C. Bhaktivedanta Swami, **705–7**
Prabhupada, Disappearance Day of A. C. Bhaktivedanta Swami, **707**
Prasadji Paramahansa, Birthday of Swami Guru, **707–8**
Purnanandaji Paramahansa, Commemoration Day for Swami Guru, **721–22**
Putrada Ekadashi, **722–23**
Radhashtami, **732–33**
Raksha Bandhan, **733–34**
Ramakrishna, Birthday of Sri, **736–37**
Ramana Maharshi, Birthday of, **737–39**
Rama Navami, **739–40**, 739i
Ratha Yatra, 171, **740–41**
Rishi Panchami, 747i, **747–48**, 908
Rukmini Ashtami, **755**
Rushi Pancham, **755–56**
Sai Baba of Shirdi, Birthday of, 399, **758–59**
Sarada Devi, Birthday of, **783–84**

Satchidananda, Birthday of Swami, **784–85**
Shaivite holidays, 397–98
Shankaracharya Jayanti, **796–98**
Sharad Purnima, 502–3, **798–99**
Sheetala Ashtami, **800–801**
Shravava Mela, **815**
Siddha Day, **817–18**
Sivananda Saraswati, Birthday of Swami, **819–20**
Skanda Shashti, **820–22**, 821i
Snan Yatra, **822–23**
Surya Shashti, **841–43**, 842i
Teej Festivals, **847–48**
Tejomayananda, Birthday of Swami, **848–49**
Thaipusam, 540, **852–53**, 853i
Tirupati Brahmotsava Festival, **862–64**
Tulsidas Jayanti, **875–76**
Vaikuntha Ekadashi, **895–96**, 896i
Vaishnava holidays, 396–97
Vaitarani, **896–97**
Valmiki Jayanti, 875, **899**
Vamana Jayanti, **900**
Varaha Jayanti, **901**
Vata Savitri, **905–6**
Vishwakarma Puja, **908–9**
Vivekananda, Birthday of Swami, **910–11**
Yogananda, Birthday of Paramahansa, **941–42**, 942i
Yogananda, Mahasamadhi of Paramahansa, **942–43**
Yukteswar, Commemorative Days of Swami Sri, **950**
Hinduism Today, 849
Hindu lunar calendar, 394–95
Hindu Renaissance. *See* Neo-Hinduism
Hiranyakashipu, 400–401, 659, 901
Hiranyaksha, 901
Hirata, Atsutane, 808
Hirneykasipu, 605–6
Hirnyakasha, 605
Hirohito, emperor, 812
Hirsch, Samson Raphael, 482
Hitchens, Christopher, 886
Hitler, Adolf, 945
Hodgson, Richard, 920
Hoeller, Stephan, 276
Hoi Ashtami, 15
Hola Mohalla, 163
Holbach, Paul Henry, 882
Holi, 162, 395, **400–402**, 401i
Holika, 400–401
Holiness, saints and, 765
Holland, 207
Holocaust, 483, 486
Holocaust Remembrance Day, 486, **944–46**
Holy Days of Obligation, **402–3**
Holy Family, Feast of the, **403–4**
Holy Innocents' Day, **404–5**
Holy Maries, Festival of the (La Fête des Saintes Maries), **405–7**, 537
Holy Mary of Perpetual Help, 684
Holyrood or the Feast of the Triumph of the Holy Cross, **407–9**
Holy Saturday. *See* Holy Week
Holy Spirit Association for the Unification of World Christianity. *See* Unification Church
Holy Thursday. *See* Maundy Thursday
Holy Trinity, doctrine of, 867–70
Holy Water, 582
Holy Week, **409–10**. *See also* Easter
Agnes, Feast Day of St., 13–14
Annunciation, Feast of the, and, 39
Ash Wednesday, 49i, **49–50**, 521
Burning of Judas, **148–49**
Good Friday, 199, **338–40**, 339i, 410, 521, 682
in liturgical year, 527
Maundy Thursday, 224, 409, 521, **567–69**
Penitentes and, **680–82**
Honen, 31, 138, 544, 804
Hong Kong
Kwan Tai, Birthday of, **507–8**
Pak Tai, Birthday of, 667
Tam Kung Festival, 845–46
Virgin Mary statue in, 561i
Wesak/Vesak, 144, 918
Hong Xiuquan, 187
Honoring Sacred Sites Day, 934
Honorius III, Pope, 312–13
Hoomi, Koot, 932
Horin-ji temple, 236
Horned God (pagan), 780
Horus, 302, 309
Hosay (Husayne) Massacre, 48
Hosay Festival (Trinidad). *See* Ashura
Hoshana Rabbah. *See* Sukkot
Hoshi Matsuri, **411**
Hourani, Albert, 437–38
Hou Yi, 581
Howe, Julia Ward, 594

Howell, Leonard, 360
Hripsime, 645–46
Hua Cheng Temple, 504
Huángbo Xiyun, 525
Huang Di, 180
Hubbard, Birthday of L. Ron, **411–13**
Hubbard, L. Ron
  background, 789–90
  birthday of, **411–13**
  Dianetics: The Modern Science of Mental Health, 248–49
  as founder of faith, 51, 168, 612
  photo of, 412i
  Sea Org, 791
  writings of, 636
Hui-yuan, 31
Human-Etisk Forbund, 886
Humanism. *See also* Unbelief
  Festivus and, 307
  Freethought Day, **320–21**, 887
  holidays of, 887
  HumanLight, **413–14**, 887
  Human Rights Day, 415
  overview of, 879, 882
  on religion, 886
  winter solstice, 927
  World Humanist Day, 887, **931–32**
Humanist Association of the Great Sacramento Area, 320
Humanist Community, 238
Humanist Manifestos, 887
HumanLight, **413–14**, 887
Human Rights Day, **414–15**, 415i
Hundred Schools period (China), 182
Hundred Years' War, 462
Hungary, 207, 764
Hungry Ghosts, 655, 877
Hupa people, 6–7
Hurle, Henry, 840
Huron people, 463–64
Hurricane Katrina, 552
Hus, John, 829
Ḥusayn, Mullá, 68–69, 72
Hussein, Saddam, 48
Huxley, Thomas Henry, 237
Hyakujo Day Observance, **416**

Iberia, 646
Ibrahim, 362–63, 417. *See also* Abraham, Prophet
I Ching (Book of Changes), 181
Icons
  Council of Nicea, 662–63
  Image Not-Made-by-Hands, 419–20
  Our Lady of Perpetual Help, 684–85
  relics and, 772
  Sacred Heart of Jesus, 757–58
  veneration of, 466
  of Virgin Mary, 725
Id al-Adha, 363, **417–18**, 442
Id al-Fitr, **418**, 442
Iglesia de San Felipe, 116
Ignatius, Patriarch of Constantinople, 466
Ignatius Loyola, 317–18
"I Have a Dream" speech (King), 555
Ikegami Honmon-ji Temple, 657
Ilmu (line dancing), 196–97
Image Not-Made-by-Hands, Feast of the, **419–20**
Imbolc, **420–21**
Immaculate Conception, doctrine of, 42, 50–51, 203, 421–22, 533–34, 562, 614–15, 717
Immaculate Conception, Feast of the, 349, 403, **421–22**, 562, 564
Immaculate Heart of Mary, 299–300, 562
Immaculate Heart of Mary, Feast of the, **422–23**
Immigration Restriction Act of 1901, 141
Imperial House of Japan, 812–13
Inca Empire, 14
Incarnation, Feast of the. *See* Annunciation, Feast of the
Incarnation of the Invisible Divine, 613
In Darkest England—and the Way Out (Booth), 315
Independence Day, 424
India. *See also* Hindu; Hinduism, festivals and holidays
  Akshay Tritiya, 18
  atheism in, 885
  British rule, 383–86
  Buddha Shakyamuni in, 129–30
  Buddhism, origins of, 133–34
  calendars and, 161–62, 393–94
  Christianity in, 200
  Gupta dynasty, 381
  independence movement, 383–86
  invasions of, 383

modern nation, 392–93
Monlam, the Great Prayer Festival, 588
New Year's Day, 395–96, 630, **632–35**
rainy season, 172–73
Saka calendar, 161–62, 393–94, 395, 630, 632–33
Sakya Dawa Festival, 777
Satavahana dynasty, 161
sun worship, 842–43
Ullam-bana, 877
Wesak/Vesak, 144, 918
Zoroastrianism in, 955, 961–62
Indian Rationalist Association, 885
Indivisible Day, **424–25**
Indonesia, 144, 918
Indra, Lord, 170, 341–42, 502, 900
Indrabhuti, Gautama, 255
Indra Jatra, **425**
Indulgences, 206–7
Indus Valley civilization, 378, 379i
Infancy Gospel of James. See Protoevangelium of James
Ingersoll, Robert Green, 425–27, 426i, 887
Ingersoll Day, **425–27**
Initiation of Avatar Adi Da's Divine Avataric Self-Emergence, 235
I'n-Lon-Schka, **427–28**
Innocent (monk), 466
Innocent I, Pope, 55
Innocent III, Pope, 589
Innocent IV, Pope, 834
Innocent XI, Pope, 590
Inquisition, 589
Institute of Scientific Atheism, 884
Institutes of the Christian Religion (Calvin), 207
Integral Yoga, 56
Integral Yoga International, 785
Interfaith contact, 608–9
Interfaith Medallion, 649
International Association of Scientologists Anniversary, **428–29**
International Association of Scientologists (IAS), 428–29, 791
International Council of Christians and Jews, 649
International Date Line, 218, 272, 443
International Day for Nowruz, 620
International Day of Prayer for the Persecuted Church, **429–30**
International Eucharistic congresses, 291
International Federation of Freethinkers, 886
International Federation of Secular Humanistic Jews, 886
International Flag Land Base, 248, 412
International Humanist and Ethical Union, 238, 413, 415, 886, 931
International Meridian Conference, 153
International Missionary Conference, 930
International Nahavir Jain Mission, 452
International Religious Freedom Act, 430
International Religious Freedom Day, **430–31**
International Society of Krishna Consciousness (ISKCON), 112–13, 331, 383, 385, 460, 606, 648, 705–7, 732, 740–41
International Woman's Day, 594
International Workers Day, 471
International Zen Association, 142
Inti, 14
Into Raymi Fiesta. *See* Summer Solstice
Ioanikiy (Joanicius), Patriarch, 292
Iran, 48, 86–87, 437, 643, 955, 962. *See also* Persia
Irani, Merwan S., 577
Iranian calendar, 651
Iraq, 22, 47–48. *See also* Shi'a Muslims
Ireland
Brigid, Saint, 709–10
Brigid of Kildare, Saint's Day of St., **128–29**
Columba, Saint, 216–17
Nicholas, Saint's Day of St., 639
Oimblc, 708
Saint Patrick's Day, **761–62**
Saint Stephen's Day, 763
Irenaeus, 897
Irene, Empress, 663
Irmina, 925
Iroquois people, 463
Isaac, 417, 475
Isabel I, Queen, 308
Isabel of Portugal, Queen, 249
Isaiah, 478
Ise Jinju Shrine, 803–4
Ise Shrine. *See* Grand Shrine at Ise
Ishmael, 362–63
Isis Unveiled (Blavatsky), 919
Islam, **431–40**. *See also* Shi'a Muslims; Sunni Muslims
Allah, 431, 432, 434, 435, 516
Báb and, 65, 67–68, 70–71

biblical material, 434–35
branches of, 436–37
Christianity and, 203, 204–5
contemporary, 438–39
Crusades, 204–5, 438, 715
dynasties, 437
in Europe, 204–5
five pillars of, 435–36
growth of, 437–39
Hinduism and, 383
Israel and, 438
jihad, 436
liturgical calendar, xxi
Mother's Day and, 594
Muhammad, Prophet. *See* Muhammad, Prophet
Muslim calendar, 157–59, 393, 440–43
New Year's Day, 442, 629
overview of, 431–32
Qur'an. *See* Qur'an
Sunni and Shi'a, divisions between, 47–48
true believers, 435
Islam, annual festivals and holy days, **440–44**
Ali ibn Abi Talib, Commemoration Days for, **21–22**
Ashura, **47–49**, 442
Data Ganj Bakhsh Death Anniversary, **241–42**
Hajj, 158, **361–64**, 417, 436, 442, 443
Id al-Adha, **417–18**, 442
Id al-Fitr, **418**, 442
important dates, 442
Laylat al-Mir'ag, 442, **516–17**
Laylat al-Qadr, 442, **517–18**, 735
Laylat ul Bara'ah, 442, **518–19**
Mawlid an-Nabi, 442, **570–72**
Muslim calendar, 157–59, 440–43
Ramadan, 158, 418, 442, **734–36**
Sai Baba of Shirdi, Birthday of, 399, **758–59**
Urs Festival, **892–93**
Islamic calendar, 157–59, 440–43
Islamic Revolution, 437, 962
Ismail, 417
Israel. *See also* Judaism
ancient origins of Judaism, 475–77, 485
Buddhism in, 141
Egypt and, 948
Hebrew calendar, 155–57, 627
Islam and, 438
modern, 483, 486
Pesach in, 687–88
Shemini Alzeret/Simchat Torah, 802
Sigd, 819
Tu B'Shevat, **874–75**
Yom HaAtzmaut, 486, **943–44**, 946
Yom HaZikaron, 486, 943, **946**
Yom Yerushalayim (Jerusalem Day), 487, **949–50**
Israeli Independence Day, 486
Israeli Memorial Day, 486
Israel Prize, 944
Italy, 107, 293, 683, 714–15
Iwashimizu Hachiman Shrine, 615
Iwashimizu Matsuri, **444–45**
Izanagi, 806
Izanami, 806

Jacob, 475
Jade Emperor, 176, 178, 191, 192, 261, 575, 667, 830, 856
Jagannath, Lord, 740–41, 822–23
Jagannath temple, 171, 740
Jahan, Shah, 438
Jahangir, emperor, 254, 558
Jain, Champat Rai, 452
Jainism, **447–53**
beliefs of, 448–50
contemporary communities, 452
divisions in, 450–52
growth of, 448
Hinduism and, 381, 447–53
migration of, 452
monastic orders, 447, 449
New Year's Day, 454, **635–36**
nine posts, 619
overview of, 447
Ranakpur temple, 448i
self-realization, 449
unbelief in, 879
Vardhamana/Mahavira, 447–48
Jainism cycle of holidays, **453–55**
Akshay Tritiya (Jain), **19–20**, 455
Diwali, 254, **255–56**, 455, 635
Gyana Panchami, **357**, 454
Kartika Purnima (Jain), 454, **495**
Mahavir Jayanti, 454, **544–46**, 545i
Mauna Agyaras, 454, **566**
Nagapanchami, **601–2**
Navpad Oli, 454, 545, **618–20**
New Year's Day, 454, **635–36**

Paryushana, 455, **672–74**
Paush Dashami, 454, **677–78**
Jain Meditation International Center, 452
Jamadagni, 671–72
Jamaica, 360–61
James, Apostle, 455–57, 772
James the Greater, Feast Day of St., **455–57**
James the Greater, Saint, 346
Jameson, Anna, 12
Janak, King, 457
Janaki Navami, **457–58**
Janardanji Paramahansa, Commemoration Days of Swami Guru, **458–59**
Janmashtami, 162, **459–60**
January celebrations
Agnes, Feast Day of St., **12–14**, 690
Avataric Divine Self-Emergence, Day of, **58–59**
Baba's Day, **78–79**
Befana, **107**
Black Nazarene Festival, **118–19**
Circumcision, Feast of the, **214–15**, 627
Evtimiy of Bulgaria, Saint's Day of Patriarch, **291–92**
Genna (Christmas, Ethiopia), 213, **332**
Hyakujo Day Observance, **416**
Linji/Rinzai Day Observance, **525**
Makar Sankranti, **547–48**, 548i
Martin Luther King, Jr., Birthday of, **554–56**
Meher Baba, Commemoration Days of, **577–78**
Nino, Saint's Day of St., **645–46**
Prasadji Paramahansa, Birthday of Swami Guru, **707–8**
Prompt Succor, Feast Day of Our Lady of, **716–17**
San Sebastian Day, **782–83**
Sava, Saint's Day of St., **786–87**
Sechi Festival, **793**
Seijin no Hi, **793–94**
Seton, Saint's Day of Mother Elizabeth, **794–95**
Solemnity of Mary, Feast of the, 215, 402, **824**
Tatiana, Saint's Day of St., **846–47**
Theophany, 527, 582, **853–55**
Thomas Paine Day, **857–58**
Three Hierarchs, Day of the, **859**
Three Kings Day, Native American Pueblos, **860–61**
Timkat, 289, 861i, **861–62**
Up Helly Aa, **890–92**
Vivekananda, Birthday of Swami, **910–11**
World Religion Day, **936–39**
Yogananda, Birthday of Paramahansa, **941–42**, 942i
Japan. *See also* Buddhism; Buddhism cycle of holidays; Shinto; Shinto cycle of holidays
Amitabha's Birthday, 31
Bodhi Day, 121, 122
bodhisattvas in, 146
Buddhism in, 138
calendars in, 161, 811
Christianity in, 808–9
Edo period, 138, 508, 807–8
Heian period, 138, 375, 802
Imperial House of Japan, 812–13
Kamakura period, 138
Ksitigarbha's Birthday, 505
local festivals, 811–12
Mahasthamaprapta's Birthday, 544
Manjushri's Birthday, 550
Meiji period, 138, 376, 655, 808
Meiji Restoration, 16, 794, 803, 810–11
Muromachi period, 138
Nehan, 623–24
New Year's Day, 812
Peter Baptist and, 690–91
spring equinox, 833
Taisho period, 138
Tokugawa period, 138, 810
United States and, 774–75
Japanese immigrants to United States, 147–48
Japa yoga, 539, 740, 895, 899
Jarvis, Anna, 594
Jaya, 901
Jayanta, 506
Jefferson, Thomas, 881
Jehovah's Witnesses, 675
Je Rinpoche, 587
Jerusalem, 127, 203, 290, 754i
Jesuits. *See* Society of Jesus
Jesus Christ. *See also* Christianity; Virgin Mary
apparitions of, 757
in art, 198i, 201i
ascension of, **45–46**, 403, 527
birth of, 701–2, 926–27
blood of, 715–16
commemorations of, 201–2

Common Era calendar and, 218
crucifixion of, 338–40
divinity of, 200–201, 202, 725, 868–69
Divino Rostro, Devotion to, **251–52**
final week of as depicted by Holy Week, 409–10
foot washing, 568–69
Image Not-Made-by-Hands and, 419
John the Baptist and, 464–65
Joseph, Saint, and, 470–72
life of, 197
liturgical year, **526–29**, 560
Maundy Thursday, 224, 409, 521, **567–69**
Passover, 156, 198, 224–25, 267, 485, 674–75
Qur'an and, 435
resurrection of, 267–69
with Saint Peter, 688–89, 689i
teachings of, 198–99
temptation of, 522i
Theophany, 527, 582, **853–55**
Transfiguration, Feast of the, **866–67**
Jewish Bible, 199. *See also* Torah
Jewish Christians, 676
Jewish Diaspora, 478
Jewish National Fund, 875
Jewish Teachers Union, 875
Jews for Jesus, 676
Jhulan Yatra, 103, **460–61**
Jie Zitui, 718
Jihad, 436
Jitō, empress, 803
Jizo. *See* Ksitigarbha's Birthday
Jizo Bon, **461–62**
Jnana yoga, 193
Joachim, 614
Joanna, 466
Joan of Arc, Saint's Day of St., **462–63**
Jodo Shinshu, 137, 138, 140, 287, 656, 804–5
Jôdo-shû, 138
Jogues, Isaac, 463
Jogues, John de Brébeuf and Companions, Saints Day of St. Isaac, **463–64**
Johanson, Donald, 238
John, Apostle, 469–70
John, Gospel of, 519–20, 565
John II Casimir, King, 231
John V Palaeologus, emperor, 419
John VIII, Pope, 230
John XV, Pope, 7
John XXIII, Pope, 37, 104, 169, 250, 333, 341, 470, 534, 554, 774, 795, 869
John of Damascus, 50
John of Matha, Saint, 340–41
John Paul II, Pope
Adalbert of Prague, Saint's Day of St., 8
Aparecida, Feast of Our Lady of, 42
assassination attempt, 299–301
Baptism of the Lord, Feast of the, 104
Basilica of Saint Anne, visit to, 696
Bridget, Saint's Day of St., 127
canonization of, 766
Catherine of Siena, Saint's Day of St., 167
Czestochowa, Feast Day of Our Lady of, 231
Divine Mercy Sunday, 251
The Divine Teacher and Model of Perfection, 766
Fatima, Our Lady of, 563
Fatima, Our Lady of and, 423
Great Mosque at Damascus, visit to, 467
Jubilee year, 473–74
Lorenzo Ruiz, 529
on Mary as Mother of the Church, 824
Mother Theresa and, 766
Poland and, 835
Rogation Days and, 749
scapular, brown, 595
Shrine of Our Lady of Guadalupe, visit to, 349
Thérèse of Lisieux, Saint and, 855
World Day of the Sick, 534
Johnson, Lady Bird, 775
John the Baptist, 34, 277, 465i, 487, 909
John the Baptist, Beheading of, 274, **464–67**
John the Baptist, Nativity of, **467–69**, 910
John the Evangelist, Day of St., **469–70**
John the Forerunner, Conception of Saint, 468
Jokhang Temple/Monastery, 524, 587
Jones, Franklin, 8, 57, 58, 58i, 613. *See also* Adi Da Samraj
Jones, Lewis E., 591
Jones, Spencer, 917
Jones, William, 384
Jopkhang Temple, 149
Josef, Akiba Ben, 225
Joseph (son of Jacob), 475
Joseph, Feast Day of St., **470–72**
Joseph, Saint, 470–72, 701–2
Joseph Emmanuel, king, 824
Joseph of Arimathea, 339, 716

Joseph the Worker, 471
Joshua, 476
Jubilee Year, **472–74**
Judah, 477, 485
Judah the Hammer, 370
Judaism, **474–84**. *See also* Judaism festivals of the year
ancient origins, 475–78, 485
Ark of the Covenent, 477, 854, 861, 909
Conservative Judaism, 482, 949
covenant with God, 475–76
in the Diaspora, 480–81
in Ethiopia, 818–19
in Europe, 481
exodus from Egypt, 475, 476i, 484, 485, 685–86
Greek and Roman eras, 478–81
Hebrew Calendar, 155–57, 627
Holocaust, 483, 486
Israel, modern, 483. *See also* Israel
liturgical calendar, xx
Messianic Judaism, 676, 839
modern community, development of, 481–82
Orthodox Judaism, 482, 754i, 943, 949
overview of, 474
Reform Judaism, 482, 949
spring equinox, 833
Torah, 199, 474–75, 479, 753
in United States, 481, 483
Zionism, 482–83
Judaism festivals of the year, **484–87**
Counting of the Omer, **224–25**, 485
Days of Awe, **244–45**, 485
Fast of Gedaliah, **297–98**
Fast of the First Born, **298–99**
Hanukkah, **368–71**, 369i, 371i, 486
High Holy Days (Jewish), 485, 753, 947
Jubilee Year, **472–74**
overview of, 484–85
Passover, 156, 198, 224–25, 267, 485, **674–76**
Pesach, 485, 674, **685–88**
Purim, 486, **719–21**
Rosh Hashanah, 156, 244–45, 485–86, 627, **752–54**, 754i, 947
Schneerson, Anniversary of the Death of Rabbi Menachem Mendal, **787–88**
Shavuot, 485, **799–800**
Shemini Alzeret/Simchat Torah, **801–2**, 837–38
Sigd, **818–19**
Sukkot, 485, 486, 801, **835–39**, 836i
Tabernacles, Feast of, 486
Tisha B'Av, **864–65**
Tu B'Shevat, **874–75**
Yom HaAtzmaut, 486, **943–44**
Yom HaShoah, 486, **944–46**
Yom HaZikaron, 486, 943, **946**
Yom Kippur, 47, 156, 244–45, 472, 485–86, **947–48**
Yom Yerushalayim (Jerusalem Day), 487, **949–50**
Jude, 105
Judge, William Q., 919
Juhannus, **487–88**
Juliana of Liège, 223
Julian calendar, 152–53, 154, 202, 217, 272–73, 526
Julian of Eclanum, 55
Julius Caesar, 152, 217, 627, 840
Julius II, Pope, 590
Julius III, Pope, 693
July celebrations
Aizen Summer Festival, **16–17**
Anne, Feast Day of St., **36–37**
Báb, Martyrdom of the, 67–68, **73–76**
Babaji Commemoration Day, **76–78**
Benedict of Nursia, Saint's Day of St., **109–10**
Bridget, Saint's Day of St., **127–28**
Cannabis Day, **165**
Clement of Ohrid, Saint's Day of St., **215–16**
Dalai Lama's Birthday, **233–34**
Death of Jean-François Lefevre de la Barre, **245–46**
Epictetus the Presbyter and Astion, Saints Day of Sts., **283–84**
Fasinada, **297**
Founders' Day (Salvation Army), **314–16**
Grotto Day, **346–47**
Indivisible Day, **424–25**
James the Greater, Feast Day of St., **455–57**
Madeleine, Fête de la, **537–38**
Mary Magdalene, Day of the Holy, **564–66**
Most Precious Blood, Feast of the, **591–92**
Mount Carmel, Feast Day of Our Lady of, **595–96**
National Day, **609–10**

Olaf, Saint's Day of St., **658**
Peter and Paul, Saint's Day of Sts., **688–90**
Pilgrimage of Sainte Anne d'Auray, **695–97**
Procession of Penitents, **712–13**
Sankt Placidusfest, **781–82**
Schutzengelfest, **788**
Tenjin Matsuri, **850–51**
Tens of Thousands of Lanterns Ancestral Memorial Service, **851–52**
Vladimir, Saint's Day of St., **911–13**
June celebrations
Aizen Summer Festival, **16–17**
Anthony of Padua, Saint's Day of St., **40–41**
Boniface of Germany, Saint's Day of St., **125–26**
Columba, Saint's Day of St., **216–17**
John the Baptist, Nativity of, **467–69**, 910
Juhannus, **487–88**
Maiden Voyage Anniversary, **546–47**
Margaret of Scotland, Saint's Day of St., **552–53**
New Church Day, **625–27**
Summer Solstice, 487, **839–41**, 924, 931
Tejomayananda, Birthday of Swami, **848–49**
World Humanist Day, 887, **931–32**
World Peace and Prayer Day, **933–35**
Jung, Carl G., 277
Juno, 535
Justinian, Emperor, 36, 211–12, 345, 710
Juya festival, 625

Kaaba, 362–64, 417, 433, 571
Kabbalah, 480
Kabinlaphom, King, 825
Kabir, 383
Kadampa order, 139
Kadmi calendar, 959
Kagyu Buddhists, 588, 935–36
Kagyupa order, 139
Kaijin Matsuri, **489–90**
Kaijin Shrine, 489
Kajari Teej. *See* Teej Festivals
Kakushinni, 287
Kali, 254, 398, 736, 800, 848
Kali Yuga, 161
Kalpa Sutra, 357, 673
Kalpa Vruksha. *See* Hinduism festivals and holidays
Kamada Ekadashi, **490–91**
Kamadeva, 903
Kamakura Matsuri, 491i, **491–92**
Kamakura period (Japan), 138
Kamakura Shogunate, 174
Kambutsu. *See* Wesak/Vesak
Kami, 806
Kami-masubi, 806
Kamsa, King, 732
Kanada Tokumitsu, 316
Kanishka, King, 381
Kaniska I, King, 652
Kanmiso-sai, **492–93**
Kannon. *See* Guan Yin, Renunciation of
Kanya Sankranti Day, 908
Kapila, 327
Karbala, Battle of, 629
Karbala, Iraq, 47–48
Karma, 449, 452
Kartavirya, king, 672
Kartika Purnima, **493–95**
Kartika Purnima (Jain), 454, **495**
Kartika Snan, **495–97**
Karwa Chauth, **497–99**, 498i
The Kashf Al Mahjub (Data Ganj Bakhsh), 241
Kashifi, Husayn Waiz, 48
Kashmir, India, 28–29
Kashyap, 605
Kashyapa, 325, 659
Kasone Festival of Watering the Banyan Tree. *See* Wesak/Vesak
Kataklysmos, **499**
Kateel Durga Parameshwari Temple, 540
Katha Upanishad, 605
Kathina Ceremony, **499–500**
Kato people, 310
Kauravas, 114, 388, 618
Kaye Bhumsa, 694
Kazahinomi-sai, 813–14
Kaza-Matsuri, **500–501**
Keats, John, 13
Kelaniya Temple, 265
Kelly, Rose, 302, 309
Kerala, India, 700–701
Kesari, 372
Keshani, queen, 327
Kevaljnana, 447
Khadijah, 432, 440
Khalsa, the Order of the Pure, 353, 540, 630
Khán, Mírzá Taqí, 74
Khán, Sám, 75
Khan, Wazir, 540

Khánum, Khadíjih, 100
Kheiralla, Ibrahim George, 89
Khlysty (People of God), 262
Khmer Buddhism, 135
Khmer Rouge, 135
Khomeini, Ayatollah, 437
Khordad Sal. *See* Zarathrustra, Commemorative Days of
Khosrau II, emperor, 281
Khrap, Stepan, 26
Khusrau, 558
Kiefer, James, 763
Kiev, Ukraine, 285i, 609
Kim, Helen, 930
Kim Gio Gak, prince, 504
Kim Il Sung, 889
Kinen-sai, 813
King, Martin Luther, Jr., 554–56, 729
King Holiday and Service Act, 556
Kintaro, 501
Kintoki Sakata, 501
Kirti Sri Rajasinghe, King, 265, 305
Kitáb al-Asmá,' 79
Kitáb-i-Aqdas, 75
Kitáb-i Panj Sha'n, 67
Kitano Tenman-gū Shrine, 615
Kitchen God, 176–77, 178
Kite Flying Day festival, 548
Kneeland, Abner, 883
Knights Hospitaller, 467
Knights of Malta, 408
Knights Templar, 307, 849–50
Knowledge Day. *See* Gyana Panchami
Kobo Daishi, 146
Kodomo no Hi, 343, **501**
Kojagara, **502–3**
Kojiki, 492, 660, 806
Kokugaku movement, 807–8
Kōmyō, empress, 816
Kongzi, 182
Korea. *See also* North Korea
  Bodhi Day, 121
  bodhisattvas in, 146
  Buddhism in, 137
  calendar, 161, 244, 343
  Chongmyo Cherye, **196–97**
  Choson dynasty, 137, 196
  Festival of the Lanterns, 918
  Great Full Moon Festival, **343–44**, 344i
  Munmyo Ceremony, **599–600**
  Ullam-bana, 191, **877–78**
  Uposattha Observance Day, **892**
  Yi dynasty, 137, 196
Koshogatsu, **503–4**
Kowalska, Helena, 250
Kripilani, Lekhraj, 78
Krishna. *See also* Hinduism
  Arjuna and, 114, 388
  as avataras, 382
  Babaji Commemoration Day, 77
  Balarama and, 102–3
  Chaitanya and, 648
  Chandan Yatra, 171
  Gaura Purnima, 331
  Gita Jayanti, 336–37
  Govardhan Puja, 341–42
  Hala Shashti, 364–65
  Holi, 400
  incarnation of Vishnu, 396–97
  Janmashtami, **459–60**
  Jhulan Yatra, 460
  Kamada Ekadashi, 490
  Mahabharata, 32
  Mauni Amavasya, 570
  Mokshada Ekadashi, 585
  Nutan Varsh, 634
  Prabhupada, Appearance Day of A. C. Bhaktivedanta Swami, 706
  Radhashtami, 732
  Raksha Bandhan, 733
  Rukmini Ashtami, **755**
  Sharad Purnima, 798
Kriyananda, Swami, 77
Kriya yoga, 77, 512, 941, 950
Kshatradharma, 353
Ksitigarbha Bodhisattva, 504
Ksitigarbha's Birthday, **504–5**
Kuala Lumpur, 852–53, 853i
Kuan Kung, 124
Kubera, 19
Kuching Bahá'í Centre, 62
Kuhon, 625
Kukai, 138
Kumari, 425
Kumbhakarna, 617
Kumbha Mela, **505–7**
Kundalini maha yoga, 247
Kung Fu, 123
Kung Li, 219
Kurtz, Paul, 886

Kurukshetra war, 114, 647
Kwan Tai, 192
Kwan Tai, Birthday of, **507–8**
Kwan Yin. *See* Guan Yin, Renunciation of
Kwan Yu, 507
Kwanzaa, 887, 927
Kyoto, Japan, 17, 508–9, 615
Kyoto Gion Matsuri, **508–9**

Laba Festival, 121–22, 190, **511–12**, 628
La Barre, Jean-François Lefevre, 245–46, 887
Labrang monastery, 149
Láhijání, Mírzá ‘Alí-Ashraf. *See* ‘Andalib
Lahiri Mahasaya, Commemoration Days for, **512–13**
Lakota Nation, 934
Lakshmann, 739
Lakshmi
  in Bengal, 19
  Chandan Yatra, 171
  Dattatreya Jayanti, 242–43
  Devi and, 398
  Diwali, 253–54
  Kojagara, 502
  lotus and, 532
  Raksha Bandhan, 734
  Sharad Purnima, 798
  Sita and, 457
Lalande, Jean de, 464
Lalemant, Gabriel, 464
La Libre Pensée, 883
Lalit, 490
Lalita, 490
Lalitavistara, 132
“Lament” (Toumansky), 97
Lammas, 277, **513–14**
Langénieux, Benoît-Marie Cardinal, 290
Lantern Festival (China), 179, 191, **514–15**
Lanterns, Festival of (Korea). *See* Wesak/Vesak
Laos, 126, 134–36, 825
Laozi, Birthday of, **515–16**, 516i
Last Supper, 567
Last Teaching of Shakyamuni Buddha, 623
Lateran Basilica, 760
Lateran Treaty of 1929, 591
Latin America, 90, 148. *See also* Brazil; Mexico; South America; Venezuela
Latronianum, 284
LaVey, Anton, 915, 916i
Lawh-i Mawlúd, 66
Law of Return, 483
Law on Civic Organizations, 137
Laylat al-Mir’ag, 442, **516–17**
Laylat al-Qadr, 442, **517–18**, 735
Laylat ul Bara’ah, 442, **518–19**
Lazarus Saturday, 274, **519–20**, 669–70
League of the Godless, 884
League of the Militant Godless, 884
Leeser, Isaac, 482
Lent, 39, 274, **520–23**, 527, 551
Leo I, Pope, 203–4
Leo III, Pope, 757
Leo III the Isaurian, 662
Leo X, Pope, 750
Leo XIII, Pope, 37, 290, 534, 693, 717, 855, 925
Lepanto, Battle of, 750
“Letter from Birmingham Jail” (King), 555
Letter to Coroticus (St. Patrick), 762
Leviticus, Book of, 224–25, 472, 801, 835–36, 947
Lewis, H. Spencer, 303
Lewis, Joseph, 886
Lha Bab Duchen, 145, **523–24**
Liang, emperor, 877
Liber Al vel Legis (Crowley), 302, 309
Licinus, emperor, 313
Lifelights Network, 785
Light of Truth Universal Shrine (LOTUS), 785
Ligouri, Alphonse de, 26–27
Line dancing (Ilmu), 196–97
Lingaraj Temple, 46
Lingka Woods Festival, **524–25**
Linji Chan, 525
Linji/Rinzai Day Observance, **525**
Lin Muniang, 574–76
Linnean Society, 237
Línjì Yìxuán, 525
Lion Dancers, 124, 178i
The Lion’s Roar of Queen Srimala, 16
Liqawent, 270
Lisbon, Portugal, 41
Literati, 185–86
Litha. *See* Summer Solstice
Lithuania, 166
Little Circle of Dharma, 141
Little Flower. *See* Thérèse of Lisieux, Saint’s Day of St.
Little Sisters of the Assumption, 51

Liturgical calendars. *See* Calendars, religious
Liturgical year (Western Christian), **526–29**, 560
Locke, Alain, 728–29
London Missionary Society, 208
Long Count calendar, 573–74
Looking Horse, Arvol, 934
Lord's Supper, 567, 641–42
Lorenzo Ruiz, Saint's Day of St., **529–30**
Losar, 149, **530–32**
Lotos, 856
Lotus, Birthday of the, **532**
Lotus mudra, 596–97
Lotus sutra, 138, 351, 636–37, 648–49, 778
Louis IX, King, 419
Louis the Pious, Holy Roman Emperor, 39
Louis XIII of France, 36, 695–96
Lourdes, Feast Day of Our Lady of, **532–35**
Lourdes, Our Lady of, 423, 533i
L. Ron Hubbard Scientology Foundation, 415i
Lucia's Day. *See* Lucy, Saint's Day of St.
Lucina, 535
Lucius II, Pope, 760
Lucius III, Pope, 311
Lucy, Saint's Day of St., **535–36**
Lugh, 513
Lughnasad. *See* Lammas
Luke, Gospel of, 37–38, 564, 668–69, 701, 708–9, 909, 953
Lumpaka, 451
Lunar calendars, xxi, 151, 157–59, 440–43, 530
Lunyu, 182
Luria, Isaac, 481, 482
Luther, Martin, 207, 557, 742, 880
Lutheran Church
  All Saints Day, 23
  Annunciation, Feast of the, 39
  Ansgar, Saint's Day of St., 40
  Ash Wednesday, 49i, **49–50**, 521
  Bartholomew's Day, Saint, 105, 106
  Benedict the African, Saint's Day of St., 110
  Boniface of Germany, Saint's Day of St., **125–26**
  Circumcision, Feast of the, 215
  Conversion of St. Paul, Feast of the, 223
  emergence of, 880
  Epiphany, 286
  establishment of, 207
  Eucharist and, 928
  James the Greater, Feast Day of St., 456
  John the Baptist, Beheading of, 466
  John the Baptist, Nativity of, 468
  Lord's Supper, 567
  Martin de Porres, Saint's Day of St., 554
  Martin Luther King, Jr., Birthday of, 555
  Mary Magdalene, Day of the Holy, 565
  saints and, 768–69
  Transfiguration, Feast of the, 866
  Trinity Monday, **867**
Lutheran Church of Denmark, 218–19
Lutheran World Federation, 210
Luxembourg, 925
Ly dynasty (Vietnam), 137

Mabon. *See* Fall equinox
MacArthur, Douglas, 809
Maccabean Revolt, 368–70, 478, 486
Macedonian Orthodox church, 215–16
MacNutt, Howard, 642
MacNutt, Mary, 642
Madan Mohan, 171
Madeleine, Fête de la, **537–38**
Madhva, 383, 388–89
Madonna and child, 201i
Madonna dell'Arco, 271, 714
Magha Puja Day, **538–39**
Magha Purnima, **539–40**. *See also* Dattatreya Jayanti
Maghi, **540–41**
Magh Mela, 570
Magic, 301–2, 309
Magnus, 658
Mahabali (demon), 900
Mahabali, King, 659, 733–34
Mahabharata
  author of, 18, 355
  Hindu and, 387–88
  Krishna and, 32
  Kurukshetra war, 113, 336
  Onam, 659
  Pandava brothers, 617, 647
  Radhashtami, 732
  Vaitarani, 896
  Yama and, 605
Mahanirvana, 623
Mahaprabhu, Chaitanya, 103, 112–13, 330–32, 648, 706, 732
Mahasaya, Lahiri, 77
Mahashivaratri, 162, 397, **541–43**, 542i
Mahasthamaprapta, 31, 351

Mahasthamaprapta's Birthday, **543–44**
Mahavamsa, 265, 702, 781
Mahavira, 255, 357, 447–48, 451, 453, 566, 635
Mahavir Jayanti, 454, **544–46**, 545i
Mahayana Buddhism
- Amitabha's Birthday, 30
- in Australia, 141
- Bodhi Day, 121
- in China, 136, 184
- cycle of holidays, 146
- in Europe, 139–40
- Guan Yin, Renunciation of, **350–51**
- Guan Yin's Birthday, **351–53**
- hell, 877
- Jizo Bon, **461–62**
- Mahasthamaprapta's Birthday, **543–44**
- Manjushri's Birthday, **549–51**
- Medicine Buddha's Birthday, **576–77**
- mudras, 597
- as reformist movement, 132
- Samantabadhara's Birthday, **777–79**
- sangha in, 131
- in Southeast Asia, 134–36, 137
- *Ullambana Sutra*, 877–78
- Uposattha Observance Day, **892**
- Wesak/Vesak, 144, 162, 623, 776, **918–19**

Mahesh Yogi, Maharishi, 385
Mahinda, 134, 265, 702–3, 780–81
Mahisasur, 239
Mahiyangana Stupa, 265
Mahmud of Ghazni, 383
Maiden Voyage Anniversary, **546–47**
Maimon, Moses ben. *See* Maimonides
Maimonides, 480, 480i
Maitreya, 30
Majic City Carnival, 552
Makar Sankranti, **547–48**, 548i
Malagawa Vihara, 304
Malayali people, 659
Malaysia, 62, 144, 918
Malcolm III, 552
Maltese Cross, 307
Mamaqání, Mullá Muhammad, 74
Mamertus, 748
Mangala, 170
Mangus IV, king, 127
Mani, 277
Mani, Commemoration of the Prophet, **549**
Manichaeism, 54, 549
Manifestation, 90–92
"Manifestations of God," 83–85
Manjushri, Wisdom Buddha, 549, 550i, 625
Manjushri's Birthday, **549–51**
Mantras, 195–96
Manusmriti, 384, 387
Maoism, 189
Mao Zedong, 181, 189
Marcellus, Archimandrite, 466
March celebrations
- Annunciation, Feast of the, **37–39**, 293, 909–10
- Ayyám-i-Há (Bahá'í Intercalary Days), **60–63**
- Bahá'í Fast, **94–96**
- Casimir, Saint's Day of St., **166**
- Doll Festival, **256–57**, 257i
- Eostara, **282–83**
- Forty Martyrs' Day, **313–14**
- Hubbard, Birthday of L. Ron, **411–13**
- Joseph, Feast Day of St., **470–72**
- Montségur Day, 277, **589–90**
- Naw-Rúz, Festival of, 81–82, 101, **620–23**, 630
- Nowruz, 323, **651–52**, 961
- Saint Patrick's Day, **761–62**
- Spring equinox (Thelema), **831–32**, 924
- World Day of Prayer, **929–31**
- Yogananda, Mahasamadhi of Paramahansa, 942i, **942–43**
- Yukteswar, Commemorative Days of Swami Sri, **950**
- Zarathustra, Commemorative Days of, **954–55**

Marchi, Michael, 684
March of Time, Lord of the, 111
Marcos, Ferdinand E., 608
Mardi Gras, **551–52**
Margaret of Scotland, Saint's Day of St., **552–53**
Mari, 199
Maria Faustina of the Most Blessed Sacrament, Sister, 250
Marian Devotion (Ligouri), 27
Marian Temples, 42
Marie de Jésus, Mother, 51
Marie Jacobe, 537
Marie Solomé, 405–6, 537
Marijuana, 165
Mark, Gospel of, 338–39, 567, 854

Marriage Supper of the Lamb, 889
Martel, Charles, 125, 437
Martin, Rabia, 577
Martin de Porres, Saint's Day of St., **553–54**
Martin Luther King Day. *See* Martin Luther King, Jr., Birthday of
Martin Luther King, Jr., Birthday of, **554–56**
Martinmas, **556–57**
Martin of Tours, Saint, 556–57
Martins de Bulhões, Fernando. *See* Anthony of Padua, Saint's Day of St.
Martin V, Pope, 55
Marto, Francisco, 299–300
Marto Age, Jacinta, 299–300
Martyrdom, theology of, 202
Martyrdom of Guru Arjan, **558**
Martyrdom of Guru Tegh Bahadur, **559–60**
Martyrdom of the Holy Templars, 277
Martyrologium Hieronymianum, 169
Martyrs. *See also* Saints (Roman Catholic tradition); Saints, celebrating the lives of (Protestant tradition); Saints, veneration of (Roman Catholic tradition)
  Adalbert of Prague, St., **7–8**
  Agnes, St., **12–14**, 690
  All Saints Day, 22
  Andrew, Saint, 34–36
  Arjan, Guru, 558
  Báb, 67–68, **73–76**
  Bahá'í Faith and, 65–66, 71
  Bartholomew, Saint, 104–6
  Brébeuf, Jean de, 463–64
  Cecilia, Santa, 13, 690
  Epictetus, Saint, 283–84
  Forty Immortals, 540–41
  Forty Martyrs' Day, **313–14**
  Gandhi, Mahatma, 554
  George, Saint, 333–34
  Holy Innocents' Day, **404–5**
  James the Greater, Saint, 346–47, 455–57
  Joan of Arc, Saint, 462–63
  Jogues, Isaac, Saint, 463–64
  Lorenzo Ruiz, 529–30
  Lucy, Saint, 535–36
  Mukte, Chali, 540–41
  Nino, Saint, 645–46
  Peter, Apostle, 169
  Peter and Paul, Saints, 688–90
  Placidus, Saint, 782
  relics and, 771–72
  Ruiz, Lorenzo, 529–30
  Saint Peter Baptist and Companions, 690–91
  saints and, 765
  Sebastian, Saint, 782–83
  Semsoun, 199
  Shi'a Muslims and, 47
  Sigisbert, 782
  Stanislaus, Saint, 834–35
  Stephen, Saint, 222, 228, 762–64
  Tatiana, Saint, 846–47
  Tegh Bahadur, Guru, 559–60
  Templars, The Day of the Martyrdom of the Holy, **849–50**
  Thomas, Apostle, 200
Marx, Karl, 884i, 884–85
Marxism, 883–85
Mary I, Queen, 207
Mary Jacobe, 405–6
Mary Magdalene, 268, 277, 537
Mary Magdalene, Day of the Holy, **564–66**
Mary Magdalene in Dos Hermanas, 750
Mary, liturgical year of the Blessed Virgin (Roman Catholic Church), **560–64**. *See also* Virgin Mary
Marymas Fair. *See* Assumption of the Virgin
Mary Queen of Scots, 553
Marysville, California, 124
Masorti movement, 482
Mass, 402
Mass in Commemoration of the Dead, 45
Master K'ung, 182
Matilda chapel, 419
Matronalia, 593
Mattathias, 369–70
Matthew, Gospel of, 866
Matthew, Louise, 92
Matthius, 953
Maudgalyayana, 877–78
Mauna Agyaras, 454, **566**
Maundy Thursday, 224, 409, 521, **567–69**. *See also* Holy Week
Maun Ekadash. *See* Mauna Agyaras
Mauni Amavasya, **569–70**
Mauropus, Saint John, 859
Mawdudi, Sayyid Abul A'la, 438
Mawlid an-Nabi, 442, **570–72**
Maximin, Saint, 537
The Maya (Coe), 573
Maya, Queen, 367

Mayan Calendar, **572–74**
The Mayan Factor (Arguelles), 572, 573
Mayasura, 494
May celebrations
  Alphabet Day, **25–26**
  Augustine of Canterbury, Saint's Day of St., **52–54**
  Báb, Festival of the Declaration of the, **67–73**, 101, 226
  Bahá'u'lláh, Ascension of, **96–99**
  Beltane, **108–9**, 915
  Chongmyo Cherye, **196–97**
  Cyril and Methodius, Saint's Day for Sts., 25, **229–31**
  Dianetics, Anniversary of, **248–49**
  Fatima, Feast Day of Our Lady of, **299–301**
  Florian, Saint's Day of St., **311**
  Great Buddha Festival, **342–43**
  Holy Maries, Festival of the (La Fête des Saintes Maries), **405–7**, 537
  Joan of Arc, Saint's Day of St., **462–63**
  Kodomo no Hi, 343, **501**
  Muktananda, Birthday of Swami Paramahansa, **598–99**
  Peace and Good Voyage, Feast of Our Lady of, **678–79**
  Procession of the Holy Blood, **715–16**
  Riḍván, Festival of, **744–47**
  Visitation, Feast of the, **909–10**
  Walpurgisnacht, 108, **915–16**
  White Lotus Day, **919–20**
  Yukteswar, Commemorative Days of Swami Sri, **950**
May Day. *See* Beltane
Ma Ying-jeo, 221i
May Queen, 108
Mazu, 192
Mazu Festival, Goddess, **574–76**, 575i
McMenain, Hugh L., 608
The Means of Prayer (Ligouri), 27
Mean Solar Day, 153
Meat Fare Sunday. *See* Mardi Gras
Mecca, Saudi Arabia, 362–64, 432–33, 440–41, 571
Medici, Catherine, 106
Medicine Buddha's Birthday, **576–77**
Medicine Buddha Sutra, 550
Medina, Saudi Arabia, 433, 440–41, 571
Meditation
  Anapanasati, 33–34
  in Bahá'í Faith, 80, 85
  Brahma Kumaris, 78
  Pratikraman, 673
  in Tibetan Buddhism, 133
  Transcendental Meditation, 385
  Zen Buddhism, 525
Medvedev, Dmitry, 610
Meenakshi, 194–95, 398, 539
Meenakshi Float Festival, 398
Meenakshi Sundareshvarar temple, 539
Meenakshi Temple, 194
Meghanada, 617
Meher Baba, Commemoration Days of, **577–78**
Mehmed II, 438
Meiji period (Japan), 138, 376, 655, 808
Meiji Restoration, 16, 794, 803, 810–11
Meiji Shrine, 256
Meitala, 691–92
Meizhou Island temple, 576
Meletius IV, Ecumenical Patriarch, 273
Mencius, 183
Mendis, Solius, 266
Menelaus, 369
Menelik II, Emperor, 628
Menendez, Josefa, 758
Mengzi, 183
Mennonites, 207, 768, 880
Menon, Balakrishnan. *See* Chinmayananda, Commemoration Days for
Menorah, 369i, 370, 371i
Merlini, Don Giovanni, 591
Meskal, 289, **578–79**
Messianic Judaism, 676, 839
Metaphysics, 185
Methodist Church, 208–9, 315, 555, 567, 769–70, 866, 921, 928
Methodist Episcopal Church, 11
Mexico, 141, 148, 347–50, 701–2
Mexico Mystique (Waters), 573
Miami, Florida, 552
Miao Chuang, King, 350
Miao Shan, 350, 352
Michael III, emperor, 229
Michaelion church, 579
Michaelmas, **579–80**
Michael the Archangel, 277, 579, 580i
Michel, Mother Saint, 717
Mid-Autumn Festival, 191, **580–82**
Middle Kingdom, 180
Middle Path, 130

Mid-Lent. *See* Lent
Mid-Pentecost, Feast of, **582–83**
Midsummer. *See* Summer Solstice
Midsummer Day, 840
Mieszko I, 271
"A Mighty Fortress Is Our God," 742
Miki Takahito, 317
Miki Tokuchika, 316
Miki Tokuharu, 316
Millenarian movements, 187
Miller, Rosamonde, 565
Miller, William, 675, 838
Million Minutes for Peace project, 78–79
Miltiades, Pope, 760
Mimamsa darshana, 388
Ming Di, Emperor, 550
Ming dynasty (China), 136, 187, 586, 640
Minnesota, 424
Miracles, Festival of Our Lady of, **583–84**
Miracles, saints and, 765, 766–67
Miraculous Medal, 562
Mirian, King, 646
Misa de Gallo, **584–85**
Mishnah, 479
Mishneh Torah, 480
Missionaries of the Precious Blood, 591
Mizuko Jizo, 461
Mizu no Kamisama, 489
Mobile, Alabama, 551–52
Modern Orthodox Kibbutz Movement, 944
Mohenjo-Daro, 379i
Mohini, 542
Mokshada Ekadashi, **585–86**
Monasticism
  Benedict of Nursia, Saint, 109–10
  in Buddhism, 131, 135, 184, 188, 499–500, 903–4, 905i
  in Church of Scientology, 791–92
  Columba, Saint, 216–17
  Franciscan order, 40–41, 909
  Franciscans of the Stricter Observance, 693
  in Jainism, 447, 449
  Martin of Tours, Saint, 556–57
Mondernists, 238
Mongkut, King, 135
Mongolia, 121, 871–72
Mongols, 204
Monica, 54, 55
Monkey King, Birthday of the, 192, 586i, **586–87**
Monkey Trial, 238
Monks, 122i
Monlam, the Great Prayer Festival, 149, **587–89**, 935
Monophysitism, 201
Montaldo, Leonardo, 419
Montantist movement, 200
Monte Cassino, 109
Montgomery Improvement Association, 555
Montmorency-Laval, François-Xavier de, 403
Montoya, Lopez de, 751
Mont-Saint-Michel church, 579
Montségur Day, 277, **589–90**
Moon, Heung Jin, 890
Moon, Hyun, 889
Moon, Hyung, Jin, 889
Moon, In Jin, 889
Moon, Sun Myung, 175, 243–44, 337–38, 670–71, 870–71, 888–90
Moravia, 230
Moravian Church, 208
Mordecai, 719–20
Morehouse College, 554
Morgan Hill, California, 375
Morisaki, 601
Moscow Patriarchate, 609
Moses, 475–76, 484, 686
Most Holy Book, 101
Most Holy Name of Mary, Feast of the, **590–91**
Most Precious Blood, Feast of the, **591–92**
"The Mother." *See* Richard, Mirra
Mother, Birthday of the, **592–93**
Mother Goddess Devi, 29–30, 239, 381–82, 398–99
Mothering Sunday, **593**
Mount Khangchend Zonga, 694
Mother of God. *See* Virgin Mary
Mother of the Big Dipper, 640–41
Mother's Day, **593–95**
Mother's Day International Association, 594
"Mother's Day Proclamation," 594
Mount Carmel, Feast Day of Our Lady of, **595–96**
Mount Govardhan, 341–42
Mount Sinai, 799i
Mucalinda, 601
Mudras, **596–98**
Mughal Empire, 383
Muhammad, Prophet. *See also* Islam
  Ashura and, 47

background, 431, 432–33, 440
fasting, 734
Hajj and, 362–64
hijra, 629
Islamic calendar and, 157
Laylat al-Mir'ag, 516–17
Laylat ul Bara'ah, 519
Mawlid an-Nabi, **570–72**
Qur'an and, 434
successors to, 21–22
Muhammad, Sayyid 'Alf, 65–67
Muhammad-Najíb Páshá, 745
Muharram, Remembrance of, 629
Muktananda, Birthday of Swami Paramahansa, **598–99**
Muktananda, Swami, 57, 59, 234
Mulian, 877–78
Munmyo Ceremony, **599–600**
Mura, 895
Murakami, emperor, 812, 851
Muromachi period (Japan), 138
Murugan, Lord, 397–98, 820–22
Mushka, Chaya, 787
Muslim Brotherhood, 438
Muslim calendar, 157–59, 393, 440–43
Musumusu, 692
Myanmar (Burma), 4–5, 134, 144, 825, 918
Myoken, 174
Myoko Baganuma, 649

Nagapanchami, **601–2**
Nagasaki, Japan, 601–2
Nagasaki Kunchi, 18, **602–3**
Nagle, Nano, 711
Nahum, 215
Nakayama, Miki, 793
Naked festival. *See* Hadaka Matsuri
Nalakuvara, 856
"Names of God," 83
Namgyal Monastery, 530
Nana, Queen, 646
Nanak, 383
Nanak, Guru, 162, 354
Nanak's Birthday, Guru, 162, 163, **603–4**
Nanakshahi calendar, 162–63, 604
Naples, Italy, 271
Napoleon III, 745
Narada, 899
Naraka, 605
Narak Chaturdashi, **604–5**
Narcissus flowers, 179
Narenda tank, 171
Narieli Purnima, **607**
Narasimha Jayanti, **605–7**, 606i
Nasik, India, 505–6
Násiri'd-Dín Sháh, 74
National Bible Association, 607–8
National Bible Week, **607–8**
National Brotherhood Week, **608–9**
National Center for Race Amity, 729
National Conference for Community and Justice, 609
National Conference of Christians and Jews (NCCJ), 608
National Council of Churches, 661, 869–70
National Council of Churches in Christ, 928, 929
National Day, **609–10**
National Day of Prayer, **610–11**, 612
National Day of Reason, **611–12**, 887
National Founding Day (Scientology), **612–13**, 791
National Liberal League, 886
National Secular Society, 883
National Shrine of the Immaculate Conception, 422
National Spiritual Assembly, 746, 936
National Spiritual Assembly of the Bahá'ís of the United States (US-NSA), 727, 729
National Teacher's Day, 220
Native Americans
Athabascan people, 703–4
Chinook people, 703
First Salmon Rites, 6, **310–11**
Hupa people, 6–7
Huron people, 463–64
I'n-Lon-Schka, **427–28**
Iroquois people, 463
Lakota Nation, 934
Osage people, 427–28
Potlatch, **703–5**, 705i
Pueblo people, 860–61
Tewa people, 106–7
Three Kings Day, Native American Pueblos, **860–61**
Native Establishment beyond East and West, **613–14**
The Nativity of Mary, 560, 561, 614
Nativity of Mary, **614–15**, 650
Natsu Matsuri, **615**
Natural selection, 236–39

Nava Durgas, 239
Navaratri, 162, 395, 398, 616i, **616–18**
Navpad Oli, 454, 545, **618–20**
Naw-Rúz, Festival of, 81–82, 101, **620–23**, 630
Nazis, 483, 944–45
Ne, Zha, 262, 856
Nehan, **623–24**, 624i
Nehemiah, 485
Nehemiah, Book of, 818
Nehru, 385
Nekong Ngyal, 694
Nemanja, Steven, 786
Nemanjic, Prince Rastko, 786
Nemi, 447
Neo-atheism, 886
Neo-Confucianism, 185–86
Neo-Druids, 924
Neo-Hinduism, 383–86
Neo-Pagan movement
  Beltane, 915
  fall equinox, **295–96**, 296i
  Lammas, 277, **513–14**
  liturgical calendar, **921–24**
  New Year's Day, 631
  Samhain, 365–67, 631, **779–80**, 923–24
  spring equinox, 833
  summer solstice, 840–41
  winter solstice, 927
Neo-Sannyas Movement, 385
Nepal
  Buddhism in, 134
  Dasain, **239–41**
  Diwali, 254
  Gathemangal, **330**
  Indra Jatra, **425**
  Navaratri, 162, 395, 398, 616i, **616–18**
  Rishi Panchami, 747i, **747–48**, 908
  Sheetala Ashtami, **800–801**
  Teej Festivals, 848
Neri-kuyo, **625**
Nero, emperor, 202
Nestorius, Bishop, 200–201
Netherlands, 639, 925
A New Book of Festivals and Commemorations (Pfatteicher), 770
New Church Day, **625–27**
New Jersey Humanist network, 413
New Laws for the Causes of Saints, 766
New Mexico, 680–81, 860–61
New Orleans, Louisiana, 552, 716–17
New Testament, Christian, 199, 201, 434–35
Newton, Isaac, 858
New Year preliminary festivals, 628
New Year's Day, **627–32**
New Year's Day (India), 395–96, 630, **632–35**
New Year's Day (Islamic), 442, 629
New Year's Day (Jain), 454, **635–36**
New Year's Day (Japan), 812
New Year's Eve (China), 628–29
New Year's Eve (Scientology), 631, **636**
New Zealand, 141, 730, 885, 923
Nezha, 192
Ngembak Geni, 653
Nian, 177
Nicene Creed, 200, 204
Nichiren, 138, 636–37
Nichiren Buddhism, 376, 648, 778
Nichiren's Birthday, **636–37**
Nichiren Shoshu, 137, 637, 657
Nichiren-shu, 637, 657
Nicholas, Saint, 212, 277, 405
Nicholas, Saint's Day of St., **638–40**, 639i
Nicholas I, Pope, 40, 230
Nicholas V, Pope, 473
Nicholas of Tolentine, Saint, 118
Nicolazic, Tves, 36, 695
Nidaros Cathedral, 658
Nigeria, 761
Night of Destiny. *See* Laylat al-Qadr
Night of Freedom from Fire. *See* Laylat ul Bara'ah
Night of Power. *See* Laylat al-Qadr
Nihon Shoki, 492, 806
Nikegami Honmon-ji Temple, 657
Nikkyo Niwano Memorial Museum, 649
Nikon, Patriarch, 262
Nimbarka, 732
Nine Emperor Gods, Festival of the, **640–41**
Nineteen-Day Fast (Bahá'í), 621
Nineteen-Day Feast (Bahá'í), 82–83, 620, **641–45**
95 Theses, 741–42
Nino, Saint's Day of St., **645–46**
Nirjala Ekadashi, **647**
Nirvana, 121–22, 375, 448, 624i
Nirvana Day. *See* Nehan
Nishi-Arai Daishi, 235–36
Nishijima, Kakuryo, 148
Nityananda, Bhagavan, 599
Nityananda Trayodasi, **648**

Niuliki, 691
Niu Ling, 261
Niwano, Nikkyo, Centennial of (2006), **648–49**
Nixon, Richard, 889
Niza, Marcos de, 860
Noble Eightfold Path, 130–31
Noche Buena, 585
Noh drama, 601–2
North America, 89, 133, 140, 208, 271, 885. *See also* United States
North Korea, 884, 885. *See also* Korea
Norway, 886
Nossa Senhora da Conceição Aparecida (Our Lady of the Conception Who Appeared), 42, 422
Nossa Senhora dos Remédios, Pilgrimage of, **650**
Novatus, 228
November celebrations
'Abdu'l-Bahá, Ascension of, **1–4**
All Saints Day, **22–23**, 275, 277, 403, 631, 774
All Souls Day, **23–25**, 275, 277
Andrew, Saint's Day of St., **34–36**
Avatar Adi Da Samraj's Birthday, **57–58**
Bahá'u'lláh, Festival of the Birth of, 82, **99–102**
Covenant, Day of the, **225–27**
International Day of Prayer for the Persecuted Church, **429–30**
Martin de Porres, Saint's Day of St., **553–54**
Martinmas, **556–57**
Presentation of Mary, Feast of the, **710–11**
Saint John Lateran, Feast of the Dedication of, **760–61**
Shichi-Go-San, **802–3**
Siddha Day, **817–18**
Willibrord, Saint's Day of St., **925–26**
World Community Day, **929**
Novena of the Heart of Jesus (Ligouri), 27
Nowruz, 323, **651–52**, 961
Nozawa Dosojin Himatsuriheld, 259
Numa Pompilius, 152
Núrí, Mírzá Ḥusayn-'Alí. *See* Bahá'u'lláh
Nutan Varsh, 634
Nyaya darshana, 388
Nyepi, **652–53**
Nyingma Meditation Center, 935

Obon Festival(s), **655–57**, 656i, 878
Octave for Christian Unity, 917
October celebrations
Adi Da Samrajashram, Anniversary of Adi Da's First Footstep on, **8–9**
Agua, La Fiesta de, **14**
Aki Matsuri, **17–18**
Aparecida, Feast of Our Lady of, **41–43**, 564
Báb, Festival of the Birth of the, **65–67**, 82, 101
Bible Sunday, **115–16**
Black Christ, Festival of the, **116–18**
Bodhidharma Day, **122–24**
Confucius, Anniversary of the Death of, **219–20**
Freethought Day, **320–21**, 887
Good Remedy, Feast of Our Lady of, **340–41**
Halloween, 277, **365–67**, 366i, 631, 780
International Association of Scientologists Anniversary, **428–29**
International Religious Freedom Day, **430–31**
Jogues, John de Brébeuf and Companions, Saints Day of St. Isaac, **463–64**
Nagasaki Kunchi, 18, **602–3**
Native establishment beyond East and West, **613–14**
Oeshiki, **657**
Peter of Alcantara, Saint's Day of St., **693–94**
Reformation Sunday, **741–43**
Romeria of La Virgen de Valme, **749–50**
Rosary, Feast of Our Lady of the, **750–51**
Samhain, 365–67, 631, **779–80**, 923–24
Templars, The Day of the Martyrdom of the Holy, **849–50**
Thérèse of Lisieux, Saint's Day of St., **855–56**
White Sunday, **921**
Oeshiki, **657**
O'Hair, Madalyn Murray, 886
Ohyama Kuinokami, 845
Oimblc, 708
O'Keefe, Daniel, 306
Olaf, Saint's Day of St., **658**
Olcott, Henry Steel, 919–20
Old Believers, 262
Old Calendarists, 155
Old Church Slavonic, 229
"Old Rugged Cross," 407
Old Testament, Christian, 199

Olga of Kiev, 911
Olsok Eve. *See* Olaf, Saint's Day of St
Omizutori. *See* Shuni-e (Omizutori)
Om Mani Padme Hum, 195
Onam, **659–60**
Onbashira, **660–61**
One Great Hour of Sharing, **661–62**
Onin War, 807
On the Origin of Species by Means of Natural Selection (Darwin), 237
Onzo Festival, 493
Open Doors, 429–30
Order of Christ, 307
Order of Saint Raphael, 276
Order of the Holy Cross, 408
Order of the Holy Savior, 127
Order of the Holy Trinity, 341
Ordinary Time after Pentecost, 528
Ordinary Time after the Baptism, 527
Ordo Temple Orientis, 309
Organization of the Islamic Conference, 414
Oriental Orthodox churches, 45, 223, 408
Origin of Suffering, truth of, 130
Orthodox Church of Serbia, 273
Orthodox Judaism, 482, 754i, 943, 949
Orthodoxy, Feast of, **662–63**
Osage people, 427–28
Osaka, Japan, 16–17, 850–51
Osaka Temmangu Shrine, 850
Osaka Yuhigaoka Gakuen Fashion Department, 16
Osaki Hachiman Shrine, 360
Osho (Rajneesh), Birthday of, **664–65**
Osho Commune International, 385
Osman I, 438
Ottoman Empire, 87, 204, 292, 438, 481
Our Lady of Antipolo, 678
Our Lady of Cures, 650
Our Lady of Good Remedy, 340–41
Our Lady of Miracles, 583–84
Our Lady of Peñafrancia, **679–80**
Our Lady of Peñafrancia Basilica, 251, 680
Our Lady of Perpetual Help, 684–85
Our Lady of Sorrows, 828–29
Our Lady of the Conception Who Appeared, 42. *See also* Aparecida, Feast of Our Lady of
Our Lady of the Rock Island, 297
Our Lady of the Rosary, 750–51
Our Lady of Valme, 749
Overport Buddhist Sakya Society, 141
Oyasama, 793

Pabhupada, Swami, 385
Pachamama, 14
Paczki Day, 552
Padmasambhava, 524
Pagan religions. *See also* Neo-Pagan movement; Wicca
  Beltane, **108–9**, 915
  Christianity and, 923
  Christmas and, 211
  in England, 53
  Eostara, **282–83**
  Europe, 780
  fall equinox, **295–96**, 296i
  Halloween, 780
  Imbolc, **420–21**
  Lammas, 277, **513–14**
  matronalia, 593
  New Year's Day, 631
  in Rome, 22–23
  Samhain, 365–67, 631, **779–80**, 923–24
  spring equinox, 833
  summer solstice, 840–41
  Up Helly Aa, **890–92**
  Yule, 924, **950–51**
Pahlavi, Reza Shah, 48
Paine, Thomas, 857i, 857–58, 881, 887
Pakistan, 800–801
Pak Tai, 192
Pak Tai, Birthday of, **667–68**
Palaeologus, Thomas, 35
Palanquins, 16–17
Palden Lhamo, 530
Palestine, 1–2, 483
Paley, William, 237
Pali-canon, 33
Pali Tipitaka, 132
Pali-canon, 132
Pallium, 13
Palm Sunday, 198–99, 409, 521, **668–70**, 669i
Pampa River, 659
Panama, 116–18
Pan-Buddhist National United Sangha, 137
Pancha Pandavas, 171
Pandava brothers, 114, 388, 647, 734
Pandav Bhim Ekadasi. *See* Nirjala Ekadashi
Panj Piare, 604
Pankaj mudra, 596–97

Pantenus, 200
Parab, Guru. *See* Nanak's Birthday, Guru
Paramahansa, Guru Purnanandaji, 115
Paramahansa, Swami Guru Bhumanandaji, 458, 721
Paramahansa, Swami Guru Janardanji, 115, 458, 708
Parameshwardas, Shri Yogiraj, 247
Paranirvana Day. *See* Nehan
Parashurama, 18
Parashurama Jayanti. *See* Akshay Tritiya
Parents Day, 175, **670–71**
Parinirvana, 623
Parks, Rosa, 555
Parliament of World Religions, 452
Parshurama Jayanti, **671–72**
Parshvanath, Lord, 601, 677
Parsons, Agnes S., 728
Parsva, 447, 451
Parthian Empire, 957
Parvata Muni, 585
Parvati
  Amarnath Yatra, 29
  Chittirai Festival, 194
  Dattatreya Jayanti, 242–43
  Devi and, 398
  Ganesh Chaturthi, 324–25
  Gangaur, 329
  Karwa Chauth, 497
  Magha Purnima, 539
  Mahashivaratri, 542
  origins of, 382
  Rishi Panchami, 747
  Sheetala Ashtami, 800
  Shiva and, 397
  Tamils and, 398
  Teej Festivals, 847
Paryushana, 455, **672–74**
Paschal Candle, 45
Passiontide, 521
Passover, 156, 198, 224–25, 267, 485, **674–76**
Path to the Cessation of Suffering, truth of, 130
Patotsav, **676–77**
Patras, Greece, 35
Patriarchate of Constantinople, 204, 609
Patrick, Saint, 761i
Paul, Apostle, 198, 222–23, 688–90, 763, 772
Paul I, Czar, 408
Paul II, Pope, 473
Paul III, Pope, 692
Paul V, Pope, 318, 333
Paul VI, Pope, 35, 104, 110, 167, 213–14, 333, 711, 726, 751, 774, 795, 824, 909
Paush Dashami, 454, **677–78**
Pavarana Day. *See* Boun Ok Phansa
Peace and Good Voyage, Feast of Our Lady of, **678–79**
Peace Tower Ceremony, 317
Pedda Panduga, 547
Pedroso, Felipe, 42
Pelagianism, 54–55
Pelagius, 55
Pelayo, 456
Peñafrancia, Feast of Our Lady of, **679–80**
Pendava brothers, 617
Penitentes, **680–82**
Penkye, 5
Pentecost, 485, 528, **682–84**, 683i
Pentecostals, 769
Penkyi Otu, 5–6
Pepin, 925
Pereira, Juana, 906
Pernet, Etienne, 51
Perpetual Help, Feast of Our Lady of, **684–85**
Persephone, 295, 420
Persia, 65, 68–71, 199–200, 719, 832–33, 901–2. *See also* Iran; Zoroastrianism
Persian Bayán, 70, 74, 80, 84
Peru, 14–15
Pesach, 485, 674, **685–88**
Peter, Apostle, 34, 198, 688–90, 689i, 772
Peter and Paul, Saint's Day of Sts., 13–14, **688–90**
Peter Baptist and Companions, Saint's Day of St., **690–91**
Peter Chanel, Saint's Day of St., **691–92**
Peter Claver, Saint's Day of St., **692–93**
Peter of Alcantara, Saint's Day of St., **693–94**
Peter the Great, 26
Petit, Berthe, 829
Pfatteicher, Philip H., 770
Phagwa. *See* Holi
Phang Lhabsol, **694–95**
Pharaoh, 685–86
Pharisees, 478–79
Pharos Church of the Most-Holy Theotokos, 419
Philadelphia Church of God, 839
Philip, Gospel of, 565
Philip II, King, 553, 691
Philip III, King, 110

Philip IV, King, 849–50
Philippines
  Black Nazarene Festival, **118–19**
  Divino Rostro, Devotion to, **251–52**
  Giant Lantern Festival, 335i, **335–36**
  Lorenzo Ruiz and, 529
  Misa de Gallo, 584
  National Bible Week, 608
  Peace and Good Voyage, Feast of Our Lady of, **678–79**
  Peñafrancia, Feast of Our Lady of, **679–80**
Philistines, 477
Philosophical Dictionary (Voltaire), 246
Phipps, William, 320
Photius I, emperor, 229
Pietists, 208
Pilgrimage of Ætheria, 409
Pilgrimage of Sainte Anne d'Auray, **695–97**
Pilgrimage of the Dew, **697–98**
Pilgrimages
  in Bahá'í Faith, 98
  Basilica of Guadalupe, 347
  Black Christ, Festival of the, 117
  of Bridget, Saint, 127
  to the Church of Notre Dame de la Mer, 406
  "Farewell Pilgrimage," 363
  Fatima, Our Lady of, 300
  Hajj, 158, **361–64**, 417, 436, 442, 443
  James the Greater, Saint, 346
  to Jerusalem, 686
  Nossa Senhora dos Remédios, Pilgrimage of, **650**
  Pilgrimage of Sainte Anne d'Auray, **695–97**
  Pilgrimage of the Dew, **697–98**
  to Rome, 472
  Romeria of La Virgen de Valme, **749–50**
  Saint Olav's Way, 658
  saints, honoring, 772
  Santiago de Compostela, 127, 456, 557
Pilgrim to the West (Wu), 586
Pinchbeck, Daniel, 573
Pistis Sophia, 565, 827
Pitra Paksha, **698**
Pius II, Pope, 35
Pius IV, Pope, 110
Pius V, Pope, 127, 405, 580, 590, 711, 750
Pius IX, Pope, 36, 37, 42, 51, 404, 421, 471, 591, 684, 696, 717
Pius X, Pope, 290, 462, 534, 590, 591, 750, 757–58, 774, 869, 917
Pius XI, Pope, 213, 231, 534, 758, 824, 906
Pius XII, Pope, 51, 104, 167, 333, 423, 471, 726, 758, 774, 855
Placidus, Saint, 781–82
Plagwa. *See* Holi
Planet Art Network, 573
Pledge of Allegiance, 424
Pleureuses, Ceremony of. *See* Good Friday
PL Kyodan, 316–17
Ploughing Day, **698–99**
Poland, 166, 231–32, 293, 834–35
Pongal. *See* Makar Sankranti
Pontius Pilate, 338
Pooram, **700–701**
Poor Fellow-Soldiers of Christ and of the Temple of Solomon, 849
Pope, Alexander, 881
Porres, Martine de, 553–54
Portugal
  Age of Exploration, 207–8
  Anthony of Padua, St., and, 40–41
  Burning of Judas, 148
  Divine Holy Spirit Festival, **249–50**
  Expectation of the Birth of the Blessed Virgin Mary, Feast of, 293
  Fatima, Feast Day of Our Lady of, **299–301**
  Fiesta dos Tabuleiros, **307–8**
  Mother's Day, 594
  Nossa Senhora dos Remédios, Pilgrimage of, **650**
Posadas, Las, 585, **701–2**
Poson, **702–3**
Postclassical Hinduism, 383
Potlatch, **703–5**, 705i
Powell, Ronald, 276
"Power in the Blood" (Jones), 591
The Power of Race Unity, 729
Poyela Boishakh, 633–34
Prabhu, Sri Nityananda, 648
Prabhupada, A. C. Bhaktivedanta Swami, 112, 113, 705–7
Prabhupada, Appearance Day of A. C. Bhaktivedanta Swami, **705–7**
Prabhupada, Disappearance Day of A. C. Bhaktivedanta Swami, **707**
Prague, 7–8
Prahalad, 606, 659
Prahlada, 400–401

Prajnaparamita sutras, 132
Prasadji Paramahansa, Birthday of Swami Guru, **707–8**
Pratikraman, 673
Prayag, India, 570
Prayers, 3, 93–94, 95
Prayer wheels (chokhor), 195–96
Preliminary Festival, 190. *See also* Chinese New Year's (Preliminary Festival)
Pre-Nicene (Gnostic) Catholic Church, 276
Presbyterian Church
- All Saints Day, 23
- Eucharist and, 928
- Lord's Supper, 567
- One Great Hour of Sharing, 662
- Reformation, 207, 208, 880
- saints and, 768–69
- World Communion Sunday, 928

Presentation of Jesus in the Temple, Feast of the, **708–10**
Presentation of Mary, Feast of the, **710–11**
Presiding Bishop's Fund for World Relief, 661
Priyadarshana, 544
Procession de la Penitencia, La (Spain), **711–12**
Procession of the Cross, 281, **713–14**
Procession of the Fujenti, 271–72, **714–15**
Procession of the Holy Blood, **715–16**
Procession of the Living Goddess, 425
Procession of the Penitents, **712–13**. *See also* Procession de la Penitencia, La (Spain)
Prompt Succor, Feast Day of Our Lady of, **716–17**
Prophets (Hebrew Bible), 475
Protestant Reformation, 206–7, 291, 553, 741–42, 768, 789
Protestants.
- *See also specific churches and denominations*
- All Saints Day, 23
- All Souls Day, **23–25**, 275, 277
- Ascension Day, 45
- Ash Wednesday, 49i, **49–50**, 521
- Assumption of the Virgin and, 50
- Augustine of Hippo, Saint, and, 54
- Bible Sunday, **115–16**
- Christ's blood, 591
- Christ the King, Feast of, 214
- the cross and, 408
- Epiphany, 286
- expansion of, 208–9
- foot washing, 569
- global fragmentation of, 209
- Gregorian calendar and, 155
- Holy Trinity and, 869
- Holy Week, 410
- International Day of Prayer for the Persecuted Church, **429–30**
- liturgical calendar, xxi
- Luther and, 557
- Midsummer Day, 840
- One Great Hour of Sharing, **661–62**
- Palm Sunday, 670
- Reformation Sunday, **741–43**
- relics and, 408
- Roman Catholic Church, relationship with, 210, 742, 769
- Saint Bartholomew's Day Massacre, 106
- saints and, 768–70
- Schwenkfelder Thanksgiving, **789**
- supernaturalism, criticism of, 880
- Trinity Sunday, 867, 869–70
- Virgin Mary and, 421–22
- World Communion Sunday, **928–29**
- World Community Day, **929**
- World Day of Prayer, **929–31**

Protoevangelium of James, 36, 560, 561, 614, 710
Proverbs, Book of, 826–27
Pryse, James Morgan, 276
Psalms and Proverbs (Hebrew Bible), 475
Pseudo-Matthew, Gospel of, 710
Pueblo people, 860–61
Pugatory, 24
Pundarika, 490
Puranas, 46
Pure Brightness Festival, 191, 655, **717–19**, 718i
Pure Land tradition, 31, 136, 184, 351, 525, 543–44, 625, 804–5
Purewal, Pal Singh, 162
Purgatory, 768
Purification of Mary, Feast of the. *See* Presentation of Jesus in the Temple, Feast of the
Purification rituals, xxiii
Purim, 486, **719–21**
Puritans, 208, 212
Purnanandaji Paramahansa, Commemoration Day for Swami Guru, **721–22**
Purnima, Guru, **355–57**

Puthandu, 630, 633. *See also* New Year's Day (India)
Putrada Ekadashi, **722–23**
Putuo Shan, 350, 352

Qá'im. *See* Twelfth Imam
Qing dynasty (China), 136
Qingming, 718i
Qing Ming Festival. *See* Pure Brightness Festival
Qin Shi Huangdi, 179
Quakers (Friends), 208, 262–63
Quebec, 36–37
Queenship of Mary, Feast of, **725–26**, 910
Quezón, Aurora Aragon, 335
Quezón y Molina, Manuel Luis, 335
Quileute people, 310
Qumran community, 479
Qur'an
  calendars and, 157
  Hajj, 363
  Islamic calendar and, 441
  Ismail in, 417
  on Jesus, 435
  Laylat al-Qadr, 517–18
  Laylat ul Bara'ah, 519
  Lord's Supper in, 642
  mandates of, 435
  Muhammad, Prophet and, 431
  overview of, 434
  photo of, 432i
  Ramadan and, 735
  revelation of, 570–71
Qutb, Sayyid, 438
Qu Yaun, 263–64

Rabbit on the moon, 581
Race Amity Convention, 728–29
Race Amity Day, 728
Race Unity Day, **727–32**
Radbod, 925
Radha, 460, 732
Radhashtami, **732–33**
Rains Retreat. *See* Vassa Retreat
Raja yoga, 78
Rajneesh, Acharya, 664
Rajneesh, Bhagwan Shree, 385
Raksha Bandhan, **733–34**
Rakshasas, 617
Rama
  altar for, 739i
  Chandan Yatra, 171
  Diwali, 253
  Gangaur, 329
  Hanuman Jayanti, 372
  incarnation of Vishnu, 396
  Kamada Ekadashi, 490
  Navaratri, 616–17
  origins of, 382
  Rama Navami, 739–40
  Tulsidas Jayanti, 875
  Valmiki and, 899
Rama, King, 388
Rama, Lord, 46
Rama IV, King, 538, 699
Rama V, King, 538
Ramachandra, Lord. *See* Rama
Ramacharitamanasa, 875
Ramadan, 158, 418, 442, **734–36**
Ramakrishna, Birthday of Sri, **736–37**
Ramakrishna, Sri, 737i, 783–84
Ramakrishna Math and Mission, 784, 910, 911
Ramakrishna Sarada Mission, 784
Ramakrishna-Vivekananda Vedanta Society, 736
Rama Lila, 616
Ramana Maharshi, Birthday of, **737–39**
Ramanavami, 162
Rama Navami, **739–40**, 739i
Ramanuja, 388–89
Ramayana (Valmiki), 372, 382, 387–88, 457, 899
Ramdas, 383
Rameswar Temple, 46
Ranakpur temple, 448i
Rashi, 833
Rashtí, Sayyid Káẓim, 69
Raski bracelets, 733
Rastafarianism, 360–61
Rastislav, Prince, 229
Ratha Yatra, 171, **740–41**
Rationalism, 879, 882
Ravana, 46, 372, 617, 739
Ravata, 4
Reagan, Ronald, 555, 610
Redemptorist order, 404
Redfield, James, 573
Reformation. *See* Protestant Reformation
Reformation Sunday, **741–43**
Reformed Church, 207, 768–69, 880

Reformed School (Tibetan Buddhism), 587
Reformed tradition, 567
Reform Judaism, 482, 949
Rehoboam, King, 477
Relics
  of Buddha, 146, 304–6
  canonization and, 767
  in Christianity, 202
  Christ's blood, 591
  of Cyprian, Saint, 229
  of Gautama Buddha, 304
  of Gregory the Great, 345
  Jesus Christ, blood of, 715–16
  of John the Baptist, 466–67
  Margaret of Scotland, Saint's Day of St., 553
  of Mary Magdalene, 537
  of Monica, 55
  overview of, 771–72
  Protestants and, 768
  of Saint Adalbert, 7
  of Saint Agnes, 12
  of Saint Andrew, 35
  of Saint Anne, 36–37
  of Saint Anne d'Auray, 696
  of Saint Augustine of Canterbury, 53
  of Saint Augustine of Hippo, 55
  of Saint Bartholomew, 105
  of Saint Benedict, 109
  of Saint Florian, 311
  of Saint George, 334
  Saint Helena and, 202, 407–8
  of Saint Nicholas, 638–39
  of Saint Olaf, 658
  of Saint Peter, 169
  of Saint Sava, 786
  of Saint Sebastian, 782–83
  of Saint Walpurga, 915
  of Thérèse of Lisieux, Saint, 856
  True Cross, 280–81, 578, 713
Religious Freedom Day, **743–44**
Religious right, 611
Remey, Charles Mason, 88–89
Republic of China (Taiwan), 136–37, 219–21, 221i, 857
Restoration (England), 208
Resurrection, of Jesus Christ, 267–69
Revelation, Book of, 579
Rice crops, 500
Richard, Mirra, 56–57, 592, 817
Riḍá', 80
Ridpath, John Clark, 476i, 477i
Ridpath's History of the World, 476i, 477i
Riḍván, Festival of, **744–47**
Rights of Man (Paine), 857
Rig Veda, 607
Rinpoche, Guru, 524
Rinzai Zen Buddhism, 138, 416, 525
Rio de Janeiro, Brazil, 552, 783
Rishi Panchami, 747i, **747–48**, 908
Rissho Kosei Kai, 649
Rivier, Marie, 711
Robinson, William, 431
Roc Day, 286
Roche, Alain de la, 750
Roderick, King, 437
Rodionovna, Tatiana, 846–47
Rogation Days, **748–49**
Rohini, 102, 364
Roman calendar, 152, 627
Roman Catholic Church. *See also* Roman Catholic Church, festivals and holidays; Saint's days
  canonization, 765–67
  Cathars and, 589
  Congregation of the Holy Cross, 408
  Cyril and, 229–30
  early challenges to, 880–81
  Eastern Orthodox churches and, 203–4, 272, 290
  in England, 290–91
  Europe and, 203–4
  foot washing, 568–69
  Gregory the Great, Saint, 345
  Julian calendar, 627
  Lent, 521–22
  liturgical calendar, xxi
  Lord's Supper, 567
  Meskal, 578
  during Middle Ages, 203–4
  Midsummer Day, 840
  Protestants, relationship with, 210, 742, 769
  Pueblo people and, 860–61
  reform of, 205
  relationship with other Christian churches, 201
  sacraments, 205–6
  supernaturalism, criticism of, 880
  Virgin Mary, veneration of, 27, 36–37, 50–51, 201, 203, 560, 562, 583, 773–74, 827–28

Roman Catholic Church, festivals and holidays
  Advent and, 10
  All Saints Day, **22–23**, 275, 277, 403, 631, 774
  All Souls Day, **23–25**, 275, 277
  Annunciation, Feast of the, **37–39**, 293, 909–10
  Aparecida, Feast of Our Lady of, **41–43**, 564
  Ascension Day, **45–46**, 403, 527
  Ash Wednesday, 49i, **49–50**, 521
  Assumption of the Virgin, **50–51**, 403, 562, 726
  Baptism of the Lord, Feast of the, **103–4**
  Black Christ, Festival of the, **116–18**
  Burning of Judas, **148–49**
  Chair of St. Peter, Feast of the, **169**
  Christ the King, Feast of, **213–14**
  Circumcision, Feast of the, 215
  Conversion of St. Paul, Feast of the, 223
  Corpus Christi, Feast of, **223–24**, 403
  Divine Mercy Sunday, **250–51**
  Easter Monday, 271
  Ember Days, **281–82**
  Epiphany. *See* Epiphany
  Eucharistic Congresses, **290–91**
  Expectation of the Birth of the Blessed Virgin Mary, Feast of, 38, **293**
  Holy Days of Obligation, **402–3**
  Holy Family, Feast of the, **403–4**
  Holy Innocents' Day, **404–5**
  Holy Week. *See* Holy Week
  Immaculate Conception, Feast of the, 349, 403, **421–22**, 562, 564
  Immaculate Heart of Mary, Feast of the, **422–23**
  James the Greater, Feast Day of St., **455–57**
  Joan of Arc, Saint's Day of St., **462–63**
  John the Baptist, Beheading of, 466
  John the Baptist, Nativity of, 468
  John the Evangelist, Day of St., **469–70**
  Joseph, Feast Day of St., 471
  Jubilee year, **472–74**
  liturgical year, **526–29**, 560
  Lourdes, Feast Day of Our Lady of, **532–35**
  Mardi Gras, **551–52**
  Martinmas, **556–57**
  Mary, liturgical year of the Blessed Virgin, **560–64**
  Mary Magdalene, Day of the Holy, **564–66**
  Michaelmas, **579–80**
  Miracles, Festival of Our Lady of, **583–84**
  Misa de Gallo, **584–85**
  Most Holy Name of Mary, Feast of the, **590–91**
  Most Precious Blood, Feast of the, **591–92**
  Mother's Day, 594
  Mount Carmel, Feast Day of Our Lady of, **595–96**
  Nativity of Mary, 614–15
  Nossa Senhora dos Remédios, Pilgrimage of, **650**
  Palm Sunday, 669–70
  Penitentes, **680–82**
  Peter and Paul, Saint's Day of Sts., **688–90**
  Presentation of Jesus in the Temple, Feast of the, **708–10**
  Presentation of Mary, Feast of the, **710–11**
  Prompt Succor, Feast Day of Our Lady of, **716–17**
  Queenship of Mary, Feast of, **725–26**, 910
  Rogation Days, **748–49**
  Romeria of La Virgen de Valme, **749–50**
  Rosary, Feast of Our Lady of the, **750–51**
  Sacred Heart of Jesus, Feast of the, 557, **757–58**
  Saint Bartholomew's Day Massacre, 106
  Saint John Lateran, Feast of the Dedication of, **760–61**
  Saint Patrick's Day, **761–62**
  saints, veneration of, **770–74**
  saints in, **765–67**
  Saint Stephen's Day, **762–64**
  Saint Stephen's Day (Hungary), **764**
  Solemnity of Mary, Feast of the, 215, 402, **824**
  Sorrows, Feast of Our Lady of, **828–29**
  Transfiguration, Feast of the, 866
  Trinity Monday, **867**
  Trinity Sunday, 867–68
  Visitation, Feast of the, **909–10**
  Week of Prayer for Christian Unity, 917
  White Sunday, **921**
  World Communion Sunday, 929
  World Day of Prayer, 930
Roman Empire, 199–200, 203, **313–14**
Romania, 35, 119–20
Romanian Orthodox Church, 284
Romany people, 405–7
Rome, 22–23, 203–4, 419
Romeria del Rocio. *See* Pilgrimage of the Dew

Romeria of La Virgen de Valme, **749–50**
Roncalli, Angelo Cardinal, 534
Roncesvalles, Spain, 711–12
Roosevelt, Franklin, 608
Rooster's Mass. *See* Misa de Gallo
Rosary, Feast of Our Lady of the, **750–51**
Rose Monday. *See* Mardi Gras
Rose of Lima, Saint's Day of St., **751–52**
Rosh Hashanah, 156, 244–45, 485–86, 627, **752–54**, 754i, 947
Rosicrucian, 303–4
Rosmadec, Sebastien de, 695
Rowzeh khani, 48
Roy, Ram Mohan, 384
Rudra, 29
Rufinus, 407
Ruiz, Lorenzo, 529–30
Rukmini Ashtami, **755**
Rulsidas, 875
Rushi Pancham, **755–56**
Russia. *See also* Russian Orthodox Church
  Andrew, Saint, and, 35
  Casimir, Saint, 166
  Christianity in, 204
  Gregorian calendar and, 154
  Immaculate Heart of Mary and, 299–300, 423
  National Day, **609–10**
  Nicholas, Saint's Day of St., 639
  Russian Orthodox Church, repression of, 25
  Tatiana, Saint's Day of St., **846–47**
  Unbelief in, 885
Russian Orthodox Church
  Alphabet Day, **25–26**
  Doukhobor Peace Day, **262–63**
  George, Feast Day of St., 333
  Julian calendar, 273
  National Day, **609–10**
  Procession of the Cross, 281, **713–14**
  repression of, 25
  True Cross, commemoration of, 408
  Vladimir, Saint's Day of St., 713, **911–13**, 912i
Ruth, Book of, 799

Sab-e Qadr. *See* Laylat al-Qadr
Sacraments, 205–6
Sacred and Legendary Art (Jameson), 12i
Sacred Congregation for the Causes of Saints, 766–67
Sacred Heart of Jesus, Feast of the, 557, **757–58**
Sacred Heart of Mary. *See* Immaculate Heart of Mary, Feast of the
Sacrifice, 181
Saddharmapundarika sutra, 132
Sadducees, 478–79
Sádiq, Ja'far, 80
Saga Dawa Duchen. *See* Wesak/Vesak
Sage Vyasa, 647
Sahaja Yoga, 385
Sahib, Guru Granth, 541
Sai Baba of Shirdi, Birthday of, 399, **758–59**
Saicho, 138
Saiedi, Nader, 621
Saint Anthony's Shrine, 41
Saint Augustine's Abbey, 53
Saint Barnabas Monastery, 334i
Saint Bartholomew's Day Massacre, 106
Saint Brigid's Cross, 128–29, 129i
Saint Casimir's Chapel, 166
Sainte-Anne-d'Auray, church of, 36
Sainte-Anne-de-Beaupré, church of, 37
Sainte-Anne-de-la-Palue, church of, 36
Saint George's Cathedral, 333–34
Saint Hill Organizations, 52
Saint John Lateran church, 473
Saint John Lateran, Feast of the Dedication of, **760–61**
Saint John's Eve/Day. *See* Summer Solstice
Saint Joseph's Academy and Free School, 794
Saint Maria Maggiore church, 473
Saint Nicholas Church, 712
Saint Olav's Way, 658
Saint Patrick's Day, **761–62**
Saint Paul's Church, 318
Saint Paul's Outside the Walls, 405, 473
Saint Peter's Basilica, 13
Saint Peter's Cathedral, 206–7, 473
Saints (Roman Catholic tradition), **765–67**. *See also* Saint's days
Saints, celebrating the lives of (Protestant tradition), **767–70**
Saints, veneration of (Roman Catholic tradition), **770–74**. *See also* Saint's days
Saint's days
  Adalbert of Prague, Saint's Day of St., **7–8**
  All Saints Day, **22–23**, 275, 277, 403, 631, 774

Alphonse de Ligouri, Saint's Day of St., **26–27**
Andrew, Saint's Day of St., **34–36**
Ansgar, Saint's Day of St., **39–40**
Anthony of Padua, Saint's Day of St., **40–41**
Augustine of Canterbury, Saint's Day of St., **52–54**
Augustine of Hippo, Saint's Day of St., **54–56**
Bartholomew's Day, Saint, **104–6**
Benedict of Nursia, Saint's Day of St., **109–10**
Benedict the African, Saint's Day of St., **110–11**
Boniface of Germany, Saint's Day of St., **125–26**
Bridget, Saint's Day of St., **127–28**
Brigid of Kildare, Saint's Day of St., 128i, **128–29**
calendar of, 773
Casimir, Saint's Day of St., **166**
Catherine of Siena, Saint's Day of St., **166–68**
Clement of Ohrid, Saint's Day of St., **215–16**
Columba, Saint's Day of St., **216–17**
Cyprian, Saint's Day of St., **228–29**
Cyril and Methodius, Saint's Day for Sts., 25, **229–31**
development of, 206
Dominic, Saint's Day of St., **257–58**
Eastern Orthodox churches and, 274–75
Epictetus the Presbyter and Astion, Saints Day of Sts., **283–84**
Evtimiy of Bulgaria, Saint's Day of Patriarch, **291–92**
Florian, Saint's Day of St., **311**
Francis Xavier, Saint's Day of St., **317–19**
Gregory the Great, Saint's Day of St., **344–46**
Joan of Arc, Saint's Day of St., **462–63**
Jogues, John de Brébeuf and Companions, Saints Day of St. Isaac, **463–64**
John the Evangelist, Day of St., **469–70**
Lorenzo Ruiz, Saint's Day of St., **529–30**
Lucy, Saint's Day of St., **535–36**
Margaret of Scotland, Saint's Day of St., **552–53**
Martin de Porres, Saint's Day of St., **553–54**
Nicholas, Saint's Day of St., **638–40**, 639i
Nino, Saint's Day of St., **645–46**
Olaf, Saint's Day of St., **658**
Peter and Paul, Saint's Day of Sts., **688–90**
Peter Baptist and Companions, Saint's Day of St., **690–91**
Peter Chanel, Saint's Day of St., **691–92**
Peter Claver, Saint's Day of St., **692–93**
Peter of Alcantara, Saint's Day of St., **693–94**
Rose of Lima, Saint's Day of St., **751–52**
Saint Patrick's Day, **761–62**
Saint Stephen's Day, **762–64**
Saint Stephen's Day (Hungary), **764**
Sava, Saint's Day of St., **786–87**
Seton, Saint's Day of Mother Elizabeth, **794–95**
Stanislaus, Saint's Day of St., **834–35**
Tatiana, Saint's Day of St., **846–47**
Thérèse of Lisieux, Saint's Day of St., **855–56**
Vladimir, Saint's Day of St., 912i, **911–13**
Willibrord, Saint's Day of St., **925–26**
Saint Stephen's Day, **762–64**
Saint Stephen's Day (Hungary), **764**
Saint Timothy's Church, 276
Saint Walburga Church, 712
Saivite Hindus
Chaturmas Vrat, **172–73**
Chittirai Festival, 194
Gangaur, **329–30**
holidays of, 397–98
Kartika Purnima, 494
Karwa Chauth, **497–99**, 498i
Magha Purnima, 539
Skanda Shashti, **820–22**, 821i
Thaipusam, 540, **852–53**, 853i
Saivya, queen, 722
Saka, Aji, 652
Saka calendar, 161–62, 393–94, 395, 630, 632–33
Sakata Chauth. *See* Ganesh Chaturthi
Sakura Matsuri, 775i, **775–76**
Sakurayama Hachimangu Shrine, 17–18, 845
Sakya Buddhists, 935–36
Sakya Dawa Festival, 144, **776–77**, 919
Sakyapa order, 139, 588
Saladin, 204, 281, 438
Salem Witchcraft Trials, 320
Sales, Francis de, Saint, 909
Salmon, 310–11

Salvation Army. *See* Founders' Day (Salvation Army)
Samadhi, 543
Samantabadhara's Birthday, **777–79**
Sambhavanath, Lord, 495
Samhain, 365–67, 631, **779–80**, 923–24
Samkhya darshana, 388
Samoan Islands, 921
Samuel, Herbert, 1, 3
Samyag Tapa, 619
Sandalwood Festival. *See* Chandan Yatra
Sandoval, Alfonso de, 692
Sangha, 43, 195
Sangha Act of 1902, 135
Sanghamitta, 265, 702–3, 780–81
Sanghamitta Day, **780–81**
Sanhedrin, 156
Sanjay, 336–37
Sankt Placidusfest, **781–82**
San Sebastian Day, **782–83**
Sanskrit language, 384i
Santa Claus, 107, 212
Santa Fe, New Mexico, 348i, 349
Santa Maria Maggiore, 405
Santanu, King, 114
Santiago de Compostela, 127, 456, 557, 711
Santi Asoka, 135
Santusita Deva, 4
Sara, Romany queen, 406
Sara, servant of Marie Jacobe, 405–6
Sarada Devi, Birthday of, **783–84**
Sarasvati, 617
Sarasvat River, 570
Saraswathi Puja, 903
Saraswati, 171, 242–43, 902–3
Saraswati, Dayananda, 384
Sariputra, 4
Sarnath, 43–44
Sarto, Andrea del, 12i, 465i
Sarton, Wallon de, 466
Satavahana dynasty (India), 161
Satchidananda, Birthday of Swami, **784–85**
Satchidananda Ashram, 785
Sati, 847–48
Saturn, 926
Satyavan, 906
Satyavata, 494
Saudi Arabia, 433, 440–41, 571
Saul. *See* Paul, Apostle
Saul, King, 477
Sava, Saint's Day of St., **786–87**
Savitri, 905–6. *See also* Surya
Sawa Dawa, 145
Sawyakta mudras, 596
Scandinavia, 39–40
Scapular, brown, 595
Schaferlauf. *See* Bartholomew's Day, Saint
Schindler's List, 945
Schneersohn, Yosef Yitzchok, 787
Schneerson, Anniversary of the Death of Rabbi Menachem Mendal, **787–88**
Schutzengelfest, **788**
Schwenckfeld, Caspar, 789
Schwenfelders, 880
Schwenkfelder Thanksgiving, **789**
Scientology, Church of
  Auditor's Day, **51–52**
  auditors in, 51–52
  Celebrity Center International, 168i, **168**
  Dianetics, Anniversary of, **248–49**
  holidays of, **789–91**
  Hubbard, Birthday of L. Ron, **411–13**
  International Association of Scientologists Anniversary, **428–29**
  lawsuits, 428
  Maiden Voyage Anniversary, **546–47**
  monasticism, 791–92
  National Founding Day, **612–13**, 791
  New Year's Day, 631, **636**
  Sea Org Day, **791–93**
  Sea Organization, 790, 792i
Scientology, Holidays of the Church of, **789–91**
Scopes Monkey Trial, 238
Scotland, 35, 207, 216–17, 890–91
Scott, Coretta, 555
Seamstresses, 373
Sea Organization, 790, 792i
Sea Org Day, **791–93**
Sechi Festival, **793**
Second Vatican Council, 210, 563, 591, 608, 708, 765, 783, 824, 917, 930
The Secret Doctrine (Blavatsky), 920
Sect of the Pure Land, 138
Sect Shinto, 808–9
Secular celebrations
  Aki Matsuri, **17–18**
  as alternatives to religious holidays, 887
  Chinese New Year's Day, 628–29
  Festivus, **306–7**
  Halloween, 277, **365–67**, 366i, 631, 780

HumanLight, **413–14**, 887
Indivisible Day, **424–25**
Juhannus, **487–88**
Kataklysmos, **499**
Kwanzaa, 887, 927
Kyoto Gion Matsuri, **508–9**
Mother's Day, **593–95**
National Day of Reason, **611–12**, 887
New Year's Day, 628
Race Unity Day, 730
Religious Freedom Day, **743–44**
Saint Patrick's Day, **761–62**
Thomas Paine Day, **857–58**
Up Helly Aa, **890–92**
World Humanist Day, 887, **931–32**
Yom HaAtzmaut, 486, **943–44**, 946
Yom HaZikaron, 486, 943, **946**
Yom Yerushalayim (Jerusalem Day), 487, **949–50**
Secularism, 879, 882. *See also* Unbelief
Secular Student Alliance, 931
Seder service, 687
Ségur, Gaston de, 290
Seijin no Hi, **793–94**
Seinfeld, 306
Seiwa, Emperor, 444, 508
Seiyu Kiriyama Kancho, 342, 411
Self-realization, 449
Self-Realization Fellowship (SRF), 77, 512, 941, 942, 950
Semsoun, 199
Seoul, Korea, 599
Seoul Chong, 599
September celebrations
Cyprian, Saint's Day of St., **228–29**
Divino Rostro, Devotion to, **251–52**
Elevation of the True Cross, **280–81**
Gregory the Great, Saint's Day of St., **344–46**
Guan Yin, Renunciation of, **350–51**
Holyrood or the Feast of the Triumph of the Holy Cross, **407–9**
Iwashimizu Matsuri, **444–45**
Lahiri Mahasaya, Commemoration Days for, **512–13**
Lorenzo Ruiz, Saint's Day of St., **529–30**
Meskal, 289, **578–79**
Michaelmas, **579–80**
Miracles, Festival of Our Lady of, **583–84**
Most Holy Name of Mary, Feast of the, **590–91**
Nativity of Mary, **614–15**, 650
Nossa Senhora dos Remédios, Pilgrimage of, **650**
Peñafrancia, Feast of Our Lady of, **679–80**
Peter Claver, Saint's Day of St., **692–93**
Purnanandaji Paramahansa, Commemoration Day for Swami Guru, **721–22**
Schwenkfelder Thanksgiving, **789**
Sivananda Saraswati, Birthday of Swami, **819–20**
Sophia, The Descent and Assumption of Holy, **826–28**
Sorrows, Feast of Our Lady of, **828–29**
Vishwakarma Puja, **908–9**
Serbian Orthodox Church, 786–87
Sergius I, Pope, 614, 709
Sergius III, Pope, 760
Serpent worship, 601–2
Serreta, Azores, 583–84
Servetus, Michael, 869, 880, 880i
Service for the Deceased Sutra, 655
Seton, Saint's Day of Mother Elizabeth, **794–95**
Setsubun, **795–96**
Seven Sisters Festival. *See* Double Seventh Festival
Seventh-day Adventist Church, 675
The Seven Valleys and Four Valleys (Bahá'u'lláh), 87
Seven Year Plan, 89
Shaftsbury, Lord, 881
Shahadah, 435
Shahenshali calendar, 959
Sháh of Persia, 65, 71
Shaivites. *See* Saivite Hindus
Shakespeare, William, 346
Shaktipat initiation, 599
Shaku, Soyen, 140
Shalivhana Saka, 161
Shamanistic beliefs and practices, 872
Shan Dao, 31
Shang dynasty (China), 159, 180–81, 667
Shani, Lord, 547
Shankara, 356i, 388–89
Shankaracharya Jayanti, **796–98**
Shankarananda, Swami, 784
Shaolin Temple, 123

Sharad Purnima, 502–3, **798–99**
Shasta people, 310
Shatrunjay, 19–20
Shavuot, 485, **799–800**
Sheba, queen of, 628
Sheetala Ashtami, **800–801**
Shemini Atzeret/Simchat Torah, **801–2**, 837–38
Shen Hui, 123
Shen Nong, 180
Sherrill, Henry Knox, 661
Shetland Islands, 890
Shi'a Muslims. *See also* Islam
  Ali ibn Abi Talib, Commemoration Days for, **21–22**
  Ashura, 47–48
  five pillars of Islam and, 435–36
  holidays of, 158
  important dates, 442
  Laylat al-Qadr, 518
  Muhammad, Prophet and, 571
  New Year's Day, 629
  overview of, 436–37
Shichi-Go-San, **802–3**
Shiel, Justin, 75
Shiji (Records of the Historian), 515
Shikhandi, 114
Shikinensengu, **803–4**
Shimogamo Shrine, 257
Shinran Shonin, 138, 146, 287, 544
Shinran Shonin, Birthday of, 31, **804–5**
Shinto, **805–10**
  Buddhism and, 806, 807, 811
  Christianity and, 808–9, 811
  Confucianism and, 805–6, 807
  New Year's Day, 812
  in postwar period, 809
  sacred texts, 806
  Sect Shinto, 808–9
  shrines, 807
  Shrine Shinto, 809
  State Shinto, 808–9
  Tsukinami-sai ritual, 806i
Shinto cycle of holidays, **810–15**
  Aki Matsuri, **17–18**
  Chichibu Yomatsuri, **174**
  Daruma Kuyo, **235–36**
  Dosojin Matsuri, **259–60**
  Hadaka Matsuri, **359–60**
  Harikuyo, **373**
  Haru Matsuri, **374–75**
  holidays of, **810–15**
  Iwashimizu Matsuri, **444–45**
  Kaijin Matsuri, **489–90**
  Kanmiso-sai, **492–93**
  Kaza-Matsuri, **500–501**
  Kodomo no Hi, 343, **501**
  Koshogatsu, **503–4**
  Kyoto Gion Matsuri, **508–9**
  Nagasaki Kunchi, 18, **601–2**
  Natsu Matsuri, **615**
  Onbashira, **660–61**
  Setsubun, **795–96**
  Shichi-Go-San, **802–3**
  Shikinensengu, **803–4**
  Takayama Matsuri, **845**
  Tohji-Taisai, **865**
"Shinto Directive," 809
Shírá-zí, Sayyid 'Alí-Muhammad. *See* Báb
Shiva
  Amarnath Yatra, 28
  Ashokashtami, 46
  Baba's Day, 78
  Bhairava Ashtami, 111
  Chaturmas Vrat, 172–73
  Chittirai Festival, 194
  Dattatreya Jayanti, 242
  Ganesh Chaturthi, 324–25
  Ganga Dussehra, 327
  Hanuman Jayanti, 372
  Holi, 401
  Kartika Purnima, 494
  Karwa Chauth, 497
  Magha Purnima, 539
  Mahashivaratri, 541–43, 542i
  Nagapanchami, 601
  origins of, 381–82
  Rishi Panchami, 747
  Shaivites and, 397–98
  Shankaracharya Jayanti, 797
  Shravava Mela, **815**
  Teej Festivals, 847–48
  Vasant Panchami, 903
Shivaratri. *See* Mahashivaratri
Shoghi Effendi
  Badí' calendar, 163
  on Bahá'í teachings, 92
  Covenant, Day of the, 226–27
  Nineteen-Day Feast, 642–43
  Seven Year Plan, 89–90

successor to 'Abdu'l-Bahá, 88
writings of, 1–2, 61, 90–91
Shogunate, 794, 802
Shoman, Queen, 16
Shomu, emperor, 816
Shonin, Nichiren, 657
Shotoku, Emperor, 359
Shotoku, Prince, 16, 367, 375
Shōwa, Emperor, 174
Showa period (Japan), 138
Shravakayana Buddhism, 132
Shravana Purnima. *See* Raksha Bandhan
Shravava Mela, **815**
Shree Shree Amandamurti, 385
Shri, 542
Shrimp trawler, 120i
Shrine of Báb, 97
Shrine of Bahá'u'lláh, 96–97, 98
Shrine of Our Lady of Peñafrancia, 680
Shrine of the North American Martyrs, 464
Shrine Shinto, 809
Shrines, Shinto, 807
Shrove Monday. *See* Mardi Gras
Shrove Tuesday, 551. *See also* Mardi Gras
Shuni-e (Omizutori), **816–17**
Shunki-Korei-Sai. *See* Higan
Shuvalov, Ivan, 846
Shvetambaras, 544–45
Siddha Charka, 619
Siddha Day, **817–18**
Siddhartha, 544
Siddhartha Gautama. *See* Buddha Shakyamuni
Siddha Yogis, 599
Sigd, **818–19**
Sigisbert, 782
Sikh calendar, 604
Sikhs
Diwali, 254
Guru Gobind Singh's Birthday, **353–54**
Guru Granth Sahib, Celebration of the, **354–55**
Kartika Purnima, 494
Maghi, **540–41**
Martyrdom of Guru Arjan, **558**
Martyrdom of Guru Tegh Bahadur, **559–60**
Nanak's Birthday, Guru, 162, 163, **603–4**
Nanakshahi calendar, 162–63
New Year's Day, 630
Sikkim, India, 694–95
Silence, 569–70
Silent Day. *See* Holy Week
Silk, 492–93
Silvester I, Pope, 760
Sima Qian, 515
Simbang Gabi Mass, 584
Simchat Torah. *See* Shemini Atzeret/Simchat Torah
Simeon, 709
Simeon the Myrrh-flowing, Saint, 786
Simpafo people, 5–6
Singapore, 62, 144, 852, 856–57, 918
Sinhalese Buddhist community, 141
Sinkyone people, 310
Sino-Japanese War, 136
Sirius star, 151
Sisters of Charity of Saint Joseph, 794
Sisters of Nevers, 534
Sisters of the Presentation of the Blessed Virgin Mary, 711
Sita, 253, 329, 372, 388, 457
Sita Devi, 739
Siuslawan people, 310
Sivananda Saraswati, Birthday of Swami, **819–20**
Sivananda Saraswati, Swami, 193, 243
Six Day War, 487, 949
Six Paramitas, 375–76
Sixth World Buddhist Women's Convention, 287
Sixtus IV, Pope, 421
Sixtus V, Pope, 590, 711, 725–26
Skanda, Lord, 821
Skanda Shashti, **820–22**, 821i
Slavery, 208, 340–41, 692–93
Slaves of Our Lady, 583
Slavic people, 229–30
Small New Year. *See* Chinese New Year's (Preliminary Festival)
Smith, Al, 608
Smith, William "Smitty," 729
Smriti texts, 387
Snake Boat Race, 659
Snan Yatra, **822–23**
Snatra Puja ritual, 635
Snow houses, 491i, 491–92
Snow Hut Festival, 491i, 491–92
Sobieski, John, 590
Society for Ethical Culture, 413
Society for Psychical Research, 920
Society for the Buddhist Mission, 139

Society of Charitable Instruction of the Sacred Heart of Jesus, 711
Society of Jesus, 317
Society of Mary, 691–92
Socinian movement, 869, 880
Soderblom, Nathan, 40
Soka Gakkai International, 140, 141, 637, 657
Solar calendars, 152, 162–63, 604, 627, 630, 632–33
Solar-lunar calendars, 151, 155, 159–61, 190
Solemnity of Mary, Feast of the, 215, 402, **824**
Solemnity of Saints Peter and Paul, 403
Solemnity of St. Joseph, 402
Solemnity of the Most Holy Trinity. *See* Trinity Sunday
Sol Invictus festival, 927
Solomon, King, 477, 484–85, 628
Song dynasty (China), 173, 504, 575
Songkran, **824–26**
Songtsen Gampo, Kind, 138
Sonoda, Shuye, 148
Sophia, The Descent and Assumption of Holy, **826–28**
Sorrows, Feast of Our Lady of, **828–29**
Soto Buddhism, 525
Soubirous, Bernadette, 421, 533–34
Sousa, Manuel B., 584
South Africa, 141, 885
South America, 208, 885. *See also* Latin America
Southeast Asia
  Abhidhamma Day, 45
  Buddhism in, 134–35
  Chinese folk religion, 86
  Confucianism and, 188
  Gautama Buddha, 825
  Hinduism, 382
  Magha Puja Day, **538–39**
  Mahayana Buddhism, 34, 134–36
  Nine Emperor Gods, Festival of the, **640–41**
  Songkran, **824–26**
Southern Baptist Convention, 218
Southern Christian Leadership Council (SCLC), 555
Southern Sung dynasty (China), 187
Soviet Union, 609, 884
Spain
  Age of Exploration, 207–8
  Annunciation, Feast of the, 38
  Burning of Judas, 148
  Expectation of the Birth of the Blessed Virgin Mary, Feast of, 293
  Guadalupe, Feast of Our Lady of, 347–48
  James the Greater, Saint, 346
  Joseph, Feast Day of St., 471–72
  Judaism in, 480
  Most Precious Blood, Feast of the, 591
  Mother's Day, 594
  Pilgrimage of the Dew, **697–98**
  Procession de la Penitencia, La, **711–12**
  Romeria of La Virgen de Valme, **749–50**
Spencer, Herbert, 237
Spencer, Peter, 11
Spielberg, Steven, 945
Spring and Autumn Annals, 185
Spring and Autumn Period (China), 718
Spring Dragon Festival, **829–31**, 830i
Spring equinox (thelema), **831–32**, 924
Spring equinox (vernal), **832–34**
Spy Wednesday, 521. *See also* Holy Week
Sri Aurobindo Ashram, 56–57
Sri Lanka
  Duruthu Poya, **265–66**
  Festival of the Tooth, 304–5
  local Buddhist holidays, 146
  Poson, **702–3**
  Sanghamitta Day, **780–81**
  Skanda Shashti, 822
  Wesak/Vesak, 144, 918
Srimad-Bhagavatam, 113, 706
Srimala, Queen, 16
Srimaladevi Sutra, 16
Sri Ramcharitra Manas (Tulsidas), 329
Sri Sarada Math, 784
Stained glass, 128i
Stanislaus, Saint's Day of St., **834–35**
State Confucianism, 186
State Shinto, 808–9
Statuary, 13
Stein, Edith, 127
Stephen, martyrdom of, 222
Stephen I, Pope, 228
Stephen of Perm, St., 26
Stephens, Robert, 238
Stephenson, Marmaduke, 431
Sthanakavasai Jain tradition, 451
St. Mary's Roman Catholic Church, 35
Stock, Simon, 595
Stoker, Bram, 915
Stolen Lightning (O'Keefe), 306

Stonehenge, 840–41, 924
Storrs, Ronald, 2–3
The Story of a Soul (Thérèse of Lisieux), 855
The Story of the Carpenter, 470
St. Peter's Basilica, 35
Struensee, Johann Friedrich von, 219
Student Day (Russia). *See* Tatiana, Saint's Day of St.
Stukeley, William, 840
Subhadra, Lord, 823
Submission, in Islam, 435
Subramaniya, Lord, 852
Subramuniya Yoga Order, 822
Suffering, truth of, 130
Sufism, 241–42, 437, 577, 892–93
Sufism Reoriented, 577
Sugawara, Michizane, 850–51
Suijin, 489
Suketumana, king, 722
Sukhavati, 30, 625
Sukkah, 836i, 836–37
Sukkot, 485, 486, 801, **835–39**, 836i
Suleiman I, 438
Sumant, 32
Sumati, queen, 327
Sumiyoshi, 601
Sumiyoshi Shrine, 489
Summer Solstice, 487, **839–41**, 924, 931
Sundareshvarar, Lord, 539
Sundreshvara, 194
Sung dynasty (China), 186, 525
Sungkyunkwan University, 599
Sunni Muslims, 22, 47, 435–36, 571, 629. *See also* Islam
Sun-tzu, 183
Sun worship, 842–43
Sun Wukong. *See* Monkey King
Sunzi, 182
Supernaturalism, criticism of, 880
Surabhi, 542
Súrah of Mulk, 69
Surangama Sutra, 543
Surin, Thailand, 279
Survivors of the Shoah Visual History Foundation, 945
Surya, 547, 842i
Surya Shashti, **841–43**, 842i
Surya Siddhanta (Kali Yuga), 161
Susano-o no Mikoto, 508
Sushila, 32–33
Suwa-no-Kami, 601
Suwa Shrine, 601–2
Suwa Taisha, 601, 660
Suzuki, Daisetz T., 140
Svetambaras, 448, 451
Svetitskhoveli Cathedral, 646
Sviatoslav of Kiev, 911
Svyatoslavish, Vladimir, 911–12
Swaminarayan movement, 634, 677
Sweden, 39–40, 535–36, 866
Swedenborg, Emanuel, 625–26
Sweet, David, 60
Switzerland, 207, 781–82
SYDA Foundation, 599
Synod of Constantinople, 663
Syria, 948
Syrian Orthodox Church of Antioch, 200
The System of Nature (Holbach), 882
Szczepanowski, Stanslaw, 834–35

Tabernacles, Feast of, 486
"Tablet of the Branch," 98
"Tablet of the Eternal Youth," 71–72
"Tablet of the Greatest Name," 80–81
"Tablet of the Youth of Paradise," 72
"Tablet of Visitation," 3, 75, 96, 98
The Tablets of the Divine Plan, 89
Tabora, Niñode, 678
Taejo, King, 599
Taho Pagoda, 16–17
Taichu calendar, 628
Tai Hsu, 136
Taiko Toyotomi Hideyoshi, 691
Taima-dera, 625
Taipei Confucius Temple, 221i
Taiping rebellion, 187
Taishō, Emperor, 174
Taisho period (Japan), 138
Taiwan. *See* Republic of China (Taiwan)
Taizi, emperor, 778
Taj Mahal, 438
Taka-mi-musubi-no-Kami, 806
Takayama Matsuri, **845**
Talib, Ali Ibn Abi, 518
Talmud, 479
Tamil Nadu, 630, 633
Tamils, 397–98, 539–40, 630, 633, 820–22, 821i, 852–53, 853i
Tam Kung Festival, **845–46**
Tanaka Tsunekiyo, 444

Tang dynasty (China), 136, 177, 180, 416, 504, 515, 586, 628
Taoism
Che Kung, Birthday of, **173**
in China, 188
Kwan Tai, Birthday of, **507–8**
Laozi, 516i
Laozi, Birthday of, **515–16**
Monkey King, 586
Preliminary Festival, 176
rabbit on the moon, 581
Tapovanam, Swami, 193
Tarthang Tulku, 588, 935
Tatiana, Saint's Day of St., **846–47**
Tatian the Assyrian, 199
Teachers' Day, 219, 221
Teej Festivals, **847–48**
Tegh Bahadur, Guru, 353, 355, 559–60
Tejomayananda, Birthday of Swami, **848–49**
Teleju, 425
Telugu-speaking people, 634
Temmu, emperor, 803
Templar Order, 849–50
Templars, The Day of the Martyrdom of the Holy, **849–50**
Temple Israel, 62
Temple Mount, 433, 440, 516
Temple of the Emerald Buddha, 538
Templeton foundation Prize for Progress in Religion, 649
Temporum Ratione (Venerable Bede), 282–83
The Temptation of Christ (Doré), 522i
Ten Commandments, 476
Tendai school, 138
Ten Days of Prayer, 625
Ten Days of Repentance, 244
Tenerife, Spain, 268i
Tenjin Matsuri, **850–51**
Tenrikyo religion, 793
Tenshozan Renge-in Komyoji, 625
Tens of Thousands of Lanterns Ancestral Memorial Service, **851–52**
Teppotsavam, 539–40. *See* Magha Purnima
Teppozu Inari Shrine, 360
Terceira, Azores, 583–84
Terepanth Svetambara Jain tradition, 451
Tertullian, 200
Tet (Vietnam). *See* New Year's Day
Tewa Native American people, 106–7
Thaddeus (Addai), 199, 419
Thadingyut. *See* Abhidhamma Day
Thailand
Asalha Puja Day ("Dhamma Day"), 44
Boun Ok Phansa, **126**
Buddhism in, 134–35
Elephant Festival, **279–80**
Kathina Ceremony, 500
Magha Puja Day, 539
Nine Emperor Gods, Festival of the, 640
Ploughing Day, **698–99**
Songkran, 825
Wesak/Vesak, 144, 918
Thaipusam, 540, **852–53**, 853i
Thampuran, Sakthan, 700
Thekong Tek, 694
Thelema, 301–3, 309–10
Thelemites, 831–32
Theodosius of Tomis, 284
Theologica Moralis (Ligouri), 27
Theophany, 527, 582, **853–55**. *See also* Epiphany
Theophany, Feast of the, 104
Theophilus of Alexandria, Bishop, 288
Theophoric metamorphosis, 85
Theosophical movement, 276, 919–20
Theosophical Society, 140, 919–20, 932
Theotokos (Mother of God), 38, 421, 560, 614, 710, 725, 824
Theravada Buddhism
Abhidhamma Day, **4–5**, 145
Anapanasati Day, **33–34**
Bodhi Day, 121
in Burma/Myanmar, 134
in China, 184
as early Buddhist tradition, 132
in Thailand, Cambodia, Laos, 135
unbelief in, 879
Uposattha Observance Day, **892**
Wesak/Vesak, 144, 162, 623, 776, **918–19**
Theresa, Mother, 766
Theresa of Avila, 471, 693
Thérèse of Lisieux, Saint's Day of St., **855–56**
Thetan, 168, 248, 412, 546, 790, 791
Thibault, Jean-Baptiste, 696
Thingyan. *See* New Year's Day
Third Order of the Franciscans, 681–82
Third Prince, Birthday of the, 192, **856–57**
Thirumala Nayaga, King, 540
Thomas, Apostle, 199–200, 277

Thomas Paine Day, **857–58**
Thomas Paine Foundation, 858
Thomas Paine National Historical Museum, 858
Thoreau, Henry D., 140
Three Hierarchs, Day of the, **859**
"Three Kings Day," 527
Three Kings Day (Epiphany), 284. *See also* Epiphany
Three Kings Day, Native American Pueblos, **860–61**
Three Magi, 103–4, 107, 284–86
Three Saints of the Western Paradise, 543
Thursday Island, 141
Tiantai school, 136
Tibetan Buddhism
  Butter Lamp Festival, 145, **149–50**, 150i
  Chokhor Duchen, **195–96**
  cycle of holidays, 145
  Dalai Lama's Birthday, **233–34**
  in Europe, 140
  Great Buddha Festival, **342–43**
  international spread of, 142
  Lha Bab Duchen, 145, **523–24**
  Lingka Woods Festival, **524–25**
  Losar, 149, **530–32**
  Monlam, the Great Prayer Festival, 149, **587–89**, 935
  overview of, 131, 132–33, 134, 138–39, 184
  Reformed School, 587
  Sakya Dawa Festival, 623, **776–77**, 919
  Tsong Khapa Anniversary, **872–74**
  World Peace Ceremony, 588, **935–36**
Tibetan calendar, 530
Tihar. *See* Diwali
Tilak, Lonmanya, 326
Tillamook people, 310
Times of London, 115–16
Timkat, 289, 861i, **861–62**
Tin Hou, Birthday of. *See* Mazu Festival, Goddess
Tiridates III, king, 645–46
Tirtha, Lakshmipati, 648
Tirthankaras, 447, 451, 453, 566
Tirumala Nayak, 194
Tirupati Brahmotsava Festival, **862–64**
Tisha B'Av, **864–65**
Tithe, 436
Ti Yin, 514
Tohji-Taisai, **865**
Tokugawa, Ieyasu, 811
Tokugawa period (Japan), 138, 810
Tolstoy, Leo, 262
Tomar, Portugal, 307–8
Tomb of Mary, 50
Tomb Sweeping Day. *See* Pure Brightness Festival
Torah, 199, 474–75, 479, 753
Torre, Pedro de la, 252
Toshitokujin, 503
Toumansky, Aleksandr, 97
Toyouke, 810
Transcendental Meditation, 385
Transfiguration, Feast of the, **866–67**
The Transformative Vision (Arguelles), 573
Transubstantiation, 205–6, 291
Treaty of Nuvarsag, 902
Treaty of Paris, 589, 716
Trinidad and Tobago, 48
Trinity, doctrine of, 725, 867–70
Trinity Monday, **867**
Trinity Sunday, **867–70**
Trinity University, 867
Tripura, 494
Tripurari Pumima. *See* Kartika Purnima
Triumph of the Holy Cross, Feast of the. *See* Holyrood or the Feast of the Triumph of the Holy Cross
Triumph of the True Cross, Feast of the. *See* Holyrood or the Feast of the Triumph of the Holy Cross
Triune God, 200
True Children, 175
The True Christian Religion (Swedenborg), 625–26
True Cross, 289, 578–79, 713–14
True Parents' Birthday, **870–71**
True Sect of the Pure Land, 138
The True Spouse of Jesus Christ (Ligouri), 27
Truman, Harry, 610, 661
Truthseeker, 858
Tryggvason, Olaf, 658
Tsagaan Sar, **871–72**
Tsong Khapa, 139, 145, 149, 587, 873i
Tsong Khapa Anniversary, **872–74**
Tsukinami-sai ritual, 806i
Tu B'Shevat, **874–75**
Tucker, Walter, 165
Tu Dam Pagoda, 144
Tukaram, 374, 383

Tulsidas, 383
Tulsidas, Goswami, 329
Tulsidas Jayanti, **875–76**
Tulsidas Ramayana, 616
Tulsi plant, 496
Tuota, Celestial King, 856
Tu/Wei-Ming, 186
Twelfth Imam, 68, 70, 74, 86
Twelfth Night. *See* Epiphany
Twin Holy Birthdays, 82, 99–102
Twin Manifestations, 101
Tyvendedagen. *See* Epiphany
Tzolk'in calendar, 573

Udhister, Maharaj, 722
Ugadi, 634
Ugadi Parva. *See* New Year's Day (India)
Uganda, 936
Ujjaini, India, 505
Ukko, 487
Ukraine, 35, 285i
Ullam-bana, 191, **877–78**
Ullambana Sutra, 877–78
Ulmann, Paulus, 788
Umā, 542
Umar ibn al-Khattab, 21
Umayyad dynasty, 203
Unbelief, xxiii, **878–88**
  atheism, 881–83
  in China, 884–85
  Darwin Day, 238
  Deism, 880–81
  early challenges to Western Christianity, 880–81
  Festivus, 307
  in France, 883
  holidays of, 886–87
  Indivisible Day, **424–25**
  Ingersoll Day, **425–27**
  in Jainism, 879
  Marxism, 883–85
  in modern West, 885–86
  National Day of Reason, **611–12**
  overview of, 878–79
  Servetus, 880, 880i
  winter solstice, 927
UNESCO World Heritage Sites, 96–97
Unification Church
  Children's Day, **175**
  Day of All Things, **243–44**
  God's Day, **337–38**
  holidays of, **888–90**
  Parents Day, **670–71**
  True Parents' Birthday, **870–71**
Unification Church, Holidays of the, **888–90**
Unitarianism, 312, 879
Unitarian Universalist Association, 413
United Buddhist Church of Vietnam (UBC), 137
United Church of God, 839
United Council of Church Women, 929
United Methodist Church, 21, 662
United Methodist Committee on Overseas Relief (UMCOR), 662
United Nations, 78, 414–15, 620
United States. *See also* Native Americans
  Aldersgate Day, 21
  atheism in, 886
  Atlantic coast of, 120
  Blessing of the Fleet, 120i, **120–21**
  Buddhism in, 140
  Freethought Day, **320–21**, 887
  Gulf coast of, 120–21
  Halloween, 277, **365–67**, 366i, 631, 780
  Haru Matsuri, 375
  Japan and, 774–75
  Japanese immigrants, 147–48
  Judaism in, 481, 483
  Mardi Gras, 551–52
  Mother's Day, 594
  National Bible Week, **607–8**
  National Brotherhood Week, **608–9**
  National Day of Prayer, **610–11**, 612
  neo-atheism, 886
  New Mexico, 680–81, 860–61
  New Orleans, 552, 716–17
  One Great Hour of Sharing, **661–62**
  Penitentes, **680–82**
  Race Unity Day, **727–32**
  Religious Freedom Day, **743–44**
  Satchidananda, Swami, 784–85
  Seton, Elizabeth Anne Bayley, 794–95
  Thomas Paine Day, **857–58**
  Three Kings Day, Native American Pueblos, **860–61**
  Unification Church and, 889
  Vivekananda, Swami, and, 910
  World Day of Prayer, 930
  World Religion Day, 936

Zen Buddhism in, 140
Zoroastrianism in, 955, 962
Unity, in Bahá'í Faith, 91–93
Universal Church, 471–72
Universal Declaration of Human Rights (UDHR), 414–15, 430
Universal Exaltation of the Precious and Life-creating Cross, 408
Universal House of Justice, 81, 88–89, 98, 101, 226, 729–30, 746, 936
Universalist Association, 312
Universal Week of Prayer. *See* Week of Prayer for Christian Unity
Universal Worthy Sutra, 778
University of Nalanda, 133
Upanishad, 384
Up Helly Aa, **890–92**
Uposattha Observance Day, **892**
Urabon service, 655
Urban II, Pope, 204, 281
Urban IV, Pope, 223–24
Urban V, Pope, 127
Urban VI, Pope, 167, 473, 909
Urban VIII, Pope, 249, 463
Urs Festival, **892–93**
Ursuline Sisters, 716–17
Uruguay, 148
U.S. Commission on International Religious Freedom, 430
U.S. Congress, 430–31
USC Shoah Foundation Institute for Visual History and Education, 945
Uthman ibn Affan, 21, 158
Uttarayana Punyakalam, 547

Vaikanasa, King, 585
Vaikuntha Ekadashi, **895–96**, 896i
Vaisakha. *See* Wesak/Vesak
Vaisakhi, 630
Vaishana community, 194–95
Vaisheshika darshana, 388
Vaishnava Hindu
Balarama and, 102
Bhagavata Purana, 605
Bhaktisiddhanta Sarasvati Thakura, Appearance Day of, **112**, 113
Bhaktivinoda Thakura, Appearance Day of, **112–13**
Chaturmas Vrat, 172
Gaura Purnima, 331
Gita Jayanti, **336–37**
Govardhan Puja, **341–42**
Hala Shashti, 365
Hari-Shayani Ekadashi, **373–74**
Holi, 400–401
holidays of, 396–97
Janaki Navami, 457
Jhulan Yatra, 103, **460–61**
Kamada Ekadashi, **490–91**
Kartika Snan, **495–97**
Mauni Amavasya, 570
Mokshada Ekadashi, **585–86**
Narasimha Jayanti, **605–7**, 606i
Nirjala Ekadashi, **647**
origins of, 382
Parshurama Jayanti, **671–72**
Prabhupada, Appearance Day of A. C. Bhaktivedanta Swami, **705–7**
Prabhupada, Disappearance Day of A. C. Bhaktivedanta Swami, **707**
Putrada Ekadashi, **722–23**
Radhashtami, **732–33**
Rama Navami, **739–40**, 739i
Ratha Yatra, 171, **740–41**
Rukmini Ashtami, **755**
Rulsidas and, 875
Snan Yatra, **822–23**
Tirupati Brahmotsava Festival, **862–64**
Vaikuntha Ekadashi, **895–96**, 896i
Vamana Jayanti, **900**
Vaishnava Prabhupada, 383
Vaitarani, **896–97**
Vajrayana Buddhism. *See also* Tibetan Buddhism
Bodhi Day, 121
Great Buddha Festival, **342–43**
Guan Yin, Renunciation of, **350–51**
Guan Yin's Birthday, **351–53**
Hoshi Matsuri, **411**
Manjushri's Birthday, 550
mudras, 597
Tens of Thousands of Lanterns Ancestral Memorial Service, **851–52**
Wesak/Vesak, **918–19**
Valentine, Saint, 898
Valentine's Day. *See* Valentinus, Feast of the Holy
Valentinus, 277
Valentinus, Feast of the Holy, **897–98**
Valerian, emperor, 228

Valit, 502, 798
Vallabha, 383
Valmiki, 899
Valmiki Jayanti, 875, **899**
Vamana, Lord, 900
Vamana Jayanti, **900**
Vannutelli, Cardinal Vincenzo, 291
Varada mudra, 597
Varaha Jayanti, **901**
Varangians, 658
Vardhamana, 447–48
Varnashrama-dharma, 387
Varshi Tapa. *See* Akshay Tritiya (Jain)
Vartan, General, 901–2
Vartan's Day, St., **901–2**
Varuna, 607
Vasant Panchami, **902–3**
Vashti, 719
Vassa, **903–5**, 905i
Vassa Retreat, 43–44, 126
Vasudeva, 102, 364
Vāsuki, 541–42, 601
Vata Savitri, **905–6**
Veda, 378–80, 604–5
Vedanta darshana, 388
Vedanta Hinduism, 910–11
Vedanta Society, 385, 736
Vedas, 494
Veda Vyasa, 18
Veeravati, 497
Vega, Osa de la, 251–52
Vegetarian Festival, 640
Venerable Bede, 282–83
Venezuela, 148–49
Venice, Italy, 551–52
Venkateshwara, 862–64
Ventura, Jesse, 424
Verigin, Peter, 262–63
Verigin, Peter Christiakov, 263
Vernal equinox. *See* Spring equinox (Thelema); Spring equinox (vernal)
Veronica, 251
Vesak. *See* Wesak/Vesak
Veurne, Belgium, 712–13
Vietnam, 137, 144, 884
Vijaya, 901
Vijayadashami, 618
Vinayak, 324
Vipassana Buddhism, 142
Virgen de los Angeles Day, **906–8**
Virgin Mary
- annunciation, **37–39**, 293, 909–10
- apparitions of, 299–300, 562, 595, 684
- in art, 201i
- Assumption of the Virgin, **50–51**, 403, 562, 726
- birth of Christ, 701–2
- Expectation of the Birth of the Blessed Virgin Mary, Feast of, 38, **293**. *See also* Annunciation, Feast of the
- Fatima, Our Lady of, 299–301
- Guadalupe, Feast of Our Lady of, **347–50**
- Holy Maries, Festival of the (La Fête des Saintes Maries), 405–6
- Immaculate Conception and. *See* Immaculate Conception, doctrine of
- Immaculate Conception, Feast of the, 349, 403, **421–22**, 562, 564
- Immaculate Heart of Mary, 299–300, 562
- Immaculate Heart of Mary, Feast of the, **422–23**
- Joseph, Saint, and, 470–72
- lost statues of, 562
- Lourdes, Our Lady of, 532–35
- Mary, liturgical year of the Blessed Virgin, **560–64**
- as Mother of God, 202–3
- Nativity of Mary, 560, 561, **614–15**, 650
- Nossa Senhora dos Remédios, Pilgrimage of, **650**
- Our Lady of Good Remedy, 340–41
- Peace and Good Voyage, Feast of Our Lady of, **678–79**
- Peñafrancia, Feast of Our Lady of, **679–80**
- Presentation of Mary, Feast of the, **710–11**
- Prompt Succor, Feast Day of Our Lady of, **716–17**
- Queenship of Mary, Feast of, **725–26**, 910
- Romeria of La Virgen de Valme, **749–50**
- Rosary, Feast of Our Lady of the, **750–51**
- Sorrows, Feast of Our Lady of, **828–29**
- statue of, 561i
- veneration of, 27, 36–37, 50–51, 201, 203, 560, 562, 583, 773–74
- Virgen de los Angeles Day, **906–8**
- visions of, 533
- Visitation, Feast of the, **909–10**
- White Dove statue, 697

Virgin of Czestochowa, 231–32
Vishnu. *See also* Hinduism
- Anant Chaturdashi, 32

Balarama and, 102
Bhairava Ashtami, 111
Chaturmas Vrat, 172
Chittirai Festival, 195
Dattatreya Jayanti, 242
Dhan Teras, 246
Diwali, 253
Ganga Dussehra, 327
Govardhan Puja, 341–42
Hala Shashti, 364
Hari, 27
Hari-Shayani Ekadashi, 373
Holi, 400–401
incarnations of, 396–97
Indra Jatra, 425
Janaki Navami, 457
Kamada Ekadashi, 490
Kartika Purnima, 494
Kartika Snan, 496
Kojagara, 502
lotus and, 532
Mauni Amavasya, 570
Nagapanchami, 601
Narasimha Jayanti, 605–6
Navaratri, 616
Nirjala Ekadashi, 647
Nutan Varsh, 634
Onam, 659
origins of, 381–82
Parshurama Jayanti, 671
Putrada Ekadashi, 722
Rama Navami, 739–40
Ratha Yatra, 740
Ugadi, 634
Vaikuntha Ekadashi, 895, 896i
in Vaishnava Hinduism, 396–97
Vamana Jayanti, **900**
Varaha Jayanti, **901**
Veda Vyasa, 18

Vishvakarma, 896–97
Vishvaksena, Sri, 863
Vishwakarma Puja, **908–9**
"The Vision of Race Unity" (US-NSA), 729
Visitation, Feast of the, **909–10**
Visits to the Blessed Sacrament and the Blessed Virgin (Ligouri), 27
Vital, Elan, 385
Vivekananda, Birthday of Swami, **910–11**
Vivekananda, Swami, 384, 385, 736, 849
Vladimir, Saint, 713, 912i
Vladimir, Saint's Day of St., **911–13**
Vladimir I, Prince, 609
Vladimir of Kiev, Prince, 204
Voltaire, 246, 881, 883
Vyas, Bhagwan Ved, 539
Vyasa, Ved, 355

Wahhab, Muhammad, 438
Wakamiya Hachimansha Shrine, 373
Wallace, Alfred Russel, 237
Walpurga, Saint, 915–16
Walpurgisnacht, 108, **915–16**
Wang Yangming, 185
Wanli, emperor, 504
Warring States period, 182, 263
Washington, George, 881
Washington Cherry Blossom Festival, 774–75
Washio Kyodo, 287
Waso Full Moon. *See* Asalha Puja Day
Waters, Donald, 77
Waters, Frank, 573
Water Splashing Festival. *See* Songkran
Wattson, Paul James, 169, 917
The Way of Salvation (Ligouri), 27
Wedgwood, Emma, 237
Week of Prayer for Christian Unity, 169, 223, **916–18**
Wesak/Vesak, 144, 162, 623, 776, **918–19**
Wesley, John, 20–21
Western Esoteric groups, 919
Western Human Potential movement, 664
Western Paradise, 31
Western Wall, 754i
Western Zhou dynasty (China), 177
White, Ellen G., 675
White, Lurana, 917
White Buffalo Calf Woman, 934
White Cloud Temple, 641
White Dove statue, 697
White Lotus Day, **919–20**
White Lotus Society, 187
White Sunday, **921**
Whit-Monday. *See* Pentecost
Whitsunday. *See* Pentecost
Whit Tuesday, 925
Wicca. *See also* Witchcraft
Beltane, **108–9**, 915
Eostara, **282–83**
fall equinox, **295–96**, 296i

Imbolc, **420–21**
Lammas, 277, **513–14**
liturgical calendar, **921–24**
New Year's Day, 631
Samhain, 365–67, 631, **779–80**, 923–24
spring equinox, 833
summer solstice, 840–41
winter solstice, 927
Yule, 924, **950–51**
Wicca/Neo-Paganism Liturgical Calendar, **921–24**
Wigilla. *See* Epiphany
Wijewardena, Helena, 266
Wilberforce, Samuel, 237
Wildkirchli cave, 788
Wilkins, Charles, 384, 384i
Willard, Frances, 594
Willibrord, 125
Willibrord, Saint's Day of St., **925–26**
Wilmington, Delaware, **11–12**
Winter solstice, 191, 211, 887, 923–24, **926–28**
Wise, Isaac Mayer, 482
Witchcraft, 108, 840, 922. *See also* Wicca
Wladyslaw I Lokietek, Prince, 231
Wojtyla, Karol, 250. *See also* John Paul II, Pope
Woman's Christian Temperance Union, 594
Women. *See also specific saints*
Ahoi Ashtami and, **15**
Aizen Summer Festival, 16–17
Buddhism and, 184
Karwa Chauth, **497–99**, 498i
Rushi Pancham, **755–56**
Teej Festivals, **847–48**
Vata Savitri, **905–6**
World Community Day, **929**
World Day of Prayer, **929–31**
Women's Inter-Church Council of Canada, 930
Woodcutting, 580i
Woolston, Thomas, 881
World Alliance of Reformed Churches, 210
World Communion of Reformed Churches, 210
World Communion Sunday, **928–29**
World Community Day, **929**
World Conference on Religion and Peace, 649
World Council of Churches, 209, 214, 769, 869–70, 917, 928
World Day of Prayer, **929–31**
World Day of the Sick. *See* Lourdes, Feast Day of Our Lady of
World Evangelical Fellowship, 209
World Federation of Buddhists, 144
World Humanist Day, 887, **931–32**
World Invocation Day, **932–33**
World Jewish Congress, 483
World Meditation Hour, 78
World Parliament of Religions, 385, 736, 910
World Peace and Prayer Day, **933–35**
World Peace Ceremony (Tibetan Buddhist), 588, **935–36**
World Religion Day, **936–39**
World's Incense Burning Day, 524
World's Parliament of Religion, 140
World Union for Progressive Judaism, 483
World Union of Catholic Women's Organizations, 930
World Union of Freethinkers, 886
Worldwide Church of God, 675, 838–39
World Zoroastrian Congress, 963
World Zoroastrian Organization, 963
Wu, Zetian, 830
Wu Cheng'en, 586
Wu Di, 123
Wutai Mountain, 549–50
Wyszynski, Stefan Cardinal. *See* John Paul II, Pope

Xia dynasty (China), 180
Xuan Zang, 586
Xunzi, 183

Yaakov, Zichron, 875
Yagneshwara, 739
Yagokoro- omoikane-no-mikoto, 174
Yahyá, 86–87
Yaks, 149
Yama, Lord, 170, 254, 604–5, 906
Yamato clan, 805
Yamuna River, 570
Yao, emperor, 581
Yaropolk of Kiev, 911
Yasaka Shrine, 615
Yashoda, 102, 544
Yavetz, Zeev, 874–75
Yazdí, Siyyid Husayn, 74
Yazid, 47
Yazid I, caliph, 629
Yehuda HaMakabi, 370
Yellow Emperor, 180
Yi dynasty (Korea), 137, 196

Yijing (Book of Changes), 181
Yin-yang, 183, 185, 260
Yoga
  Ajapa yoga, 115, 458, 707, 721
  Bhakti yoga, 103, 112, 331, 460, 605, 648
  Hatha yoga, 785
  Integral Yoga, 56
  Japa yoga, 539, 740, 895, 899
  Jnana yoga, 193
  Kriya yoga, 77, 512, 941, 950
  Lahiri Mahasaya, Commemoration Days for, **512–13**
  Muktananda, Birthday of Swami Paramahansa, 598–99
Yoga darshana, 388
Yogananda, Birthday of Paramahansa, **941–42**, 942i
Yogananda, Mahasamadhi of Paramahansa, **942–43**
Yogananda, Paramahansa, 76, 512, 950
Yoga-Vedanta Forest Academy, 820
Yogaville, Virginia, 785
Yog Maya, 895
Yom HaAtzmaut, 486, **943–44**, 946
Yom HaShoah, 486, **944–46**
Yom HaZikaron, 486, 943, **946**
Yom Kippur, 47, 156, 244–45, 472, 485–86, **947–48**
Yom Yerushalayim (Jerusalem Day), 487, **949–50**
Yoshida, Kanetomo, 807
Yoshikawa, Koretari, 808
Yoshino cherry trees, 774–75
Yoshio Iwanaga, 656
Yudhishtira, 585
Yuen Tin Sheung Tai, 667
Yugadi, 634
Yuikyogyo, 623
Yukatas, 16–17
Yukteswar, Commemorative Days of Swami Sri, **950**
Yule, 924, **950–51**
Yurok people, 310
Yukteswar, Sri, 76–77, 941

Zaccheus Sunday, **953–54**
Zahary, Pope, 125
Zakat, 436
Zambia, 61
Zao Jun, 176
Zarathustra, 651–52, 954–56, 956i
Zarathustra, Commemorative Days of, **954–55**
Zartusht-no-diso, **955–56**
Zaynab bint Ali, 47
Zechariah, Book of, 297–98
Zechariah and Elizabeth, Commemoration of Saints, 468
Zen Buddhism
  Bodhi Day, 122
  Bodhidharma Day, 122–23
  Daruma Kuyo, **235–36**
  in Europe, 140, 142
  Linji/Rinzai Day Observance, **525**
  meditation and, 184, 525
  mudras, 598
  in North America, 140
Zhi Nu, 261
Zhiyi, 136
Zhongguo, 180
Zhou dynasty (China), 180–82
Zhu Xi (Chu Hsi), 185
Ziggurats, 956
Zionism, 482–83
Zodiac signs, 159, 190, 627, 832
Zoroastrianism, **956–63**
  calendar, 958–60
  in England, 955
  Fravardegan, **319–20**
  Gahambars, **323–24**
  holidays of, 960–61
  in India, 955, 961–62
  New Year's Day, 620
  Nowruz, 323, **651–52**, 961
  overview of, 956–58
  recent history, 961–63
  spread of, 957
  Zarathustra, Commemorative Days of, **954–55**
  Zartusht-no-diso, **955–56**
Zoroastrian Seasonal-Year Society, 959
Zumarraga, Bishop Juan de, 349
Zunúzí, Mírzá Muhammad-Ali, 74
Zwingli, Ulrich, 207